AF496619

Quick drying.

Supersmooth. Ideal for grain filling.

Flexible. Ideal for repairs to all timber surfaces.

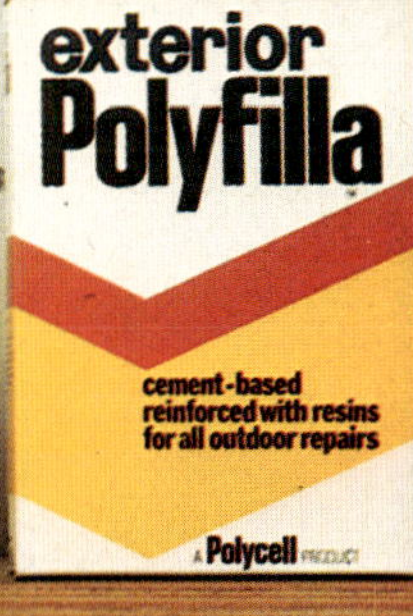

Cement based weather-resistant filler. Suitable for any size repair.

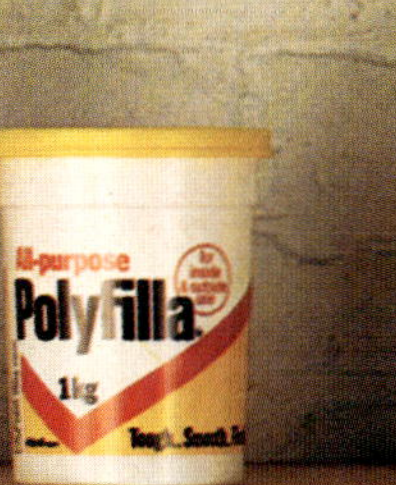

Tough enough for outside use, smooth enough for use indoors.

Polyseal Acrylic multi-purpose sealant

Multi-purpose flexible gap sealer.

Welds together torn or damaged vinyl and PVC.

Wall-papering? Do it right.

Suitable for all wall-papers, including washables and vinyls.

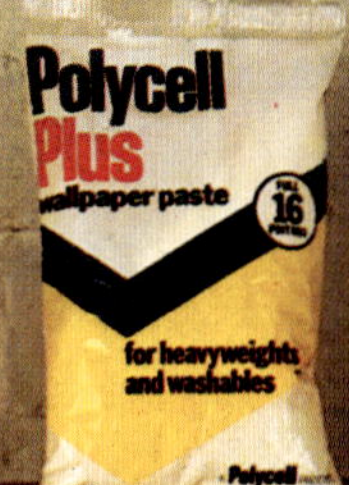

Paste for medium and heavyweight wallpapers as well as washables.

Paste for light-weight papers; fungicide free.

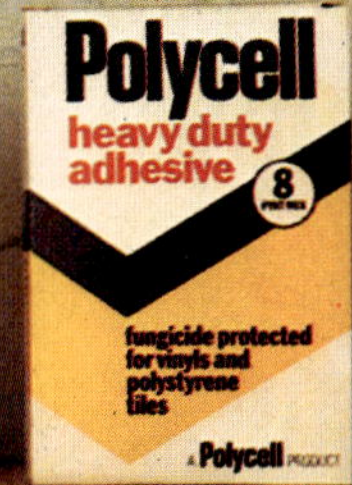

A powerful adhesive and strong fungicide for paper or fabric backed vinyls and polystyrene tiles.

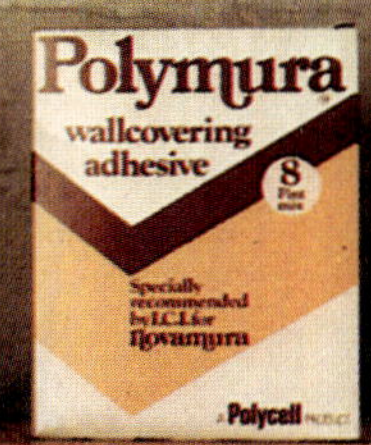

Non-drip paste recommended by ICI for Novamura.

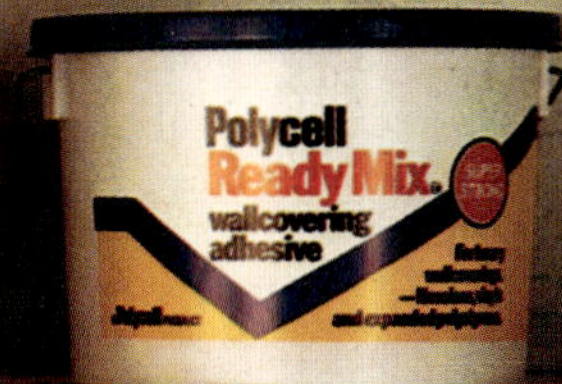

For luxury wallcoverings, paper and latex backed hessians, heavy and fabric backed vinyls and poly-styrene tiles.

Treating wood? Do it right.

Protects hard wood. Can be polished to a gloss finish.

Makes wood weather proof.

Texture painting? Do it right.

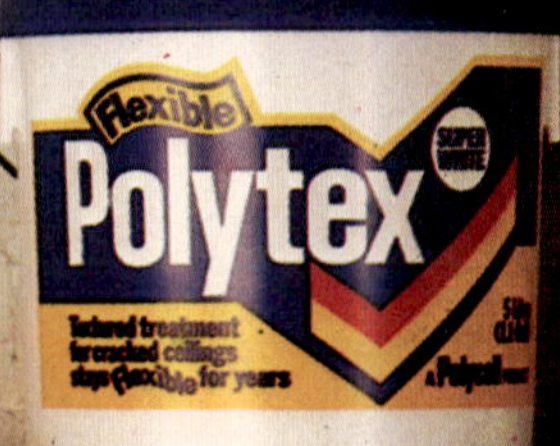

Flexible textured paint for ceilings that covers cracks for good.

Smooth-to-the-touch textured finish that repairs and decorates walls at the same time.

Handy tub of super-white grout, ready to use.

Super-white grouting cement, with a long lasting finish.

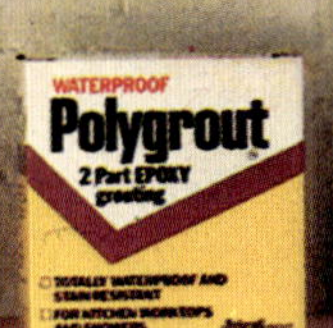

Water and stain resistant, ideal for showers and kitchen worktops.

Flexible waterproof sealant for baths and showers.

Double glazing? Do it right.

Polycell Aluminium Double Glazing

Anodised for a beautiful satin finish that will not tarnish or pit.

Polycell PVC Double Glazing

Superb insulator, white, durable and very economical.

Stripping paint and paper? Do it right.

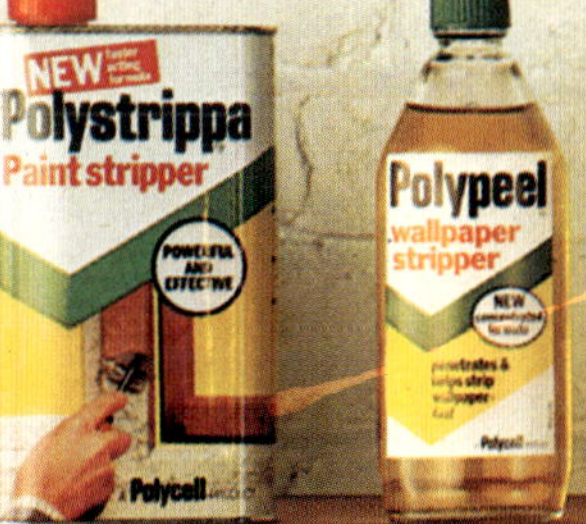

New form of paint remover that strips gloss paint back to the natural wood.

Fast-acting, non-drip paint remover. Can be rinsed away with white spirit or water.

Strips wallpapers fast and easily, available as powder or liquid.

Filling holes and cracks? Do it right.

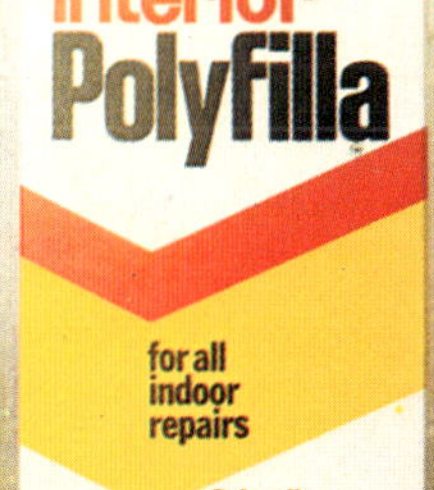

The finest filler available. Strong adhesion. Does not shrink or crack.

Preparing walls? Do it right.

Perfect for deep repairs to all building surfaces. No special skills or tools needed.

A unique brush-on plaster, ideal for large shallow areas of damage.

Seals surfaces which are powdery or porous.

Prepares porous walls and improves slip and adhesion to make papering easier.

Prevents mould for up to six months.

Preparing paintwork? Do it right.

Lightly sands and de-glosses paintwork to provide a 'key' before painting.

Cleans and prepares gloss painted surface for repainting.

For glazing wood and metal windows.

Real turpentine for cleaning high quality brushes.

High quality paint thinner and solvent.

Brush cleaner and restorer. Enables brushes to be washed out in water.

Restores hardened and neglected brushes.

Tiling? Do it right.

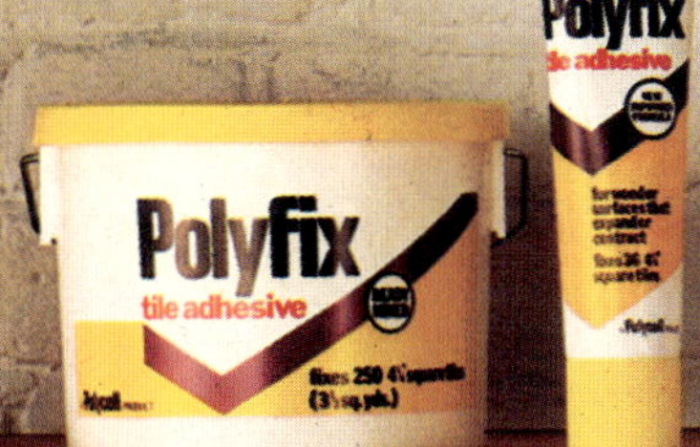

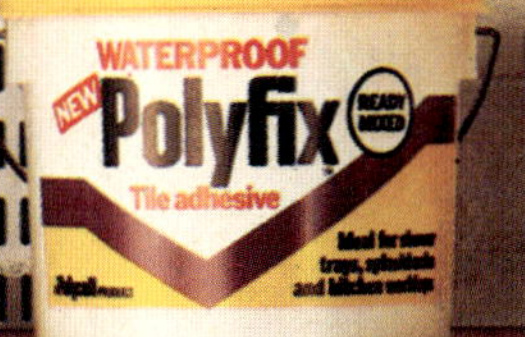

Waterproof cement for walls and floor tiles.

Economical and easy to use strong adhesive.

Fixes tiles to wood.

Ideal for showers, splashbacks and outside surfaces.

Convenient. Two products in one.

That's better!
Whatever the job, a Spear & Jackson saw helps you do it better.
And there's a Spear & Jackson saw for every job around.
Is it surprising that Spear & Jackson are the leading makers of hand saws in the whole country?
SJ
QUALITY
SPEAR&JACKSON
Spear & Jackson (Tools) Ltd., St Pauls Road, Wednesbury, West Midlands WS10 9RA.
Professional
Sovereign
Black Prince
Hardpoint
Workhorse
Sprint
DIY

TRICKS OF THE TRADE
HOME DIY

As the cost of employing a professional to make any alteration in the home is constantly increasing — whether it is to install plumbing or central heating, to renew the floors or to decorate — more and more householders are tackling these tasks themselves. With good materials, time and patience, all such jobs should be within the capabilities of the average do-it-yourselfer.

This indispensable handbook offers guidance on practically every aspect of home improvement and repair, including electrical wiring, home carpentry, domestic heating, decorating, exterior house maintenance, plumbing, flooring, soft furnishings and home security. And to help achieve a really professional finish, the book is brimming with tips and hints — the tricks of the trade — highlighted for easy reference.

TRICKS OF THE TRADE

HOME DIY

Based on the highly successful Tricks of the Trade series published by Pelham Books

CONTRIBUTORS

Larry Blonstein Geoffrey Burdett
Margaret Edwards Chris Govey
Ernest Hall W.H. Johnson
Robert Laister Helen O'Leary
F.E. Sherlock Bob Tattersall

PELHAM/GROSVENOR

Based on the Tricks of the Trade series originally published in hardback by
Pelham Books, 44 Bedford Square, London WC1B 3DU.
This omnibus edition published 1984.

Editor: Diana Briscoe
Designer/art director: Jill Coote
Design and typesetting: DP Press Ltd, Sevenoaks, Kent
Illustration: Hayward & Martin Ltd, Chislehurst, Kent
Picture research: Diane Rich, Jill Coote

British Library Cataloguing in Publication Data

Tricks of the trade.
1. Dwellings—Maintenance and repair—
Amateurs' manuals 2. Dwellings—
Remodelling—Amateurs' manuals
643'.7 TH4817.3

ISBN 0–7207–1511–3

Printed in Italy by Arnoldo Mondadori

CONTENTS

THERMAL-K-SHIELD

THE WORLD'S MOST BEAUTIFUL WINDOWS

All Thermal-K-Shield products are covered by a cast iron guarantee which protects you against faults in design, materials, manufacture or fittings for a full 10 years. This warranty offers real peace of mind because it is given by one of Britain's longest established replacement window companies. All customers' deposits are protected by the "Deposit Indemnity Fund" operated by the Glass and Glazing Federation of which Thermal-K-Shield are full members.

Although we think Thermal-K-Shield are easily the world's most beautiful replacement windows, they're actually far more than just a pretty frame.

In fact they work better and are made more carefully than any other replacement window type we know.

Not because they're made of some untried synthetic material, but because they combine two traditional materials in a brilliant new way.

Thermal-K-Shield frames are made from satin anodized or white glazed aluminium which is then clad in real Brazilian mahogany.

This warm, natural material conducts heat much more slowly than aluminium and virtually eliminates condensation on the frame.

Also, Thermal-K-Shield windows are designed to warn you of the high humidity levels which cause condensation. Each opening window has a deliberately exposed section of aluminium: when room humidity is excessive, this clever trap attracts condensation before it can harm your decorations, furnishings or health.

However, Thermal-K-Shield recognise that the only complete answer to condensation is proper ventilation, so every Thermal-K-Shield opening window is fitted with a night ventilation catch which allows you to open your windows slightly and fasten them in that position—giving good ventilation and security.

COME AND SEE THE WORLD'S MOST BEAUTIFUL WINDOWS AT YOUR NEAREST THERMAL-K-SHIELD SHOWROOM OR TELEPHONE 061-228 0728 FOR A FREE ESTIMATE.

PRESTON
59 Tithebarn Street, PRESTON
Lancs. Tel: 0772 59086

WAKEFIELD
160 Westgate, WAKEFIELD
West Yorkshire. Tel: 0924 361499

CROSBY
72 Liverpool Road, CROSBY
Liverpool 23. Tel: 051 931 3138

LIVERPOOL 18
174 Allerton Road
LIVERPOOL 18. Tel: 051 724 2791

SALE MOOR
113 Northenden Road, SALE MOOR
Cheshire. Tel: 061 905 1030

SHEFFIELD
187/189 London Road, SHEFFIELD
South Yorkshire. Tel: 0742 583447

KIRKCALDY
11 High Street, KIRKCALDY
Fife. Tel: 0592 204366

DUMBARTON
37 College Way
DUMBARTON. Tel: 0389 34482

ELLESMERE PORT
50 Whitby Road, ELLESMERE PORT
Wirral. Tel: 051-356 0920

BLACKPOOL
85-87 Abingdon Street, BLACKPOOL
Lancs. Tel: 0253 293236

POULTON-LE-FYLDE
Industrial Estate,
POULTON-LE-FYLDE
Lancs. Tel: 0253 891010

FLOORING 199

DECORATING 227

CURTAINS & BLINDS 271

UPHOLSTERY & CANEWORK 295

PICTURE FRAMING 313

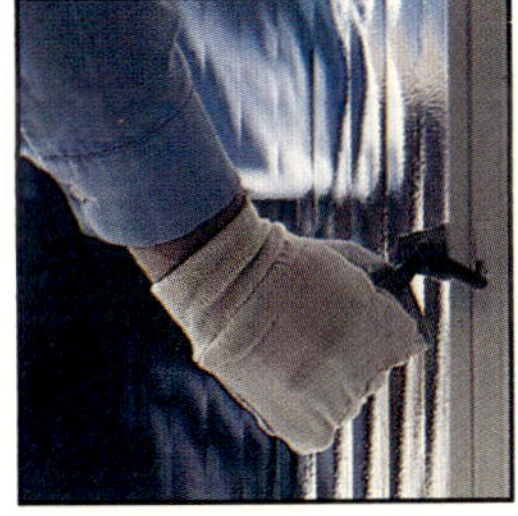

HOME SECURITY 325

FOREWORD

This book is based on the successful Tricks of the Trade series published by Pelham Books.

TRICKS OF THE TRADE – HOME DIY is designed as a compact volume, encompassing the information and 'tricks' contained in the original books, together with additional topics such as home security and designing and fitting a kitchen. It has been illustrated throughout with new diagrams and colour photographs to amplify the text.

The book is not intended for the total beginner, nor for the expert who would tackle a home extension or a complete rewiring. It is aimed at the many people who maintain their own homes and find it too expensive to call in professionals for fairly simple tasks. The book also seeks to encourage people to arrange their house maintenance on the basis that prevention is often better – and much less expensive – than cure. Many people are alarmed at the technical terms used in the trade, so every attempt has been made to explain and simplify these. The book clearly states which tasks are too complex for any but the most competent person.

The book opens with a section on tools and basic techniques plus advice on general safety and emergency first aid. The first half of the book deals with the structural and service parts of DIY: carpentry, kitchen planning, electrics, plumbing, heating and insulation, exterior maintenance and flooring.

The second half deals with the more decorative aspects of DIY: decorating (painting, tiling and wallpapering), curtains and blinds, upholstery and canework, picture framing, and finally home security – the last of which is regrettably becoming more and more important. There is also an extensive additional reading list, conversion tables and a comprehensive index.

TRICKS OF THE TRADE – HOME DIY is a complete manual for the 1980s which will become a reference book for all home-owners. The many professional tricks contained within these pages will enable the readers to make their homes safer, and more beautiful, without having to spend a fortune.

THE TOOL KIT 1

THE BASIC TOOL KIT

This comprises the tools that you really cannot do without and which you will find yourself using over and over, no matter what aspect of d-i-y you are tackling.

3m. (10ft) flexible steel tape
Check that it has a locking device and a recoil spring.

600mm (24in.) steel rule or straight-edge

300mm (12in.) steel combination square
Check ease of adjustment. It is an advantage to have a built-in spirit level.

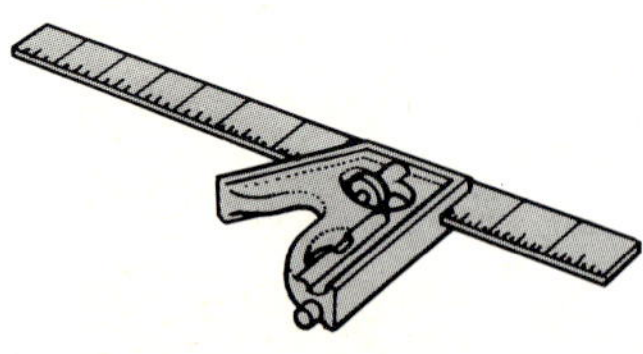

600mm (24in.) steel spirit level
Should have both horizontal and vertical phials.

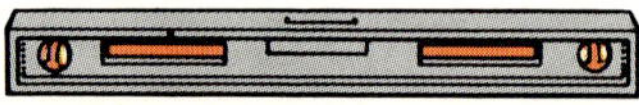

300mm (12in.) tenon saw
'Points' equals number of teeth per 25mm (1in.) 10–14 points is the best all-round size. Check for comfortable grip (wood is most comfortable) and balance.

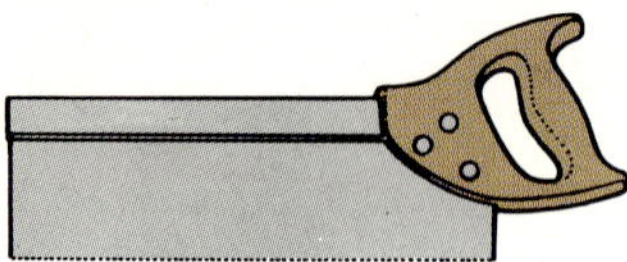

Junior hacksaw
Choose one with 150mm (6in.) replaceable blades. Keep it exclusively for cutting metal and plastic.

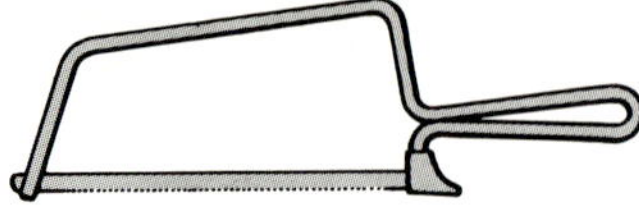

Bradawl
Used for starting drill holes and pilot holes for small screws.

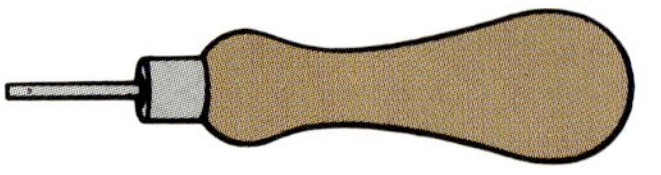

Hand drill (wheel brace)
Check that the gearing does not wobble and runs smoothly. Drill bits can be bought singly or in packs and range in size from 1.5 to 9.5mm (1/16–3/8in.). Buy them according to what screw sizes you intend using.

Screwdriver (single-slot)
Buy two to cover the most common screw sizes: i.e. 6–8 gauge and 10–12 gauge. One should have a longer blade than the other. Check they have decent-sized handles for a good grip.

Screwdriver (Phillips/Pozidrive)
A No. 2 will fit the most common sizes of screw: i.e. 6, 8 and 10 gauge.

Screwdriver (electrical)
The additional cost of a mains tester in the handle is well worth it. Check that the handle is insulated and the blade securely seated.

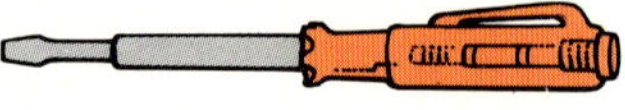

Hammer
Buy two (though you can manage with just the larger): a 450–560g (16–20oz) with steel shaft and a 'claw' head; plus a 170–280g (6–10oz) 'cross pein' or 'Warrington' head with wooden handle.

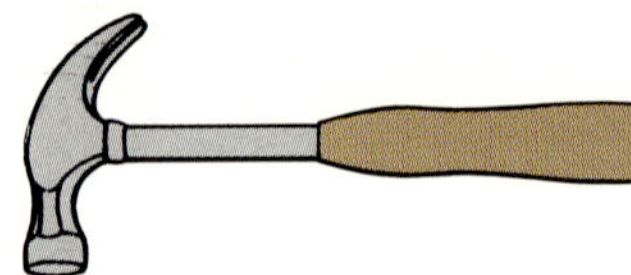

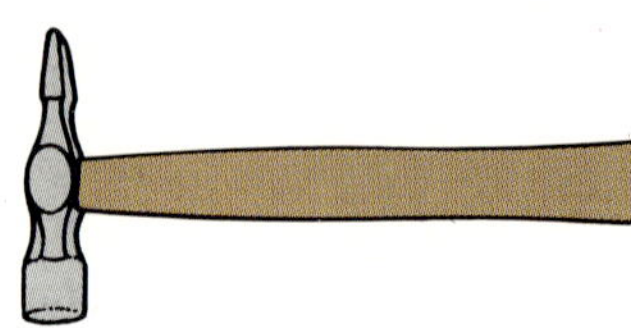

Pliers
Check the handles are insulated for electrical work and that they are not too stiff.

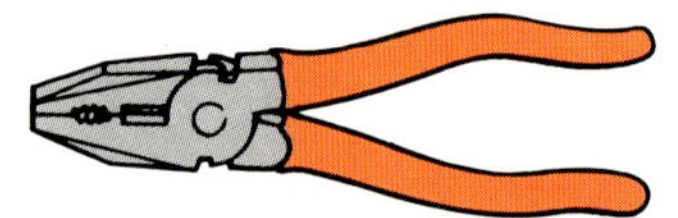

Adjustable spanner (wrench)
Buy two if you are using compression joints in plumbing. Check that the head is large enough to fit most plumbing fixings (a 200mm (8in.) should be big enough), and that the screw adjusters move smoothly.

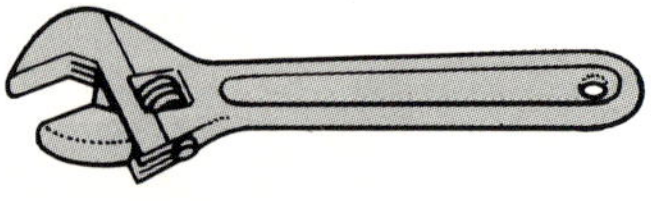

Chisel (bevel-edged)
Buy at least three: their sizes range from 6 to 25mm (1/4–1in.); unless you own a wooden mallet, buy those with plastic handles which can be used with a hammer. Check they have protective plastic caps for the blades.

Oilstone
For sharpening chisels

Bolster chisel
Essential if you have a lot of underfloor work to do.

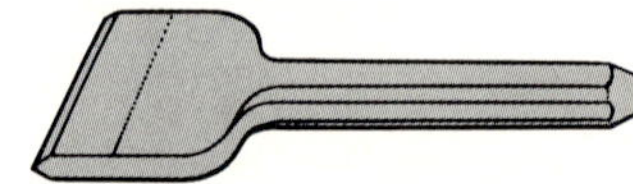

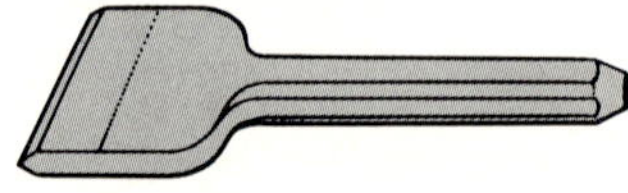

Stanley knife
Check it has a sturdy handle and a retractable blade which is easily changeable.

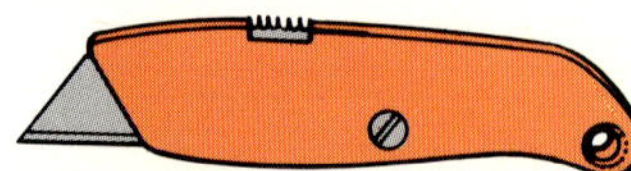

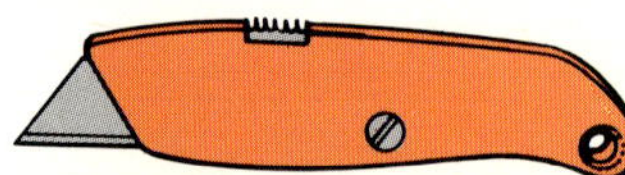

Multi-purpose trimming tool
Available in various sizes and blades for different tasks.

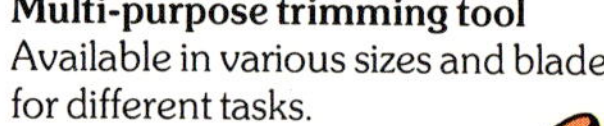

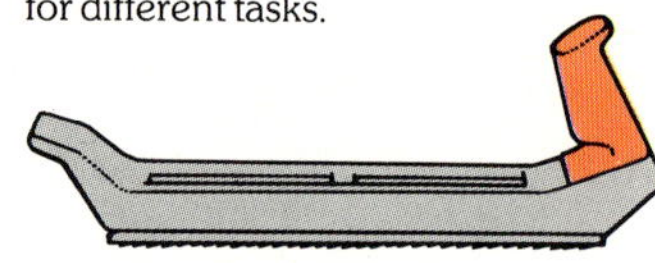

Sanding block
To wrap sandpaper around for smoothing and keying.

Ladder
Minimum height 2m. (6ft 6in.) but check you can comfortably reach your highest ceiling or the attic trap from it. Ideally buy an aluminium one with an open-leg lock and paint-tray with non-slip feet and strong struts.

OTHER ITEMS

Your basic tool kit should also contain a selection of screws and nails, stored in jars or tins; various grades of sandpaper; electrical insulating tape; waterproof sealing tape or an epoxy resin repair kit (see page 101); 3, 5 and 13-amp plug fuses; 5, 30 and 45-amp fuse wire or cartridges; carpenter's pencil; a torch (for changing fuses in the dark and finding lost screws); a plumbline (either bought or home-made); and a pair of protective industrial goggles. Use the latter whenever you are breaking up materials, working under floors or doing anything where particles may get in your eyes. It might be worth investing in a portable bench if you intend doing a lot of d-i-y.

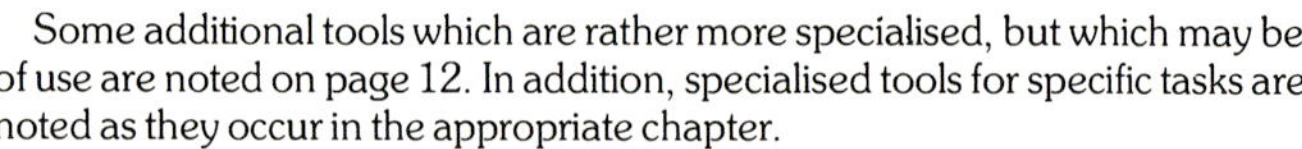

Some additional tools which are rather more specialised, but which may be of use are noted on page 12. In addition, specialised tools for specific tasks are noted as they occur in the appropriate chapter.

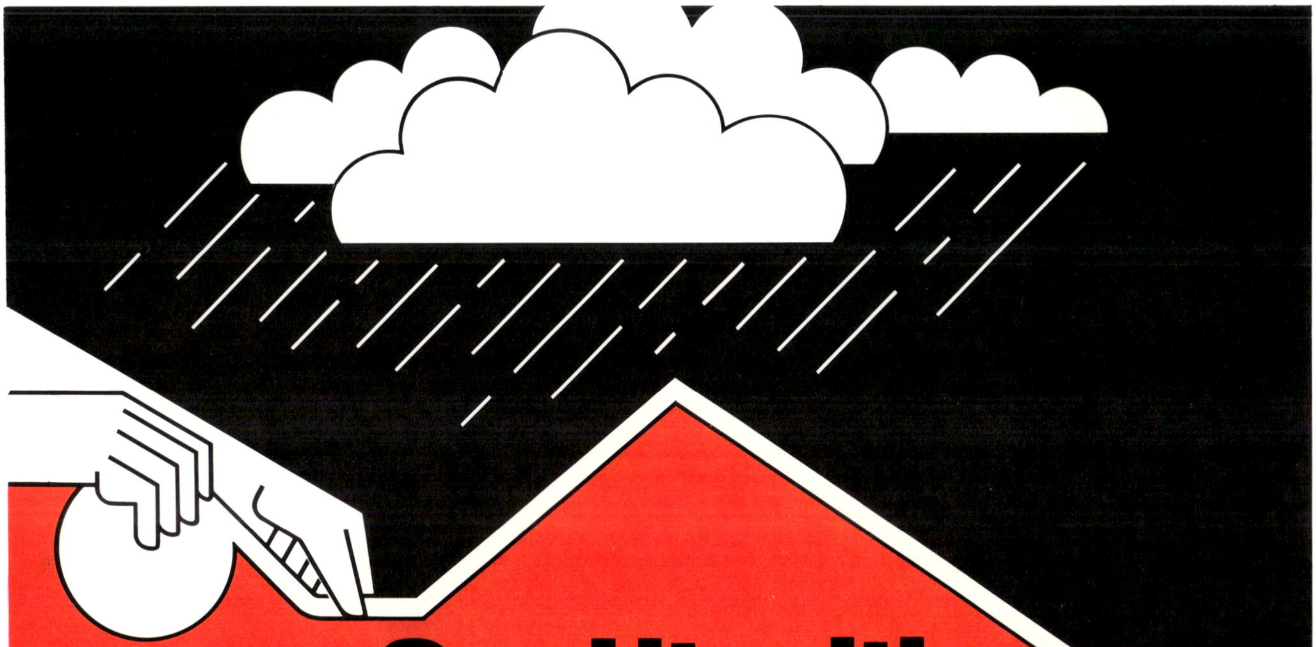

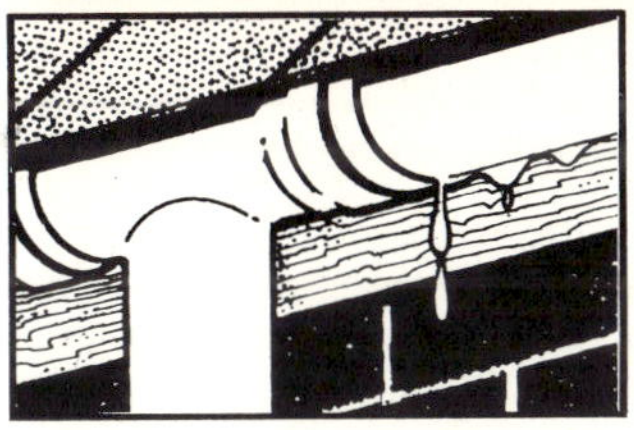

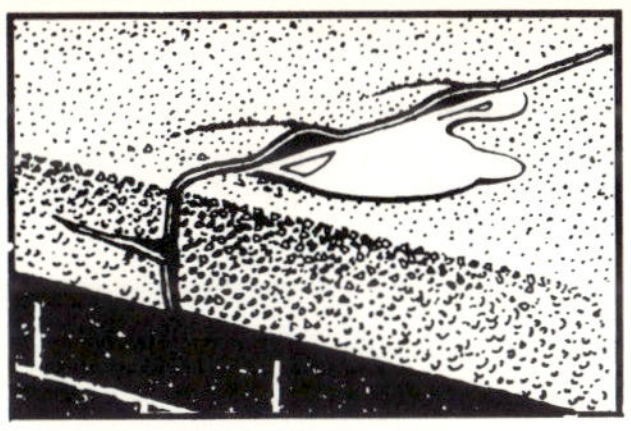

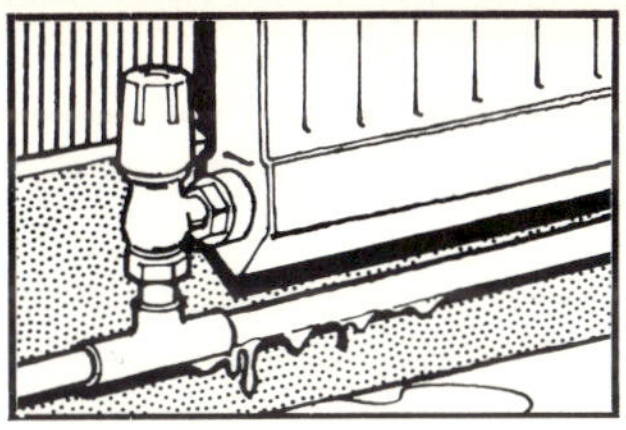

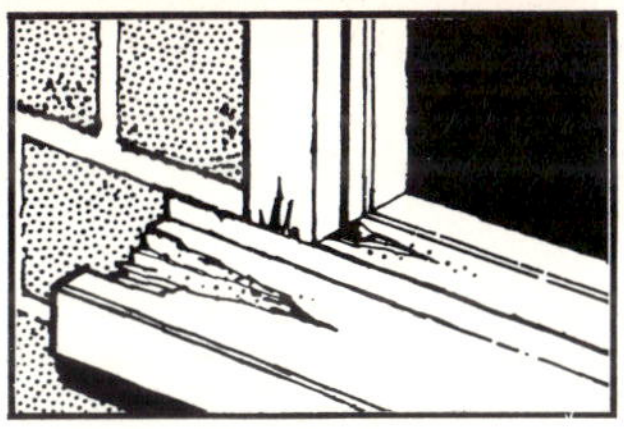

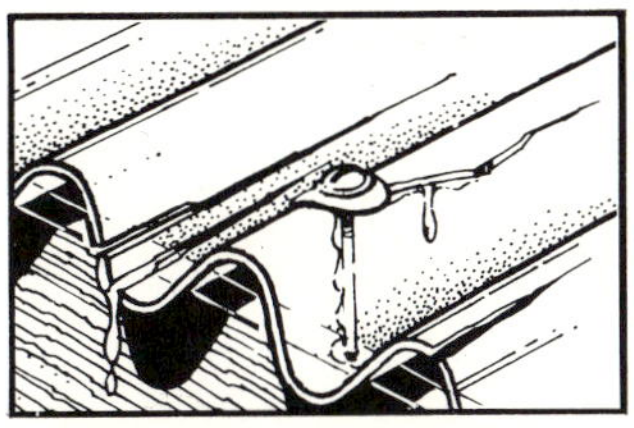

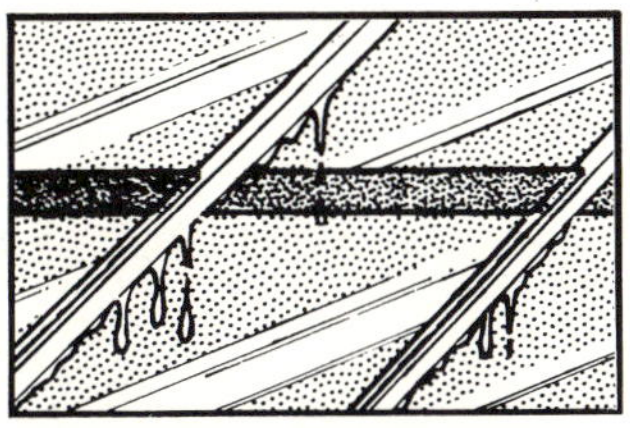

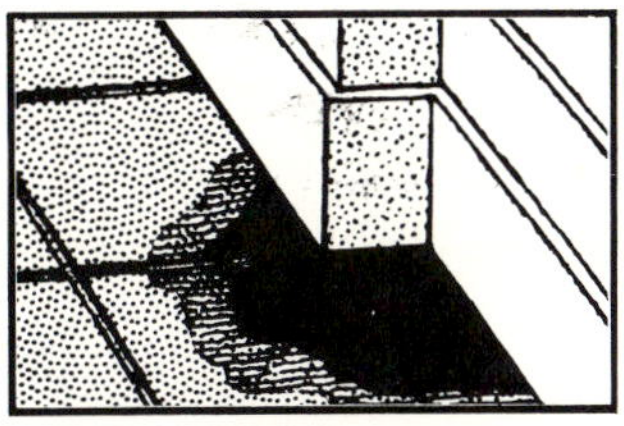

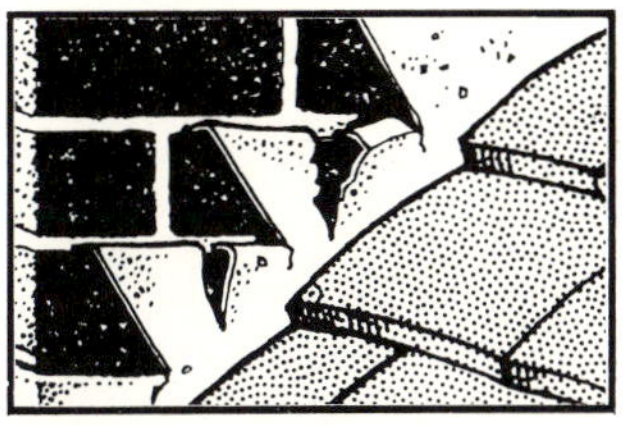

THE TOOL KIT 2

MORE SPECIALISED TOOLS

This is not a complete list of specialised tools – that could take up a book of its own – but a selection of tools which might be worth buying if you have a special interest in one aspect of d-i-y.

Panel saw
For larger sawing tasks.

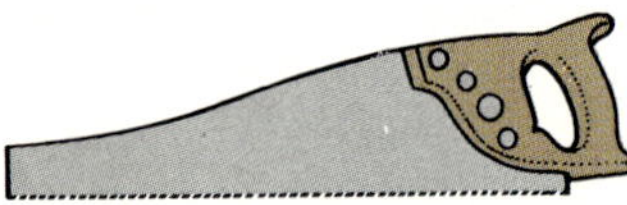

Coping saw or padsaw
For curves and sawing from drill holes.

Wooden mallet
Used with chisels.

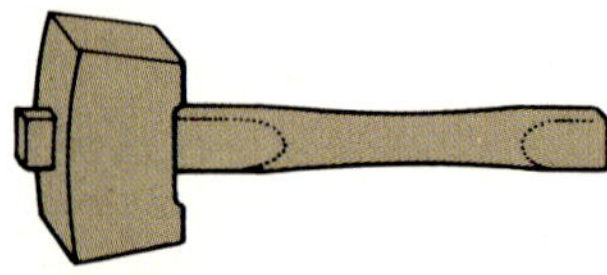

Hacksaw
Large: for cutting metals and plastic.

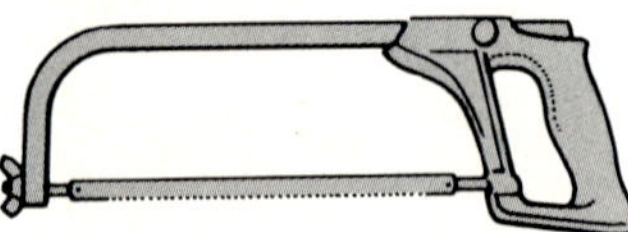

Centre punch
For starting drilling holes in metal.

Hand brace
Uses auger bits for drilling larger holes in wood.

Marking gauge
Useful for marking joints.

Nail punch

Pincers
For removing nails and trimming ceramic tiles.

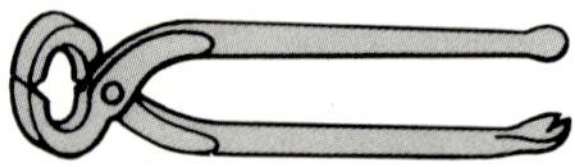

Gouge
Chisel with rounded blade.

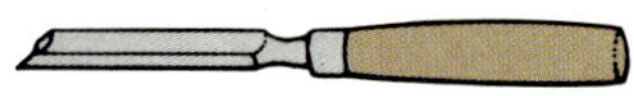

Smoothing plane
For smoothing wood.

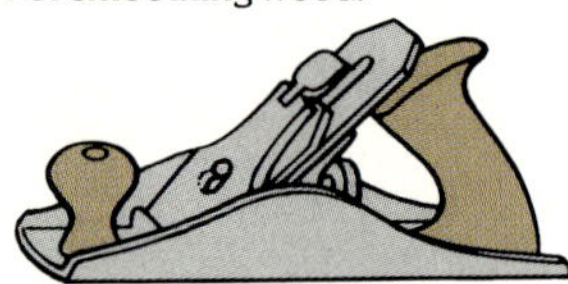

Self-grip wrench
Can be used as portable vice.

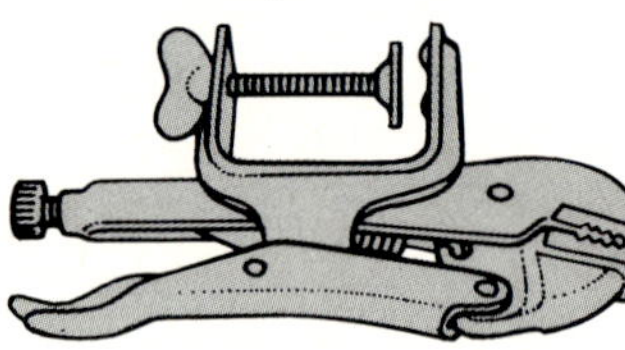

Stilson wrench
Another sort of adjustable wrench.

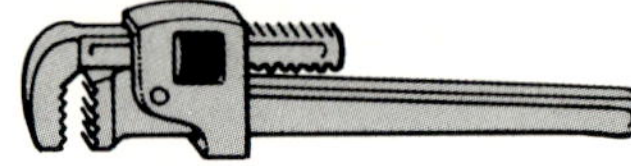

Slip-joint pliers

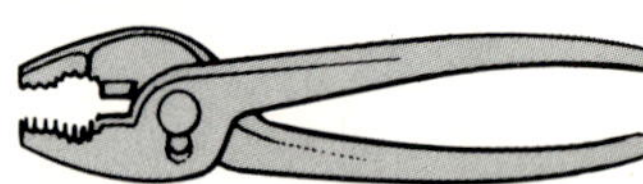

File

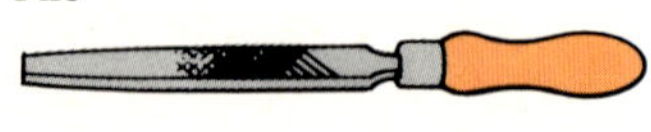

Float trowel
For spreading plaster, concrete, floor levelling compound, etc.

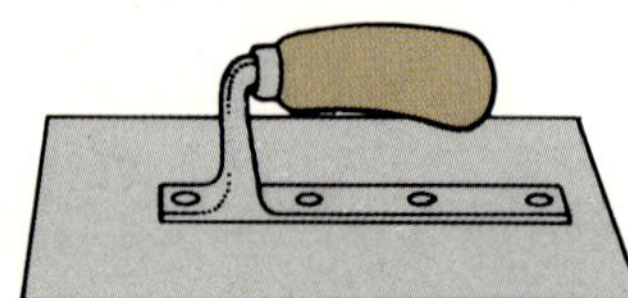

Bricklayer's trowel
Also for working in concrete.

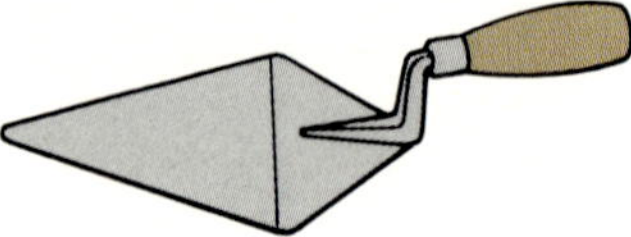

Pointing trowel
For exterior maintenance.

Club hammer
Used with cold and bolster chisels.

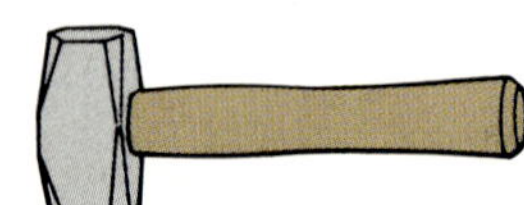

Cold chisel
For cutting rusted bolts, etc.

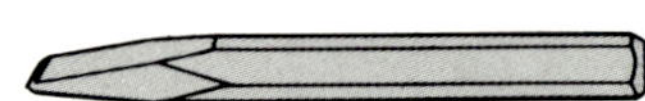

Wire strippers
For removing insulation from cable.

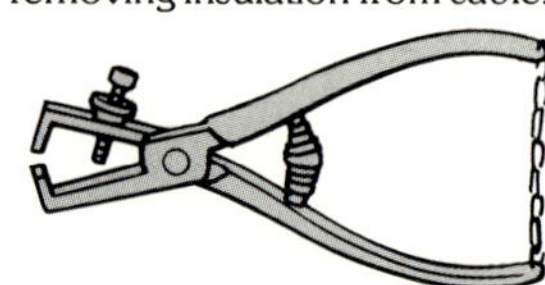

Snips
For cutting sheet metal.

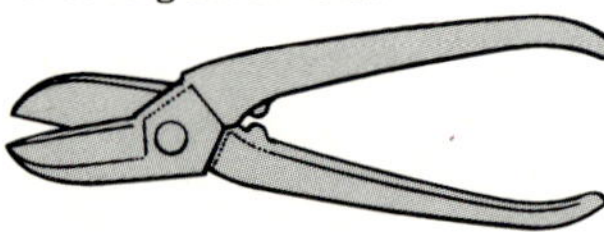

Spiral-ratchet screwdriver
Drives in screws by pumping the handle.

Crowbar or jemmy
Useful for levering.

Continuity tester
For testing circuits.

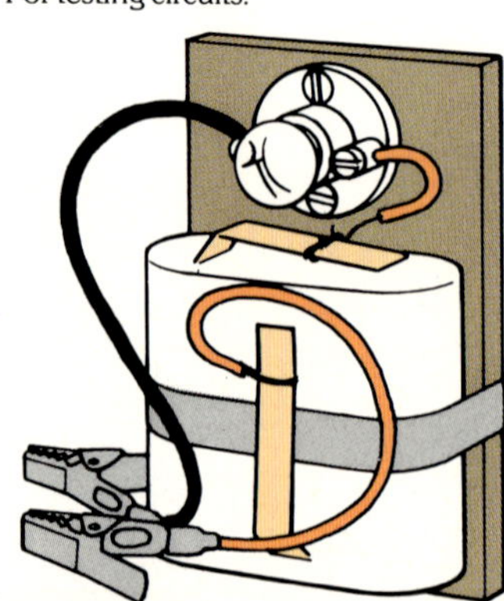

Try square
For measuring right angles.

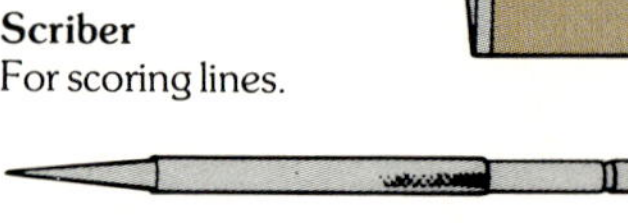

Scriber
For scoring lines.

Dividers
For scribing circles.

Countersinker
For cutting a hole for countersunk screw's heads.

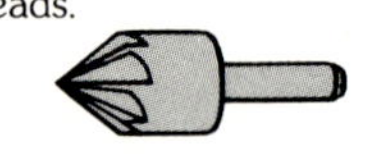

Multimeter
Measures all sorts of electrical quantities.

POWER DRILLS

Electrical drills take much of the labour out of some d-i-y tasks. However, they are bulky and cannot be used everywhere because of power limitations. Two-speed or variable drills are usually worth the extra cost because of the added flexibility. Some drills have a 'hammer' action for drilling concrete or bricks. Most drills will take attachments to perform specific tasks. Before buying a drill, you should consider carefully what you want it for and what you may want to do with it in the future. Consult the WHICH? reports for comparisons of price, versatility and attachments.

Using and maintaining an electric drill is mostly common sense. Obviously keep the cable well out of the way when using the drill, particularly with a circular saw attachment. Make sure you use a fused three-pin plug with it always. Have the drill serviced regularly and don't expect it to perform above specification – if you do, it will burn out.

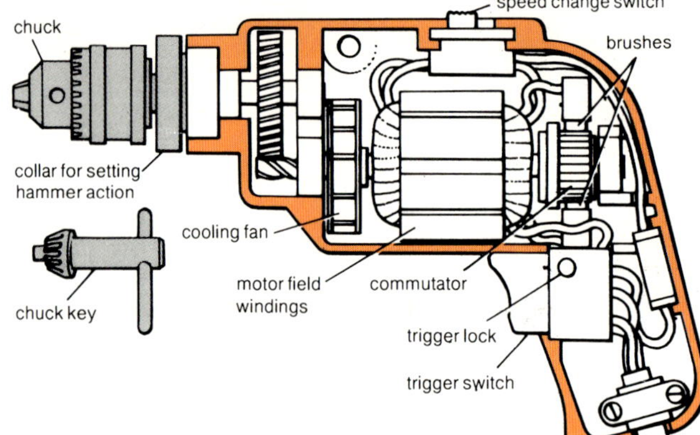

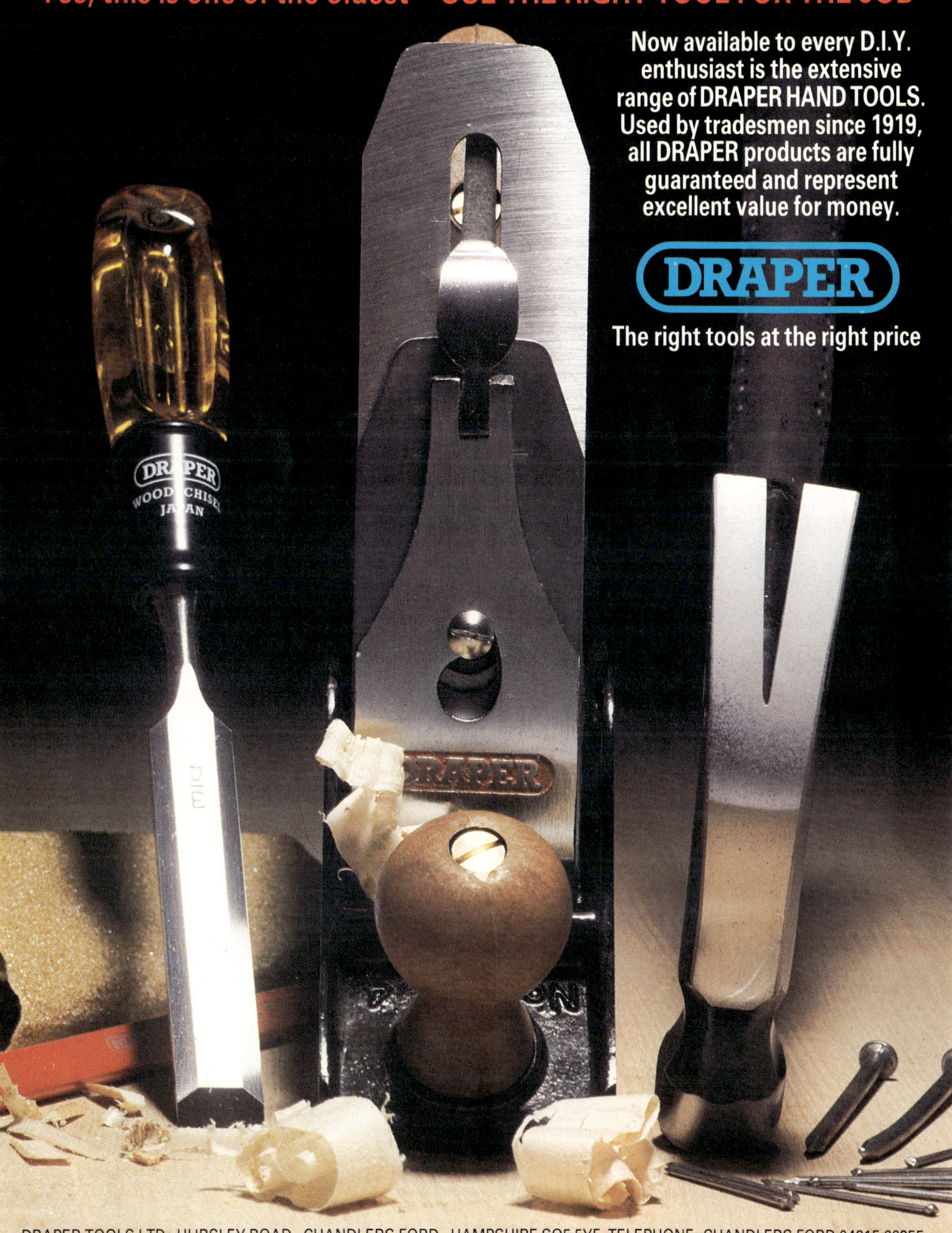
Tricks of the Trade?
Yes, this is one of the oldest - 'USE THE RIGHT TOOL FOR THE JOB'
Now available to every D.I.Y. enthusiast is the extensive range of DRAPER HAND TOOLS. Used by tradesmen since 1919, all DRAPER products are fully guaranteed and represent excellent value for money.
DRAPER
The right tools at the right price
DRAPER TOOLS LTD · HURSLEY ROAD · CHANDLERS FORD · HAMPSHIRE SO5 5YF. TELEPHONE: CHANDLERS FORD 04215 66355

BASIC TECHNIQUES

RAISING FLOORBOARDS

Various methods are used for getting rid of the tongues. Tradesmen have a special floorboard saw, but it simply isn't worth buying this tool.

It is simpler merely to chop off the tongues with a chisel. Push the blade of a bolster chisel down the gap between the boards, and strike its handle with a mallet or hammer, repeating this process along the board until you have got rid of the whole tongue.

If you have a portable circular saw, you can push the blade down the edge of the board. Switch on the motor, run the tool along the board, and it will cut off the tongue.

Take care to set its depth of cut so that the blade only just protrudes on the lower side of the tongue (not the board), which will probably be about 20mm (¾in.) below the face of the board. The teeth will then strike the timber at the best angle for cutting, and reduce the strain on the motor. It is doubly important to make this correct setting when you are working on floorboards, because the saw's blade might cut into the joists and weaken them, or strike nails, cable or plumbing pipes that may be below.

You cannot use a power jig saw precisely because you cannot adjust the depth of cut.

Whichever method you use, there is always the danger that you might strike and cut into a cable with a metal tool in your hand. Therefore it is a good idea to shut off any circuits below the floor before you begin. Plug your extension cable into a socket on another circuit.

With the tongues off you can now proceed to lift the boards. It is the same method for both sorts of boards.

HALF BOARDS

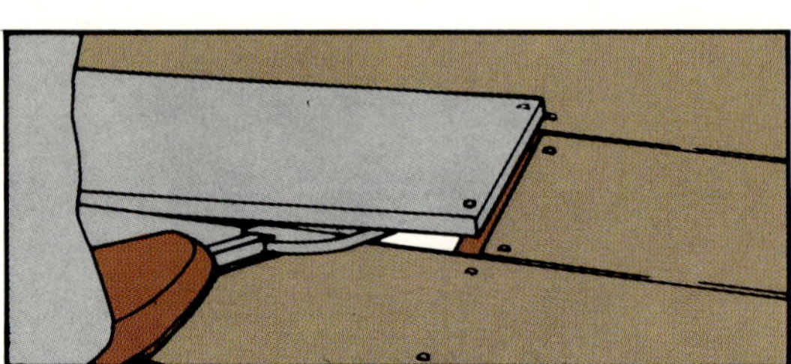

Floors are made up from random lengths of floorboard, and often it takes two or more lengths to span a room. Look for a join where two lengths of board meet and work from there. Take a bolster chisel and push it down one edge of, and slightly under, the board, near the join. Then lever. You will get better leverage if you press down hard on the handle of the chisel with your foot. Now push a chisel down the opposite edge of the board, and repeat.

It is better if you can use a second bolster chisel for this, leaving the first one in place. If not, take out the chisel from the first side, replace it with an ordinary woodworking one, and use the bolster on the opposite side.

Now push a long, thin cold chisel, or even a stout screwdriver, flat under the raised end of the board. Press down with your foot on the end of the board that is flapping free, at the same time prising up the board with the bolster chisel where it is nailed at the next joist.

You should now be able to lift up the end of the board with your hands, and push the cold chisel further along, working progressively towards the end of the board, wrenching up nails as you go, or leaving them in the joist. If the end of the board is trapped under the skirting board, wriggle it free.

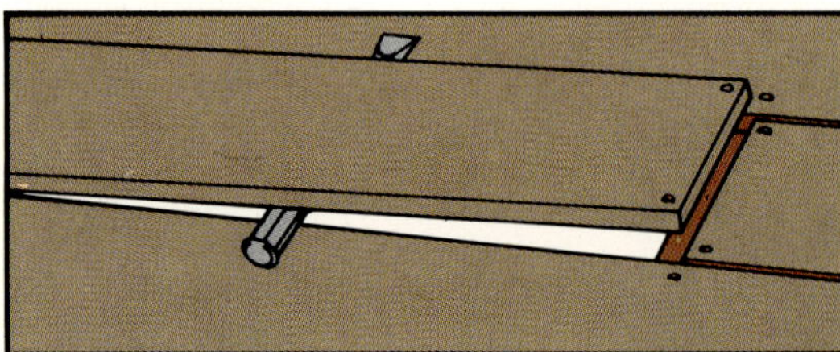

COMPLETE BOARDS

If the board you want to raise is a complete one, stretching across the whole room without a join in the middle, you will have to make a cut across its width to free it, because it will be trapped under the skirting board at each end.

Choose the point where you want to make the cut. Using a heavy hammer and stout nail punch, drive home the fixing nails at this point right through the board and into the joist below. Treat the nails on the joist on each side in exactly the same way. Now, using a chisel on each side, you can raise the board slightly over the middle of the three joists, and keep it raised by jamming an old chisel under it. This is known as 'springing a board'.

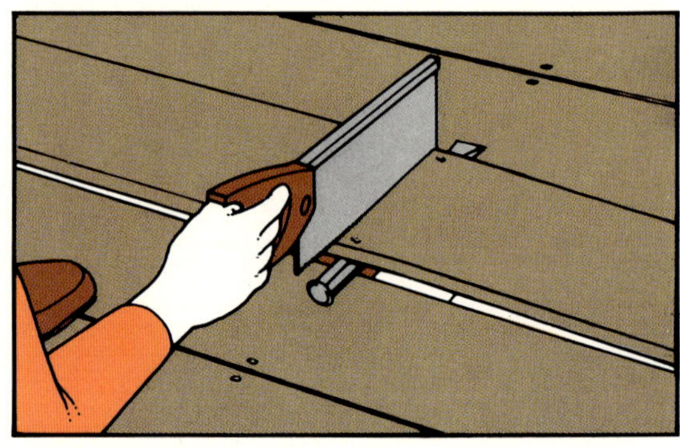

You can then saw through the board with an ordinary tenon saw, making your cut coincide with the middle of the joist. Then raise the board as above.

Why not punch all the nails right through? Then you could just pick up the board and lift it clear. If you drive nails through into the joist, you risk hitting cable or plumbing pipes, or damaging the ceiling below, therefore, this is something that you should not do.

Sometimes it simply is not practicable to spring a board because the length of board you want to raise is too short, or because it is too close to a wall. In that case make your cut across the board with a thin-bladed saw, such as a jigsaw or padsaw. Unless there is a gap between the boards, you will have to drill a starting hole, just large enough for the blade of the saw. The blade should be at an angle so that the board is cut immediately to the side of the joist at the bottom, but in the middle of it at the top. Take care that you do not cut into any pipes or cable below.

LATER PARTITION WALLS

Sometimes a board will pass right under a wall, because partition walls (see page 32) have been built after the floorboards have been laid.

To raise this kind of board, make a cross cut 100mm (4in.) from the partition, once more using a thin-bladed saw, and once again cutting at an angle sloping towards the partition. Then lift the board. A sort of deadman will be needed when you come to refix this board (see page 26).

If you need to raise a board on the other side of the partition, try not to make it the same board, but tackle the one next to it instead.

DROPPING A PLUMBLINE

Purpose-built plumblines and bobs are available but this is one item you could improvise by tying a small weight (a nut for instance) onto a length of string. An old typewriter spool is a good thing to keep your makeshift plumbline on, and it helps you to use the line properly.

Hold the spool in the palm of your hand, which you can press hard against the wall, letting the string pass over your thumb, so that the weight can swing freely. Let it do so until it stops swinging – you can steady it by jamming a knee up against it, but don't force it into an 'untrue' position. Make sure your thumb is holding the line on the pencil mark. When the line is steady, make a mark along it on the wall with a pencil held in the other hand.

You must make sure that your pencil line is directly behind the line – many draw on the line's shadow.

SNAPPING CHALK LINES

Take a length of string and rub chalk on it. Draw the string tautly across the course you want the line to take, by securing it at one end while you hold the other end firmly. Alternatively you can get a helper to hold one end. Now draw the string back, rather like a bow string, and let it go with a twang. It will mark a straight chalk line on the floor.

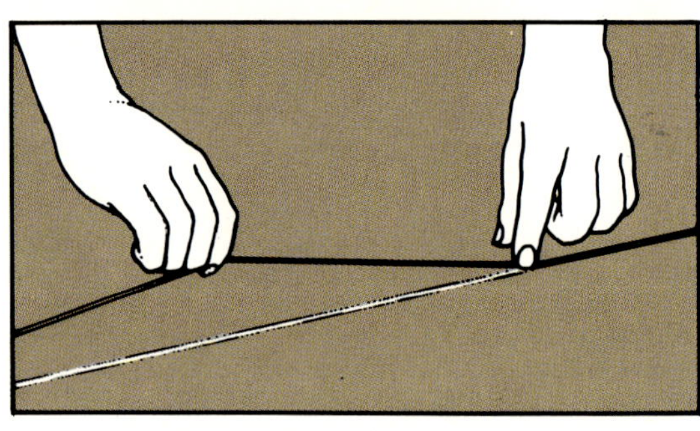

DO IT YOURSELF

FJ 50V

Jig Saw Variable Speed

Specifications

Capacity: Wood – 50mm, Steel – 3mm.
Power Input: 350W. No-Load Stroke: 0-3000.
Weight: 1.7kg.

FC 5

150mm Circular Saw

Specifications

Capacity: 0-45mm. Max. depth of cut at 90° bevel: 30mm. (45 degrees). Power Input: 710W. No-Load Speed: 4400 rpm. Weight: 2.9kg.
Other Specifications: Saw blade diameter 150mm. Blade hole diameter 20 mm. Cutting angle 0-45 degrees.

FV 12V

Impact Drill Variable Speed (Reversible)

Specifications

Capacity: Steel – 10mm, Concrete – 12mm, Wood – 25mm.
Power Input: 420W. No-Load Speed: 0-2600/min.
Impact Rate: 41600/min. Weight: 1.7kg.

FS 10

Orbital Sander

Specifications

Capacity: 92 x 184mm. Power Input: 180W.
No-Load Speed: 10000/min. Weight: 1.7kg.

INDUSTRIAL

FU-20

Planer (Rabbeting to 25mm)

Specifications

Capacity: Cutting Width 82mm. Max. Cutting Depth 3mm.
Power Input: 620W. No-Load Speed: 14,000/min.
Weight: 2.8kg.

TR-8

Router

Specifications

Capacity: Collet Chuck ¼".
Power Input: 730W. No-Load Speed: 24,000/min.
Weight: 2.9kg.

JHT-60A

Jigsaw (2 Speed)

Specifications

Capacity: Wood 60mm, 50mm with Guide Roller.
Mild Steel Plate 6mm. Min. Cutting Radius 25mm.
Power Input: 380W. No-Load Speed: 3,200/2,700/min.
Stroke: 26mm. Weight: 2.1kg.

CJ 65VA

Orbital Action Jigsaw

Specifications

Capacity: Max. Cutting Depth – Wood 65mm, Steel 6mm.
Power Input: 400W. No-Load Speed: 700-3200/min.
Stroke: 26mm. Weight: 2.4kg.

EMERGENCIES 1

Please note: This is not a complete First Aid guide and does not cover all the accidents which may occur in the home. What it does aim to cover are the accidents most likely to occur during d-i-y.

Every home should have a fully stocked First Aid Box and at least two people who know how to use it. Any materials used from the First Aid Box should be replaced as soon as possible. All serious injuries must be seen by a doctor or hospital.

Regular courses in all aspects of First Aid are run by your local branch of the British Red Cross Society, the St John Ambulance or St Andrew's Ambulance Association (look in your local Telephone Directory). You will feel far more confident of treating serious injuries correctly and effectively if you have taken a proper course on this subject. The victim will also have a better chance of survival.

First Aid is as much about common sense (i.e. what not to do), as what to do.

The six basic **don'ts** are:

1. **Don't panic** – at first look things may seem far worse than they actually are!
2. **Don't** move anyone whom you suspect has a broken limb. **Never** move someone whose spine may be injured.
3. **Don't** leave an unconscious person on his/her back (unless you suspect a fracture). **Don't** leave them alone unless it's the only way you can call for help.
4. **Don't** use a tourniquet to control bleeding – it's too dangerous.
5. **Don't** give alcohol in any form.
6. **Don't** give food or fluids to an unconscious or drowsy person (they may choke) or to a person who is likely to need an anaesthetic.

FALLS

The most common injury in d-i-y is either from falling off something or by dropping something on someone else.

UNCONSCIOUSNESS

1. Check if the person is breathing; if not apply artificial respiration at once (see Electrical Accidents: page 23). **Don't** move them if you suspect a broken back/neck (see Broken Spine or Neck).
2. If he/she is breathing with difficulty clear the airway by turning the person on his/her back, lying the head to one side and removing the blockage (false teeth, vomit, etc) with your finger.

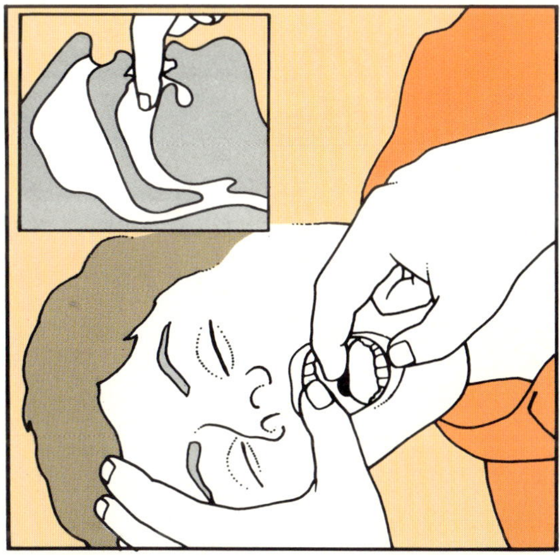

3. Call for medical aid immediately.
4. Check for bleeding and other injuries, such as broken limbs (see below). Loosen any tight clothing, particularly at neck and waist. Treat injuries.
5. Turn the person into the Recovery Position by laying the arms along-side the body and crossing the further ankle over the nearer. Place one hand under the person's head to cushion it and pull the person's further hip towards you with your other hand, resting the body on your knees as it comes over.
6. Grasp the person under the jaw and extend the chin up and backwards to maintain a clear airway. Arrange arms and legs as shown to make the letter 'K'. **Don't** leave him/her alone.

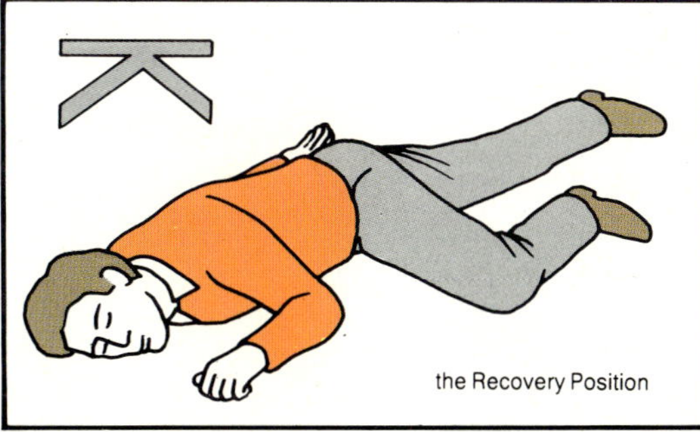

the Recovery Position

BROKEN SPINE OR NECK

The most dangerous break is in the neck or back (spine) because moving a person with such an injury can cause paralysis or death. Such injured persons should only be moved if they are in danger (i.e. from fire, gas, etc). The warning signs of a broken neck/spine are:

1. Loss of feeling and movement below the injured area;
2. Pain at the site of injury;
3. Tingling sensation in hands or feet;
4. Inability to move hands or feet, but no sign of a broken arm or leg;
5. No pain when the skin is gently pinched; and
6. Difficulty in breathing.

If any, or all, these symptoms are present you should:

1. Tell the person to lie still and cover him/her with a blanket. **Don't** try to raise his/her head or rest it on anything.
2. Get trained medical help immediately and reassure the person as much as possible.
3. If the person is unconscious, clear the mouth if accessible (see Unconsciousness).

BROKEN BONES

There are various types of broken bones but all require medical attention. Often the injured person will have heard the bone break, but other symptoms are:

1. The person cannot move the injured part and feels pain when he/she tries.
2. The area around the break is swollen, bruised or tender to the touch.
3. The limb may be deformed or in an unnatural position when compared to the other limb.

(The last two symptoms are most valuable when the person is unconscious.) If you are not sure about the injury, always assume it is broken and treat as follows:

1. If the person is unconscious, treat as above first.
2. Make the person comfortable while moving the injured part as little as possible.
3. If he/she is bleeding, treat as for Cuts (below). The most urgent task is to **stop any bleeding** – people die from blood loss, not from broken legs!
4. Send for an ambulance. **Don't** try to transport the victim yourself.

HEAD INJURIES

A bleeding face or head usually looks far worse than it actually is; the two things to check for are a fracture and foreign matter in the wound.

1. Gently feel the skull around the wound. If part of it seems to move, suspect a fracture and do not press on it. Otherwise, place a clean pad over the wound to stop the bleeding. Press down gently but firmly.
2. Cover the wound with a clean dressing. If there is foreign matter present, or you suspect a fracture, cover the area with a ring pad (see diagram) and then tie a bandage over the top to hold it in place like a pirate's headscarf.

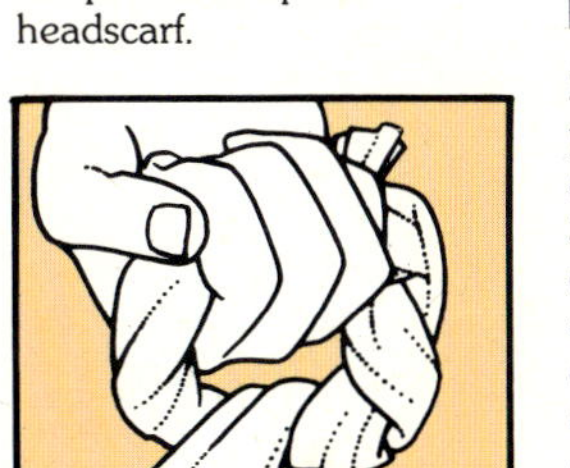

CUTS

Although a bad cut may require stitching, the two important things to consider are:

1. A puncture or stab wound can be much deeper than its surface size would warrant; and
2. Was the object that caused the wound rusty or dirty? In that case, an injection against tetanus is necessary.

The way to treat a cut is as follows:

1. **Stop the bleeding.** Apply immediate pressure with a pad of clean (if available) cloth or with the palm of your hand. Press on the wound if there is no foreign matter in it; around the edges if there is. Raise the limb if not broken.

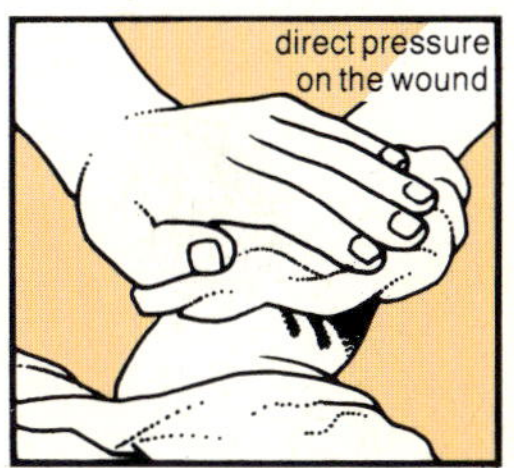

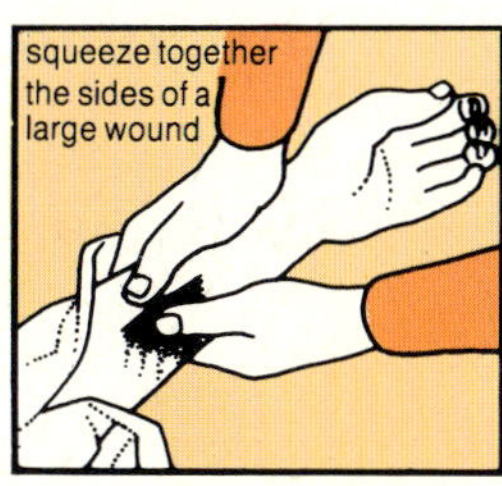

2. When bleeding stops (anything up to 15 minutes), take pad away and remove any foreign bodies that will come easily.
3. For small wounds, gently wipe the wound outwards with clean swabs soaked in warm soapy water. Use a clean swab each time. Dry around the wound with a clean swab and cover with a bandage or plaster.
4. If there is foreign matter in the wound, cover the area with clean lint, apply a ring pad (see Head Injuries) and get the person to medical attention.

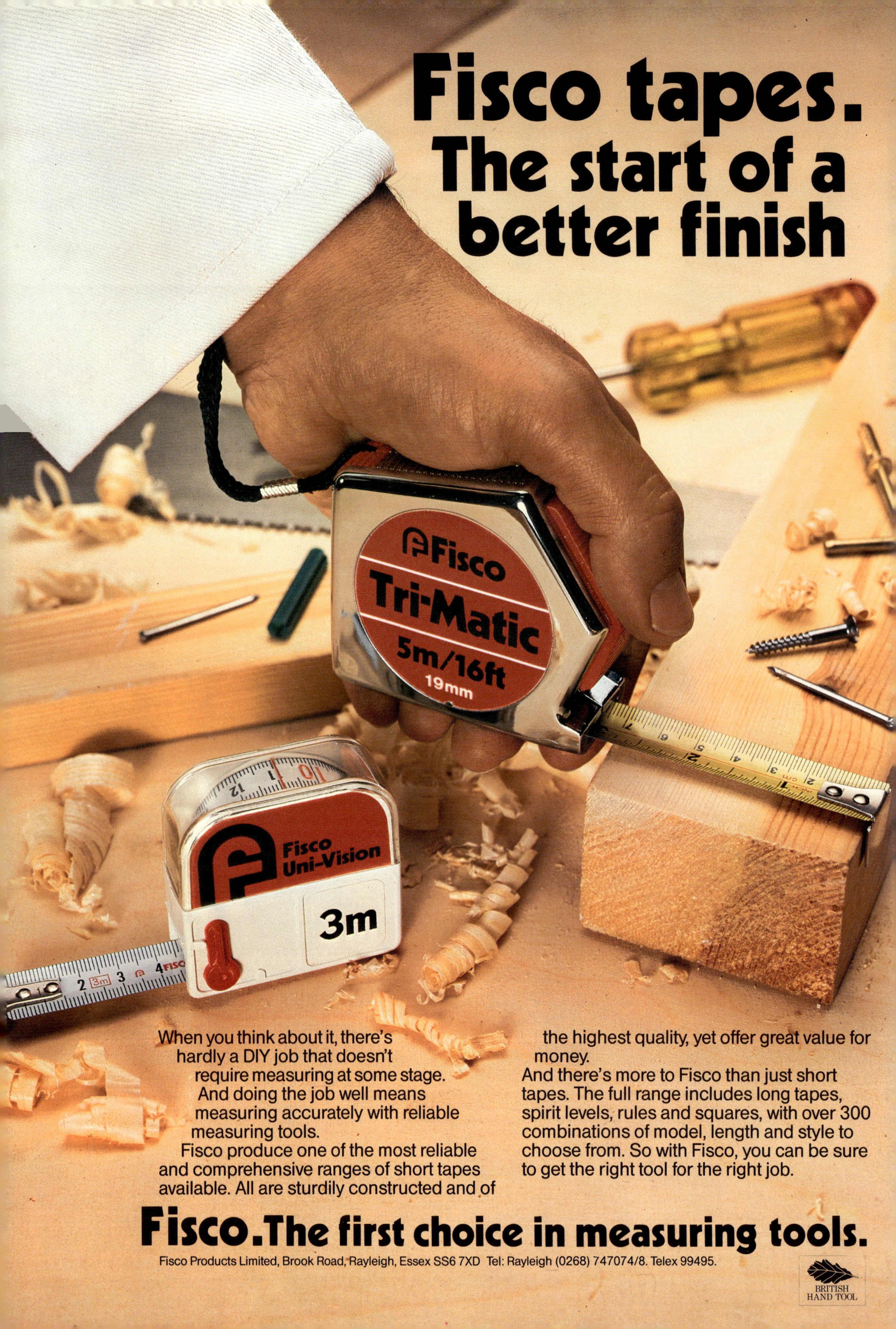
Fisco tapes.
The start of a better finish
Fisco
Tri-Matic
5m/16ft
19mm
Fisco
Uni-Vision
3m
When you think about it, there's hardly a DIY job that doesn't require measuring at some stage. And doing the job well means measuring accurately with reliable measuring tools.
Fisco produce one of the most reliable and comprehensive ranges of short tapes available. All are sturdily constructed and of the highest quality, yet offer great value for money.
And there's more to Fisco than just short tapes. The full range includes long tapes, spirit levels, rules and squares, with over 300 combinations of model, length and style to choose from. So with Fisco, you can be sure to get the right tool for the right job.
Fisco. The first choice in measuring tools.
Fisco Products Limited, Brook Road, Rayleigh, Essex SS6 7XD Tel: Rayleigh (0268) 747074/8. Telex 99495.
BRITISH HAND TOOL

EMERGENCIES 2

ELECTRICAL SHOCK

You must switch off the power before anything else! **Don't** touch the person until then. If you cannot disconnect the electricity, push or pull the person away from the source using a wooden chair or stick, or a thickly folded non-synthetic cloth. If possible, stand on a dry rubber mat. If the clothes are burning, smother the flames with a non-synthetic blanket: **don't** use water.

ARTIFICIAL RESPIRATION

Check breathing and the heart (see below: Chest Compression). If not breathing, this is what you do:
1. Put the person face up with his/her head to one side. Clear any vomit, etc out of the mouth with a finger.
2. Straighten his/her head and tilt upwards and backwards so that the crown of the head is on the ground, with one hand on the forehead and the other under the neck.
3. Raise the person's chin. Take a deep breath. Seal your lips around the mouth, pinching the nostrils shut with your fingers. Breathe into him/her.
4. Remove your mouth and watch his/her chest fall. Repeat four times quickly; then 16 to 18 times per minute (every three seconds).
5. If the person vomits, turn the head to one side and clear as before. Continue as above.

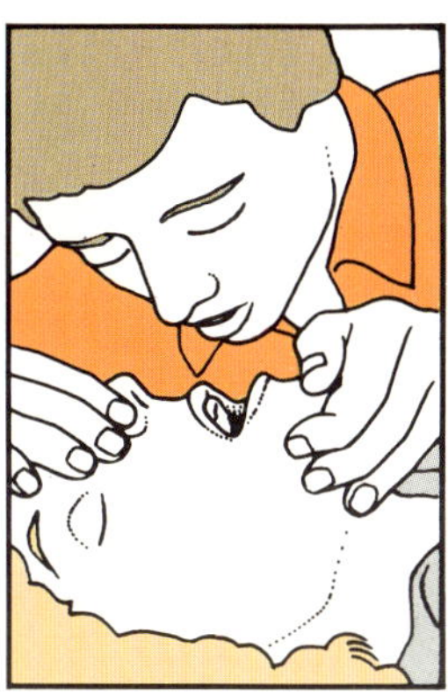

CHEST COMPRESSION

To check the heart, feel for the carotid artery (see diagram). Place three fingers on it and, pressing slightly, time the beats (about 70 per minute is normal). If you cannot feel anything, the heart has stopped. Take your time in feeling for it.

If the heart has stopped, give the first four inflations as above, then:
1. Make sure the person is on a hard surface and find the breastbone. Measure three finger's width up from its base.
2. Place the heel of one hand on this spot, thumb and fingers raised. Place the heel of your other hand on top and press down hard with straight arms so that the chest depresses 40mm (1½in.). Let the chest rise.
3. Give 15 presses, then reflate the lungs twice (see above). Repeat.
4. Check the carotid pulse after one minute. If you can feel it and the complexion is returning from blue-grey to normal, stop the compressions; otherwise you may stop the heart again.
5. For children under 10, the breastbone should be depressed 25–40mm (1–1½in.) using only one hand. For a young baby, use two fingers in the middle of the breastbone and only depress the chest 10–20mm (½–¾in.). For children you should do the depressions slightly faster, about one every ¾ of a second.

path of carotid artery

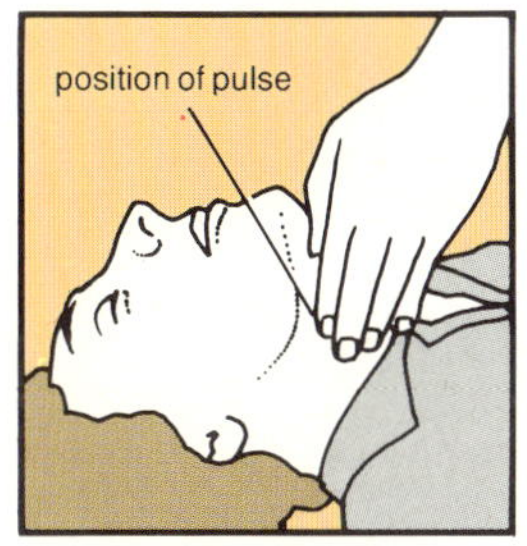

position of pulse

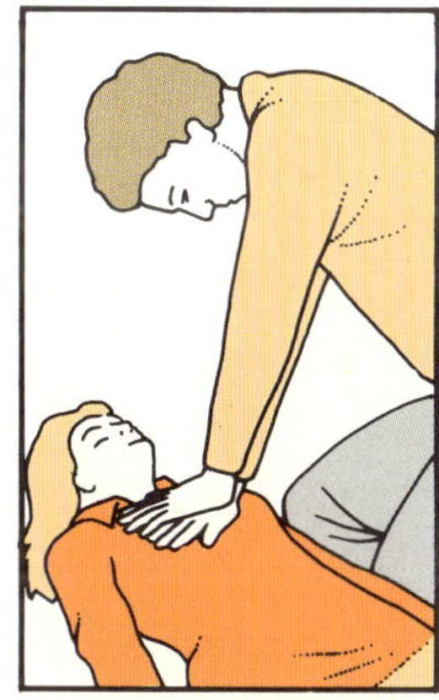

SHOCK

This is brought on by the reduction of the blood supply to the body's vital organs, following severe injuries. It is not the same as the emotional fear which comes on immediately after an injury or other unpleasant experience and from which the sufferer may recover quickly. The symptoms are:
1. Grey or pallid skin which feels damp and cold; and
2. Fast shallow breathing and a thin pulse (see right: Chest Compression).

Followed by:
3. Dizziness or fainting and blurred vision;
4. Nausea or vomiting;
5. Anxiety and restlessness, sometimes progressing to unconsciousness.

What you should do is:
1. Lay the person down and treat any injury or underlying condition which may be causing the shock. Comfort and reassure the person as you do this.
2. Loosen clothing at neck, chest and waist. Then cover the person with one blanket, or a coat. Raise (uninjured) legs slightly to return blood to the brain. Get medical aid as soon as you can, but **don't** leave the person alone.
3. If he/she is thirsty, wet his/her lips with water but **don't** give them a drink. Keep on reassuring them.
   Only give them hot sweet tea if you are sure it is emotional fear.
4. If the person becomes unconscious, turn into the Recovery Position (see page 21) unless you suspect a spine/neck injury.

GASSING

Caused by gas leaks, accidents with gas cylinders, fires involving foam furniture and from car exhausts.
The treatment is always:
1. Remove the person from the cause of the injury but **don't** risk becoming a casualty yourself. Ideally call for help before trying to rescue someone. If possible, turn off the source before entering the room, garage, etc.
2. Tie a rope around your waist so that you can be rescued if overcome. Go straight to the victim. **Don't** try to open a window; you may collapse before you get the victim out.
3. Pass your arms under the victim's armpits and grasp your wrist with your other hand. Drag the victim into the open air.
4. Place your ear close to his/her nose and mouth to check his/her breathing and observe the rise and fall of his/her chest. If the person is not breathing, apply artificial respiration (as above).
5. If he/she is breathing, turn him/her into the Recovery Position (see page 21). Continue to check the breathing regularly until help arrives.

BURNS AND SCALDS

Burns are caused by dry heat (i.e. fire), electricity or chemicals. Scalds are caused by wet heat; the treatment is the same. If the clothing is on fire; wrap a non-synthetic blanket or coat round him/her and lie them on the floor. **Don't** roll them on the floor or let them run about.

MINOR BURNS

1. Cool the injured part in cold water for at least 10 minutes, but not in a cold bath! **Don't** apply butter, creams or antiseptics. **Don't** prick any blisters.
2. Cover the burnt area with a clean dry dressing or towel and bandage it on lightly.
3. If in doubt about the damage, call a doctor or ambulance. You may have to treat the person for shock (see left).

MAJOR BURNS

1. Remove any rings, belts, and loosen tight clothing. In scalds, only remove wet clothing.
2. Cover the burned area with a dressing as for Minor Burns.
3. Give the person some water to replace lost fluids: adults should take about half a cup of water over 10 minutes; children should sip water continuously. **Don't** do this if the person becomes unconscious (see page 21).
4. Make the person lie down and treat for shock if necessary (see above). Get qualified medical aid as soon as possible.
5. A scalded mouth may swell and obstruct the airway. If the person is conscious, give him/her an ice-cube to suck.

CHEMICAL BURNS

1. If caused by a dry chemical, brush as much as possible away with a duster. **Don't** get any on yourself! Make sure the person is not lying on any of the chemical.
2. If a wet substance (e.g. ammonia, bleach, etc), wash it away with lots of water for at least 10 minutes. Take off any contaminated clothing, then treat as above. **Don't** try to neutralise the burn with another chemical.
3. For chemicals in the eye, use a gentle stream of water to flush out the cause. Turn the person so that the other eye does not get wet. Cover with a dry dressing, then a ring pad (see page 21) and bandage in place gently.
4. Get the person to hospital as quickly as possible.

CARPENTRY

FLOORS

GROUND FLOORS

Ground floors, normally of planed, square-edged boards (PAR – planed all round), are supported on, and nailed to, floor joists. These are heavy section construction timbers able to span reasonable widths and carry loads.

These joists are built-in on edge, and may be as deep as 175mm (7in.) or as shallow as 100mm (4in.). Their thickness will vary too, from 65mm (2½in.) to 75mm (3in.). The older the house, the more timber you can usually cut away. The spacing of the joists depends on the type of floorboarding, and is easily seen from the line of nail heads across the floor.

Nails must be kept to the edges of the boards if you are nailing down loose boards, as the previous owner may have notched the joist top edges to take cable runs, gas or central heating pipes.

The direction of the joist run is always across the board run, so if one board is taken up all the joists are revealed. Pipes or cables are easily threaded between joists, or below them on ground floors, but should be supported by nails or brackets.

Notching joists is not an ideal solution, but it is a common heating installation method. Notches must be as small as possible and kept central to the board run.

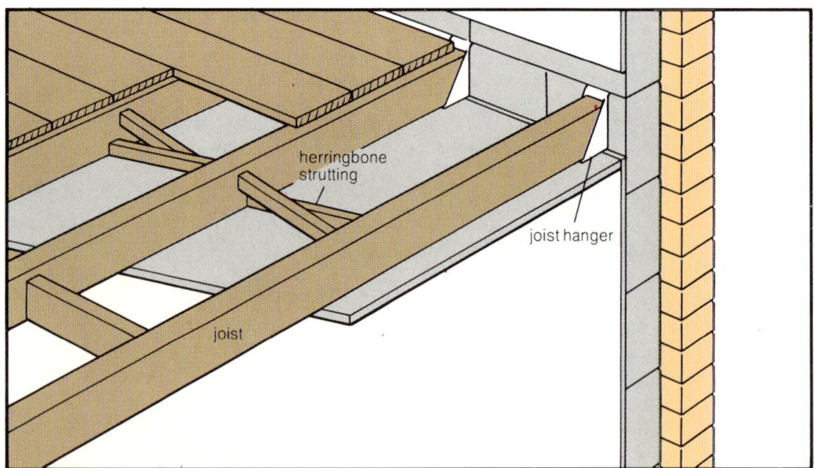

FIRST FLOORS

These are suspended floors. The joists are kept as short as possible and are deeper in section than are ground floor joists. Between them, to keep them stiff and steady, there may be herringbone struts. First floor joists may be supported on built-in metal hangers or on projecting bricks. The joist nearest the wall will always have a small gap between it and the wall.

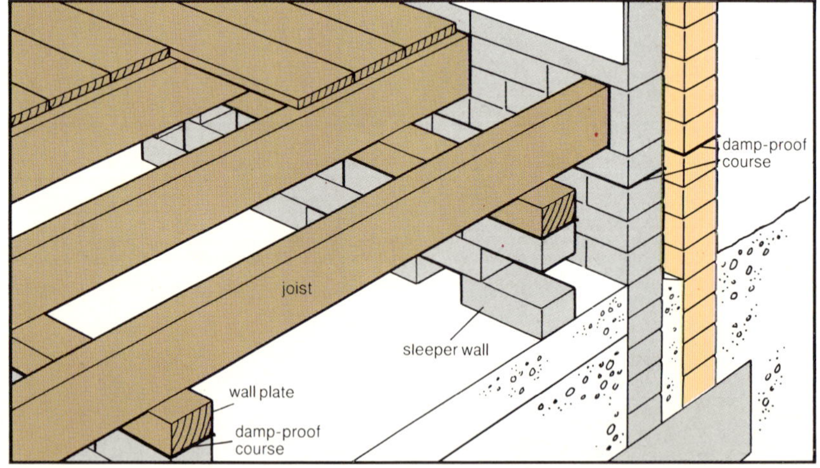

TOP FLOOR TO ROOF

Ceiling joists carry the ceiling. They are supported on wall plates at their ends and on load-bearing interior walls between the ends. The roof rafters, which are the angled pieces from the ridge, are nailed – or bolted in trussed rools – to the ends of the ceiling joists. Rafters are stiffened by horizontal purlins, which may be supported by individual struts.

FLOORBOARDS

Traditional board floors are easily worked on and repaired. They have three main drawbacks. They shrink, leaving gaps; they curl, making ridges; and their nails have a habit of standing proud as the boards themselves shrink. Some modern floors have joist support but are covered with flooring-grade chipboard.

Ideally the whole sheet should be raised when working on a chipboard floor. The joist spacing is wider, and if the sheet is reduced in size to gain access to the under-floor area, its overall strength is lost. If you have to cut through a chipboard floor, heavily batten the edges when re-laying it, screwing it down from above.

Two kinds of floorboard are used in British homes: tongued and grooved (often shortened to T and G) and square-edged. Tongued and grooved boards have a thin tongue of wood along one edge, and a matching groove along the other. When the boards are laid, the tongue of one locates in the groove of its neighbour, to form a seal designed to stop draughts and dirt coming up through any gaps that develop between the boards owing to shrinkage. For each board you need to remove two tongues before you can take up the boards – its own and that of the neighbouring one slotted into its groove.

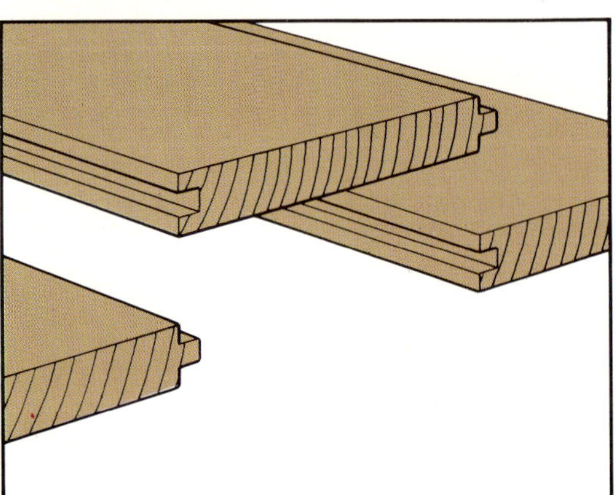

You will soon recognize the signs of a board that has been lifted before. The types of nails and patterns of nailing in a raised board may well be different. Look for short lengths of board that have been cut across their width; or if a tongue is missing from one board in a floor where all the others are tongued and grooved. If you spot a short length of board held down with screws instead of nails, that is a pretty good sign that a professional electrical job has been done below the board at some time.

A board that has been lifted once is much easier to take up a second time. If lifting such a board will suit your plans you can save yourself a lot of hard work.

STEEL TONGUED BOARDS

At one period in Victorian building, floorboards with steel tongues were used. A groove was cut in the edge of the board, and a strip of steel inserted. Such boards are a nightmare. You can cut through the steel with a hacksaw, or even perhaps an electrically-powered cutting disc, but it is a laborious job. Fortunately, steel tongues are very rare, but if you come across them it is better to forget about lifting the boards, and look for a different method.

REFIXING FLOORBOARDS

When you come to refix a board that has been raised, the usual method is to nail it back in position, using floorboard nails. On important parts of electrical wiring however, it is a good idea to fix back a short length of board with screws. This is known as a trap, and can easily be taken up if maintenance work is needed later.

When you come to refix a board cut between joists, you must use a 'deadman'. This is a short batten of timber about twice as long as the width of the board. Screw this deadman to the side of the joist. When you put the raised board back, nail it to the deadman. If you hold it hard up against the underside of nearby boards while screwing, you can be sure your replaced board will be level with the rest of the floor.

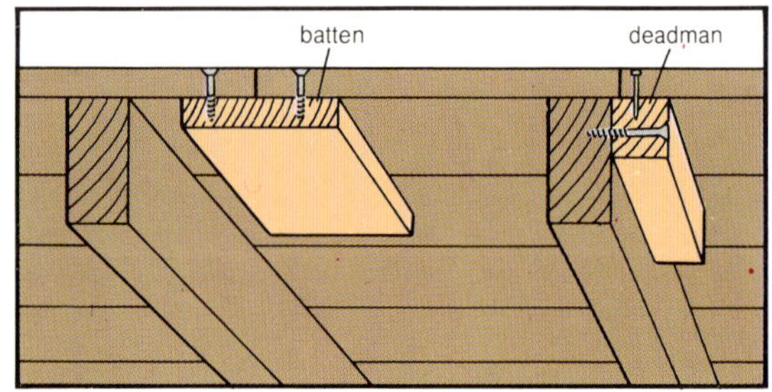

TRAPS AND SKIRTINGS

LEVELLING FLOORBOARDS

Punch in nail heads and use a coarse-set jack plane diagonally across ridged boards. If the floor is very bad, a hired sander may be the answer; but they make an enormous amount of dust. To smooth a very bad floor, lay oil-tempered hardboard, smooth side down, fully across the floor and carefully nail it at the edges. Offset each row so that you do not get a groove right across the room.

THE TRICK

Slightly dampen the underside of each board. This helps it to lie flat.

Gaps between boards may be filled with wedge-section slivers cut by an electric saw from the edges of spare boards.

FLOOR TRAPS

A floor trap should span just two joists. Usually they are positioned over the lighting cable junction for the room below, or close to the skirting for access to power cable runs under the wall or up into a box.

The two ends of the trap lid are cut centre-to-centre to two joists, and both end-on boards are cut to meet the ends of this piece. The board ends should be nailed down, but the trap screwed. If this arrangement is impossible because it is too close to a wall, use a 'deadman' (see page 26). Then screw down the trap lid.

Older homes may have a large area under the ground floor. If you can lower yourself down into it, you will be able to carry out work there without having to raise a lot of floorboards.

The way to reach this void is to take up three or four adjacent boards and create for yourself what is known as a man-access trap. Site this trap at a point where people are not likely to walk much, inside a cupboard, if this is possible. See Ceiling Traps (below) for details.

SKIRTINGS

Skirtings are fitted after plastering and are nailed to 'soldiers', which are pieces of batten of plaster thickness that have been nailed to the wall below the plaster line. These should be checked and replaced if necessary.

The new piece of skirting should be scribed to the floor line.

Raise the skirting piece on two blocks of about 10mm (½in.) thickness. Then measure the maximum height from the floor to the lower edge of the skirting. Scribing is usually done with sharp-pointed dividers: run one point on the floor and the other along the skirting to mark it.

THE TRICK

An easier way, for a one-off job, is to measure the height of the maximum gap as before and then to knock a nail into a suitable block of wood at a distance from its face equal to the measured amount. File the nail to a sharp point and use this to run along the lower edge of the skirting.

Skirtings may be nailed to the soldiers or fixed with masonry nails directly into the wall. To prevent 'bounce' when nailing, the boards must be held firmly. A short piece of floorboard is used for this; rest it on the floor and on the top edge of the skirting and put one foot on it to apply pressure.

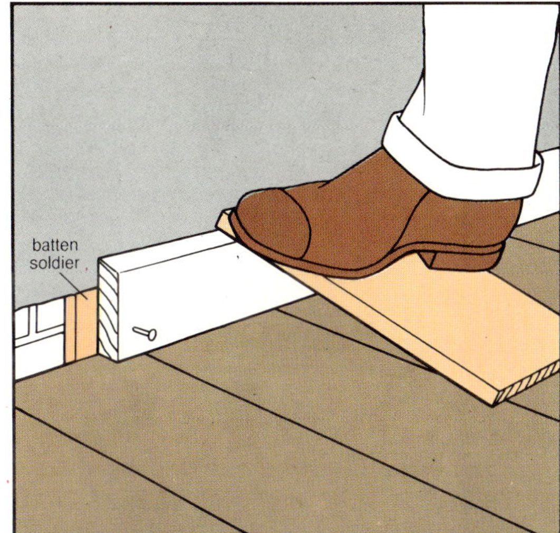

THE TRICK

To hold a bowed board back, use a strong chisel driven into a floorboard with the bevelled edge towards the skirting. Pressure towards the wall will force the skirting back.

CEILING TRAPS

A trap for roof access is essential and most houses have one. Older houses often have only small traps which can usefully be enlarged.

First inspect the loft floor. When deciding on the position of the new trap or the extension of the old one, check thoroughly that cutting through a rafter will not leave a short end supported at one point only. This may occur if ceiling joists have been run from front to back, or if short lengths have been used that terminate on an intermediate wall. If one of these short pieces is cut it will be left supported at one end only, and if any weight falls on it it will sag eventually. Other points to watch out for are pipe runs, cable runs and headroom for loft ladders.

Remove the door and the planted stops from the existing trap or chop through the ceiling plaster for a new one. Prise off the architrave that covers the joist between the ceiling and the trap frame. Then cut through the existing linings at each corner and lever them away, exposing the sides of the two joists and possibly the ends of another, depending on the trap size.

Traps should, if possible, span a double or even multiple of the joist centre distance, but if this is too wide then sub-joists may be installed. Ideally, traps should be 'trimmed', which means that the joists are jointed to form a framed opening. With alteration work this can be done by notching the trimmers into existing joists.

Cut the trimmers and sub-rafters to length and nail them together on the ground. Most traps are 'spiked' (nailed) with long, heavy nails. Use two 100mm (4in.) or 150mm (6in.) spikes at each joist. Raise the frame so formed into the opening created when selected pieces of the joists and ceiling plaster were cut away. Spike this frame into the original ceiling joists while it is held by wedges.

Line the opening with 150 × 18mm (6 × 11/16in.) PAR board, nailing it into the frame. Do the two long sides first, and then the two end pieces cut between. Use either door-stop sections or architrave mouldings to form a rebate (frame) for the trap. Mitre the corners of these pieces and nail them in with oval nails. Make good the edges of the ceiling, and cover the join with a mitred architrave. Lastly prime and paint the whole.

THE TRICK

Put a hand grip on the top of a lift-out trap for safety. You might get stuck in the loft one day.

FIXING TO WALLS 1

TYPES OF WALL

BRICK

Walls in most houses are of brick, usually the type known as 'commons'. These are fairly hard bricks, and are not intended to show. Walls built with commons are usually rendered with cement mortar, or levelled and plastered. They take plugs very securely. Facing bricks have at least one decorative face, and are therefore not rendered. They are similar in composition to commons.

DRY STUD PARTITIONS

These walls are internal partitions, built of timber studs and faced with plasterboard (see page 32). Correct fixing will enable loads to be carried.

BUILDING-BLOCK

The blocks most likely to be behind the plaster are lightweight aggregate blocks, or the ones called breeze blocks. Aggregate blocks are blue-grey in colour, with a cinder-like feel and appearance; they crumble if hit directly. Modern lightweight aggregate blocks are lighter in colour, finer in finish and more resistant to blows. Both types will take plugs and screws well and have good holding power. Nails, too, will be held reasonably well, providing that they are not too brutally driven in.

Aerated blocks are very uniform light blue/grey in colour. They are reasonably strong and have good holding properties, while being much lighter.

FIXING DEVICES

A product suitable for reasonably simple loads and applications is the Rawlplug, made of compressed fibre with a screw pilot-hole through the centre. The newer extruded plastic tubes are heavily ridged on the outer side and are claimed to suit several screw gauges. The efficiency of the hole-boring often controls the holding power of these plugs. The plastic tubes are supplied in pieces which are cut to length to suit.

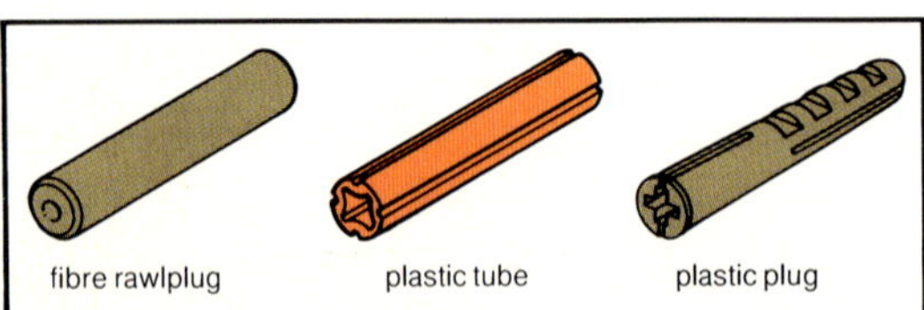

Another type of plastic plug is shaped like an extended cone, ridged and clawed on it outer surface and slightly split in length. These will take several sizes of screw.

Also available is a compound filler material based on cement and asbestos fibre which, when wetted and rolled into shape, is rammed into the hole and used as a plug. It is very effective. Other compound fillers may not use asbestos. Their main use is as a fixing plug where the hole is jagged and irregular.

THE TRICK

An alternative to the compound filler is cotton wool, slightly dampened. Roll it into a sprinkle of powder filler, such as Polyfilla. Ram it into the irregular hole and make an entrance hole with a nail.

All the above types rely on the fact that, as the tapered screw is inserted, it expands the plug material into the hole to create a firm grip and resistance to pull.

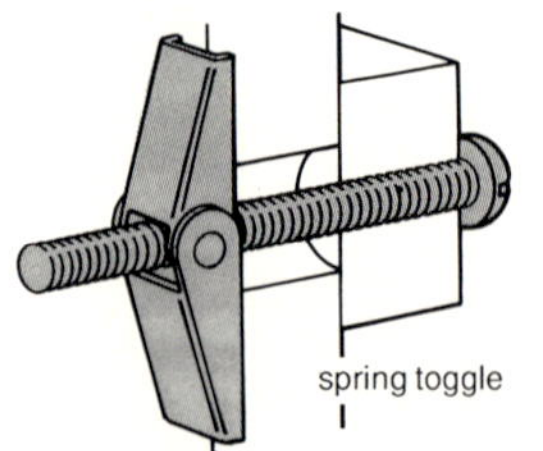

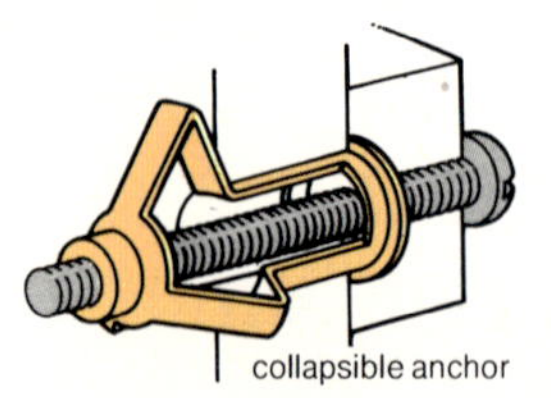

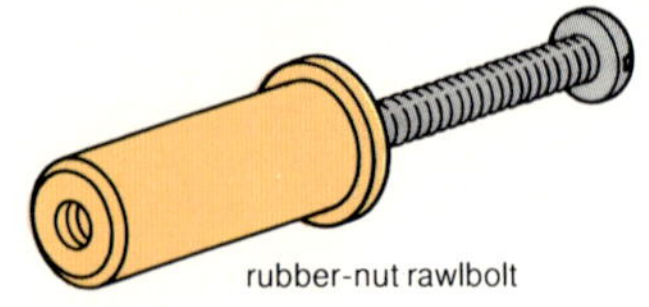

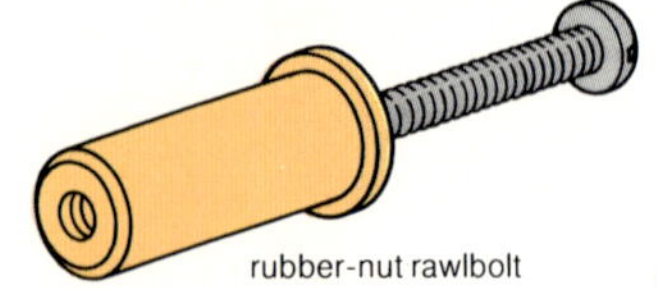

FIXINGS FOR HOLLOW WALLS AND PANELS

Solid-wall plugs rely on expansion to create their grip. If the hole has no depth there can be no grip, so the drill suddenly emerges into space. Any plug pushed into such a hole either gets lost in the cavity or is useless for fixing purposes.

Lath and plaster walls (and ceilings) will carry reasonable loads without plugging if the screws go into the lath and not into the space between the laths.

THE TRICK

Use a thin probe to locate a lath for fixing.

Two types of hollow surface fittings are the gravity toggle and the spring toggle. Neither of these devices is re-usable as each falls into the cavity when the screw is removed. A re-usable lightweight metal device is the collapsible anchor. The above types are all for fairly lightweight fixing.

For heavier jobs there are Rawlbolts. These are simply tubes of hard rubber with one flanged end and an embedded nut. They push into the wall up to the flange, and as the screw is pulled tight the tube compresses and bells out, creating a firm anchor.

The star anchor is made of hard plastic. It uses a wood screw and is lost in the cavity when the screw is removed. The anchor, screw and job are assembled and then pushed into the wall. As the closed legs clear the inner face of the wall they open slightly and are spread outwards more as the job is pulled against the outer surface of the wall.

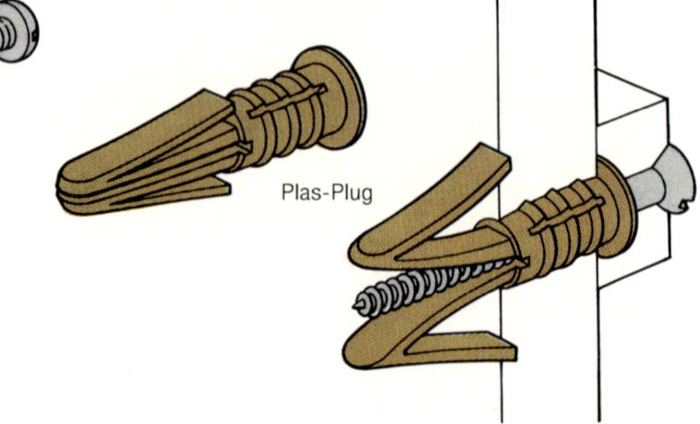

HEAVY-LOAD FIXING

Heavy loads are usually held on bolts, or nuts and bolts. Plugs for them are mostly made of cast iron, although heavy-duty plastic fittings are available for the construction industry.

The metal heavy-duty plugs are usually made in two or three split segments which are ridged on their outer faces, and held in cylindrical form by loose wire rings and light metal end caps. At the base is a cone-shaped spreader which is either bored or threaded internally to make it into a conventional nut, or is the head of a bolt that runs outwards through the plug. Where the bolt is integral to the plug, the job is pushed on to the bolt as it projects from the wall, and a washer and nut are fitted. With either type, fixing takes place as the nut or bolt is tightened – the cone-like piece is pulled up into the segments, causing them to expand and take a firm grip on the hole. To release, slacken the nut or bolt, and tap the projecting end until the core pushes back into the bottom of the hole.

Another heavy-duty fixing device is the rag bolt. This is a conventional bolt but with a short length of plain shank forged out into numerous small wings. The hole is made large and deliberately irregular. The bolt is held central and cement mortar is rammed all around it. The longer such bolts are left before loading, the stronger the fixing.

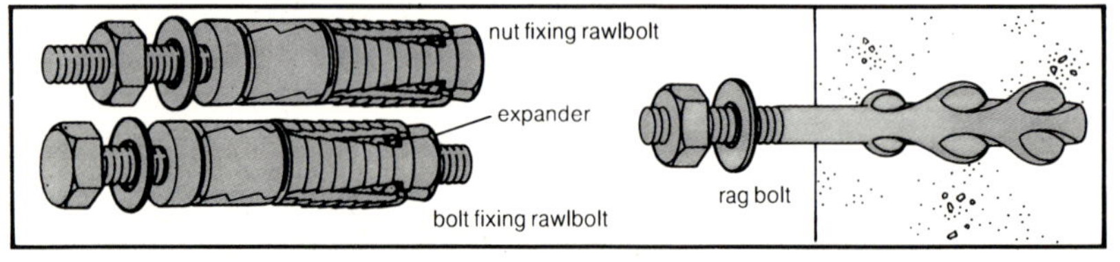

The latest hollow-surface fitting is the Plas-Plug plasterboard plug, which is a plastic plug, hollow, split and tapered, with two legs attached to its thin end. These legs face back to the larger end and, as the plug is pushed in, the legs spring out and grip the rear surface. The thicker end has heavy serrations and stays within the plasterboard. As the screw is inserted, the legs are spread wider and the serrations are driven into the plasterboard. This anchor remains in the board and may be used again in the same spot.

THE TRICK

To overcome any plugging job (even plasterboard in an emergency), chisel an approximately round wooden plug and hammer it into the hole. Pre-bore with a bradawl and the screw will spread the wood. Softwood is better than hardwood.

BURGESS POWER TOOLS LIMITED

POWERLINE

BURGESS POWER TOOLS
LEICESTER ROAD,
SAPCOTE,
LEICS LE9 6JW

TELEPHONE: 0455 272292

FIXING TO WALLS 2

1. Check the wall for condition and type. The plaster may need patching (see page 234).
2. Check the position required. Are there any projections or cable runs that must be missed?

If in doubt, shut off the power and open the socket front to ascertain the direction of the cable feed (see page 76, 85).

3. Does the job fit the wall? The wall (or shelf, etc.) may be out-of-straight. Later scribing may move the initial screw position.
4. What size plug and screw? Heavy jobs require large screws, especially if there is any pull-out load. Provided that the wall is sound and that good plugging is possible, the absolute maximum size screw required for hanging fitments is No. 10 (63mm/2½in.).

The drill, plug and screw must match. Plugs must be an easy knock-in fit and the screws should be greased.

5. Prepare the job for the screw. Mark and drill the job for the screw, selecting the drill size to give a clearance hole for the screw shank diameter. Countersink if necessary.
6. Mark the wall. Offer the job in position and mark through the holes. Use the same drill bit that was used to bore the hole in the wood – this keeps it central. Just rotate the drill to mark the wall surface (or knock it lightly).
7. Drill the wall. Having selected the screw and its plug, the drill for the wall should equal the plug diameter in size, unless you are using plastic multi-size plugs which will have the required size on the packet.

THE TRICK

On really awkward jobs, drill only one hole and plug it. Screw and check all alignments, then re-mark all the remaining holes.

MAKING THE HOLE

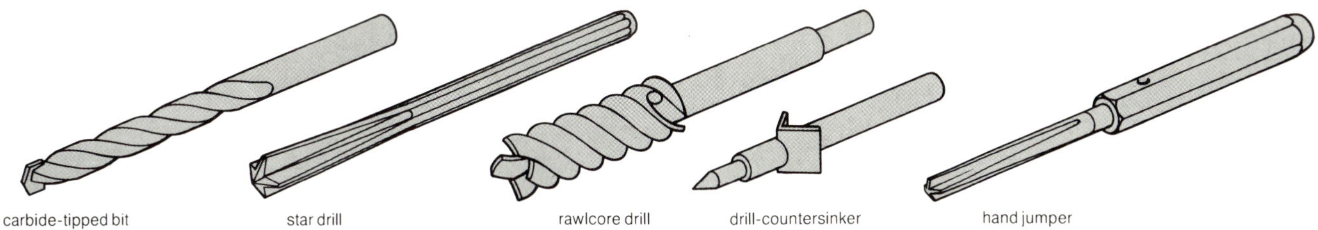

Most proprietary plugs require fairly accurate hole-drilling. The tool used most often for hole-making is the electric drill fitted with a tungsten carbide-tipped drilling bit. These bits are sold in the main plug sizes, each to suit a particular screw. Be advised by the supplier, who will indicate the correct drill, plug and screw if you describe the load and the wall. If the drill is a two-speed one, always use the slower speed for wall-drilling.

More expensive electric drills may have a hammer-blow or percussion option. These deliver high-speed end shocks to the drill bit as it turns, assisting the carbide tip to shatter the brick as the hole is made deeper. Impact drills are essential for concrete works, together with the correct carbide-tipped bit. Bricks may be prepared for masonry bolts if 'star' bits are used; strike them with a club hammer. A high-speed bit will lose its tip if pressed too hard against a stone.

THE TRICK

To overcome stones in concrete use an old-style jumper bit, which is fluted in section, very hard, and has a substantial handle to hold and to knock. Gentle but rapid blows will crack the stone and let the electric bit continue its work.

Rotate it a part-turn after every two or three blows; this keeps the bit free in the hole.

THE TRICK

Protect your face and eyes by sliding a square of wire mesh on to the jumper bit.

As the hole is being made deeper, especially in brickwork, the bit should be frequently withdrawn to remove the clogging dust. Hold the drill horizontal and square it to the wall, physically banging it into the hole whenever a hard spot is reached.

Do not press too hard on ceramic tiles (see pages 266 and 268), as cracks start very easily. Lightweight aggregate blocks, etc. drill easily, but crumble if too much pressure is used. Drill slowly, in and out, and never apply excessive pressure.

If a drill bit runs off-centre when starting, correct its cutting centre by off-laying the drill, pointing it back to the true centre. When the drill bit is back on centre, correct the drill angle.

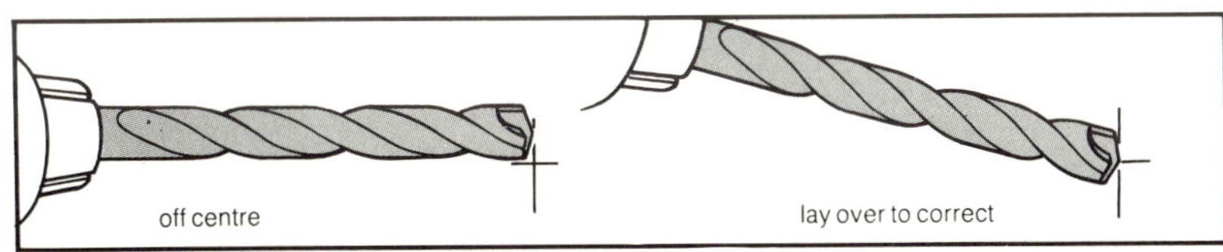

PLUGGING AND FIXING

If individual plastic plugs are being used, knock them in flush to the wall. To trim cut-off plastic plugs and traditional fibre plugs which may not go in completely flush, place a sharp chisel with its edge on the plug projection and its bevel back flush to the wall. A smart tap to the chisel and the plug shears cleanly away. All plugs should have their outer ends pushed in below wall-face level.

The entrance hole of the plug should be opened using either a nail or bradawl, which makes starting off the screw much easier.

If the job needs long, heavy screws, screw one in almost to its limit before actually fixing the job – this makes the final screwing much less arduous.

THE TRICK

Awkward jobs may be made less difficult in final fixing if a long nail or bradawl is used to locate the first plug hole. Leave it there while a second hole is aligned and screwed.

FAULTS

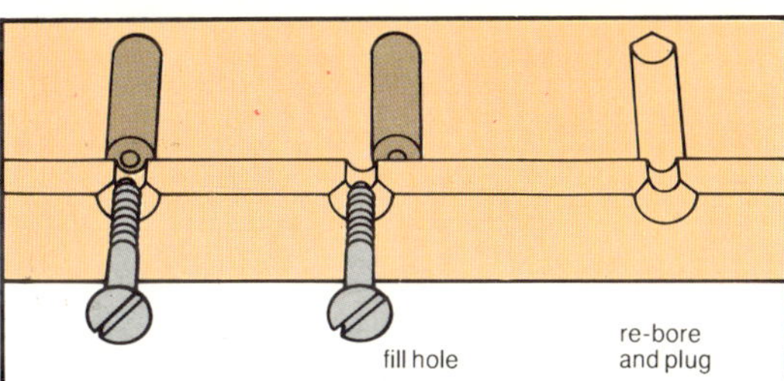

If misalignment occurs it is best to make a fresh start. It is not practical to re-plug within a few millimetres of the existing plug.

Sometimes the misalignment is so slight that the screw runs down the side of the plug. If this happens, you will feel a gritty, harsh sensation. A degree of fixing is achieved, but it will not be a strong, load-bearing job.

If re-screwing is not possible, or if the hole itself has crumbled, there are two possible solutions. A smaller plug may be driven into the centre of the existing one thus creating a tighter fit; or a large nail driven in alongside the plug will make room for a new and slightly smaller plug to be knocked in. (Once fibre plugs have been screwed into they are not easy to remove, although sometimes they may be pulled out with pincers.)

Failing a secure fix, the plug must be dug out and a compound filler plug material used. It is usually much easier to relocate the plug and screw.

Plugging ceramic tiles is slightly different. Here, if the screw and plug are the correct size, you risk that the glaze may shatter.

THE TRICK

In this instance only, you should cut the plug off short and drive it well into the hole, leaving about 5mm (3/16in.) of clear space in the tile.

PARTITIONS

These divide rooms and look like solid walls. The timber frame is covered by dry lining board (plasterboard), although older houses will have lath and plaster.

The material is usually 100 × 50mm (4 × 2in.) sawn carcase-quality softwood. The joints are half-laps, housings and notchings (see page 35). Door frames are usually built in after the studding has been erected. Check the ceiling heights and room widths with pinch rods (see page 40).

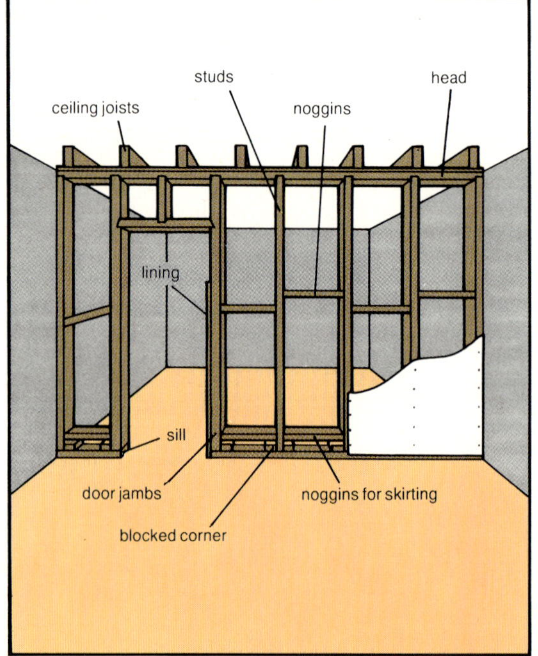

FIXING PARTITIONS

The foot plate is nailed or screwed to the flooring. The head or top is screwed through the plaster into a ceiling joist. If the partition runs parallel with the joists and in between them, 'deadmen' must be fitted from above (see page 89). To find ceiling joists, see page 81.

Fix the head or ceiling piece first, after cutting the necessary half-laps and notches. Then drop a plumb line to indicate the floor line for the foot plate. This again should be pre-cut to take the lower ends of the studs. If a door has to go through a partition, stop the floor plate at either side, allowing for the double thickness of material to be used for the door frame lining.

STUDS AND NOGGINS

The studs are knocked in plumb and then nailed obliquely to secure the fixing. Alternatively, nail framing brackets into the corners. Space the studs at 610mm (24in.) centres; first check the board widths that are available (see below).

A more economical and easier fixing is to nail offcuts of the studs to the stud and the plate to form a corner block.

Once the studs are up, insert the noggins which stiffen the studs. They may be notched in but are more usually cut-butted. Cut the noggins at about a 20° angle to the floor and stagger them up and down. Alternatively, fit them horizontal but position alternately higher or lower than the preceding piece. Nailing through the stud is easy.

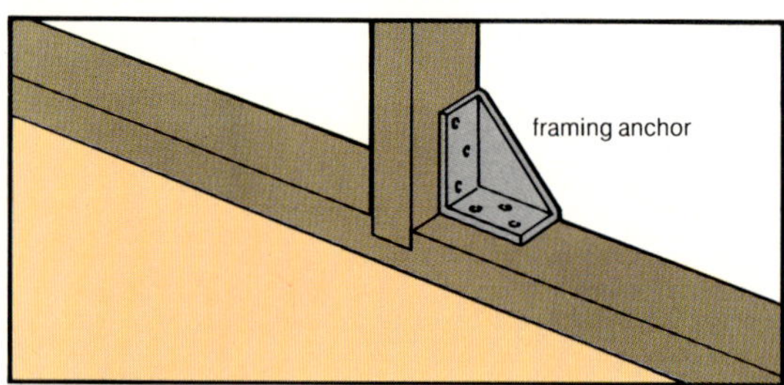

THE TRICK

Studs spring, so bolster the back of each stud with a heavy hammer or piece of metal.

The door-head piece should be notched-in, whatever the method used for the rest of the horizontal members.

The door openings should be lined with boards and fitted with stops and architrave (see page 40).

THE TRICK

As most modern doors tend to warp, especially lightweight flush doors, fit the hinge-side door stop, hang the door, and then fit the top stop and striking stop to fit the closed door.

PLASTERBOARD

The commonest board for home improvement is Gyproc wallboard. It consists of a plaster layer sandwiched between paper facings, one of which is grey and the other ivory. The ivory surface is for decoration, while the grey is for professional plastering. The edges may be square or tapered. The square edges are slightly rounded. The other has a wide flat taper to about 45mm (1¾in.) from the edge, which is about 7mm (5/16in.) thick. The whole board is 9.5mm (⅜in.) or 13mm (½in.) in thickness. For home use boards of 1.80 × 1.29m (71 × 47in.) are more easily handled than larger boards.

For use on external walls (inside), where coldness and some damp may be expected, there is a grade with a polythene film face (which goes against the wall) to act as a moisture check.

WORKING WITH PLASTERBOARD

Cut the board from the ivory side, using a fine-toothed handsaw. Short cuts may be made with a standard trimming knife, again from the ivory side.

All projections from the wall must be measured, marked, and cut while the board is lying flat. When cutting, lay it flat on stools or boxes and support it well on planks. Make the short cuts first and then the long ones.

THE TRICK

As sheet materials waver and crack, all cut edges should be supported. The easiest way is to take off-cuts of the board being cut, and nail them between two plywood strips. These 'grooves' will provide quite adequate support.

FIXING PLASTERBOARD

Strip the wall to the brickwork and fix 50 × 25mm (2 × 1in.) battens with plugs and screws or masonry pins. Spacings must leave no more than 400mm (16in.) of the board unsupported (450mm (18in.) centre to centre). Top and bottom horizontal battens are fixed first. Check all the fixings carefully to ensure that spacing and vertical alignment are correct. Pack out where necessary.

For ceilings, extra joist pieces (noggins) are fitted along all joist lines and along the room edges. The long joists are butted. Joints across the width of the ceiling are staggered and the ends are left about 3mm (⅛in.) apart for later filling.

Wall linings are cut 25mm (1in.) shorter than floor to ceiling height and the boards are pressed tightly up to the ceiling while they are being nailed.

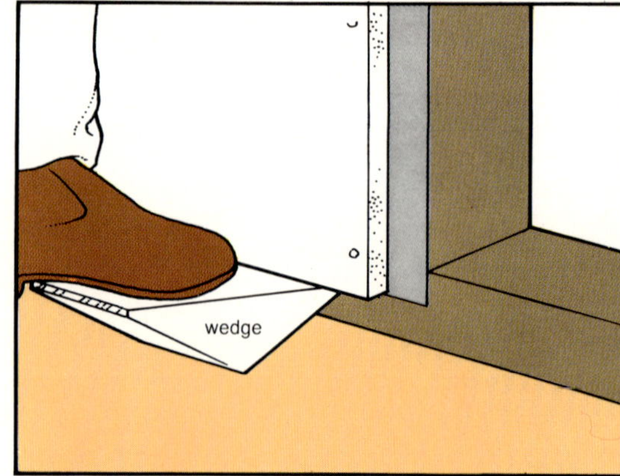

THE TRICK

Board lifters are made from an old joist end, about 225mm (9in.) long (see diagram). The apex is used downwards, with one thin end under the board. Use foot pressure on the other end to raise the board.

Plasterboard is simply nailed on to stud partitioning, ivory side out. Try to conceal as much pipe-work as possible and to run all cable along using batten space, before fixing sheets. When turning corners, the papered edge should always mask the cut edge. For scribing to walls, see Skirtings (page 27). Techniques are the same.

Nails for plasterboard are large-headed and galvanized. Drive them in with a hammer until they slightly dimple the paper surface. Nail at about 13mm (½in.) from the board edge, and space the nails at 150mm (6in.) intervals. All the edges must be nailed, and lines of nails must be used along each support batten across the board face.

Mark on a long, thin stick the centres of the studs and noggins – this will make intermediate nailing easier when the boards are fixed. Tapping with a hammer will locate the position of a stud.

JOINTS

Any construction job must be strong enough for its purpose. Strength above this merely adds weight and expense. There are certain general construction principles: all member of joints must be as substantial as possible, preserving as much strength in each part as the design allows.

Faces of joints must fit snugly together to avoid movement and to increase adhesion when glueing. Wherever possible frames should have some form of triangulation, a very simple but effective means of adding strength. Joints should also be simple in design; complexity leads to poor cutting and fitting. Wherever possible, incorporate some form of mechanical interlocking, which adds to its physical strength and makes final assembly easier.

Joints should suit the job into which they are built – the strength of a table leg joint is needed not so much to support a load as to resist failure when the table is pulled along the carpet.

CONSTRUCTION

Mortise, tenon and bridle joints should have the tenon member cut approximately one third of the material thickness and half-laps should be genuinely half and half.

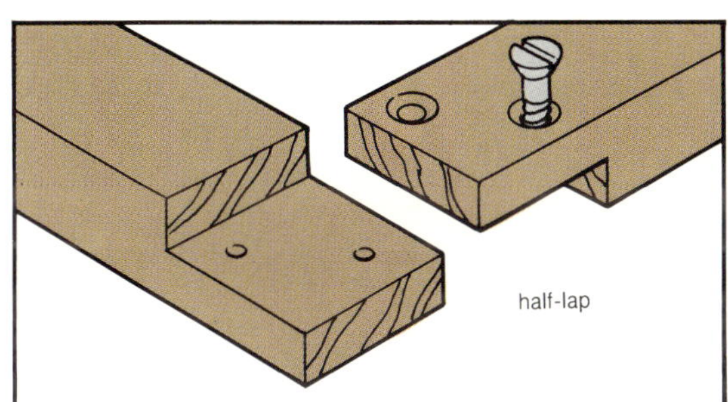

Diagonal bracing will keep a frame square if it is subject to forces that tend to distort it. Simple butt joints, held with wiggle nails (corrugated fasteners), can be considerably strengthened with gusset pieces of ply, glued and pinned. Tenons that go completely through the mortised piece can be converted into dovetailed tenons if simple tapered wedges are glued and driven into the joint.

Tenon and bridle joints may be made far more secure if square pegs are used instead of round dowels.

THE TRICK

Cut the pegs square, and use a chisel to taper the points slightly. Then knock the pegs into the holes. This gives mechanical locking.

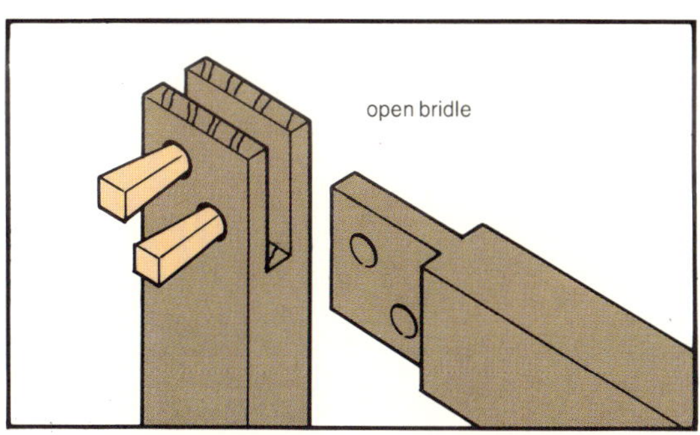

TENON JOINTS

The standard joinery joint is the mortise and tenon which has many variations to suit the application. This type of joint has maximum strength characteristics and is easy to cut. However, it must be very skilfully cut if it is to be strong, which means that in factory production it is usually machine-cut, both for reasons of accuracy and for speed of output. The home woodworker will have to cut each joint by hand, which leads to variation in accuracy. Simplifying the design by some forethought at the design stage can save time and materials.

It is sometimes necessary to add a rail to a table or frame construction after assembly and here ply keys are the solution. Cut a mortise into the side member, glue in a ply key and then glue and knock down the rail, which will have had a part-slot cut into each end.

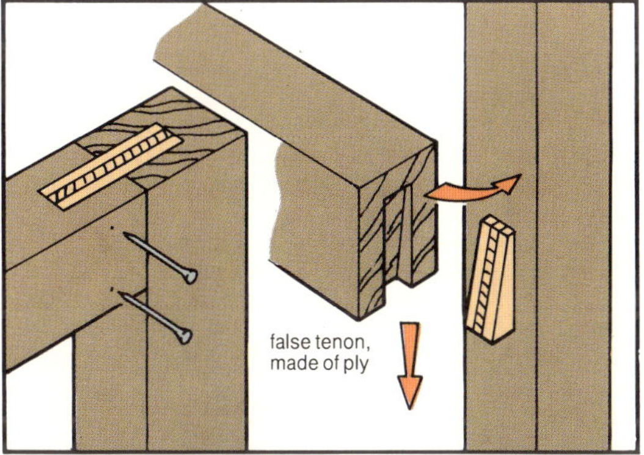

For heavy framing the tusk-tenon construction is useful, for it is in effect self-cramping. With careful design it may be used decoratively for furniture.

THE TRICK

Some jobs that require only low strength can be done by laminating plywood offcut strips across the corners.

HOUSINGS

Housings are easily cut but have low strength values so they should be used only where the load is applied in shear to the joint. However, the strength of housing joints can be greatly improved by incorporating tenons, dovetails and wedges. Remember that wood swells and shrinks. As the weather changes from dry to wet and as the house changes its temperature from warm to cold, wood will swell or shrink. The most exposed timbers will be affected most, and furniture kept indoors will move least. This is another problem to solve when joints are being designed.

Because housings are mostly used for wide boards, they tend to move the most.

THE TRICK

Any wood used for shelf-type constructions must be as dry as possible and kept for as long as possible close to the other pieces to which it is to be jointed.

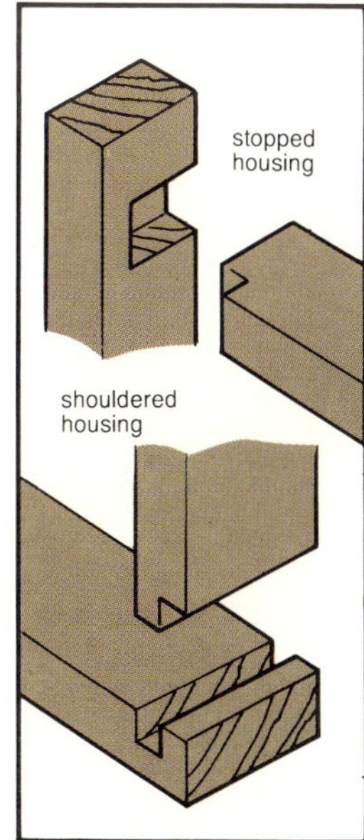

BUILT-UP CONSTRUCTIONS

If solid timber is not available, or if its stability is suspect, large items may be built-up using light framing and surface sheeting. Most suitable for this form of construction are upholstered chair sides and table end legs.

In this form of construction jointing may be kept to a minimum. Butt ends, fix with glue and wiggle nails, and then glue and pin the surface sheeting. If the surface is visible, then screw and plug it. Otherwise use modern plastic buttons to hide the screw heads.

Bear in mind strength requirements at all times during the design stage. Corner blocks improve the strength of most joints. These blocks may be square or triangular in section, and are glued in and pinned. Glue-blocked corners may be used in building quite large units, whether the material is solid wood, plywood or chipboard. If this type of construction is used, all joints must be square-cut joints and the blocks should be square, or rounded square, strips. Basic construction becomes a simple job of glueing and pinning (for small jobs) and screwing for larger ones. The strips are glued and screwed to both members of the corner to be constructed.

BOARDS AND SURFACES 1

HARDBOARD

This usually comes in a 3mm (⅛in.) thickness, either light or dark brown, or ivory-faced. Enamelled hardboards are available, as are perforated peg-boards and thicker boards up to 8mm (5⁄16in.). Available also, in specialist shops, is 2mm (1⁄10in.) board. The sheets are mainly 1.22 × 2.44m (4 × 8ft), and may be found in several lengths up to 3.66m (12ft). Sheets are commonly pre-cut to door size (see right).

Three general qualities are stocked: standard, tempered, and medium. The medium is soft, and useful for partitions which will be protected by paint or wallpaper. For most jobs use standard board; for extra strength or moisture-resistance, use tempered board.

ON FLOORS

Cut hardboard with a fine saw, and plane it with a wood plane. When levelling floors, cut large boards into two. This makes the material easier to handle and it will lie flatter. Lay it rough side upwards and offset the joins. Hardboard floors must always be protected by carpet or linoleum.

To ensure level laying, sponge the boards (rough side up) and leave them to condition for 24–28 hours. Nail securely along the edges and intermittently across the board. Hardboard may be used for shelving if the front edge is supported on a batten.

ON DOORS

To convert panelled doors into flush, cut the panels to size, plane and sand the edges smooth. Sponge over the rough face. If two boards are being treated, lay them face to face for as long as possible before fixing. This prevents them warping later and shrinks them close to the door.

Study the door before cutting to size; if you are covering the whole inner face the hinges will have to be moved (see page 40).

THE TRICK

It is best to cut boards about 35mm (1½in.) shorter and narrower than the door, and to fix them with an equal margin all round. This disguises the edge of the panel, avoids the need to move hinges and protects the edges from damage.

It pays to paint PVA glue on to the door face under the panel area and then to fix with hardboard pins (fine pins coated with copper or cadmium). Drive the pins flush but do not damage the smooth face of the board. Tip the pin heads with primer before filling any slight holes.

Usually you are warned against scratching the smooth surface, as this makes the spot porous and gloss paint will look dull on it.

THE TRICK

To repair such damage, smooth very lightly with fine abrasive paper; then apply a thin coat of shellac polish or knotting (see page 241).

PARTICLE BOARDS

These are chipboard, flaxboard and bagassé. The second two are less common – avoid them if you can, as they are more suited to factories. Flaxboard has grey-green edges and is made from shredded flax. Bagassé is darker than flaxboard, heavier and with finer particles – it is made from crushed sugar cane.

Chipboard in shops is either dense flooring quality or layer board. Use the flooring quality for this job. It can be used for furniture, but seems too heavy and solid. Its cut edges show even-size chips, closely packed.

The edges of layer board show small, sawdust-like chips on each surface, but large, loosely packed chips in the centre. Boards are available in thicknesses of 12mm (½in.) to 18mm (¾in.), occasionally 3mm (⅛in.). Sheet size is normally 1.22 × 2.44m (4 × 8ft).

Layer board is suitable for painting. For most purposes you will achieve a good finish from an undercoat and two top coats. It also makes a good substrate for melamine sheet or wood veneer.

If screwing into the ends or sides of layer board, use plastic or dowel inserts, or use a dowel driven through the face of the board or in from an adjacent edge. Face fixing is also improved if dowels are driven into the board from the side.

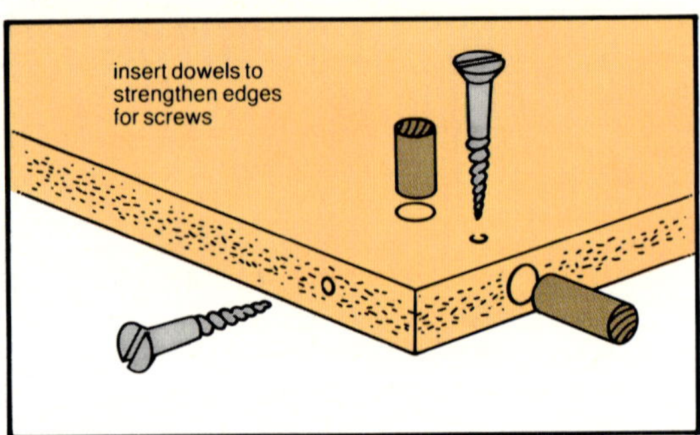

When used as a base for melamine sheet both sides should be faced, otherwise the board will curl. The curl will depend on board thickness, on its moisture content, and on the amount of glue used. If the board is a screwed-down table top, a one-face finish is sufficient. If wood veneer is used, with a wet-glue process, it is essential to veneer both faces.

Cut the chipboard with standard wood tools and plane the edges with standard planes. Keep your tools sharp, as chipboard needs sharp tools and blunts them rapidly.

THE TRICK

Invisible edges, such as door tops and bottoms, need not be edged. Rub emulsion paint well in with a finger, then paint as normal.

EDGING

Visible edges must be 'edged' with either cut, rigid laminate strips; or pre-glued iron-on natural wood veneer; or pre-glued, iron-on melamine film strip. The first is stuck on with contact adhesive; coat both board edge and strip; allow both to become tacky, and then press firmly together. Strips should be cut marginally wider than the combined thickness of the board and its facing laminate(s).

If the edging is thin melamine or iron-on real veneer, iron it on at an even speed after first testing the iron temperature and speed on a short length. The temperature and speed must balance to give correct adhesion.

THE TRICK

Immediately after ironing, use the shaft of a hammer to press down each edge. After levelling check the edges and re-iron any loose spots.

Finish with abrasive paper held at an angle on a flat block.

If the laminate strips have been cut and applied carefully, trimming is simple. Use a flat, fine file and work diagonally into the board. Tilt the file to avoid damaging the face. Tungsten cutting tools trim edges very easily – make light cuts until the edge is flush – but plastic laminate is abrasive and they do not last long.

Trimming other edges is best done with a sharp, thin-edged chisel, or a standard trimming knife. Take note of the grain direction if you are using real veneer.

More substantial edgings are made of solid wood. Plough grooves in both the lipping strips and panel, and join with a loose tongue. Glue well and plane the surface after jointing. Do not make these lippings wider than 18mm (¾in.), as they distort more than the board and the join line often shows through. Alternatively, just glue and pin the edging strip.

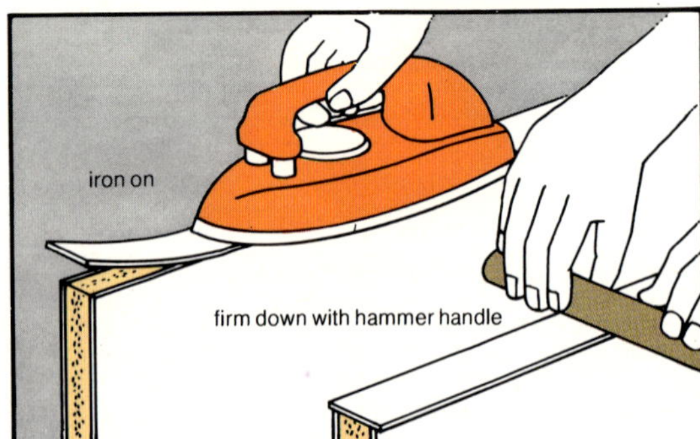

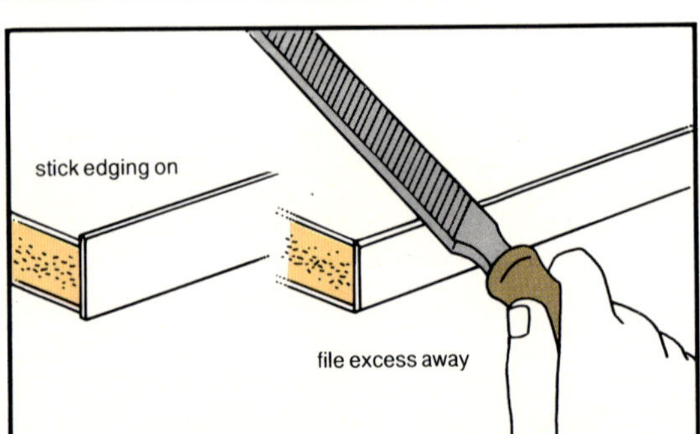

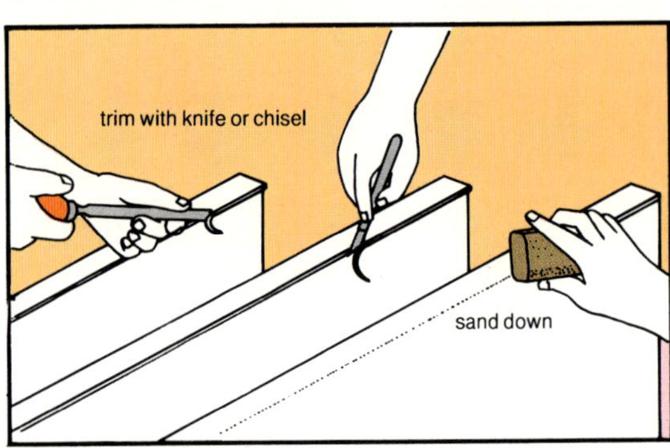

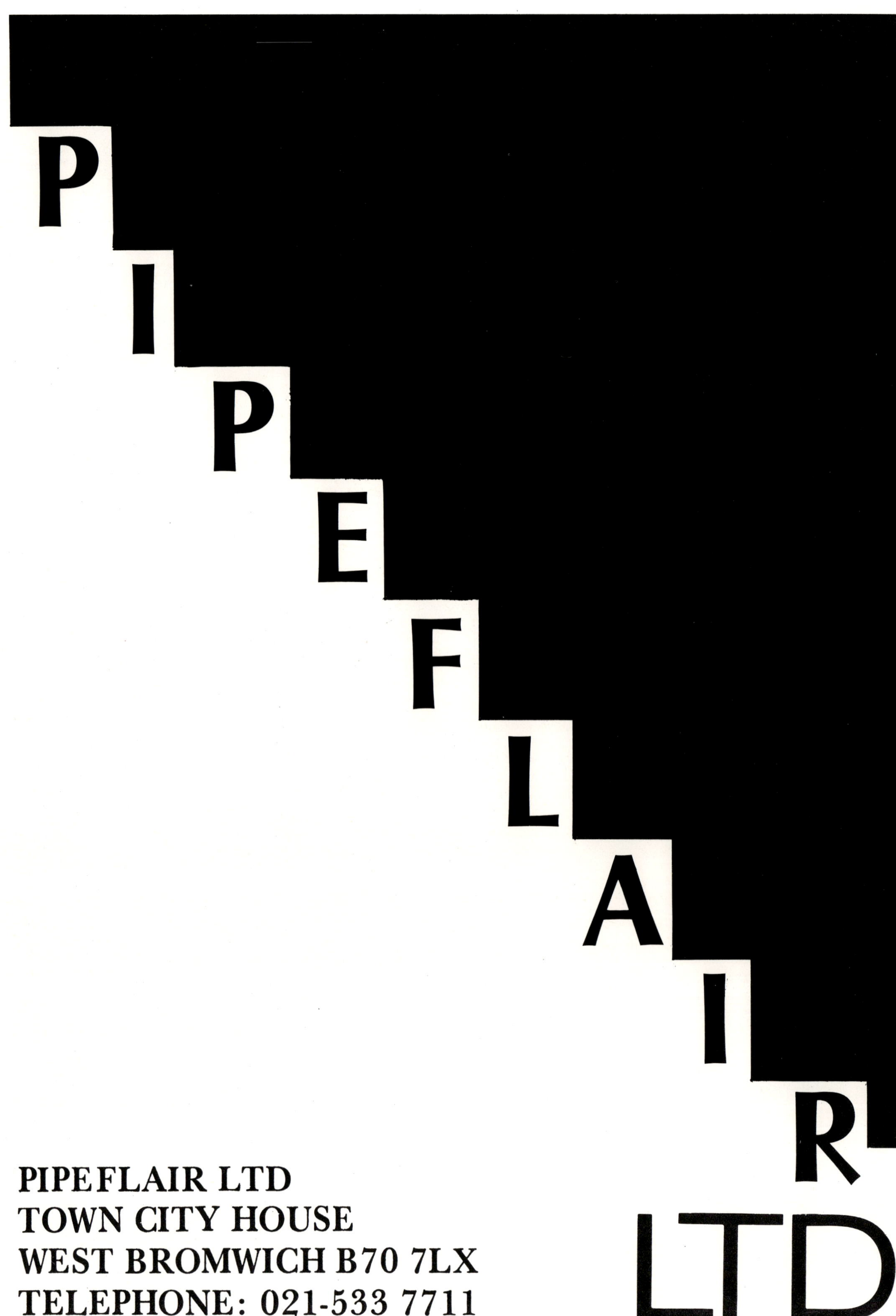

PIPEFLAIR
LTD
PIPEFLAIR LTD
TOWN CITY HOUSE
WEST BROMWICH B70 7LX
TELEPHONE: 021-533 7711

BOARDS AND SURFACES 2

RIGID SHEET LAMINATES – FORMICA ETC.

The boards are usually work-top quality, but check with the supplier. There are many grades: some are very thin and flexible, others are thicker and more rigid. Generally the thicker the board, the better is its work-surface properties.

Several kinds of adhesives will stick melamine sheet, but it is safest to use a good contact adhesive. Cut the sheet slightly oversize and apply the adhesive to both surfaces, ridging it with a serrated applicator.

For the best adhesion, the solvent must evaporate before pressing the surfaces together, so have a tea-break at this point. Usually 15–20 minutes is ample for the surfaces to get light-touch dry. Close them, pressing firmly home from the centre outwards, and ensuring accurate register as faces meet. Press down firmly all over, especially on the edges. Some adhesives are thixotropic, which means that the glued surfaces can be slid about relative to each other but very rapidly become rigid when pressure is applied. This is most useful when large or awkward laminate sheets are being laid – it gives some degree of slide before the final bond, which is an advantage over the ordinary contact adhesives that need immediate and precise positioning.

The final edging to the boards is as described on page 36: cut, glue, apply, level with a file and clean off.

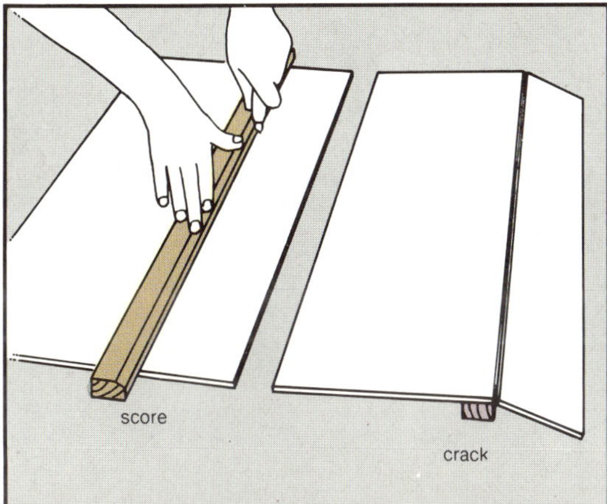

CUTTING

Plastic laminate sheet may be cut with fine-tooth wood saws: keep the saw angle low so that as many teeth as possible are in contact. Cut the board slightly oversize to allow for accidental bad register when laying.

Cutting may also be done by scribing, as with glass. Score deep lines with a strong, pointed knife and then snap the board along a straight edge. Always cut from the face side. Shapes may be fret-sawn or filed; you can nibble bits away with pliers after scribing.

Cutting is easier if masking tape is laid along the direction required; not only will the lines show up more clearly but the board will chatter less during cutting.

MELAMINE-FACED CHIPBOARD

This is perhaps the best-ever material for the home carpenter. It is consistent and easily worked. The surface, however, is not 'working' quality, since it cuts and scratches easily, so you must use it only for vertical wipe-down surfaces, or for horizontal surfaces where it is protected.

It cuts well with fine-tooth handsaws or small electric saws, but it shatters at its cut edge, so pre-cut the line using a trimming knife or marking gauge, defining both sides of the board for the saw cut. After cutting, smooth with a sharp plane and iron on the edging, trimming as before.

When buying, watch out for colour – there are lots of whites and lots of teak colours.

Use Knock-Down KD fittings and chipboard screws for assembly.

On the final finish, rub along the sharp corners of all panels with white emulsion paint (or dark brown shoe polish for dark work) – this hides any slight chips.

MINIMUM JOINT CONSTRUCTION

A simplified method of construction without jointing is possible with sections that have grooves ploughed into their faces or edges, into which you can knock standard 3mm (1/8in.) hardboard. These lengths are available in some timber yards, or can be prepared at home from planed timber using an electric saw set to cut grooves 3 × 8mm (1/8 × 5/16in.) deep. (Make two cuts or put wide 'set' on the saw.)

The lengths are cut off square (use a jig) with all ends butted. The hardboard is cut into gussets or keys, triangular in shape, measuring, according to the job, approximately 75mm (3in.) along the square edges.

To construct the job, simply offer four frame members together, glue the edges of the keys and knock them into the grooves. If the grooves do not create a tight fit, pins may be necessary through the rail and into the key. Intermediate rails may be sections with two grooves on opposing edges, two pieces placed back to back, or simply one-edged rails. Corners may be built up using sections with grooves along right-angled faces, or by glueing and pinning two sections edge to face.

CRAMPING

Most glued joints are strengthened if they are cramped during assembly. The usual G and sash cramps are expensive and are often not quite right. Simple pressure devices can be made from odd wood off-cuts from the job. Using wedges, single or in pairs as 'folding wedges', many jobs may be assembled without metal cramps.

For square frames, choose a robust batten and screw on to it two blocks, using one substantial screw in each block. These blocks must be a distance apart that equals the length across the job plus an allowance for a wedge. Simply knock up the glued job, straddle it with the batten and drive in a suitable wedge.

For heavier jobs the blocks could be screwed to a wooden floor. Large frames can be cramped across the garage floor, using bricks as spacers, and wedges to apply pressure.

Small jobs, usually cramped by G-cramps, may be closed and pressured simply, if several U-shaped pieces are cut from thick plywood. Wedges again will provide the pressure.

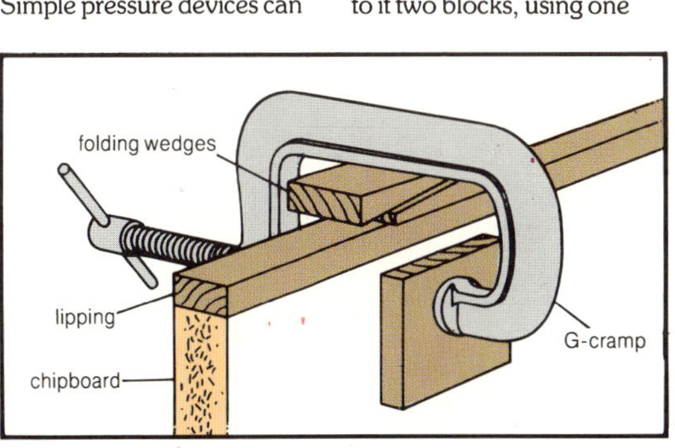

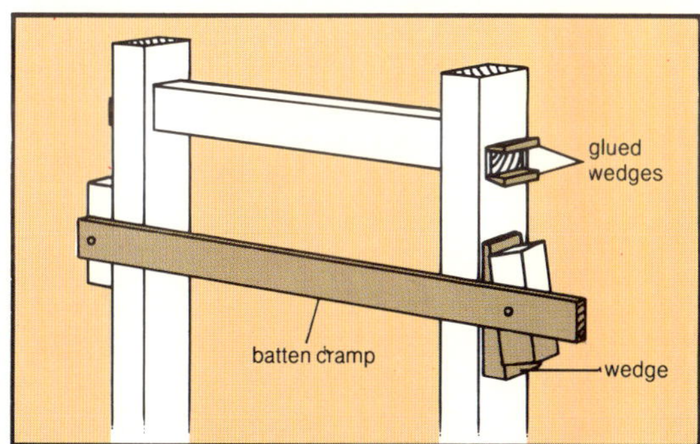

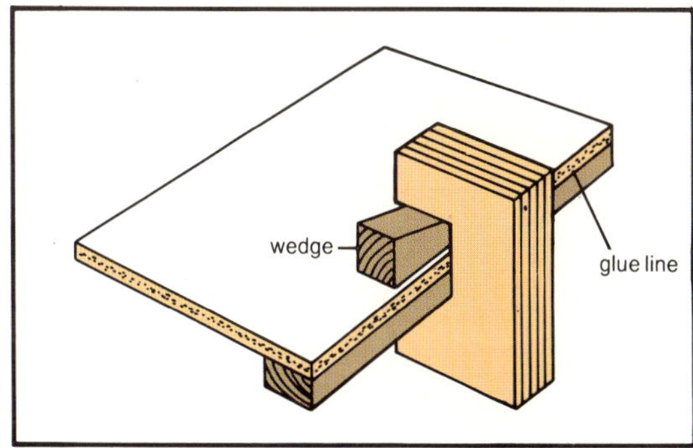

DOORS 1

When doors are made, 'horns' are left on the ends of each stile, projecting beyond the nominal height of the door. Their purpose is to aid in assembly and also to protect them from damage in transit.

Assuming you are hanging a new door on an old frame, first check the frame for size – most are standard, but some are hand-made to fit an opening. Measure the height at both ends of the frame head, and the width at various points. Check that the width is parallel. Choose a maximum-size door, because frame height may vary too. Door frames distort diagonally as a building settles.

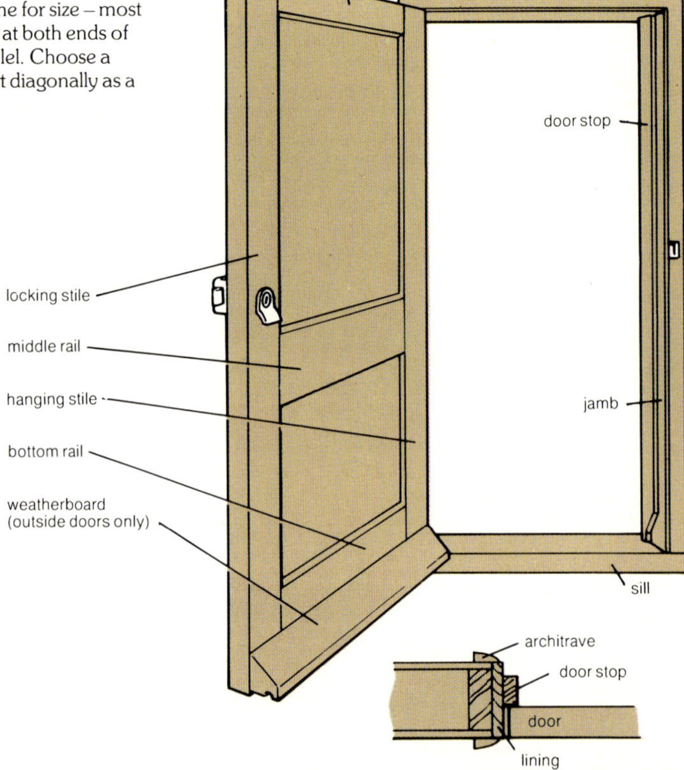

THE TRICK

Use 'pinch rods' to check diagonals, marking across the two sticks. If the diagonals vary, the frame is out of square.

Next, check for bow in the jambs. Small bows can be planed away.

Front doors are hung with decorative panel and moulded rails facing outwards. Putty rebates for glass face inwards.

PREPARATION

Offer (i.e. test) the door width, top and bottom, marking it for later waste removal. Aim for an even, loose fit. Check the door stiles for straightness and twist.

THE TRICK

Check the door for flatness before accepting delivery. Put one end on the ground and look along its top edge, down to the line of the bottom edge. If the door is twisted, the two lines will not appear to merge. Minor twist can be overcome during hanging.

Remove the bottom horns, carefully cutting them square. Offer the door into the frame. It obviously will not go right in, but wedge it while you inspect its general fit. Check:

1. Fit of hanging stile to jamb. Do stile and jamb meet in a straight line? If not, mark for correction, checking there is enough width at the locking stile.
2. Fit of locking stile to jamb. Is one out of parallel? If so, mark for removal.
3. Line of bottom rail with sill. Mark for waste removal if necessary.
4. Line of top rail with frame head line. If the frame is out of square, the gap or the waste piece marked will be tapered.

Start fitting the door by hanging the stile to the jamb. Keep in mind the general fit, as once wood has been planed away it cannot be put back. When there is a close fit, plane the bottom rail.

To plane the door edge, hold it in a cradle or other support. You will need a sharp jack-plane. An alternative method is to stand astride and grip the door with your knees.

Next, plane the locking stile until the door fits with a minimum gap. For sturdy entrance doors 4mm (⅛in.) is a reasonable allowance: i.e. 2mm (1/16in.) per side. For less heavy doors, an allowance of 6mm (¼in.) is reasonable. The frame's condition really controls the clearance; a poor frame needs more than a good one.

Finally, cut the top rail and horns to fit, then plane the top smooth. To plane top or bottom, support the door edgeways on as large a block as possible. Straddle it, and plane downwards. Use the plane edge to check your straightness.

The door should now 'push' into the frame.

THE TRICK

Use a 2p piece to act as a fitting gauge, sliding it all round.

Look carefully for tight spots. Plane off a little more, if necessary, until you get a reasonably loose fit.

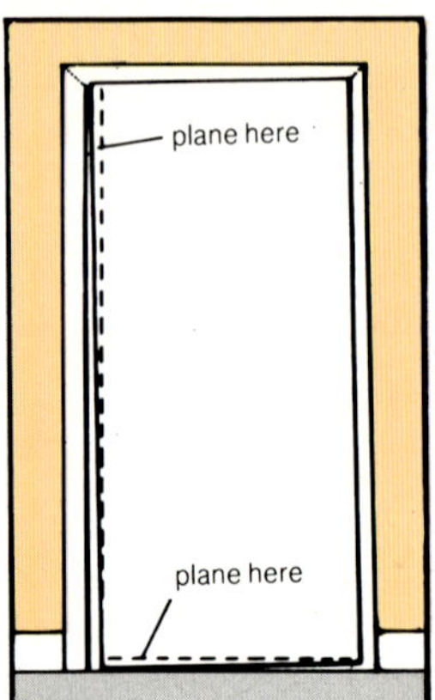

HINGES

If you intend to re-use the existing butts, take them off and inspect them. Their pivot pins may be badly worn or there may be excessive free play between the bearing points of the flaps. If cast iron, they may be cracked. Buy a new pair if you find any of these defects.

Check the recesses. If the holes are in good condition you can re-install the hinges in them. If you come across pieces of card there, the hinge flaps are too deep and had to be packed out.

Before re-fitting hinges, fit the door to the frame, using thin wooden wedges. Leave a slightly wider gap at the bottom than at the top, to allow for the door to settle. Mark across accurately from the edges of the hinge recesses onto the door edge. Take out the door and mark for the hinges.

Check the hinge position while it has at least one screw holding it to the frame. If the 'bottom' edge is above the bottom line of the recess, due to previous poor cutting, marking across will bring the door too high. The hinge bottom line is the starting-point for cutting.

THE TRICK

To allow for fall, move this bottom line down about 2mm (1/16in.) before marking the hinge top.

Chop out the recesses; make the rear slightly deeper than the front edge, but aim to leave the front edge higher than marked. This avoids trouble if you do go too deep, and makes adjustment safer. The correct depth is half the hinge thickness measured across the knuckle for a brass butt; pressed steel hinges need less depth.

If both the door and its frame are new, mark the recess position on the jamb. Use a marking gauge for the pivot centre and flap width. Remember that doors fall slightly when hung, so raise the line of the hinge slot in the jamb a fraction.

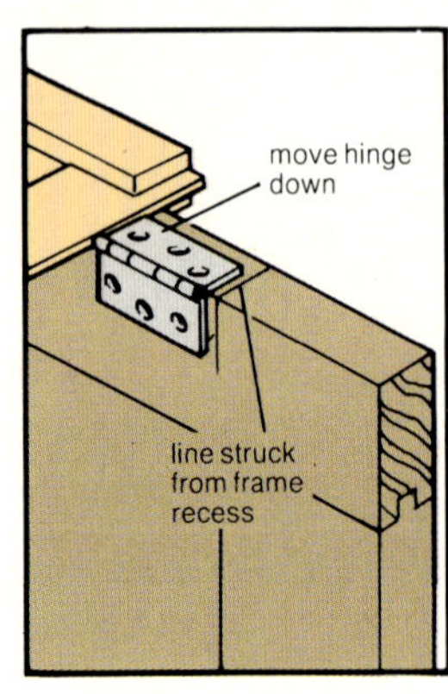

HANGING

Re-fit the hinges to the jamb, including any card packing. Use new screws and do them all up tightly, as it is unlikely that they will have to be moved.

You should make the two centre screw holes while the hinges are off. If you have not done this, have a sharp bradawl to hand. Present the door to the jamb; support it by folding wedges or a chisel, while the top hinge flap is manoeuvred into its door slot. Stab the centre hole with the bradawl, then remove the hinge flap and bore an entry. Replace the hinge flap and screw home the first screw.

Repeat this process with the lower hinge. The door should now close with a clear thump on the door stop. There should be no spring back. When satisfied, unhang the door and prime the bottom edge to prevent moisture getting in. When dry, rehang the door and screw home all the screws.

The Automatic Choice...

matic
matic
Garamatic

Now available – GARAMATIC – the ultimate remote-control automatic system for overhead garage doors.

What makes GARAMATIC so special?

Reliability The rugged positive drive system built into every GARAMATIC unit ensures a reliable and trouble free life.

Desirability GARAMATIC enables you to drive straight into a dry garage – no more fumbling in the dark, in pouring rain or freezing cold, trying to open the garage door thanks to GARAMATIC'S compact infra-red control, no bigger than a pocket calculator, operated from inside the car!

Versatility GARAMATIC is easily installed to operate most leading makes and sizes of domestic overhead garage doors.

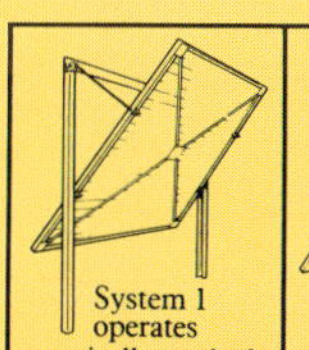

System 1 operates vertically tracked canopy doors

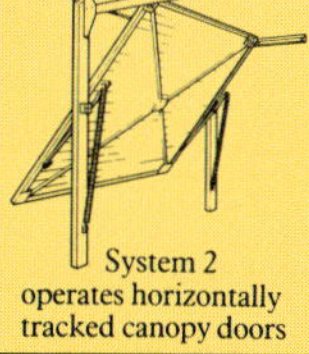

System 2 operates horizontally tracked canopy doors

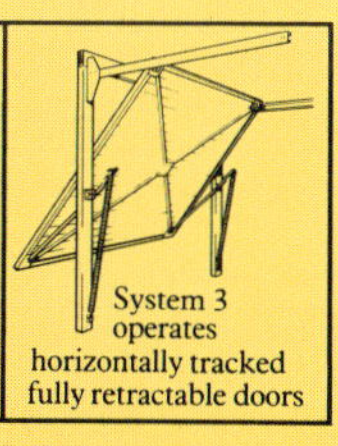

System 3 operates horizontally tracked fully retractable doors

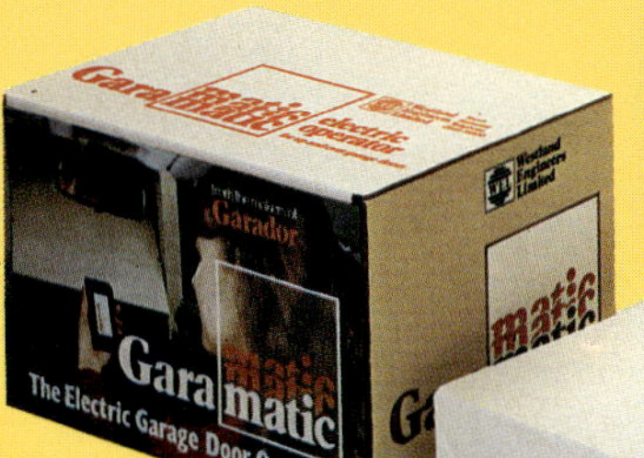

GARAMATIC –
The Automatic Choice –
only from **GARADOR**

Please send for full details

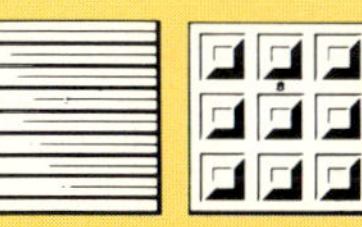

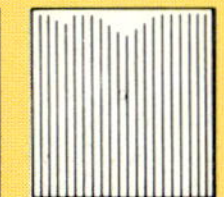

Westland Engineers Limited

PO Box 5, Yeovil, Somerset, BA20 2YA Telephone Yeovil (0935) 75200 Telex 46335

1

Elegance, style, distinction, and sheer durability are the keynotes of the new extended range of Wessex Doors. A selection of the most popular designs are shown here, but within the full range, there is a garage door to complement almost any style of house. Although being indistinguishable from natural hand-hewn timber or high-gloss painted panels, they are all hand made from tough, reinforced fibreglass which can neither rot nor rust. Most designs can be made to any required size, and come complete with balanced up-and-over mechanism.

1. Wessex Georgian
2. Antique Tudor
3. Tudor Lead Lights Mk1
4. Avonbrook White
5. Chester White with Studs
6. Georgian Lead Lights
7. Blenheim White
8. Antique Tudor Entrance Door
9. Georgian Entrance Door

2

3

4

5

8

6 7

9

All Wessex Garage Doors are specially designed to accept the **LIFT BOY** range of automatic controls. From within the comfort and safety of your car, you need only press the button on your individually-coded radio button which fits on teh sun-visor, and your door opens or closes automatically, also lighting up the garage for added convenience.

DOORS 2

RISING BUTTS

Rising butts are designed to lift the door as it is opened and so clear the carpet. As doors are heavy, the angled pivot of the hinge provides a slope down which the door can run, and so they are to some extent self-closing hinges.

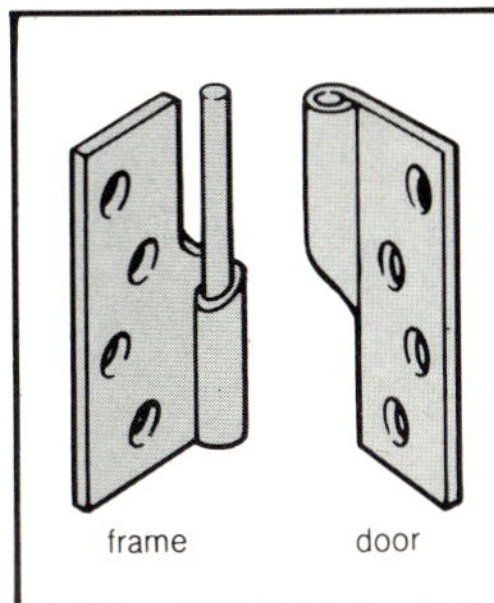

Rising butts are made in heavy cast iron or thick steel plate. They are in two parts – one carries the pivot and the other the hole for the pivot. The knuckle is left completely clear of both the frame and the door. The marking gauge is set only to the width and thickness of each flap, because each flap must be cut-in.

If the doors are close-fitting, the inner top corner of the door may need a slight 'lead' or taper cut at the hinged side. If the door top does not have enough clearance as it rises, it will not clear the frame head. It may also be necessary to chamfer the door slightly, immediately below the frame half of the hinge, to allow the door to rise.

If the door is marked accurately and the hinges cut in carefully it should be possible to drop the door on to the pivot pins after all the parts are screwed on. Do this with the door opened to a right angle.

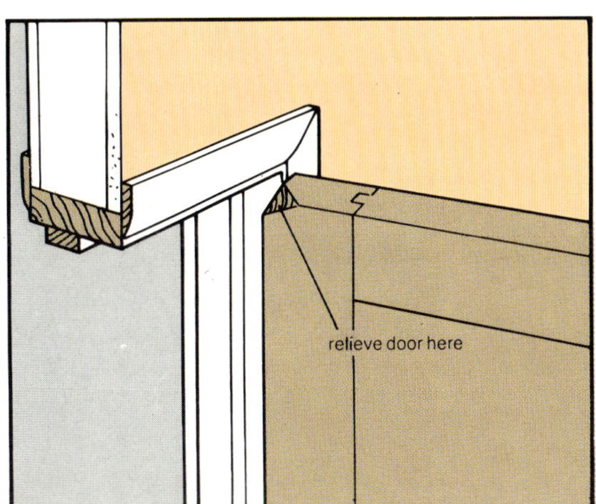

PROBLEMS

Warped doors may be sprung back if they are not so distorted that the joints have become damaged. Room doors must be removed and laid flat (somewhere in the house, to maintain their moisture content) with diagonally opposite corners supported and the up-twisted corners heavily weighted (use bricks) so that the door can be twisted in the opposite direction. Doors may need up to two weeks of the treatment.

Small cupboard doors may be distorted while still hinged. Block one corner of the door to prevent it from closing, and then wedge the other corner tight in.

CHIPBOARD DOORS

Chipboard doors tend to bow rather than to twist. For a straightforward bow, remove the door and support its two ends on battens. Load its middle with bricks to correct the shape.

If paint cans filled with water are used as weights, infinite adjustment is possible by adding or taking away water.

Chipboard doors that are bowed on the hinged edge may be pulled back by adding an extra hinge. A bowed closing edge can be corrected if a straight 'dolly' is G-cramped to it for a few days. The dolly may be a length of joist material or a ladder edge. The two high corners of the door must be packed away from the dolly before the door bulge is pulled in with the G-cramp. Try it for three or four days. If the bow persists, increase the 'anti-distortion' by using thicker packing. Be careful: chipboard cracks easily.

correcting a bowed chipboard door

DOOR HINGES

Hinges and butts tend to rust. Rusty metal is abrasive and a loose rusty screw soon makes a large hole.

The cure may be to use much longer screws of the same size when replacing the hinge. If this is not practical, bore for a 9mm (3/8in.) dowel, glue it in, and pre-bore for the screws.

If the hinge section of the stile has gone beyond use, but the stile itself is mainly sound, cut-in a dove-tailed repair piece the full thickness of the door. Make the piece at least 35mm (1½in.) thick and approximately 180mm (7in.) long. Dovetail it in, then glue and screw it firmly into place. Then recut and screw-in the hinge. The dovetail angle should be shallow; a slope of 1 in 6 is about right. If possible, very slightly wedge the cut across the door thickness so that as the patch is knocked in from the door face it keeps tightening up.

Door frame hinge positions may be repaired as above, but if an insert is cut-in it should be pocketed because of the door stop.

RUBBING AND WEDGING

Inspect the gap around the door to show you where it is rubbing. If the gap is, on average, even, you can plane it with the door hung. If the corners are binding diagonally, and there is a reasonable gap at the hanging edge, either the top or bottom hinge must be cut in slightly more deeply.

If the door blinds (rubs) along the locking jamb and there is a reasonable gap at the hinge edge, cut both the top and bottom door hinge recesses slightly deeper.

This can be done without removing the door if each is done in turn, supporting the door with wedges, and leaving one hinge screwed firmly.

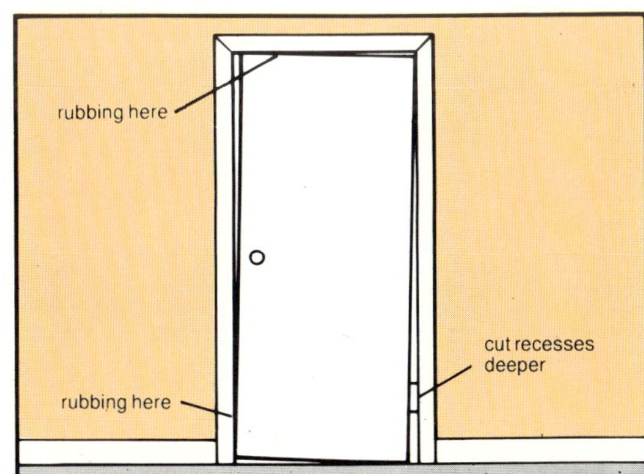

Hinge binding is identified by the screw heads meeting, indicating either that the screw is too large for the hinge or that the recesses are less deep at the back than at the front. The cure is to cut in the hinge flaps more deeply at their back edges. Never re-cut the pivot edge of the hinge more deeply unless there is a very wide gap between door and jamb, and the locking stile is rubbing.

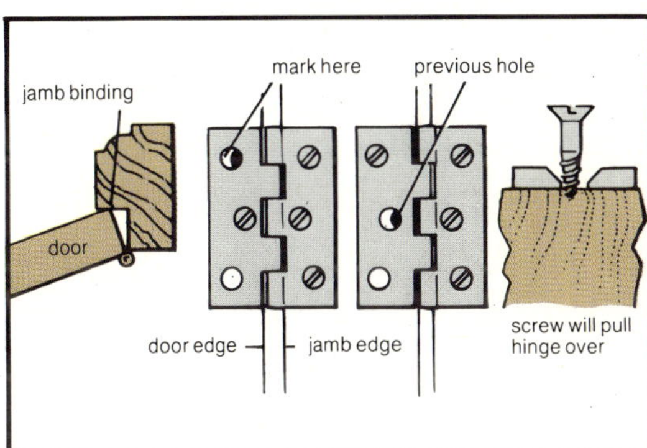

Jamb binding shows itself in two ways. The back corner rubs as it meets the door stop; so bring the hinge back slightly more into the door. Use a bradawl to mark a hole slightly to the edge of another of the hinge screw holes, and then slacken the existing screw. Move the hinge and re-screw it into the new hole, taking out the first screw as the second screw begins to hold the hinge.

The second form occurs when one of the hinge flaps has been cut-in too deeply.

Plane the door edge, if this will not make the overall fit too loose, or cut and fit cardboard packing behind the hinge flap. A sure sign of jamb binding is if the hinge knuckle appears to pull away from the door or frame when the door is pushed firmly closed.

If the door (or frame) is twisted the door will not close evenly to the stops. If the stop is cut as part of the jamb (as for most front-door frames), the hinges must be adjusted.

Doors are rigid, so that if one corner is moved forward on one hinge while the other is fixed, the door pivots on its diagonal. A door that stands proud of the closing jamb at its foot will need to be brought forward at its top hinge and vice versa.

The Brass of the Cabinet Maker

The use of brass cabinet handles and fittings dates back to the middle of the 17th century when, as today, fashion dictated direction and new types of furniture; cabinets on stands, chests of drawers and elaborate side tables were the vogue.

Prior to this time few pieces of furniture incorporated drawers and any fittings needed were made of cast iron. This material was considered unsuitable for the new, lighter pieces which were more sophisticated in design and of woods such as walnut, fruitwoods and hardwood veneers, rather than oak.

As more varied types of furniture were developed, so the demand for brass cabinet mounts quickly grew and brass casting developed into a flourishing industry.

Birmingham has been the centre of the brass founding industry in England since the second half of the 17th century and for over 120 of those years B.Lilly & Sons Limited, a Birmingham based company, has been at the forefront of the design and manufacture of high quality, brass cabinet furnishings.

Today the company offers a wide range of brass cabinet handles and fittings with many from original patterns first used by Benjamin Lilly when he founded the company in 1861.

It is this authenticity of design which makes the Lilly range ideally suited for use in restoring genuine antiques and in the manufacture of reproduction furniture.

But Lilly does not cater only for antique furniture. They offer an extensive range of elegantly designed, modern brass fittings, equal in form and quality to their more historic forerunners.

In recent years, as in many industries, the brass founding industry has experienced growing competition from overseas suppliers, but, the availability of authentic designs, the use of superior materials and workmanship, together with modern production techniques, ensures the continued success of B.Lilly & Co. Limited.

The shape of Doors to come

No photograph can ever illustrate the **'Ways with doorways'** endless list of features.

No adjective can ever describe its revolutionary construction, opening the door to an unlimited range of application. And no words can ever explain how our unique Door Gear makes the door operation so smooth and reliable.

In fact, the only way you'll ever really do this amazing system any justice is to fill in the coupon for our 'INFORMATION PACK', then become an enlightened customer.

If you can't stand the suspense,

send for your 'INFORMATION PACK' consisting of:–

- **BROCHURE – APEX 'Ways with doorways'** – 36 pages of full colour photographs showing many installations, with before and during installation history, of the most complete door system in the world – **Apex Doors & Door Gear – sliding, folding and hinged.** Applications other than doors also fully illustrated. Our brochure will become recognised Internationally, as an authoritative reference for every householder, architect and interior designer interested in Spacesaving and 'Doors as features' within homes, offices and commercial buildings. Written to appeal equally to every discerning householder, D.I.Y. enthusiast and professional.
- **'SPACE SAVING DOOR TEMPLATE'** – a full size door opening width template to enable you to study a Sliding and Folding door movement swept area and observe the solution to your Hinged door space problems on location instantly.
- **'DOOR AND PANEL SELECTOR CHART'** – simplifies your choice of door gear, doors and panels to the precise requirements of installation.
- **COMBINED – PRODUCT DATA, AND ORDER FORM.**
- **FREE ADVISORY SERVICE** – once you receive your 'INFORMATION PACK', always remember our free advisory service is only a phone call away.

No enquiry is too small.

☎ and ask for TECHNICAL or SALES.

Simply clip the coupon and return with remittance indicated thereon, to the manufacturers:–

apex Enterprises
(W & J Kern Limited),
Corporation Road, Birkenhead,
Merseyside,
England L41 1HB.
Telephone: 051-647.9323
International
Telegrams
'SLIDOR
BIRKENHEAD.'

Company & Product Profile

Since 1965 we have been a market leader manufacturing Domestic & Light Commercial Sliding & Folding Door Gear. Naturally we became aware that generally the doors available for specific purposes were inadequate.

Our customers complained of the quality and availability of the correct door for their purpose. People wanted individualism – not slabs of hardboard filled with cardboard, louvred doors, "bedrooms in boxes" (self assembled wardrobes and the like). People soon discovered that these off-the-shelf compromises were often not the value for money they had hoped for. We, therefore, decided to develop a quality alternative which evolved into a new concept in doors – a technological break-through – APEX DOORS. In combination with our DOOR GEAR and fitments, we have created the most versatile complete system ever, **APEX 'Ways with doorways'.**

Apex Doors, a unique range of brazilian mahogany doors, manufactured by Apex after 6 years development of our patented construction system and pioneering the new processes of this technological age. The result – panelled doors of dignity that would grace any home, and far excelling conventional panelled doors in strength and accuracy – enabling panels to be inserted, or interchanged, with the ease of installing electric light bulbs (a world exclusive feature).

The customer selects any of the five door designs available in most popular sizes, chooses a door finish, then separately selects the panels of their choice from our extensive range – to suit purpose and budget.

Illustrated are some of the door designs available, fitted with some of the panels. With the combination of finishes there are over 15,000 variations of design, all to complement precisely differing situations and decor. The panels can be interchanged or replaced with the simplicity of the original installation.

Apex Doors are designed specifically to complement our quality proven door gear – Sliding & Folding. Standard room opening size one piece Apex Doors are available – extending the benefits of our doors to every doorway in the home, whether they be hinged, sliding or folding.

Thanks to the versatility of our unique concept the system is suitable for room doors, room dividers, screens, partitioning, wardrobes, wall/shelving units for display/storage, wall/ceiling panelling, window shutters, and infinite other applications – limited only by the doors to your imagination.

Commercial installations recently completed include the following locations – Hotel bedrooms, Boardroom, Church, Interview-Rooms, School computer room, Restaurant, Public House, Offices, Exhibition (display screening), Shop-Front (facia), Shop display, Caravan and Boat interiors, Sports Hall.

Even if you were only contemplating the use of our Door Gear for the simple conversion of an existing hinged door to sliding or folding, using your existing door/s – or the purchase of louvred or chipboard doors, or any self assembly furniture for bedroom or lounge – our 'INFORMATION PACK' is essential reading material.

Every home owner would benefit from our comprehensive brochure – whether they propose to install our products themselves (we take you step by step through every stage of installation), or to purchase the complete professionally installed package. We guide you to the correct choice for each application – away from the pit-falls that have beset so many installations with their incorrect – door operation, door gear and unimaginative, uninspiring and often totally unsuitable doors.

We hope you will join us in benefiting from our success and the economies of our system – room doors, with panels, costs no more than a nest of very ordinary coffee tables!

Apex Sliding & Folding Doors cost less than the value of the space they save!

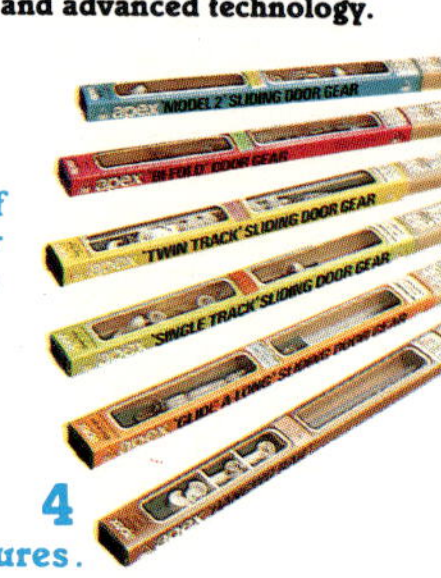

British Made.
World-wide Patents,including U.K. Patent No. 2055134,held by **J. T. Kern (Design Products)** Limited.
Licenced Manufacturers sought World-wide.

APEX 'Ways with doorways' – a revolutionary British concept – the fusion of timeless elegance and advanced technology.

Designed by you for perfection

1 You choose the door.
2 Then the finish.
3 Then the panels.
4 Then the method of installation – Sliding, Folding or conventionally Hinged.

Apex accessories of recommended door furniture, wardrobe interior fittings, matching timber trims & fitments complete the installation to perfection.

1 2 3 4

A modern variation on a classical theme. True excellence, once achieved, endures.

To: apex Enterprises (W & J Kern Limited), Corporation Road, Birkenhead, Merseyside, England. L41 1HB. Telephone: 051-647.9323.

INFORMATION PACK REQUEST COUPON

Please send me ______ INFORMATION PACK/PACKS **APEX 'Ways with doorways'.**

I enclose a cheque/postal order payable to W & J Kern Limited for £______ (£0.75 per pack) and expect delivery by return post.

PLEASE PRINT

Name Mr./Mrs./Miss ______

Position (if trade) ______

Company (if trade) ______

Address ______

Postal Code ______

Telephone ______

apex

WINDOWS 1

Any frame carrying glass is called a 'sash'. The frame (a wooden surround) is built into the house structure, and the sash is fitted to the frame. So, to fit a window (sash) means fitting one frame into another.

Sliding sash windows (those that pull up and down) normally keep out weather better than casement windows (those hinged like a door). Other windows are hinged at the top, or in the centre (they can be twisted round for cleaning). Picture windows cover a large part of a wall. Louvre windows have a series of individual panes, opening and closing like venetian blinds.

If you live in a house built after 1939, it is likely that your windows will conform to BS644 and be of a standard size which aids replacement. Before 1939 there was no standardization and windows were purpose-built for the job. Besides the standard casements and sliding sashes, a variety of other window designs may be found. The most common are the combination windows which form bay and bow windows. Dormer windows are set into the roof and do not have a specific type of sash installed (see page 171).

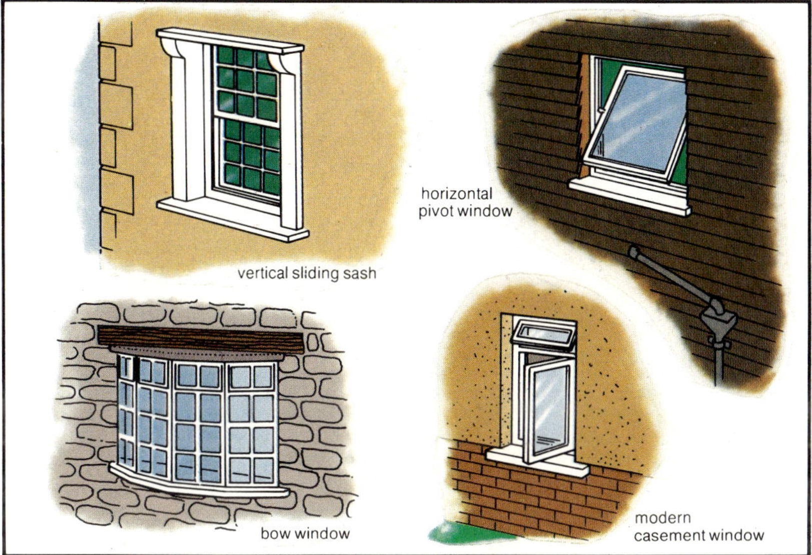

CONSTRUCTION

Window sashes are generally of wood or metal. Wood sashes are liable to rot and metal sashes will rust unless made of aluminium. Plastic sashes are not very popular, although they neither rot nor rust.

Flush-fitting sashes are fitted like doors but, as they are essentially light frames and rarely completely rigid, they are often pulled flat by the taper on the sash lock. It is sufficient to cut the combined thickness of the hinge flaps into either jamb or stile, but this is not ideal as the hinges may drop on the screw shanks.

Stormproof sashes are moulded completely on their outer edges. They have no horns left and are stormproof only because of the details of their section, and the wedging action of their catches, which pull their weather joints close. These sashes almost invariably use surface-fitting hinges, either of the type where one flap fits into a cut-out in the other, or of the Easy-Clean type.

All pressed steel butts should be fitted with their knuckles completely clear of the window (or door) and frame. Only cast iron, cast brass and folded brass hinges are set in using the pivot centre as a marker. Gauges for steel hinges are set to the flap width and the flap thickness.

THE TRICK

A useful trick with all types of hinge except cast iron and cast brass is to 'spring' them if they are not quite free. If a door is inclined to spring back, take a rod, or coin or headless nail and fix it into the hinge angle with a dab of grease. Then push the door closed. Repeat this, using slightly thicker wire, etc., until you see an improvement. A word of caution however: do this with care, because drastic action may shear the hinge knuckle or pull the screws out.

PROBLEMS

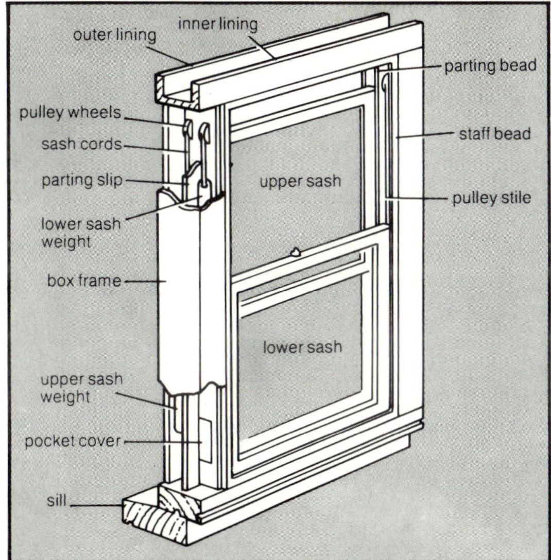

The main problems with windows tend to be caused by inadequate external protection and maintenance. Exterior painting is dealt with on page 196, interior painting on pages 250 and 251. The major problems of rotting frames or rails and loose joints are dealt with on page 52, but a very common problem, which causes much annoyance, is cord failure on vertically-sliding sashes. The result is that the window either will not stay open or will not stay closed. This how to repair it.

1. Take down the curtains and remove any window furniture – windows are heavy and there is no need to make things more difficult!
2. Prise away the staff beads on either side of the window using a broad chisel. It will have to be replaced, so don't break it if possible. Start at the centre.
3. The lower sash is now held in by its own weight and the cords only. Lean its top away from the frame and cut the (remaining) cords with a sharp knife. Gently lower the weights to the bottom of their compartments, then lift the sash out and put it somewhere where it will not get broken. Remove the old cord with a claw hammer.

THE TRICK

Do this even if only the upper sash has failed. If one cord has broken, the others cannot be much better. It is wiser to replace them all at once.

4. Prise out the parting beads which hold the upper sash away from the lower and remove it in the same way.
5. On either side of the window, there will be a small wooden cover (the 'pocket'), which allows access to the pulley stiles.

THE TRICK

If you cannot find it, tap the paint until the joint appears. Prise this off – it is sometimes screwed on – and lift the weights out bottom first. Be careful not to muddle the weights for upper and lower shashes; they are often different in weight.

6. Check that the pulley wheels are working properly and oil them. If one has jammed replace it – any builder's merchant should stock them – but make sure it is the right size.
7. Run a 'mouse' (any small weight attached to a piece of string) through each of the upper sash pulleys and lead the new sash cord through. Thread it through the eye in the weight and tie off with a figure-of-eight knot and replace in the pulley stile. Heat the end of a nylon cord with a match to prevent fraying. Cut off the other end at window sill level.

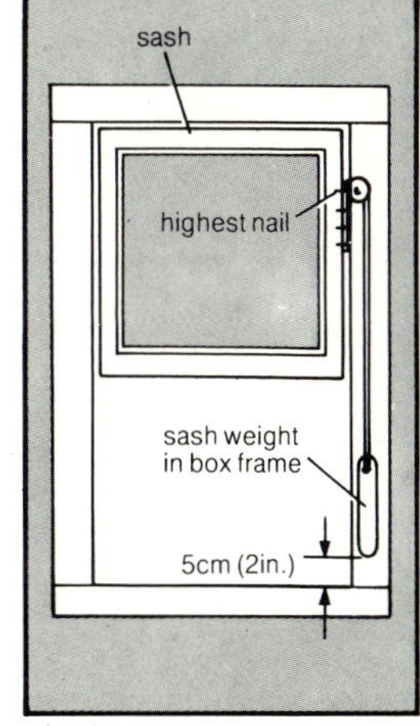

8. Support the sashes against the top of the frame and mark the centreline of the pulley wheel. This is where the highest nail will go. Rest the upper sash on the window sill.
9. Pull the weight up inside the pulley stile until it hangs just below the pulley wheel. Nail the cord onto the upper sash with the highest nail as marked, using three or four 25mm (1in.) galvanized clout nails. Cut the cord off and repeat on the other side.
10. Nail back the parting beads on either side using 35mm (1½in.) panel pins.
11. Repeat with the lower sash – you should have already marked the highest nail point (see 8).
12. Replace the pocket cover, screwing it securely in place.
13. Replace the staff beads so that their inner faces just rest against the lower sash. Use panel pins. Make sure you have enough time to complete this job – it takes longer than you think. If you are decorating, take the opportunity of having the window apart to strip and paint both frame and sash properly. Check that all joints are sound before reassembling.

WINDOWS 2

Complications in the repair of windows are that the sections are small, leaving not much room for mortise and tenons, and the glass creates a weight problem.

If the wood is usable at all, a re-wedging process may save the window before it goes too far. Prise out the existing wedges. Cut and drive in new ones, being careful of the glass. Instead of dowels, use 'star' nails to peg the tenons.

A more rigid repair can be achieved if a face-fixing corner bracket is used, but it will look unsightly. Modern stormproof sashes have so little wood at the joint that the only solution is to buy a replacement sash. If the problem is only that of a loose corner, cramp the window across the rail, then punch the existing 'star' nail through and pull it out the other side. Bore a hole, and glue in a dowel.

DIRECT GLAZING

You can improve appearance and save maintenance by removing rotted sashes and directly glazing into the former sash rebate.

Problems arise when the windows have steel-angle frames. To change these, first break out the glass – it is seldom possible to chip out the putty and re-use the glass since old putty dries hard and old glass is brittle. When the glass has been safely removed, look for the holding screws, which are often buried beneath years of rust. If the screw heads appear sound, it may be possible to unscrew them; but at this stage of their life it is not usually possible, at least with the lower ones. There will probably be three screws along each upright and two across the bottom and top. Find a heavy steel punch or tommy-bar, and with a heavy hammer simply drive the rusted screws through the frame.

Lever out the frame after securing it with rope to an interior ladder in case it pulls out suddenly. If the room is not a ground floor one, the rope is useful anyway for lowering the metal frame to the ground, running it over a high rung of the ladder.

The rebate left will be in some parts good and in others rotted and impregnated with rust. The screws will have to be chopped out. Metal frames need double rebates, one of which is only 3mm (1/8in.) deep and is not deep enough for glass (for reglazing, see pages 190, 191).

RATTLING WINDOWS

This is usually found in sliding sash windows only and is caused by ill-fitting beads. You will have to remove the staff bead (see page 51) and the lower sash (support the latter below the window but pad the glass to avoid an accident) and then re-nail the parting bead closer to the upper sash. Replace the lower sash and re-nail the staff bead closer to the lower sash so that the whole sandwich is pressed more tightly. Be careful not to make it too tight! You can use a rubber wedge to solve the problem temporarily, but the wedge will force the bead further away and so make it worse eventually.

REPLACING A WOODEN SILL

The commonest fault in wooden frames is that the sill rots because the drip groove has become blocked or regular painting has not been done.

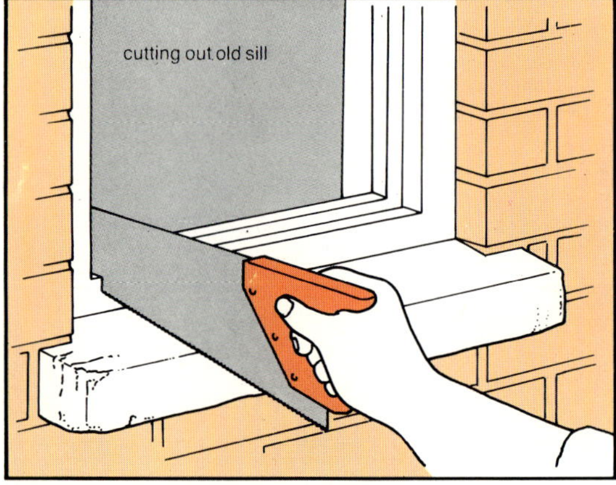

Ideally you should remove the whole frame to replace the sill, but this is a complicated operation and probably beyond the scope of most do-it-yourselfers. It is possible to replace the sill without removing the frame, although the repair is not as strong or as weatherproof. Here's what to do.

1. Buy a replacement sill from your local timber merchant – preferably made from a hardwood.
2. Remove the opening sashes, any fixed glass and the inside window sill. Put them somewhere safe, or buy new glass if the fixed glass broke during removal.
3. Cut across the sill as close to the jambs as possible vertically at each end. Then cut away the remaining timber from around the jambs and saw horizontally through the tenons at the bottom of the jambs and mullions. Remove all debris.

4. Clean away the remains of the mortar on which the sill was bedded.
5. Cut the new sill to fit the existing hole including the rebate into the brickwork. Paint it with primer (see page 195) and then cut ends of the jambs. Cut a drip groove, if there is none.
6. Slide the new sill into the hole, packing it as tightly as possible against the old frame.
7. Screw through the jambs and into the sill until the heads are countersunk. Stop the holes with filler.
8. Mortar in the gap under the sill, packing it as far back as you can.
9. Insert new pieces of wood where the jambs and mullion do not exactly meet the new sill. Glue them in place with a waterproof glue. When set, plane and sand them to an exact fit, then prime.
10. Seal all around the new sill with a mastic filler. Then re-install the sashes, glass and inside sill. Finally paint with a good outdoor gloss (see page 195).

STICKING WINDOWS

Windows generally stick because they have warped, or because of a build-up of paint on the frames, or from swelling because of damp penetration.

The cure for a paint build-up is simple. Strip back to the bare wood, then re-paint as described on pages 241 and 246.

Dampness may be coming from inside (from condensation) or from a lead. If the latter, consult pages 191 and 194. You will have to find the leak, stop it, then strip and re-paint. For what to do about condensation, see page 142.

You should strip back to the bare wood, then dry out the wood using a blowlamp. Be very careful not to crack the glass (see page 231). If there is not a 2mm (1/16in.) clearance between sash and frame, sand or plane it back to a suitable clearance. Then re-paint before any further damp can penetrate.

If the window is warped, you may be able to correct it by following the techniques given for warped doors (see page 45). Be sure to remove the glass before you start as you will surely crack it otherwise. If the hinges are badly set, again see the doors section (page 40).

FITTINGS 1

Hinges (or butts) are really pivots. They are used in a great variety of places, and an enormous range is available, to suit every kind of job. Your final choice will depend mainly on the way you want the job to swing open, and on its relationship to the other parts of the item. Good hinges are more difficult to fit than cheap ones, because top-quality cast brass butts have no free play, whereas cheaper pressed-steel butts distort easily.

BUTT HINGES

A cast brass hinge needs to be cut in very accurately, with a minimum amount showing. This is what you do:

1. Mark the hinge positions on the door. Top hinges are usually closer to the top than bottom. This applies to furniture as well as to doors. No hinge should be closer to the end than twice its length (because it would look wrong). Support the door on edge.

Use a try square on the door edge and slide the butt up to it. Mark the position of the other end using a chisel or knife edge. Square both end lines across.

gauge settings

using a gauge

THE TRICK

A joiner's door cradle made up of oddments will hold most doors. Alternatively, cramp one end to the leg of the step ladder.

2. Set the marking gauge to the centre point of the hinge pin across the width of the flap, and mark along the door edge. Repeat on the door jamb while the gauge is set (having previously marked height positions).
3. Set the gauge point to the hinge pin centre again, but across the thickness of both flaps. Gauge doors and jamb.
4. Mark all areas that are to be cut with cross-hatch pencil lines and define all cut lines with a chisel edge and a smart tap with a mallet.
5. Chisel across the width of the flaps, levering up small chip pieces. Turn the chisel flat, and remove waste. The back of the recess should be slightly deeper, on both jamb and door stile.

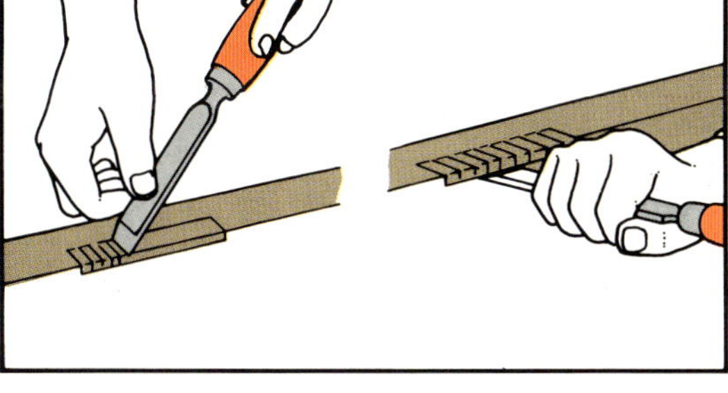

Where light items are being hinged, bolster the back of the piece that is being recessed with a solid block. This prevents splitting, should the chisel slip.

Try the hinges in all four recesses and adjust them until the pin centres are in line with the door and frame edges.

6. Carefully bradawl the centre hole of the door's hinge flap, and screw carefully with a steel screw. Brass screws look best on cabinet furniture but shear off if over-screwed.

Always pre-bore and pre-screw holes for brass screws, using a steel screw.

THE TRICK

Never use steel screws on an oak door as they corrode this type of wood very quickly; use brass or plated screws.

7. Stand the door vertical and place it within the frame, see page 40 for door hanging.

PLUG HINGES

These are the most suitable hinges for chipboard cabinets, whose doors tend to be heavy relative to their size. In order to lower chipboard weight levels, manufacturers reduce the chip contents and sometimes layer the board into a sandwich of large centre chips and fine surface chips. This makes a reasonably light board with a good top surface, but reduces its screw-holding ability.

Plug hinges spread the load by fitting into a circular recess that varies in diameter according to the size used. For chipboard faced both sides with laminate, the plug is usually about 35mm (1½in.) in diameter. The plug diameter must be matched with the boring tool purchased for the job.

THE TRICK

Plug cutters must be filed sharp before you use them – they rarely come sharp enough to cut easily.

The best type of plug cutter has a slightly raised projection forming a rim, which should be used as a depth guide. Check the thickness of the material and the depth of the plug before buying your plug cutter.

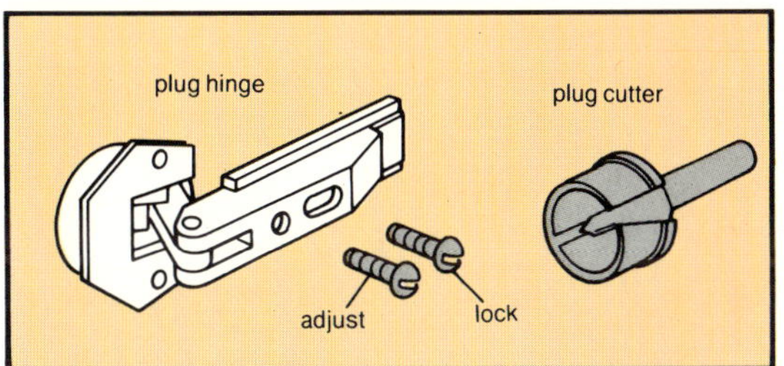

The centre point of the plug cutter should not cut through the opposing face of the board. This creates a problem, as the centre of the hole is difficult to find and to follow, especially with a hand-held electric drill. The slightest waver will cause the tool rim to contact the hard resin surface, when it will jump and tend to skid.

THE TRICK

Punch a fine centre hole with a hammer and panel pin, or drill with a fine bit; this gives a lead. As you start drilling, with the centre spur well located in the centre hole, rock the drill very slightly from side to side. This helps to break through the resin skin more easily.

Plug hinges normally have a reasonable degree of adjustability, so absolute accuracy is not essential. However, the more accurate you are, the easier the adjustment afterwards.

Inspect the hinge. Use two offcuts of the sheet material to help you visualise their relationship with hinge open and hinge closed. The outer corner of the door will always be more or less stationary. This means that if it is approximately 2mm (1/16in.) in from the outer face of the cabinet end-panel when closed, the outer face will be 2mm (1/16in.) in from the cabinet end-face when the door is open. The hinge can open the door within its own thickness, thus allowing two doors to be hung back edge close to back edge.

The hole for a 25mm (1in.) plug hinge should be bored so that the edge of the hole is about 3mm (⅛in.) from the edge of the door. This will allow the adjustment to be used fully.

As the hinges are completely concealed they can be positioned at an equal distance from the top and bottom edges of the door.

The cabinet part of the fitting is usually a plastic or die-cast metal block fixed by two short but stout screws. Look at the hinge and two sample panel pieces to judge the right distance – between 10 and 12mm (7/16 and ½in.) is reasonable for most plug hinges.

When assembling, knock the plug in using gentle blows, levelled with a wood block across the hinge. Do not insert the locking-in screw(s) until the door is hung, because any slight inaccuracy in boring, or fitting, may necessitate twisting the alignment. Use only one screw – the one nearest to the cabinet front – to hold the block until the door is tried.

When satisfied with the hang, tighten the screws. Then check how the door closes. If the doors are not in level alignment, make adjustments. When they are right, insert all the screws and tighten them. Loose plugs may be cured by smearing glue on them before insertion.

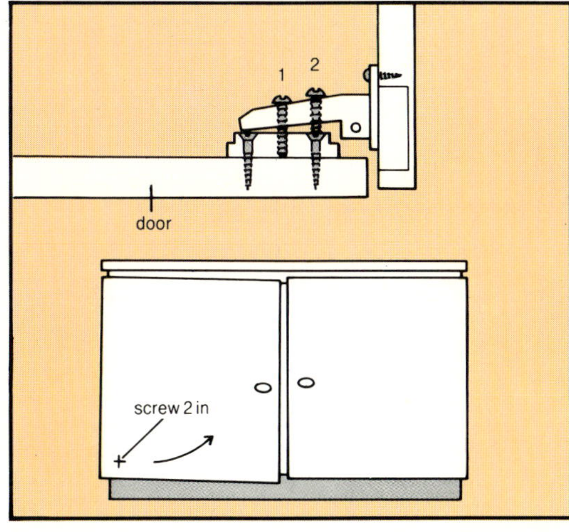

THE DISCOUNT TOOL SHOP
DO YOU NEED A NEW TOOL!
BEFORE YOU BUY A POWER TOOL OR ANY HAND TOOL, WHY NOT TAKE A LOOK AT OUR VAST SELECTION IN THE COMFORT OF YOUR OWN HOME! JUST SEND 50p TO COVER POSTAGE AND WE SHALL SEND BY RETURN OF POST OUR 200 PAGE "DISCOUNT" TOOL CATALOGUE "FREE"! WHERE YOU WILL FIND POWER TOOLS BY: BOSCH, BLACK & DECKER, ELU, MAKITA ETC. HAND TOOLS BY: DRAPER, BRITOOL, FOOTPRINT, STANLEY, KAMASA, SPIRALUX, S-I-P, ETC ETC, AND ALL AT "BIG-BIG" DISCOUNTS! 1,000s OF ITEMS FOR D.I.Y. AND PROFESSIONAL ALIKE, WHETHER IT'S SPANNERS, PLANES, WELDERS, CHISELS, DRILLS, SOCKET SETS ETC, WE'LL PROBABLY HAVE IT! SEND OFF THE COUPON TODAY — IT COULD SAVE YOU A LOT OF TIME AND MONEY!

FITTINGS 2

SURFACE-FITTING HINGES

Recess cutting into chipboard is neither easy nor practical. Layer-boards lose most of their shear strength (resistance to cracking) if this fine surface is cut. Nor can chiselling into glue and chips be done with accuracy. Screw-holding is also impaired if the fine skin is cut.

To overcome these problems, surface-fitting hinges are used. Screwed carefully, they are adequate for most chipboard work, although extra hinges are necessary on long doors. A door with two plug hinges will need three surface hinges.

Surface hinges are designed to fit round into the sides of cabinets. The two flaps fold together and the thickness of the metal gives the distance between door and frame.

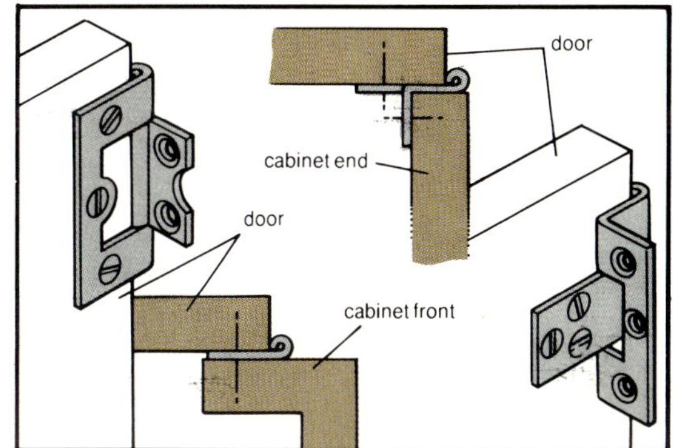

THE TRICK

Fit the frame flaps first if the door is bowed. Then the door can easily be held into the pivot of the hinge so that a mark may be made for pre-boring for one screw.

Always hang with one screw in each flap – the position may be wrong. On a tall door, fit only the top and bottom hinges. The third should be fitted only when you know that the other two are working correctly. This allows a bowed chipboard panel to be 'sprung' in.

MORTISE LOCKS

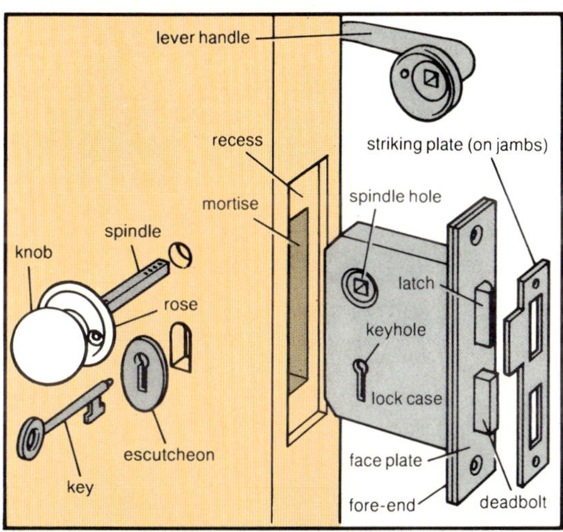

Buy the best you can afford. Check the width of the door stile, for there are deep locks and shallow locks, designed for wide and narrow stiles. Normal height for a mortise lock is somewhere between 900mm (3ft) and 1.30m (4ft 3in.) from the sill surface. If the door is half glass, the middle rail height may decide the position, as mortise locks on robust doors are often fitted into the stile between the solid wood tenons of the rail. If both mortise and cylinder locks are used, the cylinder lock is usually placed higher at approximately 1.45m (4ft 9in.). If the stile is wide enough it is better to avoid the tenons; if a large mortise is cut between tenons the strength of the joint can be lost.

Check the condition of the door jamb before deciding on the position of the lock. There may be a split or large, hard knot where the bolt-mortise must be cut. Bear in mind that screws need sound wood.

KEYHOLES AND HANDLES

Remove the lock once more and very carefully measure and mark the keyhole (if not cut), making allowance for the two face plates. Bore a hole big enough for the key shank and proceed until the drill point goes freely into the mortise and bores a small hole into the opposite side of the slot. Take a smaller bit and bore a second hole below the first. Now use a narrow-bladed chisel to open the keyhole slot downwards. Check that the key slides freely into the finished hole and on into the lock.

If you do not have a narrow chisel, use the largest bradawl you can obtain. Start the slot, then use a fine hacksaw blade to cut the slot downwards.

The lock can now be fitted and screwed into the door, attaching the outer plate with its two small screws. Check that the key moves freely.

If the door is internal and the lock has a knob-turned latch, bore through from both sides for the handle shank before you fit the lock. Doors that are to be locked from both sides need two keyholes.

FITTING

Measure the lock and mark centre lines on the edge of the door to show the centre of the lock position. Then mark the width and thickness of the lock, allowing 3mm (1/8in.) in width and 2mm (1/16in.) for easy fitting. Measure the length of the lock and mark it on the door face for reference, allowing an extra 6mm (1/4in.).

THE TRICK

Select the correct diameter drill or bit, and mark on it the required depth, using a piece of adhesive tape.

Bore full-depth holes between the length lines of the mortise, taking care to keep parallel to the door face and horizontal in height. Bore the holes as close as possible, but not so that they run into each other. Start from each end, then do the centre and finally bore out the remaining wood.

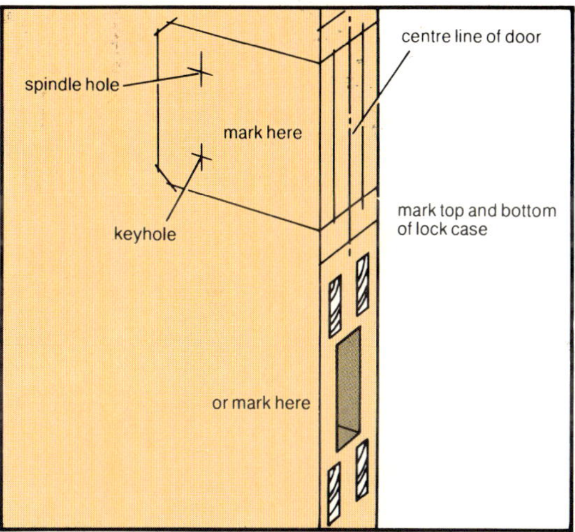

The remaining web between the holes can be removed using a strong chisel without side bevels. Lever the handle up and down to break the internal wood. A hacksaw blade can saw down each side once room is made for it. Clean out the hole until the lock slides in.

The front end of the lock may have two face plates: one integral with the casing with two holes for fixing, and another (often chromed) with two holes to take small metal-thread screws which fit into threaded holes in the casing end plate. Gently tap the lock back into the mortise, taking care not to let it get wedged, until the integral face plate is in contact with the edge of the door. Scribe a deep line round this plate and remove the lock.

THE TRICK

If a lock jams, very carefully measure the position of the keyhole on the door face and then cut it (see Keyholes and Handles). A screwdriver can be used to ease out the lock.

Use a sharp chisel to remove the wood within the marked lines to a depth equal to the thickness of the combined end plates. When the lock and its second plate are fitted, they should make a good flush fit into the door edge.

THE JAMB

Turn the bolt back into the lock and close the door, checking that no part of the lock outer face plate nor its screw-heads touch the jamb.

THE TRICK

Cover the end of the bolt with a thin coating of lipstick or a piece of carbon paper and close the door. Hold the door firmly closed and operate the key. While the key is holding out the bolt, rock the door slightly to make an impression on the jamb.

Using this as a guide, cut a shallow mortise for the bolt, testing from time to time. When it is deep enough, use the slot as a position guide to mark round and cut the shallow recess necessary for the keeper plate to lie flush within the jamb. Test the lock again and tighten all screws.

REPAIRING FURNITURE 1

CHAIRS

The most common problem with chairs is that one or more joints may come unglued and so make the chair unstable. If you want to make a lasting repair, it is essential that you should clean the joint out properly so as to give the glue a proper chance of fixing correctly. This means extracting the rung or leg or arm from its socket. The best way to do this is to use two pieces of wood as a wedge and lever; slow steady pressure is more likely to bring results than jerking.

When you have extracted the rung, etc, sandpaper off all the old glue. Wrap a piece of sandpaper round a stick which is a little smaller than the socket and clean that off too. You can use a glue solvent if you prefer, but check that it will not stain the wood first by testing on the underside of the seat or some other unobvious point.

If the rung and the socket are still a good fit, you can simply glue them back together, using a suitable glue. Do read the label and use one suitable for glueing wood together – special formulations for plastic or metal will not work nearly so well! The joint will be much stronger if you cramp it together while the glue dries. Use a G-cramp if you own one, or a batten cramp (see page 39)

THE TRICK

If not, wind a couple of turns of string around the legs, insert a stick and wind this until the joint is tight. Wedge the stick under a convenient member so that it cannot unwind – this works just as well.

If the joint is very loose, there are various things you can do to improve the fit.

THE TRICK

An easy trick is to lay two narrow strips of cloth in an X over the end of the rung after you have glued it. Make sure they will not stick out when the joint is complete. The cloth will adhere to both rung and socket, and gives the glue on both surfaces something to contact in the gap.

Use a child's paintbrush to ensure the the whole of the socket is covered properly. Just squeezing glue into the hole will not spread it.

If neither of these tricks work, you can cut a dowel to fit the old socket, glue it in place, and then bore a new hole for the rung. Alternatively, you could cut a slot in the end of the rung and insert a wedge so as to expand the end to fit the socket.

Make sure when you are glueing a leg back on that the chair is on a level surface when drying. If you have a large enough table, stand it on that. It is also a good idea to weight the seat so that the joint is pressed together as hard as possible. If using anything which might be dirty, protect the seat first.

Make sure you leave the piece of furniture in a warm atmosphere to dry. Glues function much better in warmth. It is a good idea to make sure the piece of furniture is at room temperature before starting glueing.

TABLES

There are two common problems with tables; they are wobbly legs and warped tops. Wobbly legs can either be dealt with as detailed for chairs (above), or you can glue or screw in a block or corner plate to steady them. All tables have a frame all around underneath the top, to which the latter is attached and which is called an 'apron'. Glue blocks can be cut from any spare bit of timber and glued and/or screwed into the apron. This tightens the tenons of the apron into the leg and stops the wobble. Cross-corner plates usually require a slot to be cut in the apron on either side; they then screw together like a clamp.

Warped table tops can be dealt with as for doors (see page 45) if you have time.

THE TRICK

A quicker method, which sometimes works, is to detach the top and take it outside on a fine day. Lay it concave side down on the grass and leave in the sunshine. The sun will remove moisture from the convex side, while the grass adds it to the concave side: this equalises the moisture content and reduces the warp.

You can do the same using a radiator in the winter; sponge the concave side of the table top from time to time.

To prevent the table from warping again, seal both top and bottom carefully before replacing it. Screw it down well all round and use glue blocks to strengthen the corners. If the table base is very lightweight, insert a strengthening batten down the middle.

If you have a kitchen table with a laminated top which is beginning to lift, the cure is simple. Scrape out as much of the old glue as you can, using a vacuum cleaner with a fine nozzle to get the bits out, don't crack the laminate in your enthusiasm! Then follow the instructions for glueing laminates on page 39. If you should happen to burn a hole in a laminate surface, it is almost impossible to patch it satisfactorily; you would do better to crack it off and start again. It is very difficult to cut laminate once it is glued down or to get the patch to fit exactly.

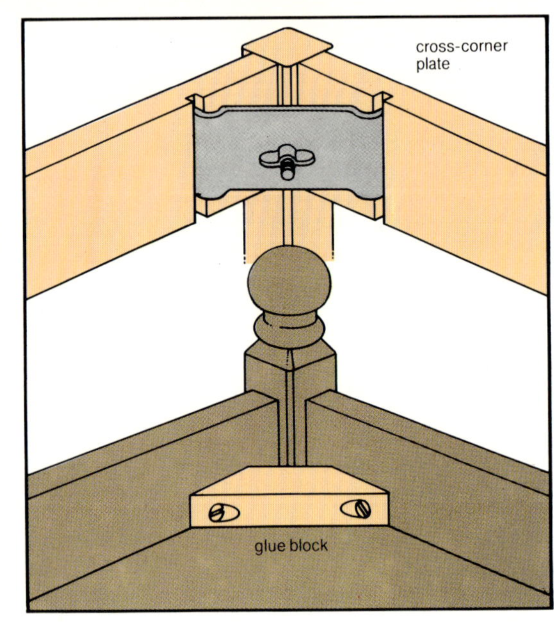

REPAIRING FURNITURE 2

DRAWERS

To prevent a drawer from falling out either buy a short metal bracket or cut a short piece of wood (about 50mm (2in.) long). Screw it onto the back of the drawer so that it lies parallel to the top, but not so tight that it cannot be moved. Insert the drawer partially, swing the stop to vertical, screw tight, and the problem is solved.

THE TRICK

If there is no sign of wear or damp, you could try sprinkling talcum powder on the rails or rubbing them with a bar of soap or candle.

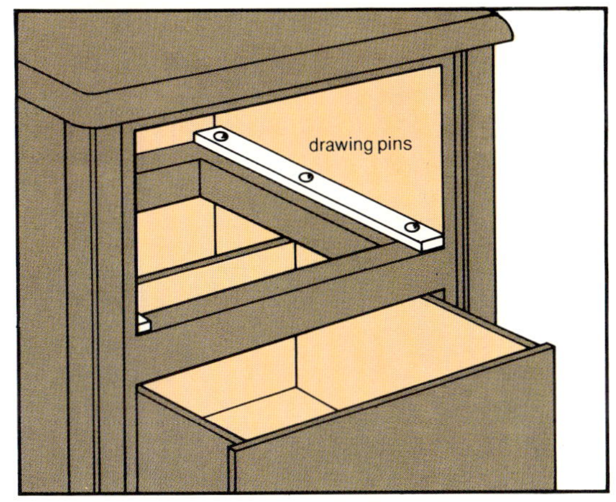

Sticking-in is rather hard to deal with as it usually means that the drawer's bottom – or the rail in the chest-of-drawers, desk or whatever – has worn badly. Take the drawer out, gently, and look at its underside and the surface on which it runs. It is usually fairly easy to see where the wear has occurred. You either have to replace the rail, nailing it on with panel pins; or you will have to build up the bottom of the drawer by glueing thin strips of wood on. Cramp and/or weight as described on page 39. It is sometimes possible to cure this kind of sticking by driving in drawing-pins on top of the rail.

However it may simply be that the wood has swollen because it is in a damp corner. Move it away from the source of damp and dry it out with a hair-drier or by running a lead with a light-socket and bulb into the drawer and leaving it switched on for 10 minutes or so.

Drawers which come apart should be glued and/or screwed back together. See page 56 for glueing techniques and page 35 for the different sorts of joints which you may encounter. Many drawers are dovetailed together. It is claimed that this joint should never require glueing or nailing, but they do come apart and if refixing, it is better to be safe than sorry.

If the handles are loose on a drawer, look on the inside to see how they are attached. Often just tightening the nut or screw will do the trick. If they are screwed into the front and do not go right through, the trick with two pieces of cloth (see page 56) will often work. Otherwise you may have to glue in a dowel and then re-bore the hole.

THE TRICK

Another trick that sometimes works is to cut a small washer of sandpaper and insert it, grit side to drawer front, between it and the handle. Obviously it must be invisible from the front.

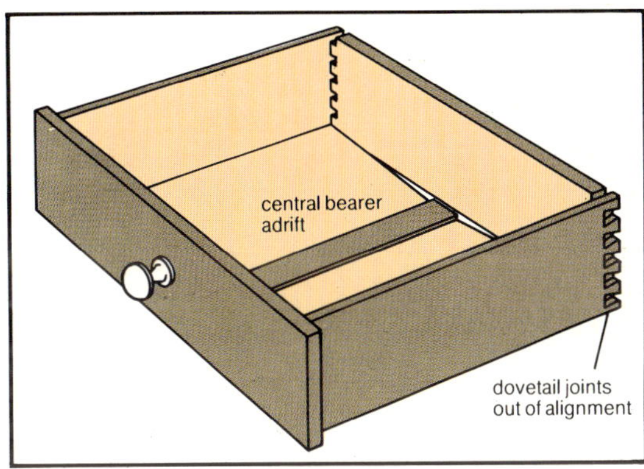

CANE, RATTAN AND BAMBOO

This type of furniture is becoming more and more popular and so a few words about repairing it would be helpful. 'A stitch in time' is the operative idea with these pieces – if you mend it as soon as a binding comes loose, it will be so much easier than if you have to re-bind a whole leg in! Use glue or a tack to hold the loose piece down. If you are glueing, hold it in place until dry with adhesive tape or bind it with string.

If you have a piece with bamboo legs which break, detach the broken member from the main piece and try to find all the large splinters. Cut a dowel to fit snugly inside the leg and glue in place. Glue the broken member onto the other end of the dowel and fit the jigsaw of splinters on as accurately as possible. Tape around the splintered part until the glue has set firmly, then coat with polyurethane varnish.

In fact, it is always a good idea to coat new cane or bamboo items with such a varnish as it prevents dirt from entering and discourages splintering to some extent.

THE TRICK

If your furniture has not been varnished, and is dirty, scrub it gently with a solution of 5g (1 teaspoon) of salt to 570ml (1pt) of hot soapy water.

If you have central heating, you may well find that your cane and bamboo furniture is drying out. Rub bamboo furniture with linseed oil from time to time; for cane furniture, get a humidifier. Smaller cane items – like baskets or trays – can be soaked with water occasionally.

If you have a cane chair where the seat has collapsed, see pages 309 to 311 which tell you all about recaning. However if the seat is simply sagging a little, you can shrink it back into shape in the following manner.

THE TRICK

Make up a hot solution of bicarbonate of soda – about 55g (2oz) to 570ml (1pt) of hot water – and soak both top and bottom sides of the seat. Push the seat upwards, so that the sag is above the correct seat level. Then wipe off as much moisture as possible and leave to dry.

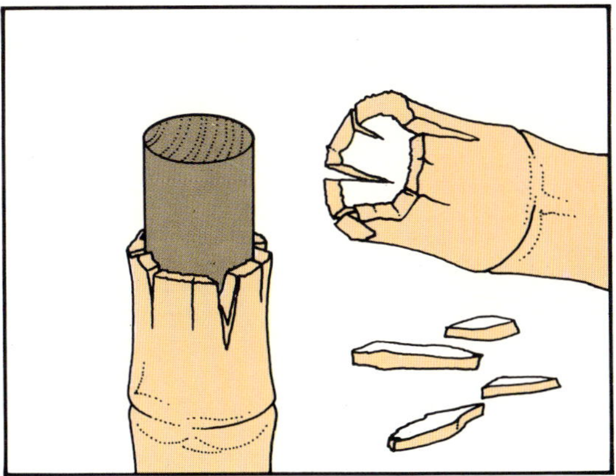

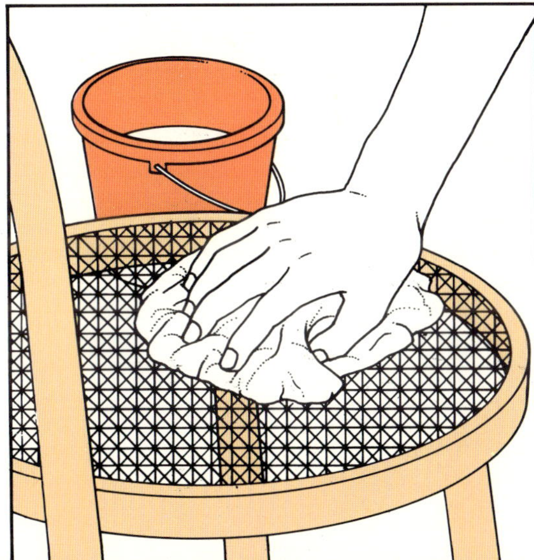

GENERAL TIPS

Dents caused by blows in new or old woodwork can be repaired with a hot iron and a wet rag. Remove any paint or other surface coating and place the wet rag over the blemish. A hot iron will drive in the steam and make the wood swell out.

If screws prove difficult to remove, first open their slots by engaging a screwdriver and striking its handle. This ensures a better grip and sometimes loosens the screw.

Sometimes a reluctant screw may be loosened by the application of a hot iron rod or hot soldering iron. This expands the screw and opens the hole a little.

NAILS AND SCREWS

NAILS

Round wire nail
(or French nail)
General purpose nail with large obtruding head.

Hardboard pin
(or soldier head pin)
Used for fixing hardboard or thin plywood. Head can be punched right in.

Stackpipe nail
(or chisel-point nail)
Used specifically to fix rainwater pipe brackets to walls.

Round lost-head nail
General purpose nail for when the head needs to be hidden.

Sprig
(or cut brad, blued cut bill)
Used for glazing, picture framing and fixing heavy lino.

Plasterboard nail
(or jagged shank nail)
Used for fixing plasterboard to supporting battens.

Cut floor brad nail
Used for fixing floorboards to joists. Shape makes splitting unlikely.

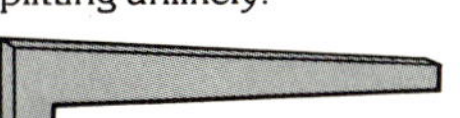

Masonry nail
Mostly used for fixing timber to solid walls (i.e. brick, concrete, breezeblock).

Tack
Made from either steel or wire. Used for fixing carpets to floors and fabrics to wood.

Panel pin
Used for cabinet making, fixing moulding and for reinforcing glued joints. Head can be punched right in.

Chair nail
Decorative nail used for trimming in upholstery work.

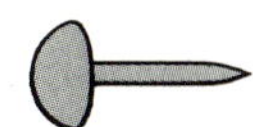

Gimp pin
Small tack used for fixing gimp and braid in upholstery work.

Cut clasp nail
Provides an extra-strong grip in wood and masonry. It is very difficult to remove, so cut the head off and drive the shank right in.

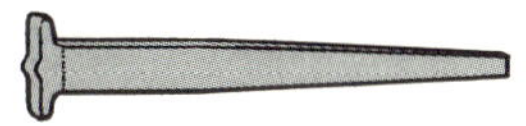

Spring head roof nail
(or galvanized roof nail)
Used for fixing down corrugated roofing – particularly iron and asbestos corrugated sheets.

Corrugated fastener
(or wiggle nail)
Used in joinery to secure corner joints.

Clout nail
(or slate nail)
Used for fixing tiles, roofing felt, sash cords and fencing. A galvanized version is available for outside work.

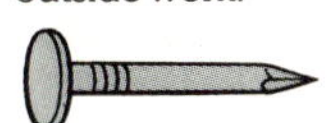

Annular nail
(or ring shank nail)
Used for an extra-firm fixing, such as floorboards or fencing slats. Also used for plywood and other boards.

Duplex head nail
(or double-head shutter nail)
Designed for temporary jobs, where the nail will have to be withdrawn. The second head makes this easier.

Oval wire nail
(or oval brad head nail)
General purpose nail for when a good finished appearance is needed. The shape of the head minimises splitting.

Alloy metal dowel
(or star nail)
Used in heavy carpentry work and for securing a mortise and tenon joint.

Staple
Used mostly for fixing wire fences to their posts and sometimes for fixing carpets. Insulated ones are used to hold surface cable runs and telephone wires.

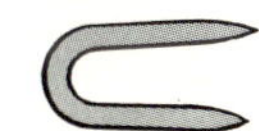

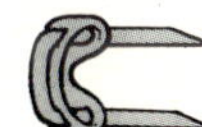

SCREWS

Types of screw slot

Slotted head

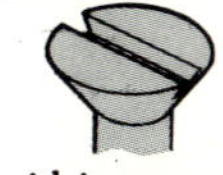

Phillips cross-head

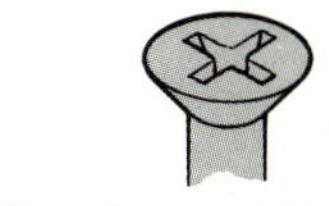

Pozidrive cross-head

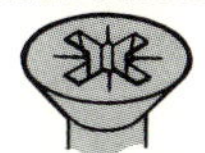

Supadriv cross-head

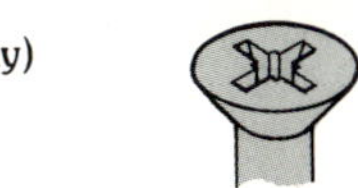

Clutch-head (one-way)

Raised countersunk head screw
Mainly used for attachments which may have to be adjusted, or even removed.

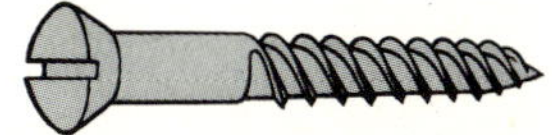

Self-tapping screw
Used for joining two thin materials, such as plastic and metal, together. As its name implies, it cuts its own thread as it is driven in.

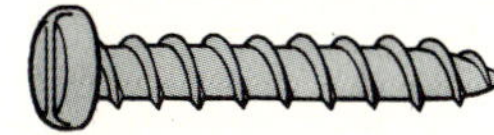

Round head screw
Mostly used for fixing thin materials which cannot take a countersunk screw, such as brackets.

Mirror screw
(or dome-head screw)
A decorative 'hidden' screw, mainly used for fixing mirrors, splashbacks and bath panels.

Countersunk head screw
The most common screw, generally used for fixing timber to timber and metal fittings to timber.

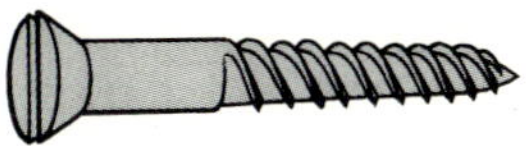

Chipboard screw
(or 'twinfast' screw)
Designed for use with chipboard, the thread goes right up to the head.

Coach screw
A heavy-duty screw driven in by a spanner. Generally found in building joinery.

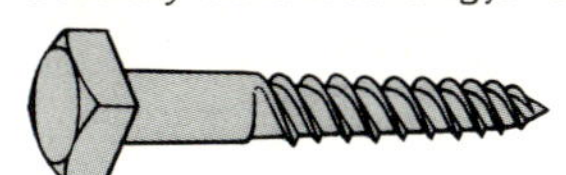

If it looks good now, think what it'll look like with your kitchen round it.

You have to be a professional to install any gas appliance.

But it doesn't take an expert to appreciate the style of New World's System One.

Its looks match anything you build around it.

Its dimensions are standard, so it also easily fits everything around it.

Inside, its Gyroflo oven can swallow a 31 lb turkey.

Its unique Sola grill grills everything placed under it evenly. Whatever the setting.

And its attractive glass-lidded hob gives you fingertip control from the fiercest of boils to the gentlest of simmers.

If you want to do something yourself, do it properly.

Look at System One in your gas showroom.

TI New World Ltd.,
Freepost, Warrington, Cheshire WA14 1BR.

DESIGNING & FITTING A KITCHEN

KITCHEN DESIGN

A kitchen is a very personal thing and every cook has a preferred layout and storage system which rarely works for anyone else. It therefore follows that a kitchen design requires far more thought than it usually is given. Few people are lucky enough to be able to design their kitchen from scratch – cost, dimensions, and fixtures like doors, windows and services may prevent you having exactly what you want even if you are proposing to gut your existing kitchen entirely. This chapter will give you some ideas about what you can do with what you've got and may suggest something you had not considered.

KITCHEN GROUND PLANS

There are five different layouts for efficient kitchens, depending on space available and preference of the user. They are:
1. The 'single-line' (i.e. one wall) kitchen;
2. The 'galley' or parallel kitchen;
3. The U-shaped kitchen;
4. The L-shaped kitchen; and
5. The 'island' site kitchen.

You may find variations on these plans (shown on this page) but most will basically conform to one of them.

'SINGLE-LINE' KITCHENS

Usually found in kitchens which have been converted from sculleries or corridors; the main catch with this layout is that it can involve more walking than is generally acceptable. Make sure that stove and sink are reasonably close together with a work surface between them and plan your storage to minimize walking.

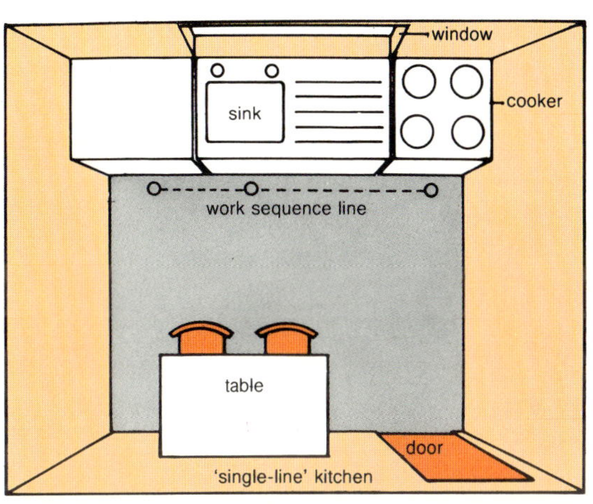

'single-line' kitchen

ISLAND SITE KITCHENS

Often the easiest answer to a kitchen with several necessary doors or items which cannot be moved and which would interrupt any proposed unit layout. You can either put the stove or sink on the island, or make it of two or three storage units sandwiched together with a continuous countertop. Make sure you have sufficient space to move round it and that, if cupboard doors are open, they do not block the passage.

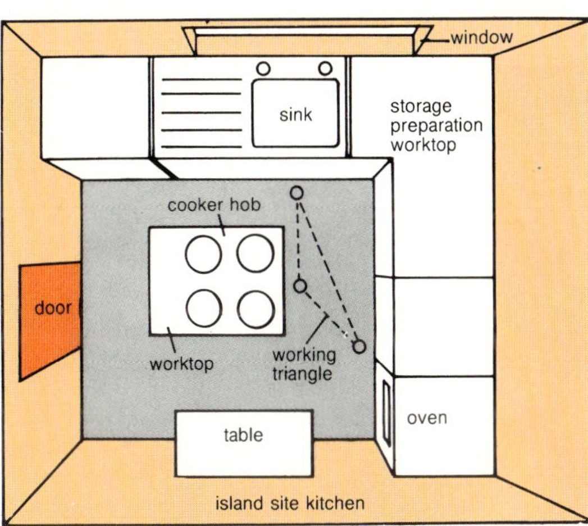

island site kitchen

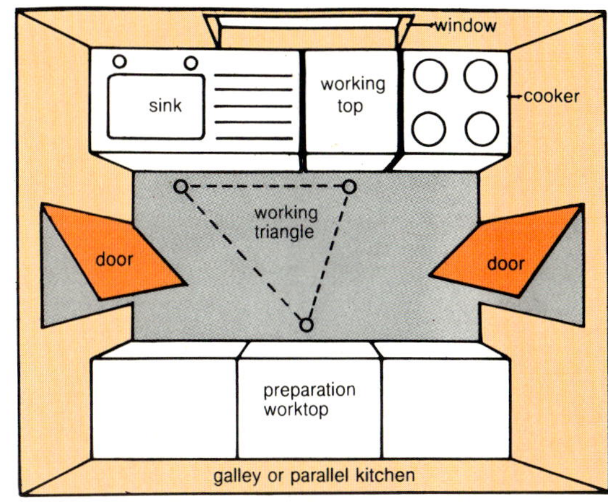

galley or parallel kitchen

GALLEY OR PARALLEL KITCHENS

The essential requirement here is a passage way at least 1.2m. (4ft) wide between the two rows of units. You should plan to position both stove and sink on the same side, so as to avoid crossing the passage way with hot dishes and saucepans. The main problem is the flow of traffic through the middle of the cooking area.

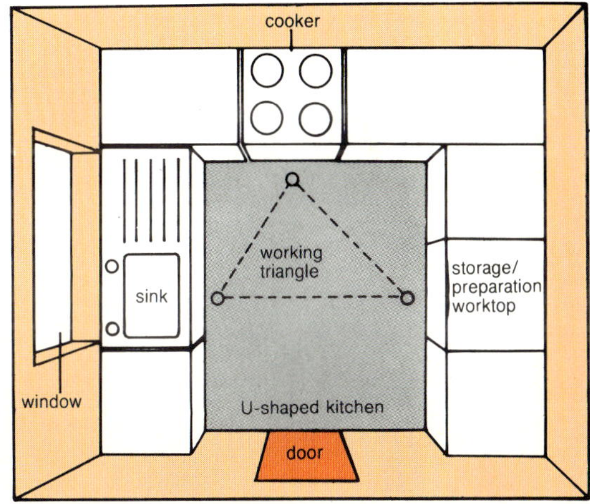

U-shaped kitchen

U-SHAPED KITCHENS

An ideal layout for a small kitchen, where the units wrap themselves around the cook on three sides. Extremely adaptable and flexible, it does require more units than the two previous designs. You could use one arm of the 'U' to separate the cooking from the eating area of the kitchen, but make sure that it does not also add substantially to the distance you have to walk.

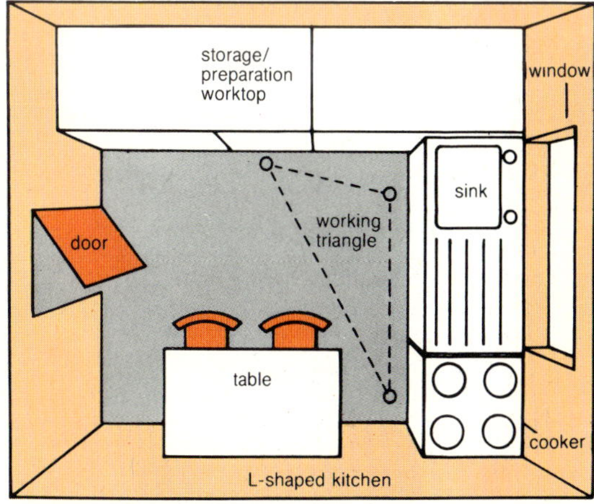

L-shaped kitchen

L-SHAPED KITCHENS

Probably the best layout for oddly-shaped rooms and large kitchens, to minimize walking, it allows for inconveniently placed doors and windows to be accommodated. It is also a good basis for later extensions of the kitchen, if you decide to spread the cost over a period of time.

DESIGN CONSIDERATIONS

A major consideration of kitchen design is conservation of energy. Research shows that most people have three major work centres in their kitchen: i.e. the sink, the stove and a food storage area. The last is often combined with a preparation surface; if not, this becomes a fourth work centre. A well-designed ground plan will site each of these areas within 1.2–1.8m. (4–6ft) of each other; no kitchen should require you to walk further than 6m. (20ft) in order to reach all three. If your kitchen does, then it is in urgent need of redesigning because you are wasting valuable time and energy while working in it.

Another consideration is exactly how you use your kitchen. Is it strictly for cooking? Does the family eat in there: sometimes, always? If so, how many do you have to seat? Do your guests come and sit in there too? Do the children play in there? Do you keep your cleaning things in there? Do you wash, dry and iron in it? Would you like to use it differently than you do now? Are you proposing to buy a washing machine, tumble drier, dish-washer, freezer, new stove, hob and oven units, waste disposal machine or any other large piece of kitchen equipment as part of this redesigning or at a later date? How much do you have to store, or would like to store in there? Does the present kitchen suffer from condensation (see page 142)? Is your present sink, stove, fridge, storage space adequate for your needs? Could you reuse and/or redecorate your present units to match the new design?

KITCHEN PLANNING

MAKING YOUR PLAN

It is absolutely essential that you have an accurate ground plan of your present kitchen, or the room which is to be converted, before you start making any plans. Use a steel tape measure to obtain accurate dimensions (including height if there is any problem there) and then draw a scale plan.

THE TRICK

Most stationery shops sell squared paper in large sheets and this is ideal. Make sure you use metric measurements throughout – all manufactured units are now made in metric sizes.

Choose a scale which will allow you to draw the plan to a reasonable working size but which will give you plenty of margin space in which to make notes and jot down other useful information, such as socket locations, water and gas pipe runs, boilers, etc. Use different colour codes for the different services.

When measuring the room, take measurements at several places, as well as along each wall. Even in modern houses, walls are seldom exactly straight and you might well find a bend which would spoil the line of a run of units. The location of windows and doors should also be marked accurately. Take the measurements to the edge of the door or window mouldings, not to the actual gap. Be sure to indicate which way they open.

EQUIPMENT

Measure carefully each piece of equipment that you are proposing to retain in your new kitchen and cut out a piece of thin card (file dividers are ideal) to the correct scale.

THE TRICK

Write on it what piece it is and its accurate dimensions. This should always be in the order: length × width × height. It is important to check that a worktop run will fit.

Do the same for any new equipment you intend buying – you can get the dimensions from the manufacturer's brochure. If you are going to buy new units, cut out several pieces to match the full unit and half unit sizes. You can then move them around until you get the best layout.

This exercise is worth doing even if you are intending to go to a kitchen supplier who will do the whole job for you. If you can get a clear picture in your mind of what the end result should be, the company's designer will find it much easier to produce a suitable design. Equally, if you say that you want to do 'X' but cannot see how it can be accommodated, the designer may well be able to spot the answer. The most difficult brief for any designer is from a person who has no idea what he or she actually wants in the end!

ALTERATIONS

When you start shuffling your unit and equipment pieces around, have a look at the kitchen ground plans shown on page 63 to see which layout looks both pleasing for you to work in and possible in the space available.

Remember that it is inadvisable to put a stove under a window because of the dangers from draughts and that you should not have to carry hot items right across the kitchen: i.e. the stove and sink should not be opposite each other. Cooker hoods are more efficient if they vent to the outside, so this may fix the cooker position if you have a bad condensation problem.

It is probably a good idea to work out your 'ideal' layout and then modify it to fit. Budget is an overriding consideration, but it is possible to move doors, knock down walls and generally improve the space available. For instance, if you have a separate larder, is this really necessary? Does it have load-bearing walls, or could you knock them down and incorporate the space into the kitchen proper? Major works may be subject to the Building Regulations; check with your local Town Hall before getting too far. This is particularly the case if you want to build an extension.

If you want additional equipment, does it have to go in the kitchen? Could you buy a combination fridge/freezer instead of two items? Could you keep your cleaning equipment elsewhere (under the stairs perhaps)? Are you storing things like paint in the kitchen which could go in the garage? If you have an old fireplace, can you utilise the flue for the boiler, venting the cooker? Could you stack your tumble drier on top of the washing machine? If you want a hob, why not use an under-the-counter oven instead of the tall oven unit? Could you incorporate a fold-away ironing board? Buy units which include plinth drawers for extra storage? If you have a very narrow kitchen, why not buy units with sliding doors?

FLOORS, WALLS AND CEILINGS

Kitchen floors are often badly worn and therefore uneven; check them with a spirit level. If they are badly worn, consider using a levelling compound and then laying hardboard over the top (see page 203). Sheet vinyl is probably the best flooring for a kitchen; avoid seams as much as possible – if you have a big kitchen, consider using an extra-wide vinyl (see page 211). Kitchen carpets, which repel stains, are available; carpet tiles are another practical alternative.

Walls are probably best tiled around work surfaces and sinks because they can so easily be wiped clean, while resisting water and heat. Tiling the gap between unit top and the bottom of wall cupboards is very popular.

If you decide to hang wallpaper, make sure it is a washable vinyl or equivalent (see page 252) because it will last much longer.

If you have a condensation problem, consider using an anti-condensation paint (see page 142).

If you have a very high ceiling in your kitchen, or if it is in bad condition, you might consider installing a false ceiling. Lighting is a problem in kitchens (see right) and an illuminated suspended ceiling (with fluorescent lamps above it) will diffuse light without harsh shadows. If you have a lot of pipework near the ceiling, it would also conceal that. The individual tiles can be removed and washed, which makes it much easier to keep clean than the average kitchen ceiling.

SERVICES

Make sure that you plan and install all new sockets, plumbing, etc before you start putting in the units. Work out carefully what your requirements will be, and consider the little extras which may make life simpler in the future. For example, you may not own a washing machine, but it is worth getting a plumb-in point installed if you are doing some plumbing work.

Make sure you have enough sockets installed: it is worth having them placed above the worktop level when intended for items such as kettles, toasters, blenders, etc. Five sockets are usually considered the necessary minimum.

THE TRICK

If you are having any gas work done, do have a bayonet connection put on the cooker as this allows you to disconnect and reconnect the cooker without calling out the Gas Board.

LIGHTING

It is absolutely vital that all kitchens should have ample light on all work surfaces. You should never find yourself working in your own shadow; if you are, you should do something about it quickly otherwise you are heading for a nasty accident. If you have wall cupboards, fluorescent lights attached to their undersides will provide convenient lighting.

If you want to use spotlights (see page 91), be sure that you install enough to ensure that all areas are properly lit. If you do not connect them all to one switch, you can have your mood lighting and still work in safety.

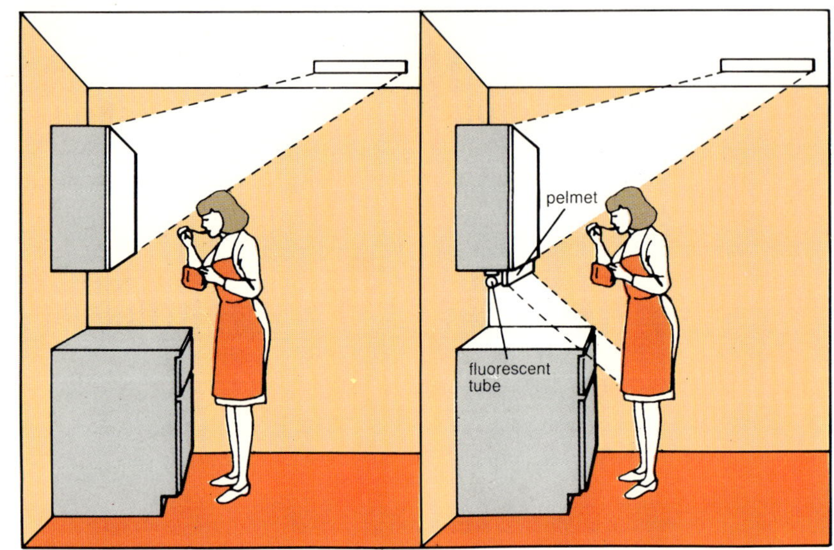

PERSONAL REQUIREMENTS

As we said earlier, kitchen layout and design is a very personal thing. Take your time in deciding what you want; don't be rushed into choosing a layout or equipment and be sure to choose a colour scheme which is agreeable to you. After all, you are going to have to live with it for years, so get it right to start with.

GREENFIELD SYSTEMS

Made in Great Britain
Made in Great Britain

BUILDING A KITCHEN

Draw the final layout carefully and use it to plan out the dimensions of the fittings. The working surface height should be 900mm (3ft) above the floor but can, of course, be varied. Pay particular attention to the cabinet doors. Decide which way they should open and the hinges to be used. The end and central dividers, made from veneered chipboard, are the same no matter how long the unit is. The basic framework can then be fitted with cupboards, drawers and other fittings to suit the planned layout.

Location of the central dividers must allow for any fitted sink, cooker hob or other fittings. They should be positioned, if possible, so that standard panel widths can be used for the main cupboard doors and so that ready-made drawers will fit snugly in between them. Design the working surface as a completely independent part of the cupboard unit so that it will simply drop over the unit to cover fixing screws and joints. Avoid joints in the laminate covering wherever possible.

Drop-in sinks are ideal for flush laminate tops as they can be located anywhere. To accommodate the conventional sink and draining board, design the base unit to allow the top to drop neatly into position. Where a working surface abuts this type of sink, the joint must be completely sealed using a flexible purpose-made sealant.

BUILDING THE BASIC UNIT

After making an accurate drawing showing the dimensions and locations of shelves and drawers, cut the end and centre dividers from a panel of material of the correct width. Mark and saw out the plinth recess (ends) and batten recesses (dividers). Cover the visible cut edges of the plinth recess with an appropriate edge trim. Cut the two top horizontal cross members from 75 × 25mm (3 × 1in.) softwood. Use these to measure the length for the full-length base shelf, cut to the same width as the ends.

It would be necessary to cut away the top part of one divider to make room for the sink. Measure the sink depth and mark it on the drawing so that you know where to position the divider and how much to trim off.

This system can be extended and modified to suit almost any kitchen unit required, with or without fixtures. Drawer, false fronts and cupboard doors are surface fixed to hide the divider edges.

CONSTRUCTION

Lay the ends and dividers together on a flat surface, back edge to back edge in pairs and, using a soft pencil, carefully mark the location of the base shelf and any intermediate shelves. Refer to your drawing to locate all battens supporting shelves or drawers. Next mark the location of dividers on both softwood cross-members and on the base shelf.

Drill and fit end battens to the base shelf, then fix the shelf by screws from the underside to all the dividers. Fix the softwood cross-members to the dividers. Fix the ends by screws to the base shelf through the batten, also to the cross-members.

Cut the back from enamelled hardboard with dimensions taken direct from the assembled unit. The back may be either pinned or fixed with screws, after any necessary cut-outs have been made for waste fittings and tap connections. If the back is cut squarely (use a T-square), the frame will automatically be square if the back edges line up.

For the plinth, simply paint a piece of plain chipboard with two coats of black plastic laminate after assembly. Cut the plinth and screw battens along the top and two sides. Fix it to the ends and base shelf with screws.

Fit a blanking plate opposite the sink to conceal the underside of the bowl. Now fit cupboard doors and drawers to the unit. Build drawers from purpose-made plastic components faced with plastic veneered chipboard panels to match the main unit. To fit the fronts accurately, first fit the drawer and runners in the unit and then hold up and fit the fronts in turn starting from the top and working down. In this way each front can be levelled with the one above. Full details are included with the plastic kit parts.

Hang the doors using either the lift-off or lay-on type of hinges. Fit shelves after main construction using purpose-made removable plastic supports.

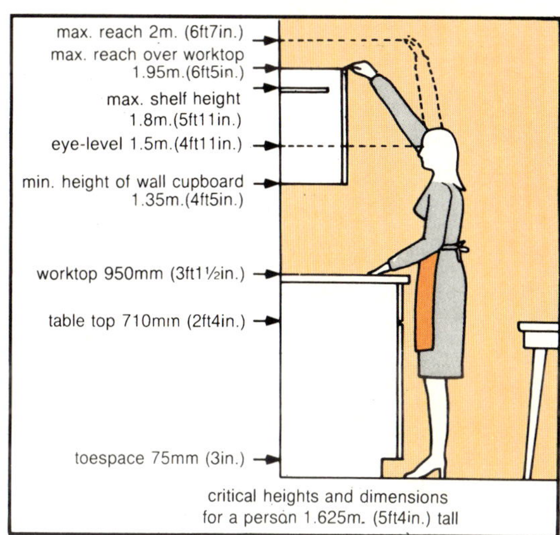

critical heights and dimensions for a person 1.625m. (5ft4in.) tall

ON-SITE FIXING

Place the unit without its top in its final position. Check levels in both directions using a spirit level. Generally it is the front to back level that will need some adjustment by trimming the bottom edge of the ends. Mark any additional holes for plumbing and cut them before the unit is finally fixed.

Once the unit is firmly and accurately sited, fix it to the wall with four screws, fitted through the back and into wall plugs. The top, including the sink, is the last component to be fixed. In kitchens with more than one inserted unit, it is best to fit all the bases first, then fit the worktop continuously over everything.

WORKING TOP

With the units in place, measure for the countertop. Cut it from 20mm (¾in.) thick blockboard which is much more resistant to warping than chipboard. If possible, plan it so it can be cut from one sheet of blockboard. Where joins are necessary then these should be arranged over the centre of a cupboard area, so that a strengthening block may be fixed to the underside. Note that the working top is designed to project approximately 25mm (1in.) over the top front edge with a lip of a strip of 25mm (1in.) square softwood.

With the blockboard cut to shape, fix the edge lip with screws from the underside. Make sure that the softwood strip lines up perfectly with the edge of the blockboard. Plane off where necessary.

Face the visible edges of the top with a strip of plastic laminate (see page 36). Take care that the trim does not bridge any internal curves. Cut the laminate for the countertop to shape allowing an approximately 5mm (¼in.) overlap all round. Glue into position and finish (see page 39). When cutting the aperture for an inset sink, bore holes at the corners and join them with jigsaw or padsaw cuts.

A	= base board	H	= top shelf (½ size)
B	= end	J	= cross rail
C	= divider	K	= worktop
D	= base supports	L	= fascia
E	= bottom shelf	M	= drawer
F	= top shelf	N	= cupboard door
G	= bottom shelf (½ size)	P	= hardboard back

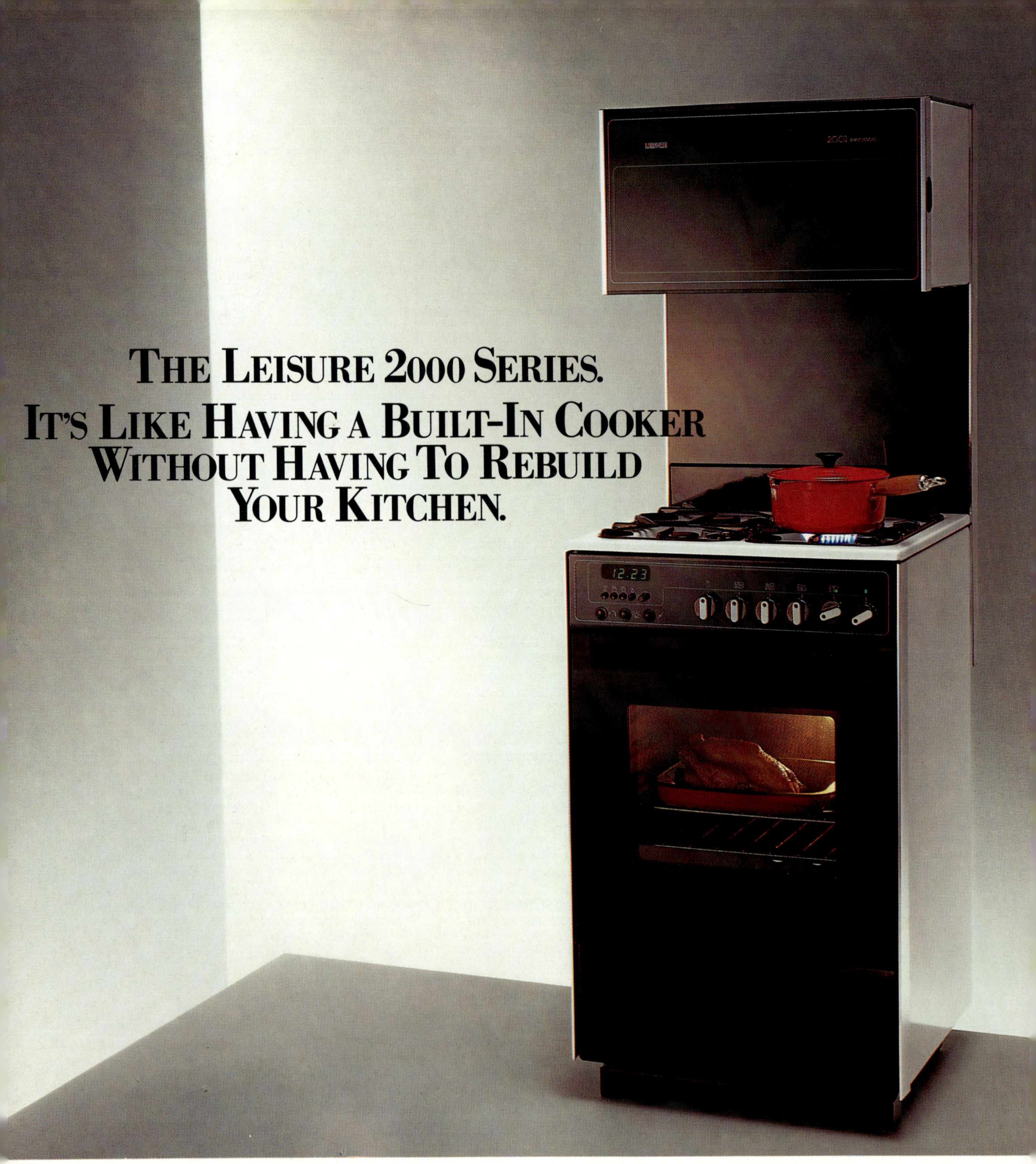

The Leisure 2000 Series.
It's Like Having A Built-In Cooker Without Having To Rebuild Your Kitchen.

Although there are hundreds of cookers from which to choose, there are only two options.

Either an inexpensive free-standing cooker without all the time saving gadgets you really need.

Or a sophisticated built-in cooker that demands an expensive kitchen refit.

Fortunately, now there's the Leisure 2000 series. A range of beautiful freestanding gas cookers, that give you all the features of a built-in cooker without the cost.

The Leisure 2001, for instance, has a grill centre that includes not only a rotisserie, but also the unique Leisure Rotoaster (a built-in sandwich maker and kebab turner).

There's also an electronic clock plus automatic controls programmed by microchip.

If you would like the advantages of a quality built-in cooker without having to rebuild your kitchen, why not call in to your local gas showroom today?

Or fill in the coupon at the back of this book.

From all the cookers available there may be two options, but there's only one choice.

LEISURE

Advanced Kitcheneering.

Leisure
A member of the Glynwed International plc group of companies.

KITCHEN SAFETY

You are more likely to have a serious accident in your own home, than you are outside it. Of all the rooms in the house, the kitchen is the one where you are most likely to meet disaster.

Make sure that major appliances are serviced on a regular basis. Gas and Electricity Boards have service departments.

Keep poisons well out of the way of small children. Remember that bleach, methylated spirits, metal polishes, ammonia, dry-cleaning fluids, etc. are all poisonous. Never transfer such liquids into other bottles – particularly drinks bottles – unless they are carefully labelled and kept most securely.

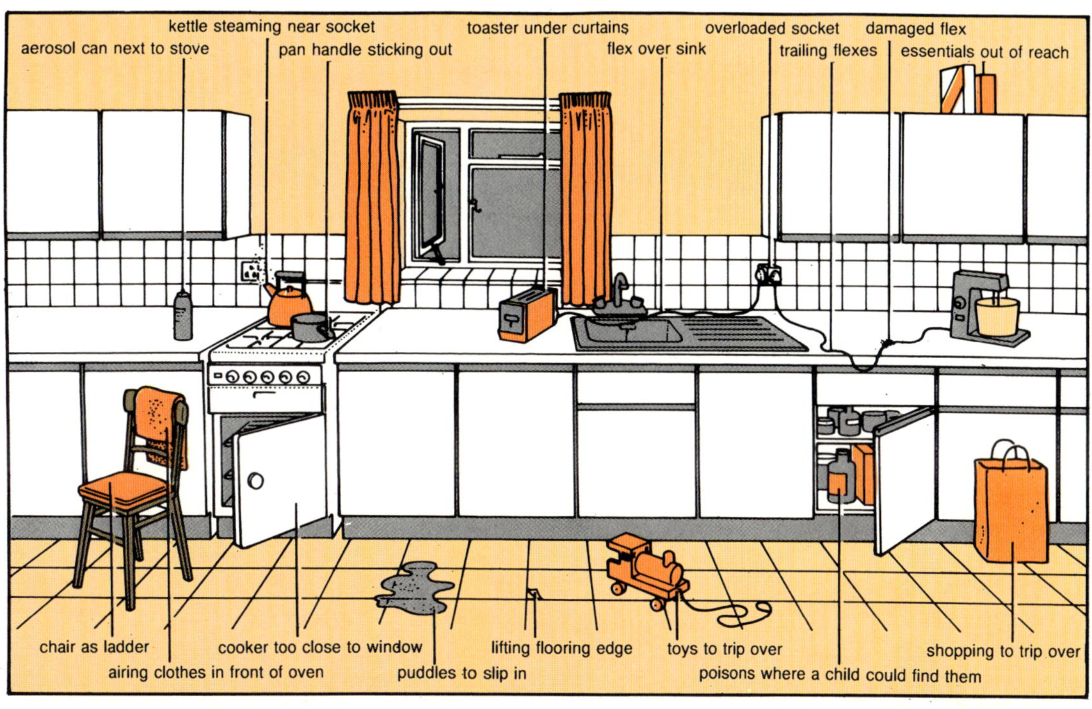

GAS

Never go looking for a gas leak with a lighted match, candle, etc. Never switch on a gas stove if you can smell gas (however faintly) unless there is some good reason for it. It is much safer to telephone the Gas Board and ask them to come and inspect to make sure that nothing is wrong.

If you do have a gas leak, turn off the gas at the meter, check that all fires, stoves, the boiler, etc. are switched off. If you can do it safely, open the window in the room where the leak was so as to clear the room of fumes. Don't let anyone smoke, use lighted flames or switch on electrical points until the leak is mended.

ELECTRICITY

Never forget that a faulty appliance can kill. Don't continue to use malfunctioning equipment – get it mended. Make sure that all plugs are correctly connected (see page 75) and check flexes for wear at least once every six months. Always use the correct weight of fuse, to avoid overloading the item.

Don't use adaptors in the kitchen and don't overload a socket. It is easy to change a single socket to a double one (see page 85) and much safer. As suggested on page 64, when redesigning a kitchen, make sure you have as many sockets as you will need: if necessary, run a new ring main specifically for the kitchen. Make sure that cookers, etc. are properly wired into circuits of the correct voltage using fused connector units (see page 86).

Avoid flexes trailing along worktops if at all possible – install extra circuits if necessary and never drape flexes across sinks or round taps – the smallest flaw in the insulation could kill you.

Never fill irons, kettles, etc. when plugged in. It is most dangerous. You should also not immerse any piece of electrical equipment in water. If this does happen by accident, place the item in a warm dry atmosphere and allow to dry out completely. If you use it before it is properly dry, it will probably blow a fuse.

Make sure you understand how items like blenders, coffee grinders, microwave ovens, irons, and other kitchen electrical goods are supposed to be operated. Read the instruction booklet carefully and keep it somewhere handy so that you can check if you are not sure you are doing the right thing. If you don't understand something, go back to the shop and ask for a demonstration.

If something stops working, switch it off and disconnect it before you start investigating. Never try to dislodge something in a blender, etc. with a finger while it is still running. Try to buy items which have positive safety points, like coffee grinders that only work when the lid is in place to avoid damage from the blades.

Always switch off at the mains when you have finished using an item. An inquisitive child could be badly hurt if the power is left connected.

FIRES

Hot fat is a major source of danger in any kitchen. Never deep-fry with the pan more than half full of fat, and always have a suitable sized lid to hand to cover it in case it catches fire. Don't tip wet food into hot fat; always dry it on a kitchen towel first. Never leave a chip pan unattended or allow it to overheat – if it starts smoking, turn the heat down at once. Never move it if on fire.

You are strongly advised to buy a fire blanket and hang it on the wall near the stove. When opened out and thrown over a fire, it will prevent oxygen from reaching the flames and so smother them. Powder extinguishers are efficient in a kitchen fire but require regular servicing and refilling – a fire blanket is cheaper and easier.

Don't forget that you should never use water on a fire caused by hot fat or electricity – it will only make matters worse.

Never hang clothes to dry over a stove or the oven door. Never leave anything flammable on or near the stove – particularly not aerosols which can explode when overheated.

If you decide to have curtains or blinds in your kitchen, make sure there is no danger of them being blown onto the lighted stove and preferably use a non-flammable material like glass fibre to make them. Never use an electrical item like a toaster under a curtain or, indeed, under wall cupboards.

If an electrical item catches fire, turn it off at the socket if you can. If you cannot reach the socket, turn the whole circuit off at the consumer unit (see page 75) and then unplug the item.

It is not advisable to keep polishes, paint strippers, or other chemicals in the kitchen unless they are in a well ventilated cupboard. If in a warm confined space, they may overheat and explode. For the same reason, don't leave aerosols in the direct sunlight on a regular basis. Never try to burn aerosols – they will explode.

If you are unlucky enough to have a fire, don't panic. If it is a minor fire try to deal with it as detailed above. If it is too big, make sure the windows and doors are shut and phone the fire brigade. Don't breathe in smoke unless to escape: the air is often purer near ground level, so get down and crawl.

FALLS AND SPILLS

Never stand on a chair to reach a high cupboard – use a proper stepladder or a step stool. Organise your kitchen so the things you use regularly are in a convenient place that does not require climbing.

If you have small children, never leave saucepan handles where a child could reach up and pull – always turn them into the centre of the stove (this is a good precaution to take at any time in a small kitchen) and consider buying a saucepan guard to fit around the hob.

Don't overfill the cupboards that small children can reach – a tower of tins can hurt a lot. Also don't try to carry too much at one time – better two trips than dropping the lot!

If you spill water or fat on your kitchen floor, do wipe it up immediately as it could cause a nasty fall – especially if you have elderly people around. Keep the floor free from obstructions and, if your children play in the kitchen, train them never to play in the cooking area and to pick up toys – particularly those with wheels.

If you have mats in your kitchen, make sure they have a non-slip backing. If you have an edge where vinyl meets carpet, install a suitable edging strip (see page 212). If the seams of the vinyl start lifting, resecure them with adhesive or small nails.

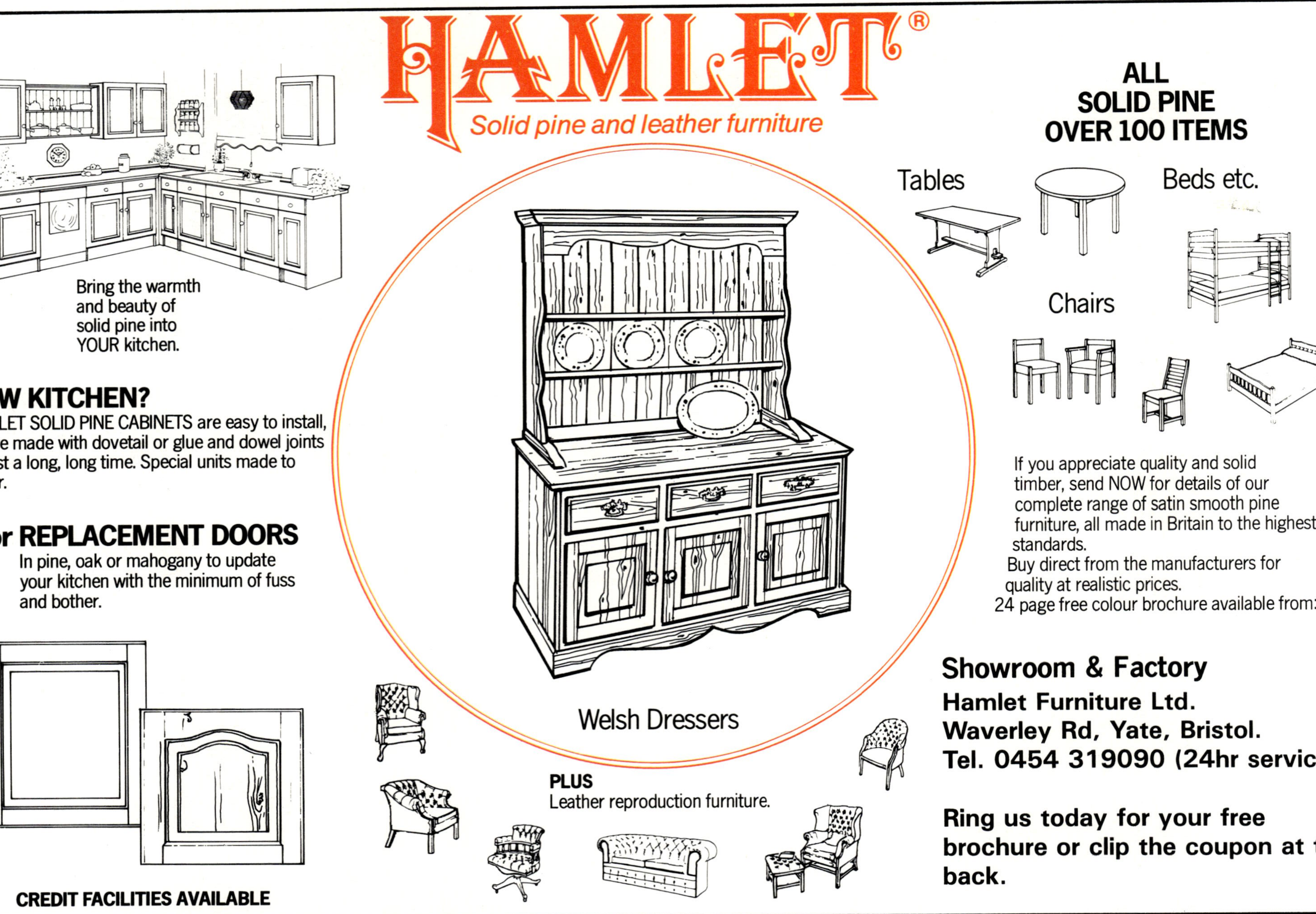

HAMLET®
Solid pine and leather furniture
ALL
SOLID PINE
OVER 100 ITEMS
Tables
Chairs
Beds etc.
Bring the warmth
and beauty of
solid pine into
YOUR kitchen.
NEW KITCHEN?
HAMLET SOLID PINE CABINETS are easy to install, all are made with dovetail or glue and dowel joints to last a long, long time. Special units made to order.
or REPLACEMENT DOORS
In pine, oak or mahogany to update your kitchen with the minimum of fuss and bother.
CREDIT FACILITIES AVAILABLE
Welsh Dressers
PLUS
Leather reproduction furniture.
If you appreciate quality and solid timber, send NOW for details of our complete range of satin smooth pine furniture, all made in Britain to the highest standards.
Buy direct from the manufacturers for quality at realistic prices.
24 page free colour brochure available from:
Showroom & Factory
Hamlet Furniture Ltd.
Waverley Rd, Yate, Bristol.
Tel. 0454 319090 (24hr service).
Ring us today for your free brochure or clip the coupon at the back.

ELECTRICAL WIRING

MAINS ELECTRICITY

Electricity comes from the generating station to the boundaries of your home by what is called the street cable. The service cable brings it on to your land and into your house. In urban areas the street and service cables run underground, but in the country they are likely to be overhead.

Whichever way it enters, it will end up at what is known as the service terminal box. This box has a fuse that protects the whole installation, and also allows engineers from the local Electricity Board to shut off the supply (electricity) when they need to work on the system. Close by the service terminal box, and mounted on the same board, is the meter. If you have a dual-rate meter that makes a lower charge for electricity used during the night, there will also be a time clock.

Up to and including the meter, the installation is the property and the responsibility of the Board. If anything goes wrong, it is up to the Board to carry out repairs. You must not tamper with the Board's installation; indeed both meter and service terminal box are sealed to prevent your doing so. Beyond the meter, however, the system belongs to, and is the responsibility of, whoever owns the building. This is known as the 'consumer's installation'.

THE CONSUMER'S INSTALLATION

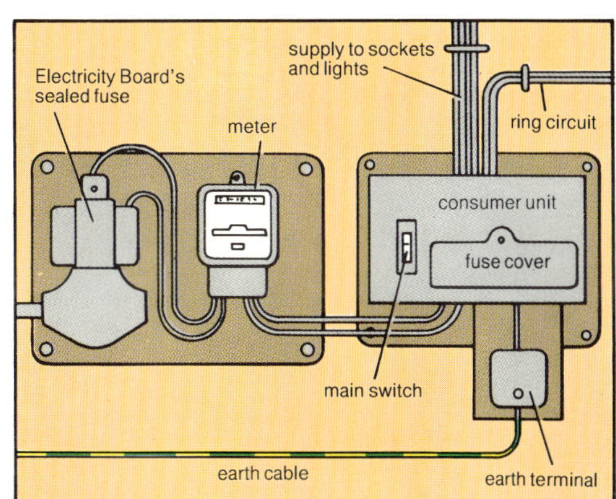

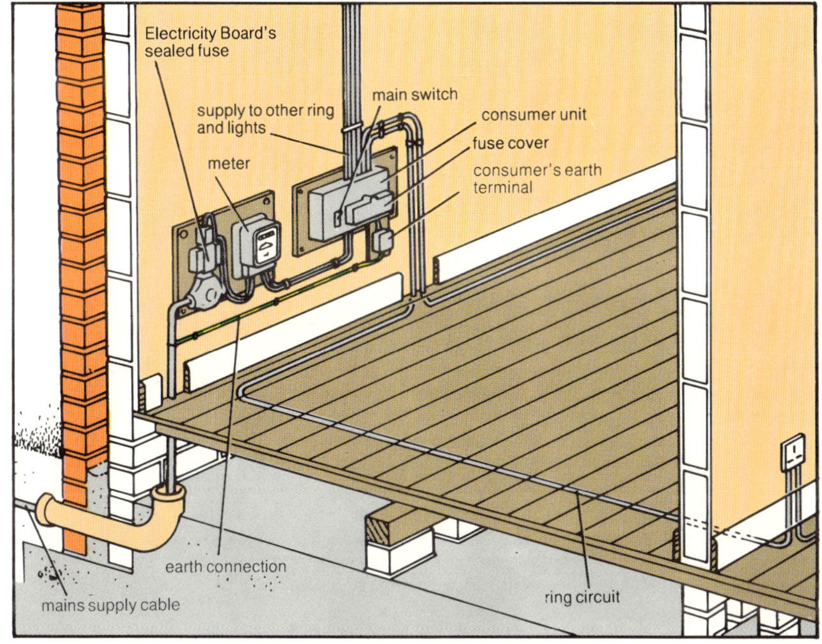

Electricity is carried around your home to the various points where it is needed – the lights, socket outlets, the cooker and so on – by cable. The cable used for most modern house wiring is flat PVC-sheathed and insulated two-core and earth (see page 79). This is the type you must use for all the jobs described in this chapter, except for the rare exception where we state otherwise.

If your electrical system was installed some time ago, you may find that you have the old fashioned cable – round, and either rubber or fabric covered. If you do, it is a sign that your whole installation is on the point of requiring complete renewal, because this kind of cable will be getting near to the end of its useful life, and could be dangerous. Unless you are really skilled, renewing the wiring of a house is a job for a fully qualified electrical contractor and you should call one in.

Various sizes of cable are used, according to what kind of circuit is being served. We will tell you what size of cable you should use for each job.

THE CONSUMER UNIT

At the heart of every modern electrical installation is the consumer unit, which houses the fuses controlling the various circuits in your home and a mains switch. This switch enables you to cut off the supply of mains electricity to the whole house. It is a double-pole switch which has two live and two neutral terminals, enabling both poles of the circuit to be switched off or isolated.

The consumer unit is placed on the wall, usually next to the meter, and cables – a live one with red PVC insulation and a neutral one covered in black insulation – pass to it from the meter. These (round) cables are meter leads. They have an outer sheathing, as well as the inner PVC insulation.

The third cable is insulated in green (or green and yellow) PVC, but has no outer sheathing. This is the earthing lead. It runs to either an earthing terminal clamped directly to the metal sheath of the Board's service cable, or to a composite terminal fixed to the meter board and connected to the service-cable clamp by a short earthing lead. The old method of fixing the earthing lead to a clamp on the mains water pipe is no longer permitted as the sole method of earthing.

Live In relation to a conductor, it means that a difference in voltage exists between the conductor and earth. In domestic installations, this is usually 240 volts.

Neutral This, in relation to a conductor, means that, as the neutral pole of the electricity network is earthed, there is no significant voltage between that neutral pole and earth.

WIRING REGULATIONS

Every electrical installation should conform to the requirements of the Institution of Electrical Engineers' Wiring Regulations and any alterations or additions to an installation should comply with the regulations. Although not a statutory document the regulations are recognised by all official bodies. Provided the work you carry out complies with the current regulations, the Electricity Board will connect it to the mains electricity supply. However 'good workmanship using proper materials' is essential for any wiring work to comply with the regulations. If the workmanship is bad, or poor or unsuitable materials are used, the Electricity Board can refuse to connect the wiring to its mains.

The current (15th) edition of the Wiring Regulations was published in 1983. Although the requirements do not differ very much from the 14th edition (1966), new terms have been adopted so that the regulations harmonise with other countries. It may be some years before they become familiar to the general public but those related to domestic wiring are listed below. All the advice given in this chapter complies with the 15th edition.

1. Both 'live' and neutral poles of an electrical circuit on the mains are classed 'live'. The former 'live' pole is renamed 'phase', the 'neutral' remains 'neutral'. The terminals of plugs, socket outlets, and other wiring accessories (as well as electrical appliances) will in future be marked P, N and E instead of L, N and E.
2. The earth wire of a circuit, formerly termed the earth continuity conductor (ECC), has been renamed the circuit protective conductor (CPC).
3. Current-operated earth leakage circuit breakers (ELCB) are renamed residual current devices (RCD) or residual current circuit breakers (RCCB).
4. Voltage-operated earth leakage circuit breakers are renamed voltage protective devices (VPD) or voltage protective circuit breakers (VPCB).

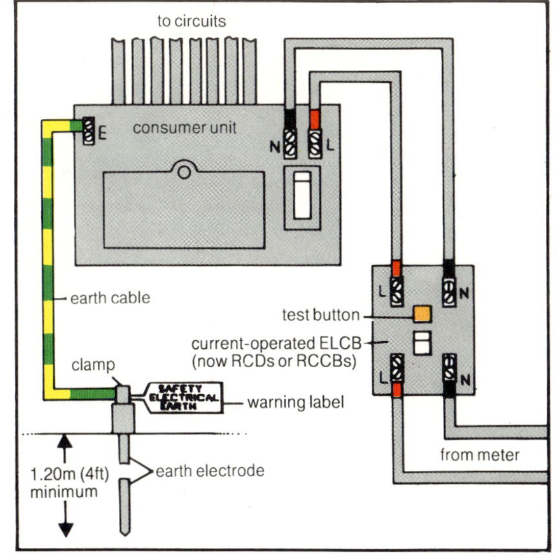

THE CIRCUITS

The electrical system of your home is divided into a number of separate circuits. There are two reasons for this, the first of them economic. You need a smaller, and therefore cheaper, size of cable for supplying the lights than for taking electricity to a cooker.

The second is that, if a fault develops in one circuit, the whole house is not deprived of electricity.

two-way switches

separate lighting circuits on ground and first floor

LIGHTING CIRCUITS

A lighting circuit is wired in 1mm cable (i.e. 1sq.mm is the cross-sectional area of live and neutral conductors), governed by a 5 amp fuse in the consumer unit. The average small home usually has two lighting circuits: one for upstairs and the other for downstairs. The reason is that, if a fault develops in one circuit, the whole house is not plunged into darknesss.

There are two basic types of lighting circuit: the most common in modern installations is known as the 'loop-in' system; the other is the joint-box.

THE LOOP-IN SYSTEM

The loop-in system consists of a length of cable running from the consumer unit to each of the ceiling roses; it is 'looped-in' or connected to each rose in turn. The rose must be a special one with terminals to accommodate the loop-in. The loop-in wiring circuit is not one continuous length of cable going round the house. To cut down on the amount of wiring needed, some lighting points are serviced from a branch line of cable, running out from one rose. You can have only one branch line from each rose. Another cable runs from each rose to the light switch (see page 80).

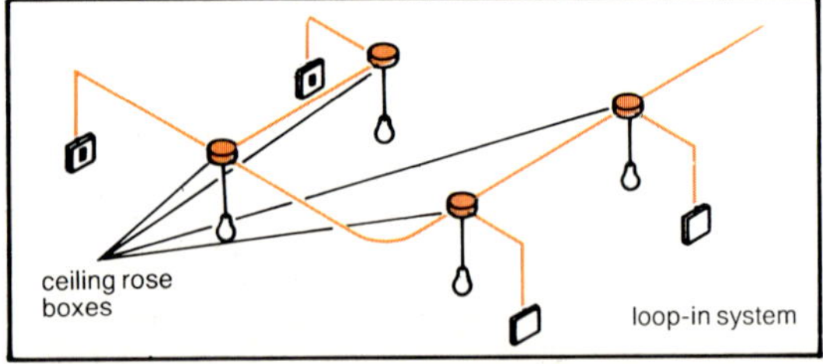

THE JOINT BOX SYSTEM

In the joint box system, the cable runs to a series of small, round, four-terminal joint boxes, instead of the ceiling roses. There is one joint box for each lighting point. Two additional cables leave the joint box – apart from the incoming and outgoing mains cables – one to the light, the other to its switch (see page 80). The joint box will, if possible, be hidden out of the way.

The loop-in system is preferred nowadays. Modern lighting systems are generally of this type because all the joins are made at the ceiling roses, and so are easily accessible for work on the circuit, or to add another light. A loop-in circuit is also quicker and cheaper to install in the first place – joint boxes add to the cost and take time to fit. Nevertheless, there are situations where the joint box has advantages; so you sometimes get a hybrid system.

At one time the cable used for domestic lighting was just twin-core: i.e. it had no earth wire. Now an increasing number of shades and fittings are made in metal, and the importance of adequate earthing even on lighting is recognized. As a result, all modern lighting circuits are earthed. If yours is not, you should add an earth wire.

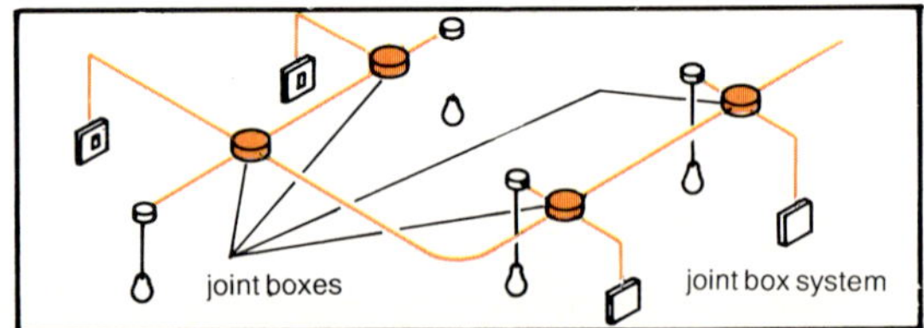

THE RING CIRCUIT

The ring circuit is the one used to take electricity to the power socket outlets or points. The ring circuit is suitable for supplying appliances up to a rating of 3 kilowatts, which means everything from a table lamp, up to and including fires or room heaters. Anything above that rating – cookers and water heaters, for example – must have its own circuit. (For radial power circuits, see page 78.)

A ring is a single circuit of 2.5mm cable running in a loop from a 30 amp fuseway in the consumer unit, and back to it, supplying a number of socket outlets on the way.

A 30 amp circuit will allow 7,200 watts of appliance to be switched on at one time. As two electric heaters could easily tot up to 6,000 you can see that during winter you could get dangerously near to the limit, with the risk that the cable might get overloaded and the fuse would blow. Since a 30 amp rewireable fuse requires 60 amps to blow it, the circuit wires would get very hot before the fuse snaps.

Such dangerous overloading is unlikely, because the regulations state that you must have a separate ring for every 100sq.m (or 1,000sq.ft) of floor area of your home, thus limiting the number of heaters, the biggest consumers of electricity in the home, that are likely to be switched on. It is usual in small homes to have one ring for upstairs and one for the ground floor.

At one time, each socket outlet had its own circuit with its own exclusive wiring back to its own separate fuseway. There were three different sizes of socket, each with its own rating. The sockets and plugs were not interchangeable, obviously highly inconvenient. It could be dangerous too if the wrong plug was fitted. Some homes still have this form of wiring. If yours is one of them, identifiable by sockets using round pin plugs, you ought to get it rewired immediately. The advantages of the ring are, first, that you can have as many socket outlets as you wish. This is true not only when first installed, but also you can easily add sockets later on. Secondly, there is only one shape and size of plug, which means that the plugs are freely interchangeable. This is not dangerous because the fuse protecting the appliance is in the plug itself, although the circuit has its own fuse back at the fuseway.

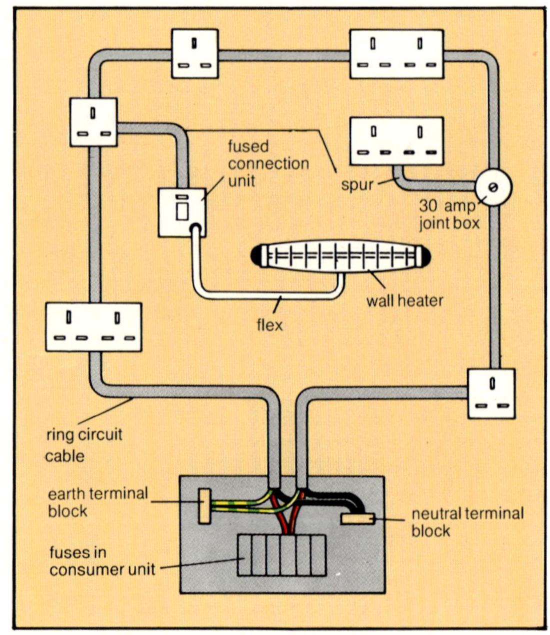

SPURS

A ring circuit can also have branch lines, known as 'spurs', serving sockets in remote parts of the house to reduce the amount of cable used. A spur should supply one outlet only, which may be a single or a double socket outlet or a fused connection unit.

FUSED CONNECTION UNITS

The fused connection unit (see page 86) is for use with appliances that it is convenient to have permanently wired, e.g. the fridge, washing machine, tumble drier and dish-washer.

The switch of a fused connection unit is a double-pole one, unlike that of a socket outlet which is only single-pole.

The fuse for a permanently wired-in appliance is, incidentally, in the connection unit itself. The rating of fuses is 3 amp for up to 720 watts, 13 amp for between 720 and 3,000 watts.

OTHER CIRCUITS

Appliances with a rating of more than 3,000 watts must not be connected up to a ring circuit, but must have their own. This is a safety precaution to avoid the possibility of an overload. These 'radial' circuits start at the fuseway, go to the appliance, and end there.

Examples of appliances needing a radial circuit are electric cookers, immersion heaters, instantaneous water heaters and electrically heated showers.

THE CONSUMER UNIT

A combined double-pole mainswitch and fuse-distribution board, it is available in various sizes from 2-way to 10-way. Each 'way' represents a separate fuseway; each fuseway supplies a separate circuit.

The consumer unit is the only mainswitch and fusegear needed in a normal domestic installation. The fuseways can be fitted with fuse units containing rewirable or cartridge fuses, or with miniature circuit breakers (see page 78). Some consumer units are fitted with a circuit breaker (see page 79) instead of a mainswitch.

It is from the fuseways that the various circuits go out to supply electricity to the lights, power points, water heater, cooker and so on of your home. A fuse is a weak link deliberately introduced into a circuit so that it will 'blow' should anything go wrong, thus cutting off the supply of electricity before damage can be caused. The fuse is housed in a fuseholder in the fuseway of the consumer unit and you need a fuseway for each of the circuits of the house.

The rating of the fuse – the amperage, as it is sometimes (incorrectly) called – varies according to whether the circuit will be supplying lighting, or power circuits. Modern fuseholders are colour-coded so that you can see at a glance what fuse they carry. The colour takes the form of small dots on the outside of the holder. This is the colour coding:

5 amp	white	30 amp	red
15 amp	blue	45 amp	green
20 amp	yellow		

It is extremely dangerous to insert into a fuseholder a fuse of a rating higher than that required by the circuit. The circuit could then overheat before the fuse blew and might result in a fire or other damage. If you insert a fuse of too low a rating it will blow as soon as you switch on the electricity. See page 76 for fuses for lighting, power and radial circuits.

A consumer unit can have from as many as ten fuseways. Until now the average number in British homes has been six, but eight is becoming more commonplace. If you ever have a completely new electrical system installed, and are in a position to choose the size of the consumer unit that goes with it, make sure you plump for one that is big enough. As a rule of thumb, you want a fuseway for every circuit you start off with, plus two, or perhaps even more, spares.

FUSEWAY CONNECTIONS

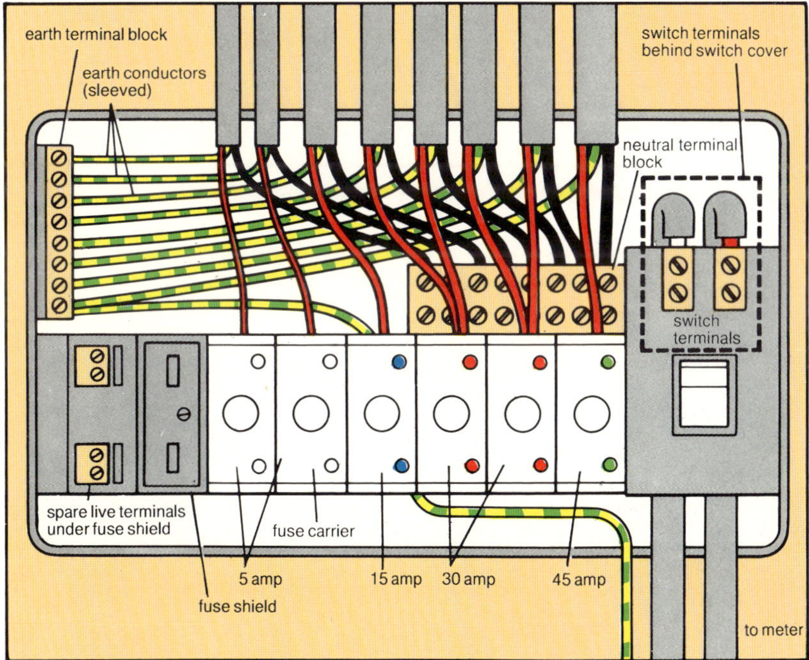

For many of the jobs you will tackle, you have to connect the cable of a circuit to a fuseway in the consumer unit.

Only the live wire is connected directly to the fuseway; neutral and earth wires are grouped in separate terminal blocks. Having discovered the correct fuseway, you will see clearly to which point on the blocks the neutral and earth wires go.

The diagram shows how to make the connections at a typical fuseway. Other types may differ slightly in layout, but the principles are usually the same. However, if you do not understand exactly what you are doing, it is better to leave the job to an electrician.

INSTALLING A SWITCHFUSE UNIT

When you need a completely new circuit and find that there is no spare fuseway in the consumer unit to which you can connect it, you have to install a new mainswitch and fuse unit – known as a switchfuse unit. This is a 1-way consumer unit having a double-pole switch and a single fuse unit which is connected independently to the mains supply by the Electricity Board. You are not allowed to make this connection yourself.

The switchfuse is screwed to the wall near the consumer unit, on the meter side. The circuit cable is fed in through the entry hole and connected to the terminals marked load – the red wire to the L terminal and the black to the N, and the earth wire to the earthing terminal.

You now need two lengths of 16mm single-core PVC-sheathed cable, one black and one red, for wiring the switchfuse to the mains. One end of these cables is inserted in the 'feed' terminals of the switchfuse. The other is for connecting up to the meter by officials of the Electricity Board.

Electricity Boards nowadays are reluctant to connect more than one pair of meter leads to their meters, for they feel this is turning the meter into a form of joint box. Instead they require a multi-way service connector box into which the various meter leads are connected and out of which the final cables to the meter are run. Some Boards fit this and make no charge. Some charge and others may require a contractor to fit it.

A simple way out is to loop the new meter leads of the switchfuse out of the mains terminals of the existing consumer unit; these terminals being designed for looping. However, you must call in an Electricity Board engineer to withdraw the service fuse while you make the connection. This is, in any case, a job a do-it-yourselfer should tackle only if he/she is very experienced in electrical work.

First your switchfuse unit needs to be properly earthed, and you do this with a short length of 6mm green and yellow PVC-insulated earth cable. One end is connected to the earth terminal of the switchfuse and the other to the earthing terminal of the whole installation, which is usually near the meter. If you cannot find this, connect the earth wire to the earthing terminal of the consumer unit.

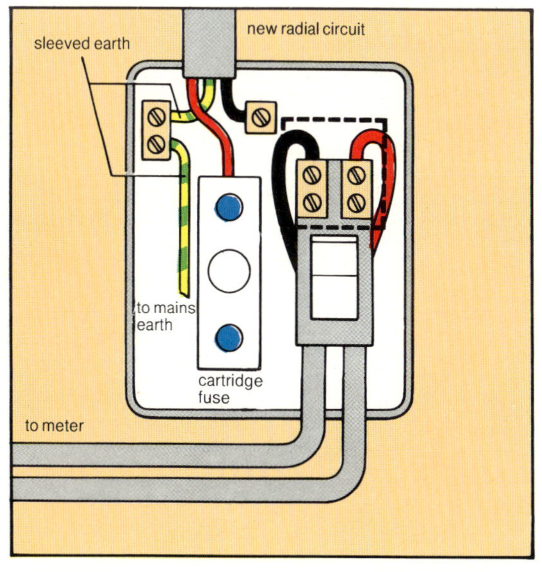

CIRCUIT FUSES

Circuit fuses are to protect each circuit from excess current in the event of a fault or serious overload. These are contained in the fuseholder of the appropriate colour for the current rating (see page 77). The fuses can be rewirable, in which case the fuse is a length of fusewire, or of the cartridge type, the cartridge itself then being coloured according to its current rating. Rewirable- and cartridge-fuse units, and their fuseholders, are not interchangeable. Cartridge fuses are more reliable than fusewires, and require less excess current to blow than do the equivalent fusewires.

The overwhelming majority of fuses in British homes are the rewirable type. The advantage is that, if a circuit fails, by looking at the fuseholder you can see at a glance whether the fuse has blown or not. However, it is much easier to take out and replace a cartridge fuse.

Older installations have two, or even several, mainswitch and fuse units. At one time there was a different tariff for electricity according to its purpose – lighting, cooking, heating and so on – so each of the main switches had its own meter. Later the flat rate was adopted, and so separate mains units became unnecessary. Many of them are still in use, though nowadays connected to just one meter. Electrical installations with these mainswitch units are out of date and should be modernized.

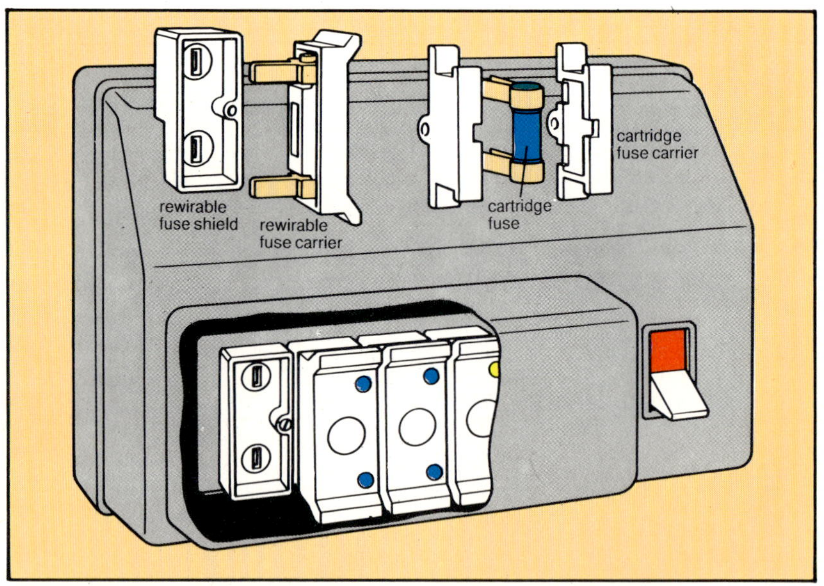

MINIATURE CIRCUIT BREAKER

A miniature circuit breaker (MCB) is a single-pole switch which trips (switches off) automatically, when excess current due to a fault or overload occurs in a circuit. It operates with less current than a fuse and when fitted into consumer units in place of fuses ensures greater protection. To restore power, all you have to do is switch on again, although you cannot do this until whatever fault caused the trip has been rectified.

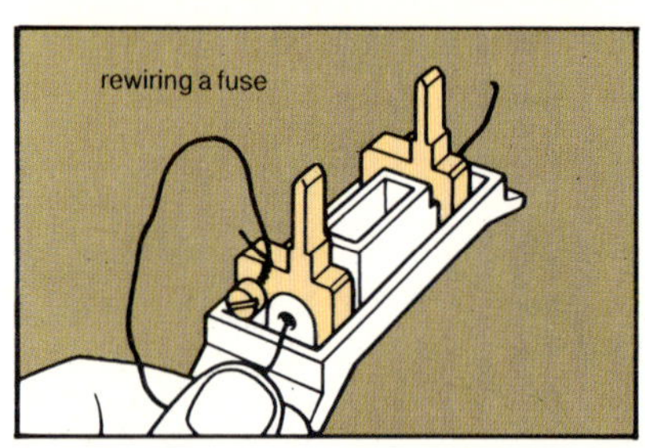

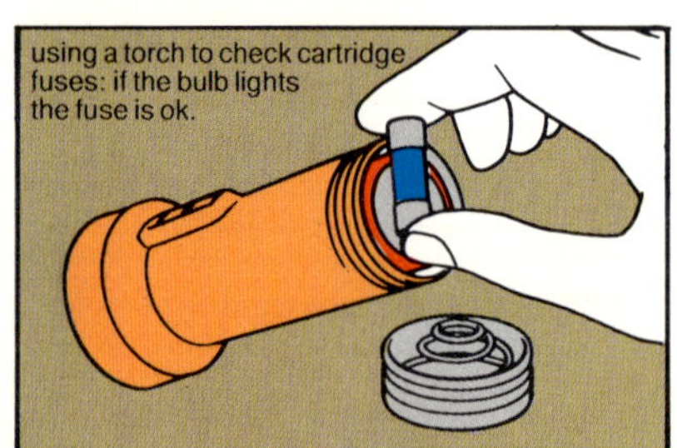

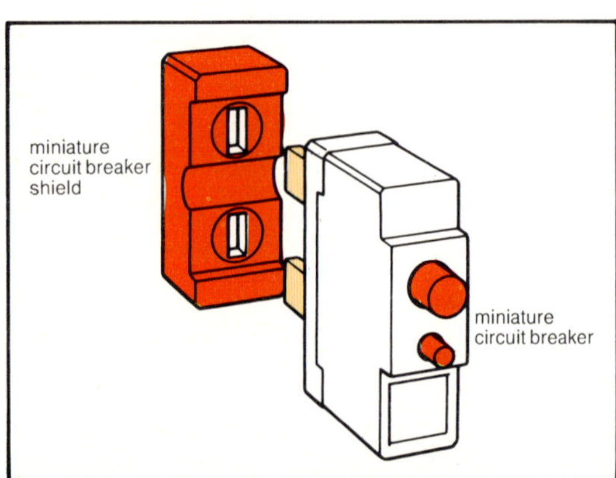

IDENTIFYING CIRCUITS

Do you know which fuse in your consumer unit governs which circuit? In good installations they will be marked, but if not there is an easy way to find out.

Switch off the power, take out one fuse, and restore the power. Then go round the house switching on every light and plugging portable appliances into each socket, to find out which one will not work. Those that do not are, of course, on the circuit of the fuse that you have taken out. Do this with each fuse in turn, and very soon you will have mapped out your system. Check the bulbs work first!

1	COOKER	45A
2	DOWNSTAIRS RING MAIN	30A
3	UPSTAIRS RING MAIN	30A
4	STORAGE HEATERS	20A
5	IMMERSION HEATER	15A
6	DOWNSTAIRS LIGHTS	5A
7	UPSTAIRS LIGHTS	5A
8	CELLAR, HALL + LANDING LIGHTS	5A

THE TRICK

Make the necessary notes on the back of the consumer unit cover so that you will have the information immediately available next time you need it.

RADIAL POWER CIRCUITS

A radial power circuit is similar to the ring circuit in that it supplies an unlimited number of 13 amp socket outlets plus fused connection units for fixed appliances having individual loadings not exceeding 3000kW. Instead of the circuit cable returning to the fuseway in the consumer unit from the last socket outlet, the cable terminates there.

There are two versions of the circuit: the 20 amp version is limited to an area not exceeding 20sq.m (700sq.ft); the 30 amp version is limited to an area not exceeding 50sq.m (1765sq.ft). The 20 amp version is wired in 2.5mm twin and earth PVC-sheathed cable from a cartridge or rewirable circuit fuse or an MCB of 20 amp current rating. The 30 amp circuit is wired in 4mm twin and earth PVC-sheathed cable from either a cartridge circuit fuse or an MCB of 30 amp current rating, but not from a rewirable fuse.

A radial power circuit is excellent for supplying a number of socket outlets in a small area, such as a kitchen, to supplement those supplied from the ring circuit.

CHECKING LIGHTING CIRCUITS

According to the regulations the loading on a typical domestic lighting circuit must not exceed 1200 watts. In most homes the load will be well below that limit, but it is always as well to check.

How can you do this? Simply look at how many lights there are on a circuit, and count the number of bulbs in them. Tot up the wattage of each bulb to give the loading. Bulbs of 100 watts and over should be taken at face value; those under should be counted as 100 watts each. How do you determine how many lights there are on a circuit? Switch on all the lights in your home and check that all the bulbs are working. Go to your consumer unit, switch off the main, take out the fuse governing your first lighting circuit (see left), then switch on again. Go round the house noting which lights are out. These are the lights on that particular circuit. Do the same with the second and third (if there is one) lighting circuits in turn.

SWITCHING OFF

The most important safety rule is that you must always switch off with the master switch at the consumer unit before starting work. Never take any chance on this. Before you touch any part of the electrical system of your home always ask yourself: did I switch off first?

There is, however, no need to deprive the whole house of electricity. All you need do is switch off the main, take out the fuse controlling the circuit on which you want to work, and then restore the power.

THE TRICK

Before you begin work switch on a light or plug in a portable appliance to make sure the circuit is dead.

By shutting down just one circuit, you can still have lights fed from another circuit if you are working after dark. But beware, you may grow so accustomed to the circuit being dead that you may move on to another and forget that this is live. So we repeat – before starting always ask yourself: did I switch off?

EARTHING & WIRING

EARTHING

The connection of all appropriate metalwork to the general mass of earth is via suitable earth electrodes. Should a live conductor come into contact with earthed metalwork, the almost unimpeded flow of earth leakage current to earth will also flow through the live conductors up to the point of fault and therefore through the fuses. This causes the fuse to blow and isolates the faulty section from the mains.

An earthing clamp is a copper strip attached to a fastener containing a terminal, used for clamping earth conductors to a cable metal sheathing to provide an earthing point.

An earthing rod is a copper-coated steel rod with an earth clamp and terminal at the top end, at least 1.2m (4ft) in length. This is driven into the soil where no conventional earthing terminal or means of earthing can be provided by an Electricity Board.

PROTECTIVE MULTIPLE EARTHING SYSTEM

Recently a new system of earthing is being adopted by Electricity Boards where appropriate and where conventional methods of earthing are not possible. The system is termed Protective Multiple Earthing (PME).

The Electricity Board connects the consumer's earthing conductor to the neutral pole of the supply system and, at the same time, connects it to an earthing rod driven into the ground on the consumer's premises. As the neutral pole is already connected solidly to earth at the nearest 'street' transformer, this method is superior to connecting it to the metal sheathing of the Board's underground service cable.

Before an Electricity Board will provide PME, it requires that all extraneous metalwork, including the water and gas mains pipes, be bonded to earth.

CIRCUIT BREAKERS

For safety in the garden, earth leakage circuit breakers (ELCB) or residual current circuit breakers (RCCB) are available.

These give protection against electric shock if a machine develops a fault or if you accidentally cut through the flex. They work by automatically monitoring the circuit and sensing any leakage of current to earth. If leakage occurs, they quickly cut off the power.

To comply with new regulations, outdoor equipment must be protected by an RCCB.

You can buy a socket outlet RCCB which protects only this socket.

There are two types of portable RCCB. One is a kind of adaptor with a lead and ordinary 13 amp plug. The other is an RCCB that is actually built into a 13 amp plug.

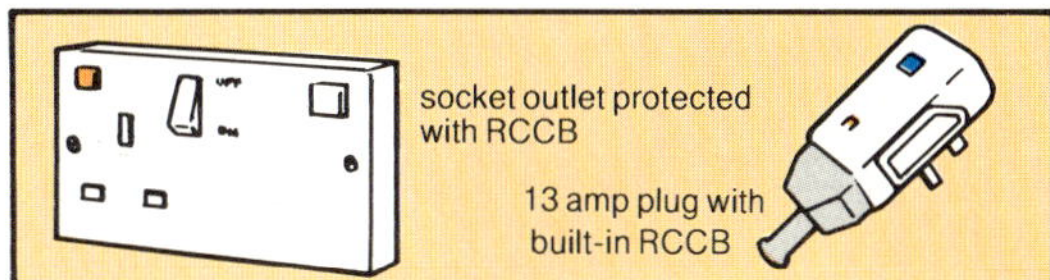

CABLE OR FLEX?

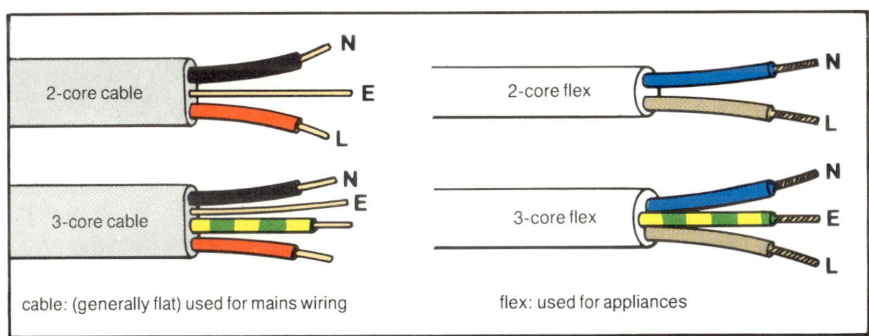

cable: (generally flat) used for mains wiring

flex: used for appliances

To an electrician, the wires that carry electricity around the house are known as 'cable'. The wire that is attached to an appliance, or to a light, is a 'flex'. The two wires inside the cable, which actually carry the current, are properly called the conductors. These are insulated: the live conductor is covered in red PVC and the neutral one in black. Note that the brown/blue colour coding applies only to flexes. Cable wiring still keeps to the old colour code.

The third wire is the earth – which is a strand of bare copper. However, a green and yellow PVC sheathing should be slipped over this before it is connected to its terminal, to guard against its coming into dangerous contact with a current-carrying terminal. The sheathing should cover the whole of the exposed earth wire.

Since this regulation did not become compulsory until 1967, you may well come across earth cable that has not been so treated.

THE TRICK

If you see bare copper wire connected to a terminal, it is certain to be an earth – the live and neutral wires have PVC insulation fixed on during manufacture.

WIRE STRIPPING

The outer PVC sheath is best cut with a small knife from the cut end. Draw the blade along the cable, making sure that it cuts in between the wires forming the inner core. Avoid cutting the insulation of the conductors. Hold the inner wires apart so they are protected from the blade. Peel the sheath back, and cut it across its width.

Now bare the ends of the conductors. If you cut into the core, its current-carrying capacity is reduced.

How much sheathing you remove depends on the type of connection. At a socket outlet, or any other accessory that is fitted to a box, you must strip off at least 125mm (5in.) and preferably even 150mm (6in.). This stripped portion then lies loosely within the box so that it can easily be withdrawn if you want to work on it. At a ceiling rose, remove the outer covering of only that part that will lie within the rose. Remove only 12mm (½in.) of insulation from the inner conductors to allow them to be connected to terminals.

THE TRICK

Or buy a pair of wire strippers, which are quite cheap. The strippers have a dial to select the depth of cut appropriate. This ensures the inner core is left unharmed. Put the wire in the jaws of the stripper, press the handles and you will cut the plastic, which can then be pulled off.

FUSED PLUGS

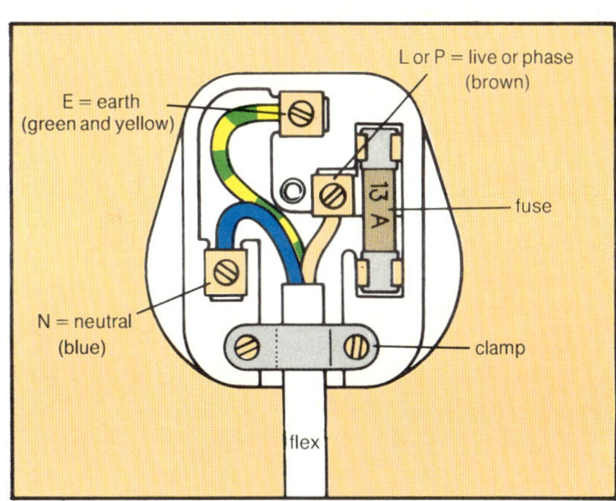

The 13 amp fused plug is the standard plug used in the U.K., available in moulded plastic and in unbreakable 'rubber' versions. Other versions, with neon indicators, are available. Plug cartridge fuses are made in various ratings: 3 amp (red or blue) for lamps and appliances up to 720 watts rating; 13 amp (brown) for appliances of 720 to 3000 watts loading. These two sizes are all that are needed to comply with the regulations but other ratings (2, 5, and 10 amp) are also made; these are black in colour. Some fused adaptors and some round-pin plugs are fitted with cartridge fuses labelled BS646. These fuses are smaller than those for the 13 amp plug, and will not make adequate contact if fitted.

WIRING UP A PLUG

Many do-it-yourself electricians make unsafe connections by stripping off too much of the outer PVC sheathing of the flex. The end of the flex from which the sheathing has been removed should be contained entirely within the plug. The clamp, which holds the flex securely in place where it enters the plug, should grip fully sheathed flex, not three separate wires.

So to get it right you should remove 50mm (2in.) of sheathing from the end of the flex and 12mm (½in.) from the individual conductor, in order to make a proper connection at the terminals.

It is, of course, imperative to connect the wires to the right terminals: the brown wire goes to the live terminal (marked L); the blue wire to the neutral (N); and the green and yellow wire to the earth terminal (E).

Some appliances are what is known as double insulated, and therefore do not have a green and yellow earth wire. In that case you forget about the earth, and merely connect up the live and neutral wires.

JOINT BOXES

A joint box is a moulded plastic circular box containing three or more terminals and having a screw-on cover. For lighting circuits, a 4-terminal box of 10 or 20-amp current rating is normally used, but 6-terminal boxes are also available. In a ring circuit, 3-terminal 30-amp joint boxes are used, primarily for connecting spurs to the ring cable.

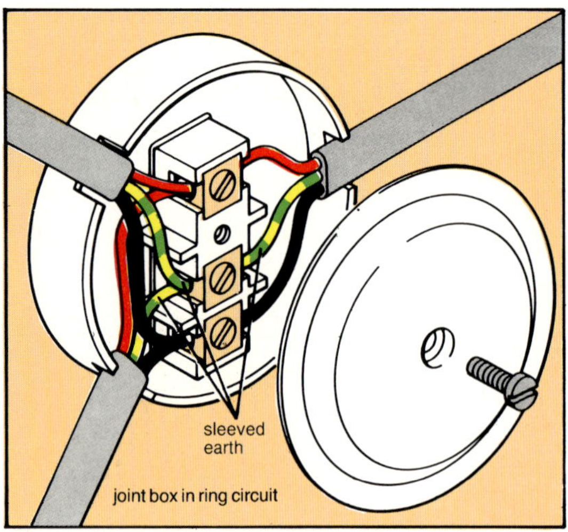

joint box in ring circuit

RING CIRCUITS

The joint box is mounted on a length of timber fixed between two joists about 75mm (3in.) from their top edge. Unscrew its top and lay the ring cable across it. Mark with a ballpoint where it touches the middle of the terminals, and strip 35mm (1½in.) of outer sheathing on each side to reveal the inner wires.

Next strip about 12mm (½in.) of insulation from the middle of the exposed red and black wires.

Having stripped the cables, connect the red and black wires to the outer two terminals of the box. The bare earth goes to the centre terminal. Remember that the regulations state that you should slip green and yellow PVC sleeving over an earth wire before connecting it up.

Without severing the wire, you take two pieces of sleeving, slit them along their length, and slip them over the wire, leaving a length of wire between them to be fixed to the terminal. Hold them in place with sticky tape.

The wires of the spur are connected to the same terminals as those of the ring. Slip a length of green and yellow sleeving over the earth. Finally, screw back the joint box cover.

THE TRICK

It might be easier to do all this stripping if the cable were cut in two, but the regulations recommend that you should avoid breaking cable whenever possible.

WIRING FROM THE MAIN FUSE BOX

If the most convenient point to tap into the main for your new spur is the fuseway of the ring itself, switch off at the main, and track down which fuseway supplies the ring. Connect your spur to this.

LIGHTING CIRCUITS

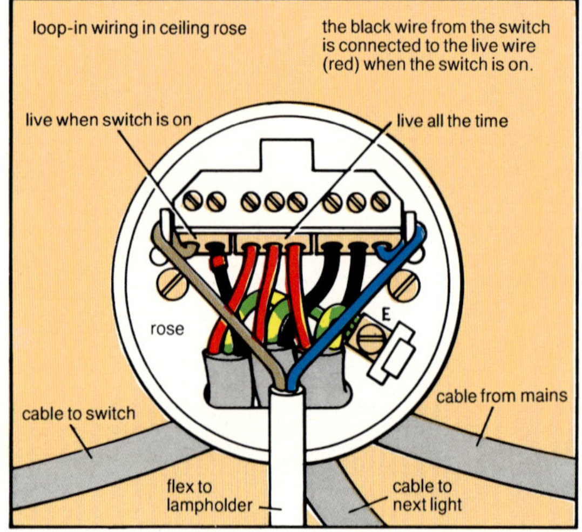

cable from mains
cable to next light
N
E
joint box
L
cable to rose
sleeved earth
cable to switch
rose
switch
flex to lampholder
joint box wiring

Traditionally, joint box lighting systems have had their own special rose, with just three terminals, but nowadays retailers normally stock only loop-in roses. The reason is that the loop-in rose can be used for either system (whereas the joint box rose can not).

To tell whether a rose is wired on the joint box or the loop-in system, unscrew its cover (having switched off at the main) and look how many wires enter it. A joint box rose will have only one set – live, neutral, and earth (the last may be missing) – wired up to three terminals. A loop-in rose will have a much more complicated arrangement of terminals, and two or three sets of wires.

Having located a convenient joint box, run a cable from the box to a new joint box, and from this second box run a cable to the light and switch drop (very important: see page 87). To add a fifth cable; the red wire is connected to the live terminal, the black to the neutral, and the earth to the earth terminal. If your box differs from the diagram, connect the red to the terminals already carrying most red wires, and the black to those holding most black ones.

Sometimes the joint box will be too small to connect another cable. In that case insert your new joint box in one of the feed cables, making connections as before. The feeds will be those connected up to the main red and black terminals in the existing joint box.

In a home where the wiring was installed later, first locate the cluster of joint boxes. The likeliest spot is under the landing floor (see page 14). Provisionally choose a joint box and trace its feed cable back to the consumer unit. Check that the red wire of the cable actually finishes at a 5 amp lighting circuit fuse. If it does not, look for a 5 amp lighting fuse in the consumer unit, and trace the cable from it back to a junction box under the landing floor.

If you cannot find a joint box, look for a lighting mains cable under the raised floorboard, and insert a joint box in it. From this box run a cable direct to your new light position, fitting a loop-in rose there. From your new rose, run a switch drop.

TESTING FOR SPURS

Let's return now to that requirement about only having one socket outlet on a spur. How do you know whether the outlet on which you are working is on a spur or not? When you remove the face plate of the outlet you should see two sets of red, black and earth wires. Occasionally you will come across only one set. Then you will know that the socket is on a spur, for it is at a dead end. Here is a test to determine whether an outlet with two sets of wires is on a ring or a spur.

THE TRICK

With the current switched off, part the two red wires (if they are twisted together) and connect one lead of a battery and bulb tester to one red wire and the other lead of the tester to the other red wire. If the bulb lights, the cable is part of a ring; if it does not, the cable is a spur.

Let's assume your cable is a spur. You can find out whether a socket with only one set of wires is on that spur by this simple test.

THE TRICK

Making sure the current is off, connect the red and black wires of this socket together and connect the leads of the tester to one set of red and black wires at the first socket. If the bulb lights, the two sockets are on the same spur.

For this test to be reliable you must make sure that at the first socket you are working on the right set of wires: i.e. those going on to the next outlet on the line, and not the cable that leads back to the main ring. It might be an idea to carry out the test on both sets. Make sure the black and red wires are no longer connected before you restore the power.

CABLES 1

UNDER THE FLOORBOARDS

Cable can be hidden under the boards of a timber floor or in conduits set in concrete floors, but these must be installed while the concrete is being laid.

The cable can go parallel to, or across the joists. In the former case, if there is a ceiling below, the cable can lie loosely on top of the plaster. Beneath a ground floor room, it can be fixed with clips to the side of a convenient joist. Where the cable is unlikely to be disturbed (when there is no access to the space below the floor) the regulations permit the cable to lie loosely on the earth of the foundations.

Cable passing across the joists should go through holes bored in their sides at least 50mm (2in.) from the top of the joist. The holes constitute all the fixing the cable will need. Where this is not possible, the cable must be protected by metal. You can buy metal inserts for this at electrical shops.

It is worthwhile sitting down with a pencil and paper looking at where the various cables start and finish, and working out the best routes for them to travel. If you are tackling a major job, and have several cables to deal with, it may be that you can alter the routes slightly and, by using a little more cable, accommodate more than one cable under just one board.

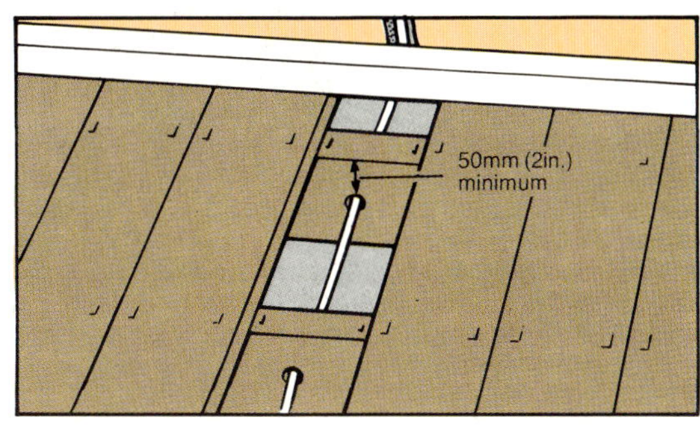

INSIDE WALLS

A hollow partition is an obviously convenient place for hiding cable passing from one floor to another or going from a wall switch to a ceiling rose. To gain access to it, if the wall is on the upper storey of your home, climb into the roof space and you will see where its top finishes. If it is on a lower storey, you will have to lift up the floorboards directly above the wall to find its top.

The top of the hollow will almost certainly be covered by a horizontal frame member and you will have to bore a hole through this – make it 25mm (1in.) in diameter so that you will have plenty of room to feed the cable through. The cable will not fall down into precisely the spot in the void where you want it, and you will find it difficult to push it there accurately.

THE TRICK

The trick is a device called a 'mouse'. A 'mouse' is a heavy object such as a large nut. Tie it to a piece of string, and drop it down the hollow until it reaches the spot where you want it. If the cable is to pass up the wall, you tie the 'mouse' end of the string to it, and haul it up. If you want to drop it down the void, fasten it to the free end of the string, and pull downwards.

One snag you might quickly come across is that there may be horizontal frame members inside the hollow at the halfway stage, and perhaps elsewhere.

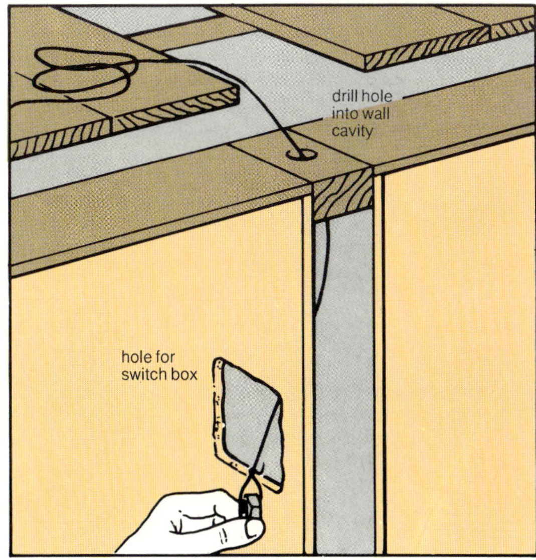

THE TRICK

The trick is to bore a hole in the outer face of the plaster just above and another one just below the horizontal frame member – the length of string from your 'mouse' that has dropped down the hole will tell you exactly how far from the top of the wall the frame member is. Cut a channel in the plaster and the frame member; pass the cable out of one hole, along the channel and into the second hole.

Finally, make good the holes with filler. This process will have to be repeated at every horizontal member that blocks the path of your mouse.

Inside cavity walls, use the hollow wall techniques. However, inside the cavity are small strips of metal, known as wall ties, which span the gap to hold the two leaves together. You may strike one of these with your mouse, but it should be possible to skirt round them.

If a vertical drop in a cavity is more than 4.6m (15ft), the regulations say it must have an intermediate fixing. To comply with this, you take the cable out of the cavity through a hole in the wall under the first-floor boards, and secure it to a joist.

If your home has cavity wall insulation, you cannot pass cable down the cavity.

ABOVE THE CEILING

You can run cable above the ceiling of the top storey. Here, obviously, would go cable feeding the ceiling roses. If you have a loft space above your top-storey ceiling, then running cable will present no problems. Your only worry will be to avoid putting your foot through the ceiling.

THE TRICK

To prevent this, you ought to take up a stout piece of timber, place it across a joist or two, and stand on that.

Cables in the roof can be installed running at right angles to the joists, or parallel to them. In the former case, you need not go to the trouble of boring holes in the sides of the joists. Carry the cable over the top of the joists, fixing it with clips so that it hugs them closely.

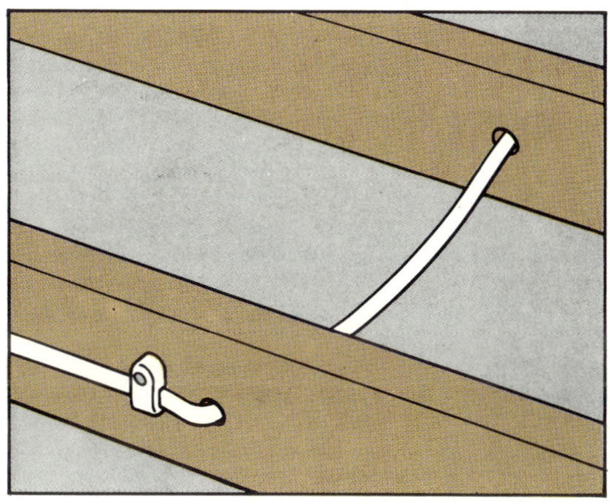

If the cable is in a spot where it is likely to be stepped on by anyone going up into the loft, it needs protection. You could thread it through holes drilled in the sides of the joists, but it is quicker and easier to use plastic capping or channelling on top of the joists. This will save you having to use clips to hold the cable in place.

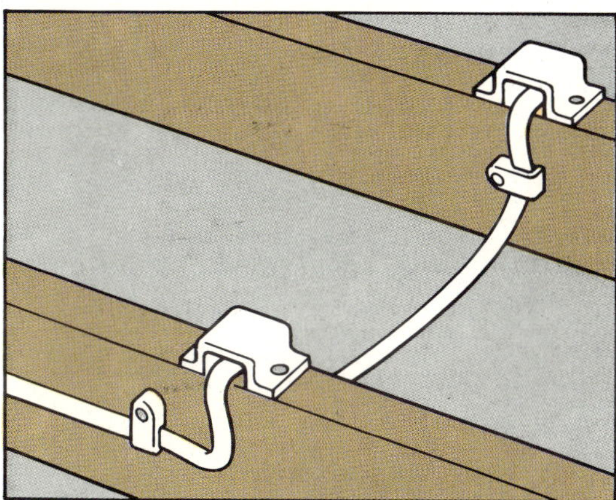

A cable running parallel to a joist should be tucked down well at ceiling level close to the joist, and will need few fixings because the loft insulation will help to protect and keep it in place.

If you do not have a loft, you can gain access from the room below to pass cable in the void above a ceiling, especially if your cable run will be parallel to a joist.

You cut a hole in the ceiling at the start of the run, feed the cable through it (see page 82), and bring it out through another hole bored at the other end. When finished, you make good the holes with filler. This can be done across the joists, but it is very difficult.

How do you know which way the ceiling joists run if you can't actually see them? Look at the floorboards to determine which way the floor joists lie. It's almost certain that the ceiling joists will be in the same direction. To make sure, tap the surface of the ceiling with your knuckles. You will get a hard sound below the joists, and a hollow one when you touch the space between.

CABLES 2

BURIED IN PLASTER

If you want to conceal cable running in a solid wall, you must bury it in the plaster.

The type of plastic-covered cable used for home wiring can be buried like this, without the need for any conduit or other protective covering. It might sound a little risky, but in fact the cable is much less at risk below the plaster than on the surface.

First cut out a channel known as a 'chase'. On a bare wall draw a line, using a straight-edge and the blade of a Stanley knife, along the course you want the chase to take, and then another parallel to it but the thickness of the cable away. If there is paper on the wall, trim away a strip about 25mm (1in.) wider than the cable before you cut the lines in the plaster.

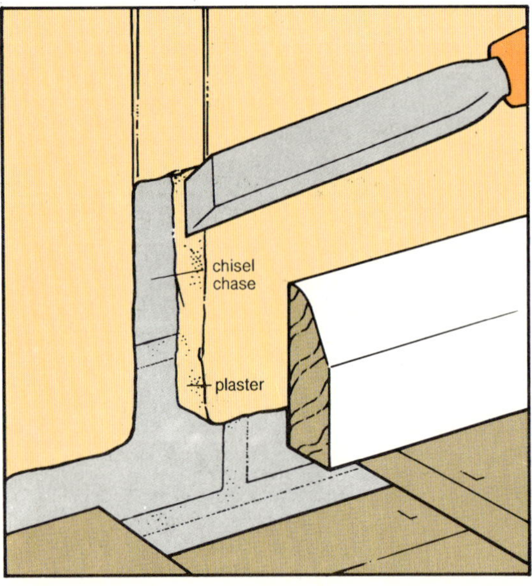

Cut out the chase with an old wood chisel, or screwdriver. First run the blade of the chisel or screwdriver along the grooves cut by the knife, using a straight-edge to ensure greater accuracy. Then chop out the plaster to the brickwork, or whatever forms the wall structure.

When the chase is deep enough, place the cable in position and make good with plaster filler.

THE TRICK

If it will be some time before you tackle the making good, you can hold the cable in place with a few dabs of contact adhesive.

THE TRICK

If you want to run cable in two adjacent rooms, it might not be necessary to cut a chase in both. Just make a wider chase in one room to take both cables, then feed the cable for next door through a hole bored in the wall.

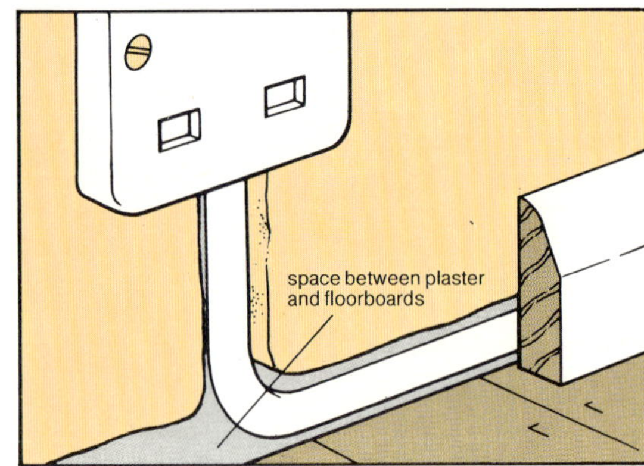

In many houses, however, the coating of plaster will be fairly shallow, and you will have to chop into the masonry behind it. For this you use a bolster chisel. How difficult this will be depends on what the wall consists of.

Architrave is the term given to the moulded timber that frames a door opening, etc. If you prise it off, you will see a small gap between the wall edge and the timber that lines the opening – it is this gap that the architrave is there to cover neatly. Cable you want to hide can be pushed into the gap, and then covered up as the architrave is replaced.

Architrave is normally just nailed in place, and if you jam a bolster chisel between it and the door frame, you will easily prise it off. Just nail it back again when you have finished.

Cable can also run behind the skirting board, in much the same way as behind an architrave. Plaster is very seldom carried right down to the floor level of a room. If you remove the skirting, you will find plenty of space behind it for a cable.

FIXING CABLE TO WALLS OR CEILINGS

Sometimes you will end up fixing cable to the surface of a wall. In that case, the cable must be securely fixed in place. You can use plastic clips, which have steel pins so that they can be driven into masonry or timber. Hold the cable in place, or get a helper to do it for you, place the clip over the cable, then hammer home the pin, making sure it does not damage the wire.

Otherwise use the buckle clip; this fastens rather like the buckle on a belt. This clip is fixed in place first, the cable is laid in the open buckle, and then the buckle is fastened. Whichever type you decide on, choose a clip suitable for the size of cable you are using.

It is important to make a surface fixing such as this very neat, and to do that you must make a truly vertical or horizontal line on the wall. If you are using plastic clips, the line should be just to one side of the cable run; for buckle clips it should be right in the middle of it. The clips should be at intervals no greater than 400mm (16in.) for vertical runs and 250mm (10in.) for horizontal ones. Do not allow the cable to twist while you fix it; kinks are hard to get out.

If you are forced to use surface-run cable on a ceiling, the best method is to use trunking or channelling.

THE TRICK

If you decide on channelling, stick the cable to the ceiling temporarily first, using an adhesive, then cover it with the capping. When using trunking, first fix its base firmly to the ceiling, lay the cable inside it, and use matchsticks to give temporary support until the cover is fitted.

MOVING CABLE HORIZONTALLY

Whether you are running cable under a floor or above a ceiling there are occasions when you have to make it travel quite a distance without being able to gain access to the whole run. How do you get the cable to go where you want it? Take a length of stout wire, and bend the end of it into a sort of hook shape. The cable is doubled up at the end to make a loop, and is then fed into one hole. The hooked wire is then pushed from the other hole, and located in the loop of the cable. Then the cable is pulled along to where you want it. This process is given the graphic title of 'fishing for cable'.

There may also be occasions when 'fishing' is the most convenient way of moving cable vertically as an alternative to 'dropping a mouse'. You can move cable horizontally by pushing it, using a long cane or cobweb brush.

THE TRICK

Another dodge involves using a length of rigid plastic pipe, or electrical conduit. Thread the cable through the pipe, which you then pass under the floor or above the ceiling. Fasten the cable at one end – the coil end if you are feeding cable from a reel – and pull out the pipe at the other. The cable will then be left in position.

As you try to pass the cable along, you may come up against an obstruction – possibly a piece of solid timber, rather like a joist, but running in the opposite direction. You may also meet 'bridging': a couple of crossed battens designed to keep the joists correctly spaced apart. Such obstacles are often in the centre of the room, and under a partition wall. If the obstruction is solid, you have to lift a board on each side of the obstruction, but you can often wriggle the cable round it.

MOUNTING BOXES 1

Every switch, socket outlet or other wiring accessory, except those having an integral box or backplate, must be mounted on a box. This encloses the unsheathed ends of cables, and in some instances houses a cable connector. Some boxes also contain the earth terminal.

1. One-gang box. Used for mounting a single accessory.

2. Two-gang box. Used for mounting a double socket outlet and some special accessories, such as 45 amp and 60 amp double-pole switches for cookers, etc.

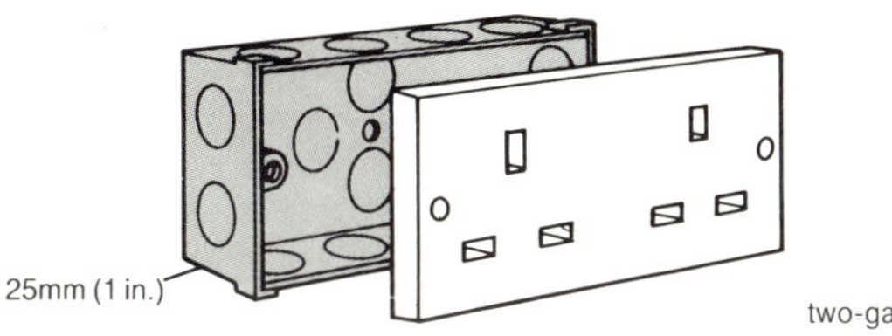

two-gang

3. Dual box. Similar to a 2-gang box, but slightly wider with screw fixing lugs in its centre. Used for mounting two 1-gang accessories on one box.

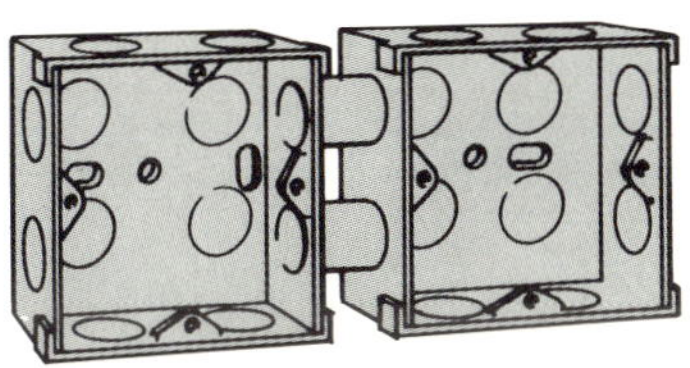

dual-gang

4. Lighting switch box. A shallow box solely for lighting switches. Fitted with cable entry grommets, one adjustable screw fixing lug and an earth terminal.

5. Architrave switch box. A knock-out box about half the standard width; also used as backing box for some wall lights.

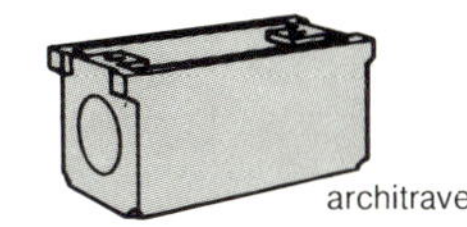

architrave

6. 'BESA' box. A conduit box having one or more conduit and cable entries. Circular with two screw fixing lugs at 50mm (2in.) centres, used for mounting wall lights and spotlights.

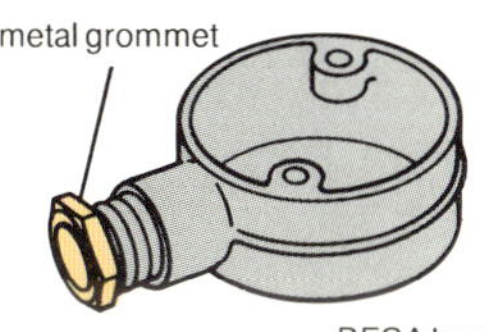

BESA box

Boxes for surface mounting in the home are usually white plastic. In work places, they are often metal, which is less easily damaged. Boxes for flush mounting are always metal, either aluminium alloy or black-coated steel. These are cheaper than the plastic ones.

Wherever possible, always plump for flush-mounted boxes (see page 84). They are more difficult to install, but are neater and safer.

In a plastic box, the holes are often 'knock-outs': i.e. they are made of very thin plastic, converted into holes by pushing them out with a screwdriver. Some plastic boxes have push-out sections on top and bottom to allow for surface-run cable. A metal box has 'knock-out blanks': i.e. a circular section held by thin strands of metal. Push this out and you have a hole of the right size.

Cable entering a metal box risks being chafed, and its internal conducts exposed. A rubber or plastic grommet – available at electrical shops – should be pushed over the edges of the hole.

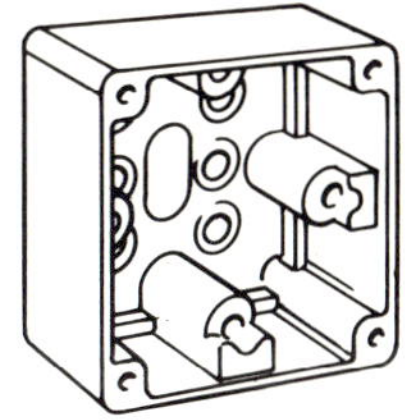

surface-mounted one-gang

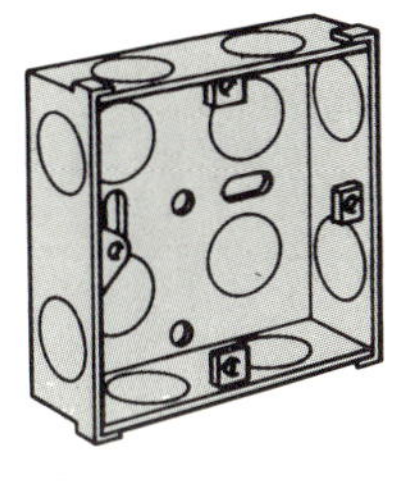

flush-mounted one-gang

SURFACE-MOUNTED BOXES

Fixing a surface-mounted box to a wall presents few problems. Drive two No. 8 woodscrews through the holes in the back into wall plugs. The holes are drilled in the wall, preferably with an electric drill. An out-of-true wall accessory looks unsightly. Make sure the box is truly horizontal, or parallel to an adjacent feature such as a door frame.

Place the box in position and mark the position for the plugs through the 'push-outs'. Use a bradawl to make a starting hole in which to locate the bit of your drill so that it will not skid. Push the plugs in, and screw the box to them. When the box is in place, check that it looks horizontal. If it does not, you can correct matters as follows.

THE TRICK

One trick is to use a No. 6 screw instead, pushing the fixing down or up by inserting a matchstick into the plug hole, between plug and masonry.

If the box is way out, there is no need to start completely from scratch. There are usually several 'push-outs' in the back of the box; take out one screw, and drive it through another 'push-out' and into a wall plug, this time making sure your positioning is correct. Some boxes have elongated slots. With these it is easy to slacken off the screw and make minor adjustments.

THE TRICK

The wall may be a material where it is difficult to get a firm fixing with wall plugs. Cement (or glue) a thin piece of wood, slightly smaller all round than the box, to the wall surface and screw the box to the wood.

TILED WALLS

If you want to fix a box to a tiled wall, make sure that its visual relationship to the pattern is true. Boxes are usually centred where four tiles meet. Tile is not an easy material to drill, because the bit tends to skid.

THE TRICK

One trick to avoid this is to press hard on the drill bit, and move the drill around without switching on the motor. You will cut through the glaze, and so the point of the bit will be turning on rough material in a small hole.

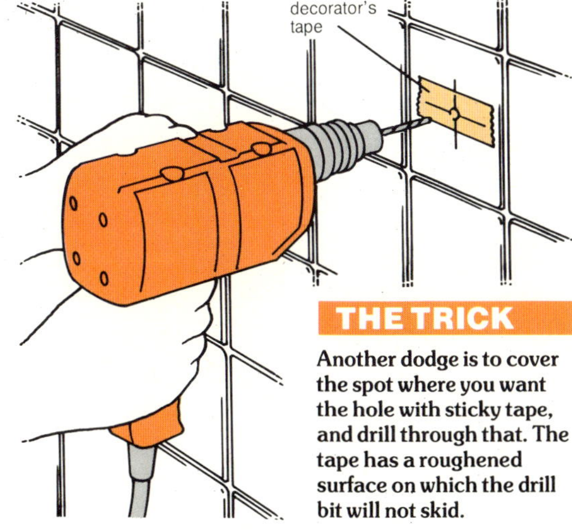

THE TRICK

Another dodge is to cover the spot where you want the hole with sticky tape, and drill through that. The tape has a roughened surface on which the drill bit will not skid.

HOLLOW WALLS

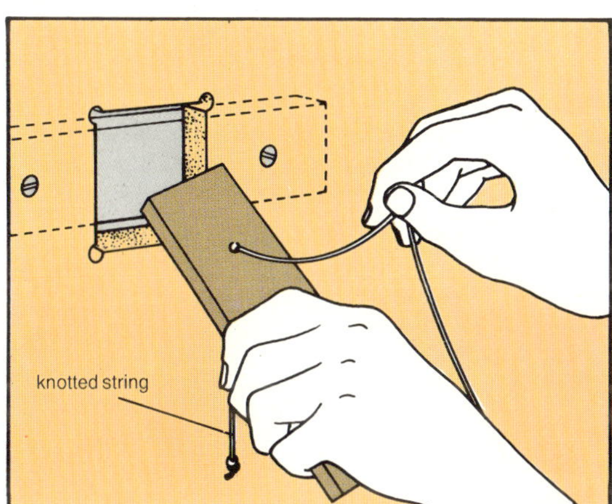

Probably the biggest problem occurs when you want to screw the box to a hollow wall. The best solution is to screw the box to one of the solid timber uprights.

How do you locate the uprights? They will probably be at intervals somewhere between 300–400mm (12–16in.). Go along the wall tapping it with your knuckles. You will notice a distinct difference with a 'solid feel' as you tap the uprights themselves and a 'hollow feel' in the space between. Upright spacings are usually regular.

If there is no upright in a suitable position, you must use a 'deadman'. This is a batten fitted behind the lath and plaster surface. Drill a small hole in the batten, thread a length of string through, and knot one end so that you can pull the batten along. Insert the batten into the wall, then draw on the string to position it correctly. Drive ordinary woodscrews through the plaster and laths into the batten behind. You can then fix your box by woodscrews driven into the deadman.

When dealing with a modern hollow wall, it is better to use the studs, and screw the box to one of these. Locate them as above. As the studs in a modern wall are spaced as much as 600mm (2ft) apart, it is likely there will not be a convenient one, so it may be easier to make a fixing to the plasterboard using cavity wall fixers or alternatively by using flanged plastic boxes.

MOUNTING BOXES 2

FLUSH–MOUNTED BOXES

Choose your box with care, they come in four depths. Easiest to accommodate is the 17mm (about ⅝in.) box; known as the 'plaster depth box'. Even if the plaster on your wall is too thin, you will not have to chop out much brickwork to make the hole deep enough. This box can take only 5 amp lighting switches.

Standard boxes are usually either 25mm (1in.) or 35mm (1½in.) deep. Modern accessories have a face plate with a fairly deep bevel. Because of this the 'works' do not stick out so far at the back, so they will usually fit into the 25mm (1in.) box. Before buying any accessories, check that they are shallow enough for the 25mm (1in.) box. If not you will have to fit a 35mm (1½in.) one.

There is a specially deep 47mm (1⅞in.) box for when that extra space would be very handy, even if it is not absolutely necessary. Never try to fit one of these boxes in a thin partition of, say, breeze block.

SOLID WALLS

It is not easy to get a flush-mounted box level, but you can now buy boxes in which one of the threaded lugs for the accessory's fixing screw is adjustable, so that you can alter the position of the face plate.

If the wall is papered, place the box on the paper, making sure (with a spirit level) that it is truly horizontal; then draw round its outline with pencil. Using a sharp Stanley knife, and a straight-edge to guide it, cut through the paper all along the pencil lines, and peel off the paper. A painted wall is dealt with in much the same way.

Chop out the plaster down to the masonry below, using a bolster (or cold) chisel. If it is a plaster-depth box, place it in the hole to see if there is enough room. If any part of the box stands proud, you will have to chop into the brickwork until you have a good fit.

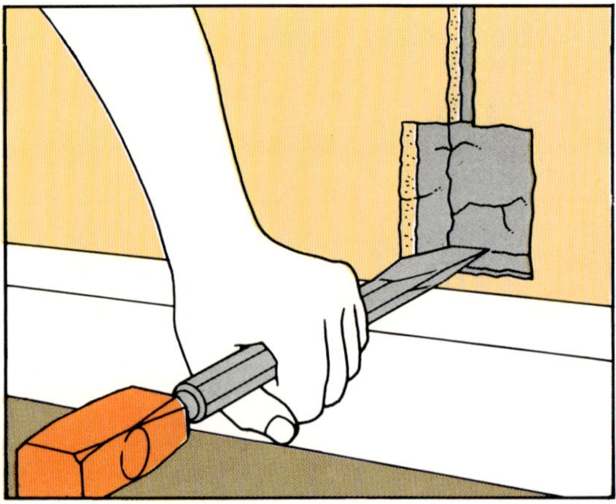

It is a good idea to place the box at this stage into the hole and check that it is horizontal. It does not matter if the hole is too deep, as the edge of the face plate will cover up any gap.

Cutting out is done with the chisel at an angle of at least 45 degrees; not only will you chip off the masonry more easily, but also there is less chance that you will damage the structure.

When you think you have penetrated enough, push the box in for a final check. The bottom of the hole must be perfectly flat, so that the box will not wobble in use.

THE TRICK

Cut out the hole a bit too deep, then cover the bottom of it with cement. Push the box in, and excess cement will ooze out of the bottom. Withdraw the box, clean off the excess, then wait for the cement in the hole to set.

When you are satisfied with the hole, the box is fixed with No. 8 woodscrews, driven into wall plugs. This is your last chance to make the box horizontal.

With a little care you should not damage the wall much. Remember that the face plate will cover up any damage near the edge. Making good should be done before the electrical connections are made.

HOLLOW WALLS

If your hollow wall is of plasterboard, fixed to a timber framework, then sinking a flush box is easy. Buy special lugs that clamp on to the side and are then fixed to the plasterboard.

A lath and plaster wall presents much greater problems, and you should aim to fix to a stud. Begin by cutting through the laths with a padsaw; you will have to drill a starting hole. You will then have exposed the stud. The hole will probably not be deep enough, so cut a notch in the stud. Make the notch with a tenon saw and chisel (see page 39). The bottom must be true and flat, so that the box will lie level with the surface.

The difficulty is that, the end of at least one lath will now be flapping. The plaster on top will keep it stable to a certain extent, but you have weakened the wall.

THE TRICK

To repair it, after you have fitted the box, chop off plaster each side of it, and slide a short length of thin timber vertically behind the laths. Place an identical piece on top of the laths, and drive screws through into the timber behind. Cover over the top timber with plaster or filler.

stud

TILED WALLS

Walls clad with ceramic tiles are the trickiest of all to cope with if you are thinking of sinking a flush box in them. If you have spare tiles, the best course is to hack the existing ones off the wall, chop out the holes for the box in the wall behind, cut four spare tiles to shape and stick them in place. If not, you are taking a big risk. Otherwise, it is best to install a surface box, or find another spot not covered with tiles.

THE TRICK

If you still want a flush box on tiles, you could draw the outline box in pencil on the tiles. Just inside and all round the perimeter drill a series of holes through the tiles with a masonry bit. You can then remove the 'waste' without causing any damage to tiles left on the wall. This is a long and tedious process.

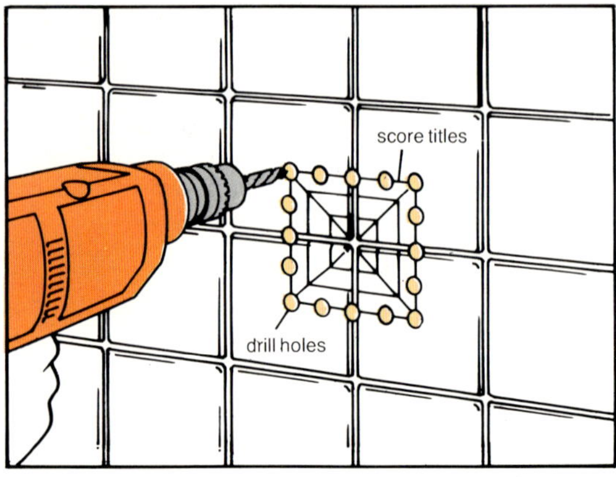

NEW SCREWS FOR OLD

The threaded lugs on mounting boxes were once made in imperial sizes. The lugs have now been metricated, so what happens when you want to fit a new accessory to an old box? With an old metal box, just drive home the new metric screws, and they will tap their way in.

On a plastic box with a brass inset, you must use the correct screw. Try to force a metric screw into an imperial thread, and the brass inset will be wrenched out making the box useless. It is the same with BESA boxes, used as the backing for some light fittings.

On imperial screws, the thread goes right through to the end; on metric ones the last few twists at the end are omitted.

EXTRA SOCKET OUTLETS

The easiest way to add extra socket outlets is to take out an existing single socket and put a double in. The only time you cannot do this is when there are two sockets on a spur (see page 80). Since 1983, only one socket outlet is permitted. If a spur supplies only one socket, this may be doubled.

There are four possibilities for conversion:

1. If the single socket is flush, you can make the double surface-mounted using a shallower box;
2. You can let the new double socket be flush;
3. If your present single outlet is surface-mounted, you can put a surface double in its place; or
4. You can use a flush fixing for the new double.

There is only one set of terminals on the back of a double outlet, although there are two sockets. The red wire goes in the L (or P) terminal, the black in the N and the green or green and yellow in the E.

FLUSH TO SURFACE-MOUNTED

Switch off power and take out the two screws holding the socket face plate.

Withdraw it from the box. You will see three pairs of wires fixed to the terminals: two live, two neutral and two earth. There are two if it is part of the ring. Withdraw these wires and discard the socket. Knock out the push-out in the back of the plastic 2-gang box, draw through the cable projecting from the flush box, then screw the double box in place. Use the screws from the discarded single socket, as you know they will fit the lugs of the flush box.

Now connect up the wires to the terminals on the new double socket, then fix it to the box with the screws provided. To fit flush-mounted boxes, see page 84; then wire as above.

THE TRICK

A more economical conversion, instead of fitting a double socket, is to install two singles side by side, using those that would otherwise be thrown away.

They will need to go to a dual box (see page 83). With two single sockets mounted side by side, there will be two sets of terminals to which you must connect. So one socket must be looped-in to the other: i.e. one socket must be connected to the circuit, while a short length of 2.5mm cable runs from its terminals to those of the second.

Instead of having a length of cable, it is better to take 150mm (6in.) of cable and remove all the sheathing. Run the red wire between the two L/P terminals and the black one between the two Ns.

THE TRICK

You will probably find it more convenient to buy a 150mm (6in.) length of insulated earth wire and use it instead of the bare copper wire.

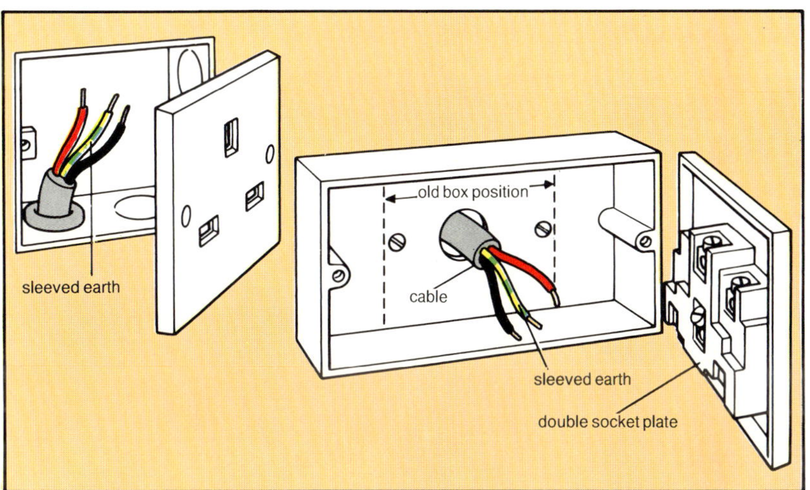

INSTALLING NEW SOCKETS

If you cannot substitute a double for a single, you must install a completely new outlet. When doing so, make sure it is a double. It is strictly against the regulations to install a socket outlet in the bathroom. The only socket permitted there is one for use exclusively with electric razors (see page 92).

The easiest way of getting your new socket outlet is to install a spur. Remember that you can have only one double socket; the cable to use is 2.5mm two-core and earth PVC-sheathed.

WIRING FROM A SOCKET

Begin by looking for a convenient socket to make your connection. First carry out the test described on page 80. The socket can be in the next room as two sockets on a dividing wall back to back or side by side, make an admirably economical and disturbance-free installation.

This need not be on the same floor. A cable can run the short vertical distance between floors. You will now have a downstairs socket on the upstairs ring – or vice versa. This is important to bear in mind when you want to shut down a circuit by removing the fuse.

Having determined which socket you will use, run the new spur cable to it. If the socket is flush, switch off the ring and disconnect the wires from the terminals and withdraw the screws, so you can take the box out. This is necessary so that you can remove a knock-out to allow the spur cable to enter. You may find it easier to 'fish' for the spur cable (see page 82).

Replace the box in position, drawing the wires through the appropriate holes. The wires of the new spur go in exactly the same terminals as those of the ring (see below). There will now be three wires in each terminal instead of two.

When adding an extra single-strand conductor, make sure that the terminal screw grips all of them. Screw the face plate back in place.

THE TRICK

You will find that, while the old stranded conductors go in more easily if twisted together with pliers, solid (i.e. single-strand) conductors should be inserted side by side.

SITING THE SOCKET

Always begin by installing the socket as, until it is in position, you can never be entirely sure exactly where your cable should run. The socket can go at any point on the wall that suits you; but it should always be at least 150mm (6in.) above a floor or worktop so that you can insert and withdraw plugs freely. A socket is, of course, screwed to a box fixed to the wall (see pages 83–4).

Run cable from the box to where you propose to connect it to the ring. Connect the three conductors in the cable to the socket terminals as above. Before connecting up the earth, slip a green and yellow PVC sleeving over it. You must make absolutely sure that you have connected the right wire to the right terminal, otherwise your installation will be very dangerous. There are three points to connect up a new spur to the main:

1. At the terminals of an existing socket outlet;
2. At a joint box inserted into the ring circuit cable;
3. At the ring circuit fuseway in the consumer unit.

You should choose what will create the shortest cable run.

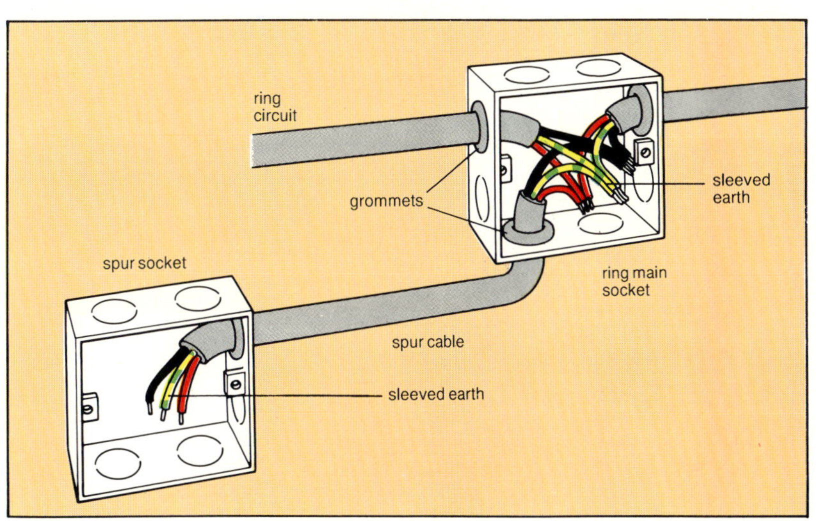

FIXED CONNECTIONS

FUSED CONNECTION UNITS

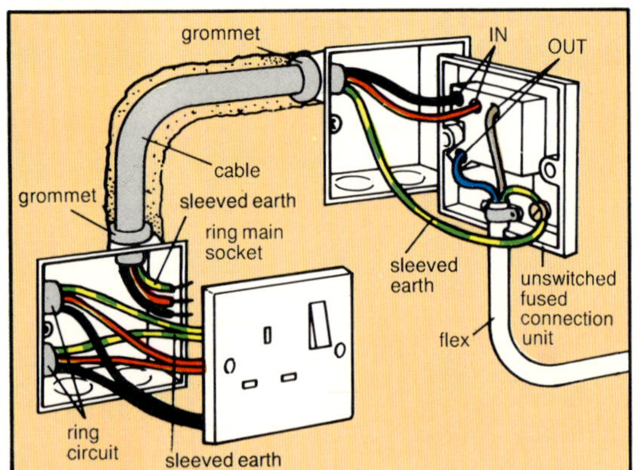

Many appliances are permanently wired-in to the ring circuit via a fused connection unit. The mains cable goes to a set of terminals marked 'feed': the red wire to the L/P terminal, the black to the N, and the bare copper wire to the E, a short length of green and yellow PVC sheathing being slipped on first. The flex goes to the other terminals labelled 'load'. The brown wire is fixed to the L/P terminal, the blue to the N, and the green and yellow to the E. In some cases both earth wires are fastened to the same terminal – which may not be labelled, but it is always clear which one it is. Do not confuse the 'feed' and 'load' terminals, or the switching will not work properly, which could be dangerous.

Connection units are fitted to a box, and may be flush- or surface-mounted. The flex may reach the terminals via an inlet hole on the face plate, or if concealed it can go though a hole in the box.

If your unit does not have a switch, there is no need to disconnect the appliance from the main. All you need do is remove the fuse. In some models, it is under a retractable cover held on the face plate by a small screw.

Double fused connection units are not available, but you can have a twin installation by fitting two connection units to a dual box (see page 83).

INSTALLING A COOKER

A cooker must have its own radial circuit connected to a cooker control unit, so if your home does not already have one, you must install one.

The control unit fits to a box, and may be flush- or surface-mounted. The cable supplying the control unit must be 6mm twin core and earth PVC-sheathed, and must run from a separate 30, 45 or 60 amp fuseway in the consumer unit. Some cooker control units offer just switching facilities, but others also have a socket outlet, intended for an electric kettle.

A cooker control is usually fixed to the wall about 1.50m (5ft) above the floor, and by the regulations within 2m (6ft 6in.) of the cooker, so that it can easily be turned off in an emergency. It does not have to be on the same wall as the cooker. If you are fitting a new control unit remember to place it within this distance from the site you have chosen for your cooker. A cooker you intend to wire up to an existing control must be placed within the required 2m (6ft 6in.). Otherwise move the control unit.

Low down on the wall behind the cooker you should fit a terminal cooker box on a mounting box, which can be flush or on the surface. This installation method allows the cooker to be disconnected easily from the terminal box. Use the same size cable as in the main circuit to connect this to the cooker control; it can be either surface-run or concealed.

A cooker does not come with a flex and you need a length of cable of the same type to connect to its terminal box (somewhere on the back). Leave a little slack so that the cooker can be pulled out for cleaning.

The cooker control unit and the cooker terminal box are wired up just like the fixed connection units (see above). The 'feed' terminals of the control take the supply cable coming in from the consumer unit. The 'load' terminals take the cable running onto the terminal box. In the terminal box, the 'feed' terminals take the cable from the control unit, while the trailing cable from the cooker is wired to its 'load' terminals.

Wired up as described, your cooker has a circuit which is permissible under the regulations for a cooker up to a rating of 12kw, plus a kettle socket.

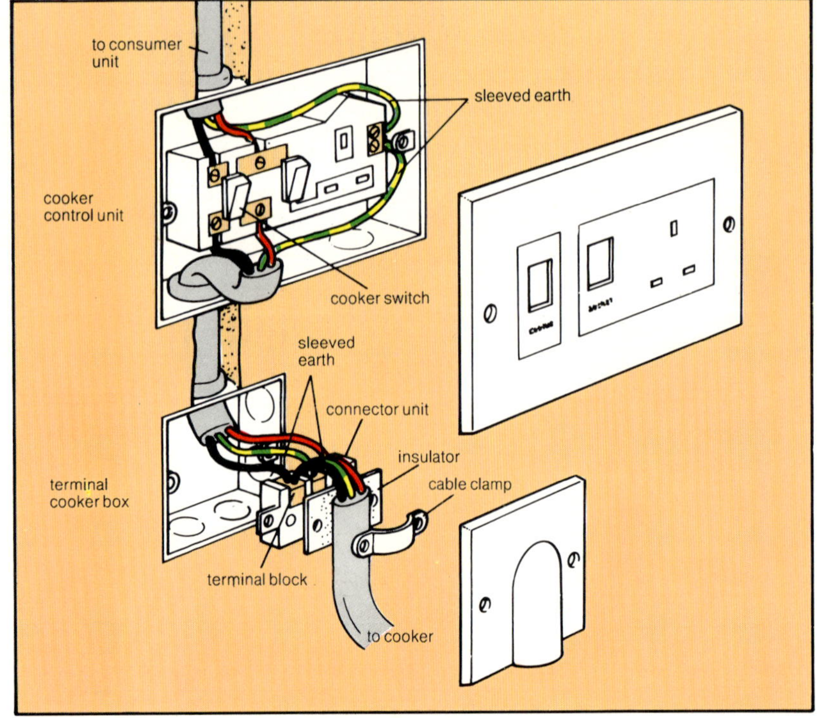

SPLIT-LEVEL COOKERS

Built-in split-level cookers (separate hob and oven) need have only one control unit, provided that both sections are within 2m (6ft 6in.) of it. The only difference, is that two appliances have to be connected up to one control. You can either run two cables from the control to each section of the cooker: each cable would be connected to the same 'load' terminals in the control unit. Or run one cable from the control to a cooker terminal box and run the hob cable from this box. Then loop-out another cable from the same 'load' terminals as the hob cable to a second cooker terminal box to feed the oven.

If one part of the split-level cooker is more than 2m (6ft 6in.) from the control box, you will have to install a second cooker control unit. Your circuit would then be: cable from the mains to the first control, cable looped out to the second control, separate cables running from each control to separate connection boxes – one for the hob, one for the oven.

INSTALLING A FREEZER

A freezer needs its own circuit that can be left live, when the rest are shut down. If you install a fused connection unit for the freezer and wire it back to a spare fuseway in the consumer unit, then you can turn off the mainswitch, take out all the fuseways except the one for the freezer, and restore the power.

The best method is to run the freezer circuit from a switchfuse (see page 77). This is connected independently to the mains supply, so that the freezer circuit is not affected when you switch off the rest of the mains. Begin by installing the new fused connection unit near the site for your freezer. Run a length of 1.5mm twin-core and earth PVC-sheathed cable back to the switchfuse unit. If you have installed a freezer in an outhouse or garage, you must follow the instructions for taking power outside (see page 94).

WIRING FOR LIGHTS

In diagrammatic form the theory of lighting would show the neutral wire passing directly to the light. The live wire would go to the light via the switch.

When the switch mechanism is on, current can pass along this live wire to the lighting point, and the bulb comes on. When the switch is off, the flow of current is stopped, and the lights are turned off. Confusion arises because of the way this is accomplished with the loop-in system in practice. The mains cable (containing live, neutral and earth wires) goes direct to the ceiling rose, and all three wires are connected to terminals there. A further cable, again with all three wires connected to terminals in the rose, leaves the lighting point and goes to the switch. This latter cable is known as the switch drop.

The confusing point is that both the conductors (other than the earth) in the switch drop are live. However, one of them is covered in black PVC insulation, the colour of a neutral wire, because you cannot normally buy twin-core and earth cable in which both conductors are red. (Cable with both conductors in red is manufactured but is sold specifically for use as switch drops in large contract work.

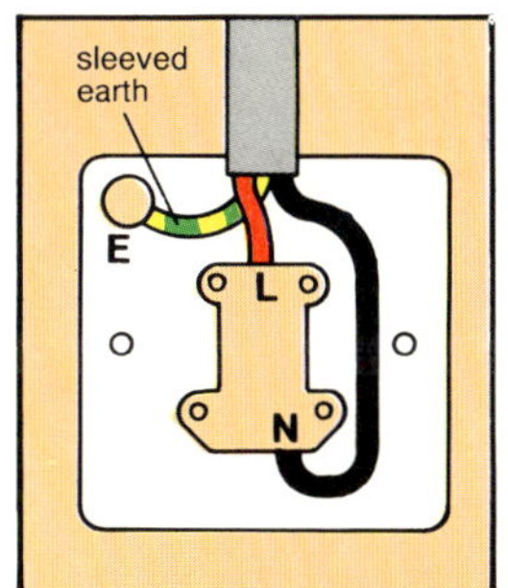

It is deliberately kept out of the retail shops, because it might prove a hazard in unskilled hands.)

When you look inside a loop-in rose you may not know which is the black live wire from the switch drop. It is important that whenever you are working on a ceiling rose you should wire up to the correct terminal.

A rose in a system wired on the joint box principle will not present this confusing picture. There will be only one set of wires inside it and each of these (live, neutral and earth) will be of the correct colour. The switch drop, with its confusing live black wire, will be connected up in the joint box that supplies the rose (see page 80).

THE TRICK

It is good practice when lighting is being installed for this 'black live' wire to have a piece of red sticky tape fixed to it so that anyone subsequently working on it will recognize it straightaway for what it is. (Similarly the regulations require that there should be red tape on the black wire at the switch.)

THE TRICK

Whenever you disturb the terminal connections at a ceiling rose, it is a good idea to make a note or label the wires so that you can put them back correctly.

TWO-WAY SWITCHING

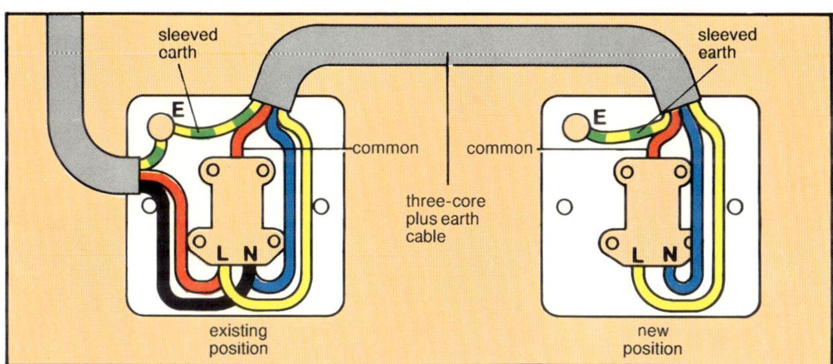

If you live in a two (or more) storey house you probably already have one set of lights controlled by a two-way switching system. Those on the hall and landing can be turned on and/or off both at the top and bottom of the stairs. However, it can be useful to have two-way switches in other parts of the home. The most obvious instance is the bedroom, where it is very handy to turn off the light at a switch near the bed as you settle down for the night.

Two-way switching is accomplished by means of special switches. Disconnect the existing one-way switch and dispose of it. In its place fit a two-way switch, connecting up the existing wires to it as shown. There will be no need to disturb the earth wire on a square-plate switch, for it is connected to an earth terminal on the box itself. Fit the box for the second two-way switch in the position you have chosen for it.

Between the two boxes you run a special cable which is three-core plus earth. The three insulated cores are red, yellow and blue respectively, the colours for three-phase power circuits in industry. The cable is 1.5mm and PVC-sheathed. Connect the wires up to the switches as shown, and screw the switches to their mounting boxes.

You may find a different wiring pattern in two-way switches already installed. A one-core cable and earth will run from the mains feed to a common terminal (labelled 'C'), and a two-core cable to L1 and L2. This two-core runs to the L1 and L2 of the other switch, and a one-core returns from the second common terminal to the light (or joint box).

Ceiling switches (see page 91) also come in two-way switches. They form a quick and convenient way of fitting an extra light switch in a bedroom without upsetting the decorations, particularly if you have concealed lights or other unusual lighting treatments.

TWO-WAY SWITCHING FOR AN OUTDOOR LIGHT

If your exterior light is outside the back door – to light the way to an access door for the garage, for instance – it can be useful to have two-way switching, with the second switch out of doors, so that you can turn off the light after you have locked the back door, and found your way to the garage. The switch is also useful when you want to come and go on foot via the side entrance.

This kind of switch can be fitted without running cable out of doors. The two switches are fitted back to back on an exterior wall – the inside one in the kitchen, say, and the other outside near the back door. A short length of 1.5mm, three-core plus earth, PVC-sheathed cable connects the two switches. The inside one is a normal two-way rocker switch; the outside one must be a weatherproof two-way switch such as the MK 'Seal'. The wiring is as above.

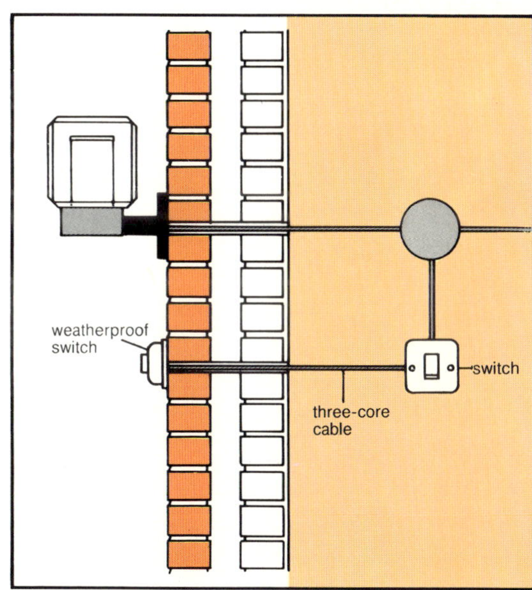

It is possible, of course, to have a second light at the back of the house operated from a one-way switch, but so that you can get away with using ordinary PVC-sheathed lighting cable, make sure that all your runs are inside the house, with the cable passing through the wall to switch and lamp. Wiring out of doors must be done in PVC-covered, mineral-insulated, copper-sheathed cable, and fixing this involves a lot more work (see page 93).

THE TRICK

An outdoor switch near the front door is not to be recommended as it might attract children or vandals.

SPECIALISED SWITCHES

DIMMER SWITCHES

This is an electronic device used with tungsten-filament lighting (such as ordinary electric light bulbs) to vary the intensity of the light output from full brilliance down to zero. Dimmers cannot normally be used to control fluorescent lighting, but by using modified dimmers and an extra transformer in the lighting fitting, this is possible.

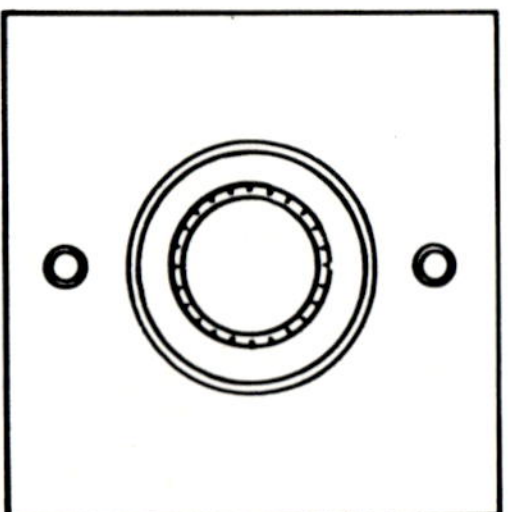

One- or two-way combined dimmer and on/off switch

There are many different types of dimmer switches and you should take a careful look at what is available before buying one. Ask for advice at the shop. It is usually more convenient not to have to reset the dimmer each time the light is turned on; therefore it is probably worth the extra cost to have an ON/OFF switch as well as the dimmer

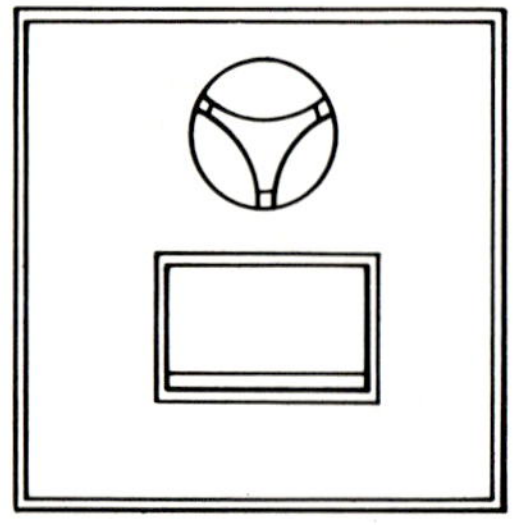

One- or two-way dimmer with separate on/off switch

knob. Most dimmers are designed to fit the basic one-gang, flush- or surface-mounted box, so there should be no need to install a new one. If your light switches are of the old-fashioned round variety, you will have to install a modern square mounting box (see pages 83–4).

There are various specialised dimmers to cope

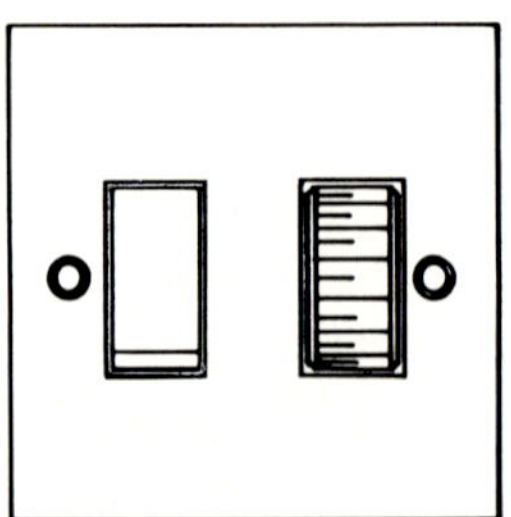

Milled-edge drum dimmer with separate on/off switch

with specific situations, such as for spotlights or dimming lights on a two-way switching system. You will have to fix a dual-gang mounting box (see pages 83–4) to take the dimmer switch and the two-way switch. If you have a two-gang switch – for instance, to control ceiling lights and wall lights in your sitting room separately – you will have to install two dimmer switches: one for the wall lights and one for the ceiling light. You cannot run both off the same dimmer unless they are wired to the same ON/OFF switch. There is now a dimmer unit which will perform this task.

INSTALLING A DIMMER SWITCH

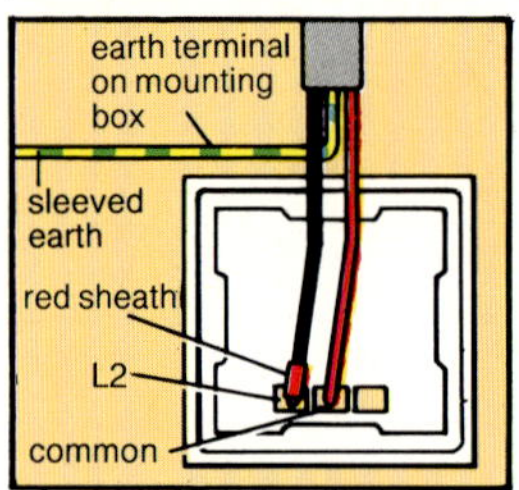

Begin the installation by removing the face plate of the existing switch from its box by withdrawing the screws. Disconnect the wires from the terminals and discard the switch. One of these wires will be red, another black, and a third one green, or green and yellow. The last of these is the earth, but although the other two are colour-coded for live and neutral, they are in fact both live.

Now connect these wires to the terminals on the back of the dimmer switch. The exact layout of these switches varies from make to make, so you should follow closely the instructions that come with it. Fix the dimmer switch to the box with the screws provided, and the job is finished. The diagram shows how the wiring for the two-way dimmer switch is connected.

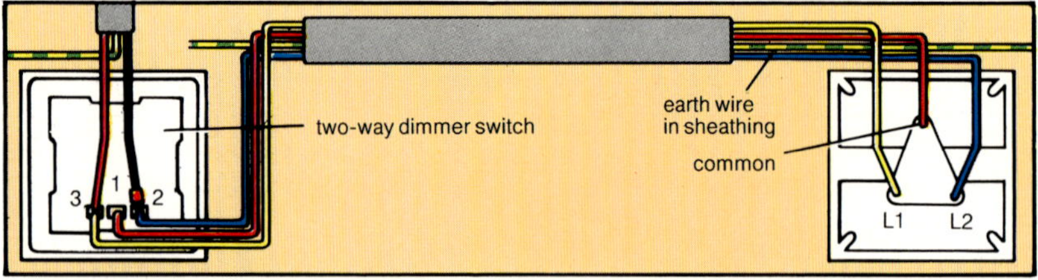

DIMMER SWITCH FAILURE

This is usually caused by overloading the unit or by the failure of a light bulb which destroys the semi-conductor by a short circuit. A 200-watt dimmer is fine for a simple ceiling light; but if you want to run four or more wall lights from it – each with 100-watt bulbs – it is obviously not going to be able to cope for very long. If you are not sure how to calculate the wattage level, read page 78 on Checking lighting circuits. Don't forget that, though you may have planned for 60-watt bulbs, someone else may install 100-watt ones.

TIME SWITCHES

There are two main reasons for installing time switches: they are, firstly, economy and, secondly, protection. The first is usually in connection with water heating or central heating and requires permanent fixtures; the latter can often be dealt with more efficiently by means of moveable plug-in switches. Time switches vary immensely in complexity and ability and you should consider precisely what you want it to do before you make a purchase.

IMMERSION HEATERS AND CENTRAL HEATING SYSTEMS

You could consider a time switch if you are installing an immersion heater (see page 95) and/or central heating and are not using an economy rate tariff supply because neither are needed on a full-time basis. It is pointless to heat water to the same temperature day and night or to heat your home through the day when everybody is out at work or at school. It is also extremely expensive! A properly insulated hot-water cylinder should keep the water hot all day, so that it only needs to be boosted just before baths, etc, are required (see page 137).

The most basic time switch simply turns itself on and off twice a day. The most complicated has a seven-day cycle with the potential to have different 'On' and 'Off' times each day. Even the most basic time switch has an over-ride facility so that you can turn on during an 'Off' period.

You should install a time switch for an immersion heater between a double-pole switch and the heater (see page 95). This is so that, when you go away, you can switch off completely without having to mess around with the time switch settings. You will, of course, have to reset it when you return.

The wiring in of a time switch is shown in the diagram. Don't forget to slip the sheathing over the bare earth wires before attaching them to the earth terminal.

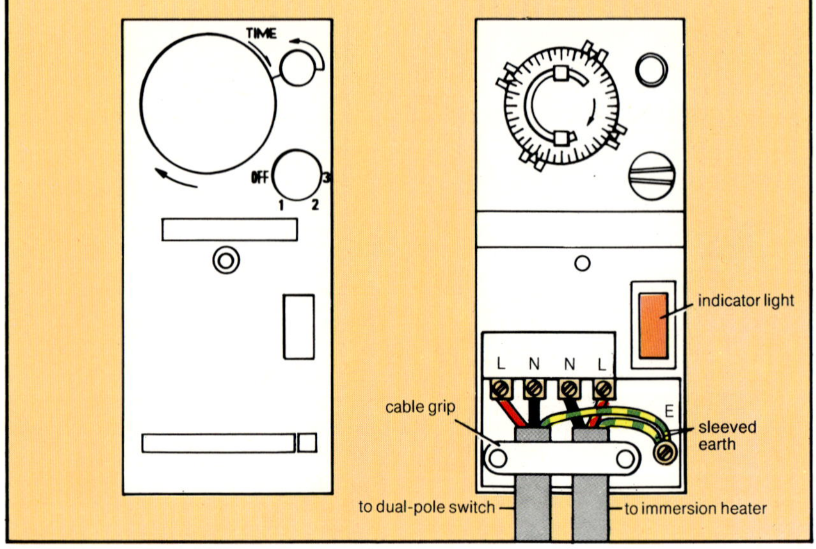

THE TRICK

Leave yourself a note to remind you to reset the time switches but not somewhere where a potential burglar might spot it! Time switches also have to be reset at the start and finish of Summer Time.

PROTECTION

It is possible to obtain highly complex systems which will control every room in your home to a specified programme; but these are extremely expensive and should be installed by the experts who design them. They also require a fair amount of specialised servicing. Unless you have valuable possessions or have other reasons, they are not worth the cost. For a full discussion of some less expensive ways to protect your home, see the chapter on Home Security starting on page 326.

CEILING LIGHTS

Most fixed lights on a circuit are 'plain pendants'. They consist of flex hanging down from a ceiling rose, and supporting a shade held on the lampholder.

FIXING A CEILING ROSE

If you want to install another ceiling lighting point, you must have a ceiling rose. The rose must be very firmly fixed, because it has to hold the weight of whatever light fitting you choose. Most ceilings are of plasterboard, or lath and plaster, fixed to joists above. On both, the rose cannot be positioned at random as you will not get a safe enough fixing. The best place is directly below a joist. The fixing screws can then go through the plaster and into the timber beyond. There should be enough space to push cable down the side of the joist and into the rose.

THE TRICK

You can always use a carpenter's chisel and mallet to cut a notch on the underside of the timber.

To fix a rose, decide on its position and make the necessary holes in the ceiling through which to feed the cable. Unscrew its cover, then drive 35mm (1½in.) woodscrews via two of the fixing holes through the plaster, and into the joist beyond. The fixing holes may be push-outs, as may the hole in the base for threading the cables through.

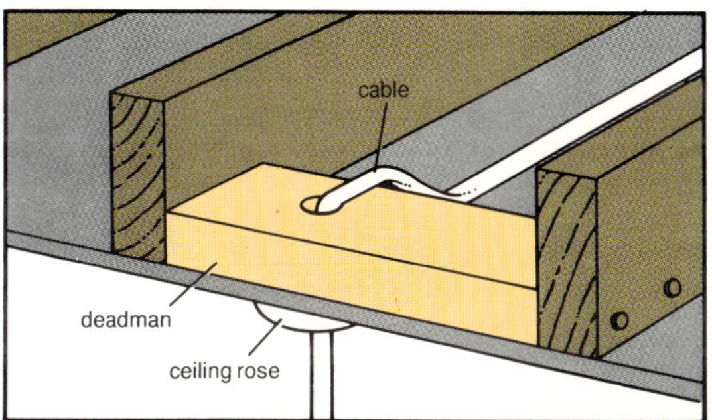

THE TRICK

If you insist on having one between joists you have to make use of a 'deadman' (see page 83). A ceiling deadman should be about 10 × 25mm (4 × 1in.) long with a hole drilled in the middle to let the cables through. It is much simpler if you can raise the floorboard upstairs or gain access via the loft.

Some ceilings, especially in modern flats, are of concrete. Fixing a rose to these is merely a matter of driving the fixing screws into wall plugs inserted in holes drilled in the ceiling.

EXTRA CEILING LIGHTS

You must decide if the new light should have its own independent switching. Most lights do have their own switch, but if a room has two or more ceiling lights it is often convenient to have them all controlled by one switch. A new light in a room that does not presently have one will usually need to be independently switched. In all cases, the wiring must be done in 1mm, twin-core and earth, PVC-sheathed cable.

Adding extra ceiling lights is relatively simple if you have a loop-in system. You install a rose, then run cable from it to the nearest existing rose, at which the connection to the main is made. It is usually most convenient to tap into the rose already in the room. It is essential to do so if you want both lights in the room to work off one switch. If you are installing a light in a part of your home that doesn't have one at present, then the rose in a nearby room will be the best. Make the connections at the existing rose as shown. Your rose may differ slightly from this, but you should see how to make the connections. If you are in any doubt, call in an electrician. If the new light is to be controlled by the switch of the existing one then connect the red wire of the new cable to the SW terminal, the black wire to the N and the earth wire to the E terminal, at the existing rose. The connections at the new rose are simple, as is shown.

If the light is to be independently switched, then at the existing rose the red wire of the new cable goes to the LOOP terminal instead of to the SW one. The black still goes to the N terminal. The new rose will be wired up and you must also install a switch (see pages 80, 83–4, 87). When fitting the lighting flex to the rose, make sure its brown wire goes to the SW terminal, its blue to the N, and earth to E. Some roses have terminals marked FLEX.

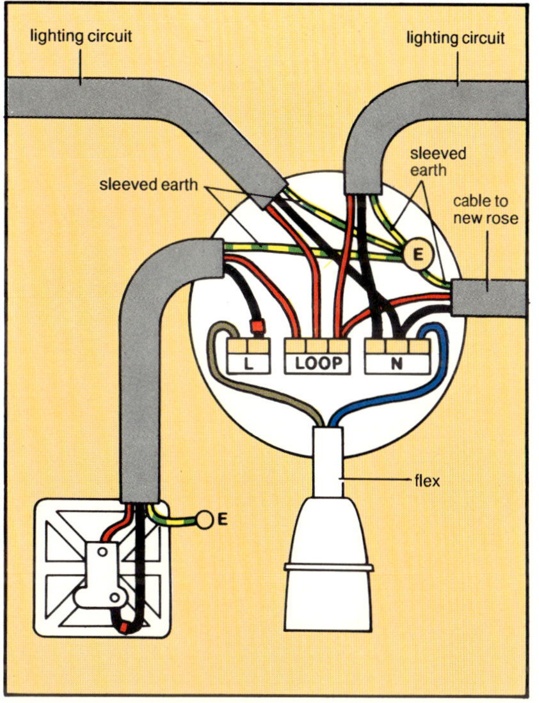

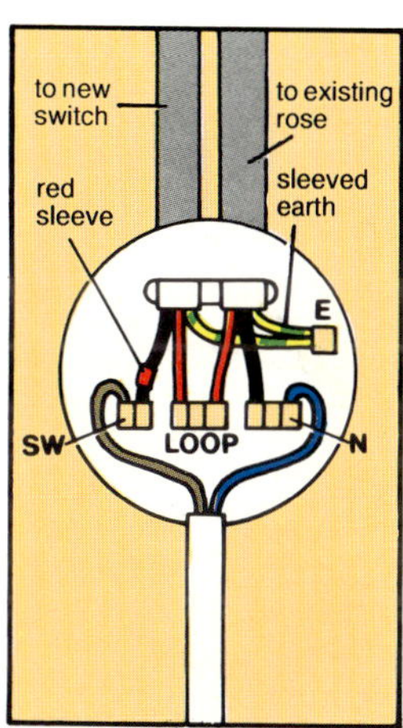

Even with a loop-in system, it may be that the nearest ceiling rose is too far away for convenience. In that case you will have to introduce a joint box. Trace the mains cable back to a convenient spot, and there insert a joint box (see page 80).

MOVING A LIGHT

To reposition an existing lighting point, remove the existing rose, and draw its cables back into the ceiling void. Let's assume you have a loop-in system. Take care not to separate the various wires joined together – tape them up temporarily if you wish. In particular note which is the main red loop wire. Cable must be run to the new light position and connected to the existing wires by means of a 4-terminal 10 amp joint box.

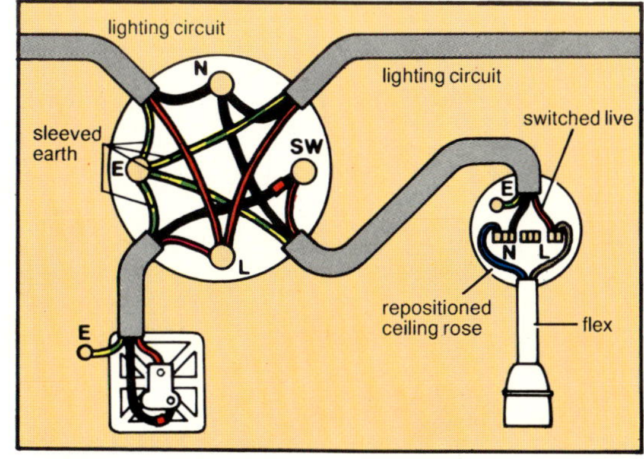

The black wire of the new cable goes into a terminal containing two or more black loop wires. The new red wire goes into a terminal with the single switch wire (black, but with a red identification sleeve). The earth wires go together. The existing red loop wires should go in one terminal, and no new wire should be connected to them.

(In a joint box system, the rose will have only red, black and earth wires. At the joint box you connect red to red, black to black, and earth to earth, leaving one terminal spare.) The rose in its new position is connected up as for independent switching.

CLOSE-CEILING FITTINGS

Modern close-ceiling fittings are complex and take the place of flex and rose. The best way of installing them is as described for moving a light (left). Remove the existing rose and dispose of it. Just above its former position, fit a 4-terminal 10 amp joint box and run a new heat-resisting cable to the light fitting. Connect this latter cable to the fitting by means of a plastic connection block. Most modern fittings come complete. If yours does not, buy a block and cut off a 3-terminal section with a knife. The fitting itself is held in place with wood screws.

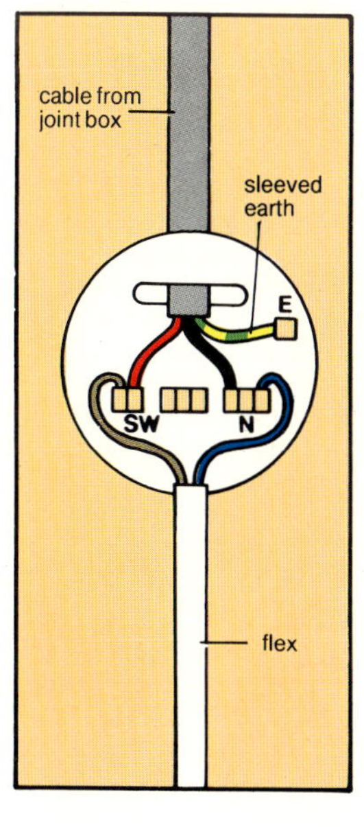

WALL LIGHTS

One way of dispensing with that boring lighting arrangement of having just one pendant fitting in the centre of a room is to install wall lights. They were a feature of many suburban houses built in the 1930s, and because they help to create decorative and efficient localized lighting effects they are becoming popular once more.

The first thing is to decide on their position. Many people fix one in each of the chimney breast alcoves. Others also fit a couple on a long wall. In any event, the normal mounting height is 1.5m (5 ft) above floor level, but this can be varied slightly according to the design of the fitting, and your own tastes. In very tall rooms it is a good idea to place the light much higher.

Some wall lights are designed to fit to a mounting box. It is the BESA box intended primarily for accepting conduit (see page 83). The box is sunk into the wall flush with the plaster, and the light fitting mounted to it. Other fittings incorporate a box into their design, because the connections of the wall light to the mains cable must be made in a non-combustible chamber, as with switches and sockets.

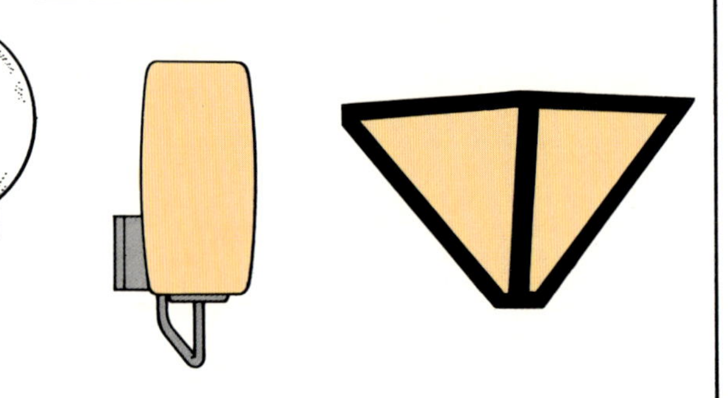

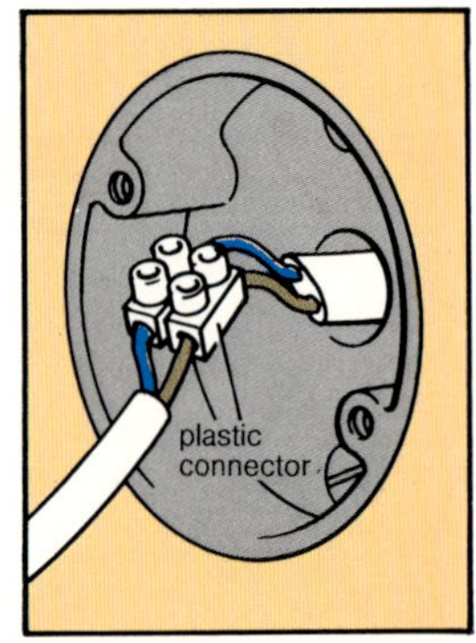

WIRING

The wiring for wall lights should be done in 1mm, twin-core and earth, PVC-sheathed cable. Now what are the wiring arrangements to be? One possibility is that you dispense with the existing ceiling light completely, and have your new wall lights controlled by its switch. In that case all you need do is run cable from each wall light to the position of the rose. The existing light fitting should be removed, and the rose itself dismantled and dispensed with. The exact method of doing this will vary from make to make, but usually it is obvious how to do it.

The new cable from the wall lights is connected up to the existing circuit by means of a four-terminal 10 amp joint box. In essence it is just like moving a light and you should follow the procedure outlined on page 89.

If, alternatively, you wish to keep the centre light, but have its switch control the wall lights too, so that all come on and off together, then run the new cable from the wall light back to the ceiling light. There it should be connected in the rose to exactly the same terminals as the light flex – red to brown, black to blue, and earth to earth. In other words, there is no joint box.

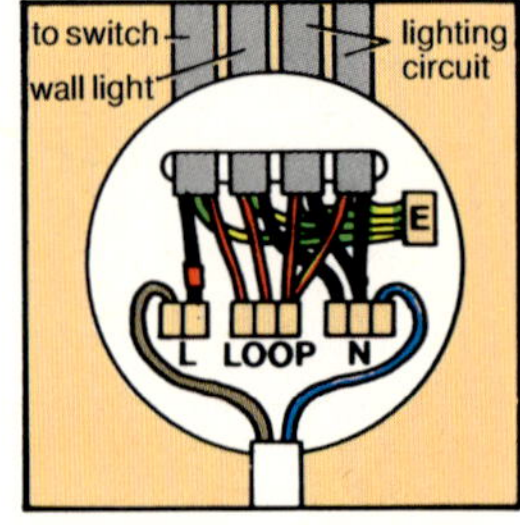

SEPARATE SWITCHES

If you want to have the wall lights separately switched and still keep the centre light, the easiest way is to buy wall lights that have their own switch. Then cables to the wall lights are connected to them with a two-terminal plastic connector in an architrave box, the earth terminal of which is used to join the earth wires, as shown. In a loop-in system, the other ends of the wall-light wires are connected to the three-terminal blocks of the rose, black with black, red with red, and earth wire to earth terminal (covered with a sleeve, of course) as shown. You can, of course, also tap the mains feed of the lighting circuit directly, using a three-terminal joint box.

The snag about wall lights with their own switches is that you have to walk across the room to turn them on and off. It's much more convenient to have them governed by a switch just inside the room door. In any event, not all fittings have their own switching, and even those that have may not be suitable for connecting directly to the live wires of a lighting circuit – check on this point when you buy. The regulations require that this sort of light should have a separate isolating switch – the conventional room lighting switch is quite suitable.

There are several ways of installing switched lights, but probably the easiest of all is by means of a four-terminal joint box. Once again, trace the existing mains cable to a convenient point and there install the joint box. There will be four cables – two to the mains, one to the light and the other to the switch as shown.

Probably the most convenient of all would be to convert the existing room switch into a two-gang arrangement – one for the centre light, the other for the wall lights. In that case remove the existing switch, and fit a two-gang switch in its place.

Note that in the diagrams only one wall light cable is shown. Where you have two or more wall lights, it is best for the cables from each to be connected to the same terminals of the new joint box.

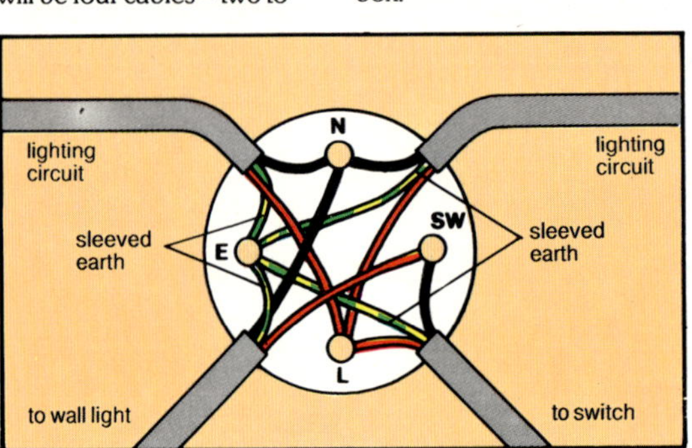

SWITCHES

Plateswitch. The name given to the modern lighting switch and most other switches because of its face plate design, which is usually of moulded plastic.

Rocker switch. Most switches are rocker operated, the rocker being of piano-key style. Originally switches were termed dolly switches because of the dolly-like 'knob'; this pattern was superseded by the toggle-switch, and finally the rocker pattern was developed.

One-way switch. A normal lighting switch having two terminals, enabling a light to be switched On and Off from one position only.

Two-way switch. Similar to the one-way, but with three terminals. It provides a change-over action for use in a two-way switching circuit, enabling the light to be switched On and Off from two different positions. A two-way switch may be used for one-way switching, when two only of the three terminals are used.

Intermediate switch. A four-terminal switch inserted into a two-way switching circuit, which enables a light to be switched On and Off from three positions (or even more when additional intermediate switches are inserted into the circuit).

One-gang switch. The standard square plateswitch containing one switch only, which can be one-way, two-way or intermediate.

Two- and three-gang switch. These are also the square plateswitch assembly but contain two and three switches respectively on the one plate. All switches in each assembly are two-way, these being wired for one-way or two-way working as required. Assemblies of four- to six-gang switches are also made, which have an oblong face plate for mounting on a two-gang box.

OTHER LIGHTING

SPOTLIGHTS

Spotlights can be mounted at any level on either the walls or the ceiling. If hung on the wall, they are wired as for wall lights (see page 90); if hung on the ceiling, cable should be passed through from above as described on page 89. They usually have a circular base which therefore requires to be fixed to a BESA box (see page 83).

Some spotlights are designed to be fitted to a lighting track which can be screwed to either wall or ceiling and which provides a power point for up to 3120 watts (depending on what type of circuit it is connected to). The track itself is formed from aluminium and contains conductors for live (phase) and neutral, plus an earth strip. The track is sold in standard lengths, but you can buy a coupler which join lengths together. It is possible to run small appliances, such as an iron, heated rollers, or a radio, from the track by fitting flexible cord adaptors into it, and fitting the equivalent adaptor to the appliance in place of a normal three-pin plug. If this is required, you must wire the track into a spur from the nearest ring main (see page 85).

THE TRICK

Check before running the track from a ceiling rose that you are not overloading the lighting circuit. Remember that most spotlight bulbs are 100 or 150 watts, which could take you over the 1200 watt level quite quickly (see page 78).

The regulations require that every spotlight and wall light should be under the control of an isolating switch, even when an integral switch is part of the fitting. This is so that you can work on the fitting safely.

There are many different types of spotlight on the market, producing different results when in position. You should consider carefully whether you want the light to illuminate one specific item; to throw a general light on a specific area; or merely to provide overall visibility. You should also consider where you are proposing to mount the spotlight as different lights will cover different areas from the same position (see diagram). Ask the salesperson to advise you what is most suitable for what you want to do if you want a specific effect.

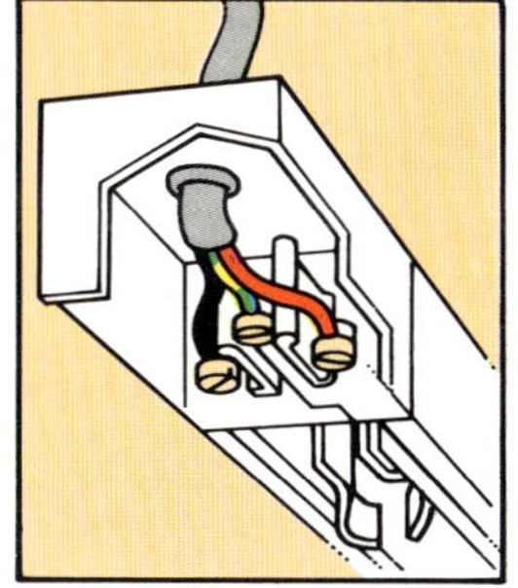

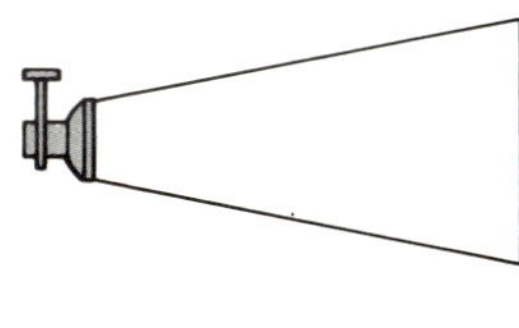

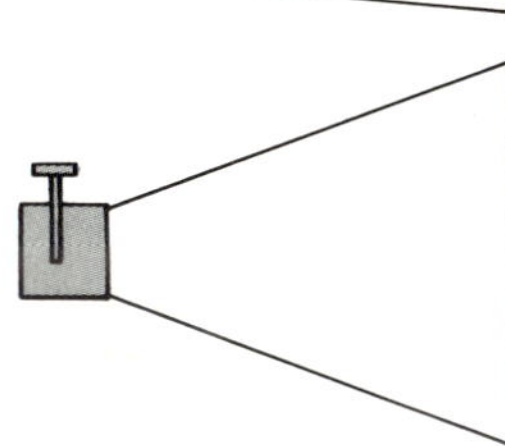

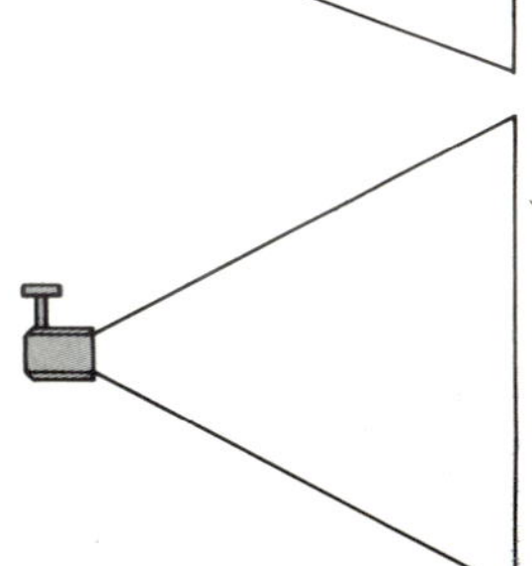

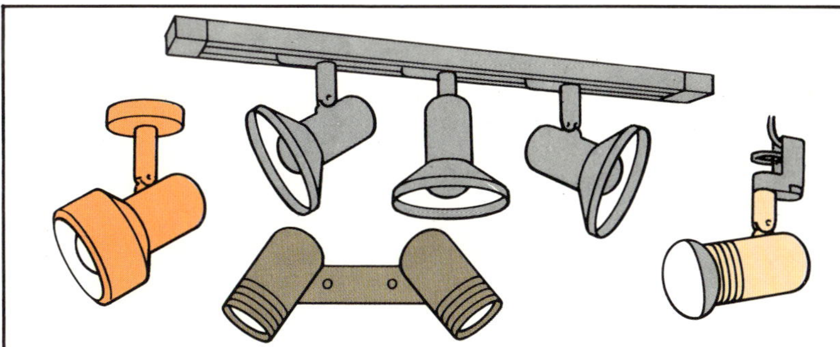

FLUORESCENTS

A fluorescent tube is a glass tube, coated on the inside with a metallic salt, and filled with very low pressure mercury vapour. This vapour, when heated, discharges ultra-violet which, when filtered through the coating, gives off a flood of light which reduces form and shadow in comparison to a normal light bulb. The tubes are available in different colours and you should ask the salesperson which colour would be most suitable for the intended use. The tube gives off about 10 watts per 300mm (1ft) of tube.

The tube is mounted in a plastic or metal holder which can be screwed to a wall or ceiling and is wired in as for a ceiling rose (see page 89). There are two different sizes of tubes, so be sure to get the right one for your holder. The holder contains a two-pin tube holder at each end, plus a 'starter' which heats the cathodes inside the tube, and a 'choke' which provides a limited voltage surge to start the discharge process.

THE TRICK

If the lamp refuses to light even after you have changed the tube, the starter may have burnt out – especially if the tube has been flickering badly.

A new starter can be bought from any electrical shop and usually just screws in like an electrical bulb.

The holder may have a Perspex diffuser over the tube to avoid glare, or a baffle may be used. Some designs have a reflector on each side to reflect the light downwards. Fluorescent lights are extremely economical to run and the tubes last considerably longer than most light bulbs. The disadvantage is that the light flattens out a room (though this is not always a bad thing) and can heavily distort colour (pink in particular) which makes it unflattering to the people in the room.

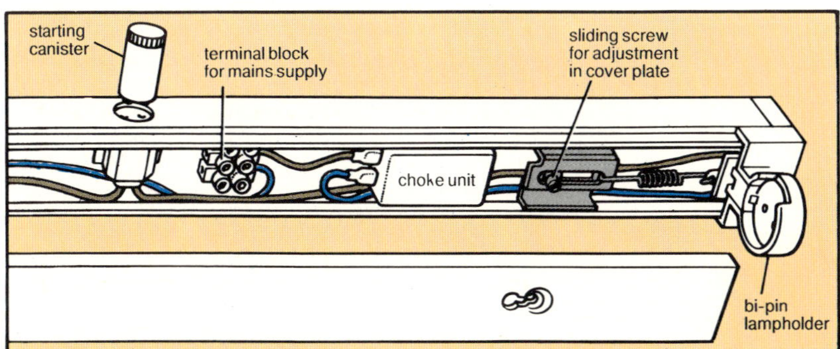

LIGHTS UNDER SHELVES

A very popular idea in modern lighting schemes is to install lights under shelves, or under the wall cupboards in a kitchen. These lights are better connected to the ring, rather than the lighting circuit.

The trick is to install a switched fused connection unit as a spur from the main ring circuit, and connect the light to it. If you want to run more than one light from the connection unit, you can connect the cable for each light to its load terminals, or loop-in the lights to each other.

CEILING SWITCHES

Cord-operated ceiling-mounted switches are fixed in a similar way to ceiling roses. These switches are to be found mainly in bathrooms, and indeed is the only type of switch allowed in bathrooms. If you want a bathroom light to be controlled by the normal rocker switch, the switch must be outside the bathroom – on the landing for instance. This is because a person who is wet is much more likely to be seriously affected by an electrical shock than one who is dry.

However, there is no reason why you should not have ceiling-mounted switches in other rooms of your home should you want them. The wiring is shown in the diagram; its main advantage outside the bathroom is that it avoids having to run cable down walls to the conventional switch.

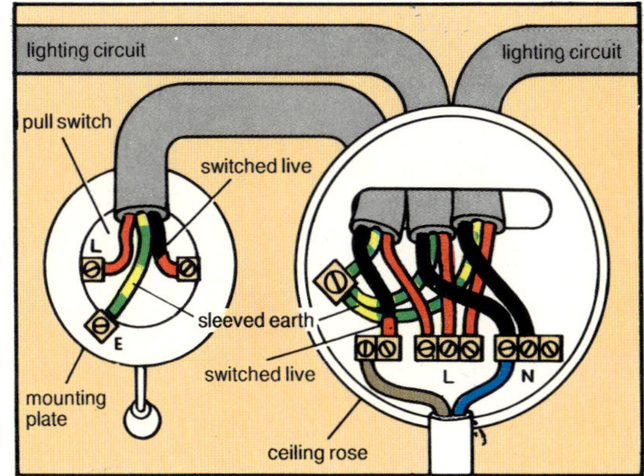

SHAVER SOCKETS

The lead of an electric razor has a special two-pin plug that will not fit into an ordinary socket. The plug is specially moulded on at the factory so that it cannot be disturbed. Therefore you must have a special socket outlet for it. There is an important safety reason for this, as it is dangerous to fit an ordinary socket outlet in a bathroom, and strictly against the wiring regulations. It is so much easier to get an electric shock when you are wet. So, if you want to use your electric razor in your bathroom you must fit what is known as a shaver supply unit, and it must be manufactured to British Standard BS3052.

These units incorporate a transformer that isolates the razor from the earthed mains supply, so that there is no risk of your getting a shock if the razor develops a fault. A razor supply unit will take only a razor plug, and there is a cut-out that limits the current to about 0.2 amps, so that no other appliance could work off the socket. You can also buy a strip light incorporating a shaver outlet designed to be fitted over a mirror; but if you install it in the bathroom it must comply with BS3052.

BATHROOM OR BEDROOM

It is probably more convenient to shave with an electric razor in the bedroom, and this may relieve pressure on the bathroom during the morning rush. A shaver socket is in effect a cheap way of increasing your bathroom facilities. Women also use electric shavers as beauty aids, and they would probably find a shaver outlet in the bedroom more convenient. Probably the overwhelming reason in favour of a bedroom installation, however, is that it works out much cheaper. An outlet suitable for installation there costs little more than a quarter of the price you would have to pay for one suited to the bathroom.

For the bedroom – or any other room except the bathroom – you buy a shaver socket outlet. It is important to get this terminology right. A shaver supply unit, manufactured to BS3052, is for the bathroom; a shaver socket outlet is for elsewhere. This latter has the same standard two-pin socket and thermal cut-out as the bathroom job, and also a 1 amp cartridge fuse to protect the cut-out but it has no transformer. This type of outlet is fitted to a standard one-gang socket mounting box, which may be flush or surface, and is designed to be connected to the lighting circuit by means of 1mm, two-core and earth, PVC-sheathed cable.

INSTALLATION

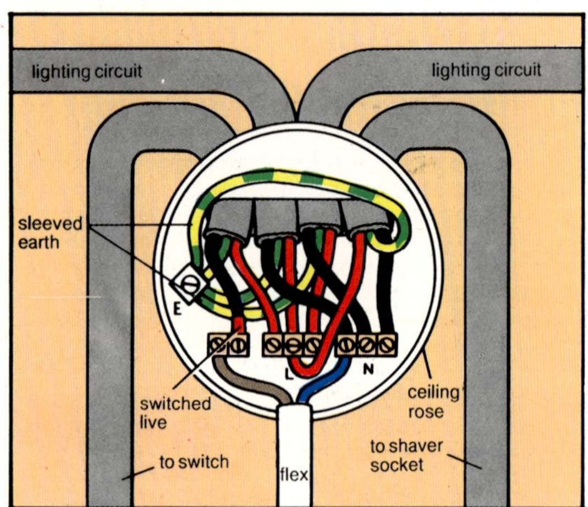

The installation can be very easily carried out in an upstairs room if you site the outlet low down on the wall, which will involve a minimum amount of disturbance and cable runs. You tap into the light of the room below, which means lifting a couple of floorboards. If you have a loop-in lighting system, you connect to the loop-in terminals of the rose. Otherwise, insert a joint box in the lighting circuit and run a cable from it to the shaver outlet. If the socket is mounted on a hollow wall, you can bring the cable up inside it, with practically no disturbance to the decorations. Even on a solid wall, however, you will have to chase out only a small channel.

If there is no lighting circuit handy, you can connect your razor socket to a ring circuit. The way to do that is to install a 13 amp fused connection unit with a 3 amp fuse as a spur from the ring, and wire the socket to that.

A shaver supply unit for the bathroom can also be flush or surface-fitted, and it is fixed to a mounting box, just like a switch or socket outlet, but in this case usually a special type. If you are surface mounting the unit, you use a plastic box, making sure it matches the colour of the supply unit itself. For flush mounting, a 50mm (2in.) depth metal box is used. That is quite a lot to cut out of a wall however, especially an internal partition one, and you might burst through the other side. As an alternative, you can use an ordinary two-gang socket outlet box, which is only 35mm (1½in.) deep. You then need a 20mm (¾in.) thick plastic spacer, which goes between the razor unit and the box, and must be fitted before any connections are made. The spacer is visible, so must be the same colour as the unit.

The wiring of a shaver supply unit is carried out just like that of a shaver socket outlet. It, too, may be fed from a spur of the ring circuit, or from the lighting circuit. The cable is connected to terminals on the back of the razor unit. As a safety measure the earth strand of the cable should be wired to the earth terminal on the box itself, and a short length of earth cable run from this terminal to the E terminal on the back of the unit.

If there is roof space over the bathroom, the simplest method is to run a length of 1mm, two-core and earth, PVC-sheathed cable from the room's loop-in ceiling rose (or any other that may be handy) across or along the joists, through a hole pierced in the ceiling, and down the wall to the shaver unit.

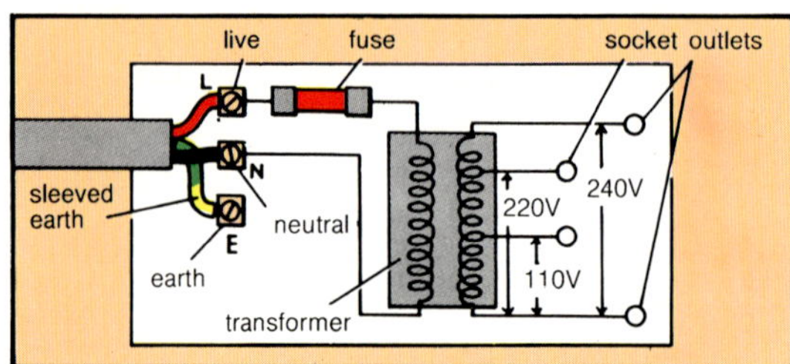

OUTDOOR LIGHTS

If you would like an exterior light near your front door, it is a simple matter to fit one, taking the current from the ceiling rose of a nearby light. The same is true if you would like one on your patio for summer evening parties, or near your back door to light your way to the coal bunker or dustbin on a dark evening. Here we talk about fitting a light at the front door, tapping into the hall rose. The method is similar for the other installations.

You can, of course, have an independently switched outdoor light with a joint box system, by following the instructions on page 89 about adding an extra light.

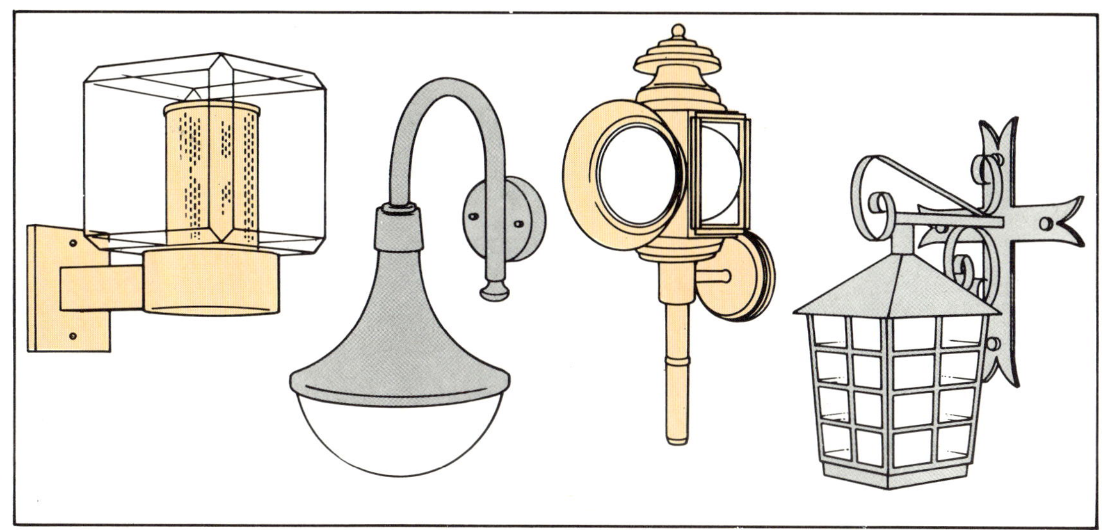

INDEPENDENTLY SWITCHED

If you have a loop-in system, it is easy to have the outdoor light independently switched. You do so by introducing a joint box element to your circuit.

This is the arrangement to adopt. You need a four-terminal joint box, from which will radiate three lengths of 1mm, twin-core and earth, PVC-sheathed cable. One length will go to the hall light, another to the new outdoor light, and a third to the new switch for the outdoor light. The diagram shows how the connections should be made at the joint box. Note that both leads from the switch are, in effect, connected up to the live circuit, and so the black wire should have red adhesive PVC tape fixed to it.

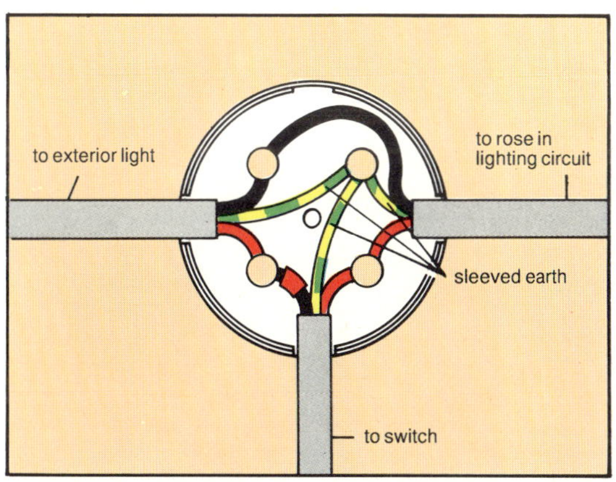

As for the connections at the rose of the hall light, they should be as follows: where there are three terminals and an earth, you will notice that one has no flex wire from the bulb holder attached to it. Connect up the red wire of your new cable to this terminal, and the black wire to the terminal containing two or more black wires as shown.

SWITCHED WITH EXISTING LIGHT

If you have a rose of this type, and want to have the outdoor light switched in conjunction with that in the hall, forget about installing a switch and joint box. Run cable from the hall light to the porch light, and make your connections to the terminals carrying the flex of the hall light.

Most loop-in roses have a bank of three terminal blocks in line. In that case, connect the black wire of the new cable to the outer 3-terminal block and, where the new light is to be independently switched, the red wire to the centre 3-terminal block, which has no flex from the hall light as shown. The red wire should go to the outer two terminal blocks if the new light is to be switched in conjunction with the hall light. For two-way switching, see page 87.

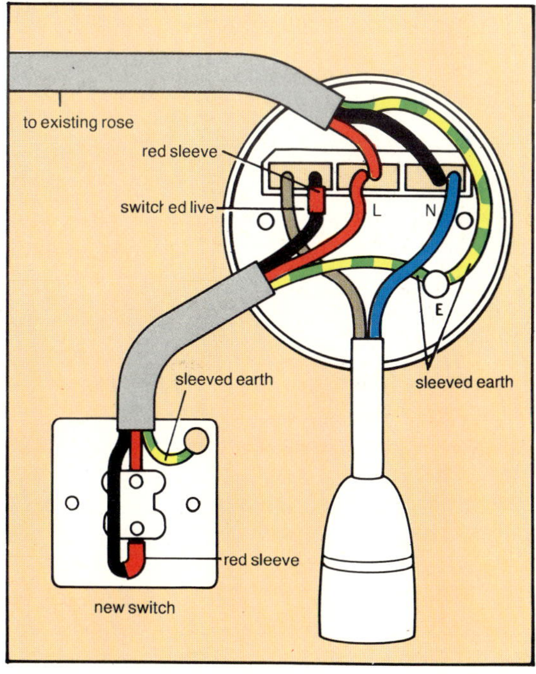

WIRING

Most of the wiring described will run below the floor of the room immediately above the hall. The joint box will be fitted in this void, and you will find it easy to push the new cable down through the hole immediately above the hall rose, in order to make the connections to it. The cable from the joint box to the new switch will emerge into the hall from the ceiling above, and can be surface-run or concealed.

What about the cable to the light? It really depends on what type of light fitting you have chosen. (It goes without saying that this must be one suitable for exterior installation. It is against the regulations to fix an interior light out of doors.) If the light is to be a wall-mounted lantern, the cable to it comes down from the void above the ceiling, runs down the wall (in any of the ways outlined on pages 81–2) and passes out to the exterior through a hole in the wall directly behind the fitting. If you bring the cable down the wall inside the house, even in a channel cut in the plaster, a very deep hole will have to be drilled through the wall to carry the cable outside, and you will have to buy a long and expensive drill bit to do this. Here is a simple way to do it.

THE TRICK

Aim to run the cable in the middle of a cavity wall. The exit hole from the cavity to the outside can be cut in a mortar joint, using a long, thin cold chisel – a tool it is well worthwhile buying if you intend to do any amount of electrical work.

What if your house does not have cavity walls?

THE TRICK

Your chisel will be about 300mm (1ft) long, so you can still cut your way from the outside through a considerable proportion of the wall. Finish off the hole by working from the inside of the house. The cable can be brought down the wall from the ceiling to this hole either surface-run or in a channel cut out of the plaster.

Your fitting may, however, be designed to go on the ceiling of a porch. In such instances the path to be chosen for the cable will depend on the construction of the porch. For example, there may be a void over the porch ceiling where the cable can be run. In some instances, you will be able to bore a hole in the room above just below its floorboards to make a short cut to the light fitting. Devise a route to suit your own particular installation.

The exact method of fitting the light will depend on the type you have bought. Usually, however, you have to fix a back plate to the wall or ceiling, and the light itself is attached to it. In some cases the cable is connected directly to the lampholder, but nowadays it is usual for the fitting itself to have a short length of cable to which a plastic connecting block is attached. Usually the procedure to be followed is obvious from an examination of the fitting, and often full instructions are given.

POWER TO OTHER BUILDINGS

Most people with a garage like to use it not merely as a place to park the car, but also for general household storage and as a workshop. An attached garage, built as an integral part of, and at the same time as, the house itself, usually has an electricity supply from the start. This is often not the case with a detached garage, especially one built on as an afterthought. Taking power to this kind of garage is a big but not impossible project.

GARAGES

A good scheme for a garage workshop would be to install a light and a socket outlet, which you might as well make a double while you are about it. Since there will be no plaster on the walls of your garage, a neat flush fitting of all the accessories is out of the question, so the best thing is to make them surface-mounted, and all the wiring surface-run. You can have your accessories in plastic, although many people feel that industrial-type metal ones, designed for surface mounting, are more appropriate in a garage. Grey PVC-sheathed cable seems more suitable with industrial metal accessories.

Basically, what you have to do is take power from the house out to the garage, via cable that must go at least 500mm (20in.) below ground. Make sure there are no sharp stones, etc. on the bottom of the trench, or the soil with which you fill it in, since they might damage the PVC covering of the cable and cause corrosion. The cable must be 4mm, twin-core (there is no earth wire), PVC-sheathed and insulated armoured cable. It has an overall PVC covering to stop the armour from corroding.

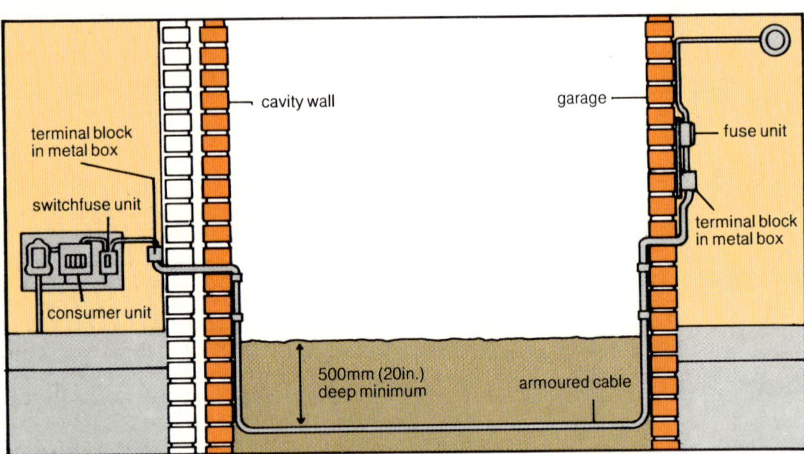

Although twin-core armoured cable is commonly used for the underground section of the outdoor extension, with the wire armour serving as the earth conductor, Electricity Board engineers now tend to regard the wire armour as having insufficient electrical conductivity to make it a satisfactory earth conductor. Instead they require the cable to be three-core, the third core being used as the earth conductor. The core colours are red, yellow and blue respectively; so use the red for the 'live', the blue for the neutral and the yellow as the earth conductor. Enclose the ends of the earth conductor in green/yellow sleeving. The wire armour, although not the circuit earth conductor, must be bonded (connected) to earth at one or both ends.

This cable rises from the trench at each end to go up the house and garage walls, to which it is fixed with clips at 300mm (12in.) intervals. It enters both buildings by means of a hole that you must bore with an extra long masonry bit, or by using a long, thin cold chisel (see page 93).

THE TRICK

With cavity walls, it is better to bore the hole in the outer leaf from the outside of the house and the inner one from inside, to reduce the risk of getting brick dust in the cavity between them, which might introduce damp into the structure.

GARAGE WIRING

The wiring in the garage must be controlled by a mainswitch and fuse unit which you will probably want to position high up on the wall. From this, 4mm, twin-core and earth, PVC-sheathed and insulated cable will lead to the socket outlet. The rest of the circuit – i.e. the lighting – is in 1mm, twin-core and earth, PVC-sheathed and insulated cable which of course, has to be joined up to the 4mm cable via an essential 3 amp fuse. This joint must be in a non-combustible chamber, which is best provided by a fused connection unit fitted with a 3 amp fuse. Run 4mm cable from the socket outlet to this unit, and connect it inside to 1mm cable, which you then run to a loop-in ceiling rose fitted to the ceiling, or more likely the roof, of the garage. To control the light you need a switch, which you should position at a convenient height on the wall, just inside the door so that you can use it on entering. If there are two doors to the garage, for instance a personal one at the side in addition to the main ones through which you drive the car, you might want two-way switching, with an additional switch fitted near the other door. Wire up the switch, or switches, to the rose (see page 87).

The mainswitch and fuse unit controls the whole installation. Power is supplied to that via 4mm, twin-core and earth, PVC-sheathed and insulated cable, which has to be joined to the armoured cable coming in from outside. Once again, the joint must be made in a combustion-proof chamber; this must be of metal – no matter what type you have used throughout the rest of the installation – because it forms the earthing of the whole circuit. So fit a metal mounting box to the wall, as close as possible to the point where the armoured cable enters the garage. Fit a screwed gland to the end of the cable, having removed some of the outer PVC covering so that you get a good connection.

THE TRICK

If the box has a black enamel finish as most do, instead of the less common galvanized finish, scrape off the enamel around the knock-out hole to provide a good electrical connection between the screwed gland and the box and, therefore, effective earth continuity.

Instead of the usual rubber grommet, secure the gland in one of the box's knock-out holes with a locknut and bush: this is the earthing arrangement. The cable of the inner wiring is joined up inside the box to the armoured cable by means of a three-way terminal block, or a couple of 30 amp insulated connectors, but its earth wire goes to the terminal on the box itself – the exterior cable has no earth to which it can be joined. Cover up the face of the box with a blanking-off plate.

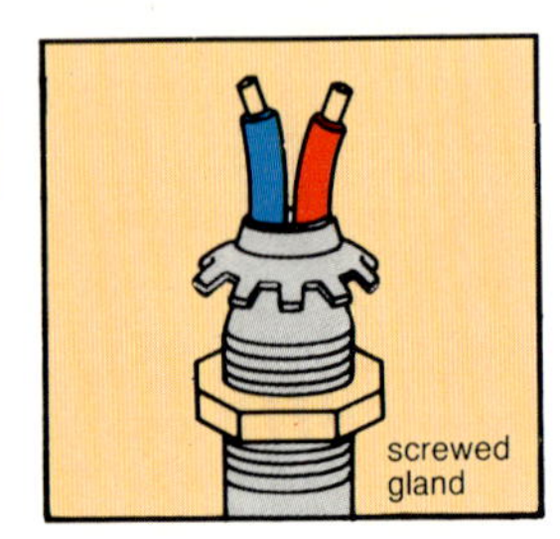

A similar arrangement must be adopted inside the house where the armoured cable is connected up to 4mm, twin-core and earth, PVC-sheathed and insulated cable, which is then run to a spare fuseway in the consumer unit. If there is no spare, connect a new switch fuse unit (see page 77). Inside the house, however, you may want the metal box to be hidden under the floorboards.

SHEDS AND GREENHOUSES

All the above information has been related to a garage, but you might want to have your workshop in a timber garden shed. If you have a greenhouse, you might need electricity there too; to power electric heaters and so on, as well as giving light.

The wiring for these buildings is exactly the same as for a garage, the only difference being that – depending on the construction of its foundations – you might be able to bring the cable indoors by running it under the walls, which would involve a slight extension of the trench.

IMMERSION HEATERS

The simplest has just one element; when you switch it on, it will heat all the water in the tank. You must choose a heater to match the size of the cylinder, so that it will have a long enough element to reach somewhere near the bottom of the cylinder, otherwise you will not have enough hot water. The snag with this type of heater is that you have to wait for the whole tank to be warmed up before you get hot water; with a large cylinder that can take a long time.

To avoid this, install a dual-element heater. This has, in addition to the long element, a short one that warms up just the water near the top of the cylinder which is where the draw-off point is. Hot water is lighter than cold and always floats to the top of a tank, so this heated water will not be dispersed throughout the rest of the tank. Dual-element heaters have switches marked 'bath' for full-tank heating, and 'sink' for part-tank.

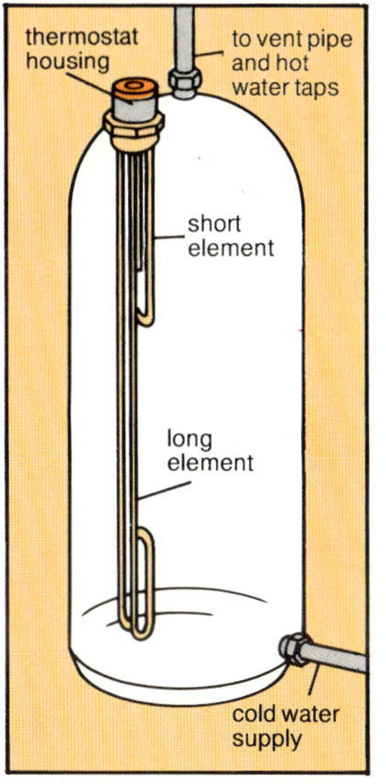

Since an immersion heater element is almost as long as the tank is tall, you need a lot of space above the tank to drop the heater into it. In some homes there is not enough headroom, then the heater must be fitted horizontally near the bottom of the tank. Here again, though, you will have to heat the whole tankful of water, no matter how little you need. So it is a good idea to fit a second, horizontal, heater, say a third of the way from the top of the tank. Thus the bottom heater would be wired for 'bath' heating, and the top one for 'sink'.

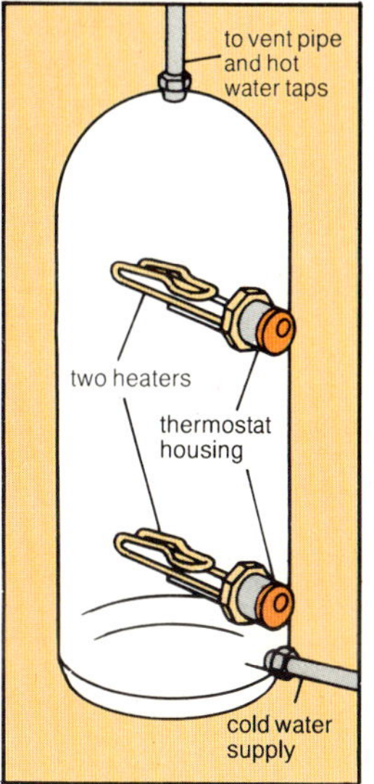

Immersion heaters are rated as 2 and 3kw. The more powerful the heater you buy, the quicker your water will be heated. Although a more powerful heater will cost more to buy, it will not cost more to run.

Installation of an immersion heater falls into two parts – the plumbing (see page 114) and the electrics.

WIRING UP

An immersion heater needs to be controlled by a switch. This has to be near the tank, but it can be inside or outside the airing cupboard. A water heater must have its own circuit, because it is a continuous load and would overload the ring circuit.

Run a length of 2.5mm, two-core and earth, PVC-sheathed cable from the switch back to the consumer unit, ready for connection when the work is completed to a spare fuseway. This should be fitted with either a 15 or 20 amp fuse. If there is no spare fuseway you must install a separate switchfuse unit (see page 77).

The connection from the heater terminals to the switch is made by heat-resisting three-core flex. As this is an appliance flex, rather than mains cable, its live wire will be brown, its neutral one blue, and its earth green and yellow.

IMMERSION HEATER SWITCH

Now let us move on to the switch. This should be 20 amp double-pole (if you ask for a switch specifically made for an immersion heater you will be given one of the correct rating) and it is best to choose one with a neon pilot light, so that you can see at a glance when the power is on. The switch is fitted to a box in the normal way.

If you have fitted a heater with a single element, or a double one that has its own integral bath–sink change-over switch, the wiring is simple. On the back of the switch face plate you will see the appropriate terminals. The mains cable goes to the feed terminals – the red one to L, the black to N, and the bare copper earth wire to E, after a length of green and yellow sleeving has been slipped on to it. The heater flex goes to the load terminals – brown to L, blue to N and green and yellow to earth.

Some dual-element heaters do not have an integral changeover switch, and for these – and when you have installed two separate horizontal heaters – your control switch, as well as being a double-pole on–off, must also offer these changeover facilities. In such cases the wiring is slightly more complicated, for you have two flexes – one from the sink element, or top heater, and the other from the bath element, or bottom heater. The diagram shows how to wire up a typical switch.

THE TRICK

The airing cupboard is a long way from the point where you most often use hot water – the kitchen sink. So it will save a lot of walking if you have a switch near the sink.

You can run the cable from the fuseway to a switch in the kitchen, then on upstairs to another one at the airing cupboard. This latter switch is then left on all the time – it acts merely as an isolator for shutting off power to the heater during an emergency or when maintenance work is being carried out. The main switching on and off of the heater will be done at the sink.

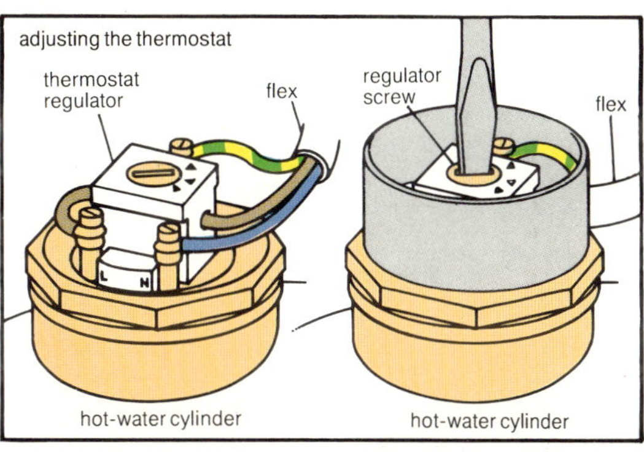

THE TRICK

Another – though more expensive – possibility is to have a two-point switching system, for which you need two special switches. Then either switch will turn the heater on or off (rather like the two-way lighting switching) and both pilot lights will go on and off together when either switch is operated.

If your selection of sink or bath operation is done by a separate switch, rather than by an integral one on the heater, it is up to you to decide whether the changeover switch shall be in the kitchen or near the airing cupboard.

THE TRICK

Another possibility if your heater is not supplied via an economy rate tariff circuit, is to install your own time switch, which will turn the heater on and off automatically in the morning. It can be set to operate twice a day, so that the heater is switched on again in the evening (see page 88).

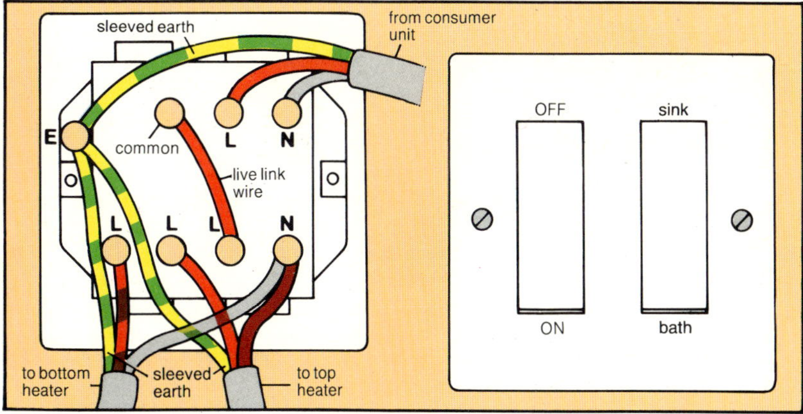

TERMINALS AND THERMOSTAT

Immersion heaters vary slightly in their construction, but the terminals are on the top of the heater, under the cap. There you will also find the thermostat (unless the heater is the rare kind with a non-adjustable thermostat) and you should set this to suit your family's convenience.

THE TRICK

Remember that the lower your setting, the lower your electricity bill: 71°C (160°F) is the recommended setting for a vertical heater and 60°C (140°F) for a horizontal one.

Once you have connected the flex to the heater terminals, replace the cap that covers them. If in the future you want to remove this cap for any reason, always first turn off the switch controlling the heater, otherwise you can get a severe and probably fatal shock.

PLUMBING

PICTURE your new bathroom with a suite from the Balterley Bathrooms Collection. Spoil yourself with choice that's almost beyond dreams.

There is a rich selection of suites decorated with the Grecian Key motif, in Balterley Gold or Balterley Platinum to give the ultimate in opulence.

And there are suites adorned with floral garlands in a variety of delicate pastels.

Bathrooms with platinum.

Bathrooms with roses.

For details of the Balterley Collection contact: Balterley Bathrooms, Silverdale Rd, Newcastle-under-Lyme, Staffs ST5 6EL, Tel: (0782) 633118, or see the Collection on display at your local Balterley Approved Studio. **Accrington** Broughtons, 18–20 King St. **Andover** Dolphin Home Improvements, 1 The Broadway. **Ashton-under-Lyne** Ashton Discount Warehouse, 147–149 Stamford St. **Atherton** J Moss & Co, Bolton Rd. **Barnsley** Bathroom and Shower Centre, 25 Sheffield Rd. **Bedford** Martel Distributors, 27 Roff Ave. Bathroom World, 26 St. Cuthbert St. **Blackpool** Graham Shaw Bathrooms, Dickson Rd. **Bodmin** Creative Home Interiors, 85 Fore St. **Bolton** Bolton Bathroom Centre, 136–138 Tonge Moor Rd. **Boston** G P Gallichan, 37 Fenside Rd. **Bury** C Parkinson, 125 Bell Lane. **Birmingham** Plan Four, 1199 Coventry Rd, Hay Mills. V A L Products, Hurst St. **Blythe** Bradleys, 40 Regent St. **Bournemouth** Cee Jays, Charminster Rd. **Bradford** Bradford Bathrooms & Kitchens, Unit 1, Hartley St, Wakefield Rd. **Camberley** Layzell Bathware, 149 London Rd. **Cambridge** Eaton Studio, Burligh St. **Carlisle** Live In Style Design, Lord St. **Chaddesden** Peerless Home Centre, 488–492 Nottingham Rd. **Chester** Deva Warehouses, Unit 4/5, Central Trading Est, Saltney. **Chester Le Street** Les Marshall, 35 Middlechare. **Clitheroe** S S Moore, York St. **Denton** Interior Design Centres, 11–15 Stockport Rd. **Dudley** The Dudley Bathroom Centre, 144 Wolverhampton St. **Eaton Socon** Anglia Interiors, The Green. **Harlow** A Eleven Heating Supplies, 50–51 Burnt Mill, Burnt Mill Ind. Est. **Hayes** B S P Plumbing Supplies, Coldharbour Lane. **High Wycombe** Modern Kitchens & Bathrooms, Wye Ind. Est. London Rd. **Horley** E & B Engineering Sales, 71–77 Brighton Rd. **Hornchurch** Wallace Scott, 47 High St. **Ilkeston** G W Atkins, 59 Bath St. **Irthlingborough** LEA Kitchens & Bathrooms, 18 High St. **Keighley** Keighley Plumbers Merchants, Temple St. **Lancing** Leaney & Osborne, 41 Penhill Rd. **Leicester** R E Doughty, 44 Wood Gate. Kitchen Plus, 37 Holbrook Rd. **Leigh** Classic Ceramics, 243–245 Wigan Rd. N Owen, 175 Firs Lane. **Leighton Buzzard** Bathroom Kitchen & Tile Centre, 46–48 Hockliffe Rd. **London** F M S, Selfridges, Oxford St. Hunt Kennard, Canal Wharf, Horsendon Lane, Perivale. Interdesign, Station Approach, Sheene Lane, Mortlake. Luxury Living, 152 Clapham Manor Rd, Clapham. **Malvern** Malvern Building Supplies, Bond St. **Manchester** Nu Feenix, 22–34 London Rd. Walkden Bathroom Centre, Bolton Rd, Walkden. John Whiteley & Sons, 1326 Ashton Old Rd, Openshaw. **Market Deeping** Robert Stone, 48 High St. **Nelson** Ainsworth & Dent, Leeds Rd.

MAINS WATER & SEWERS

All domestic properties must legally be provided with an adequate supply of 'potable' (drinking) water. This is usually the task of the local Water Authority which distributes water via the 'mains' system. The mains are tapped via a 'communicating' pipe and stopcock (which are the property of the Water Authority) and connected to the 'supply' pipe which is the property of the householder. Another stopcock in the supply pipe is known as the 'main stopcock' and is the principal means of turning off the water. It is vitally important that you should know where your main stopcock is, and that it is in good working order (see page 102).

Soiled water and waste products are removed from domestic properties by means of 'soil' or 'waste' pipes which connect to the drains. The whole of this system is the property of the householder. The drains then connect with the sewers which form a network of publicly owned and maintained pipes which remove all sewage to a plant where it can be treated. The sewage system is the responsibility of the local urban or rural council.

Some private dwellings are not connected to the main sewers, in which case the drains will run either to a cesspool or to a septic tank. A 'cesspool' is a water-tight, underground receptacle where all soiled water and wastes can be stored until removed by the local council or a private firm.

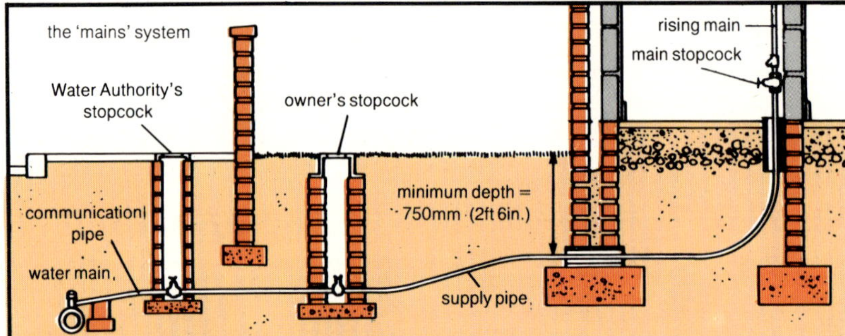

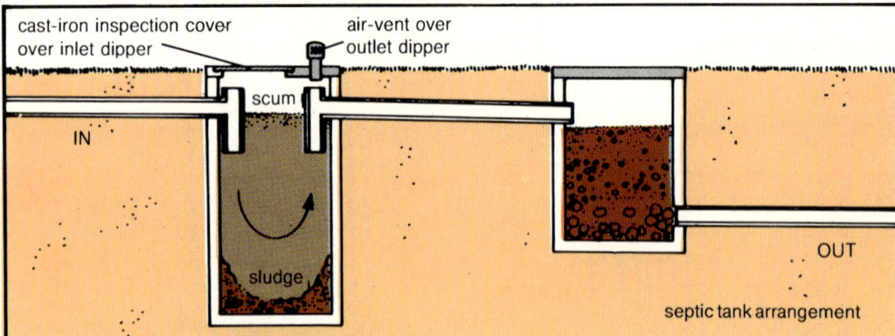

A 'septic tank' is more like a small sewage works; it breaks down the waste into a highly purified liquid form which can then be disposed of. Septic tanks usually have two chambers: the first takes the new waste; the second contains a filter bed. Septic tanks require little maintenance apart from emptying the sludge about once a year unless the system is very heavily used.

THE TRICK

If you do have a septic tank, avoid using too much disinfectant or detergent, otherwise the action of the bacteria will be slowed up and the tank becomes blocked.

BUILDING REGULATIONS

Most new plumbing work is covered by either the Building Regulations (or their local equivalents) and/or by the local Water Bye-laws. Any plumbing work, apart from normal repair or replacement, should be submitted to your local Building Control Officer and to the local Water Authority. Failure to do this may result in prosecution and a hefty fine.

THE TRICK

It is often possible to obtain a grant from your local council for installing an inside lavatory or a bathroom. It is vital that you should apply before you start the work; no council will give a grant for work already in progress.

TRACING DRAINS AND MAINS

You should know exactly where your drains run outside the house and which pipes inside the house contain mains water.

Always write down such information, and make sure everyone in your household knows where the information is.

THE TRICK

Check all the stopcocks and gate valves in your home to discover what each one does. Write on a small label what its function is and tie it to the stopcock or valve in question.

Know where all the inspection chambers for your drains are – the Building Regulations state they should be within 12.5m (41ft) of drain junctions; where drains change direction or gradient; and at intervals of not more than 90m (295ft) on a straight run.

WASTE SYSTEMS

There are two principal waste disposal systems found in Great Britain today. The older is known as the 'two pipe system'; the more modern is known as the 'single stack system'.

THE TWO PIPE SYSTEM

Introduced in the 1920s it was the result of the introduction of general indoor plumbing. The wastes were removed by two vertical stack pipes: the first, termed the 'soil pipe', removed all wastes from the lavatory; the second, termed the 'waste pipe', drained the bath, wash basins and bidets. The difference between the two pipes is that the soil pipe is vented by extending it above the eaves, whereas the waste pipe has a hopper head at first floor level, into which the various branch pipes (from bath, basin, etc) discharge. The soil pipe discharges directly into the drains but the waste pipe goes via a trapped gully.

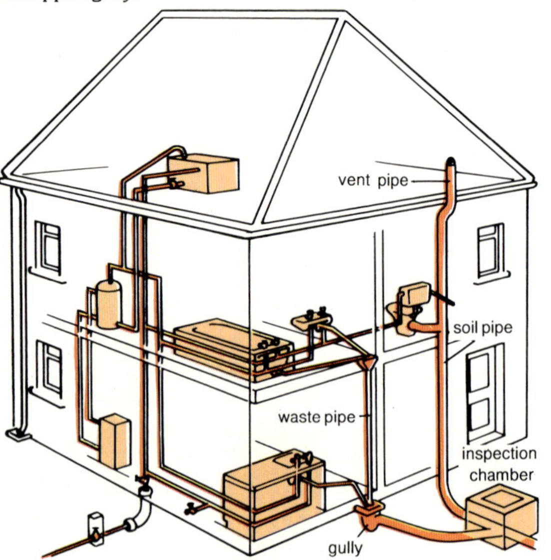

THE SINGLE STACK SYSTEM

Introduced in the early 1960s it involves piping all wastes into a single pipe which discharges directly into the drain without a trap. The top of the pipe must finish not less than 900mm (3ft) above the level of any opening windows in order to vent legally. The purpose of 'venting' is to prevent the downrush of waste from a branch pipe from sucking the water out of the 'traps' in basins, baths, lavatories, etc. These 'traps' are chambers where water is trapped (often in a U-bend) to prevent unpleasant smells from entering the house.

Lavatories at ground level in both systems, often discharge directly into the main drain; while sinks, washing machines, etc will discharge into an open gully at ground level, which connects via a water trap, with the drain.

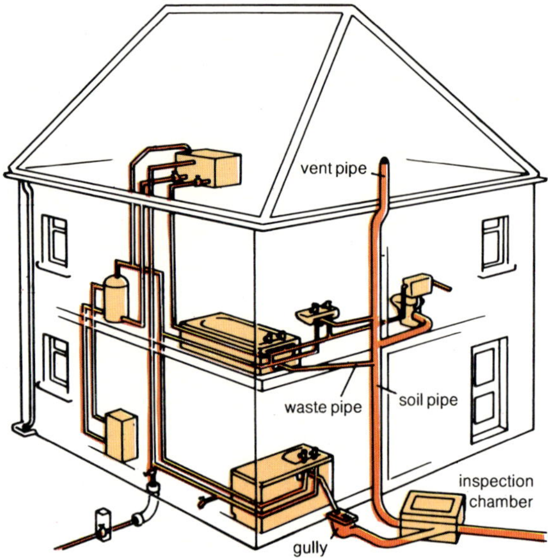

EMERGENCIES

LAVATORIES

PAN LEAKAGE

Leakage from a lavatory-pan outlet when flushed, is a serious fault demanding immediate attention.

It is usually upstairs-lavatory suites that are affected. The joint between the pan outlet and the socket of the branch soil-pipe is often made with putty which then dries and shrinks. This, combined with settlement of the floorboards, produces the leak. Fortunately it is easily remedied.

You need a tin of non-setting mastic filler and a roll of waterproofing building tape. Rake out the existing jointing material with a screwdriver and make sure that the space between the pan outlet and the soil-pipe socket is dry and clean.

THE TRICK

Bind two or three turns of the waterproofing tape round the pan outlet and caulk down hard into the soil-pipe socket. Fill in the remaining space between outlet and socket with the non-setting mastic. Bind another couple of turns of waterproofing tape round the completed joint.

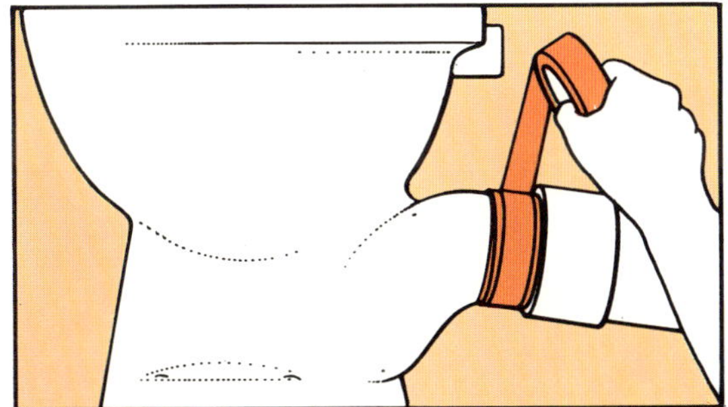

PIPES

DEALING WITH A FREEZE-UP

If water freezes in your system, deal with it promptly. At first there will be a small ice-plug; neglected, this will quickly spread.

A rough indication of its position can be obtained by noting which parts of the plumbing system have ceased to function. If, for instance, water is flowing into the cold-water storage cistern but no cold water is reaching the bathroom, then the ice-plug must be in the cold-water distribution pipe between the storage cistern and the bathroom.

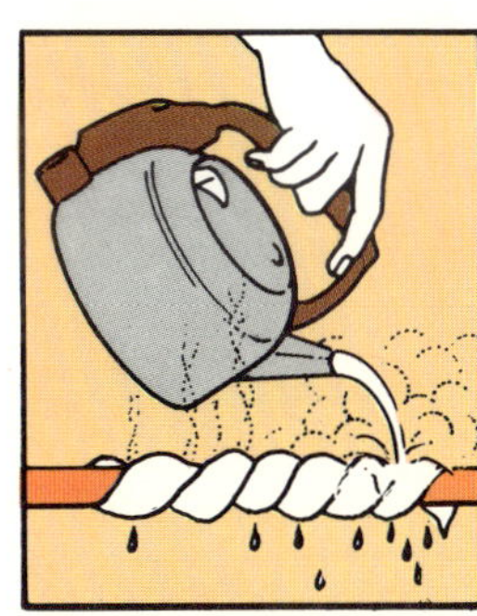

THE TRICK

Strip the lagging off the affected pipe and apply cloths, soaked in hot water, or a filled hot water bottle. A hair drier can direct a stream of warm air to an inaccessible pipe.

Modern copper piping is a good conductor of heat. Warmth will travel along it to clear a blockage some distance from the point of application.

A BURST PIPE

The first indication may be water dripping through a ceiling. Don't attempt to find the cause before you have taken immediate steps to limit the effects.

Turn off the main stop-cock (see page 102) and open up all the taps in the house. This will drain the system and prevent serious flooding. It might be wise, too, to let out the boiler or switch off the central heating. The chances are that you can switch on again when you have located the burst – but it is best to err on the side of safety. Only after doing this should you go to find the cause of the trouble.

If you have copper pipework (see page 118), the leak is probably caused by one of these joints pulling apart. It can easily be remade.

Lead pipe often splits when frozen. The orthodox method is to insert a new piece of lead pipe, fixing it with wiped soldered joints.

This is not really a d-i-y job!

The householder can however make a temporary repair which – while not approved by the local water authority – could well prove to be as effective as the approved method.

THE TRICK

You will need an epoxy-resin repair kit. Knock the edges of the split together with a hammer and clean the pipe with wire wool or abrasive paper. Mix up the filler and butter round the pipe, over and into the split and for 50–75mm (2–3in.) on either side of it. While the filler is still plastic, bind round it a fibreglass or nylon bandage. The filler will now ooze through the bandage, so butter on a further layer of filler.

Within a few hours the filler will have set and you can let water run through again. When the joint has set thoroughly, it can be rubbed down to give a neat 'wiped joint' appearance.

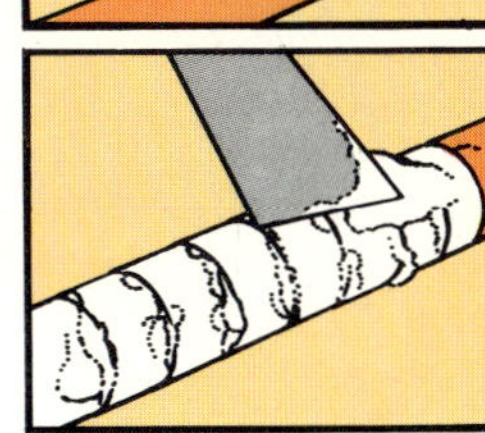

LEAKING BALL-FLOATS

A leaking ball-float will make itself apparent by a heavy flow of water through the overflow pipe. This 22mm (¾in.) pipe cannot cope indefinitely with the water flowing into a cistern at mains pressure. Before long the cistern will overflow, the remedy is to install a new float.

THE TRICK

Tie up the float arm so that water cannot flow in. Unscrew and remove the leaking ball. Enlarge the leak sufficiently to drain off the water inside it. Screw it back onto the float arm and slip a plastic bag over it, tying the mouth of the bag securely round the float arm.

LEAKING BOILERS

A leaking boiler is among the most catastrophic plumbing emergencies that a householder is likely to have to face. Everyone should know how to minimize the mess and to limit the amount of damage.

First: turn off the main stopcock (see page 102) and open up all the hot and cold taps. Switch off the immersion heater and put out the boiler fire. Get the garden hose and connect one end to the drain cock beside the boiler. Take the other end to an outside gully and open up the drain cock. Make sure that water is running freely through the hose.

You can now mop up the flood in confidence that the system is draining and that very soon the flow will cease.

It will – quite obviously – be several days before a new boiler can be fitted. While you are waiting, the hot-water system will inevitably be out of action but there is no reason why the remainder should not be used.

If there is a gate valve in the cold-water supply pipe to your hot-water cylinder, simply close this valve, open up the main stopcock and refill the cold-water storage cistern. However, there probably will not be a gate valve. You will have to find some other way to cut off the water supply to the hot-water system.

There are probably two distribution pipes near to the base of the cold-water storage cistern in the roof space. One will supply the hot-water storage cylinder and the other the lavatory-flushing cistern and the bathroom cold taps.

THE TRICK

Trace the hot-water cylinder pipe back to the cistern and push a cork of suitable size into its inlet. To guard against the cork breaking in the pipe, screw an ordinary wood screw into the cork before inserting it – leaving 6mm (¼in.) or so projecting from the cork.

Having isolated the hot-water cylinder, you can open up the main stopcock and allow the cold-water storage cistern to refill.

STOPCOCKS

Screw-down stopcocks resemble taps in all respects and can be regarded as bib-taps set into a run of pipe. Since they are rarely closed, their washers seldom need changing. This is fortunate since to cut off the water supply to the main stopcock it is necessary to seek the help of the local water authority.

Leakage past the gland is a more common fault and should receive immediate attention. Adjustment or renewal of the gland packing is carried out exactly as for taps (see page 104). Turn the stopcock off before attempting to renew the packing.

JAMMING

Jamming, as a result of long disuse, is a common fault in stopcocks. You attempt to turn it off and find that it is apparently immovable. Applying penetrating oil and trying again, over a period of several days, may free it, but – in the kind of plumbing emergency that demands the closure of stopcocks – you won't have several days to spare. The best course of action is to make sure that stopcocks do not jam.

THE TRICK

Make a point of turning them on and off several times about twice a year. When you open it for the last time, open it up fully, then give the handle just a quarter of a turn towards closure.

OTHER VALVES

Mini stopcocks, operated by means of a screwdriver or the edge of a coin, are sometimes fitted into pipe runs just before they connect to taps or ball-valves. These permit water flow to be reduced if required. They can also cut off water supply to one tap without having to drain the whole system.

Gate valves resemble screw-down stopcocks in appearance and are used to control the flow of water at low pressure. The waterway is closed by a metal plate or 'gate' When the valve is opened, this gate rises into the upper part of the valve. Gate valves give a metal-to-metal seal that is less watertight than that of a screw-down stopcock. When open, however, they give an absolutely unimpeded flow of water. They may be fitted in central heating systems to enable sections to be isolated and in the cold-water distribution pipes from the cold-water storage cistern to the hot-water storage cylinder and to the bathroom cold-water taps.

REPLACING A STOPCOCK

It should be stressed that these instructions have been given on the assumption that you have a 15mm or ½in. copper rising main. Fitting a stopcock into a lead or galvanized-steel rising main is not a d-i-y job.

Turn off the stopcock. Drain the rising main from the cold tap over the kitchen sink. There may be a drain-cock immediately above the main stopcock. If there is, open it and drain from there too.

Hold the stopcock up to the point that you have marked on the rising main. You will be able to see from outside the compression joint how far the pipe ends will project inside. Mark these two points on the rising main and cut the section between them squarely out of the main. If there was no drain-cock immediately above the main stopcock, a pint or two of water will flow out as you do this. Be prepared.

Unscrew and remove the cap nuts and olives from the 'run' of the stopcock. Slip first a cap nut and then an olive over the end of the upper length of cut pipe.

THE TRICK

Push them up the pipe and use a spring clothes-peg to stop them from slipping down again.

Slip a cap nut and olive over the lower end of cut pipe in the same way. Use a clothes-peg to prevent them from slipping.

'Spring' the two ends of the rising main into the body of the stopcock. There is sufficient 'give' in a length of copper tubing to make this easy.

An arrow engraved on the body of the stopcock indicates the direction of water flow. It is vital that this arrow should point away from the rising main. If it is fitted the wrong way round, water pressure will force the jumper down onto the valve seating and no water will be able to pass through it.

Apply waterproofing compound to the pipe ends and to the olives. Remove the clothes-pegs, push the olives up to the joint body and tighten up the cap nuts using two wrenches (see page 118). Turn the new stopcock off. Open up the main stopcock and check for leaks. There should not be any but, if there are, tighten up the compression cap nuts a little more.

To turn off the water supply to the cold tap over the kitchen sink, and any garden tap, you must turn off the main stopcock (see page 100).

In most cases the bathroom cold taps will be supplied from the cold-water storage cistern, probably situated in the roof space. This cistern will also supply the hot-water system and the hot-water taps. To cut off the water supply from any tap supplied from a main storage cistern, there is no need to turn off the main stopcock.

THE TRICK

Place a slat of wood across the top of the storage cistern and tie the float arm of the ball-valve to it so as to prevent water flowing into the cistern through the ball-valve.

You can now open the taps to drain the cistern.

When changing the washer on a hot-water tap, there is no need to drain all the hot water from the hot-water cylinder, provided that the bathroom cold taps are supplied from the storage cistern.

THE TRICK

After tying up the cistern ball-valve, open up the bathroom cold taps only. Open up the hot taps only when water ceases to flow from the cold ones. A pint or two of water will drain off and then flow will cease.

The storage cylinder will remain full of hot water. This is because the supplu pipes to the hot taps are taken from the vent pipe above the hot-water cylinder.

Multikwik show you how to connect a W.C. pan firmly quickly and easily

The original Phetco Multikwik push-fit self-sealing connector takes all the hassle out of connecting a W.C. Pan.

Simple diagrams and instructions given here makes choosing and fitting the right type of connector 'plumb' easy!

Multikwik connectors are designed to give a water tight seal without a sealant.

HOW A MULTIKWIK WORKS

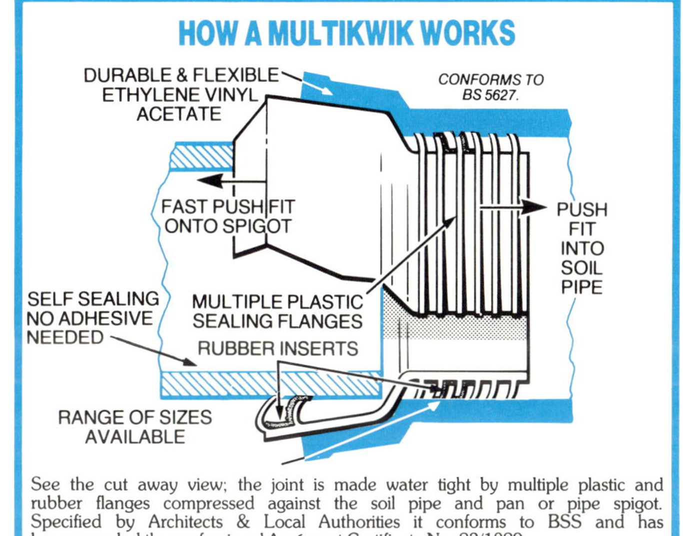

See the cut away view; the joint is made water tight by multiple plastic and rubber flanges compressed against the soil pipe and pan or pipe spigot. Specified by Architects & Local Authorities it conforms to BSS and has been awarded the professional Agrément Certificate No. 83/1089.

EXAMPLES OF CONNECTORS

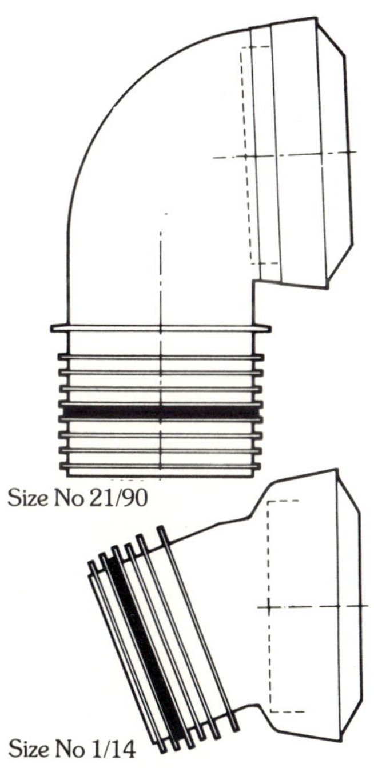

Size No 21/90

Size No 1/14

STAGE 1 Check outside diameter of W.C. pan spigot and inside diameter of soil pipe. Note any other relevant dimensions; select the correct size connector to suit.

STAGE 2 Align the W.C. pan spigot with the connector socket and push through the sealing flanges to joint. NB the rubber and plastic sealing flanges fold inwards as shown to ensure a positive seal.

STAGE 3 Offer the W.C. pan and connector up to the soil pipe, having ensured that the inside of the soil pipe is reasonably clean and smooth. If the inside surface is rough, the lubricant supplied should be smeared over these surfaces.

STAGE 4 Just push the W.C. pan and connector firmly into the soil pipe. No sealant is required.

STAGE 5 Check that the W.C. pan is sitting correctly and then complete the installation according to the sanitary-ware manufacturers instructions.

Go along to your **Local DIY Store** or **Builders Merchants** and ask for the Phetco **Multikwik by name**, it is the original W.C. Connector. **Only Phetco** offer the widest range of connectors and extension pieces available.

In case of difficulties please get advice from the Manufacturer:

PHETCO (ENGLAND) LTD.,
26a High St., **TOTTON**, Hants.
Tel: Southampton (0703) 869077

TAPS

REWASHERING

The need to rewasher is indicated by a constant drip when the tap is turned off. First turn off the water to the tap (see page 102). Use a reliable wrench to remove the headgear. The jaws of the wrench must fit tightly and securely to the 'flats' of the headgear. The longer the wrench handle, the more leverage you'll obtain.

You should be able to unscrew and raise an easy-clean cover by hand. If you use a wrench on it, pad the jaws well with cloth. With the tap fully opened, it is possible to slip the jaws of the wrench under the cover to grip the flats of the tap.

If the jumper is resting on the valve seating, the washer is secured to the jumper by a tiny nut. This is sometimes difficult to undo.

THE TRICK

Apply a drop of penetrating oil. After a brief interval, secure the jumper firmly in a vice and tackle the nut with a spanner of the correct size. If the nut still seems to be immovable, you can buy a new jumper and washer complete from any d-i-y store.

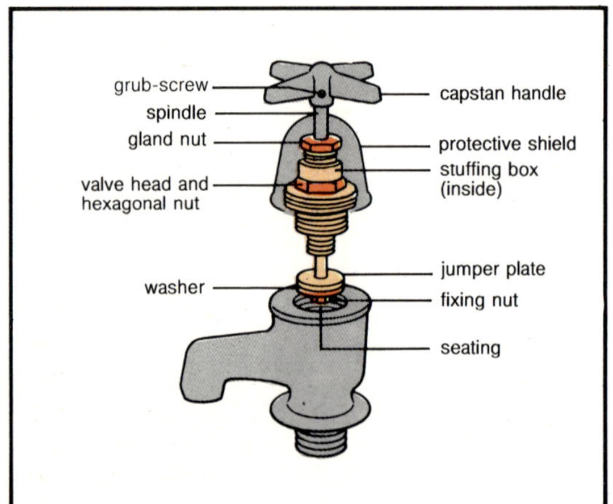

Make sure that your new washer, or washer and jumper set, is the right size.

When renewing the washer of a bathroom tap, or the kitchen hot tap, the jumper may not be resting on the valve seating when the headgear is unscrewed. It is 'pegged' into the headgear so can be turned round and round but cannot be removed. Make a really determined effort to unscrew the retaining nut.

THE TRICK

If it seems firmly welded in position, insert the blade of a screwdriver between the plate of the jumper and the headgear and forcibly break the pegging. Now you can remove the jumper. Buy a new jumper and washer complete, but, before inserting it in the headgear of the tap, 'burr' the stem with a rasp or coarse file so that it gives an 'interference fit'.

TAPS WITH SHROUDED HEADS

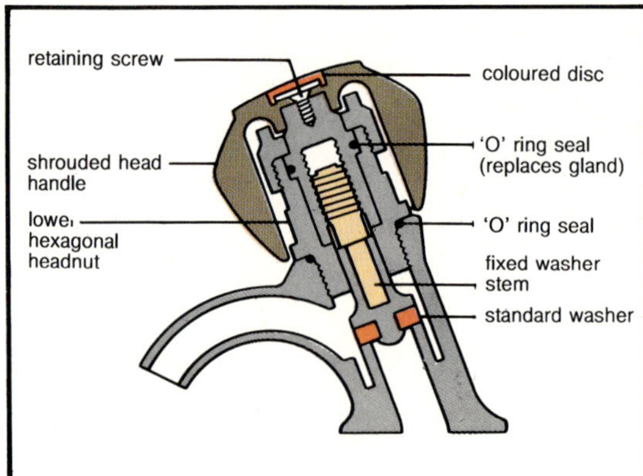

The way in which the head is removed depends upon the make of the tap. The commonest method has a retaining screw concealed under the plastic HOT or COLD indicator at the top of the head.

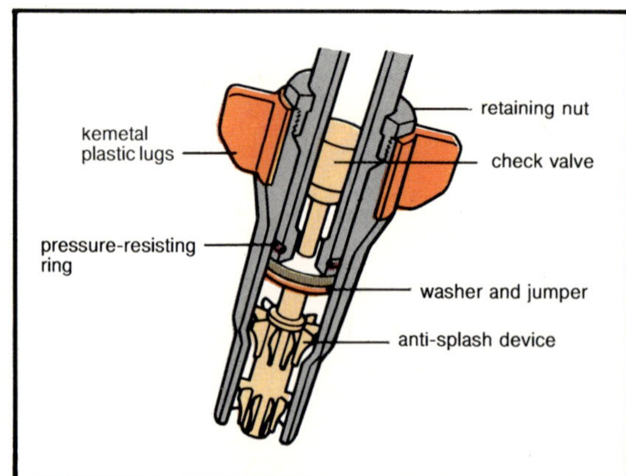

THE SUPATAP

The 'supatap' is the trade name of a tap of totally different design from those already described. One of its main attractions is the ease with which washer changing can be carried out without cutting off the water supply. Supataps are turned on and off by turning the actual nozzle of the tap. Kemetal plastic 'ears', or lugs, are fitted to the nozzle to make this possible.

First unscrew the retaining nut at the top of the nozzle. Turn the tap on – and keep on turning. Water flow will increase at first but will then suddenly cease, just before the nozzle comes off in your hand, as a check valve within the body of the tap falls into position.

Tap the nozzle outlet on a hard surface. Turn it upside down and the anti-splash device, with the washer and jumper inside it, will fall out. Prize the washer and jumper out and press in the replacement. Reassemble the tap.

THE TRICK

When you screw the nozzle back into position, remember that it has a left-hand thread. Overlook this and you'll wonder why 'the thread won't bite'.

FAULTY VALVE SEATINGS

If a tap begins to drip again almost immediately after it has been rewashered, this indicates that the valve seating has become worn and is no longer giving a watertight seal. The best solution is to purchase and fit one of the nylon washer and seating sets available in handy packs from most d-i-y shops.

The tap is dismantled (after cutting off the water supply of course) and the new nylon seating placed squarely over the old metal one. The new plastic washer and jumper unit is placed in position in the headgear of the tap, which is then reassembled. All that remains to be done is to turn the tap off – hard! This will force the new seating into position over the old one. The tap may continue to drip slightly for a short while. However, after a week or so, the new seating will settle into position to give a watertight seal.

The valve seatings of supataps cannot be reconditioned in this way. However, a simple tool is readily available from the manufacturers.

TROUBLES WITH THE GLAND

An escape of water up the spindle is a fault most likely to be encountered in the kitchen taps. There are two common causes: detergent seepage and back pressure from a hose.

The first move should be to adjust the gland packing nut. If the tap has an easy-clean cover, remove the tap handle and cover to gain access to it.

Crutch and capstan handles are secured to the tap spindle by a tiny grub-screw. Remove this and put it in a safe place. The handle may now be removed – perhaps with the help of a few gentle taps from underneath.

THE TRICK

A useful tip for removing a stubborn handle is to unscrew the easy-clean cover and open the tap up fully. Raise the cover and insert two pieces of wood between the base of the cover and the body of the tap. Now try to turn the tap off. The upward pressure of the cover will force off the handle as you turn it downwards.

There is no need to turn off the water supply unless you adopt this course of action.

To adjust the gland nut, give it half a turn in a clockwise direction. Turn the tap on and see if flow up the spindle has ceased. If it has not, tighten again.

Eventually, all the adjustment will be used up and the gland will need to be repacked. Unscrew and remove the gland packing nut. Rake all existing packing material out of the gland with a penknife. Repack with household wool steeped in Vaseline. Caulk down hard before replacing the gland nut and tightening it.

Very modern taps are likely to have 'O' ring-seals instead of a conventional gland. If they leak, replacement of the 'O' ring provides a simple cure.

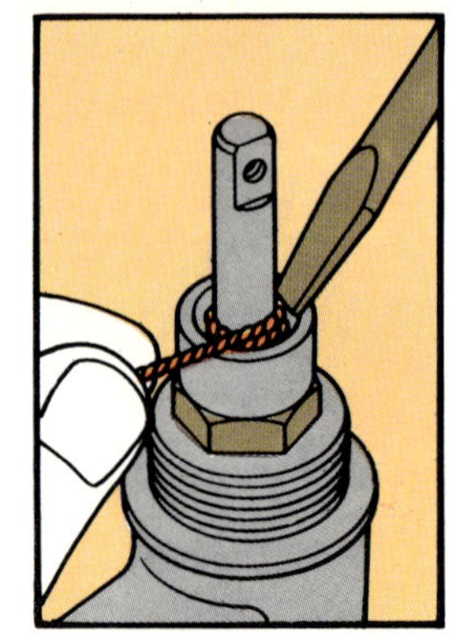

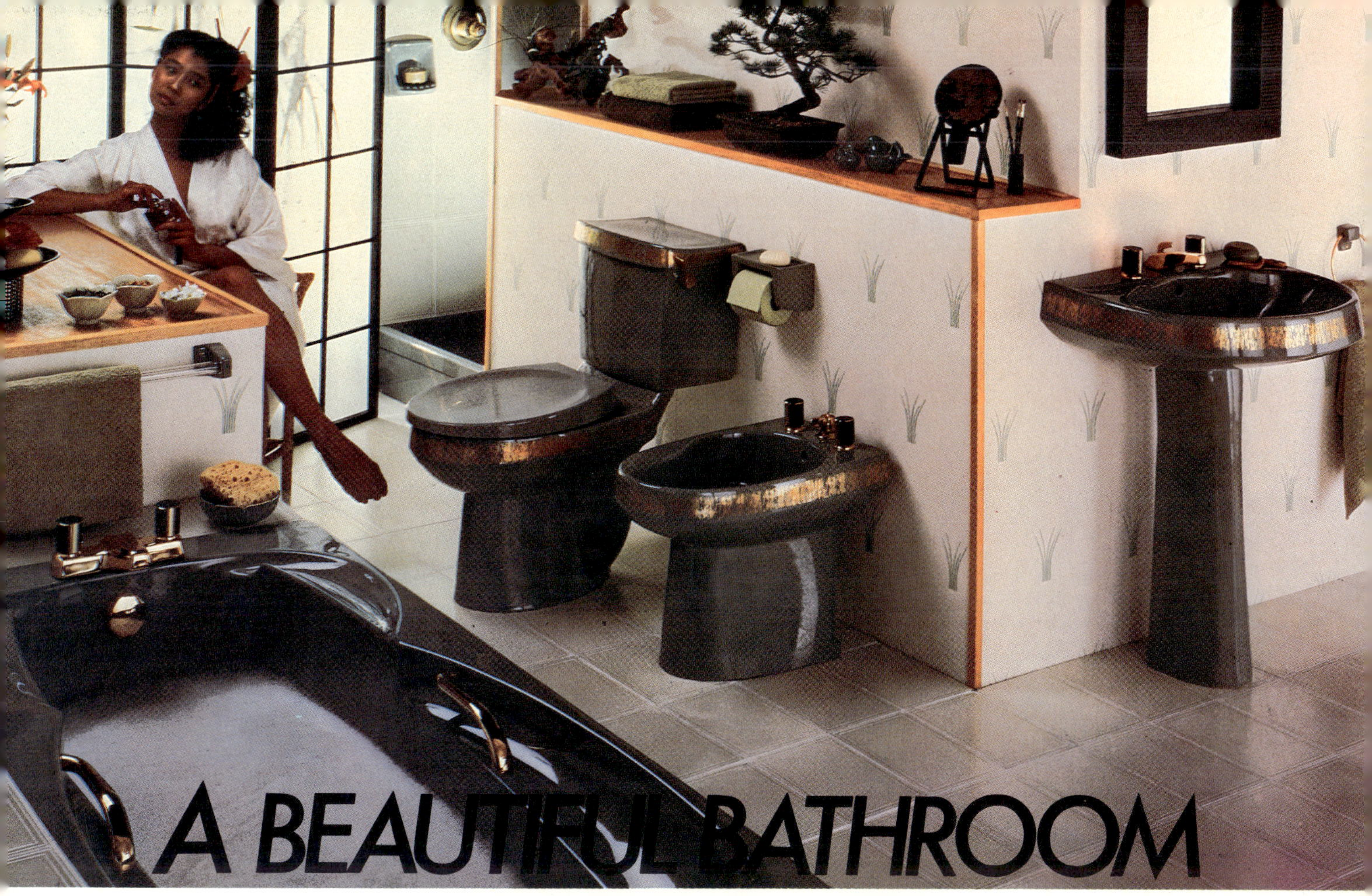

A BEAUTIFUL BATHROOM MADE EASY.

It's so easy for you to give your bathroom a beautiful new look with Armitage Shanks.

That's because quite simply our range of top-quality bathroom fittings and accessories, in the superb selection of Armitage Shanks colours, will suit every single style, size and shape of bathroom imaginable – giving you just the right effect you are looking for.

Take our washbasins, for example.

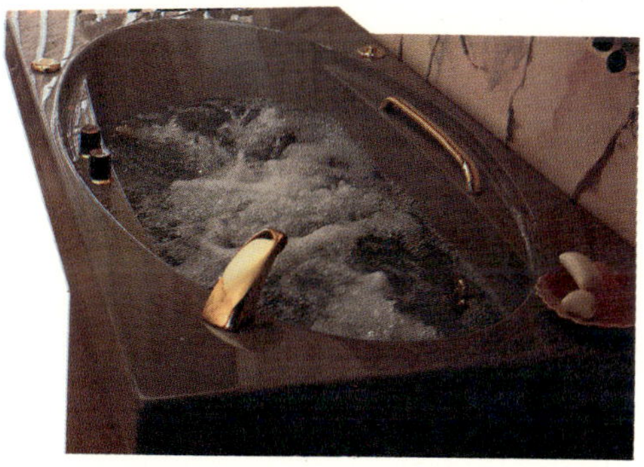

Armitage Shanks are able to offer you an excellent selection that includes traditional pedestal basins, space-saving cloakroom models, and complete luxury vanity tops.

Then there's a superior range of elegant vanity units – they are ideal for both bathroom and bedroom locations.

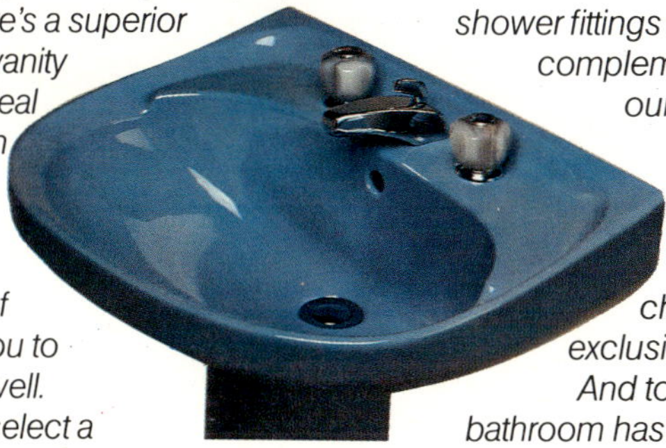

We've an extensive range of quality w.c.'s for you to choose from as well.

You can select a modern, stylish close coupled w.c. with cistern attached, or either a floor or a wall mounted w.c. with the cistern concealed.

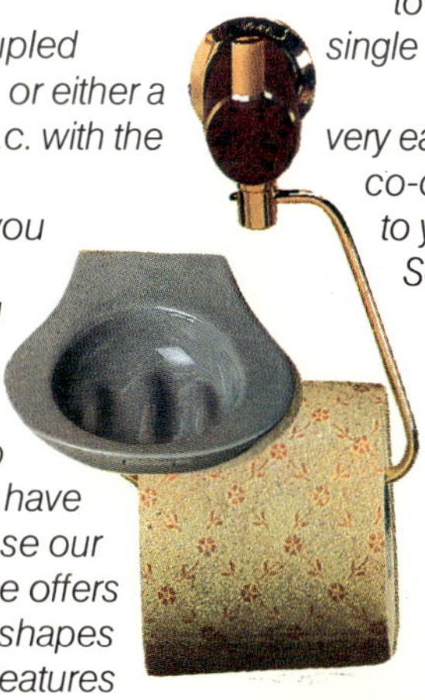

And of course if you include a bidet to match you will have a stylish and practical addition in your bathroom.

When it comes to choosing your bath you'll have no problems that's because our fully comprehensive range offers you many different sizes, shapes and attractive and useful features to take your pick from.

Perhaps you need to save space in your bathroom, you can do just that with a shower bath, or maybe you want to add a touch of originality with our unusual corner bath, and if you're after complete bathing luxury there's nothing better than having an Armitage Shanks Whirlpool bath.

Our Starlite range of taps and shower fittings is specially designed to complement every single one of our suites, with an excellent selection of co-ordinating handwheels from contemporary chrome-plated through to exclusive tortoiseshell.

And to make sure your bathroom has the perfect finishing touch, there's our range of accessories, from soap holders to towel rails, all made to match every single one of our beautiful fashion colours.

Only Armitage Shanks make it so very easy to create your own beautifully co-ordinated bathroom that's designed to your own special and exclusive taste.

So why not get full details today.

For your FREE copy of our lavish 24 page brochure, post the coupon at the back of this publication.

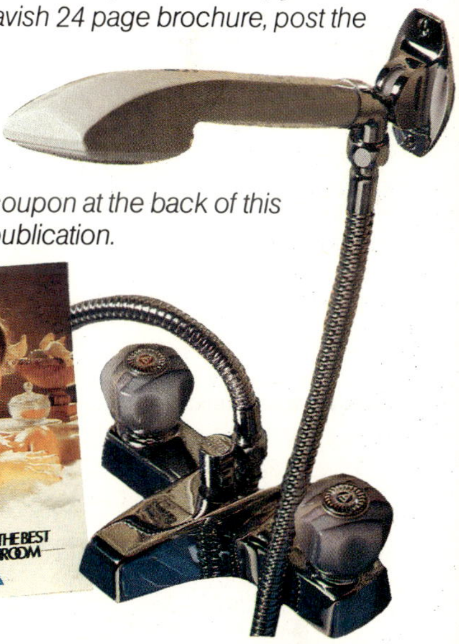

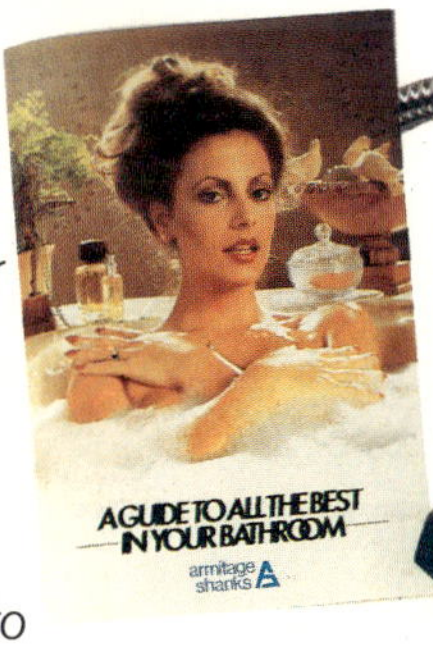

armitage shanks

All the best in your bathroom

Armitage Shanks Ltd.,
Armitage, Rugeley, Staffs. WS15 4BT
London Showroom: The Better Bathroom Centre,
303/6 High Holborn, London WC1V 7LB.

BALL-VALVES

A ball-valve maintains the required water level in open tanks and cisterns. Ball-valves supply water to lavatory-flushing cisterns, the main cold-water storage cistern and the small feed and expansion tank of an 'indirect' hot-water system (see page 124).

The essential feature is a float, connected to the valve by a rigid arm of metal or plastic. As the water level falls, the float falls with it. This opens the valve and allows water to flow into the cistern. When the water has reached its former level, the float arm closes the valve and stops water flow.

The two types most likely found are the 'Portsmouth' and 'diaphragm' or 'Garston' valve.

PORTSMOUTH BALL-VALVES

The Portsmouth valve is the older type. Always made of brass or gun-metal, the float arm pushes a washered plug to and fro horizontally in the valve body. When the valve is closed the washer is pressed firmly against the seating to ensure a watertight joint.

Washer failure is the commonest fault, indicated by a steady drip from the overflow pipe of the cistern.

RENEWAL

To renew the washer, first cut off the water supply (see page 102). Some Portsmouth valves have a screw-on cap on the end of the valve body. This must be removed. With a pair of pliers, pull out the split pin on which the float arm pivots; remove the float arm.

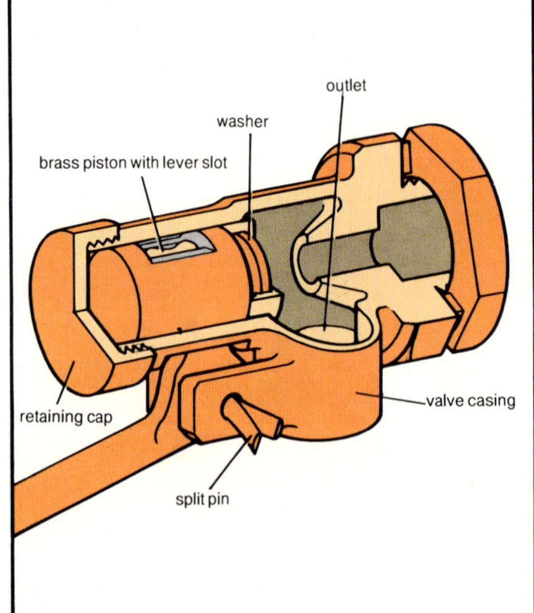

THE TRICK

Have a spare split pin handy. If the old one has been in use for some years it may break.

Insert a screwdriver into the slot in the valve body from which the end of the float arm has been removed, and push the plug out. Be ready to catch it as it comes out!

The plug is in two parts: a body and a retaining cap that holds the washer in place. Insert a screwdriver through the slot in the plug and unscrew the retaining cap with a pair of pliers. If this proves difficult don't struggle too long. Pick out the old washer with a penknife and force the new one under the flange of the retaining cap. Make sure that it lies absolutely flat under the flange.

Clean the plug with fine abrasive paper. Wrap another piece round a pencil to clean the inside of the valve body. Apply a light smear of vaseline to the plug before inserting it.

Corrosion and hard-water scale may cause jamming. If this happens, dismantle the valve, renew the split pin, then clean the plug and interior of the valve body as suggested above.

NOISE PROBLEMS

Noisiness is another failing of Portsmouth valves. Apart from the rushing of incoming water, there may be heavy banging (water hammer), or a steady drumming or humming noise as the cistern refills.

Householders are frequently unable to trace the latter sound. It occurs after they have drawn off hot water and can often be alleviated by turning on the cold-water tap. (This reduces water pressure and diminishes the flow of water through the valve.) This drumming is the result of ripple formation on the surface of the water as fresh water flows in.

The more serious water hammer arises from the valve bouncing on its seating, because of the ripples, when nearly closed.

In the past it was usual to reduce these noises by fitting a 'silencer tube'. They are now banned by water authorities.

THE TRICK

Try this: take a small plastic flowerpot and drill two holes near to the rim. Tie a loop of string through each hole. Slip the loop over the float arm, so that it is suspended 50–75mm (2–3in.) below the float. This will prevent the float from bouncing. If it works, replace the string with nylon cord or copper wire that will not rot.

You should also ensure that the rising main is securely fixed to the roof timbers. This is especially important when replacing an old galvanized steel storage cistern with a plastic one.

Finally, consider replacing the existing valve with a diaphragm valve.

EQUILIBRIUM VALVES

Portsmouth valves are classified as high-pressure (HP), low-pressure (LP) or full-way, depending upon the diameter of the nozzle orifice. This is usually stamped on the valve body.

Mains water pressure can vary greatly during the course of 24 hours. The answer is to fit an 'equilibrium' ball-valve. This resembles the conventional Portsmouth valve, but has a channel drilled through the plug permitting water to flow through to a watertight chamber behind it.

A Portsmouth valve opens under the influence of two forces: the float arm and water pressure in the main. With an equilibrium valve, pressure is equalized and the valve opens solely via the float arm. This lets the valve have a much wider orifice without leaking when water pressure is high, and it refills rapidly when pressure is low.

DIAPHRAGM OR GARSTON BALL-VALVES

The diaphragm, Garston or BRS ball-valve was developed in an attempt to produce a silent and effective valve free from corrosion and scale troubles.

The diaphragm valve has a nylon nozzle, which resists scoring by grit and gives a smooth even water flow. The nozzle is closed by a largish rubber diaphragm. As the water level rises, a small plug presses this firmly against the valve nozzle. This plug, which is the only moving part, is protected from water, scale and corrosion by the diaphragm. Its demountable nozzle makes it possible to convert the valve from high-pressure to low-pressure use, or vice versa, in seconds.

A poor flow from a diaphragm valve will usually be caused by the diaphragm jamming against the nozzle or by debris lodged within the valve. Before dismantling the valve, cut off the water supply. Once the problem is removed, a miniature waterfall will make it all but impossible to reassemble.

The valve is dismantled by turning the large knurled retaining nut. The diaphragm can then be picked out with a screwdriver and any debris removed.

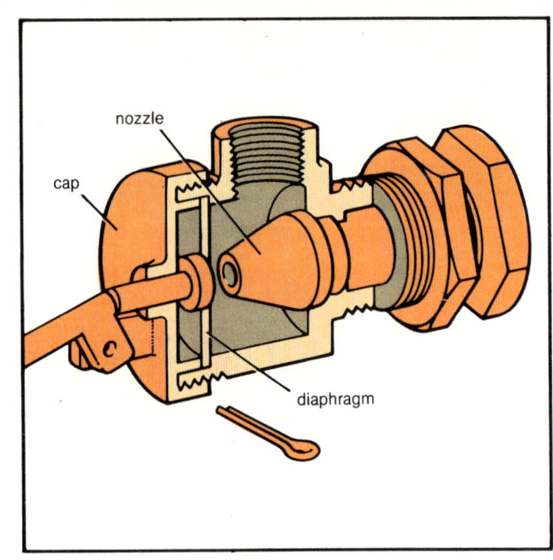

WATER LEVEL ADJUSTMENT

Diaphragm valves always incorporate some kind of screw control that raises or lowers the float to adjust the water level in the cistern.

Where a control of this kind is not provided, the water level can be adjusted by bending the float arm. Unscrew and remove the float. Take the float arm in both hands and gently bend the float end upwards to raise or downwards to lower the water level. Screw the float on again and check that your adjustment is satisfactory.

THE LAVATORY SUITE

A common fault of the 'direct action' flushing cistern is a failure to flush promptly, instead, two or more sharp jerks are required.

If this happens you should remove the lid of the cistern and check the water level. There may be a mark on the cistern wall to indicate the correct level. If there is not adjust the ball-float so that the level of water is about 15mm (⅔in.) below the bottom of the overflow outlet.

SIPHONING

If the water level is correct, the trouble lies within the siphoning mechanism. When the flushing level is operated, a metal disc is raised within the dome of the siphon. This throws water over the inverted U-tube above it into the flush pipe, thus starting the siphonic action. The metal disc has holes in it to permit water to flow through freely once the siphonic action has begun.

When the disc is raised these holes are closed by a valve – usually a thin, plastic diaphragm. This flaps up to allow water to pass upwards through it, but is held down firmly by the weight of water as the disc is raised.

If the diaphragm is no longer effectively closing the holes, it becomes increasingly difficult to throw water over into the flush pipe to start the siphonic action.

To renew this diaphragm you must withdraw the siphoning mechanism from the cistern. Tie up the float arm (see page 102) and flush the cistern to empty it.

Unscrew the nut that connects the threaded 'tail' of the siphon to the flush pipe and disconnect the flush pipe. You will need a good wrench to unscrew the large nut immediately beneath the base of the cistern. Have a bucket handy to catch the pint or so of water left in the cistern. Once the nut has been removed, you can withdraw the siphoning mechanism. It is wise to buy a new diaphragm before beginning the job.

THE TRICK

Buy the largest. Scissors will cut it to size. It should be big enough to cover the disc and touch – but not scrape on – the walls of the siphon dome.

Although most flushing cisterns are dismantled as described, there are a few where the siphon mechanism is secured by bolts. Very modern ones may have the flush pipe thrust into the cistern past a watertight 'O' ring-seal.

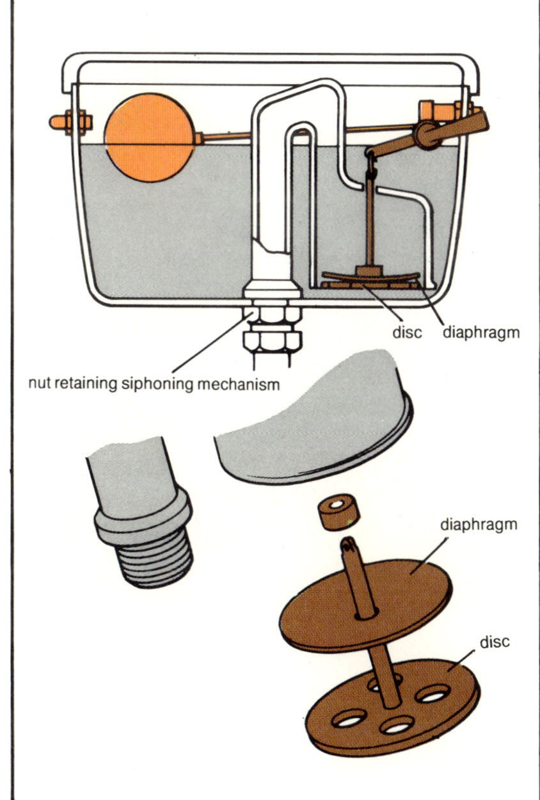

BURLINGTON CISTERNS

This kind is invariably made of cast iron and has a well in its base. In this stands a heavy, iron bell, to the top of which is connected the chain-operated flushing lever. A stand-pipe, connected to the flush pipe, rises inside this bell and extends, open-ended, to a point about 30mm (1¼in.) above full water level.

It works by raising the bell and releasing it. It forces water inside it and over the rim of the stand-pipe as it falls into the cistern well. This starts the flushing action. The bell has lugs at its base that permit water to pass under the rim once siphonic action has begun.

Its principal fault is a tendency to 'continuous siphonage'. The main cause is an accumulation of debris in the cistern. The lugs sink into this debris, so air cannot pass under to break the siphon after flushing.

Contributory causes may be a ball-valve that refills too rapidly and the slow wearing away of the lugs at the base of the bell.

Cleaning out the base of the cistern thoroughly will usually effect a cure. It may be necessary to reduce the flow through the ball-valve inlet by partially closing a stopcock in the water supply pipe. In others it may be necessary to build up the bell's lugs with an epoxy-resin filler.

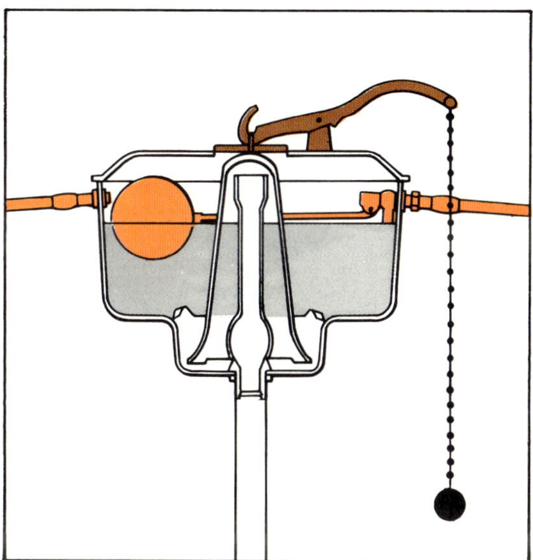

CONDENSATION

Both kinds of cistern may be affected by condensation, which occurs when warm, moist air comes into contact with the cold surface of the cistern. Lavatories situated in bathrooms are most prone to this trouble, as the air in bathrooms tends to be both warmer and damper. Improved ventilation gives the most certain answer. In serious cases it may be worth fixing an electric extractor-fan in the bathroom window.

Insulating the cistern's surface will also help. Iron Burlington cisterns can be painted externally with two or more coats of insulating anti-condensation paint. Plastic cisterns have a built-in insulation that renders them less liable to condensation.

THE TRICK

Empty the cistern and dry it thoroughly. Line it internally with strips of wafer-thin expanded polystyrene sheets (used as an insulating lining under wallpaper). Use an epoxy-resin adhesive and allow to set thoroughly before refilling the cistern.

Two small final points on condensation: run a couple of inches of cold water into the bath before you turn on the hot tap. Second, do not drip-dry washing over the bath.

CLEANSING THE LAVATORY PAN

When the flush is operated, two streams of water should flow round the flushing rim with equal force to meet in the centre of the front of the pan. There should be no 'whirlpool effect' as the pan empties.

Check the level of the water in the flushing cistern A full 9l. (2gal.) flush is essential for thorough cleansing.

Check that the flush pipe connects squarely to the 'flushing horn' of the lavatory pan and that no jointing material or other debris is obstructing the inlet to the pan. If you have an old-fashioned 'rag and putty' joint, replace it with a modern rubber cone flush-pipe connector (see page 109).

Check with your fingers, or with a mirror, that the space under the flushing rim of the pan is free from flakes of rust and other debris.

Check that the pan outlet connects squarely with the socket of the branch drain or soil-pipe.

THE TRICK

With a spirit-level, check that the pan is set dead level. If not, loosen the screws that secure the pan to the floor and pack underneath with linoleum or similar to make level.

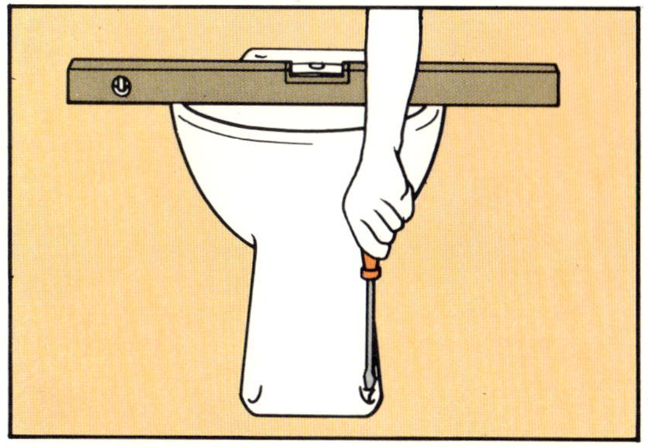

Whatever the job in hand, use Pro-Techs.

The first-ever range of specially designed DIY gloves.

The trick of any successful DIY job, as any professional will tell you, is to use the right tools for the job.

Yet it's surprising how few DIY-ists use the right gloves for the job.

Particularly when you think of the hell hands can go through.

That's why they need protecting.

And that's why Marigold have designed Pro-Techs.

The first-ever range of specially designed DIY gloves for professionals and enthusiasts alike.

Whatever the job in hand, get your hands on a pair of Pro-Techs.

You'll find them at larger DIY stores everywhere.

We think you'll find them just the trick.

PRO-Techs

Marigold®

LRC Products Ltd., North Circular Rd., E4 8QA.

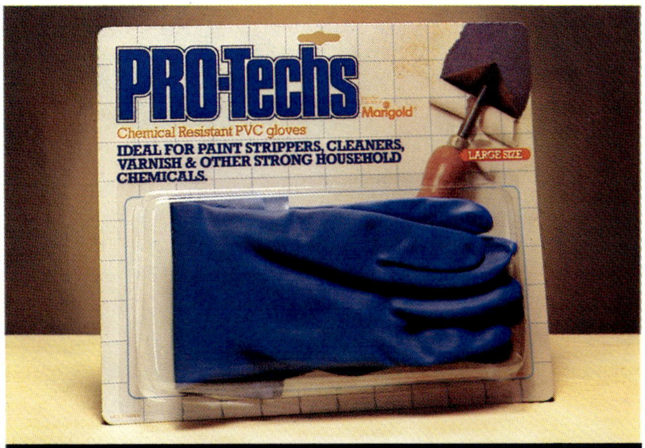

PVC Pro-Techs.
A chemically resistant glove that protects hands from harmful paint strippers, wood preservatives and the like.

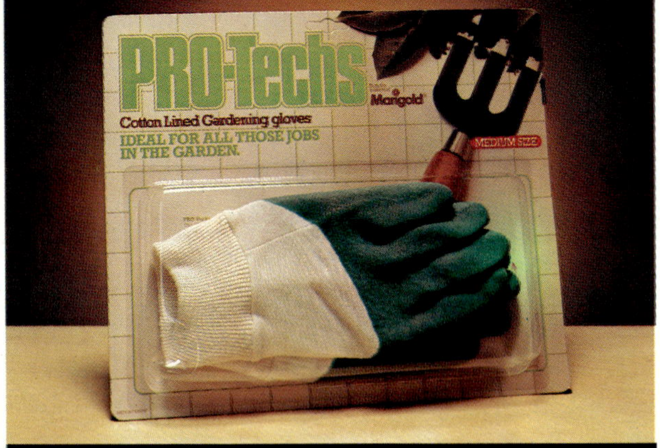

Gardening Pro-Techs.
A hard-wearing cotton lined latex glove that prevent green fingers from becoming grazed fingers.

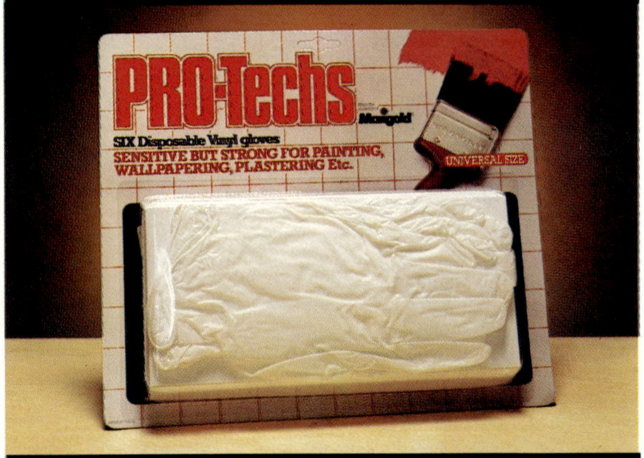

Disposable Pro-Techs.
A sensitive yet strong vinyl glove for those messy one-offs like painting and decorating.

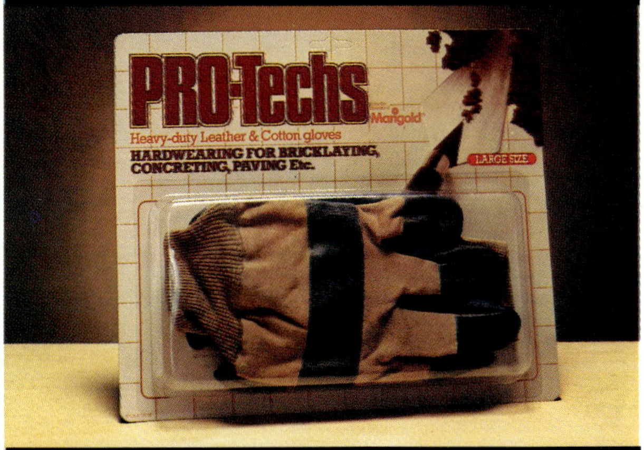

Heavy-Duty Pro-Techs.
A super rugged leather and cotton glove that can tackle – and tame – the heaviest manual work.

RENEWING LAVATORIES 1

LOW-LEVEL CISTERNS

Many competent d-i-y enthusiasts have purchased a standard low-level flushing cistern complete with short, wider-diameter flush pipe – usually sold as a 'flush bend'. They cut off the water supply, disconnect and remove the old high-level cistern and replace it with the new cistern and the flush bend – only to find that the new cistern is overhanging the lavatory pan by a few inches. Quite apart from the discomfort of using a lavatory suite with the flushing cistern thrusting at one's shoulders, it will be found to be impossible to raise the lid and the seat completely.

The pan of a conventional low-level lavatory suite is normally situated 50–75mm (2–3in.) further from the wall behind it than that of a high-level suite. This is to enable the low-level cistern to be accommodated.

Until recently the only way in which a high-level suite could be converted to low-level use was to bring the lavatory pan 50–75mm (2–3in.) forward into the lavatory compartment. Modern plastic drain connectors and extension pieces have made this a less difficult task. However, it is still a daunting job and in some cases, involves the replacement of a perfectly satisfactory lavatory pan.

In a small bathroom, bringing the pan forward – even such a small distance – can mean that it is unacceptably close to the bathroom washbasin. The washbasin too must be moved – possibly to a position that will make it impossible to open the bathroom door!

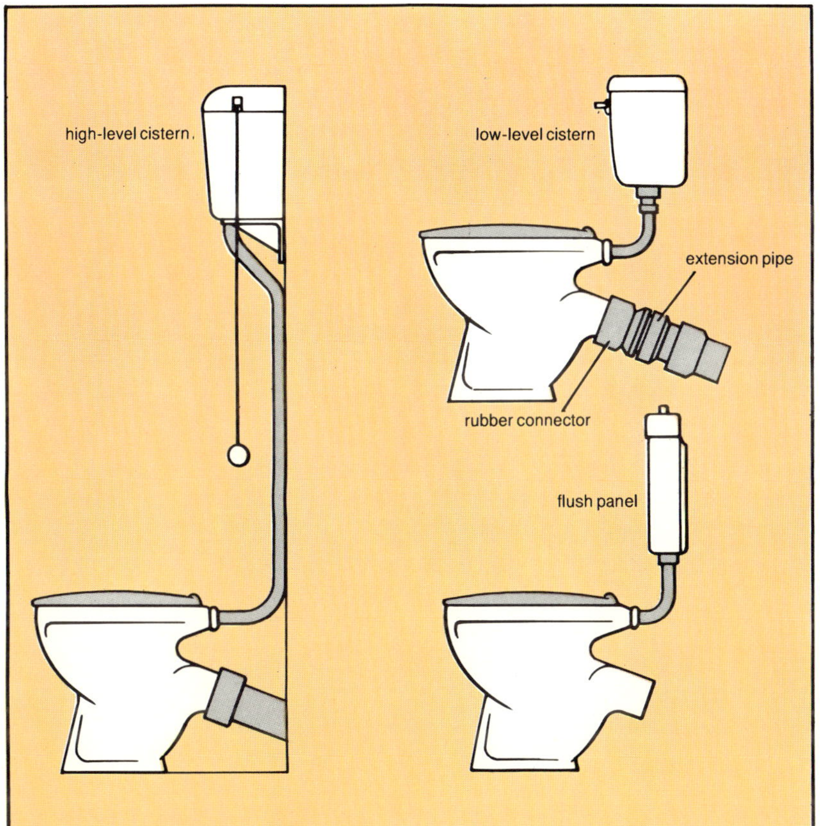

FLUSH PANELS

During recent years, slim-line flushing cisterns, or 'flush panels', have developed that simplify high- to low-level conversion. In most cases the same lavatory pan can be used, in its existing position.

With a flush panel, the flushing inlet of the lavatory pan can be as little as 130mm (5¼in.) from the wall behind it compared with the 200–300mm (8–9in.) required by a conventional low-level cistern. In order to accommodate the full 9l. (2gal.) of water required for an adequate flush, these slim-line cisterns are rather wider than conventional ones. Before purchase, make sure that there is sufficient width of unobstructed wall behind the pan.

RUBBER CONE JOINTS

If the high-level suite was installed before 1939, it is possible that the flush pipe will be connected to the lavatory pan with a 'rag and putty' joint. These are unhygienic and should be replaced with a new rubber cone joint. The larger end is pushed over the flushing inlet to the lavatory pan, while the end of the flush bend is pushed into the smaller end so that it connects squarely with the inlet.

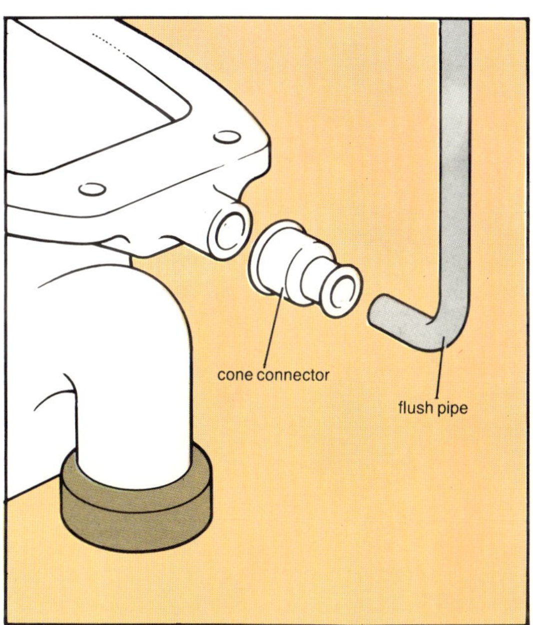

THE TRICK

If necessary, both ends of the cone can be bound round with copper wire to ensure watertight connections.

REPLACING UPSTAIRS LAVATORY PANS

A pan with a crazed or cracked surface is a potential health hazard and should be renewed, whether or not conversion from high-level to low-level is planned.

The pan of an upstairs lavatory suite will probably be connected to the branch soil-pipe with a putty or mastic joint. The pan itself will be fixed to the wooden floor of the bathroom or lavatory compartment with brass screws.

Disconnect the flush pipe from the pan. Undo the brass screws that secure it to the floor and pull the pan forward.

THE TRICK

If you move the pan from side to side as you do so, its outlet should come out of the socket of the branch soil-pipe without too much difficulty.

Clean all existing jointing material out of the soil-pipe socket and place the new pan in position, making sure that its outlet goes squarely into the centre of the socket.

PAN TO SOIL-PIPE JOINTS

You have a choice of methods for making the joint between the outlet of the new pan and the branch soil-pipe. You can bind two or three turns of waterproofing building tape round the pan outlet and caulk down hard into the socket. Fill in the space between outlet and socket with a non-setting mastic and complete the joint with another two or three turns of building tape.

On the other hand, the use of a modern plastic push-on drain-connector – such as the 'Multikwik' connector – is less messy and gives a neater completed finish.

It is vital that the pan should be set dead level. Check this with a spirit-level and, if necessary, pack slivers of wood or pieces of linoleum under the lower side to bring it level.

Use a rubber cone connector (see above) to connect the flush pipe to the flushing inlet of the new pan.

THE TRICK

Slip lead washers over the non-corroding fixing screws before you insert them into the holes at the base of the lavatory pan to secure it to the floor. These will protect the ceramic surface when you drive the screws home.

RENEWING LAVATORIES 2

REPLACING GROUND-FLOOR PANS

Renewing a ground-floor lavatory pan can be a good deal more difficult than an upstairs one because the pan is likely to be cemented to a solid floor. The S-trap outlet will probably be connected to the branch drain with a cement joint.

Disconnect the flush pipe from the pan. With a hammer, break the lavatory pan outlet behind the trap. Loosen the front part of the pan from the floor by driving a cold chisel between its base and the floor. Pull the front part of the pan forward out of the way.

You will now be left with the jagged end of the pan outlet projecting from the socket of the branch drain. Stuff a wad of cloth or newspaper into the hole to prevent fragments of cement and ceramic material from going down the drain.

Attack the protruding end of the pan outlet with a hammer and a small cold chisel. Work carefully, keeping the blade of the chisel pointing towards the centre of the pipe.

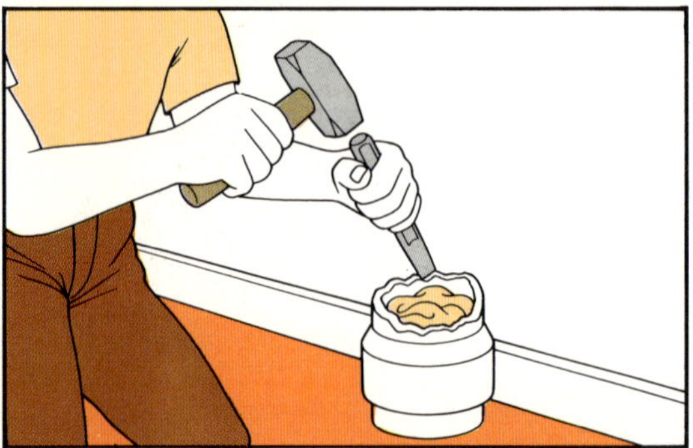

THE TRICK

Break down the outlet right to its end at one point and then the rest of it will come out fairly easily.

Attack the jointing material in the same way. Make every endeavour not to break the drain socket, although, if you do, the situation is not entirely hopeless. The push-on drain-connectors (see page 109) can be used in a drain with or without a socket. Having cleared the socket, carefully remove the wad of cloth or paper, doing your best to make sure that no debris falls into the drain.

INSTALLING THE NEW PAN

The new lavatory pan should not be cemented to the floor. Secure it with fixing screws only. Chisel all existing cement mixture from the floor to obtain a smooth surface.

Place the new pan in position with its outlet projecting squarely into the socket of the drain. It must be positioned centrally with an equal space between the outside of the pan outlet and the inside of the socket all round.

If you have managed to break the socket in your efforts to clean it out, you will have to use a push-on plastic drain-connector. If the drain socket is intact, you can use a drain-connector, a mastic joint (see page 109) or, you can make another cement joint. However the joint is made, the floor must first be prepared for the fixing screws.

If you are making a cement joint, the pan must be finally fixed to the floor first. With either of the other joints the final securing of the pan to the floor should be completed after the joint is made.

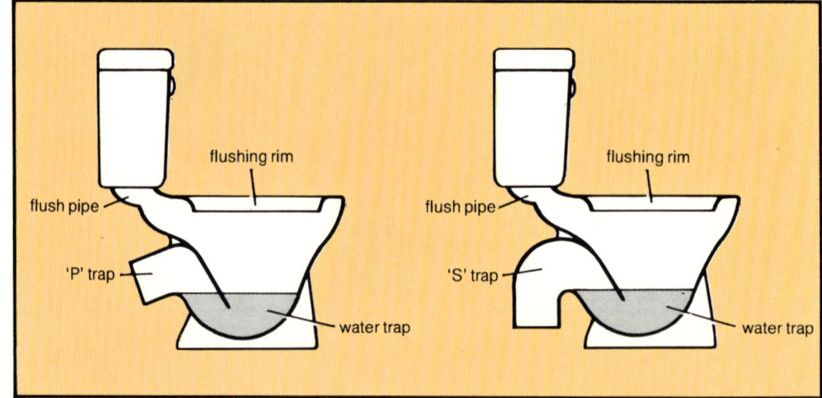

THE TRICK

With the pan in position, mark through the screw holes to the floor with the refill of a ballpoint pen. Use a refill because the holes will probably be too small to allow the actual pen to pass through them.

Remove the pan; drill and plug the floor at the four points marked. It is now important that the pan should be placed back in exactly the same position as before. Marking the position of the pan on the floor before you remove it, and probing through the screw holes to ensure that the plugs are directly beneath them, will ensure this.

Slip lead washers over the screws, insert through the holes into the plugs and screw firmly home. Check the level with a spirit-level and pack underneath with linoleum as necessary.

THE CEMENT JOINT

Dampen some newspaper and caulk down hard into the space between the pan outlet and the drain socket. This will prevent jointing material squeezing through the joint into the drain – a frequent cause of drain blockages.

Make up a mixture of two parts of cement to one part of clean, sharp sand. Fill the space between pan outlet and drain socket with this mixture, making sure that there are no 'voids'. Finish off to a neat, angled fillet at the top of the socket.

THE TRICK

A cement joint of this kind must be left absolutely undisturbed for 24 hours. Do not disturb in any way – even to fix the lid and seat, or to connect the flush pipe.

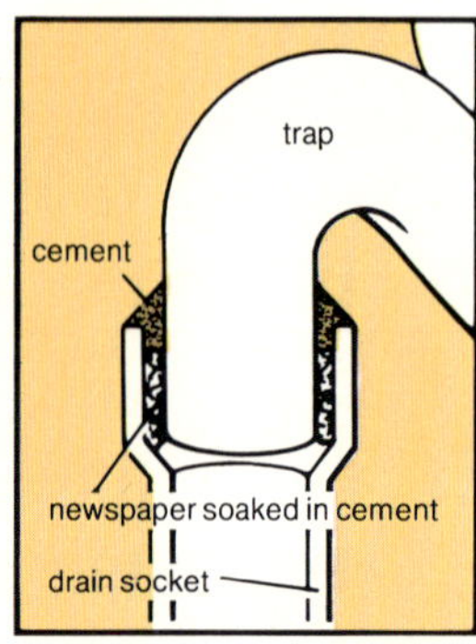

DOUBLE-TRAP SIPHONIC LAVATORIES

Where silent and efficient operation is an overriding consideration, consider replacing the existing lavatory suite with a close-coupled double-trap siphonic model.

With this kind of appliance the flushing cistern and lavatory pan form one unit. There is no flush pipe – not even the short one of a low-level suite – to be seen. Flushing does not depend, as with the common 'wash down' lavatory, upon the weight and momentum of the flush water. Siphonage is employed to empty and cleanse the pan.

The pan outlet has two traps instead of the one trap fitted into a conventional lavatory. A short length of pipe or 'pressure-reducing device' connects the air space between the two traps to the outlet of the flushing cistern.

When the cistern is flushed, water rushing past the end of this pipe sucks the air out of the air-space between the two traps creating a partial vacuum. At this point, atmospheric pressure (i.e. the weight of the atmosphere above the lavatory suite) pushes out the contents of the pan. If working properly, the water level in the pan can be seen to fall before the arrival of the flushing water, which serves largely to wash the sides of the pan and to recharge it.

When considering a suite of this kind, it must be remembered that the new suite will project several inches further into the room.

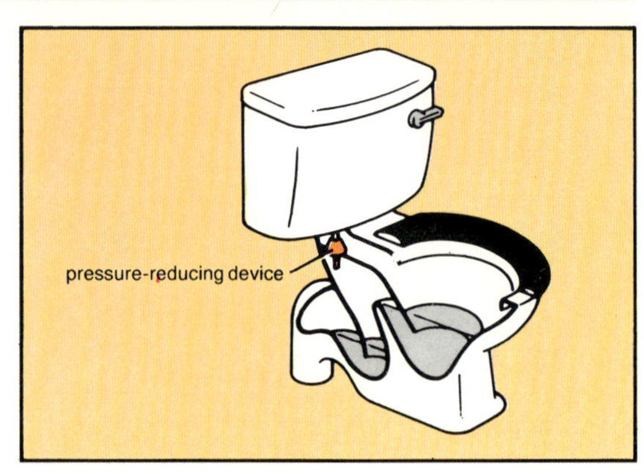

THE DRAINS 1

BLOCKED WASTE-PIPES

Let's take, first of all, that part of the drainage system that is above the ground. Any blockage that occurs will almost certainly be in a branch waste-pipe taking the waste from a sink, bath or washbasin to an external gully or to the main soil- and waste-pipe (see page 100). It will probably be in the 'trap' (the bend in the pipe immediately beneath the appliance) which is designed to retain a certain amount of water and thus to prevent drain smells coming back into the room.

Sink wastes, are particularly prone to blockages. Having completed a pile of washing-up, you pull out the sink waste plug – and nothing happens! The sink remains full of water.

FORCE CUPS

A blockage of this kind can usually be cleared quickly and easily by means of a force cup or sink waste plunger. This consists of a hemisphere of rubber or plastic mounted on a wooden handle. Every householder should have one.

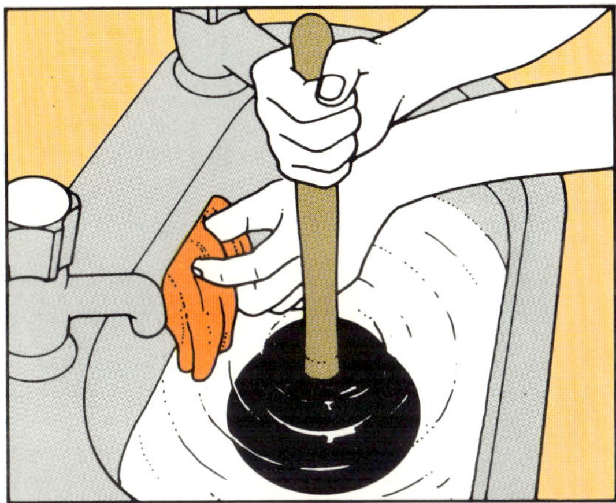

THE TRICK

Place the force cup squarely over the sink waste outlet. With one hand hold a damp cloth firmly against the overflow outlet and, with the other, plunge the handle of the force cup sharply downwards four or five times.

Since water cannot be compressed, the effect of this is to convert the column of water in the upper part of the waste-pipe into a ram which should displace the blockage. The overflow outlet must be blocked to prevent this force being dissipated up the overflow.

You may merely move the obstruction further along the pipe. If you do not immediately remove the blockage, keep on trying.

CLEARING THE TRAP

If you still cannot clear the waste pipe, you will have to gain access to the trap. Place a bucket underneath it before you attempt this.

The traditional U-trap has a screw-in cap at or near its base. The entire lower section of the more modern plastic or chromium-plated bottle-trap can be unscrewed and removed. When you open up the trap, the entire contents of the sink will flow out – hence the importance of the bucket underneath it.

Probe into the trap and waste pipe with a piece of wire. Expanded curtain wire can be very helpful. The chances are that you will find a solid object – a sliver of wood, a piece of bone or something similar – wedged across the pipe.

If you have to unscrew and remove the access cap of a trap, you might break the washer that provides a watertight seal when the cap is screwed home. A temporary washer can be improvised by binding a rubberband tightly round the thread of the cap before replacing it.

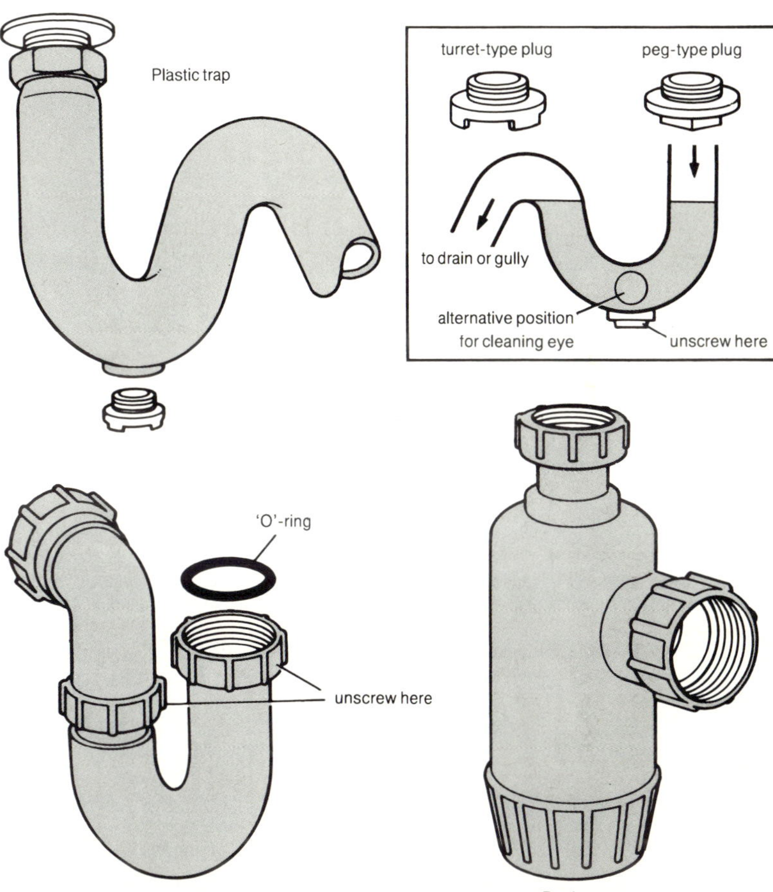

LAVATORY BLOCKAGES

BATH AND BASIN BLOCKAGES

Blockages in bath and basin wastes can nearly always be cleared by plunging. It is not unusual to find that blockages are caused by hair caught in the grid. Try probing through this.

THE TRICK

A straightened out paperclip or hairpin can make a useful tool for this. You may be surprised at the amount of hair, quite invisible from above, that is nevertheless suspended from the grid and is effectively blocking the outlet.

The outlet of a lavatory pan is unlikely to block except as a result of misuse. Floor cloths, scrubbing brushes and plastic toys have all been known to be 'flushed round the bend'.

A blockage is indicated by the water level in the pan rising almost to the flushing rim when the cistern is flushed. It may then, very slowly subside.

An obstruction of the trap can usually be cleared by plunging, but a special drain plunger is best for this purpose. This is a 100mm (4in.) diameter rubber disc screwed onto the end of a drain-clearing rod.

THE TRICK

It is not the kind of tool that most of us keep, but an old-fashioned mop – or even a bundle of rags tied, very securely, to a broom handle – can be used in an emergency.

Alternatively, a length of flexible wire can be passed round the trap to find and dislodge the obstruction.

However, before attempting to clear an apparently blocked lavatory-pan outlet in this way it is wise to check on the underground drains (see page 112). It is there that the cause of the trouble may be found.

THE DRAINS 2

THE UNDERGROUND DRAINS

Access to the underground drains is obtained by raising the cast-iron manhole covers that you will find in your driveway or in the path at the side of your house.

The cover should have two hand-holds to make it easy to lift but these could have corroded.

THE TRICK

In any event you will find it easier to raise the cover if you first run a screwdriver blade, or the sharp corner of a spade, between the cover and the frame in which it rests to remove the accumulation of dirt that will have found its way there. You can then – if there are no handles – use the spade as a lever to raise the cover.

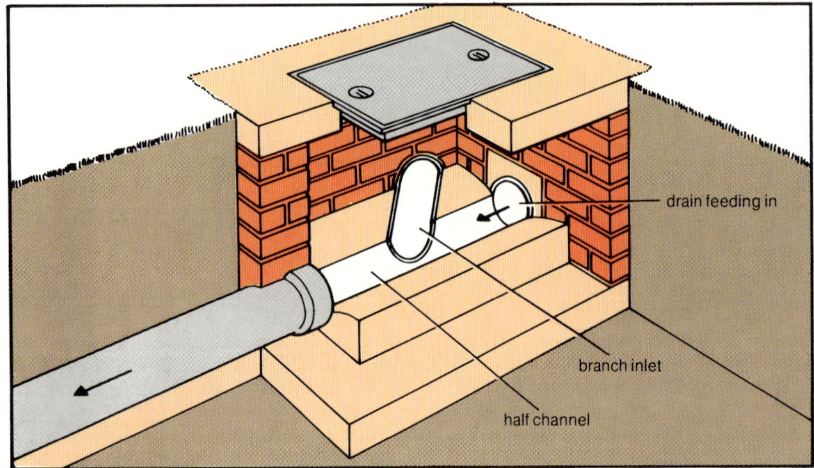

Underneath you will find the drain manhole or inspection chamber, which is a rectangular pit, with walls of brickwork or concrete, and a cement-rendered base through which runs the half-channel of the drain.

Inspection chambers should be provided at all major changes of direction of the drain and at all points at which a branch drain joins the main drain. You will see branch drains entering the chamber through the wall and sweeping round in a 'three-quarter bend' to join the main drain 'in the direction of flow'.

A blockage may be indicated by a lavatory that fails to flush properly, a flooded yard gully or water oozing out from under a manhole cover. With a flooded yard gully, first try raising the grid. It could be that the trouble is due simply to this being clogged with leaves and other debris.

Raising the manhole covers will give you a good idea of the position of the blockage. If one manhole is flooded and the next one is empty, then the blockage must lie somewhere between the two.

You will need a set of drain rods or sweep's rods to clear it. Screw two or three rods together, push one end into the flooded manhole and feel for the half-channel at the bottom. Push the rods along the half-channel into the drain in the direction of the empty manhole. Screw on more rods as necessary and keep pushing until the obstruction is dislodged.

THE TRICK

To help push the rods along the drain, or to extract them afterwards, you can twist them in a clockwise direction. NEVER twist in an anti-clockwise direction. If you do, the rods will unscrew and will be left in the drain.

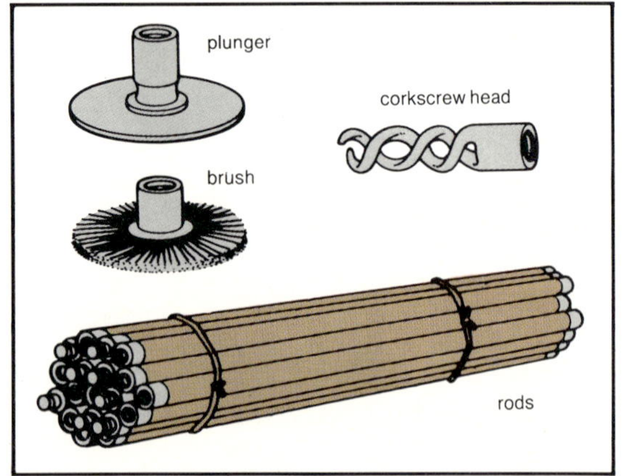

THE INTERCEPTING TRAP

It used to be the custom to provide the household drains with an 'intercepting trap' to disconnect them from the public sewer. It is many years since these traps have been installed in the drains of new dwellings.

You can check if your house has an intercepting trap by raising the cover of the inspection chamber nearest to the public sewer. This will probably be situated just inside the front gate of your home.

At the end of this chamber the half-channel will appear to discharge into a hole, filled with liquid. Immediately above the 'hole' (actually the inlet to the trap) will be a large stoneware stopper. This stopper seals off the rodding arm which permits the length of drain between the trap and the sewer to be rodded to clear any blockage that might occur.

THE FRESH-AIR INLET

Near the manhole there may be a 'fresh-air inlet'. This is a length of drain pipe connected to the manhole and terminating at ground level in a metal box with a grille at the front. A mica flap, hinged at the top, rests against this grille.

Fresh-air inlets are ineffective, it is better to remove the metal box and seal the inlet.

CLEARING THE TRAP

It can usually be cleared by plunging.

Assuming that you have some drain rods and a 100mm (4in.) drain plunger, screw a couple of rods together and screw the rubber plunger disc onto the end of them. Feel for the half-channel at the bottom of the manhole and move the plunger along until you can feel the inlet to the intercepting trap.

Plunge down sharply three or four times. Unless you are very unlucky there will be a gurgle and the water level in the manhole will fall rapidly as the released sewage flows through to the sewer.

THE TRICK

After clearing a drain, hose down the sides of the manholes and let the household taps run for half an hour or so to flush the drain through thoroughly.

PARTIAL BLOCKAGES

An unpleasant smell apparent just inside the front garden of a house is usually due to a partial blockage of the intercepting trap. A sudden increase in pressure inside the sewer may cause the stopper to fall out of the rodding arm into the trap to cause a blockage.

Sewage will begin to flood the manhole but will not be noticed because, when it reaches the level of the rodding arm, it can flow down that arm to the sewer. Within the manhole, however, it will become more and more foul until the smell, escaping from the fresh-air inlet or from under the cover, attracts the attention of the householder.

If this does happen, fish around with a broom handle until you can move the stopper away from blocking the trap. When the sewage level has subsided, flush drain thoroughly as before. It is always wise to seek the cause of recurring drain blockages.

THE TRICK

Phone, or write to your local council and ask the Environmental Health Officer if he will advise.

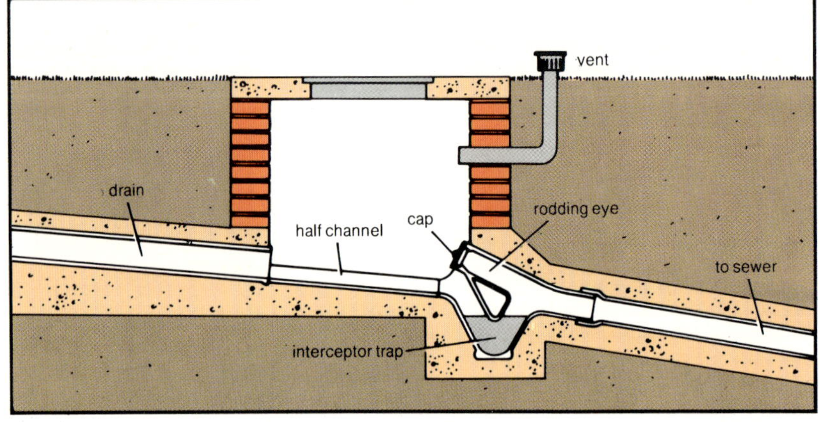

THE COLD-WATER STORAGE CISTERN

Is the cold-water storage in your roof space made of galvanized mild steel? If it is, is it showing signs of corrosion? These are patches of rust round pipe connections, a light 'dusting' of rust on walls or base, or even warty growths protruding into the cistern from the walls.

The tendency of galvanized-steel to corrode has increased with the use of copper supply and distribution pipes. The result is an electro-chemical, or 'electrolytic', action that may take place between the copper pipes and the zinc coating of the galvanized steel.

A galvanized-steel cistern to which copper pipes have been connected may reproduce the conditions of an electric cell if the water supply is slightly acid. The zinc coating of the galvanized steel will dissolve away and the steel beneath will then be unprotected from corrosion.

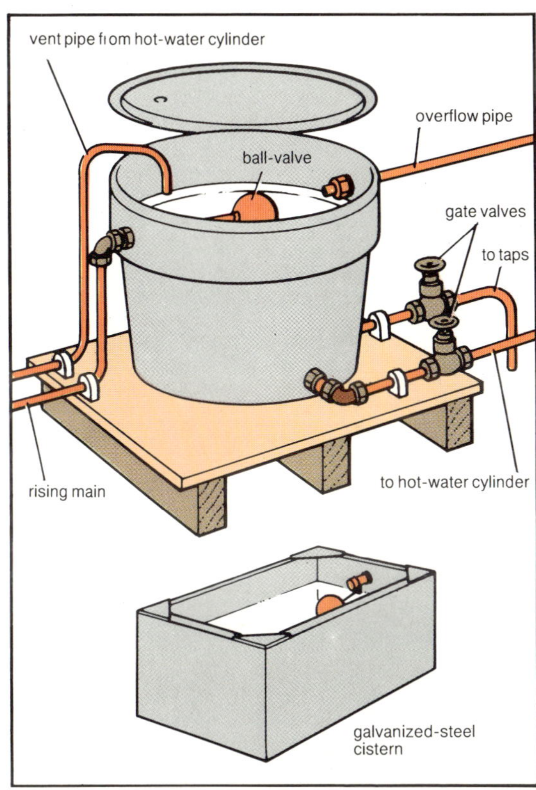

TREATING CORROSION

If your cistern is already showing signs of corrosion, you can eradicate this and protect the cistern indefinitely by internal painting. Cut off the water supply to the cistern and drain it from the bathroom taps (see page 102). You will find that the distribution pipes taken from the cistern are connected 50–75mm (2–3in.) above its base. This means that you will have to bale – and mop – out the last 4l. (1gal.) or so.

THE TRICK

Before proceeding it is best to disconnect the rising main, the overflow pipe and the distribution pipes from the cistern. This is because it is in the immediate vicinity of the tappings made for these pipes that rust is most likely to develop.

Dry the walls and base of the cistern thoroughly and remove every trace of existing rust by means of wire brushing or with abrasives. If you use a wire brush, wear goggles to protect your eyes.

Removing the rust in this way may have left deep pitmarks in the walls of the cistern. It could even have produced holes that penetrate right through the walls in places. Fill in any such holes or pit-marks with epoxy-resin filler. Allow to set and rub down to a smooth surface.

Finally, apply two coats of a tasteless and odourless bitumastic paint. When ordering, stress that it must be non-tainting. This treatment will give several years' protection against even the most corrosive water supply. It can be repeated if necessary.

PREVENTING CORROSION

A new galvanized-steel cistern can, of course, be protected in the same way at the time of installation.

THE TRICK

Rub down the walls and base of the new cistern with abrasive paper to provide a key, and apply the paint after the holes have been cut for the pipe connections but before these connections are made.

ANODIC PROTECTION

Another way the cistern can be protected is by means of a sacrificial magnesium anode.

Anodic protection depends upon the same electro-chemical principle which produces electrolytic corrosion.

All metals have a fixed and known 'electric potential' and, in the conditions of the electric cell, it is the metal with the higher potential that dissolves away. Zinc has a higher potential than copper – but magnesium has a considerably higher potential than either zinc or copper. A sacrificial anode therefore consists of a lump of magnesium which is in electrical contact with the walls of the cistern, by being submerged in the water.

As electrolytic action takes place the magnesium dissolves away – is 'sacrificed' – and the zinc coating of the cistern walls is protected. One well-known anode is sold as a lump of magnesium to which is attached a copper wire. A clamp is provided at the other end of the wire.

To fix, scrape the rim of the tank thoroughly down to the bare metal at the point at which the clamp is to be fitted. This will ensure a good electrical contact. Place a batten of wood across the tank and hang the anode over it so that it is suspended well below the surface of the water.

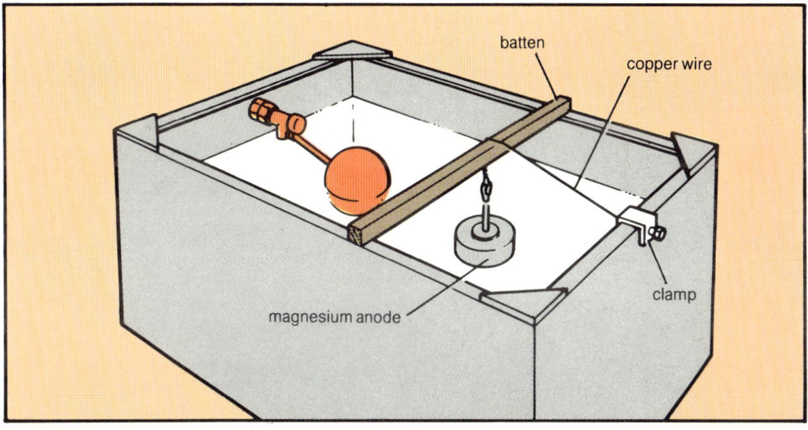

FROST PROTECTION

Modern means of heat conservation may make the plumbing installations in the roof space more vulnerable to frost. Insulating above the bedroom ceilings with fibreglass blanket or vermiculite loose-fill (see page 130) will prevent the roof space receiving heat lost from the rooms below. This may have protected the plumbing in the past.

Pipe-runs in the roof space should be kept well away from the eaves and should be as short as possible. They should be thoroughly lagged and care should be taken to extend the lagging round the bodies of ball-valves and gate valves. Only the handles of gate valves should protrude from the lagging.

The cold-water storage cistern should be provided with a dust-proof cover and the walls, but not the base, should be lagged with fibreglass or expanded polystyrene tank-lagging units.

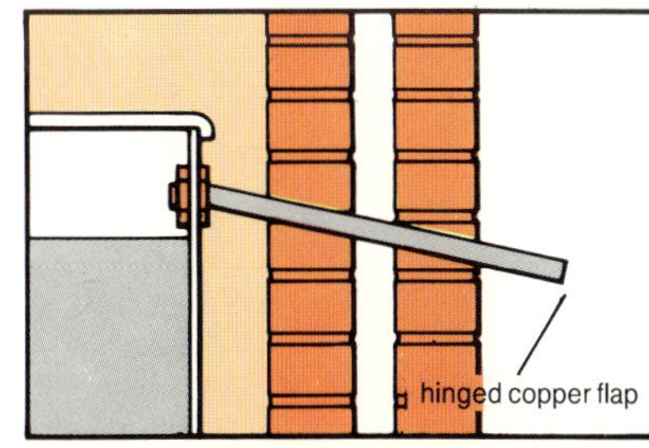

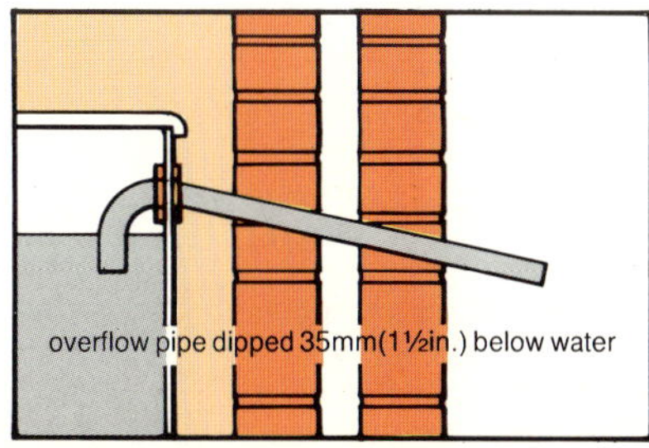

THE TRICK

Omitting lagging from the base of the tank and leaving the small area of ceiling immediately beneath the tank uninsulated will mean that some warmth will penetrate upwards from the room below.

It used to be the practice to fit a hinged copper flap on the outlet of the cold-water storage cistern's overflow or warning pipe to prevent cold draughts from blowing up it into the roof space. The modern method of protection is to turn the overflow pipe over inside the cistern so that it dips 25–30mm (1–1¼in.) below the surface of the water. The water thus provides a trap that prevents draughts from blowing up the pipe. Plastic gadgets are available for screwing onto the inlet of an existing overflow pipe to provide this protection.

HOT-WATER STORAGE TANKS

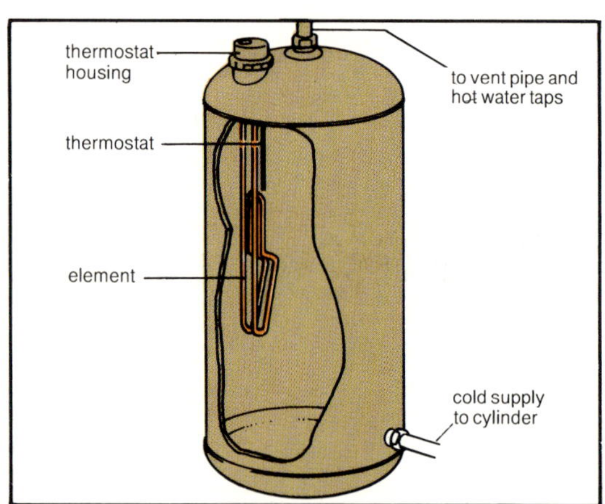

The essential feature of a cylinder storage hot-water system is a closed hot-water container, usually – but not necessarily – a copper cylinder, which is supplied with cold water from an open storage cistern at a higher level. The distribution pipe that takes the cold water from the storage cistern to the cylinder should be at least 22mm (¾in.) in diameter and should connect to the cylinder 25–30mm (1–1¼in.) above its base.

A vent pipe, sometimes incorrectly called an 'expansion' pipe, rises from the apex of the cylinder and is taken upwards to terminate open-ended over the cold-water storage cistern. It is from this vent pipe, above the level of the storage cylinder, that the hot-water distribution pipes are taken to the kitchen and bathroom hot taps.

The water in the storage cylinder may be heated solely by means of a thermostatically controlled electric immersion-heater, or solely by means of a solid-fuel, gas or oil-fired boiler. Commonly, a combination of the two methods is used.

ANODIC PROTECTION

Galvanized-steel tanks are also liable to attack from corrosion and they cannot be protected by internal painting in the same way as a cold-water storage cistern. Such a tank can, however, be afforded anodic protection. Anodes provided for hot-water tanks normally consist of a lump of magnesium mounted on the end of a metal rod.

To install, tie up the ball-valve of the cold-water storage cistern and drain the hot-water system from the taps and from the drain cock beside the boiler (see page 102). When the system has been completely drained, undo the bolts that secure the hand-hole cover and remove this cover. Drill a 6mm (¼in.) diameter hole in the middle of the cover and screw on the metal rod so that, when the cover is replaced, the magnesium anode will project into the centre of the tank.

When a new galvanized-steel tank is installed, make sure that every trace of metal dust or shaving, resulting from cutting holes for the tappings, is removed before the tank is filled with water.

THE TRICK

A magnet will help with this, or you can wipe the entire interior surface with a piece of dough. Any trace of metal dust or shaving left in the tank will become a focus of corrosion and will lead to the rapid failure of the tank.

If you have a galvanized-steel hot-water tank of this kind, the pipes connected to it will be either of galvanized mild steel or of lead. Never replace or extend them with copper tubing. To do so will invite electrolytic corrosion. Heavy galvanized-steel tubing is not really suitable for d-i-y use but, if you need to extend such a system, you can safely use stainless-steel tubing.

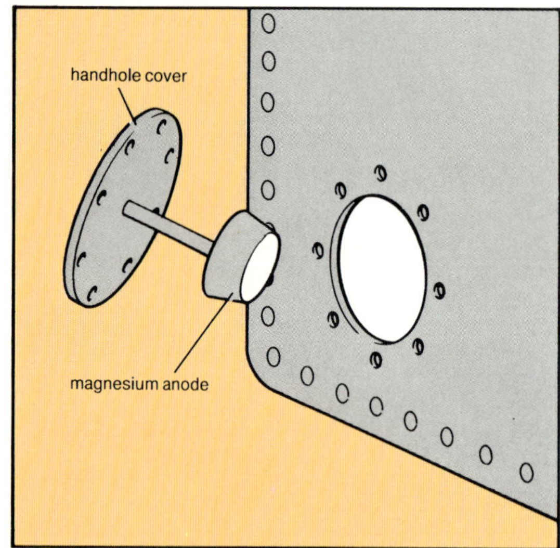

PLUMBING IN AN IMMERSION-HEATER

An immersion heater is a good auxiliary way of providing hot water when the weather is too warm to light the boiler, or the central heating is out of action. The plumbing is quite simple: a hole must be cut in the tank, a flange fixed into the hole, and the heater itself threaded into the flange.

There can be difficulties, however, if your home has a radiator system of central heating, in which case your hot cylinder will be the indirect type (see page 124). If you have an indirect heater it is best to ask the manufacturers for advice, or even leave things to a plumber.

Begin the installation by draining the cylinder via a drain cock, which you will find somewhere near the bottom of the cylinder or perhaps on the pipework near the boiler (see page 102). You cannot drain the cylinder by turning on a hot tap because the draw-off point is at the top of the cylinder. For a top-fitted heater only a small amount of water need be drained off, but for a side-mounted one the tank must be practically empty. If it does not exist, a drain cock should be provided on the cold-water supply pipe just before this reaches the cylinder.

CUTTING THE HOLE

Some cylinders nowadays come with a hole already cut and covered up by a blanking-off boss. Unscrew the boss, and you will find a flange fitted beneath it ready to take the heater.

However, if you need to make the hole yourself the ideal tool is a tank cutter, which you fit to a carpenter's brace. Few do-it-yourselfers, however, own a tank cutter, and they are too expensive to buy for just one job, so try to hire one.

THE TRICK

Alternatively, cut the hole with a padsaw-type hacksaw. Make a template of the flange (some come with one supplied), place it on the tank, and draw round it with a pencil. Drill a starting hole for the saw-blade, then cut out the circle.

THE TRICK

Another method is to drill a series of holes all round the circle, just inside the line. Push in the metal, and smooth off with a file.

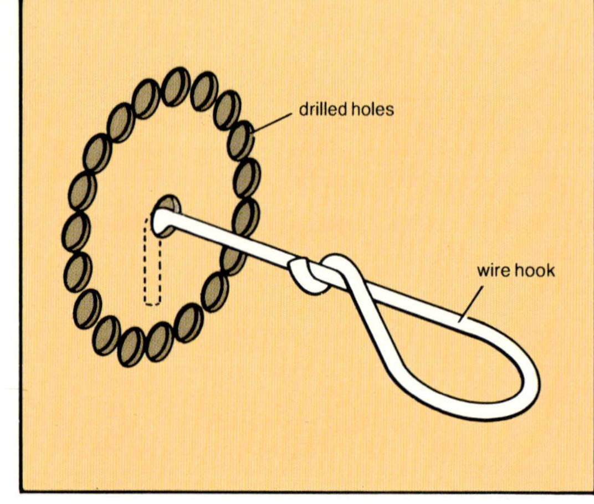

FIXING THE FLANGE

The easiest type of flange to fit is a solderless one. You place it inside the tank and fix it by tightening up an outer ring using either a ring spanner, or a wrench. To make the fixing watertight, there is an inner and an outer washer.

THE TRICK

One problem is the possibility of dropping part of the flange inside the tank: you will never get it out again once you do so. Tie a length of string to the flange, anchoring the free end on a nearby pipe or airing cupboard shelf, just in case.

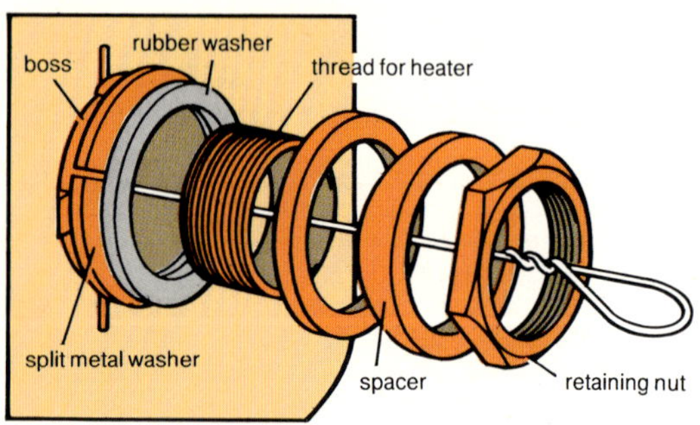

With the flange in place, take hold of the heater, remove the cap that covers the terminals – it is usually held in place by a small screw – and screw the heater into the threaded hole of the flange.

If your hot-water tank is the galvanized, rectangular kind, lift off the inspection cover, and examine it carefully. If you see any signs of corrosion (see page 113), you need a new tank. There will probably be sediment in the bottom of the tank, which you should scoop up first. Choose a site for the heater that will avoid any pipes inside the tank, and fit your flange. This will be easier than with the cylinder type of tank, because you can put your hands at the back of it. See page 95 for the electrical wiring details.

BOILERS

A 28mm (1in.) flow-pipe runs from the upper tapping of the boiler to a tapping about one quarter of the distance from the top of the hot-water cylinder. A return-pipe connects the lower (return) tapping to the return tapping of the boiler.

When the boiler fire is alight there is a constant circulation of lighter, heated water from the boiler and heavier, cooler water from the lower part of the storage cylinder. Hot water, because it is lighter than cold, rises to the top of the cylinder. It is thus always available.

It is impossible to drain the cylinder and boiler from the hot-water taps, so a drain cock must be provided. In a boiler, this should be fitted to the lowest part of the return-pipe from cylinder to boiler.

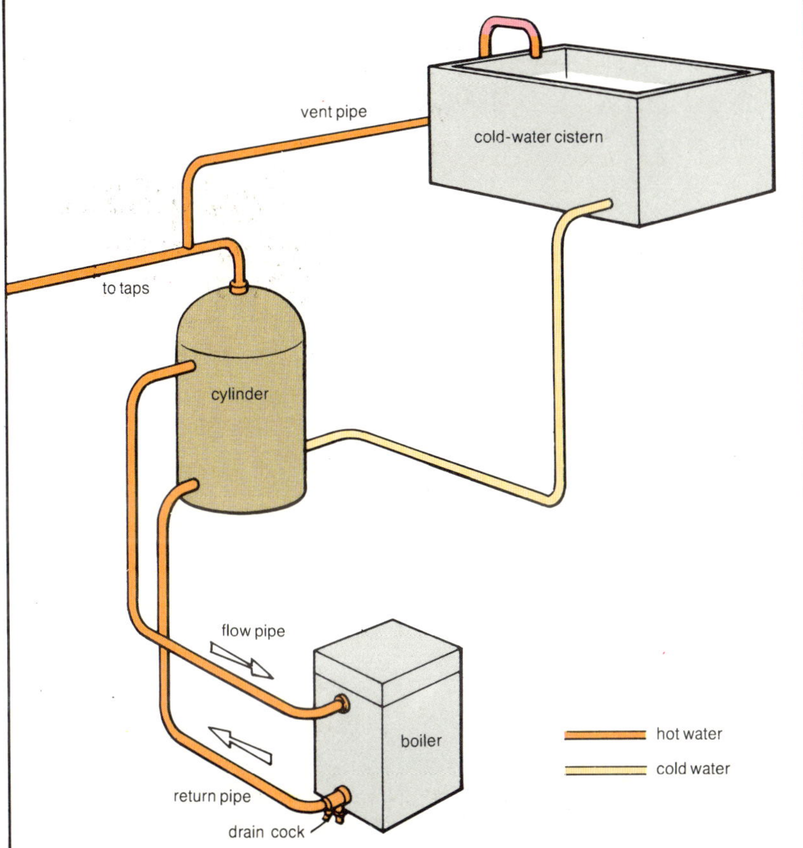

BOILERS WITHOUT DRAIN COCKS

It sometimes happens that, to cut costs, the drain cock is omitted from a cylinder hot-water system. How, in such a case, can the system be drained? It cannot be done without creating some mess but this can be cut to a minimum.

Tie up the ball-valve of the cold-water cistern and drain the hot- and cold-water supply pipes (see page 102). Undo the large nut that connects the vent pipe to the dome of the cylinder. Have a bowl and cloth handy as you do, as some water will be spilled.

Next siphon out the storage cylinder: fill a garden hose with water and arrange for someone to squeeze one end tightly closed over a yard gully, while you thrust the other end deep into the cylinder via the tapping at the apex of the cylinder dome. Release the yard end and water will flow from the cylinder until it is empty.

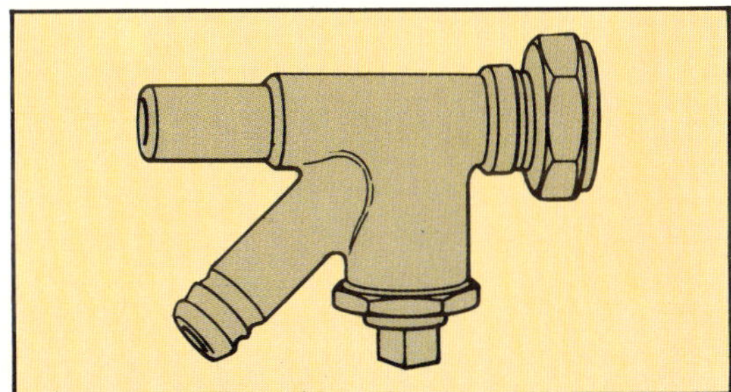

THE TRICK

The hose should not fit too tightly into the tapping. If it does, air will be unable to enter to replace water siphoned off; a partial vacuum will be created and the copper cylinder will collapse.

To drain the flow- and return-pipes and the boiler itself you must undo one of the couplings on the return-pipe. Have a bowl or bucket handy, although unless these pipes are unusually long there will be only a few pints of water to flow away.

Draining a hot-water system in this way is certainly not a job that most people would wish to tackle more than once.

THE TRICK

Before refilling, cut the return-pipe from cylinder to boiler at its lowest point. Purchase a drain cock with compression junctions for connecting to 28mm (1in.) tubing and fit it into the return-pipe at this point (see page 102).

SCALE

The formation of hard-water scale or fur on the internal surfaces of boilers and on immersion-heater elements is a serious problem in many parts of the country. Areas affected are those with a 'hard' water supply.

Hardness is due to the presence of dissolved bicarbonates and sulphates of calcium and magnesium. When such water is heated to about 70°C (160°F) carbon dioxide is driven off and they are changed into insoluble carbonates which precipitate out as boiler-scale.

Boiler-scale insulates the water in the boiler from the heat of the fire. You notice that the water in the cylinder takes longer to warm up, so you pile on more fuel or increase the draught. More scale forms and eventually alarming sounds can be heard as overheated water is forced through ever-narrowing channels.

Boiler-scale also insulates the metal of the boiler from the cooling effect of the circulating water. Eventually the metal of the boiler will burn away and a leak will develop.

BOILER CORROSION

PREVENTION

It is obvious that everything possible should be done to prevent scale formation. Scale does not begin to form until the water temperature rises above 60°C (140°F).

THE TRICK

In hard water areas set the immersion-heater thermostat to this temperature.

If you have a boiler, you should endeavour to restrict the temperature of the circulating water to this level. (You are unlikely to be successful in controlling a solid-fuel boiler to this extent.)

A mains water-softener will reduce all water entering your home to zero hardness and will eliminate absolutely all risk of scale and other hard-water problems, however, mains water-softeners are rather expensive.

Certain phosphates of sodium and calcium (sold as 'Micromet') in the hot-water system will prevent scale formation. Micromet does not soften water, its action is to stabilize the chemicals that cause hardness so that they will remain in solution when the water is heated.

Micromet crystals are placed in a basket of plastic mesh suspended in the cold-water storage cistern 70–100mm (3–4in.) below the level of the ball-valve inlet. Minute quantities of the chemical are dispensed into the hot-water system. The crystals must be renewed at half-yearly intervals.

Rusty red water running from the hot taps – particularly after a large volume of water has been drawn off – could be the result of corrosion in the cold-water storage cistern or, in a galvanized-steel hot-water tank. If these are free from rust, then corrosion must be taking place in the boiler. This is serious, as a rusting boiler will eventually leak as surely as will a scaled-up boiler.

The remedy for corrosion in a boiler is to convert the system to 'indirect' hot-water supply (see page 124).

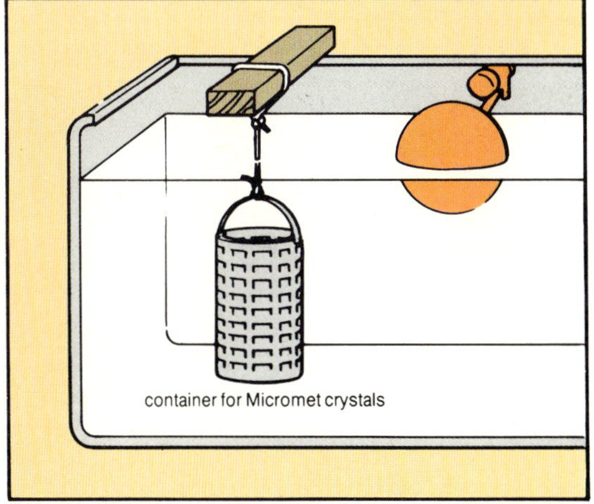

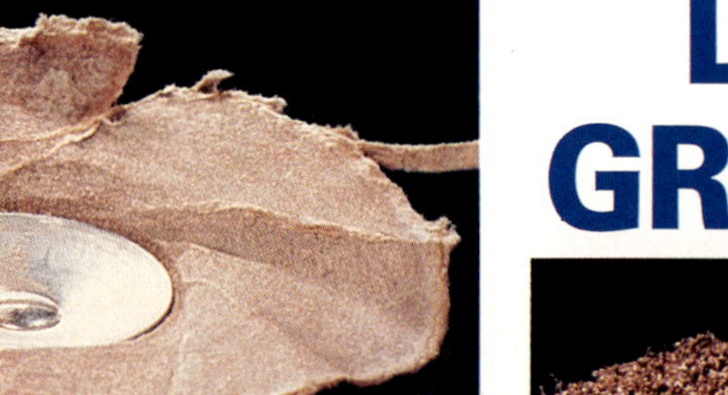

THE DISC IS DEAD

LONG LIVE GRIP 'N' SAND

GRIP 'N' SAND

Gives up to 50 TIMES longer life than standard sanding discs!

* Replacement Discs available
* GRIP 'N' SAND is best used at a slight angle
* For fine finish use light pressure — for heavier sanding increase pressure
* GRIP 'N' SAND will fit any electric drill
* To clean — remove disc, knock dust free or hold disc under running water
  Oil based paints and varnishes can be removed with thinners

No more:— Locking screws, torn or creased discs, damaged work pieces.
Simply press disc to pad. Re-usable, easy to clean.

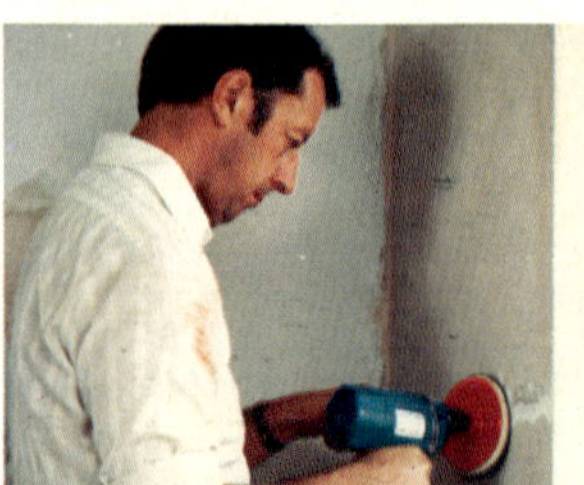

GRIP 'N' SHINE — an easy to use polishing system for use on the car, wooden and leather furniture and floors. The Polishing Bonnet is a mixture of pure wool and synthetic material to prevent burning which often occurs in bonnets of 100% synthetic material.

GRIP 'N' SAND and GRIP 'N' SHINE are available from DIY stores or by contacting:

Tex Abrasives p.l.c., Hermes Works, Greenstead Road, Colchester, Essex, CO1 2SR. Tel. (0206) 867181

PIPES

AIR LOCKS

A common failing of cylinder hot-water systems is the presence of air locks. These may occur when the system has been drained and refilled, or they may recur regularly during normal use. The symptoms are a poor flow, accompanied by bubbling and spluttering from one or more of the hot-water taps. It usually is not too difficult to clear an air lock.

THE TRICK

Connect one end of a length of garden hose to the nozzle of the cold tap over the kitchen sink and the other end to the hot tap giving trouble. Turn both taps on full.

The cold tap over the kitchen sink is connected direct to the rising main and the mains pressure will blow the air bubble out of the system.

If the trouble recurs, you should look for the explanation. A common cause is a pipe of too small a diameter feeding the hot-water storage cylinder. This pipe should be at least 22mm (¾in.) if it is to replace hot water drawn off from the hot tap over the bath.

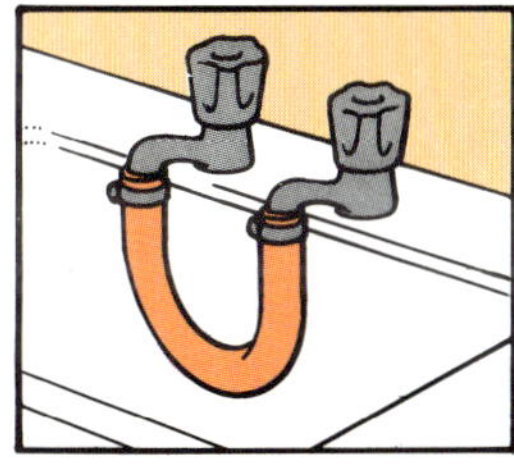

If it is smaller the water level will fall in the vent pipe when the bath taps are turned fully on. Eventually the level will reach the horizontal run of pipe supplying hot water to the bathroom. Air will enter this length of pipe and an air lock will develop.

Other possible causes are too small a cold-water storage cistern or a sluggish ball-valve.

THE TRICK

To check on this, climb up into the roof space and watch the cold-water storage cistern while someone is running off water for a bath. If the cistern empties before enough water has been drawn off for the bath, then this will be the cause.

Either the ball-valve needs to be overhauled or renewed, or a larger storage cistern is required.

FROST DAMAGE

When water freezes and turns to ice, it expands and increases its volume by something like 10 per cent. Hence the frozen and burst pipes that accompany any prolonged period of severe frost.

Such periods of severe frost are relatively rare in the British Isles. Because of this we have, in the past, tended to regard frost precautions fairly casually. It has been the need for energy conservation, rather than anxiety about frozen pipes, that has made us take insulation seriously in recent years.

Frost precautions should really be incorporated into the design of the house and its plumbing system. Intelligent design is more effective than the most thorough lagging.

Frost rarely penetrates more than 300mm (1ft) or so beneath the soil in this country, so the 'service pipe', which brings water from the Water Authority's main to the house (see page 100), should be at least 800mm (2ft 6in.) beneath the surface of the soil throughout its length.

Inside the house this pipe is usually referred to as the 'rising main'. A branch will be taken off it to supply the cold tap over the kitchen sink and it will then rise, by the most direct route, to supply the cold-water storage cistern in the roof space.

It used to be considered very important that this pipe should rise against an internal wall of the house. Cavity-wall infilling and other means of thermal insulation have made this less important in modern dwellings than it was in the past. If you live in an older house and the rising main rises against an exposed external wall, lag it thoroughly with fibreglass pipewrap, or with foam plastic or expanded polystyrene pipe-lagging units.

THE TRICK

Make sure that the lagging extends behind the pipe. It is from this direction – from the cold wall – that the danger will come (see page 142).

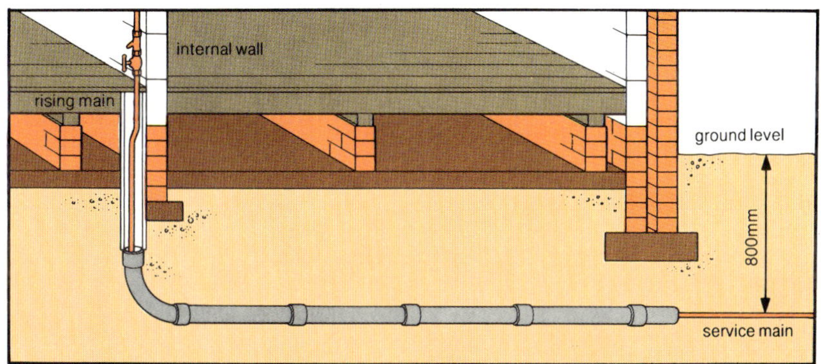

WINTER HOLIDAYS

If you leave your home empty for more than a few days during a time when frosts are expected, the plumbing system must be protected. Not even the most efficient lagging will afford more than a day or two's protection from severe frost.

If you have a reliable automatic central-heating system leave this on under the control of a 'frost-stat' – a thermostat that will switch the heating on when the temperature drops to a predetermined level.

If you have no central-heating system and a direct cylinder hot-water system, the entire system should be drained before you leave home. Turn off the main stopcock, open up all the taps and drain the hot-water system from the drain cock beside the boiler or, if the cylinder is heated by electricity only, from the drain cock at the base of the cylinder's cold-water supply pipe. Leave a large notice by the boiler and the immersion-heater switch: 'SYSTEM DRAINED – DO NOT LIGHT OR SWITCH ON UNTIL REFILLED.'

THE TRICK

Incidentally, when refilling the system on your return it is a good idea to connect one end of a length of hose to the cold tap over the kitchen sink and the other end to the drain cock of the hot-water system Open the tap and the drain cock and the system will fill upwards, pushing air in front of the rising water. This will reduce the risk of air locks forming.

The primary circuit of an indirect hot-water system and any central-heating circuit should not be drained. To leave a system of this kind empty is to invite corrosion (see page 124).

Manufacturers of corrosion-inhibitors make anti-freeze solutions that can be added to enclosed primary and radiator circuits to protect them from frost. Automobile anti-freeze should not be used.

For emergency work on pipes, see page 101.

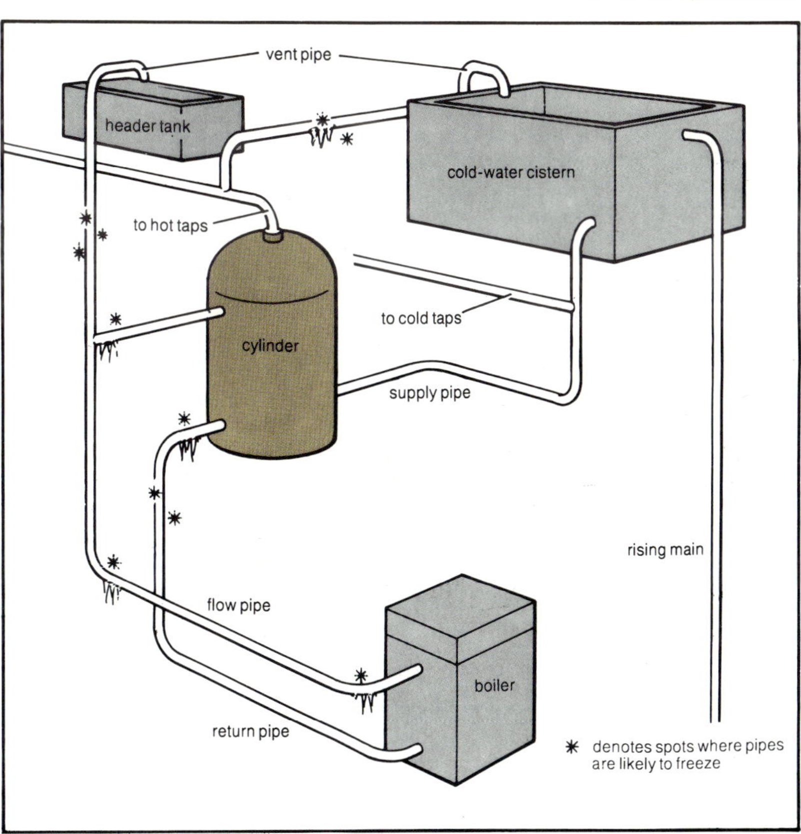

HANDLING PIPING 1

COPPER TUBING

The almost universal use of light-gauge copper tubing in post-war plumbing installations has done most to bring domestic plumbing within the scope of the home handyman.

Half-hard temper copper tubing, as used for domestic water supply and distribution, is available in a variety of sizes but those most likely to be required for d-i-y work are 15mm, 22mm and 28mm. (These are the metric equivalents of ½in., ¾in. and 1in. diameter tubing.) The discrepancy between, for instance, 15mm and ½in. is because the metric measurement is of the external diameter of the tubing. The old Imperial measurement was of the internal diameter.

To join lengths of copper tubing and to connect this tubing to taps, stopcocks and ball-valves, the home plumber may use either non-manipulative (Type 'A') compression fittings or soldered capillary joints and fittings. Compression fittings are more expensive but can be used with confidence by the complete novice.

COMPRESSION FITTINGS

A compression coupling, used for joining two lengths of copper tubing, has a joint body with, at each end, a soft copper ring or olive and a cap nut. Make sure, with a file, that the tube ends have been cut squarely and that all 'burr' resulting from cutting has been removed. Unscrew the cap nut from one end of the joint and slip it, followed by the olive, over one of the tube ends.

THE TRICK

Smear the olive and the tube end liberally with boss white or some similar jointing material.

Push the tube end into the body of the joint as far as the tube stop. Now push the olive and the cap nut up to the joint body. Screw on the cap nut hand-tight. Repeat this process with the other length of tubing and the other end of the coupling.

Finally, use two wrenches or two spanners of appropriate size, to tighten up the two cap nuts. This will compress the soft copper olive against the pipe wall to make a watertight joint.

Most manufacturers insist that with their compression joints a jointing agent is not needed. However, you will find that all professional plumbers use it. It will take up any unevenness in the tube end and ensure a watertight joint at the first attempt.

After a little practice you will probably find that there is no need to remove the cap nut and olive and put them separately over the tube end. You will be able to loosen them and then push the tube end home through them. In the early stages, however, it is wise to make the joint as suggested.

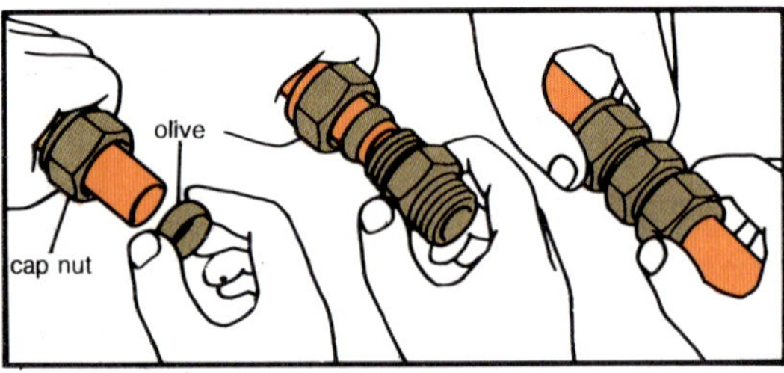

There is a wide range of compression joints and fittings available. There are 'tee' junctions for connecting branches to existing pipework, reducing fittings for connecting small-diameter pipes to larger ones, a variety of bends, and fittings for connecting copper tubing to the threaded tails of taps and ball-valves.

If – as is quite likely – you need to connect new metric-sized tubing to existing imperial pipework you will find that 15mm and 28mm fittings can be used, without adaptation, with ½in. and 1in. diameter tube. Adaptors are necessary for connecting 22mm tubing to old ¾in. pipes but these are readily obtainable.

At some stage you will undoubtedly need to cut a piece of copper tubing to length. This can easily be done with a hacksaw. Square off the end and remove any 'burr' with a file afterwards. For a big job, a tube cutter which incorporates a reamer for the removal of burr, is a worthwhile investment. It will ensure a square tube end.

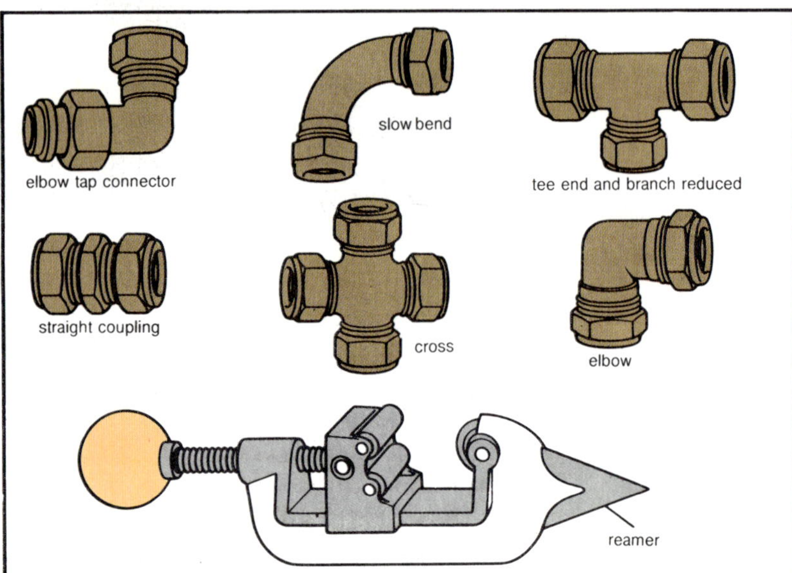

SOLDERED CAPILLARY FITTINGS

Solder capillary fittings are available in two forms; 'integral-ring' and 'end-feed'. Integral-ring fittings incorporate, within a built-in groove, sufficient solder to complete the joint. A separate roll of solder wire is necessary to make an end-feed joint.

Preparation of the pipe ends is as for a compression fitting Clean these ends, and the bore of the joint, with wire wool and smear an approved flux over the tube ends and round the inside of the joint. Thrust the tube ends into the joint as far as the tube stops. Then, with the joint firmly supported, apply the flame of a blow torch, first to the tube in the vicinity of the fitting and then to the fitting itself.

With an integral-ring fitting, the solder in the ring will melt and will flow, by capillary action, into the narrow space between the wall of the tube and the inside of the joint.

With an end-feed fitting, solder-wire must be held at the mouth of the fitting as it is heated. This too will flow into the narrow space between tube and fitting to complete the joint.

In both cases the joint is complete when a bright ring of solder appears all round the mouth of the fitting. Once made, the joint should be left undisturbed until cool enough to touch. Where – as with a coupling or a tee junction – two or more joints are to be made, these should all be made at the same time.

An exact fit is more important with capillary fittings than with compression ones. 15mm, 22mm and 28mm fittings cannot be used with ½in., ¾in. and 1in. Imperial tubes. However, adaptors can be obtained for this purpose.

Although a variety of compression and capillary bends are available it is possible – and much cheaper – to make easy bends in 15mm and 22mm copper tubing by hand, using a bending spring of the correct size to prevent the walls of the tube collapsing as you do so.

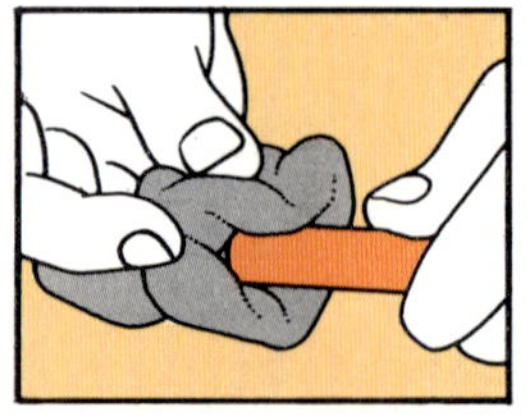

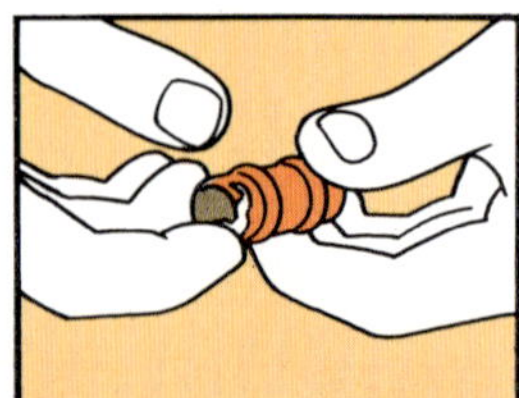

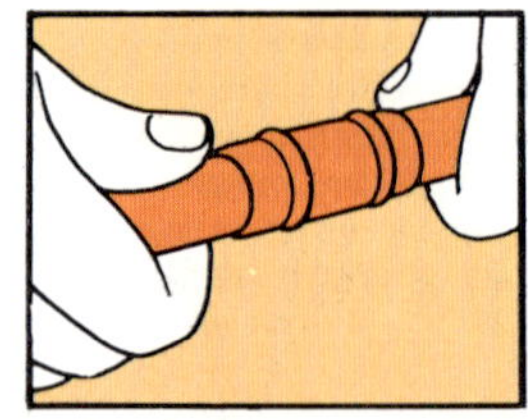

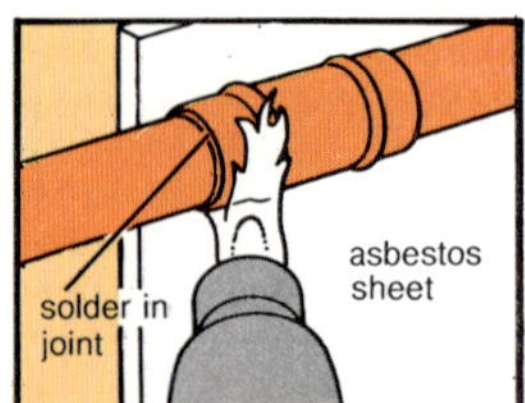

THE TRICK

Grease the spring thoroughly to facilitate removal and insert into the tube to the point at which the bend is to be made. Bend over the knee, overbending at first by a few degrees and then bringing back to the required shape. To withdraw the spring, insert a bar through the loop at the end. Twist to reduce the spring's diameter – and pull. Never attempt to tap or 'dress' the tube until the spring has been withdrawn. If you do you may find that the spring is immoveable.

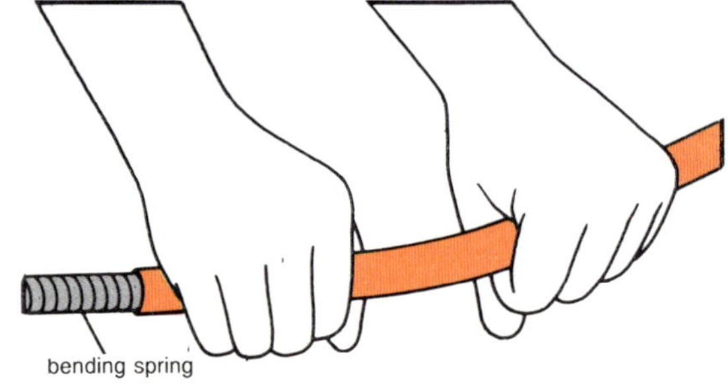

HANDLING PIPING 2

PVC TUBING

PVC tubing has been used increasingly domestically in recent years. It is useful for branch waste-pipes from baths, sinks and washbasins, but can also be used for main soil- and waste-pipes, roof drainage, underground drains, overflow pipes, hot- and cold-water supply, and central heating circulating pipes. It is relatively cheap, light, easily handled and completely free from risk of corrosion.

When ordering, it is probably safest to ask for PVC tubing for sink, bath or basin waste or for overflow pipe as many stockists still use the familiar Imperial sizes. It may be referred to by either its internal or its external metric dimension. PVC tubing is easily cut with a hacksaw.

PVC tubing can be joined by compression joints, by solvent-welding or by ring-seal joints. Solvent-welding must always be used for cold-water supply pipes but compression fittings useful for a short length of waste or overflow pipe. Ring-seal joints must always be used on main soil- and waste-pipes and in underground-drainage systems because they can expand when warm wastes run through them.

Compression joints resemble copper tubing (see page 118) except that a rubber sealing-ring is used instead of a copper olive. Loosen the cap nut, slip the pipe end in as far as the tube stop, and tighten up the cap nut again.

Solvent-welding PVC

tubing is the equivalent of using soldered capillary joints. Before beginning, check whether any printed instructions issued with the fittings vary slightly from what follows.

Cut the tube end squarely and remove all swarf and burr with a file. Insert the tube into the socket and mark the depth with a pencil.

THE TRICK

Roughen the pipe end and the interior surfaces of the socket with fine abrasive paper. (Steel wool will merely polish the surfaces.)

Degrease the roughened surfaces, using clean absorbent paper and a cleaning fluid approved by the manufacturers. With a brush, apply an even coat of solvent cement to the pipe end and the inside of the fitting. Use lengthwise strokes, applying a slightly thicker coat to the tube end than to the socket surfaces.

Immediately insert the tube and hold in position for about 15 seconds. You may then remove surplus cement but you should not otherwise disturb the joint for about five minutes. The pipe should not be brought into use for at least 24 hours.

PLUMBING IN AN AUTOMATIC WASHING-MACHINE

An automatic washing-machine needs hot and cold water – so two supply pipes have to be tapped. Provision must also be made for drainage. The simplest solution is to hook the outlet hose over the kitchen sink. Where it cannot be done, a stand-pipe outlet will get rid of the waste water.

Assuming you have the usual 15mm (½in.) copper rising main and a similar hot-water pipe supplying the kitchen sink; for the cold-water connection, turn off the main stopcock, drain the rising main and insert a 15mm (½in.) compression tee at a convenient height.

Drain the hot-water pipe as well. Cut the hot-water pipe and insert a compression tee at the same level as the tee inserted in the rising main.

Insert lengths of 15mm (½in.) copper tubing into the tees' outlets. These should be sufficiently long to take the water supplies to within about 300mm (1ft) of the machine. Fit the other ends into the compression inlets of purpose-made washing-machine stopcocks. These have back plates for screwing to the kitchen wall and outlets designed for connection to a washing-machine hose.

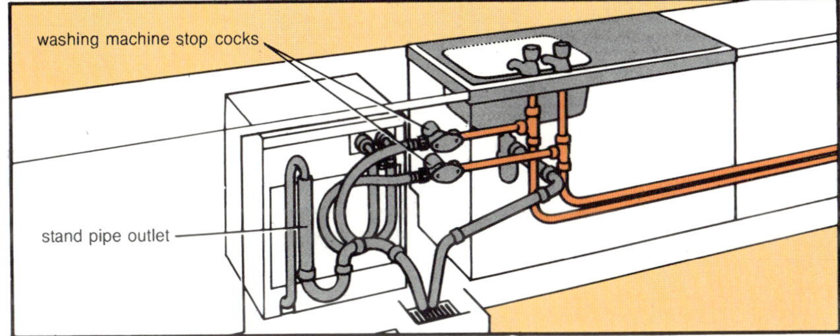

PROBLEMS

The hot and cold supply pipes to the kitchen sink probably run closely parallel to each other. This means that the branch supply pipe from the further of these will have to be bent round the other main supply pipe.

There may be enough give in the nearer supply pipe to take the branch supply from the further one to the washing-machine without bending it. In any event two easy bends can be made in the branch pipe without too much difficulty (see page 118).

However, the washing-machine hoses can be connected direct to the main hot and cold supply pipes.

'KONTITE THRU-WAY VALVES'

Kay & Co. Ltd, of Bolton, manufacture the 'Kontite thru-way valve'. These can be fitted into kitchen hot and cold supply pipes and connected directly to the hoses of the washing-machine.

The thru-way valve has been designed to make fitting particularly easy. It has Kontite compression joints at each end but one has not been provided with a tube stop. This means that the valve can be slipped into position without having to 'spring' the cut ends of the supply pipe.

You must, of course, cut off the water supply and drain the pipes before fitting this valve. Cut a 28mm (1⅛in.) segment out of the supply pipe at the point the valve is to be fitted.

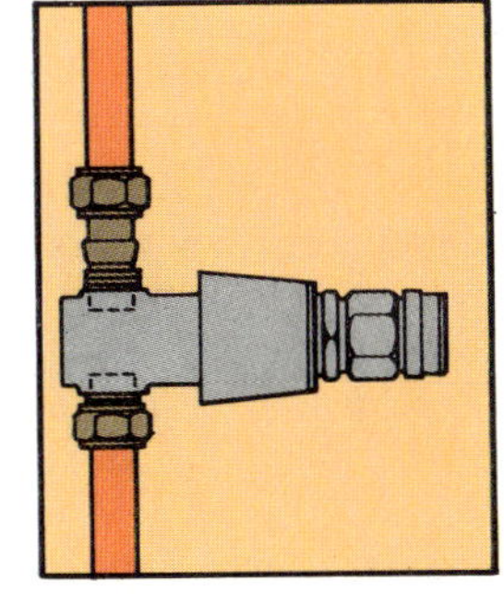

OPELLA HOSE-CONNECTORS

Opella plastic hose-connectors can be fitted without cutting the supply pipes, although they must be drained before you begin.

Prepare the section of the supply pipe by removing any paint and rubbing down with fine abrasive paper. Carefully drill a 8mm (5/16in.) hole in the centre of the front of the pipe.

THE TRICK

You will find that your drill is inclined to slip, so make a 'pilot dent' by tapping a nail onto the tube.

Make sure that the hole is central and do not let your drill bit go through the back of the pipe.

Position the back-plate of the hose-connector behind the hole. Make sure that the rubber seal is in position round the small pipe projecting from the front plate. Push this pipe into the hole and tighten up the screws that connect the front and back plates.

Drill the wall behind the back plate and secure with the wall plugs and screws provided. Bind PTFE thread sealing tape round the threaded tail of the tap body to ensure a watertight joint and screw into place. Its direction can be adjusted by removing one or more of the washers provided on the tap tail.

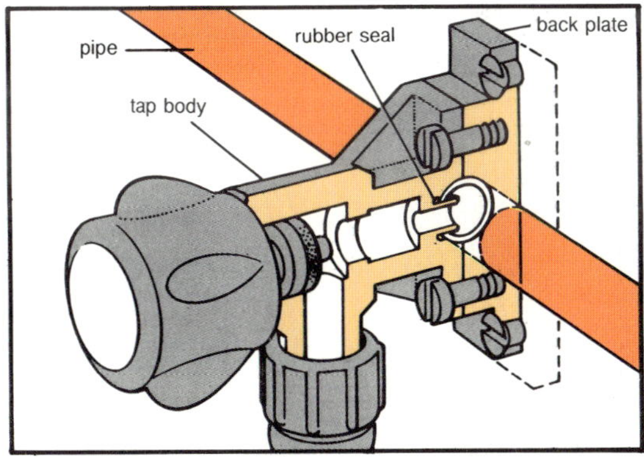

STAND-PIPE OUTLET

If you want a stand-pipe outlet, these are available from makers of PVC tube and fittings. It should be 600mm (2ft) long and have an internal diameter of at least 35mm (1⅓in.). This will allow the hose to hook in without giving an air-tight fit. The stand-pipe must be securely fixed to the wall by pipe clips.

Where the outlet is taken to a yard gully, a trap at its base is not absolutely essential. A trap must be provided where the waste has to be connected to a main soil- and waste-pipe.

Before making a connection to a soil- and waste-pipe, you should always consult the local Building Inspector.

BARTOL PLASTICS LIMITED

SINKS AND BASINS

SINKS

Deep, ceramic 'Belfast pattern' sinks with wooden draining-boards retained their popularity until well into the 1950s, so you are quite likely to encounter one. You will replace it with a modern sink unit having either a stainless-steel or enamelled-steel sink top with integral drainer. Unless price is an overriding consideration, stainless steel is better.

THE TRICK

To avoid unnecessary disruption, fit the taps, waste and trap to the new sink before removing the old one.

You may decide to fit individual pillar-taps or a mixer. If you decide on a mixer, be sure to specify a 'sink mixer' when ordering.

MIXERS

Bath and basin mixers are simply two taps with a common spout. Both hot- and cold-water supplies to the bathroom are under equal pressure. The kitchen hot-water supply comes, via the cylinder, from the cold-water cistern. The cold supply comes direct from the main.

It is illegal to mix water from the main and water from a storage cistern. Sink mixers are therefore made with two separate channels inside – one for hot water and one for cold. Mixing takes place after the water has left the nozzle.

Slip flat plastic washers over the tails of the taps or mixer, and insert these tails into the holes provided at the back of the sink. Looking underneath, you will see that the shanks of the tap tails protrude through. Slip 'top hat' or 'spacer' washers over the tails before you screw on and tighten up the back nuts.

TRAPS

Modern stainless-steel sinks are provided with combined wastes and overflows, the overflow outlet being connected to the waste by a flexible tube. The flange of the waste is usually bedded down into the waste-outlet hole of the sink on a bed of non-setting mastic, although a flat plastic washer is sometimes used.

The trap screws onto the threaded tail of the waste. Traps can be obtained in either brass or plastic.

THE TRICK

A trap with a telescopic inlet will connect the outlet to any existing branch waste-pipe which takes the sink waste to an outside gully.

REMOVING THE OLD SINK

Remove the draining-board and unscrew the large nut that secures the trap to the waste outlet. You may now be able to lift the sink off its cantilever brackets. However, you will probably have to chip away, with a cold chisel and hammer, a cement joint connecting the sink to the tiled wall behind. The sink is very heavy. Don't attempt to lift it and take it outside without help.

THE TRICK

Cut the cantilever brackets flush with the wall with a hacksaw rather than attempt to dig them out.

Unscrew and remove the old trap from the waste-pipe, unless you think you can use the old trap with the new sink.

Cut off the water supply to the two existing sink taps and drain the supply pipes to them (see page 102). Unscrew and remove the taps. Extricate the copper supply pipes from the plaster with a cold chisel and hammer, and pull them forward to supply the new taps.

INSTALLING THE NEW SINK

Measure carefully the distance from the floor to the tails of the taps when in the unit. Measure that distance up the water supply pipes and cut them off squarely. You will probably have to cut another 25mm (1in.) or so off, but better too long than too short.

Place the new sink unit in position. To connect the tap tails to the supply pipes you will need two 15mm (½in.) swivel-tap connectors (sometimes called 'cap and lining joints') with a compression inlet. Insert the 'lining' of the tap connector into the tail of each tap and screw up the cap nut. The lining is provided with a washer that will ensure a watertight joint without any other jointing material.

Measure the water supply pipes against the compression inlets of the tap connectors. Cut them as necessary and connect up the compression joints (see page 118). Restore the water supply and check for leaks.

If the water supply pipes are of lead, get a plumber to connect the tap connectors as wiped soldered joints will be necessary.

Screw the trap onto the waste outlet, connect this to the waste-pipe and make good the damage to the wall and tiling.

BASINS

Ceramic basins may be 'pedestal' or 'wall hung' Pedestal basins take up more room but can conceal the plumbing. Modern pedestal basins are always supplied with a concealed bracket. They should never be supported only by the plumbing and the pedestal.

Ceramic basins normally have a built-in overflow. A slotted waste connects this to the main waste outlet.

THE TRICK

When fitting it is important to make sure that the slot in the metal waste coincides with the outlet of the built-in overflow.

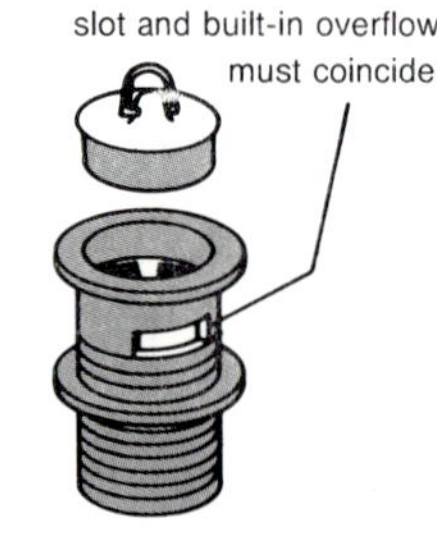

Plastic or chromium-plated brass bottle-traps, rather than simple U-traps (see page 111), are normally fitted to basin outlets. They take up less room and are neater. Either individual pillar-taps or a basin mixer may be fitted – provided that the bathroom cold supply is taken from a main storage cistern. Check on this before purchasing a conventional basin mixer.

As ceramic basins are made of relatively thick material, the shanks of the taps will not protrude when installed. A flat washer should be used between the basin and the back nut of the tap.

THE TRICK

When screwing up the back nuts, make sure that the taps are secure, but do not overtighten. Ceramic basins are easily broken.

Vanity units (enamelled pressed-steel basins set in a piece of bathroom or bedroom furniture), are plumbed in exactly the same way as sink units.

RENEWING TAPS

Renewing the washbasin taps can be more difficult than it appears, as the back nuts can be extremely difficult to undo. They are inaccessible and often become virtually welded in position. A cranked basin spanner will make it easier and penetrating oil will help to loosen them.

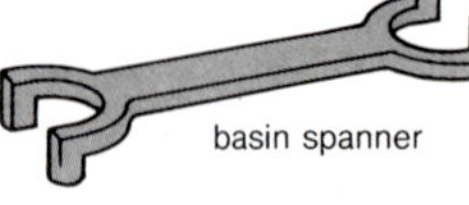

If you still cannot move them, do not risk damaging the basin. Disconnect the water supply and waste-pipes. Remove the basin and turn it upside down on the floor. You will now get a much better grip on the back nuts.

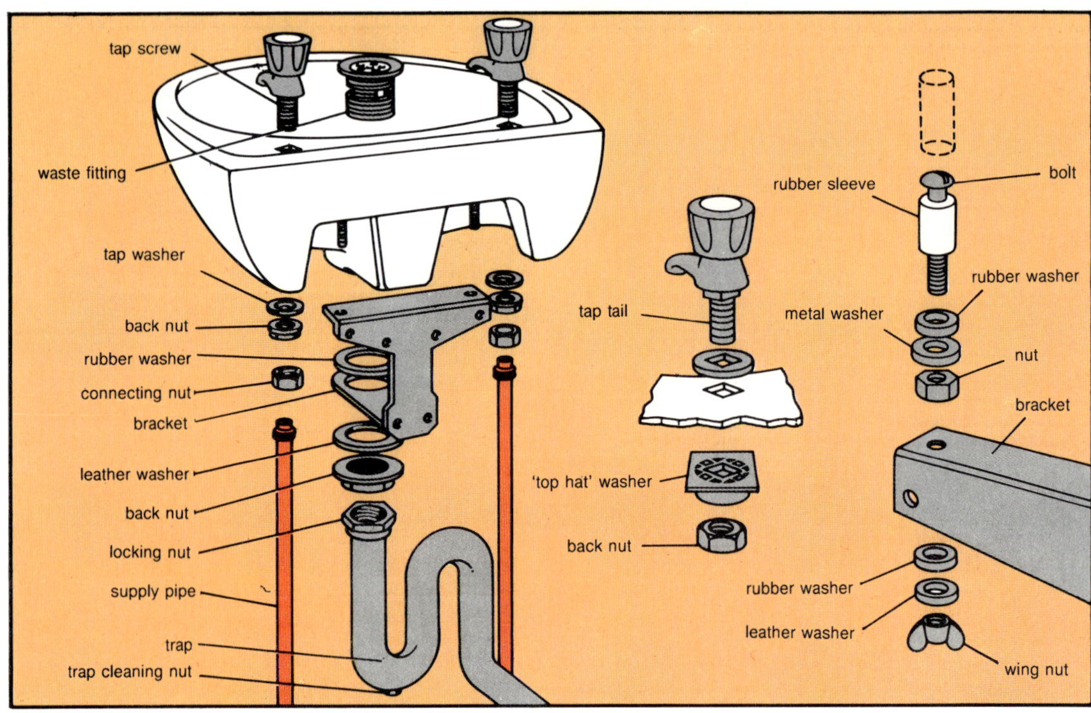

BATHS

WHICH TYPE?

Baths may be made of enamelled cast-iron, enamelled pressed-steel or acrylic plastic. Your existing bath will almost certainly be of enamelled cast-iron. These baths are strong and hard-wearing – but they are also very expensive, heavy and difficult to install. The thick material tends to conduct away the heat of the water.

Pressed-steel baths are cheaper and lighter but they are fairly easily damaged in storage and installation.

Probably the best would be a modern acrylic plastic bath. These are light, relatively cheap and, having good qualities of insulation, are economical and comfortable. They are tough and hard-wearing. The colour goes right through and any surface scratches can easily be polished out.

They are easily damaged by extreme heat. A lighted cigarette placed, even momentarily, on the bath rim can cause permanent damage. Exercise extreme care when using a blow torch in the vicinity of one of these baths.

INSTALLATION

An acrylic bath will be supplied complete with a wooden or metal frame or cradle, and complete instructions. This cannot be assembled until the old bath has been removed. However, to avoid prolonged disruption, it is a good idea to fit the taps and waste before removing the old bath.

Although individual bath taps may be preferred, bath mixers are extremely popular. Many incorporate a shower fitting. A flexible metal hose rises from the top of the mixer to terminate in a shower sprinkler intended for attachment to the bathroom wall. A control knob is provided to divert water from the mixer nozzle to the shower sprinkler when required. Bath taps and mixers are fitted in exactly the same way as sink taps and mixers (see page 122).

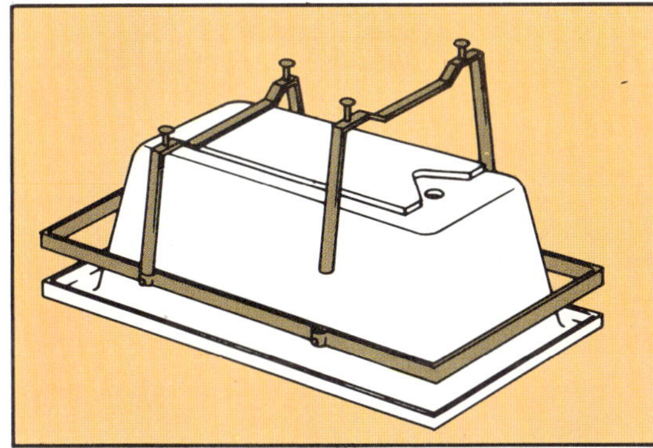

Modern baths have combined wastes and overflows, the overflow being connected to the bath trap by means of a flexible hose. Always use plastic traps and waste-pipes with acrylic baths. Rigid metal fittings could damage the plastic material when the bath fills with warm water and therma movement takes place.

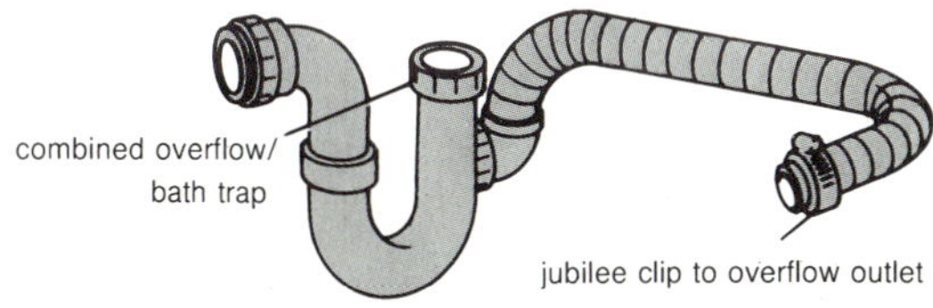

REMOVING THE OLD BATH

Having fitted up the new bath with its taps and waste outlet, you can proceed to the really difficult part of the job: removing the old bath. Strip off the bath panels and have a good look at the water supply, overflow and waste-pipes. They will be in dark, inaccessible and very confined space between the foot of the bath and the wall. Cut off the water supply and drain the pipes.

The bath overflow may be connected to the bath's trapped outlet. In an old installation the overflow pipe will probably be simply taken through the bathroom wall to discharge into the open air outside.

THE TRICK

If this is the case, the overflow pipe should be sawn across, flush with the wall, with a hacksaw.

Although the supply pipes will be inaccessible, it should not be too difficult to undo the cap nuts that connect the water supply pipes to the tails of the taps. Do not attempt to undo the back nuts securing the taps to the bath. Disconnect the bath trap from the waste-pipe leading outside.

THE TRICK

Before trying to remove the bath, lower it by means of the screw adjustment on each of the four feet. This will make it possible to move it without damaging the wall tiling.

The old bath will be very heavy indeed. Don't rush the job.

FITTING THE NEW BATH

Assemble the cradle or frame of the new bath, exactly in accordance with the manufacturer's instructions, and place in position. The cradle will prevent the bath from creaking or sagging when filled with hot water.

It may be that the water supply pipes will be in such a position that you can connect them by means of a compression and cap-and-lining connector, to the tails of the taps without too much adjustment. Don't forget that the old pipes will be 22mm (¾in.) Imperial size. You will need a conversion fitting (see page 118) to connect to a metric joint.

THE TRICK

If the pipes are too short, or are otherwise difficult to connect to the taps, Ucan 'copperbend' can prove very useful. This is obtainable in 400mm and 350mm (15¾ and 11¾in.) lengths with or without a swivel tap connector (cap-and-lining joint) at one end.

Cut your supply pipes to length, fit a length of copperbend with swivel tap connector to each supply pipe. The copperbend can easily be bent to reach the tap tails at exactly the right point.

THE TRICK

Make the connections in the right order: the further tap first, then the overflow and waste-pipe, and finally the nearer tap.

Do not fit the bath panel until you have restored the water supply and have checked for leaks.

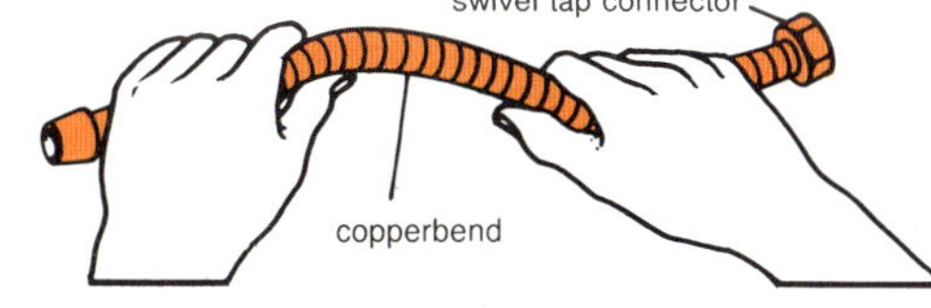

RE-ENAMELLING

If you have an old cast-iron bath, with enamel, this enamel may have been chipped. If so, you can repair it with bath enamel paint. A bath with baked-on enamel cannot be repaired thus. You will need about 285ml (10 fl.oz) of bath enamel for a normal-sized bath.

Start by removing the chain, etc from the waste-cover. Wash the bath down with hot water and detergent. Then rub the bath down, using wet-and-dry paper (see page 231) dipped in water, until the surface is completely smooth. Rinse away all debris and dry the bath off. Wipe the inside of the bath with white spirit to remove any trace of detergent, then dry again. It is very important that it should be completely dry before painting.

The paint should be applied with a medium flat varnish brush (see page 237) and as thinly and evenly as possible. Paint the bottom of the bath first, then the sides, using long cross-strokes to avoid runs, etc. Paint the rim last and leave to dry overnight.

Apply a second coat as above; then leave to dry for 48 hours. Replace the chain and fill the bath with cold water. Leave this in for 48 hours. It is advisable for the first week back in use, to run some cold water in before you run the hot.

THE TRICK

To prevent any water dripping into the bath from the taps, it is a good idea to hang empty jars under them. Make sure the jars do not touch the wet paint.

OTHER WATER HEATING SYSTEMS

INDIRECT HOT-WATER SYSTEMS

The most permanently effective way of eliminating boiler-scale is by installing an indirect hot-water system. With this system, the domestic hot water is heated indirectly by a heat exchanger or 'calorifier' within the cylinder. The flow- and return-pipes between boiler and cylinder are connected to this calorifier. This closed system, referred to as the 'primary circuit', is supplied with water from a small – say 23l. (5gal.) – 'feed and expansion tank' in the roof space.

An indirect system's immunity to hard-water scale is because the water in the primary circuit circulates repeatedly through the boiler and cylinder, and cannot be drawn off except when the whole system is drained. Only the very tiny losses of water due to evaporation are made up from the feed and expansion tank.

When the primary circuit is first filled and the boiler lit, a minute amount of scale is deposited on the boiler's internal surface. This will exhaust the scale-forming chemicals in the primary circuit. Therefore, as this water continues to circulate, no more scale will form. There may be some scale formation in the outer part of the hot-water cylinder, but this will be minimal. The cylinder water will become quite hot enough for all domestic purposes but will rarely reach the high temperatures at which boiler-scale is precipitated.

If central heating is to be combined with hot-water supply, an indirect hot-water system is essential. An indirect system is also recommended where the local water supply is hard or corrosive.

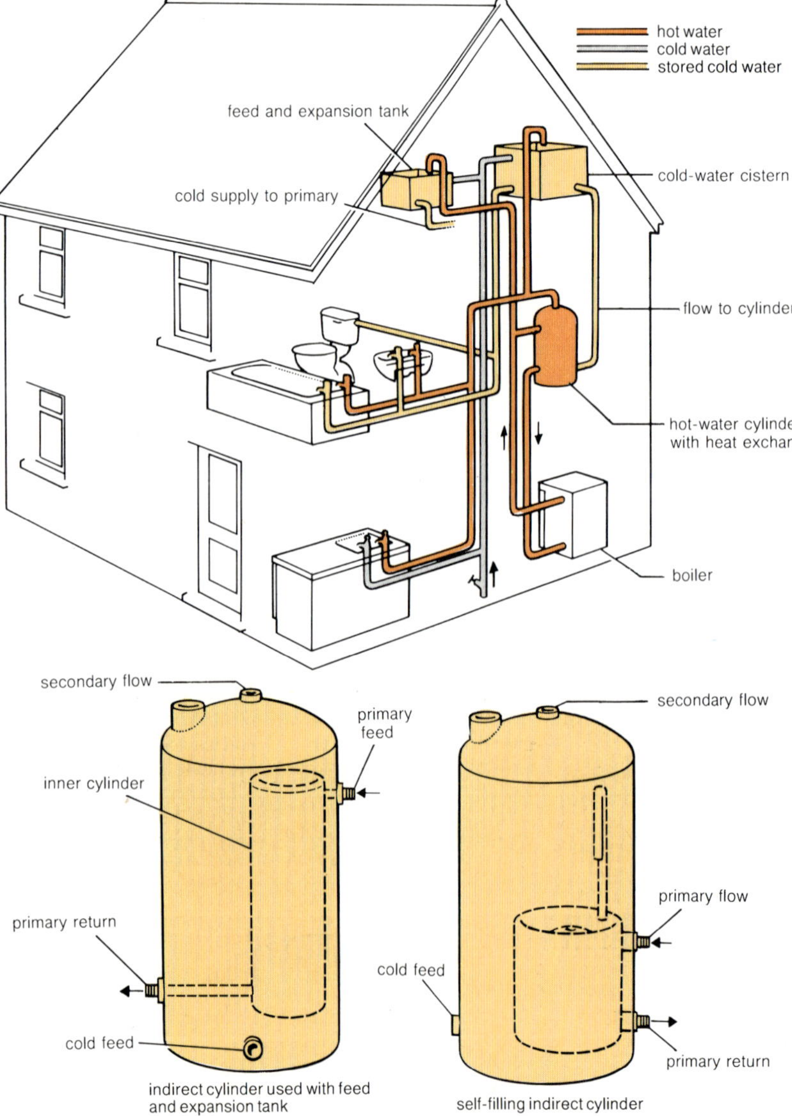

indirect cylinder used with feed and expansion tank

self-filling indirect cylinder

INSTANTANEOUS WATER-HEATERS

Gas multi-point instantaneous water-heaters provide an alternative whole-house hot-water system to the cylinder storage system. These are supplied with water direct from the rising main. Water is heated 'instantaneously' as it passes through a system of small-bore copper tubing within the appliance. Small, single-point heaters are also available.

Small, instantaneous electric water-heaters can be useful in supplying warm water for hand-washing to a lavatory compartment or for providing a shower.

Heaters of this kind give a lower rate of delivery than a cylinder storage hot-water system. They only heat the water that is actually used and can be economical in a house occupied for only a few hours each day. The maintenance of these appliances is not a d-i-y job.

SELF-PRIMING CYLINDERS

Patent 'self-priming' indirect cylinders do not have a separate feed and expansion tank. The heat exchanger consists of a specially-designed 'inner cylinder'. When the system is first filled with water from the main cold-water storage cistern, water overflows from this inner cylinder into the primary circuit. An air lock then forms in the inner cylinder to prevent water in the primary circuit returning to mix with the domestic hot water. The inner cylinder is also designed to allow for the expansion of the water in the primary circuit when it is heated.

Self-priming cylinders give a less positive separation of primary and domestic hot water than a conventional indirect system. However they do provide a simple and relatively cheap means of converting an existing direct-cylinder hot-water system to indirect operation.

CORROSION

Small-bore and microbore central-heating systems are based on an indirect cylinder storage hot-water-supply system. It used to be thought that such systems would be free of internal corrosion. This has not proved to be the case. Some air will always be present, it may enter through minute leaks or dissolve into the surface of the water in the feed and expansion tank.

The first symptom is that the radiators become cool at the top, and need venting more frequently.

THE TRICK

If your radiators need frequent venting, apply a lighted taper to the vent valve, if the escaping gas burns with a blue flame, it is hydrogen – a product of corrosion.

The other product of corrosion is a black iron-oxide sludge, called 'magnetite'. This obstructs circulation at the bottom of radiators and is drawn through the system to the magnetic field of the circulating pump. Its abrasive qualities often cause an early pump failure.

PREVENTION

Corrosion in central-heating systems can be prevented by the introduction of a chemical-corrosion inhibitor into the feed and expansion tank when it is first installed. To introduce an inhibitor into an existing system, it must first be thoroughly flushed out.

The boiler must be turned off or let out and drained (see page 115). Open up the drain cock but do not tie up the ball-valve of the feed and expansion tank. Allow water to flush the system through.

THE TRICK

With a padded mallet, tap the surfaces of all radiators – begin at those furthest from the boiler – to free adhering magnetite. Flush the system for at least 20 minutes after the water coming from the hose outlet appears to be clean.

Go to the feed and expansion tank and get a helper to stand by the boiler drain cock ready to turn it off. Hold up the float arm of the ball-valve to prevent water from coming into the tank. When empty, signal your helper to turn off the drain cock. Introduce the inhibitor into the tank and release the float arm to enable the system to top up.

Light the boiler and switch on the circulating pump for at least an hour to ensure that the inhibitor penetrates the system.

Note that, when the central-heating system is cold, there should be only 50–75mm (2–3in.) of water in the feed and expansion tank. The water in the primary circuit expands when heated and flows into this tank to rise above the level of the ball-valve float.

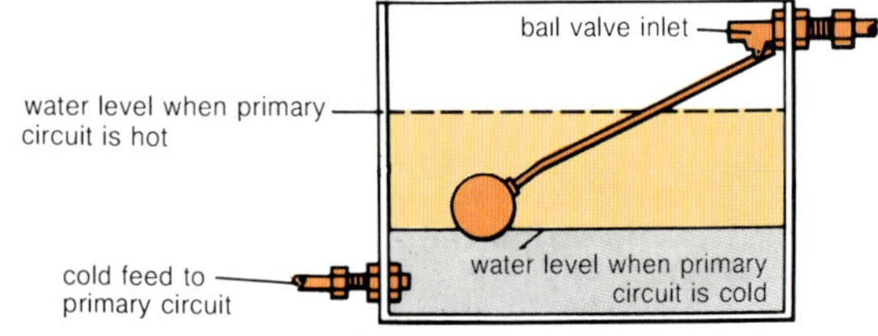

HEATING & INSULATION

INSULATION

In a straight choice, insulation has priority over heating. If you can afford only one of the two, it must be insulation. The better the insulation, the less need for a high standard of heating; ideal insulation would need no artificial heat at all, but that is beyond our reach. Insulation is for the most part not a particularly controversial subject, with the exception of double glazing (see page 134).

For almost twenty years, domestic central heating ruled alone as the answer to indoor chill, but now common sense has produced two good and permanent reasons why you should reconsider the way you achieve a satisfactory standard of indoor comfort. Cost is the obvious one; the other is the predicted exhaustion of those fossil fuels.

So prevention of heat loss from buildings has come to the fore. It is important to keep two things in mind:

1. Insulation is now more important than heating and demands priority in your thinking, your spending and your timetable; and
2. The more thorough your insulation the less important, and less costly to buy and run, is the heating.

Insulation has no running cost, and money spent on it is money saved forever; the key to a better standard of living lies here more than in all the rest. The first building (A) shows the average distribution of heat loss from a typical middle-aged semi-detached house not specially insulated. Note features such as the high heat loss from walls because of their large area, and the lesser loss from windows despite the ease with which heat passes through glass. The second building (B) shows the reduction in heat loss after proper treatment, through roof, walls, floor, windows and by draughts. If the amount lost before insulation is taken as 100 per cent, the total loss now comes to only 42 per cent. In other words you will have saved more than half the heat previously lost.

Do check with your local council before embarking on major works of insulation; you may be eligible for quite a substantial grant towards the cost. However, if the work is in hand when you apply, you will not receive anything. Mortgage companies are usually reasonably favourable towards a mortgage extension for such works, because it will increase the value of the property.

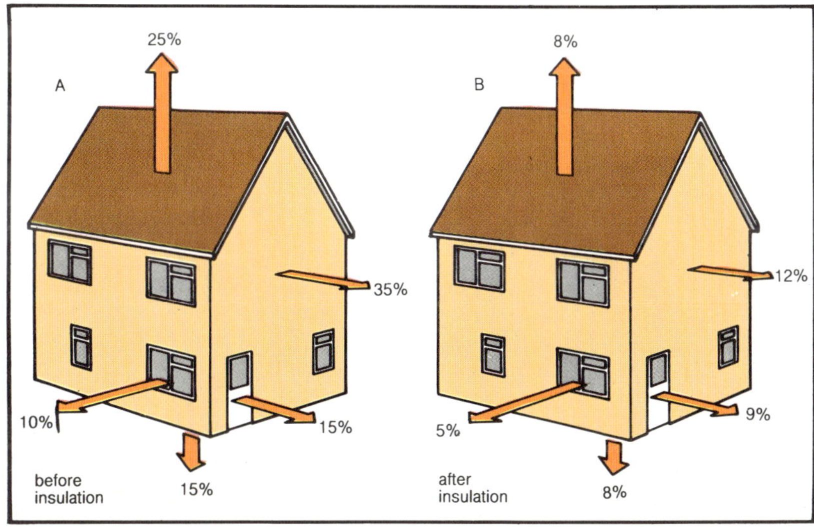

FURTHER INFORMATION

The following associations will be able to give you much more detailed information than is possible in this book.

Insulation Glazing Association (IGA)
6 Mount Row, London W1Y 6DY (01-629 8334). No IGA member will try to persuade you that double glazing will save 50 per cent of your fuel bills.

National Association of Loft Insulation Contractors (NALIC)
P.O. Box 12, Haslemere, Surrey GU27 3AN (0428 54011).

National Cavity Insulation Association (NCIA)
Same address.
This organization deals with cavity wall insulation by any approved method; the majority of members use foam injection. There are some reputable operators who do not belong to either of the two associations above but, unless you know one personally, use a firm which is a member.

Eurisol-UK
St Paul's House, Edison Road, Bromley, Kent BR2 0EP (466 6719).
Known also as the Association of British Manufacturers of Mineral Insulating Fibres, this organization will answer any questions to do with insulating using glass fibre or rock or mineral wool. Although the material is the same, they are not contractors and so do not overlap with NALIC (see above). Eurisol-UK are imaginative and forward-looking, and believe in insulating to the higher standards of tomorrow.

Gas or Electricity Showrooms
Get a brochure from your local showroom. It will show you the main points to insulate, their relative importance and broadly how to go about it.

The Building Centre
26 Store Street, London WC1E 7BT (01-637 1022).
One of a small number of building centres in major cities, any of them worth a visit. This one is the oldest and the best. It has a showroom, bookshop and information centre.

QUICK TRICKS

The following pages will give you a comprehensive idea of the recommended methods of improving your insulation, but you may want to try to do a few things quickly while waiting for your grant application to be processed or to save money for something like cavity wall insulation.

You are probably all too aware of where the worst draughts come from, but it is worth locating them accurately. Use a lighted candle, held 50–75mm (2–3in.) away from window frames, skirting, etc to locate them. Do be careful not to set fire to anything while doing this! If there are skirting draughts, there is a quick and cheap way to cure them (see page 136).

If you have ill-fitting windows, there are various things you can do without replacing them totally or going to the expense of double glazing. First establish, by the candle test, whether the draughts are coming from the casement itself or from the frame which has gaps between it and the walls: you will be surprised how much can come through a seemingly minute hole. Mark the affected areas with light pencil lines, then fill the cracks with a proprietary filler and filling knife (see page 234 for techniques).

THE TRICK

Alternatively, use a caulking gun and a suitable mastic filler. The latter is better for filling the gaps on the outside of window frames as it can spread and fill quite a large width in one pass.

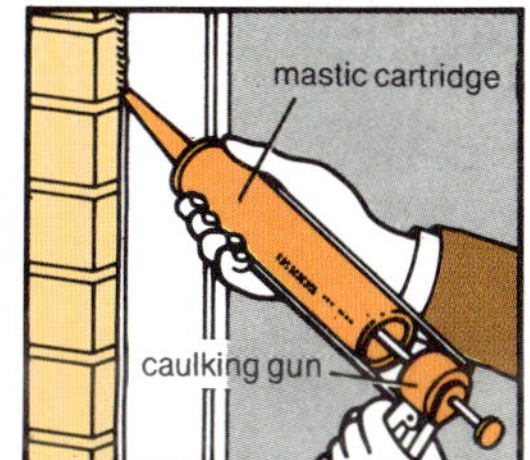

It is always worth doing both inside and outside if you have a draughty frame – water can always get in where wind does.

If it is the sashes which are letting in draughts, you should reposition them and relocate the beads (see page 51–52). However, if it is the middle of winter or you don't feel you can cope and cannot afford a carpenter yet, you can do a very effective job with plastic insulating tape (see page 136). A strip along the head and the foot of the frame, plus a strip where the sashes overlap, will improve matters greatly.

You can also do a cheap form of double glazing with clingfilm by stretching it over the existing glazing bars. The clingfilm will only stick properly if the frame has been recently painted. Try to keep a 20mm (¾in.) gap between the film and the glass.

A more effective form of this is a heavyweight clingfilm which is attached to the window frame with double-sided adhesive tape. Then use hot air from a hair drier to stretch the film to a sheer transparent surface. This can be removed at the end of the winter or left in place.

Another cheapish way of improving window insulation is to buy curtains with thermal or metallic linings. Alternatively you can make your own detachable linings from this fabric (see page 277) or buy them made-up.

LOFT INSULATION

Start with loft insulation because it is cheapest, easiest and quickest. If no such work has been done before, it could earn you at least a 50 per cent grant from your town hall. Insulating the hot water cylinder, and pipes in the loft, comes into the same category. However, make sure to enquire before you start. Loft-insulating materials are classed as either loose-fill or blanket type.

LOOSE-FILL INSULATION

Loose-fill (vermiculite and Micafil are the same thing) is light, not abrasive to handle, and has to have its top levelled off, but in other respects behaves rather like a liquid. If the ends of the channels formed by the joists are not blocked with wooden end stops, the substance will flow away.

Ventilation holes must be drilled in the soffit board in order to provide ventilation in the attic, which in future will be cold and more liable to condensation, with resultant damage to timbers. This ventilation feature applies to every form of loft insulation.

THE TRICK

An easy way to level the substance, having decided what depth you want, say 100mm (4in.), and knowing the depth of the joists, say 150mm (6in.), is to cut a piece of stout card 50mm (2in.) deep by the width between the joists. Fasten this to a wooden handle and run it along the joist tops.

BLANKET INSULATION

This is made of glass fibre or mineral wool and sold in rolls of stated length, width and thickness. To decide what you need, for length measure from end to end of one channel between the joists and multiply this by the number of channels. The width is simply the width of the channel, from inside one joist to inside the next, plus about 50mm (2in.). However, just in case the builder had his own ideas, measure more than one width. As regards thickness you have a choice between wisdom and cost. Here are the figures, to help you decide.

Building Regulation requirement	100mm (4in.)
Prudent minimum	160mm (6½in.)

Remember that with all insulation you spend now in order to save ever after.

LAYING THE INSULATION

THE TRICK

Wear long gloves, or gloves and long sleeves, and a mask all the time.

Take into the loft a few boards that span the joists, to kneel on and a pair of large, heavy-duty scissors or a carving knife. Another useful gadget is a piece of flat board not wider than the joist channel width, attached to the end of a long broom handle.

Take a roll of fibre to the channel furthest from the hatch. With its free end pointing to the eaves, unroll it along the channel. Using the gadget described above, make the end reach but not over-reach the channel end, and tamp it lightly so that it lies flat without wrinkles or bunching up. Unroll the fibre along the whole channel, tamping lightly, to finish at the joist end as before.

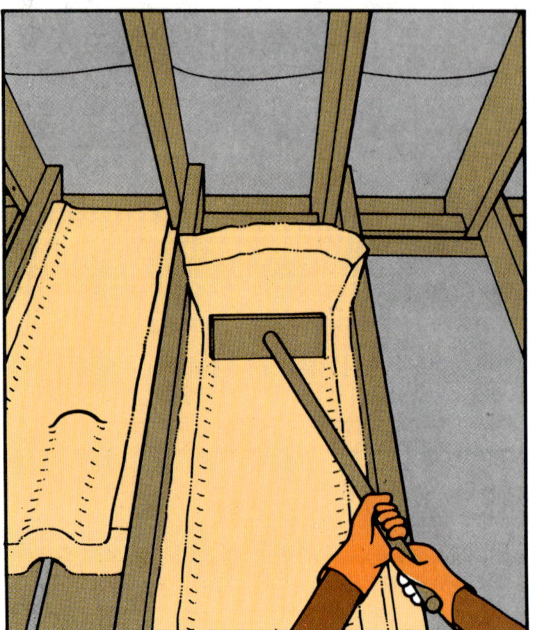

THE TRICK

The roll should be slightly wider than the channel, as described above, to allow for a small amount of tuck-in along the sides as an insurance against leaving any gaps.

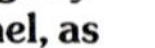

Deal with any non-standard channels, such as might occur at a gable end, by filling in with cut strips.

Be very careful with electric cables, and do not cover over any electrical fittings, such as lighting fixtures, which might be in the path of the insulation. Water pipes which run at low level in one of the channels should be included in the cover – i.e. the insulation will cover them. For individual plumbing insulation, see page 137.

It may seem very wrong to have a draught, even a wind, in the attic, but that is no more than you must have at the other end of the house, under the ground floor. Continuous ventilation is essential, if you are to avoid dry rot in the timbers. To ensure ventilation you must have clearances on one side of the house – the prevailing windward side if possible – for air to enter, and similar provision on the opposite side for it to get out again.

insulation and ventilation in the eaves

Don't forget to check, and (if necessary) treat this area for woodworm and dry rot before installation, particularly if it is relatively inaccessible at normal times. This is not a do-it-yourself job (see page 203). The special spraying techniques, along with the necessary safety precautions, are available only from specialist firms.

OTHER ROOF INSULATION

If there is not enough room to carry out an insulation job as described above, you must apply it underneath the ceiling of the room below. Different materials are needed – generally slab or tile insulation which can be stuck on or screwed through the ceiling to the underside of the joists.

Flat roofs create yet another problem. They are usually felt-covered, and the felt can deteriorate, letting in rain and wetting the timbers. Small amounts of moisture will be evaporated by the warmth rising from the room but, if you insulate the underside of the roof, you will cut off that supply of warmth and a wet roof will remain wet, with serious consequences. If you want to insulate a flat roof, take specialist advice.

WALL INSULATION

The walls of a building lose most heat because they present the greatest area; they must therefore rank high on the list for treatment.

SOLID WALLS

Insulation may be applied to solid walls inside or out, or both. A householder can do it himself, or employ a general or specialist contractor.

EXTERNAL METHODS

For external application, there is no such thing as a magic paint which is a good insulator, so turn away from such advertisements. Acceptable methods can be described as direct and indirect. In the direct method a new wall of considerable thickness, up to 100mm (4in.), is added to the existing wall, and all rainwater pipes, etc repositioned. Such a system is Disbotherm, which the makers frankly state costs about 10 times as much per unit area as cavity insulation.

An indirect method is one which wards off cooling winds and rainwater which absorbs heat in evaporating; it is very useful for walls on exposed sites, on the windward side. It consists of cladding the wall in a material such as slates, ceramic or cedar tiles, or timber in the form of bargeboarding. Very often a handyman can, with help, undertake this work. Even a tall, fairly dense hedge can be helpful in very windy places, by deflecting direct winds.

INTERNAL METHODS

For internal application, the only objection to a thermal inner lining is that it encroaches into the indoor space, but this is largely imaginary, as it is rarely more than about 50mm (2in.) thick. Before fitting a thermal inner lining, make sure that the outside wall is not likely to let rain through, for instance via bad joints or broken brick. Self-colour walls can be treated with a sealing compound (FEB or Lillington, for instance) which will hold back surface water. Walls which can take colour will benefit from an application of Snowcem, Sandtex or a similar cement-based agent.

With nearly all insulating materials effectiveness is geared to thickness, so the more you can put on the better. There are many proprietary boards and similar rigid forms of insulation which will be explained in the shop and by the manufacturers.

The easiest to apply is the expanded polystyrene tile or sheet; try to get a fireproof grade. Dealers sell cartons of suitable adhesive; spread it like butter at each corner and in the middle, then press each tile firmly to the wall, making sure that it sticks all the way.

THE TRICK

Tiles usually have chamfered edges, and if you do not want these edges to show as a pattern put the chamfer inside, facing the wall.

Because the tiles are thin, and therefore of limited effect, it is best to wait a day and then stick a second layer on top of the first. The finished job has a somewhat fragile surface and will dent if furniture is pushed against it. It may be painted with emulsion paint, or papered using heavy-duty paste.

INSTALLING MINERAL WOOL

A more substantial job would use a sandwich, with loft insulation-type mineral wool as the filling. The 'bread' is the wall on one side, and hardboard or any similar board on the other (inner) side. When you are deciding on the thickness of material, remember that it also has a sound-insulating effect.

Make sure the wall is quite dry, and free from mould. If in doubt, wash it down with diluted Jeyes Fluid and leave to dry.

Paper the wall with aluminium cooking foil instead of paper. An ordinary, general-purpose paste will do. This serves two useful purposes: aluminium is itself an insulator of the reflective type, and it is also a guarantee that no moisture can penetrate the wall and thus the insulation.

Next fix vertical battens to the wall, using a masonry drill, plastic plugs and wood screws. These battens must run from floor to ceiling, and are best at centres from 600mm to 1m. (2–3ft). The minimum section to use is 25 x 25mm (1 x 1in.). It would be better to make your sandwich at least 35mm (1½in.) deep.

Now put on gauntlets and apply the filling, either mineral wool or glass fibre, so that the entire area is filled thoroughly but not tightly packed.

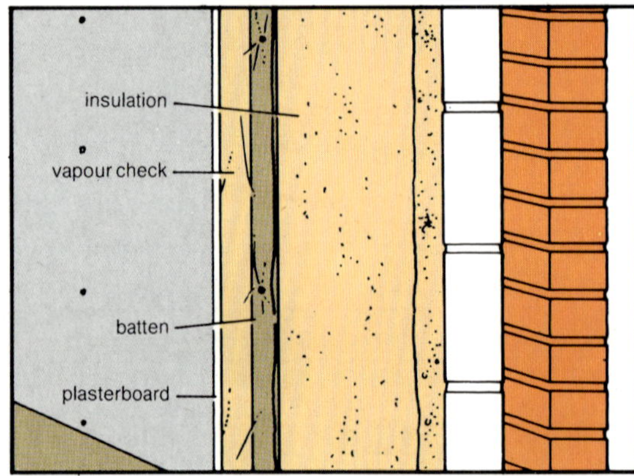

THE TRICK

Encourage it to remain in place by putting rough dabs of adhesive on the wall, helped if necessary by strings laced from batten to batten and kept in place with drawing pins. These can remain in place afterwards.

Last comes the cladding. Hardboard, softboard and plasterboard are all suitable materials, or you can achieve an instant timbered effect by using a faced ply. In all cases make sure that the sheets butt closely to each other and to the floor, ceiling and adjacent wall. Air from the room must not be allowed to get behind the cladding. In all cases except ply, tape the seams and joins before papering or painting.

THE TRICK

If using ply, it will look better if you make a join using matching timber strip.

In the case of taped sheets it is preferable to cover them with lining paper before painting, in order to achieve a smooth finish.

CAVITY WALLS

Most houses in Britain have cavity walls, for which only one form of treatment is worth considering: i.e. cavity filling, by foam or pellets or mineral wool fibres, applied by a contractor who is a member of the NCIA (see page 127). It is not a job you can do yourself. If you are offered a choice between foam and fibre, just go on the estimate; there is next to nothing to choose between the two methods, provided that the contractor is an NCIA member. If you are actually building your own house, you can insert rigid insulation, usually mineral fibre board, as work progresses.

WINDOW INSULATION

Although normal windows are responsible for a relatively small heat loss – around 10 to 20 per cent – they are the greatest obvious nuisance. This is because they have a high heat loss per unit area, which cools the air touching them. Thus cold down draughts come off them and water condenses, making them stream with condensation. In addition they often leak real draughts through badly fitting frames. Unhappily the cost of treatment by proprietary double glazing is high. It is in fact unlikely to be cost-effective, which means that the cost will not be paid back by savings in heat formerly lost for many years.

What are the characteristics of good double glazing? The insulator is not the glass at all, but a slice of still, dry air approximately 20mm (¾in.) thick. The glass is the casing around it. Any departure from those three conditions – still, dry and 20mm (¾in.) – means reduced effectiveness; although for some forms of proprietary unit, thinner sections have to be made for practical manufacturing reasons. One of the proprietary windows, which can be slid into and out of position and usually has a gap of 75–100mm (3–4in.), breaks all the rules and is only moderately effective. However it acts quite well as a sound insulator and is useful for windows overlooking a busy street.

Remember that double glazing badly done achieves nothing at all. There are three choices:

1. To let a contractor take over the supply and installation;
2. To buy proprietary double-glazed windows from one of the firms which supply them; or
3. To tackle the job from scratch using extra single panes.

If you decide to use a contractor, he should, for your protection, be a member of the IGA (see page 127).

FITTING PROPRIETARY DOUBLE GLAZING

This is well worth considering in terms of what you pay for the benefit that you will receive. The general method is to examine the window frame closely and repair any flaws, rotten wood, or bad joints into the wall (see page 52). Measure the area which will be available when the existing window is removed.

Then contact the chosen manufacturer or a stockist and find out what is the nearest size that can be supplied. For instance, a timber infill may be required in the lowest 50–75mm (2–3in.) to accommodate the locking device. This will be explained by him. Plain aluminium frames have proved a nuisance in the past because the conductivity of the metal causes increased condensation on the frames. Consequently a new method of construction has been invented, with a plastic insert between the inside and outside. This is the type of window to buy.

When the new window arrives, remove the old one, and make any adjustments to the dimensions of the opening, for instance by adding fillets to close the area. Make all joins good.

Finally, fasten the new window in position, following the instructions carefully. You must achieve a tight fit and tighten the frames down evenly so as to avoid any wind or warp in the frame of the new window. Don't forget to paint the surround.

THE TRICK

Double-glazed windows are in most cases aluminium-framed, and do not need painting; however, if you want to change their appearance apply a good metal primer first (see page 241).

FITTING EXTRA PANES

An extra pane of glass can be fitted in front of the existing one but ensure that the three conditions mentioned above: still, dry air and about 20mm (¾in.) gap, are fulfilled.

Examine the existing window. Check for soundness of wood (see above), condition of paintwork, and state of putty holding the pane in. Take whatever action is indicated; in particular make sure that the surface of the frame where the new pane will go is smooth and level, without burrs or paint lumps.

WOODEN FRAMES

Measure up for the new pane, which should extend

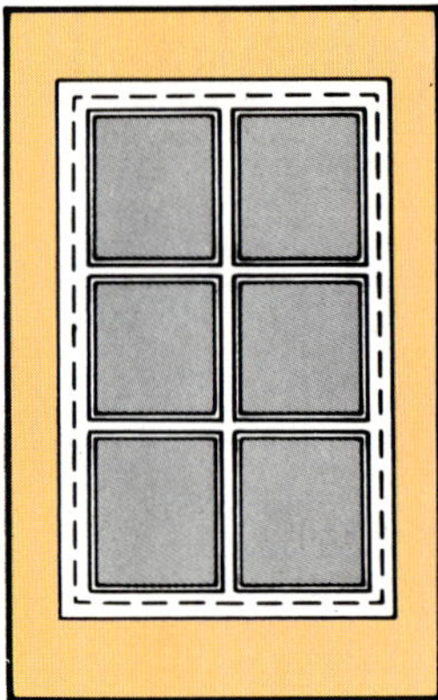

roughly halfway across the wooden frame on each of the four sides, thus giving a good area of contact for the glass while leaving plenty of room for whatever fastening is used.

The whole object is to form an airtight seal between glass and wood. On very plain surfaces double-sided adhesive tape is satisfactory, but such surfaces are rare. Plastic insertion strip is better, if you can mitre the corners.

In both these cases there must be a method of securing the pane to the wood. You can use simple rebated picture framing for

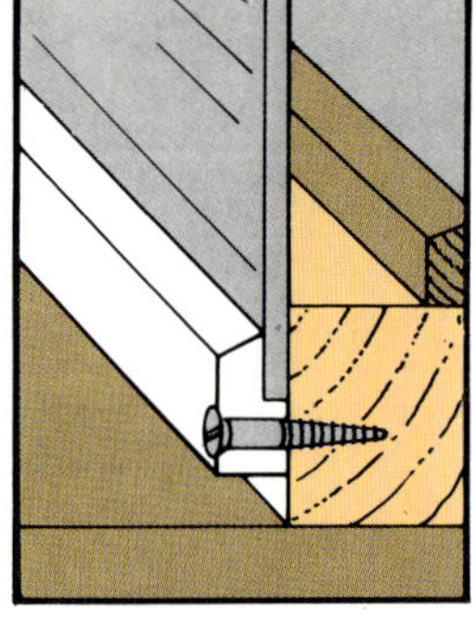

instance, with mitred joints at the corners.

A good idea is to use a proprietary sealing strip, which is a plastic channel to hold the new pane, with a profile into which engage a series of screw-on holding-down clips. An incidental advantage of this material, which you can buy at d-i-y shops and ironmongers, is that it can be dismantled, if the outer pane gets broken, simply by undoing a few screws.

The dry air requirement is accomplished at the time of fitting the new pane. If you can do the job in hot, dry, weather that is sufficient; but at any other time you have to create your own climate.

THE TRICK

Rig up a portable electric fire so that it looks straight at the window from about 1m. (3ft) distant, and leave it on until the window is quite warm and dry. Make sure that the new pane also is dry, remove the fire after switching it off, and quickly secure the pane in place.

METAL FRAMES

For a metal-framed window the method is the same but you are denied the easy way of simply pushing in a few wood screws. Instead, you must mark off for screw holes, drill and tap preferably blind holes of about 6BA, and finally secure with studs of the same rate; e.g. 6BA. Thin frames will not take blind holes – drill them oversize to the fasteners, and use bolts with nuts.

If you imagine double glazing is going to cure condensation, you will most probably be mistaken. Good double glazing will halve the heat loss expected through single glazing, but it is still greater than through an uninsulated wall.

With a Polycell DIY Double Glazing kit you don't need special tools or expertise to achieve professional results. So you can dispense with expensive installers.

Now let's dispense with some of the myths.

"DIY systems don't work." Wrong.

Polycell kits are made to the highest professional standards.

In fact, when tested by the Agrement Board (the Independent Test Authority for Building Products), they were found to be just as effective at reducing draughts, heat loss and noise as manufacturer installed sealed units.

But, compared to manufacturer installed secondary systems, they're almost half the price.

That probably explains why they have already been installed in over a million windows.

"DIY systems don't open and close." Wrong.

Many DIY systems don't. But Polycell kits open and close, vertically, horizontally or hinged to match your window, just like manufacturer installed systems. So they're safe in the event of fire.

"DIY systems look awful." Wrong.

Not Polycell kits. Only Polycell offers you a choice of uPVC or satin anodised aluminium.

uPVC has an attractive white finish that will never peel, crack or discolour. It is also a superb insulator, easy to work with and very economical.

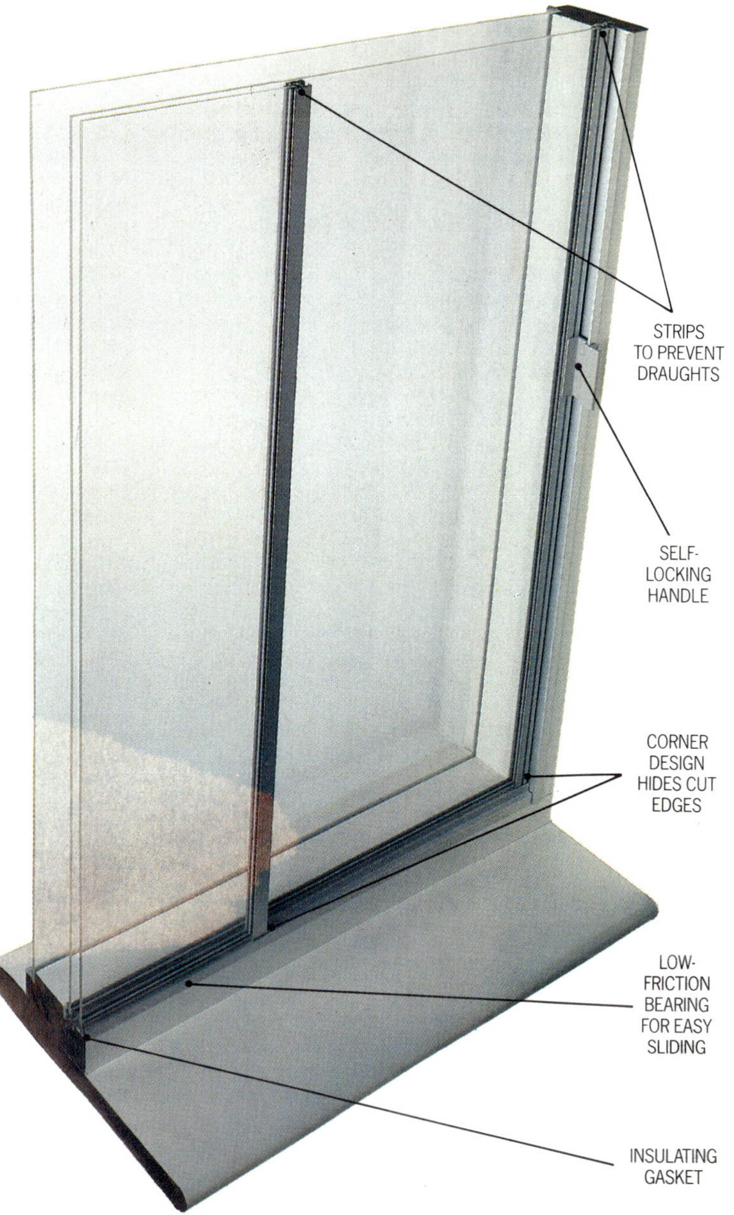

Cut the cost of double glazing by half. Don't pay the installers.

Polycell's aluminium kits are anodised for a beautiful satin finish which will not tarnish or pit, unlike some DIY systems.

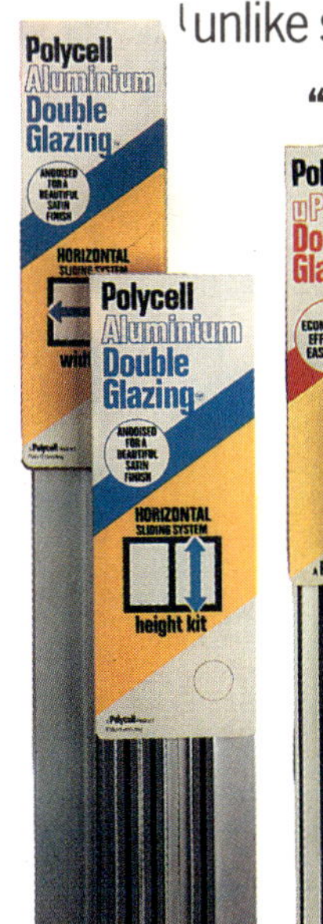

"The kits must be hard to install." Wrong.

You'll find Polycell kits fit like a glove.

This is not surprising. After all, they have been designed and developed by the leaders in DIY.

Which is also why they're easy to install, even for a beginner.

Measure the size of your window and buy a height kit and width kit to the next size up. Then follow the simple instructions in every kit.

"I'll still make a mistake." Wrong.

You only need to be able to use a drill, a hacksaw and a screwdriver. And our kits don't need mitred corners, which can be difficult to cut.

They're even designed to mask small errors in measurement or cutting without affecting looks or performance.

"I can do a professional job with Polycell Double Glazing." Right.

Polycell. Do it right.

FLOOR AND DOOR INSULATION

FLOOR INSULATION

Suspended wooden floors at ground floor level lose heat in two ways, and must be treated for both. Heat is conducted downwards, and cold draughts often rise up from below. Too much risk is involved in insulating below floor level; this is what has to be done on the top level.

Examine the surface for split and damaged boards and cracks. If they are bad, it is far better to replace them than to try patching. If a substantial number of boards has to be replaced, it is worth getting a quotation for putting in a solid floor, with a waterproof membrane. Solid floors lose less heat and are not dependent on continuing draught in the subfloor.

Take up a board or two and make sure that the wood underneath is sweet and dry. It is best to have a contractor spray it against dry rot and woodworm.

If you discover small cracks, loss of tongues in tongued and grooved boards, and so on, a smoking string will show up the entering draughts. Be sure to use a natural fibre string (e.g. hemp), which will smoulder when lit; avoid synthetic strings.

These gaps should be filled either with a bought filling substance or with one you can make yourself for nothing from old newspapers.

THE TRICK

To make papier mâché, tear the newspaper into shreds, put them in a large saucepan and add a little water and a couple of dessertspoons of plain flour. Boil the mixture until the paper has disintegrated and turned into a pulp.

Force the pulp into the gaps and crevices – an ordinary mason's trowel is a useful tool for the job. Leave the top edge slightly proud of the floor level, and allow to dry. When dry, bring it back to floor level with coarse glasspaper on a block. No further treatment, such as stain or varnish, is needed because the floor will not be left bare.

It is a desirable intermediate step to cover the entire floor in ordinary-grade hardboard. Make each sheet fit snugly, and finally tape all the joins. This is not only a great help towards insulation, but also makes a level floor out of an uneven one, eliminates rough edges, and so prolongs the life of underfelts, etc (see page 203).

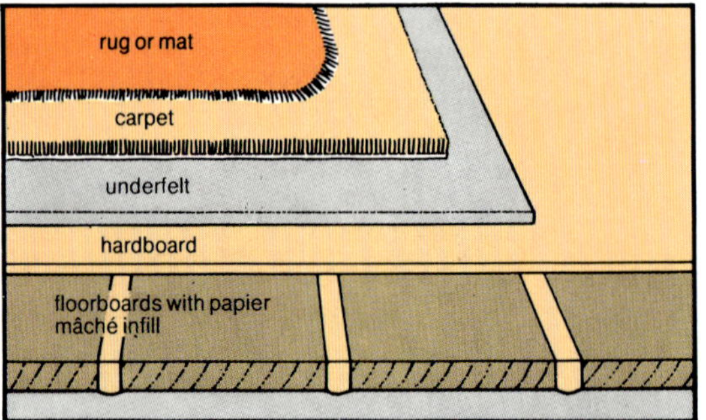

The bulk of the insulating will be done by the next layers, and so a great deal depends upon having a good-quality underfelt and a good-quality carpet. If both are 'fitted': i.e. covering the entire floor, so much the better. Finally you can put rugs on parts of the floor over the carpet; they will do more than protect the carpet from spilt drinks as they will contribute to the total insulation.

Floors above ground level do not, of course, require to be insulated, unless there is a garage or lock-up shop beneath. Even in flats you can benefit from what the people below spend on heating; only a need for soundproofing might lead to treatment on the lines described.

SKIRTINGS

If your skirting boards do not fit tightly to the floorboards, and so let in draughts, there are two things you can do before resorting to the ultimate in removing and repositioning all the skirtings. You can make up some more of the papier mâché described above and force it into the crack between skirting and floor using the same technique as filling cracks (see page 234). Alternatively, you can buy a simple wood beading from any builder's merchant.

This should be fixed with panel pins to the skirting board (not to the floor). Press it down hard with a piece of wood or a screwdriver (see page 27) while nailing on.

THE TRICK

To establish where the draughts are coming from, hold a lighted candle about 50–75mm (2–3in.) from the join and run it along. The flickering will indicate places requiring attention.

DOOR INSULATION

A glass door might be seen as a special kind of window (see page 134), and there is no reason why glazing should not be doubled on a door. Nor is there any reason why thin wooden panels should not be doubled, with insulation infill.

Doors are generally notorious for the way they leak draughts. Doors, window frames and floors are the principal sources of the cold draughts which attack heating and it calls for good detective work to trace them all. They fall into various categories: some are really bad and require surgery from a joiner; others can be repaired with fillers: plastic wood, Sirapite or putty, depending upon the situation.

Doors also shrink and leave gaps which should be filled with draught excluder. The number and types of draught excluder have increased greatly: many are plastic, in which case they

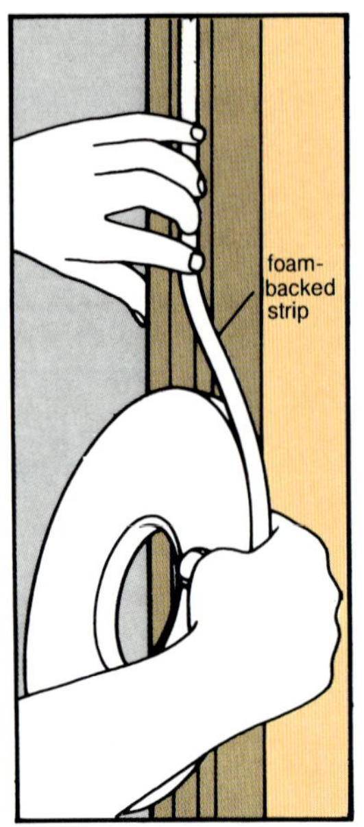

should be examined occasionally for wear. There is also an angled copper strip type. It is best to ask advice at your local d-i-y shop, choosing what is suitable for the gap size and situation and its expected life.

Most internal doors can be successfully insulated with self-adhesive foam-backed plastic strip which comes on a reel. This perishes fairly easily and should be inspected regularly for wear. The secret of applying it successfully is to make sure that the surface to which it is to be applied is really clean and dry.

To exclude draughts from underneath a door, apply self-adhesive plastic strip incorporating felt ribbon to the bottom of the door. Make sure that the bottom of the felt fits snugly against the floor, otherwise you might as well not bother to use it.

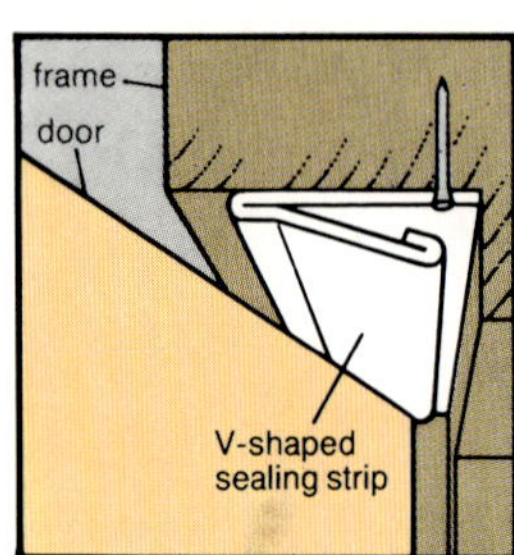

Attaching the V-shaped metal seals is slightly more complicated, but is longer lasting and somewhat more efficient. The important things to remember are that corners should be mitred so that the two adjoining strips do not bind and that the same applies where cuts are made to accommodate hinges or locks. Mitre the narrow side only to 45° at the angle where the lintel meets the jambs (see page 40). At locks and hinges, mitre both sides of the strip and nail through both to prevent splitting. Use a pin push to insert the nails if you own one; if not, start the holes with a bradawl, then use a hammer and nail punch.

Another source of draughts on a front door is the letter-box. Use the candle test (see above) to check. If there is a draught, buy and install an internal letter-box flap or draught reducer.

PLUMBING INSULATION

COLD WATER CISTERNS

The most important thing to remember about insulating cold water cisterns in the roof, if you are insulating the rest of the loft at the same time, is not to push the fibreglass or Micafil under the cistern. If you do, you will cut off all rising warmth from the house below and the cistern will probably freeze, however well you insulate it.

The easiest way to insulate a cold water cistern is with glass fibre roll, preferably the sort with paper bonded to one side (because it is easier to handle). If you can buy glass fibre which is as deep as the cistern do so, because it is easier to apply. It is advisable to insulate the pipes leading to the cistern before you start on the cistern itself (see below).

Start wrapping from the bottom of the cistern and secure with at least two strings (more if you are doing the whole cistern with one width). If you are doing the job by yourself, a bit of insulating tape will hold the glass fibre in place while you are positioning the other side.

THE TRICK

Don't pull the strings too tight, otherwise you will crush the insulation and lessen its effectiveness.

If you need to apply another layer above the first, do so now. Again use two strings to hold it in place. Try, if you can, not to tie the bottom string of the second layer at the same height as the top string of the first layer.

Your cold water cistern should already have a lid. If it does not, cut a piece of plywood to about 25mm (1in.) larger all round than the cistern's top. Then cut a piece of polystyrene to the exact size of the cistern's top and nail it onto the plywood. This will give you a close-fitting lid which is resistant to condensation (see pages 140 and 142). Then cut a piece of fibreglass to overlap the cistern lid by about 150mm (6in.) all round. If you need to join two pieces together, use insulating tape. Do not tie this down.

EXPANSION PIPES

If you have an expansion pipe over the cistern (more likely with central heating expansion tanks), you must make some provision for letting it overflow back into the tank.

THE TRICK

The easiest way is to buy a largish plastic funnel and cut a hole for it in the lid under the expansion pipe. Use insulating tape to seal it into place.

POLYSTYRENE

You could make an insulation cover for your cold water cistern from sheets of expanded polystyrene which is available from most builder's merchants in sheets ranging in thickness from 6mm (¼in.) to 75mm (3in.). In this case, the thicker the better, and also the stronger, so use 75mm (3in.) thick if you can get it.

Make the box about 50mm (2in.) larger overall than the cistern itself and use polystyrene cement to join the sides together. In this case, do not lag the pipes to the cistern until after the box is in place, because you can cut the holes for the pipes very accurately with a sharp knife. Glue the cutouts back onto the main box with polystyrene cement.

For the lid, cut two pieces of polystyrene: the first should be to the overall size of the finished box; the second should be to the inner dimensions of the box. Glue the two pieces together carefully and trim the smaller section with a sharp knife to produce the optimum fit.

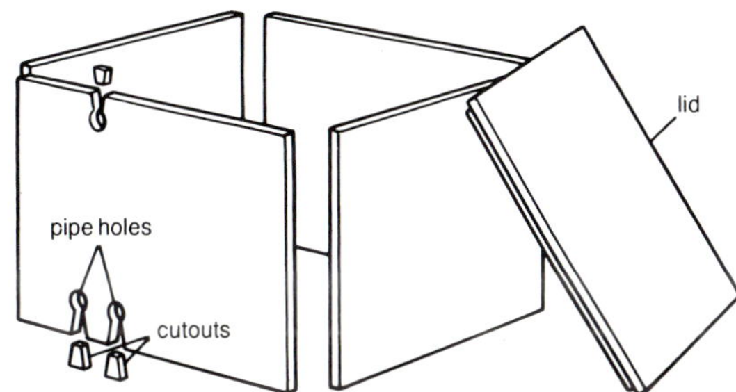

You can insulate a cold water cistern with Micafil granules, but only if it is resting on boards: do not use this method in a loft where it is resting on the rafters. You should build a hardboard box so that there is a 50mm (2in.) gap all round between it and the cistern. Cut holes for the pipes, then, when the box is in place, tape over the gaps so that the granules do not fall out. Carefully fill the gap with the granules, making sure not to get any in the cistern. You can either make a tray for the lid and fill it with granules, or cut a polystyrene lid as described above.

LAGGING PIPES

FELT LAGGING

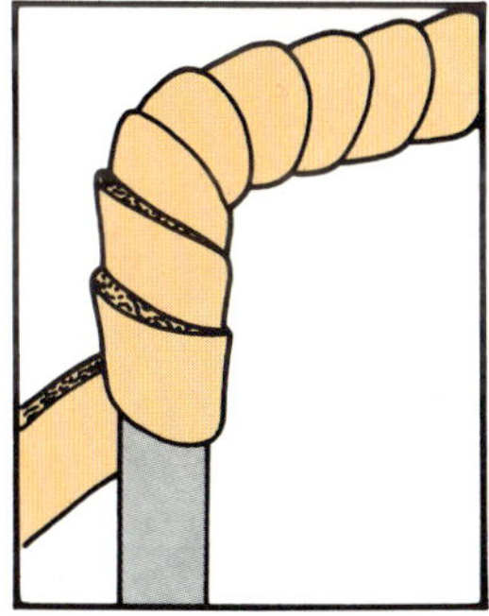

Strips of felt for lagging pipes come in rolls of 75mm × 3.6m (3in. × 12ft). It is applied rather like a bandage and should overlap on each turn by about half the width of the strip. This is particularly important when going round bends as they are both the most vulnerable points for frost and the most likely to be underwrapped.

Always start lagging at the cistern or tank. Make three turns around the pipe and tie in place with a string. When you come to the end of a strip, overlap the new strip one complete turn of the old one and again tie in place with a string. Take a turn round the neck of any stopcock or gate valve you may pass. Make sure you do all the pipes; the overflow is just as important as any other.

FOAM PLASTIC TUBING

Usually supplied in 900mm or 1.8m. (3 or 6ft) lengths, this can be bought in sizes to fit any pipe diameter between 6mm (¼in.) and 75mm (3in.). It is important that you buy the right size for maximum effectiveness. It can be cut to length with scissors.

Again start at the cistern or tank. Open the lagging and spring it over the pipe pushing it up so that it butts firmly against the tank or cistern. Use plastic insulating tape to secure the sides together. At bends, push the edges together and secure first with a strip of tape along the length of the tubing, then with pieces around the pipe. At joins in the tubing, wrap tape around the pipe so that it overlaps both pieces of tubing. The same remarks apply about doing all the pipes.

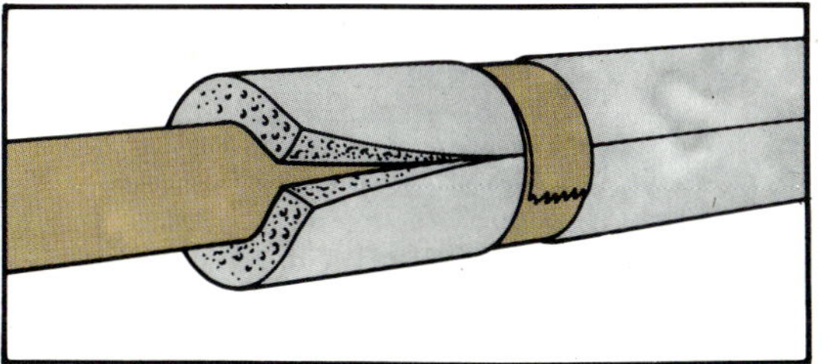

HOT WATER CYLINDERS

One of the quickest and easiest ways to improve your insulation is to fit a hot water cylinder jacket. Measure the cylinder's height and circumference, then go to any hardware shop and buy the correct size.

THE TRICK

If you want to really improve your insulation, buy another one two sizes larger at the same time and install it over the top of the first one as below.

To install a jacket, simply thread all the loops of the jacket pieces onto the collar (or a piece of string) and tie this around the pipe at the top of the cylinder. Smooth the pieces down the sides and arrange them so that they overlap and cover the whole cylinder. Fit the first belt near the top and the second near the bottom of the cylinder and tie off any excess length in case the belts slip. Readjust the pieces if necessary.

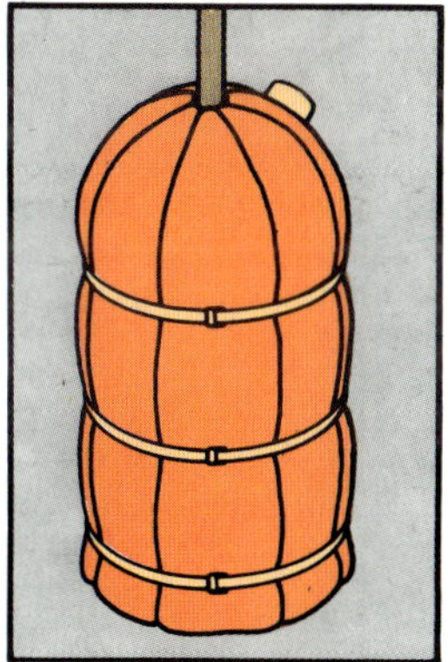

If you have bought a second (larger) jacket, repeat this operation arranging the pieces so that their joins come in the middle of the pieces of the under jacket.

THE TRICK

Remember that, if you have an immersion heater or a cylinderstat, you must not cover them up. If you do, they will overheat and burn out.

Condensation — A Growing Problem

The theory of condensation is well known. Whenever warm moist air meets a cold surface, condensation normally occurs. The effect is uncomfortable, and it can also result in expensive structural damage. Surface condensation leads to damp, unhealthy living conditions and can appear in relatively new housing just as it can in older dwellings. Mould grows on wallcoverings, furniture, bedding and clothing, causing acute discomfort which many families seem unable to improve. And that is not an end to the problem.

A second and less well understood form of condensation is interstitial. This occurs as vapour pressure drives water vapour through all except completely impermeable materials. As vapour reaches colder conditions condensation may take place even where surface condensation is absent.

Yet condensation need never happen — and can be cured.

The answer is to achieve a proper balance between three elements: heating, ventilation and insulation . . . which is where Coolag is proving to be the one reliable name to turn to.

Coolag offers the ideal insulation for condensation control and prevention of heat loss. Properly applied, a balance can be achieved which can ensure that neither form of condensation will continue.

Most building materials are porous. Water vapour can therefore pass through

with condensation as the dew point is reached. Hence, unless the building is allowed a proper cycling of air and correct insulation, a build up of water may occur.

Conventional insulating materials are relatively soft and not suitable as surfaces for walls and floors in homes and, as most insulants are themselves porous, they will allow warm moisture-laden air to penetrate the cold structure behind where condensation may take place.

The insulant quickly absorbs the condensed water and its insulation value is degraded. A suitable insulant for internal lining must therefore have a rigid wearing surface and be impermeable to moisture vapour.

Purlboard is a Coolag insulant which offers this important benefit. Developed by ICI, Purlboard is widely specified throughout the building world. It's as easy to use and as versatile as ordinary plasterboard and offers outstanding thermal performances. No other material can give the same insulating efficiency as the Coolag foam.

Whether you're wanting to insulate an existing wall or you're building a new extension on your house, Coolag Purlboard is the natural choice.

Purlboard's general purpose backliner makes the material suitable for plaster-dab bonding, adhesive bonding or mechanically fixing to studding or battens. A lot will depend on the suitability of the background and your own preference. Purlboard is easily cut with a sharp knife or fine tooth saw.

Available with both Square Edge Grey plasterboard for direct plastering and Taper Edge Manilla plasterboard for taping and decoration, Purlboard lends itself to DIY applications.

Purlboard, the easy way to insulate your home.

Fixed using standard building and DIY methods, full, easy to follow instructions are available.

Flat Roofs — the easy way

April 1982 saw amendments to parts of the 1976 Building Regulations dealing with insulation requirements of domestic dwellings. It had been known for some time that insulation placed at ceiling level had, in many instances, been susceptible to moisture accumulation. Warm, moisture-laden air, from rooms below had been condensing within the insulation, not only reducing its efficiency but also contributing to more serious condensation problems. In an attempt to alleviate these dangers the 1982 amendments insisted that where insulation was to be placed at ceiling level cross-ventilation must be provided.

In flat roof construction this created practical difficulties. If cross-ventilation was achievable it was often awkward and costly. In many cases it was simply non-viable.

Coolag Purlboard's answer to these problems is Purldek. It is no secret that Purldek is enjoying ever-increasing success as more and more builders discover it really is not only the easy way of complying with the regulations, it is the easiest way of putting an insulated roof on a new extension.

Purldek consists of an exterior grade plywood directly laminated to 50mm of rigid polyurethane foam with an aluminium foil completing the sandwich. Supplied in 2400 × 1200 sheets, Purldek is light to handle and easy to use. It is simply laid on top of the roof joists and nailed into position, ready to be finished with any standard felting system.

Correctly applied, it complies with all the latest building regulations without the necessity to cross-ventilate.

Fixed using standard building and DIY methods, full, easy to follow instructions are available.

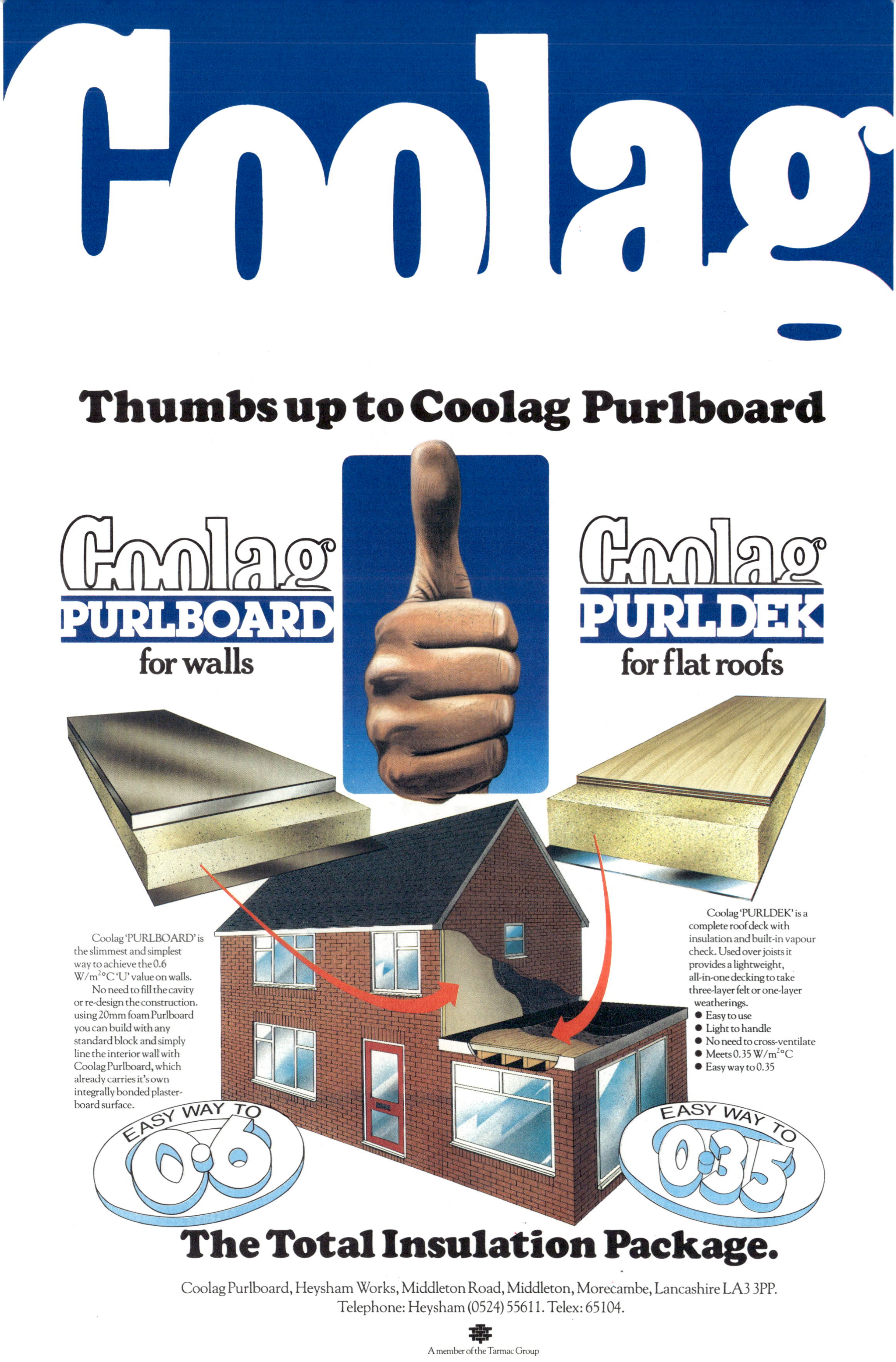
Coolag
Thumbs up to Coolag Purlboard
Coolag PURLBOARD for walls
Coolag PURLDEK for flat roofs
Coolag 'PURLBOARD' is the slimmest and simplest way to achieve the 0.6 W/m²°C 'U' value on walls.
No need to fill the cavity or re-design the construction. using 20mm foam Purlboard you can build with any standard block and simply line the interior wall with Coolag Purlboard, which already carries it's own integrally bonded plaster-board surface.
Coolag 'PURLDEK' is a complete roof deck with insulation and built-in vapour check. Used over joists it provides a lightweight, all-in-one decking to take three-layer felt or one-layer weatherings.
● Easy to use
● Light to handle
● No need to cross-ventilate
● Meets 0.35 W/m²°C
● Easy way to 0.35
EASY WAY TO 0·6
EASY WAY TO 0·35
The Total Insulation Package.
Coolag Purlboard, Heysham Works, Middleton Road, Middleton, Morecambe, Lancashire LA3 3PP.
Telephone: Heysham (0524) 55611. Telex: 65104.
A member of the Tarmac Group

DAMP AND CONDENSATION 1

RISING DAMP

Rising damp is caused by the water in the ground around the building rising up the walls by what is known as 'capillary action'. The major barrier to this action in most buildings is what is known as the 'damp-proof course' or dpc. This is a non-permeable barrier, ideally positioned about 150mm (6in.) above ground level. All buildings meant for human habitation built since 1875, have been required to have one incorporated, but many early ones are perishing because of the materials from which they were constructed.

Rising damp is more likely to occur in a house built of fairly porous bricks and where the mortar was a straight sand:lime mix with no concrete added. However, the most common cause is that earth or gravel has been allowed to pile up along the outside wall so high that it goes above the damp-proof course. When this happens, the moisture in the earth can penetrate straight into the porous bricks above the damp-proof course and thence penetrate the inner wall. This problem is also liable to occur if you lay a new path around the side of your house (see page 193).

THE TRICK

If the path looks as if it is going to go above damp-proof course level, you must dig away existing earth or concrete until a suitable depth is reached.

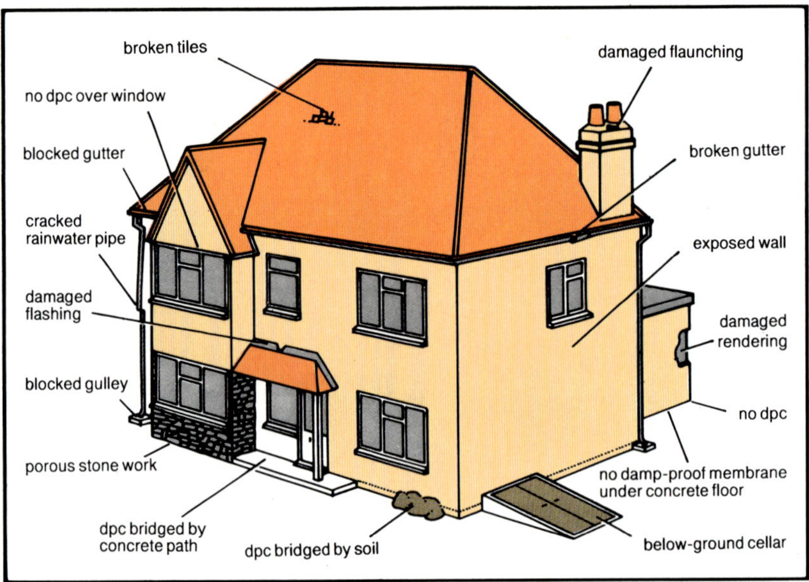

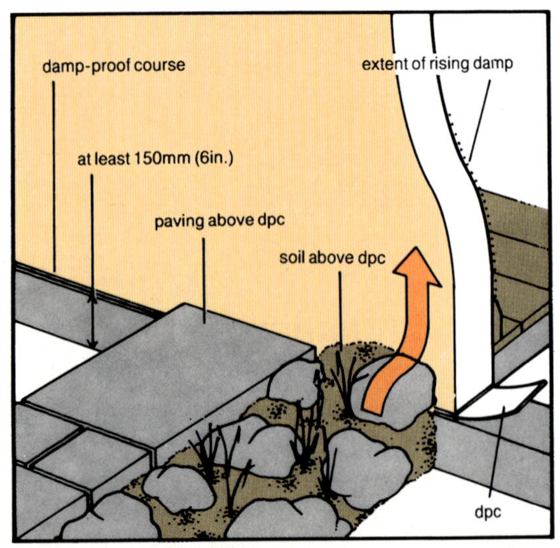

Penetrating damp usually occurs when water lands on the outside wall of a building and penetrates through to appear as a damp patch on an inner wall. It is often caused by inadequate maintenance which results in large quantities of water running over the same bit of wall. It also occurs when a wall is badly exposed to driving rain. The best way to cure the latter problem is to render the wall in some way (see pages 187–88). Efficient and regular exterior maintenance of the property will minimise the risk from gutters, falling damp from window sills, or broken rainwater pipes.

Another cause of penetrating damp is the bad positioning of ties in cavity walls. If these slope towards the inner wall, they can provide a bridge for water to flow across. This can also happen if mortar or plaster is dropped into the cavity

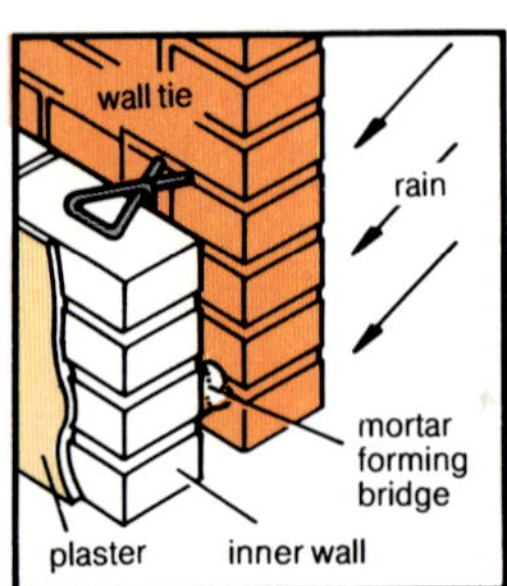

during construction or later improvements. This is why it is so important not to knock bits into the cavity when doing electrical or plumbing work – you may be causing a serious problem for the future. Really all that can be done to cure this fault is to knock a hole in the wall and remove the offending debris. If the ties are badly positioned, this is a job for a builder.

An isolated damp patch well away from floor level is quite likely to be caused by penetrating damp; likewise on the upper storeys. If it is near floor level, it could either be rising or penetrating damp.

DAMP-PROOF COURSES

The earliest damp-proof courses were made of slate – some of these have gone soft and crumbly, but many have lasted well, depending on the type of slate used. Later on a layer of bitumen or felt was used; you sometimes find sheets of lead or copper have been installed. Nowadays thick black polythene is commonly used. This is much the same sort as is recommended for use under chipboard floors (see page 225).

If you decide that the damp-proof course is at fault, if it is only a small section that has failed, it is possible to replace it yourself. You have to remove all obstacles, such as skirting boards, pipes, cable, etc, and then cut right through the mortar in both walls with a special type of chain saw. You should not do more than about 1m. (3ft) at a time, otherwise the wall might settle and cause structural damage. You then insert the new membrane, and then wedge the gap so that you can fill it with mortar. It is a difficult and complicated process and is probably better done by a builder. If the damage is extensive, or if there is no damp-proof course at all, you should call in a professional to install a new one.

There are other methods of installing a damp-proof course, but the only sure cure is to insert a new membrane. The best of the other methods appears to be an injection of water-repellant chemicals, which is fed into the wall slowly over a period of days. Another formulation is pumped in at fairly high pressure. They seem reasonably efficient in walls where there is not a severe pressure of water incoming and providing they are properly applied. Most companies which use them will give a 20 or 30 year guarantee with the work. It is not a d-i-y process.

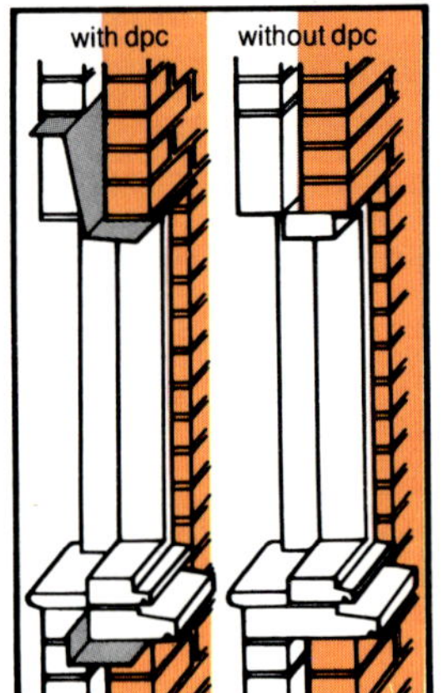

Damp-proof courses are also required around any breaks in an exterior wall, such as round doors and windows. If the original builder has omitted it, or if it has partially perished, that annoying leak round your bay window may well be explained. To repair or replace it, requires removing the whole frame door or window; if this seems too much, call in a builder.

DAMP METERS

A very useful instrument which is well worth buying – basically it tests the dampness of interior walls. Run off batteries, it has a two-pronged fork for sticking (gently) into the plaster or woodwork and two lights. One indicates normality, the other lights up when the fork touches something damp.

THE TRICK

Remember that a wall can be damp even if there are no visible signs of it.

This instrument also works on concrete, so test your downstairs solid floors as well. A failure of the membrane under the floor may be providing an entry point for damp.

DAMP AND CONDENSATION 2

CONDENSATION

This is the most pervasive and most difficult to cure of all the damp conditions. This is because it arises inside the building, not outside, and has many different causes – not just one. Condensation is basically water vapour: it 'condenses' onto walls, windows, surfaces, etc when the air in the building is 'saturated' and can hold no more. This saturation point is directly related to the internal temperature of the building – hot air can absorb water vapour more quickly.

There are four main factors involved in condensation problems. They are:

1. The heat of your home;
2. The ventilation;
3. The thermal insulation; and
4. The amount of moisture you create.

The last is perhaps the most important, because your moisture production rate produces the water vapour. To cure condensation you must either reduce water vapour, increase the heating of your home, or both. But ventilation is the key.

KITCHENS

Kitchens are prime producers of water vapour from cooking, washing up, washing and drying clothes, etc. There are various things you can do to minimize water vapour production, one of the simplest is to keep the kitchen door shut so that the vapour does not pass into the rest of the house.

You could also try using saucepan lids as much as possible.

A cooker hood fitted over the stove and vented to the outside will cut down on both moisture production and on general kitchen smells. They usually plug directly into a 13-amp socket (see pages 83–5) and the best models have two or three speeds.

An extractor fan set into the kitchen window will provide additional ventilation, although it does not need to be switched on all the time. Again such fans usually work off a 13-amp socket. You will have to cut the window glass to make a hole for the extractor fan (see page 190). Very often, if you just run the fan for ten minutes after a steamy job, this will cure any condensation.

THE TRICK

If your kitchen is unheated, or if you use a free-standing gas or paraffin stove, consider installing an electric fan or convection heater or an oil-filled radiator.

The reason is that these free-standing stoves produce about 570ml (1pt) of water vapour for every 2.8l. (5pt) of paraffin burnt. This is quite a substantial input. It would also be worth you insulating any pipes in your kitchen with foam tubing (see page 137).

Tumble driers give off a fair amount of water vapour, particularly at the beginning of the run. They should be vented to the open air; if yours is not, you should either arrange for it to be connected or (if it is not the type to require this) consider changing to another model.

Anti-condensation paint is sometimes useful where the condensation is only a mild problem. It provides an insulating film between the warm humid air and the cold surface. However it will not absorb condensation.

HUMIDITY

Do not get carried away trying to reduce humidity in your home, particularly if you have central heating and antique furniture. Hot dry air is ruinous to well seasoned wood, as any antique dealer will confirm. Lack of humidity can also be a problem if you own a piano – it will not stay in tune long if the air gets too dry.

THE TRICK

Pot plants or a bowl of water near a radiator will often provide sufficient moisture to compensate without adding to your condensation problem. You can also buy humidifiers to hang over the radiators which work quite well.

BATHROOMS

The bathroom is the other room in your home where large quantities of water vapour are regularly generated. Showers are particularly bad in this respect and may often cause mould to appear on walls and ceilings when installed.

THE TRICK

There is not much you can do about cutting down steam from a shower, but if you like hot baths, try running 50mm (2in.) of cold water into the bath before you turn on the hot tap. This will reduce steam substantially.

Again an extractor fan might be worth fitting if the bathroom is very badly ventilated. Don't forget that if you do install one, you must wire it into a fused connection unit (see page 86) and the controlling switch must be outside the bathroom (see page 91). It is illegal to install a socket in a bathroom as well as being extremely dangerous.

If your bathroom is unheated, consider installing an electric towel-rail or a radiant wall-fire. The latter should be positioned high up on the wall, preferably out of reach of anyone in the bath, and should be operated by a pull cord switch. It is advisable to install a normal rocker switch for such a unit as well; this must go outside the bathroom. An electrical towel-rail should be wired into a fused connector unit. You will find, if you switch the heater on about 30 minutes before you intend to use the bath or shower, that the room will have heated sufficiently to minimize vapour production.

If you keep your hot water heated to the recommended temperature of around 60°C (140°F), the vapour production will be lower than if you heated it to, say, 71°C (160°F).

OTHER ROOMS

To lessen condensation problems in other rooms, you will have to start improving insulation, unless you are heating the rooms by paraffin stoves. Insulation of various parts of the structure of the building is discussed on pages 127 to 137.

As regards wall insulation, you can reduce condensation by installing inner linings which are lightweight and therefore warm up and cool down considerably faster than the masonry wall behind them. For a cavity wall, nail 20mm (¾in.) square battens to the wall at suitable intervals (see page 32). You can then either use a special vapour-check plasterboard, or staple polythene sheets over the battens before nailing on the ordinary plasterboard. For a solid wall, you should use insulated plasterboard (see diagram below and page 132).

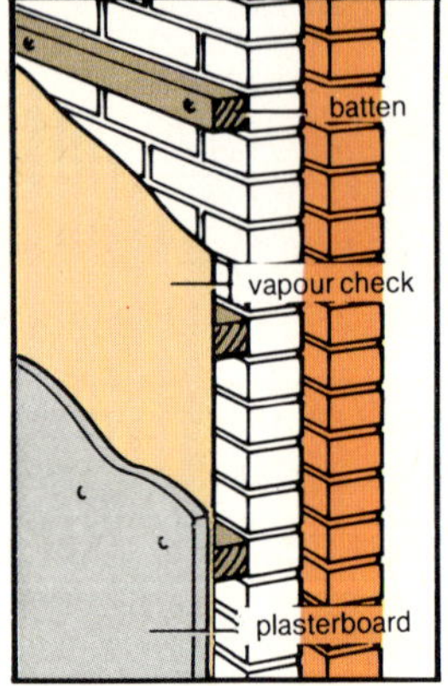

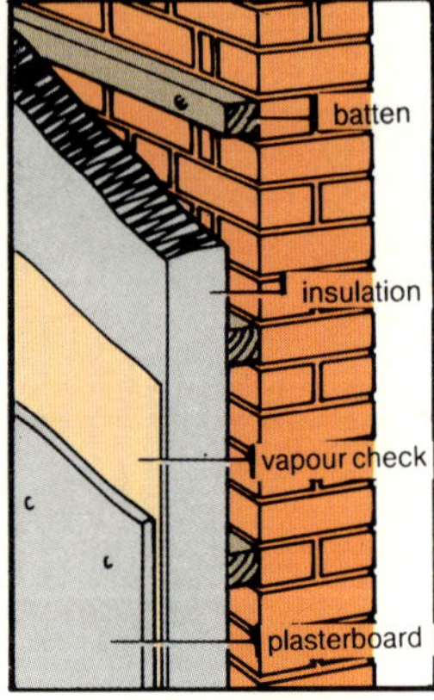

HYGROSCOPIC DAMP

This is an unusual type of damp where moisture is absorbed from the surrounding air, but may appear in modern houses. It is the result of using a particular sort of plaster (called 'Carlite') in the wrong place and is a builder's error. It is designed for use on walls which will not get damp, and on them it works perfectly satisfactorily. However, if used on a solid external wall, it will suck moisture in from the damp brickwork and produce a crystalline deposit on the inner surface. The only cure is to hack off the plaster and replace it with one designed for such a wall.

The Great Escape

can stop at your front door

Excluders for every door of every home!

R.N. Bradley

Brook Sawmills, Bradshaw Brow, Bradshaw, BOLTON BL2 3EY Telephone Bolton (0204) 51821/2/3

A MEMBER OF THE DRAUGHTPROOFING ADVISORY ASSOCIATION

CENTRAL HEATING SYSTEMS

PUMP-CIRCULATED SYSTEMS

SINGLE-PIPE AND TWO-PIPE SYSTEMS

In the single-pipe system, one pipe leaves the boiler and, after travelling all round, returns via the pump to the boiler.

In the two-pipe system, the pipe which leaves the boiler (the flow pipe) goes around the circuit until it reaches the last radiator, and then stops. A second pipe, which starts at the outlet of the first radiator, goes back to the boiler. This second pipe picks up all the outlets from the radiators, while the first pipe only supplies their inlets.

With the single pipe, which acts both as supplier and as exhaust, the water entering each radiator gives up some heat and so falls in temperature. Thus the water in the single pipe gradually falls in temperature as it goes around the circuit. This fall can be calculated and, at the lowered temperature, succeeding radiators have to be proportionately larger in order to perform as required.

In the two-pipe system such dilution does not occur, and any fall in temperature in the flow pipe is only nominal. Consequently all radiators may be calculated on the same water temperature basis. This helps them to work better while taking up less room. Overall they also cost less, and this can be offset against the extra cost of pipe. The two-pipe system is superior and should be used whenever possible.

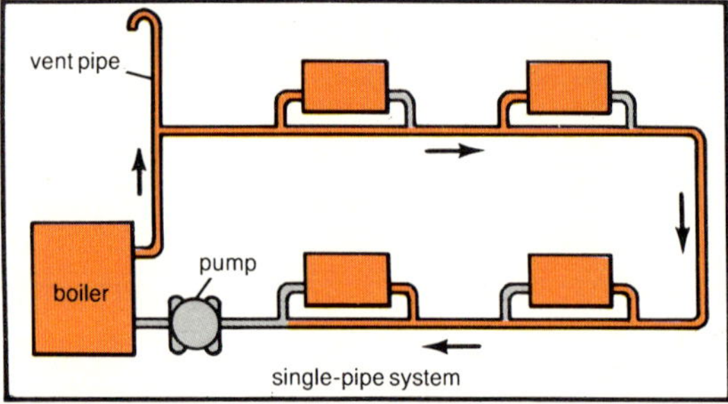

single-pipe system

MICROBORE SYSTEM

The microbore system has to deal with a different set of circumstances. It has a main flow pipe, led a comparatively short distance to a manifold. There is a return pipe with the same length of run. After that small pipes, usually of 8mm, 10 or occasionally 12mm (5/16, 3/8 or 1/2in.) diameter, run 'out and home' from the flow manifold to the radiator and to the return manifold. Each appliance has its own pair of small or microbore pipes.

It is easier to run a circuit using microbore; in fact it resembles running an electric cable. Microbore copper pipe can be unrolled as you go, hand-bent to all curves, hidden behind skirtings, and even run inside picture rails. It is also quite easy to kick it, stand a table leg on it, shut it in a door, etc; any of these could ruin it.

Microbore is not just a matter of pipe size and arrangement. Any appliance needs a given quantity of heat in order to do its job, so a very small pipe needs to pass as much water as a much larger pipe. It can do so only if more pressure is applied to pump more water through it. This means that a more powerful pump is needed. Another snag is that smaller bores get blocked more easily than larger pipes; consequently microbore systems call for greater care regarding scale, rust, etc. Microbore systems use the same boilers, radiators, etc as other systems.

HOW THE TWO-PIPE SYSTEM WORKS

The two-pipe system with gravity domestic hot water circulation system combined, is likely to be the best buy for quite a long time to come. The hot water primaries (flow and return pipes) should take the most direct, most nearly vertical route possible.

THE TRICK

It is best if the hot water cylinder is located above the boiler position, not at the other end of the house.

The heating flow and return are not under any such constraint, and long horizontal runs are quite in order. Loops, which are not allowed in gravity circuits, may be made, though it is best to make them upwards. To go past a door, for instance, it is better to travel up and over than down and under, solely because the system cannot be fully drained if there are traps.

vent pipe · flow pipe · return pipe · boiler · pump

two-pipe system

All four tappings (connection points) on the boiler are shown in use. It is quite acceptable to use only two, one flow and one return, or three (these would usually be two flow and one return). Unless a boiler is known to have an internal barrier, it could be bad practice to use opposite return ports when the heating return is pumped. The water under pump pressure can easily overcome the gentler gravity flow through the other port and cause reversed circulation in the primaries. On the other hand it could be difficult to combine a continuous gravity flow into a flow which is stopped and started by a pump (see diagram below). It is sometimes argued that the cold feed pipe can be combined with the vent pipe quite safely. The argument is most often used by installers wanting to cut a few cost corners. Circumstances could arise in which this would be anything but safe, if only because the two functions of cold feed and venting work in opposite directions. Two separate pipes are needed.

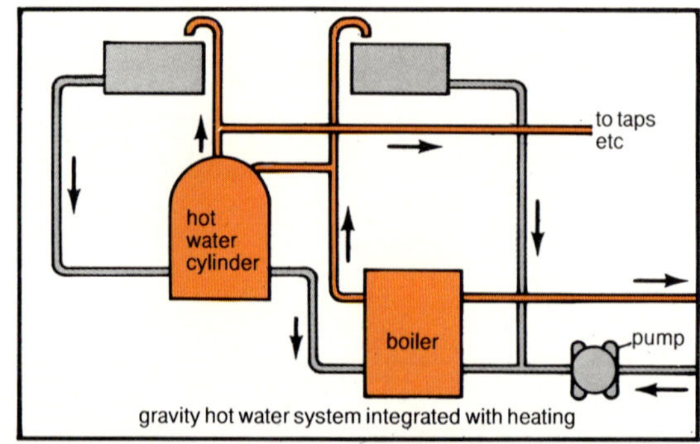

gravity hot water system integrated with heating

PUMPS

The pump is usually positioned on the return pipe to the boiler. If you buy a 'small-bore unit', which is among other things a boiler with pump attached, that pump is on the return side. The pump could go on the flow side, but only when the vertical distance between the overhead cistern and the highest point in the system to which water is pumped is less than the 'head' of the pump.

THE TRICK

Every pump states its 'head': it will pump *x* litres (or gallons) per hour against a head (or to a height of) *y* metres (or feet).

For the average house, a standard pump will do as much work as is required. If its maximum output is not required, there are ways of reducing it. Many pumps have a built-in regulator, which partly closes an internal damper. If a pump is not equipped with one, use the outlet valve as a throttle. Regulate the speed of water flow through the system so as to obtain a 10°C (20°F) temperature drop, from boiler outlet to boiler inlet across the circuit. You should then check that there is no sign of 'pumping over': i.e. water being pumped out of the overflow over the cistern when the pump is at work. This can quickly lead to corrosion; if it does occur, the pump performance must be further reduced until the fault is cured.

All pumps should be fitted with a stopvalve on inlet and outlet, making them easy to remove for servicing.

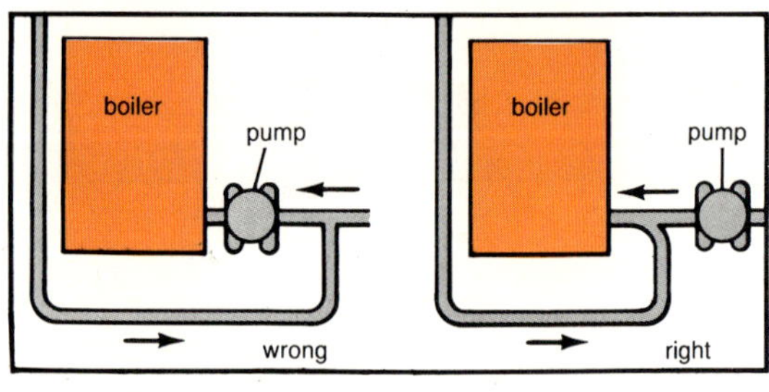

GRAVITY SYSTEMS

In these, gravity circulates the water: a pump can do it better! There are two situations in which a gravity system is still useful. One is on the domestic hot water side of a combined central heating system. The other is the remote country cottage, miles from a power cable, which need not thus be denied central heating.

TEMPERATURE CONTROLLERS

THERMOSTATS

A room thermostat senses the temperature of a room and decides whether the required temperature has been reached or not. In wet systems it controls the circulating pump, in warm air systems the circulating fan. The setting imposed on this thermostat controls how much heat you have.

BOILER THERMOSTATS

This thermostat is present in even the simplest systems, except in solid fuel back boiler installations. A boiler thermostat may be electric or non-electric, though the latter is less common now. Most boilers in the UK are gas-fired, but electric control valves compactly fulfil all the necessary operations for the boiler to work, and also act as central receivers for other controls, such as the boiler thermostat and the clock. With electric control systems, every controller is a switch, which stops or starts an operation by making or breaking the electricity supply to the principal control. This is simplified for the installer or user, to become a plug-in point.

THE TRICK

Never set the thermostat below 60°C (140°F), otherwise you will encourage flue corrosion.

If you have a direct hot water system, change it into an indirect system (see page 124).

THE TRICK

In the meantime, if yours is a hard water district, do not set the boilerstat much above 60°C (140°F).

There is often some advantage in using a boilerstat for seasonal heating control. In the most severe weather the boilerstat set at 90°C (190°F) will make more total heat available, and each radiator will give more heat. In milder weather it will behave more uniformly if the boilerstat is at 65°C (150°F). You might choose two other settings in between, for normal near-freezing weather, and for average winter weather.

RADIATOR THERMOSTAT

Instead of a room thermostat which acts for the whole house, it is advantageous in all but cost to control each radiator independently. A system of this type usually has a permanently running pump stopped only by a clock, but a roomstat may be used in addition, set higher than the highest radstat setting.

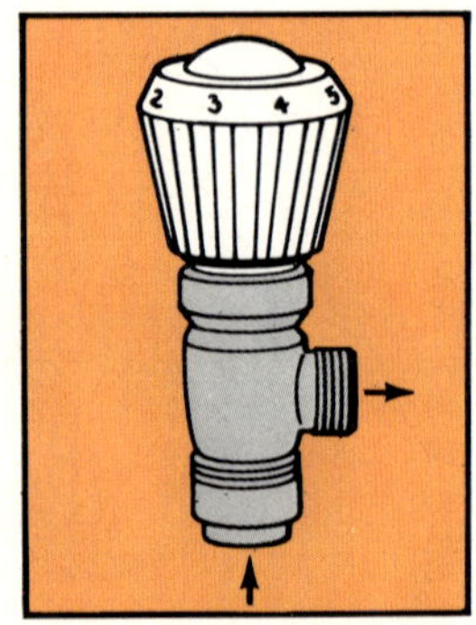

ZONE CONTROLLERS

Between the broad control of a single roomstat and clock, and the individual control exercised by radstats, there is a middle-of-the-road method of controlling by zones. In its most useful form this means upstairs and downstairs zones, the day area and the night area. These need to operate at different times, and usually at different temperatures. These differences are regular features and therefore well suited to automatic control.

The control is carried out by an electromagnetic valve in the heating pipeline to the zone or floor. The actuator is a zone roomstat, or both a roomstat and clock.

Caution: suppose that you have a zoned system, with both or all zones fully controlled; also a cylinderstat on the domestic hot water system. There are bound to be times when all of them are at 'Off', and this will happen suddenly.

THE TRICK

It is imperative therefore that any such system must be worked by a fully automatic boiler, also capable of shutting down at once. It must not be connected to a solid fuel boiler, or a crude oil-fired boiler.

CYLINDER THERMOSTAT

If you want to run a fairly high boiler temperature, but also want to limit the hot water temperature, you have to choose between them. With a cylinderstat, however, you can select a hot water temperature at any level below boiler temperature, thus achieving both objects. Cylinderstats may be electric or non-electric. The electric models take several forms, and may be integrated into more complex control systems. The non-electric ones work on the principle that too high a temperature in the water expands a wax-filled bellows, causing progressive closure of a valve through which water flows from boiler to cylinder.

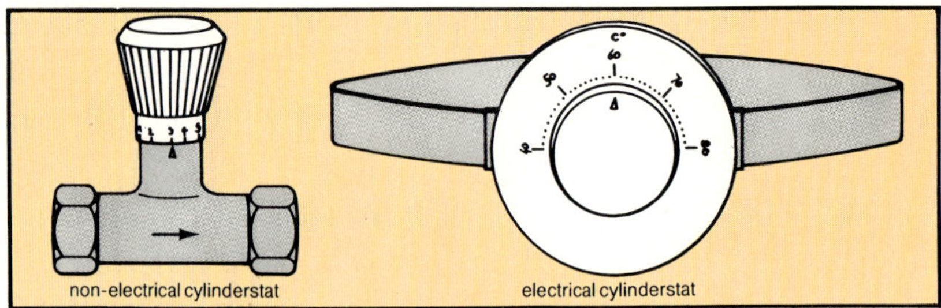

non-electrical cylinderstat
electrical cylinderstat

FROST OR LOW LIMIT THERMOSTAT

This is a safety device, which is mechanically similar to a roomstat, but operates at a low range and has a cut-in point commonly set at 2°C (36°F) up to 4°C (40°F). It is entirely dependent on being correctly placed and incorporated into the system.

THE TRICK

Its position must be the most exposed part of the heated area, for instance near a boiler sited in an outhouse, near a garage radiator, or beside the cistern in the attic.

It is then wired into the control system so that when it comes into circuit it overrides any form of control which might be in an 'Off' position. The purpose is to bring the heating to work despite everything if there is a danger of freezing in any part of the circuit. Its greatest usefulness would be if you are away at Christmas.

PROGRAMMERS

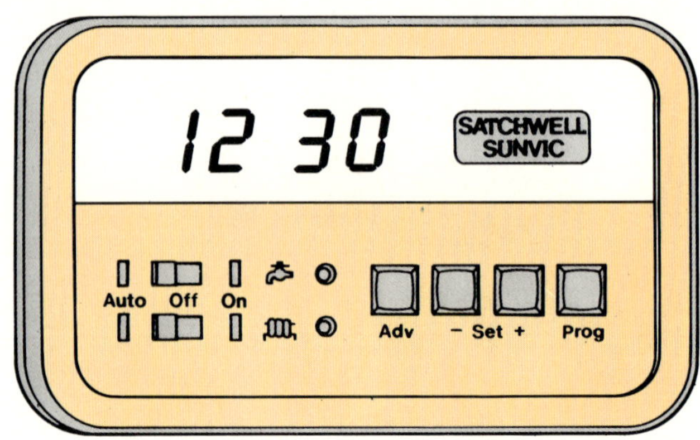

A programmer is a set of multiple switches in one case, which include the clock and sometimes (for boilers) the boilerstat, and a number of 'programmes'. These enable you to decide whether you will have, at times which the clock will arrange for you, domestic hot water with or without central heating once, twice, or all day, or non-stop. This it might do in a number of choices from four to twelve or more. However, most people rarely use more than four.

With the common system, you may have domestic hot water without central heating, but not the other way round. If you want complete freedom of choice you must have a system in which the primaries, which produce domestic hot water, are pumped.

FURTHER INFORMATION

For anything to do with installation of services – heating, hot water, etc. – you can ask at gas or electricity showrooms.

The Heating and Ventilating Contractors' Association (HVCA)
Esca House, 34 Palace Court, London W2 4JG (01–229 5543)
A trade association whose members between them span the whole field of heating, etc. HVCA gives very good guarantees, without cost to the customer, against any failure by its members to perform satisfactorily. Contractors who are HVCA members usually advertise that fact, but if in doubt ask at head office for local names. Be sure to tell them the type of work you have in mind, because they have many specialists among their members.

RADIATORS 1

PANEL RADIATORS

The common kind of radiator has dimples or vertical furrows on its surface, which are simply a means of increasing the real surface area by comparison with the 'picture frame' area. This is done because heat output depends upon surface area, among other things, and heat output is what radiators are about. Panel radiators range from about 250mm (10in.) tall to 900mm (36in.) or more, and from about 450mm (18in.) long to 6m. (18ft) or more.

An association called MARC has created a stable and reputable system of measuring radiator outputs.

THE TRICK

Do not buy a radiator unless it is made by a firm subscribing to MARC and carrying their swing ticket.

Radiator output is measured under standard conditions which are stated, and there is a simple formula supplied for converting that output to other sets of conditions, though this is rarely needed in practice.

Radiator output enables you to choose the right size radiator for the calculated heat loss of the room where it is to go. The sum of all radiator outputs indicates the size of the boiler which will be needed.

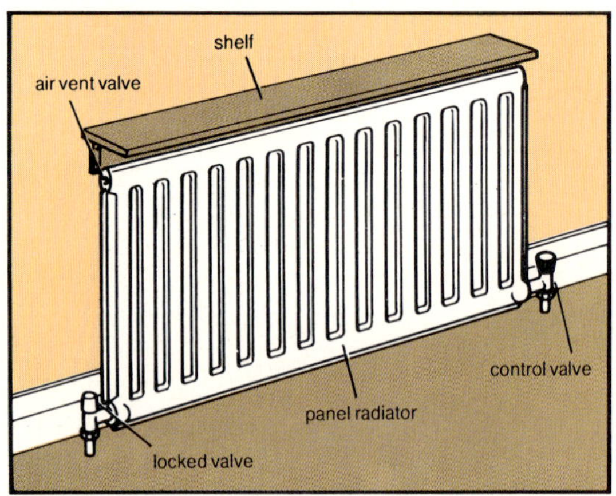

SHELVES AND REFLECTORS

There has been a certain amount of talk about putting reflectors behind a radiator – either home-made ones of kitchen foil or bought ones. They are claimed to increase their efficiency. It is probably worth using it with radiators on external walls.

An addition with more reason is the radiator shelf. Any radiator not under a window should have a shelf to prevent discoloration of the wall. The rising warm air stream off the radiator carries airborne dust and the charred remains of minute living cells, which tend to condense on the first cooler surface, hence brown stains on walls above radiators.

THE TRICK

A shelf should be 25mm (1in.) or so longer at each end than the radiator, up to 25mm (1in.) deeper, and fixed at 65–70mm (2½in.) over the top of it. The junction with the wall must be filled with a sealing strip to be airtight.

POSITIONING

Radiators must not depend upon the connecting pipes for support. The makers supply brackets of adequate strength, and complaints about brackets almost invariably reveal that the fault was in connecting the brackets to the wall. If you drill into solid brick and use plastic plugs, the screws supplied with the brackets should prove equal to normal demands.

Some radiators are still made with four connections, one at each corner. Connections are usually 15mm (½in.) tappings. One of the top ones, usually on the downstream side, is for the air-bleed valve, itself usually 3mm (⅛in.) gas thread in an adaptor. The arrangement of top inlet, opposite bottom outlet is best for performance, but rather unsightly because of the length of exposed pipe. It is more common to fit both inlet and outlet to the bottom tappings. This has been further simplified by a combination fitting which allows inlet and outlet to use just one tapping. This is well suited to microbore installations.

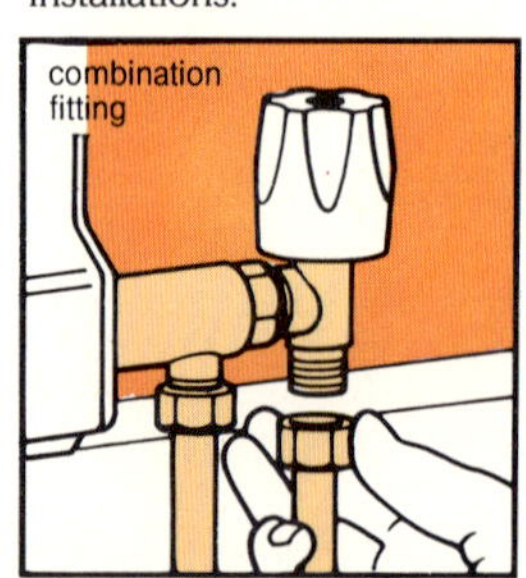

THE TRICK

Radiators should stand under single-glazed windows, so that the rising stream of warm air can counteract the falling stream of cold air off the glass.

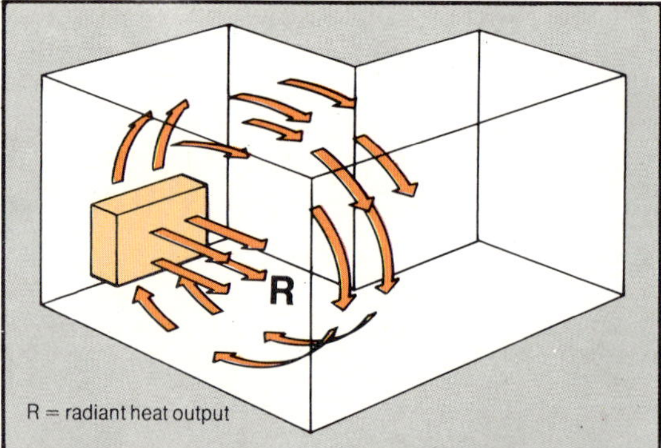

If you have double glazing this is irrelevant, so consider positioning the radiator as near as possible to the rising pipework. If an inside wall is readily available it will be about 5 per cent better than an outside one. The bottom of the radiator should be just above skirting board level, which allows air to travel under and up behind the radiator.

A radiator should never be boxed in, put behind a screen, or in any way prevented from having its own clear view of most of the room. Heat is given out by a radiator in two ways. Up to half is radiation, which is what you get from a gas or electric fire, but at lower temperature. The rest is convection, a current of warm air which travels up the back and front of the radiator and leaves from the top, deflected outward by a shelf if one is fitted. It then has to bend at the ceiling and, still at high level, go to another wall where it is bent downwards and then cycles back to the radiator. A lot of diffusion takes place, so that warmth is more widely distributed than the description suggests. Nevertheless a single radiator fitted in, for instance, the smaller alcove of an L-shaped room has little chance of producing an even temperature in the whole room.

VALVES AND KEYS

Every radiator, and indeed every heat emitter of whatever kind, should be equipped with valves on inlet and outlet. In normal use one acts as a balancing valve, to regulate the share of the total circulating water the radiator takes. The other is for regular on/off use. In less ordinary circumstances (a leaking radiator, or when you paint behind it), both valves are used, to isolate and remove the radiator without interfering with the rest of the system, draining and so on.

An ancillary piece of equipment which you should insist upon getting with a radiator is the air vent key. A radiator, particularly with both connections at the bottom, is ready made for air pockets, but it is easy to get rid of them.

THE TRICK

You should bleed every radiator at regular intervals until you have established whether it is justified, or whether the system will tolerate a much longer interval between operations.

Do not paint panel radiators with metallic paints as these substantially reduce heat output. You can use any other kind of paint, and any colour. After three or four coats strip them off, then prime and start again.

PLAIN-FRONTED RADIATORS

There are, of course, heat emitters other than panel radiators. The most likely type of modern radiator to be seen has a plain front – obviously a simple metal sheet. Behind that, and welded to it, are tube coils through which the hot water passes. This kind of radiator behaves like a panel type and should be treated in the same way. Its difference lies in installation.

Because the resistance to flow is quite high, this pattern must be connected to a two-pipe system, in which resistances are treated in parallel, not in series, to use an electrical analogy. Radiators of this type are imported, which means that they do not come under the auspices of MARC and cannot benefit from their test procedure.

RADIATORS 2

SKIRTING HEATERS

The Americans make much use of an admirable type of radiator which promotes a better room heating pattern than any radiator discussed so far. This is the skirting heater (US: baseboard heater) which runs unobtrusively along the line of the skirting board and produces a broad sweep of warm air. Among other advantages is its remarkably good vertical gradient, sometimes called the hot head/cold feet syndrome. The reason it has not caught on in Britain is cost; wet central heating has been tied to minimum costs, and skirting heaters were never allowed to compete with radiators. However, they are recommended to anyone prepared to pay for results. Most skirting heaters can have their output modulated by means of a damper which controls the amount of air which can pass over the gilled tube heating element.

FAN CONVECTORS

Another good appliance for vertical temperature gradient relies upon power to achieve its results. This is the fan convector. Air is ejected, usually obliquely downwards, by a fan which is controlled by a room thermostat and often by a clock as well. As the output is negligible when the fan is stopped, this arrangement provides control with maximum economy and effect. Because of the thermostat click, it is not recommended for bedrooms.

All these devices must remain visible; the warm air output must have freedom to follow its pattern. A skirting heater must not be hidden behind anything. A fan convector must not discharge its powered air stream direct at a heavily padded armchair. Both these appliances, and ordinary convectors, give off negligible radiation. Consequently the freeway is required only where the warm air stream runs: in ordinary convectors this is upwards; in fan convectors forwards and for most purposes downwards. (You often have a choice, with variable louvres.)

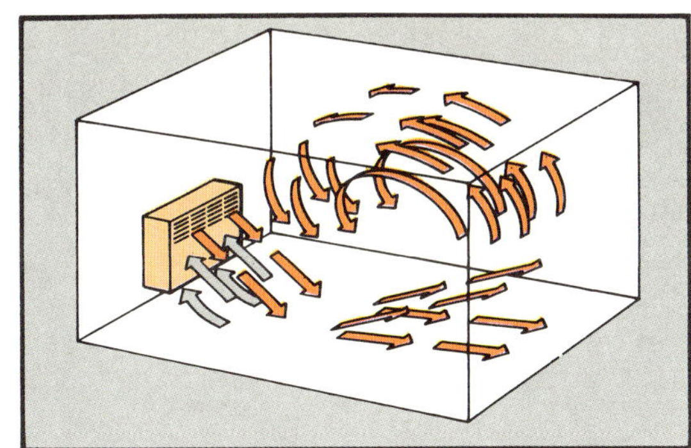

Fan convectors, and ordinary convectors which have a coil of pipe as the heat source, require a two-pipe system. The fan convector incorporates a room temperature thermostat, and often a three-speed selection switch as well. Choose the speed which will enable the convector to work most of the time, instead of being shut off for 40 minutes in every hour by its own radiator thermostat.

REMOVING A PANEL RADIATOR

You may require to remove a radiator because it has sprung a leak and you need to replace it, or in order to paint behind it. Some radiators are designed to swing down without having to remove them. If you are not sure about this, consult the installers or play safe and remove the radiator completely. It is possible to paint the back of a radiator using a radiator brush with a long handle.

Check how many valves the radiator has: if two (one at each end), close both; if only one, you will have to drain the central heating system first (see page 115).

Close the control valve so that it is fully off. Take the cap off the locked valve at the other end and close it also using an adjustable spanner. Count how many turns were required to close it completely and make a note of it.

Either remove the carpets from under the radiator, or lay down plastic sheeting to protect them (the radiator water may contain rust which will stain your carpets irreparably). Place a basin under each of the valves and loosen the union joints at each end as gently as you can. Try not to distort the pipes.

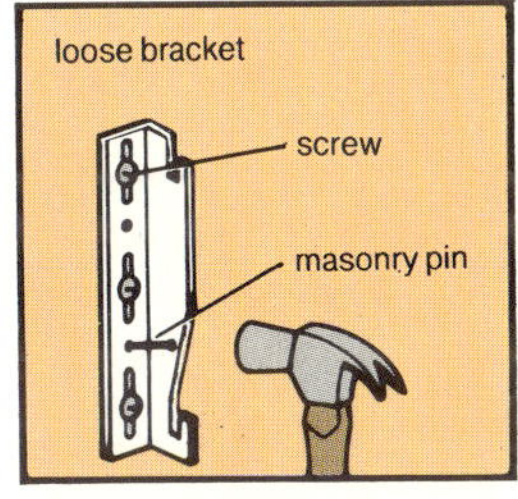

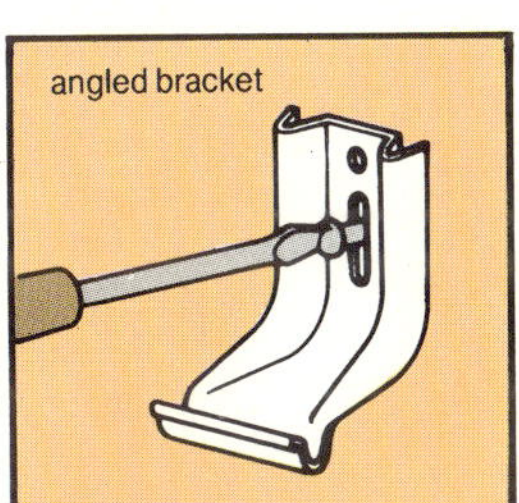

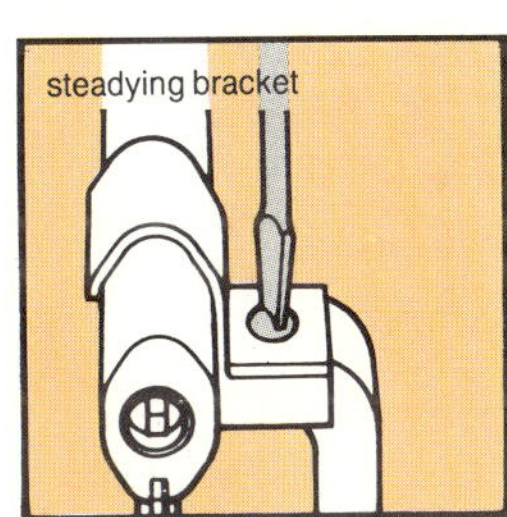

If the radiator is held on the wall with angled or steadying brackets, loosen them carefully. Remember that large radiators can be very heavy, especially with some water left in them and arrange for help if you don't think you can manage alone. Lift the radiator off its brackets and tilt it so that the remaining water runs into one of the basins. Lay it on some plastic sheeting on the floor in the middle of the room or lean it against another wall, so that any drips will not cause stains.

THE TRICK

If you intend installing a new radiator, do not reuse the air vent valve or union connectors from the old one; buy new ones.

Smear the threads of the new union connectors with jointing compound (see page 102) and wrap plumber's hemp into them; alternatively use PTFE tape.

Screw the union connectors into the appropriate radiator sockets and tighten. Install the end-plug and air vent valve in the same way. Rehang the radiator and tighten the steadying or angled brackets. Spread jointing compound and the hemp or tape around the threads of the valve unions; tighten the unions onto the valve unions.

Open the locked valve with your adjustable spanner by the number of turns that was needed to close it (see above). Refit the valve's cap. Refill the expansion tank if you have drained the system, then open the control valve. Unscrew the air vent valve with the key (see page 148) and hold a basin under it. When water begins to flow out, close the valve.

If you are re-installing a radiator, it is safer to use new union connectors; however you do not need a new end-plug or air vent valve.

JAMMED CONTROL VALVES

Jammed control valves are usually caused by either over-enthusiastic turning or accumulated paint. Chip the latter away gently, then apply paint stripper (see page 231) to remove the final layer. Over-enthusiastic turning is rather harder to deal with. First make sure you are turning it the right way: anticlockwise (to the left) to open; clockwise (to the right) to close.

Remove any plastic cap to the valve otherwise it will be damaged. Get two adjustable or stilson spanners and grip one on the valve's body to counter the leverage of the other on the shank.

THE TRICK

Tap gently on the end of the shank spanner with a hammer – don't use brute force directly unless nothing else will shift it.

If you're not in a hurry, try some penetrating oil – that might well free it.

JAMMED VENT VALVES

This may well be because you are trying to use the wrong sized key.

THE TRICK

Take an impression of the plug (use Plasticine, Blu-tac, dough) and, if the key is the wrong size, take the impression to an ironmonger to get a correct one.

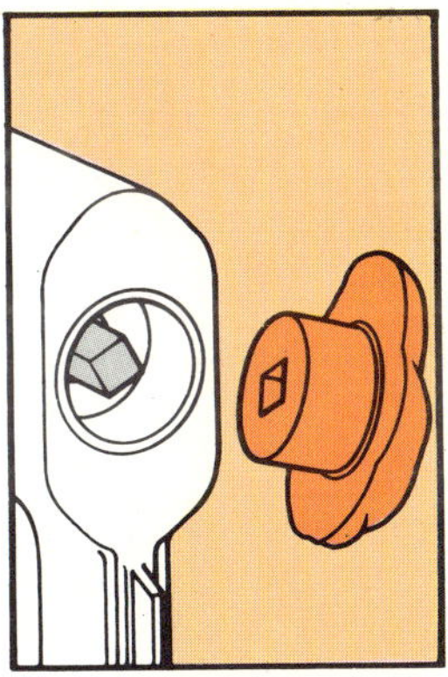

If accumulated paint is the problem, use paint stripper as above.

If you can manage to get the key onto the shank, you can probably shock the valve free by gripping the key with an adjustable spanner and tapping the end with a hammer. You are only aiming to break the threads' adhesion so don't hit it with all your strength! Be ready to catch the dirty water which will flow out when you open the valve further.

HEATING BY WARM AIR 1

All types of central heating and a large proportion of other forms of heating achieve their effect through warmed air. In most cases this is second-hand, as for instance in a radiator on a wet system. The hot water warms the radiator, and the radiator warms the air; it is the air, not the radiator, which warms us. That, however, is not what is meant by warm air heating, which has air as the primary medium: it is air which receives heat from the heater, without any other medium in between.

The use of air instead of water has many instant attractions of the sort that make air-cooled car engines popular. There is no strongly made retaining system, no corrosion of pipes and passageways, no freezing problem, and no soggy mess if the medium leaks out of the system.

A typical room could be served by hot water heating in a 20mm (¾in.) pipe, but the same service in warm air would need a duct of section about 150 × 200mm (6 × 8in.). Nobody wants to live with a thing that size running down the hall or across the ceiling. As a result, a full ducted system is feasible in most houses only if incorporated during design and construction; i.e. in new houses, where the ducting can be 'lost' in the structure.

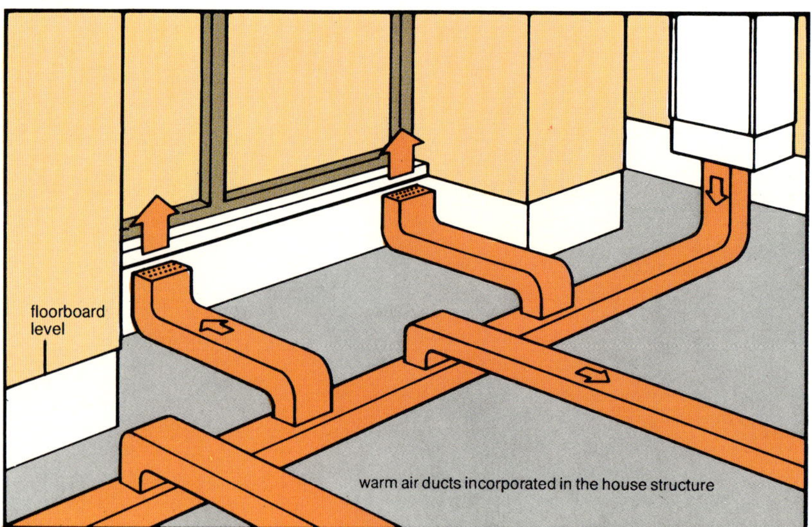

warm air ducts incorporated in the house structure

STUB DUCT SYSTEMS

A stub duct system differs from a full duct system in having only short or stub lengths of duct, which discharge warm air to a limited number of points, from which the air has to find its own way around the house. Clearly it is important to choose the best site for the heater.

WHAT TYPE OF HEATER?

All types of air heater which are adapted to connect to a duct on at least the air outlet side may be used. They all incorporate a fan, to move the air through the unit and to push it through the ducts, but not all fans are of the same power.

THE TRICK

If you go to buy a unit, make sure to ask whether the fan is intended to serve a full duct or stub duct system.

Most Electricaire units are suited to stub ducts and there are some units, such as the Thorn gas-fired one, in which the fan speed is adjustable to suit the duct resistance. This will deal with both stub ducts and full duct systems of varying lengths and complexities.

WHERE TO POSITION THE HEATER

The heater can go almost anywhere except in a bathroom, or in a bedroom on account of the click when the thermostat cuts in or out. It is often helpful to make a list of places where air should discharge: for example, into the hall so that there is drift to upstairs; into the living-room because that is where comfort is most needed; into a dining-room if you use it regularly, or a study if that has priority. Don't forget that, in some cases, you could rear a stub duct to feed upstairs, say on to the landing or the main bedroom. There is no objection to taking more than one exit from a duct; each exit is going to be fitted with a damper, so that air discharge can be stopped, started and controlled in quantity. Comfort with economy depends on making constant use of these dampers, and shutting off air flow when it is not needed.

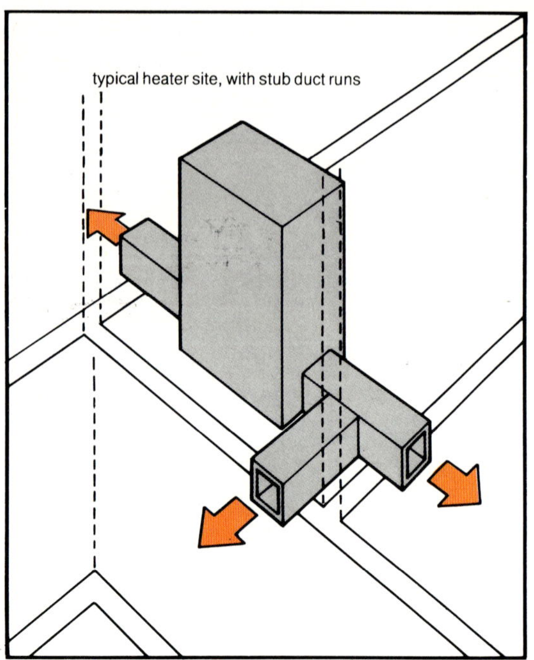

typical heater site, with stub duct runs

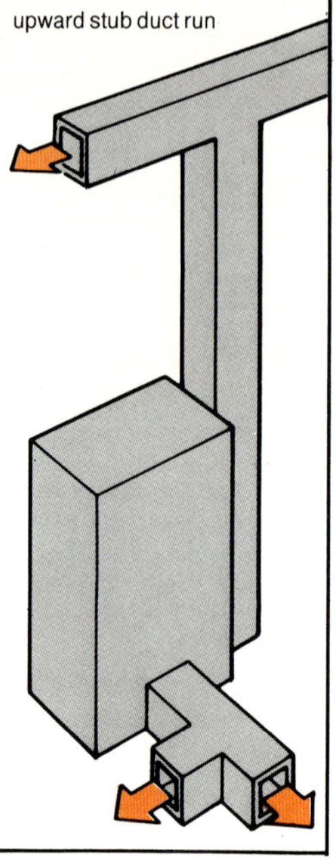

upward stub duct run

DUCTS

A short length, or even a wall length, of duct could be run against a wall and hidden under a bench seat. In critical conditions it could be led under the floor for most of its length, since there is no objection to dips as there might be in water-filled pipe.

THE TRICK

Where ducts pass through walls, the gap should be made up with soft filling (e.g. mineral wool packing) because a certain amount of expansion movement will take place.

The ducts are usually made of galvanized sheet steel, and can be bought with bends and other fittings from a good builder's merchant. The use of rigid glass fibre, once common, is now suspect because of the greater emphasis on fire resistance nowadays, but this material does make excellent insulation over the steel.

In the trade a mitre tool is used to cut V strips in a sheet of material, so that there is only one longitudinal joint to be taped. A good handyman with a sharp tool should be able to do the same.

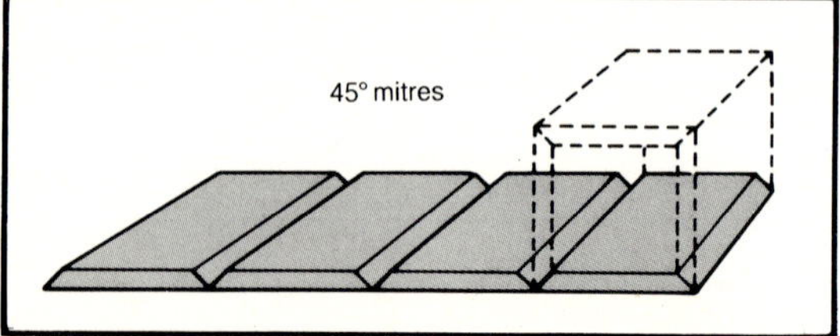

45° mitres

THE TRICK

In case of error (i.e. a too sloppy or too tight fit) simply cut through the grooves and fit all sides separately, taping them on.

Metal ducting should always be insulated on the air flow (but not necessarily on the return) side. If there is a danger of damp or wet, it must be waterproof-wrapped as well.

What size should the ducts be? Just follow these simple rules:

1. It is pointless to make any outlet bigger than the outlet on the heater itself, but it could be disadvantageous to make it much smaller because the emerging air might make a noise. Perhaps the best idea is to make each outlet equal to the outlet size on the heater. This is ideal when only one outlet damper is in use; if more than one is being used, the air is proportioned by the use of the terminal dampers.
2. Duct sizes must allow for connection between duct and damper, and duct and heater; both pieces of proprietary equipment will be in standard sizes.
3. The heater must be the right way round on the chosen site. Imagine what would happen to your scheme if any of the heaters were turned through 180°.

It switches on when you wake up

and warms up at once...

You can change the programme

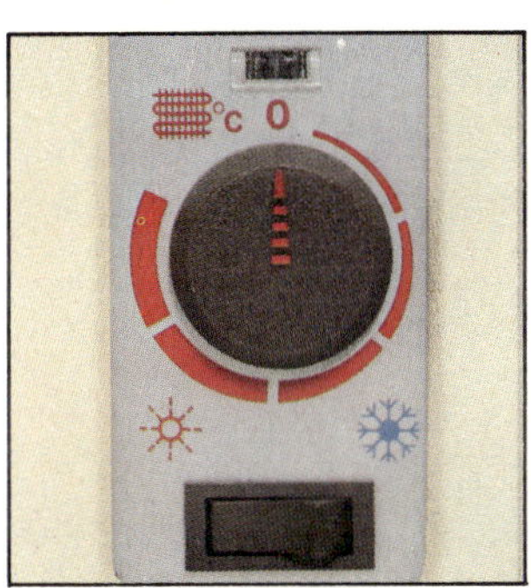

and turn up the volume.

Myson Fan Convectors -the Hi-Fi of heating

Before you decide on just radiators for your central heating, listen to this.

It's as easy to fit a Myson Fan Convector. It'll warm up from cold in a quarter of the time a radiator takes – so it's ideal for bedrooms, hallways and kitchens. Its circulation of warm air will heat every corner of the room. It's instantly controllable, because it has a three-speed fan and variable thermostat built-in. And it'll take up far less wall space than a radiator of the same output. *There's even a Kickspace model that fits in the gap under kitchen units.*

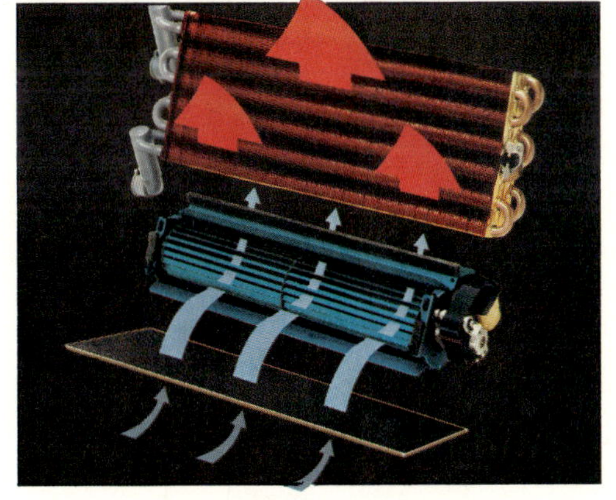

How a Fan Convector works
Hot water from your boiler flows into the fan convector like an ordinary radiator and into a very efficient finned heat exchanger. Air is then drawn over the element by the whisper-quiet fan and gently circulated to every part of the room.

MYSON

Myson Domestic Products Limited,
Ongar, Essex CM5 9RE.
Telephone: Ongar (0277) 362222.
Telex: 99356.

HEATING BY WARM AIR 2

CHOICE OF FUEL

There are only two serious contenders – gas and electricity. Gas is superior in being instantly controllable and to fine limits, its appliances being moderately sized and of moderate weight. Its principal disadvantage is that it demands a flue, either a conventional or balanced type. Electricity needs no flue and is a true 'go anywhere' unit. Gas-fired units with a conventional flue must have a return air duct. With all other units the system would benefit from one, but it is not essential.

There is, however, one drawback to electricity: once there was a wide choice of Electricaire units, but now there is only one, excluding any second-hand ones which might be available. In their heyday they were served by an off-peak tariff which included a voluntary three-hour middle-of-the-day boost, but the off-peak tariff has now become Economy 7, seven hours only, at night; a customer who wants a mid-day boost must take it at standard tariff, which is generally unacceptable because of the high price of electricity. The net result is that any heater of this type now gives a reduced performance because it can store less. The available unit is vertical, which means that the weight is concentrated.

On doubtful floors it is a good idea to trim out the floorboards and raise a concrete plinth direct from the subfloor.

This is a moderately crude application, well suited to the operational habits of the electrical unit if you can get a satisfactory one. However, a gas-fired unit is not only much more readily available but, in balanced-flue form, quite easy to accommodate in most situations. In both cases the ratings are few and standard, and the object is to choose one which is over, not under, your estimated requirement. The supplier can help you.

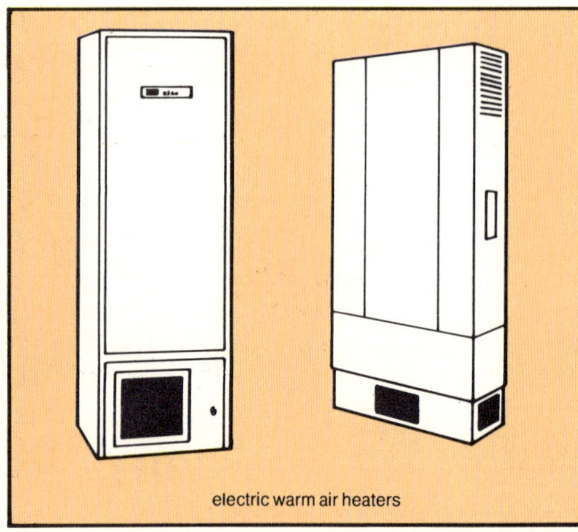

electric warm air heaters

DUCTLESS HEATERS

The free flow (ductless) heater is a type of appliance which makes almost no technical demands, but in return can only be described as crude, though sometimes surprisingly effective.

The earliest form of ductless heater was known as a 'brick central' and was literally a brick structure inside the house with an air heating furnace, often oil-fired, inside it. Air was allowed in at low level, and out, considerably heated, at higher levels. The warm air then had to find its way around the house, and in many cases did so with considerable success.

This cumbersome structure was overtaken by a long list of mainly imported metal air heaters which are scarcely heard of any more. The one survivor resembles a large gas fire but is in fact oil-fired and can have a back boiler. It will give off enough warmed air to heat a three-bedroomed house, all generated in the living-room. Open doors encourage drift, or a fan may be set in the wall to push some air into the hall from where it will circulate more widely. The description makes it sound more crude than it is, and many users claim to be very satisfied.

gas-fired warm air heaters

SETTING UP

First, a brief reminder of the points discussed so far, in the order of doing them:

1. Select a suitable heater. If electric, put it wherever best suits the duct runs. If gas, compromise between the best duct run and the requirement for a flue, either conventional or balanced.
2. Decide how the ducts will run, their size, and the positions of the outlet dampers. You will also need to insulate them.
3. Plan for a return duct, assuming that you want one. The main reason would be to achieve maximum re-circulation of warmed air. This may sound very desirable, but take care: it would, for instance, be a mistake to recirculate air from a room in which smokers congregate. It is illegal to take it from a kitchen or lavatory.

All is now ready to assemble the physical items of the system. Power must be supplied to run it, as must the means to control it. In the case of a gas-fired unit, you should employ either the local gas people or a CORGI-registered installer.

Important note: Because of the Gas Safety Regulations, the house-holder is entirely responsible, in law, for the safety of any d-i-y gas installations. If anything should go wrong, the consequences could far outweigh any expected saving in doing the job yourself.

For the person of average practical ability it is easier to make a successful job of an electrical installation. It must conform to the requirements of the 'IEE Regs': the Institution of Electrical Engineers' Regulations for the Electrical Equipment of Buildings: check these before starting (see page 75).

The essence of the electrical installation is a separate supply from the off-peak meter, serving only the heater. The supply will be twin and earth, and both the cable size and the fuse rating will be specified by the manufacturer or supplier of the heater.

If you are not already connected for the Economy 7 tariff you will have to make an application for connection. This will in all probability mean that the Electricity Board will test your installation to see that it conforms to the regulations and is electrically safe. There is no charge for changing meters.

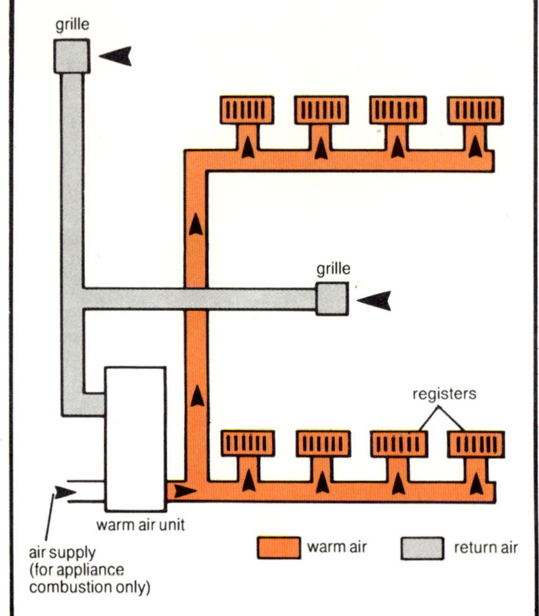

THE TRICK

Gas or electric, it is best to have the fan controlled by both a clock and a room thermostat so that conditions of comfort are reached when they are wanted.

That apart, the method of operation differs. Gas models are always at the ready, and will give their rated output indefinitely, on demand.

THE TRICK

Electric models, however, have to be programmed in advance so that the estimated amount of heat is stored overnight for the next day.

DIRECT HEATING 1

GAS

Our coal is estimated to have at least another three hundred years' life. Gas from the North Sea may not last more than this century, but very probably gas in another form, from coal, will take over, so there is no need to worry about future continuity of supplies. The nature of official testing has brought about a welcome uniformity, so that, faced with a choice between two approved appliances, you may safely choose on personal preference alone. The other more worrying aspects have been taken care of on your behalf.

INSTALLATION

The installation of gas-fired appliances of all kinds is a matter for experts, and you should have the job done for you, either by gas authority staff or at least by an installer who is registered with CORGI. There are legal penalties for contravening the Gas Safety Regulations, and the householder is liable no matter who did the job. However, the installer will have to consider various basic points: if you consider them first, you may not ask him for the impossible.

The internal gas supply must be capable of passing enough gas to the appliance. This, as it happens, is rarely a problem. It is most likely to arise when one pipe from the meter has several branches off to other appliances, a large proportion of which may well be on at the same time. This usually calls for a larger-diameter feeder.

The gas pipe to the appliance must be thoroughly gas-tight. It should run where it cannot sustain mechanical damage by being tripped over, hit by moving furniture, etc. It is best run concealed: i.e. under floors.

The gas supply pipe must terminate in a stopcock with a union connection on the outlet side so that the appliance can be shut off and if necessary removed without disturbing the rest of the gas supply.

The floor beneath a gas fire rarely poses any problems. If the fire is wall-mounted and you want to run the carpet beneath it, this is fine so long as the fire's burner bar is not less than 250mm (10in.) above the floor. Floor-standing fires are usually in the hearth.

Flue and chimney arrangements are very important. The flue pipe off the fire must be connected to a flue or chimney. It could with advantage be connected to a flue liner inside a conventional chimney. The flue, chimney or flue liner must have a Gas Council-approved type of terminal fitted.

In any case the hearth front must be closed off, except for a very small area, such as a slot about 150 × 25mm (6 × 1in.) near the bottom of the plate or board used to seal off the front. This has the dual function of controlling the operation of the chimney and preventing the escape of warmed air. The flue off the gas fire passes through a slot cut in the board.

The board used for sealing off the hearth must be non-flammable. If the existing board is asbestos it should be replaced with a mineral fibre equivalent. Do not cut the old asbestos – the dust is extremely hazardous.

FURTHER INFORMATION

First try the local showroom. Smaller ones often cannot handle other than routine questions, in which case ask for a name and phone number at the regional head office. It is better to make your own enquiries.

Showrooms can deal with safety, installation, testing for known or suspected leaks, and spares for most appliances for up to 15 years. They can give you names of CORGI-registered installers, and the address of the Gas Consumers' Council if you wish to complain about the gas industry.

LOG-EFFECT GAS FIRES

Some people like to see a flicker reminiscent of the open coal fire, however artificial that flicker obviously is. For those who want it, there are gas fires which incorporate a section giving no warmth but have moving lights in it; there is also a fire entirely composed of ceramic logs on to which gas flames play. Originally the efficiency of these fires was poor, on a par with the old open coal fire. Some rapid changes have been made which bring moderate efficiency to some models, but there is still a conflict between energy conservation and a pleasing visual effect.

WOOD

The stoves designed for burning wood which are often advertised in the glossy magazines are mainly of Scandinavian origin, with at least one from Eire, and are not covered by any approvals scheme. They are fairly high-priced, and in Britain, where timber is no longer commonly available, are probably most useful and economical to those who have permanent access to a supply of free or cheap timber. You should satisfy yourself on at least two points before buying: is the wood-burning appliance going to conform with the Clean Air Acts in a smokeless zone, if you live in one?; and what advice is given about possible flue troubles with the light tars of low boiling point which might condense in cool flue pipes, causing blockages?

It is equally important to note that, however cheap the wood, it may not be used on any of the NCB-approved fires and room heaters unless the makers specifically say so. It is perfectly legitimate to ask them, since they will not necessarily mention this possibility.

OIL

This fuel does not make a significant contribution to this form of single appliance heating. The safety aspect of the paraffin stove, which used to be a drawback, has long since been dealt with by making every unit self-extinguishing if overturned.

No amount of development work can get away from the fact that each gallon (4.5l.) of paraffin burned produces a gallon of water in vapour form. This, from a flueless apparatus, is the raw material of condensation, and all too often the paraffin stove bought to provide the warmth which will counteract condensation is itself the chief cause of that nuisance. Paraffin heaters are fine in tool sheds and the like but rarely indoors.

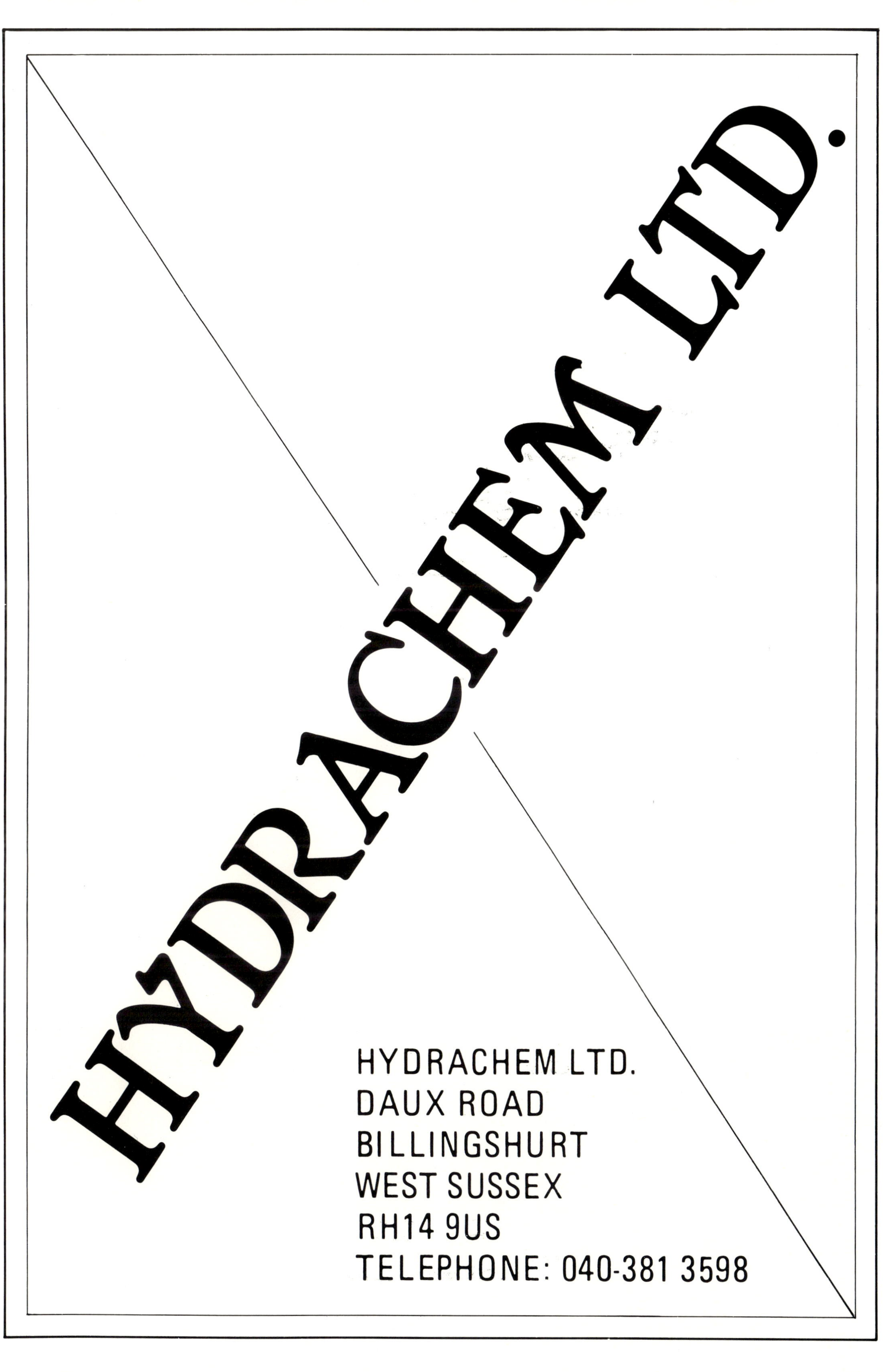

DIRECT HEATING 2

ELECTRICAL OFF-PEAK HEATING

Almost by definition, this involves energy storage, because the input or actual use occurs for the most part while people are asleep, and the results stored for use on waking. Electricity at the Economy 7 tariff is used – see page 152. If you are starting a heating system, you can buy good, second-hand storage heaters pretty cheaply: watch the local paper's small ads.

You must wire each unit back to the board, using cable suitable for 13 amps, with a double-pole wall-mounted switch near the heater (see pages 75 and 76). The Board will have to change your meter for an Economy 7 meter and clock (see page 152).

Operation of storage heaters is not like any other apparatus. Heat control is anticipatory, in that you decide the day before whether you will need more or less heat next day.

Some heaters have extra insulation to limit natural output, and a means of accelerating heat output when required. This might be by a mechanical damper which lets air travel up the hollow core; or, better, it might include a fan which blows air over the hot core when required. A fan lends itself to control by both clock and room thermostat, and so this is well suited to a household where the living-room is not occupied until evening, by which time a natural output-type heater would be running down.

THE TRICK

Do not leave objects on the top or even leaning against the sides. As well as the fire risk, you will probably blow the overheat fuse and shut the unit down.

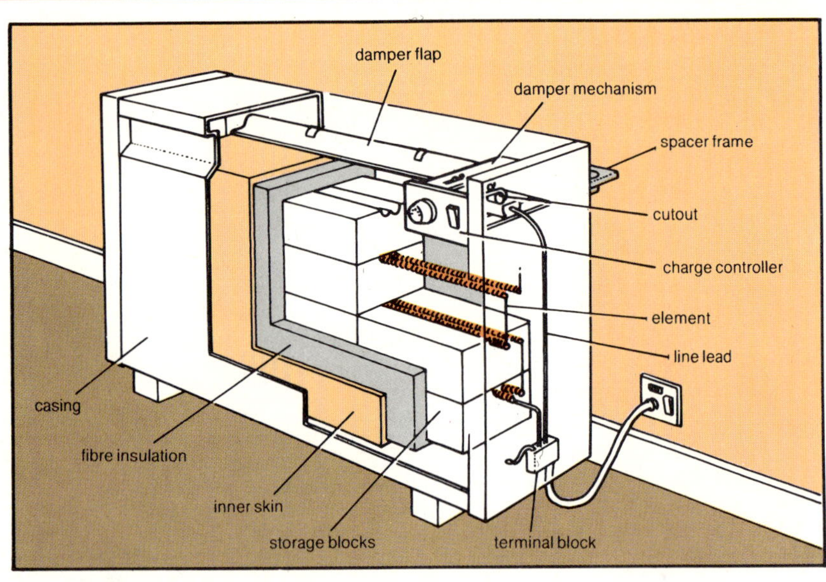

FURTHER INFORMATION

Go to the local showroom first. Many retailers sell electrical goods, and some of these will guide you through the regulations. However, for safety, always consult the Electricity Board (through the showroom) when it is a case of satisfying the IEE Regs. There is also an Electricity Consumers' Council.

SOLID FUEL

Most solid-fuel room heaters now incorporate the advantage of hopper feeding, which can make the appliance run for 10 hours without attention. They are usually offered in two forms, built-in or free-standing: i.e. mainly recessed into the fireplace opening, or standing in front of the chimney-breast front line. The latter have a decorative casing all over. Designs vary widely.

If one of these types could be suitable, consider the following points:

1. Make sure that you have a working chimney, and sweep it (see page 159).
2. Measure your fireplace opening, width, height and depth (back to front).
3. Go either to a good builder's merchant, or to an agent of the NCB or SFAS (usually a fuel merchant selling appliances).
4. Make a shortlist of those appliances which are suitable for your size of room. If with boiler, can it handle the heating load as well as making domestic hot water? A qualified salesman can usually answer this.
5. Ask whether a flue liner is advised. The answer might depend upon examination of the chimney. It is an extra cost, but a flue liner is the instant answer to nearly all possible chimney troubles, and might even cure marginal cases of down draught.
6. Ask to see, and if possible borrow, the maker's installation instructions for the appliance you like best. Read these carefully so that you know what is going to be involved in connecting the flue pipe into the chimney; in sealing the appliance into the hearth if inset; in sealing off the hearth opening; and in providing the standing area for the appliance if it is freestanding. It is not usually permitted to stand these appliances on a wooden floor.

THE TRICK

If there is no hearth slab, and no specific instructions, consult the Building Regulations (try the public library or town hall.)

7. Do not buy an appliance which does not have NCB approval. No NCB agent will offer you one, but there is no control over what is imported and sold by local distributors.

ADDING A CHIMNEY

If you have no chimney, all is not lost. An external chimney of precast blocks can be built onto a gable end; or a flue pipe can be run, either mainly internally or mainly externally.

THE TRICK

A flue run mainly indoors is better, not only because it eliminates over-cooling but also because it gives up some useful warmth.

There are, however, very stringent rules about how it is to be run, particularly when passing through ceilings and roof. These are set out in the Building Regulations. Any flue pipe must terminate above ridge level, and have an approved-pattern terminal fitted.

CHOICE OF FUEL

One important factor will be the kinds of fuel suited to the appliance. Both the type and the size of fuel, where it applies, will be given. You can choose on price, or best availability – consult the merchant. All solid fuels tend to degrade in store.

THE TRICK

Don't put the slack in the dustbin – it is always useful for banking up a fire, or with hopper-fed appliances introduced to mix with the graded fuel until it is used up.

The object is to keep degradation to a minimum. Store under cover and try to avoid storing in too much depth, where the weight will crush the lower layers. Although you feed into the store at the top, arrange to withdraw from the bottom, so that the lower layers do not suffer progressive degradation. Bunkerage note: 1 ton coal occupies 1.2cu.m. (42cu.ft); coke, 2.3cu.m. (80cu.ft).

FIREPLACES 1

A fireplace consists of four basic parts. Their correct names are the surround, which is the vertical part on the wall around the fire opening; the hearth, fixed on the floor in front of the surround; the fireback, which forms an enclosure inside the opening at the back and sides of the fire; and the fire itself, in which the actual fuel is burned. Taking the breakdown a little further, there are, in fact, three hearths: the decorative bit that you actually see is the superimposed hearth, sometimes called the decorative hearth. Behind it is a small slab of concrete on which the grate sits, and this is the back hearth. The superimposed hearth rests on a slab of concrete inset into the floor, which is known as the constructional hearth.

This is how a fireplace works. If air is warmed it rises, so when you start a fire in a fireplace (with the old-fashioned method of paper and sticks, firelighters, or the more modern gas ignition), you heat the air immediately above the fuel, and it rises up the flue. To replace this air, more is drawn into the fire opening from the room. This new air, in turn, is heated and rises up the flue. As it passes over the coals, it causes combustion to increase, which steps up the flow of air, thus increasing the combustion even further. It is a self-perpetuating process, and is the one that caused old-fashioned fires to create such fearsome draughts. These are much reduced, if not eliminated altogether, when you install a modern appliance.

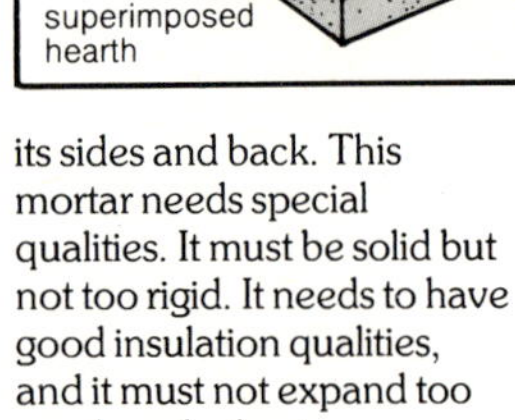

DAMAGED FIREBACKS

There is not much to go wrong with a fireplace. The most common – indeed, perhaps the only likely – fault is that the fireback will become damaged under the intense heat of the fire, and will then need to be replaced.

Heat is, in fact, the great problem with fireplace installation. Not only does it in itself impose a strain on the components, but also it causes them to expand and contract – and moreover different materials expand at different rates. Damage can be caused unless you can prevent them from crushing up against each other.

Fitting a replacement fireback in a normal installation is a task within the scope of the do-it-yourselfer, but it becomes a much more complicated job when there is a back boiler. This section only deals with fireplaces.

REMOVING THE OLD FIREBACK

First you will have to get rid of the old fireback. To gain access to it you will probably need to remove the grate. Old-fashioned ones merely stand loosely on the back hearth. Before you can lift a modern appliance clear, you will have to withdraw the fixing screws that hold it down to the back hearth, and break the cement pointing at its sides and base.

THE TRICK

Under the cement at the sides, you will find short lengths of asbestos rope. Take care of these for you will need them when you refit the fire. Avoid creating asbestos dust, for this is a health hazard.

The fireback will need to be wrenched free, or indeed broken up on the spot. Stick a small crowbar or bolster chisel behind it to do this. Lift it clear, then break up and shovel out the mass of cement and rubble you will find behind.

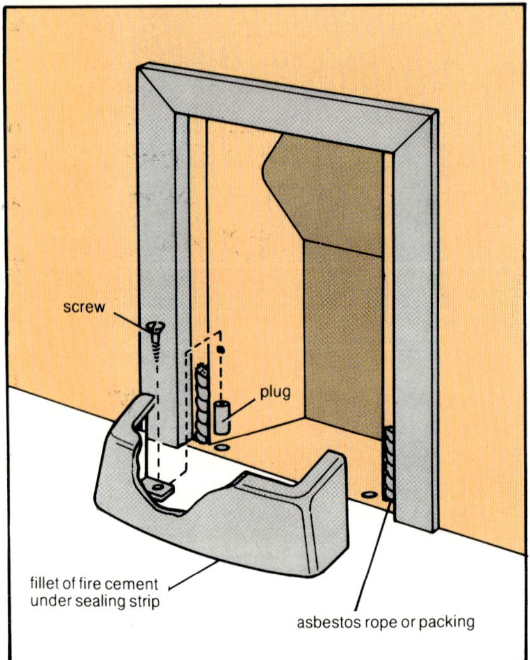

INSTALLING THE NEW FIREBACK

Fire openings are manufactured to a standard size, so you should have no difficulty in buying a fireback to fit. The fireback has a break line near the top and when you hit this it will split in two. It is installed in two parts so that it can expand under the heat with less likelihood of damage.

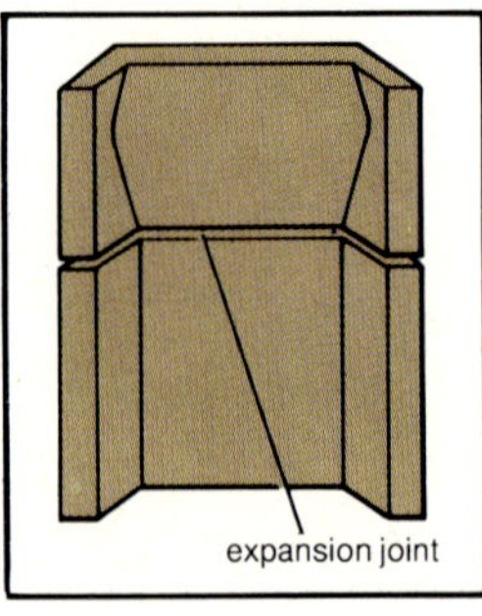

The new fireback should stand on the back hearth, and should be positioned just far enough forward that it lightly compresses the asbestos rope which you will find at the top and sides of the back of the fire opening. They will form an expansion buffer.

It is fixed in place by a mortar with which you plaster the whole void round its sides and back. This mortar needs special qualities. It must be solid but not too rigid. It needs to have good insulation qualities, and it must not expand too much under heat.

THE TRICK

You will best achieve these results with a mix of four parts of vermiculite to one of lime.

Even so, there will be a certain amount of movement caused by the heat, and a small expansion gap should be left to compensate for this.

THE TRICK

The best way to create such a gap is to wrap two layers of ordinary corrugated cardboard round the rear of the fireback before the mortar is poured in. This will normally char away as the intense heat comes into play, and leave just the right space. However, it does not matter if it stays there unaffected by the warmth.

Be careful not to make the mortar too wet: it should be damp rather than soggy. Pack it in well and bring level with the top of the fireback.

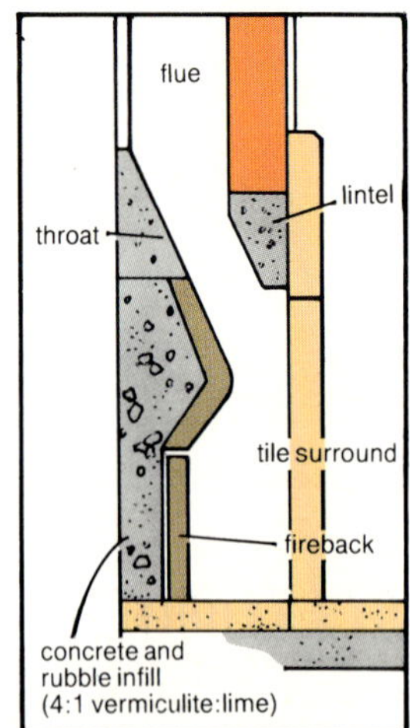

Over the fire opening at the back of the surround, you will see a lintel, the centre section of which slopes upwards. You must now add extra mortar to the top of that, behind the fireback, and this should be parallel to the slope in the lintel. This extra mortar is called the 'flaunching'. With the lintel slope, it forms a 'throat' through which smoke and combustion gases pass up to the flue. The flaunching should be as smooth as you can make it because a rough surface will cause friction which can impede the flow of gases.

REPLACING THE GRATE

Finally replace the grate. If you have an old free-standing grate, it is a good idea to fit a modern one. The supply of air to this can be regulated at the turn of a handle, and thus is more economical. It also causes fewer draughts, and allows you to choose whether you want it to be burning brightly as you settle down in front of the fire in the evening, or merely idling at other times of day.

The manufacturer of the appliance will probably supply an instruction sheet; you should follow this closely. Usually, however, you have to screw the appliance in place, and this you should do by driving its fixing screws into metal plugs, which are non-combustible. The plugs will go into holes drilled in the concrete of the back hearth. The meeting point where the sides of the appliance meet the fireback should be sealed with asbestos rope, supplied with the grate and later pointed with fire cement.

THE TRICK

The rope will need to be held in place before you complete the pointing. Use isinglass for this.

Don't seal the appliance to any steel surround the fire opening may have, but you do need a tight seal between the bottom of the appliance and the hearth, and you can do this with fire cement. A modern appliance, removed to repair the fireback, is replaced in the same way.

FIREPLACES 2

REMOVING UNWANTED FIREPLACES

If you regard your fireplace as redundant, removing it is not a difficult job, although it is a strenuous one.

The surround is held to the wall by screws driven into wall plugs through lugs on each side, and occasionally the top, of the surround. The screws are hidden under the plaster because the fireplace is installed before the plastering.

Chip off a 25mm (1in.) wide band of plaster all the way round the surround, using an old chisel (or screwdriver) and hammer, until the fixing lugs are revealed. When you have found the screws, withdraw them in the normal way. The surround can then be lifted clear. You will need a helper for this. The superimposed hearth is bonded to the constructional hearth by cement. You must break this bond, before it can be lifted clear

THE TRICK

The best tool for freeing the superimposed hearth is an ordinary garden spade. It has a sharp blade that you can push between the two hearths, and a long handle that allows you to assert maximum pressure. A couple of timber wedges to push under the top hearth as the bond starts to break are also very useful.

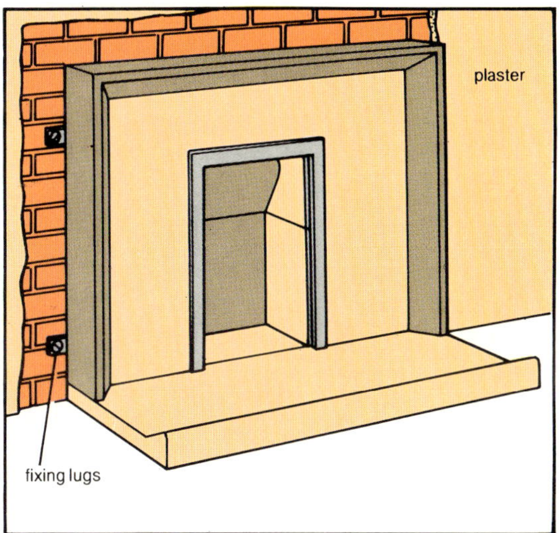

FILLING THE OPENING

There are various ways of blocking off the recess; whatever method you decide to use, you must remember to allow for:

1. The chimney flue must be permanently ventilated at the point of blocking; and
2. The chimney must be left open at the top.

The least satisfactory way is to install a ventilated roof to the recess and use it for storage, because you must leave some sort of ventilation in that roof, yet it must be strong enough to hold any debris that falls down the chimney. If you do decide to do this, make sure that you do not disturb the lintel and – if you share the chimney with the house next door – be careful not to take too much off the back of the fireplace, or you may find the contents of your cupboard being roasted!

Another method is to square off the plaster around the hole and fix a wooden frame in it. You can then attach a plywood or plaster-board cover and install a small metal or plastic ventilator just above skirting board level. Fill in any gaps around with wall filler. If the fireplace backs onto another which is still in use, or if you want to plaster over the recess, be sure to use plasterboard.

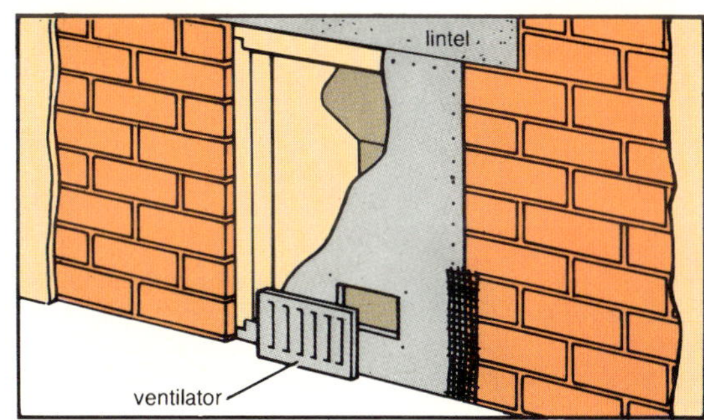

The most satisfactory solution is to brick up the gap completely, placing an airbrick just above skirting board height. This ensures that any debris from the chimney will be safely contained and provides a good surface for plastering over. To do this, you should start by chopping back the plaster so that you can chop out the half bricks left around the fireplace, using a cold chisel and club hammer. Be careful not to disturb the lintel. Make up a mortar mix of 1:1:6 cement:lime:sand. Add water to make it a putty consistency.

Lay a bed of mortar 12mm (½in.) deep on the hearth concrete and start laying bricks by buttering one end with mortar and placing it against the last brick of the existing wall. Put some mortar on top if you have to slot it into a half brick's hole. Repeat until you reach the other side. Tap each brick into position with the handle of the trowel. Repeat on each layer (course) until you reach the top of the recess. Use a spirit level and a straight-edge to ensure that each course is level and that the wall does not bulge outwards. Don't forget to put the airbrick in at the right place. Clean off any excess mortar on the wall's face.

When the mortar is dry, plaster over the brickwork and set a ventilator grill over the airbrick.

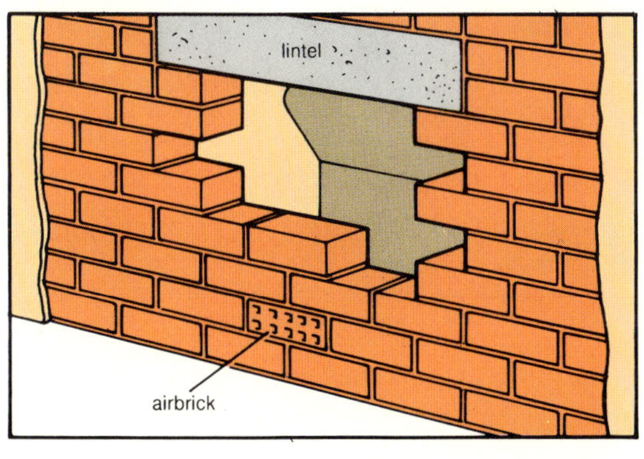

SMOKING CHIMNEYS

If your chimney is not allowing smoke to escape up itself, there are various things which may be wrong. The most common answer is that it is dirty or that it is partially blocked by a bird's nest or misplaced brick, etc. Get it swept professionally (try the Yellow Pages) and the problem may well disappear.

If the fireplace has not been used for some time, you will want to test whether it will work properly.

THE TRICK

Just screw up a few old newspapers, place them on the back hearth, and set fire to them. Watch from both inside and out of the house, whether smoke is going up the chimney properly or not. You will not be breaking any smokeless zone rules with a short test like this.

Another cause may have been your over-enthusiastic draughtproofing efforts. The fire warms the air which rises up the chimney carrying the smoke and fumes away. If no fresh air is coming into the room, the fire will not burn properly. Check that the air vents in the hearth are clear and that all air bricks outside are clear. Otherwise you can try cutting a small hole in the floorboards on either side of the hearth or dismantling some of your draughtproofing.

If a chimney has not been used for some time, it may have got cold. In that case the rising hot air will not get to the top, but will fall back into the room below. This should clear fairly rapidly, but try to reduce the down draught as much as possible by opening and/or closing doors and windows. Remember every fireplace has its own peculiarities and experiment.

If the bricks of the chimney have become porous, or if the basic chimney design is bad, you will have to call in a builder. This also applies if the chimney leans sideways or bows outwards!

THE TRICK

You may get problems if you install a sunken grate where there was a barred one before; if the surface of the throat is uneven or if it is too large, in which case there is inadequate suction. For all these, consult a builder.

Because of the Clean Air Acts the modern open coal fire has to meet stringent tests, for design and operation, to qualify for NCB approval. Efficiency is three or four times better, and we no longer live with a smoke problem, mainly due to the use of relatively smokeless fuels such as Welsh steam coal, briquettes, semi-cokes such as Coalite and Rexco, and other prepared fuels. Anthracite is not very suitable for the open fire since it needs a high draught to keep it alight, but certain models can even burn house coal, the traditional open fire fuel, in spite of its high smoke content. An internal-flue gas circulation deals with the smoke, and the appliance tends to be known as the Smoke Eater.

DESIGN CALCULATIONS

At an early stage somebody has to decide how much warmth a house needs, and this will determine the size of the equipment needed to supply it. That person might be any of the following:

A design engineer. These can be engaged independently, or they might be employed by a firm such as the ones which will sell you the equipment to a design which they make from your particulars.

An installer. Reputable installers are able to make the basic calculations. Installers sometimes tend to get into a rut in such matters as 'margin', which is the percentage added to the calculated total heat requirement, in order, it is said, to cope with emergencies. The most likely undeclared emergency is an error in their own calculations. A common margin is 10 per cent, but as much as 30 per cent is sometimes used.

There is some excuse for using a margin only with solid fuel heaters and boilers (to cover the gap between rated and real output) but it would be better done away with altogether. The basis of design is still an outdoor temperature of −1°C (30°F), whereas the average winter temperature is considerably better than that. This means that, most of the time, such a designed system is too big.

Yourself, using an 'aid'. A suitable aid might be a circular calculator of the sort made by Mears. One circle slides over another, and windows show what figures you are using and what conclusions are reached from them. Because the parameters and the actual dimensions alter, calculations deal with each room separately; then you add up the subtotals.

Yourself, working from first principles. There is nothing to beat this method; but why bother?

THE TRICK

You do not have to work from first principles even though you go through all the motions, as there is a standard procedure – in several versions – set out in tabular form.

On that form you fill in all the details, dimensions, U values, air changes and so on. The form helps you to process these, line by line, until you reach a conclusion.

HEAT LOSS SHEET

Design outdoor temperature −1°C

1. Room 2. Design room temp. (°C) 3. Design temp. diff. (°C) 4. Room length (m) 5. Room width (m) 6. Outside walls, long (m) 7. Room height (m)						
	Area	U value	kW	Area	U value	kW
8. Outside walls, total 9. Windows 10. Outside doors 11. 9 + 10 12. 8 − 11 13. Unwarmed wall 14. Unwarmed floor 15. Unwarmed ceiling 16. Reqd. air changes 17. Room vol. 18. Air heat loss 19. Total heat loss 20. Allowance 21. Design heat loss						

If using imperial units: Design outdoor temperature is 30°F; physical measurements are in feet, and areas in ft². U values are imperial; heat loss in Btu/h.

Acknowledgement is made to Newnes Technical books in whose 'Beginner's Guide to Central Heating' *by W. H. Johnson the Heat Loss Sheet first appeared.*

HOW TO USE THE HEAT LOSS SHEET

Each room must be calculated independently.
The outside design temperature is usually taken as −1°C.
The immediate results from lines 9 to 15, and 18, are in watts. Divide by 1000 to enter in table.

Complete lines as follows:

1. Identify room, as kitchen, bedroom 1, etc.
2. Design temperature for that room.
3. Difference between 2 and outside design temperature.
4. } Longest wall and other wall.
5. }
6. Total of outside walls.
7. Height of room.
8. 6 × 7.
9. Area of windows, and U value. kW column is area × U value × line 3.
10. Outside doors, as for windows line 9.
11. Add areas of 9 and 10.
12. Subtract line 11 from line 8 (area). Add U value of walls. kW column, area × U value × line 3.
13. If next door is a room or space at lower temperature heat will pass. Enter partition area, and U value. kW column, area × U value × line 3. If next door is unheated, assume halfway to cold.
14. 4 × 5 × floor U value. kW column, area × U value × line 3.
15. As 14 but for ceiling.
16. Air changes, average 1.5 per hour.
17. 4 × 5 × 7.
18. Lines 17 × 16 × 3 × 0.33. (For Btu/h use 0.02, not 0.33.)
19. Add all the kW column figures.
20. An allowance may be up to 10% of line 19. Allowances are not usually recommended except in the case of selective heating, or where rapid warm-up is wanted and means exist to cut back to a 'normal' rate (as with thermostatic radiator valves).
21. Sum of lines 19 and 20 if applicable.

HOW TO MAKE THE CALCULATIONS

Calculations by any method do not manufacture information. You supply the information and they process it. Consequently the end result cannot be better than the information you put into it. No one would expect you to measure your rooms wrongly, but what do you know about air changes?

THE TRICK

The simple answer is to use 1½ per hour for every room except the bathroom (3) and kitchen (2).

These presume normal or average house occupation. If you have five or six friends in five nights a week, all heavy smokers, you should reconsider 1½ for the living-room

U VALUES

More important than air changes are the U values. The U value is thermal transmittance; it is a measure of how much heat will pass through a given material (wall, window, roof, panel, etc.) in unit time over unit area, when there is a 1° temperature difference between one side and the other. All talk about unit time, etc. is not meant to confuse. It enables one definition to cover both imperial and metric versions of U.

The imperial U value is measured as Btu/ft² h °F, and the units are, as well as Btu, square feet and hours and degrees Fahrenheit. The metric U value is W/m² °C, thus using watts, square metres and degrees Celsius (centigrade). As watts are equal to joules per second, the time interval is in this case one second. The relationship is:

1 Btu/ft² h °F = 5.7 W/m² °C.

Just to give an idea of what U values look like, here are some brief examples:

	m.	imp.
External wall, plastered, 275mm (11in.) unventilated cavity	1.7	0.30
Window, single-glazed	5.7	1.0
Window, double-glazed	2.9	0.50
Pitched roof, tile on board and felt	2.0	0.35
Suspended ground floor	1.7	0.30
Solid ground floor on earth	1.15	0.20

It is obvious that the lower the heat transmittance (U value) the better for you. Not only will you lose less heat, but if you are putting in heating, less heat lost means less plant to replace it. Less plant means less cost, that being one of the payoffs for what you spend on insulation. Accordingly, when you are calculating to select heating apparatus you want to get the U values right.

For traditional situations every book will give a table of U values; but in the now important area of reduced U values due to modern and varied methods of increasing resistance to heat transmission, the situation is less clear-cut.

THE TRICK

Take cavity insulation – here you would be well advised to ask the contractor to tell you the U value in the light of his own experience and method. An informed guess, by the way, is 0.6 (0.11).

The loft is the place most likely to have been done by yourself, so that there is nobody to ask for a figure. To show the dramatic effect which loft insulation can have, here is an example of one insulated to the 1976 Building Regulations requirement, which was a blanket 80mm (3in.) thick.

Blanket	W/m² °C	Btu/ft² h °F
80mm (3in.)	0.6	0.11
140mm (5½in.)	0.25	0.04
180mm (7in.)	0.20	0.035

This shows what the bold step of almost doubling the insulation thickness can achieve – a saving of 66 per cent in lost heat.

CHECKING CALCULATIONS

Supposing that somebody else does the calculations, how can you check them? It will be very difficult unless you 'speak the language'. You can ask for explanations of particular points and, if you spot it, seize on any attempt to introduce a margin. Look at some of the U values, either comparing with the brief list above, or with a more detailed list from a more comprehensive book.

There is one almost empirical and certainly rule-of-thumb test you can apply. It will tell you nothing except whether any room has been blatantly over-calculated, as it relates to an average room which has had no insulation treatment. The single condition is that it is to living-room standard, at about 21°C (70°F).

THE TRICK

Find the volume of the room, height by width by length, in feet. Multiply this by 5 and the answer is in Btu/h. It is not worth translating that into metric, although you can turn the Btu/h into kW by knowing that 10,000 Btu/h equals 3 kW.

The answer you get is almost certain to be higher than you now need, even without insulation. So at least you can make sure that your house is not being overtreated to a vast degree.

Whatever the job in hand, use Pro-Techs.

The first-ever range of specially designed DIY gloves.

The trick of any successful DIY job, as any professional will tell you, is to use the right tools for the job.

Yet it's surprising how few DIY-ists use the right gloves for the job.

Particularly when you think of the hell hands can go through.

That's why they need protecting.

And that's why Marigold have designed Pro-Techs.

The first-ever range of specially designed DIY gloves for professionals and enthusiasts alike.

Whatever the job in hand, get your hands on a pair of Pro-Techs.

You'll find them at larger DIY stores everywhere.

We think you'll find them just the trick.

PRO-Techs

Marigold®

LRC Products Ltd., North Circular Rd., E4 8QA.

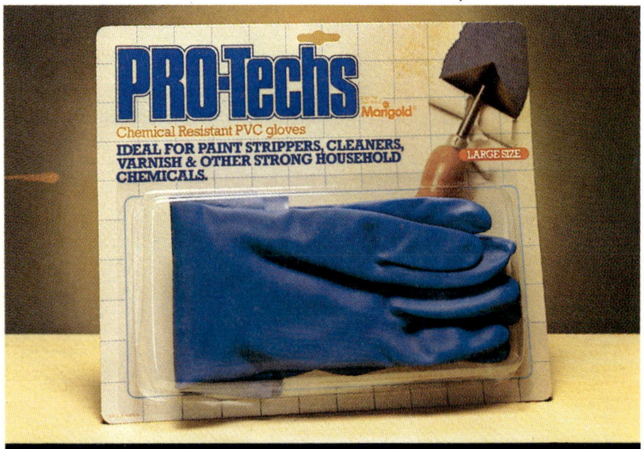

PVC Pro-Techs.
A chemically resistant glove that protects hands from harmful paint strippers, wood preservatives and the like.

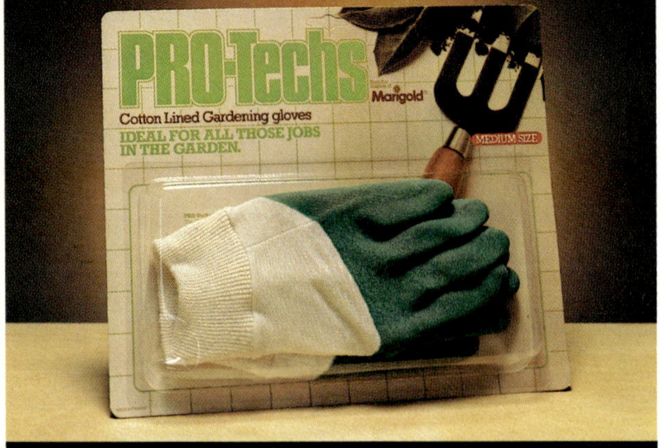

Gardening Pro-Techs.
A hard-wearing cotton lined latex glove that prevent green fingers from becoming grazed fingers.

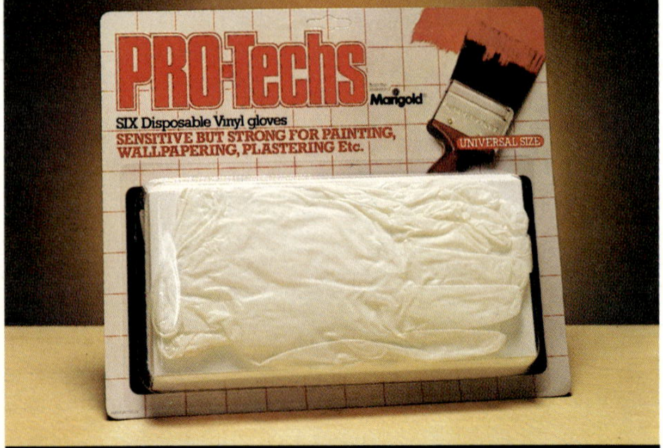

Disposable Pro-Techs.
A sensitive yet strong vinyl glove for those messy one-offs like painting and decorating.

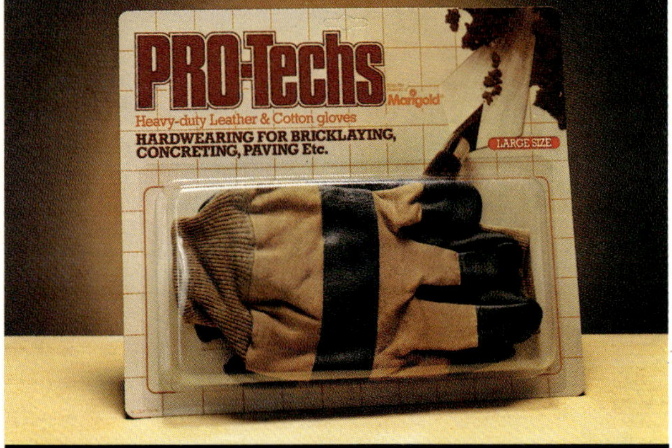

Heavy-Duty Pro-Techs.
A super rugged leather and cotton glove that can tackle – and tame – the heaviest manual work.

EXTERIOR MAINTENANCE

1. ROTTEN, DECAYED WINDOW FRAME.

2. BRUSH ON RONSEAL HARDENER.

3. SMOOTH RONSEAL HIGH PERFORMANCE WOOD FILLER INTO SHAPE.

4. INSERT RONSEAL WOOD PRESERVATIVE TABLETS INTO THE WOOD.

THE MOST COMPLETE CURE FOR WET ROT EVER INVENTED.

You can't solve wet rot by painting over it. In a couple of months time you'll have the same problem back again—only worse.

What you need is the Ronseal Wood Repair System—the most complete cure for wood rot ever invented. It solves the problem simply and effectively, and you save money by not having to replace costly timber.

Here's how you do it. Clear the rotted wood back to a sound surface and paint on Ronseal Wood Hardener.

It strengthens the decayed wood and forms an effective seal against any further water penetration.

Then, simply apply Ronseal High Performance Wood Filler for a smooth, non-shrink, non-crack, ready-to-paint finish.

And to help prevent wet rot recurring, insert Ronseal Wood Preservative Tablets.

That's the Ronseal System. Simply the most complete cure ever for rotten problems.

For more details write to Sterling Roncraft, FREEPOST, East Molesey, Surrey KT8 9BR. Or fill in the coupon at the back of the book.

Ronseal is a registered Trade Mark

GENERAL POINTS

CHECKLIST

You should make regular inspections of the outside of your home to look for signs of damage. Good times to do so are after a gale and at the beginning and end of winter. It is a good idea to take a pair of binoculars to allow you to check up on the higher parts of the house. Here are some of the things you should be on the look out for.

1. **Chimneys:** Are any pots broken or missing, and are there cracks in the flaunching?
2. **Roofs:** Look for broken and missing slates or tiles, or moss growing on the roof. Include all visible flashings in your inspection.
3. **Flat roofs:** Keep an eye open for any faults in the felt on these. Check the verges for lifting felt.
4. **Gutters and downpipes:** Make sure these are in good order, that there are no damaged or missing sections, and that the gutters are not sagging, which would allow water to overflow. Clear any debris likely to cause a blockage.
5. **Gullies and hoppers:** Keep clear of any debris likely to cause a blockage. Improvise a cover if blockages persist.
6. **Walls:** Inspect the bricks themselves for signs of damage and the mortar between them to see if it needs repointing. On rendered walls, look for cracks and defective patches.
7. **Damp-proof course:** Never allow anything to be piled against the walls to form a 'bridge' that would by-pass the damp-proof course and introduce damp higher up in the walls. If you spot any faults in the damp-proof course, they should be attended to right away.
8. **Airbricks:** These should never be blocked off or the foundations might get damp.
9. **Windows:** Any damaged panes should be replaced, (even if there is only a slight crack), and defective putty renewed. The gap between frame and wall should be well pointed.
10. **Doors:** Open and close these to ensure they function properly. Look out for rotting sills and bottom rails.
11. **Gates and fences:** Repair any damage to these. Watch for leaning fence posts and add supports.
12. **Paths and drives:** Repair loose or missing paving slabs, and fill holes in concrete.

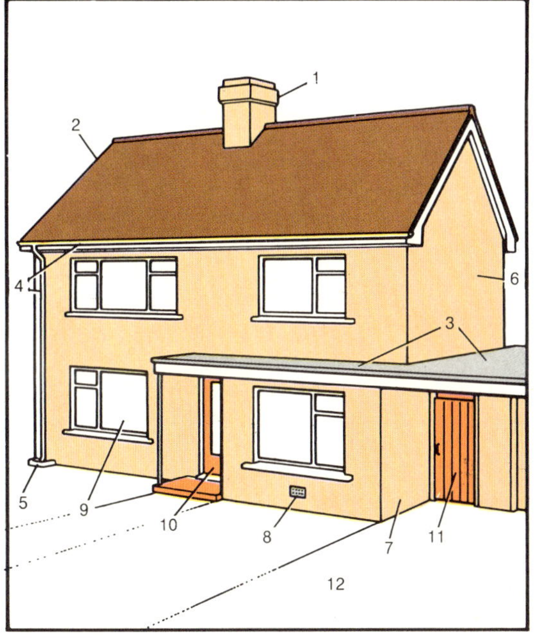

THE HIRE OF TOOLS

If you intend to do any amount of d-i-y, it is well worth your while investing in a proper set of tools to cover most contingencies (see pages 10 and 12). However, there are many tools which are useful for one specific task, but which it is hardly worth you buying as you will use them only once – or so infrequently as to be nearly the same. There are also the large and expensive items – such as concrete mixers and steam wallpaper strippers – which you would probably not want to store anyway.

The hire tool trade has become much more aware of the needs of the do-it-yourselfer in recent years and is providing many more of the items which a do-it-yourselfer may lack. Find the names of the local tool hire firms by consulting the Yellow Pages.

THE TRICK

If you are intending to do a lot of work, or want to buy only a minimum tool kit, it is a good idea to phone round and ask them to send you a catalogue (many companies now have one) and a price list giving the various hire options.

Most companies will hire by the day, the week and the month; there is often a substantial reduction for a longer period of hire. Always inquire about this and whether they have a special weekend cheap rate. The company will require a sizeable deposit when you collect the item which will be returned when the item is. If you want the item delivered or collected, there will almost certainly be an additional charge.

Most hire companies, who are well aware that people tend to hire equipment which they have not used before, have a set of printed instructions explaining how to use it properly and any dangers that may not be foreseen by the user. If you are hiring something you have not used before, always ask for a set of instructions and read them through before taking the item away. If there are not instructions, ask for a demonstration and keep asking questions (and taking notes if necessary) until you are clear what to do and what not to do. All shops should be willing to do this – after all, a broken tool is an unhirable tool. It also establishes the fact that the tool was in working order when it left the hire company – you don't want to be blamed for someone else's damage!

If you are considering painting or papering a staircase, it is a good idea to contact local hire companies and scaffolding companies too, to check if they have any scaffolding specifically designed for staircase work. The ladder system (shown on page 169) is perfectly adequate for the task, but you might feel happier on a system designed specially for such work. Scaffolding boards and towers can often be hired from local scaffolding companies; it is worth comparing prices. A scaffolding company will probably require a larger deposit however.

THE TRICK

It is always worth booking the tool required a few days in advance. Nothing is more annoying than planning a weekend's work around a tool which is not then available.

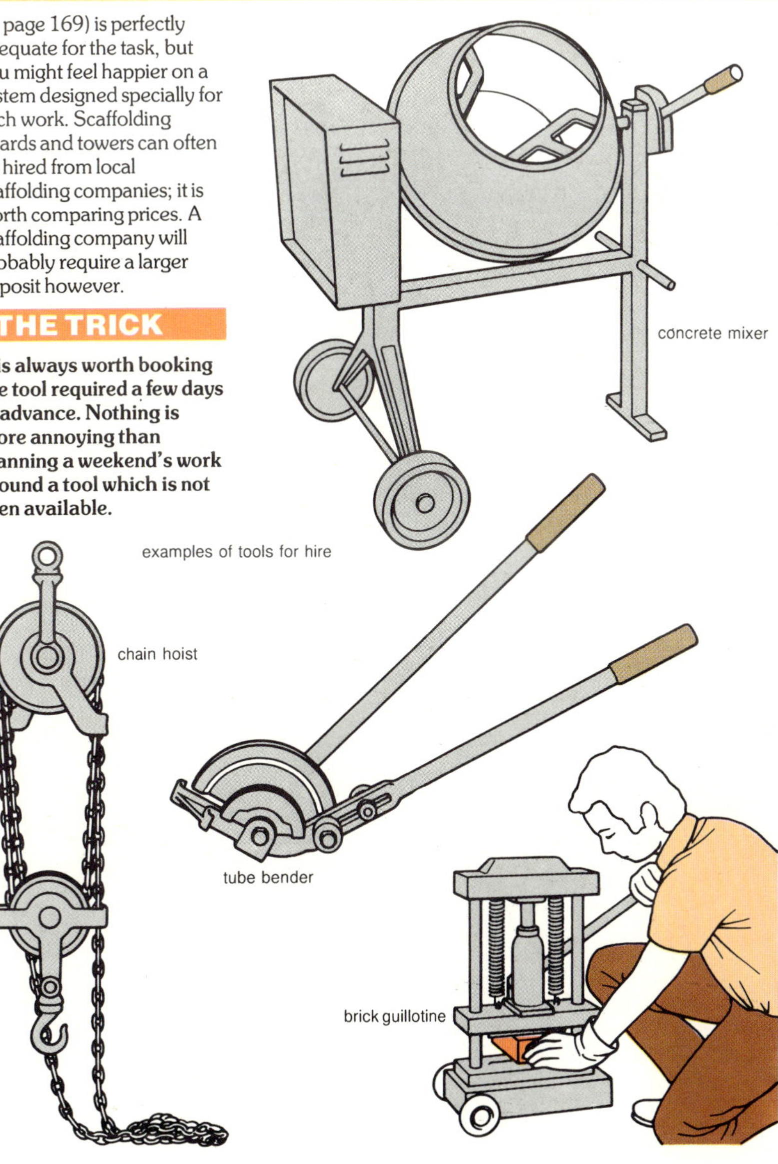

examples of tools for hire

THE REGULATIONS

Two completely different sets of regulations govern building work in England and Wales: they are the Town and Country Planning Act, and the Building Regulations 1976 with 1st and 2nd Amendments. (Scotland and Northern Ireland have their own, not always identical Regulations). These rules apply with equal force to alterations and to new buildings. Even if you are a do-it-yourselfer working on your own property you must obey them.

The rules are administered by two entirely different departments of your local authority – the Planning Department in the case of town planning, and the Building Control Officer's Department for the Building Regulations. Just because permission to proceed is given under one set of rules, it does not follow that you have been granted – or will automatically get – it for the other.

It is vital always to get permission before you begin work, because otherwise your local authority can require you to restore the building to its original condition at your own expense – or do the work for you and send you the bill. These Regulations should not be considered as interfering with personal liberty; they are a means of ensuring that building work is carried out in a proper sound manner, and that our homes are healthy and safe.

TOWN AND COUNTRY PLANNING

These will concern you very deeply if you ever propose to do any heavy structural work.

For most minor work around the house, you can go ahead without the say-so of anybody. However, where you intend to build an extension, alter your home structurally (e.g. by turning two rooms into one or dividing up a room), turning a house into flats, etc, your work must comply with the Building Regulations. Not only must you get permission, but also the Building Control Officer will inspect the work as it proceeds.

The Regulations are designed to ensure that materials and methods of construction are suitable for the job in hand. The Building Control Officer will be concerned to see that the building will be structurally stable; that stairways, etc; are sound; that proper damp and weather-resistance precautions have been taken; that there is sound and heat insulation; that rooms are of the correct height and well ventilated; that flues, fireplaces and heating appliances are properly installed, and that there is adequate drainage and connection to sewers or cesspools.

The Regulations themselves are complex, and almost impossible for the layman to understand. If you are erecting a prefabricated building and/or using other similar manufacturer's products, you can be reasonably certain that they will comply. Otherwise, consult your local authority and ask their advice. The Building Control Officers should be as helpful as the Planning Officers.

LISTED BUILDINGS

Certain buildings are listed as being of historical or architectural interest – you will have been told if your home is one of these. In such cases, you will not be allowed to do anything which alters the external appearance of the house, and restricted in what you can do to alter period features indoors.

Certain areas are designated as 'conservation areas'. In these, there will be restrictions on what you can and cannot do. For instance, planning permission may be required for development that would be permitted without it elsewhere.

COVENANTS

On some older houses in Britain, restrictive covenants rule against certain alterations being carried out. Even if you could get planning permission and Building Regulation approval, you would not be able to go ahead. Your solicitor, when you bought the building, should have checked out the situation on covenants.

THE BUILDING REGULATIONS

Planning, as far as the home handyman is concerned, will not concern him/her all that much. Planning permission is needed for what is described as development work – i.e. putting up a new building – or altering an existing building extensively – e.g. turning a house into flats. It is also, theoretically, required if you want to add on an extra room or convert a loft. However, if you do not raise the height of the building, you can now extend a house by up to 70cu.m. (2472cu.ft), or 15 per cent of the original size of the house to a maximum of 115cu.m. (4060cu.ft) – whichever is the greater. Few do-it-yourselfers are going to put up a building bigger than that. Note the phrase 'original size': any existing extension, unless built before 1948, does not count as part of the original house.

You will need permission if you propose to build in front of the present building line (although a small porch is usually allowed); also if the extension would be to a house on a corner site so that it faced a side road.

Garages, small sheds, greenhouses, etc, do not normally need permission, although you might require it for the drive leading to the garage.

THE TRICK

You will need the consent of the Highway Authority for your drive to cross a footpath.

Fences and walls which do not exceed 1m. (3ft 3in.) at the front of the house and 2m. (6ft 6in.) elsewhere are permitted, unless you live on an open-plan estate which the builder was allowed to develop on condition there were no boundary walls.

If you are in any doubt about the need for planning permission, go and talk to the Planning Officers at your town hall. You will find them very helpful. If the alteration involves the use of a prefabricated building (it might if you proposed to build an extension or garage), the manufacturer will advise you on planning requirements, and even help you to submit an application.

SKIP HIRE

If you are proposing to hire a skip for your rubble, etc, and to park it on a public highway, you should check with your local council whether you require a Skip Licence. This usually does not cost anything and is obtainable from the Council. However without it, you may be prosecuted for obstructing the public highway. You will find skip hire companies in the Yellow Pages under 'Waste disposal services'.

VAT

VAT has to be paid on all building materials and tools and on services such as the hire of equipment. A tax rebate can be claimed on zero-rated building work i.e. the construction of a new house or a genuine home extension carried out by a builder, not a do-it-yourselfer, but there are no VAT concessions on repairs or maintenance.

Builders, like all other businessmen, list VAT as a completely separate item in the price – they have to in order to make their returns of tax paid to the Customs and Excise. As a result you may find that when you go shopping for materials, or hiring equipment, at places that are mainly used by builders the price you are quoted will not include VAT, so always make a point of asking whether the figure you have been given includes VAT or not. Otherwise you may get a nasty shock when the bill is presented, for there could be an extra percentage you were not expecting.

In DIY and home improvement retails outlets – as, indeed, in all shops – VAT is normally included in the advertised price.

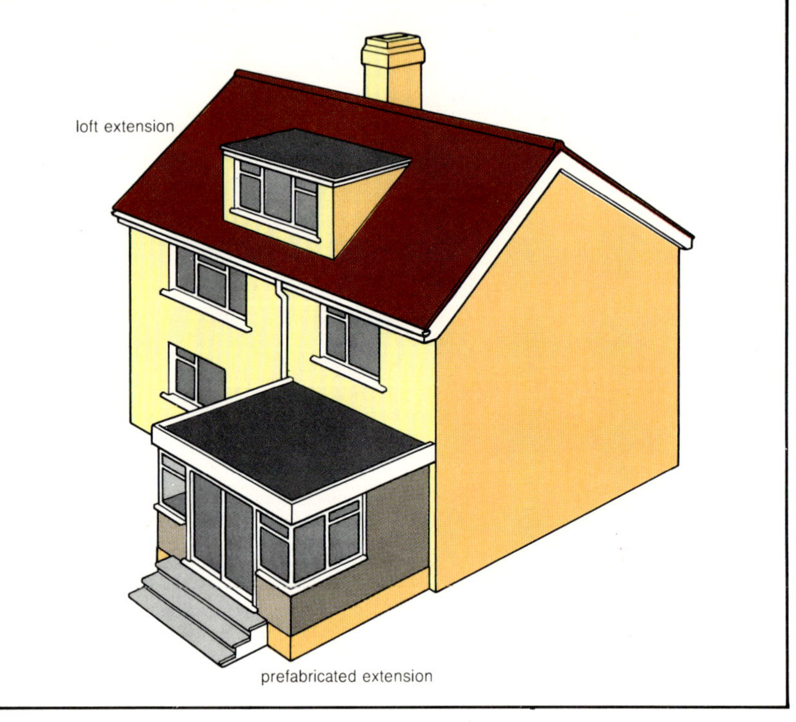

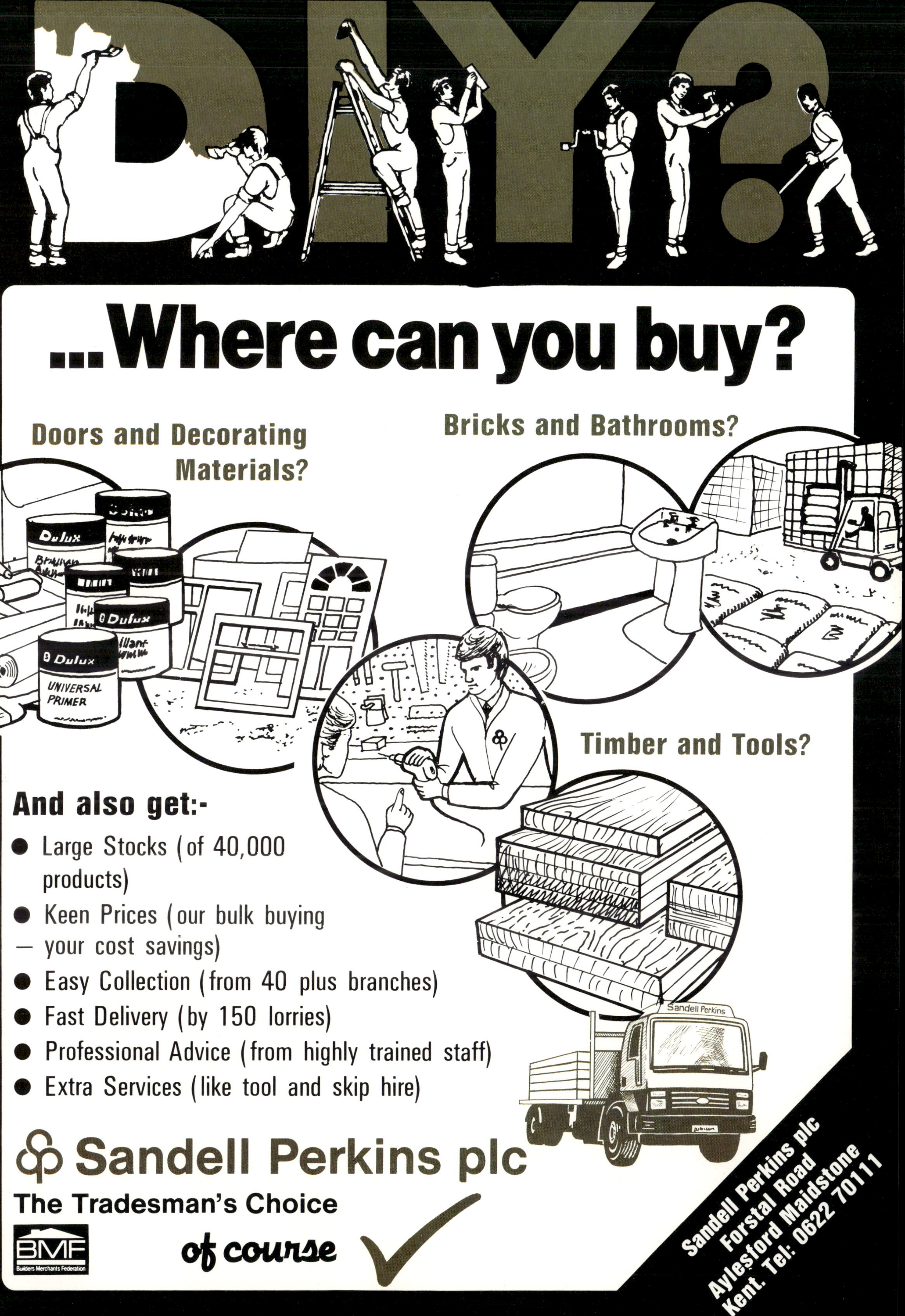
DIY?
...Where can you buy?
Doors and Decorating Materials?
Bricks and Bathrooms?
Timber and Tools?
Dulux
Dulux
Dulux UNIVERSAL PRIMER
And also get:-
● Large Stocks (of 40,000 products)
● Keen Prices (our bulk buying — your cost savings)
● Easy Collection (from 40 plus branches)
● Fast Delivery (by 150 lorries)
● Professional Advice (from highly trained staff)
● Extra Services (like tool and skip hire)
Sandell Perkins
Sandell Perkins plc
The Tradesman's Choice
BMF
Builders Merchants Federation
of course
Sandell Perkins plc
Forstal Road
Aylesford Maidstone
Kent. Tel: 0622 70111

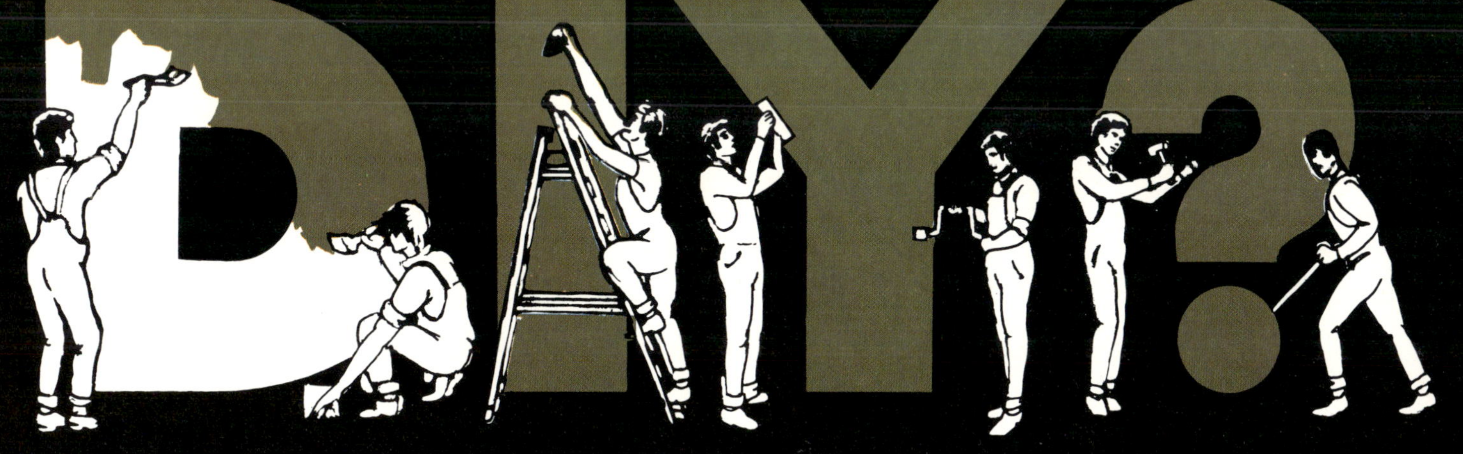

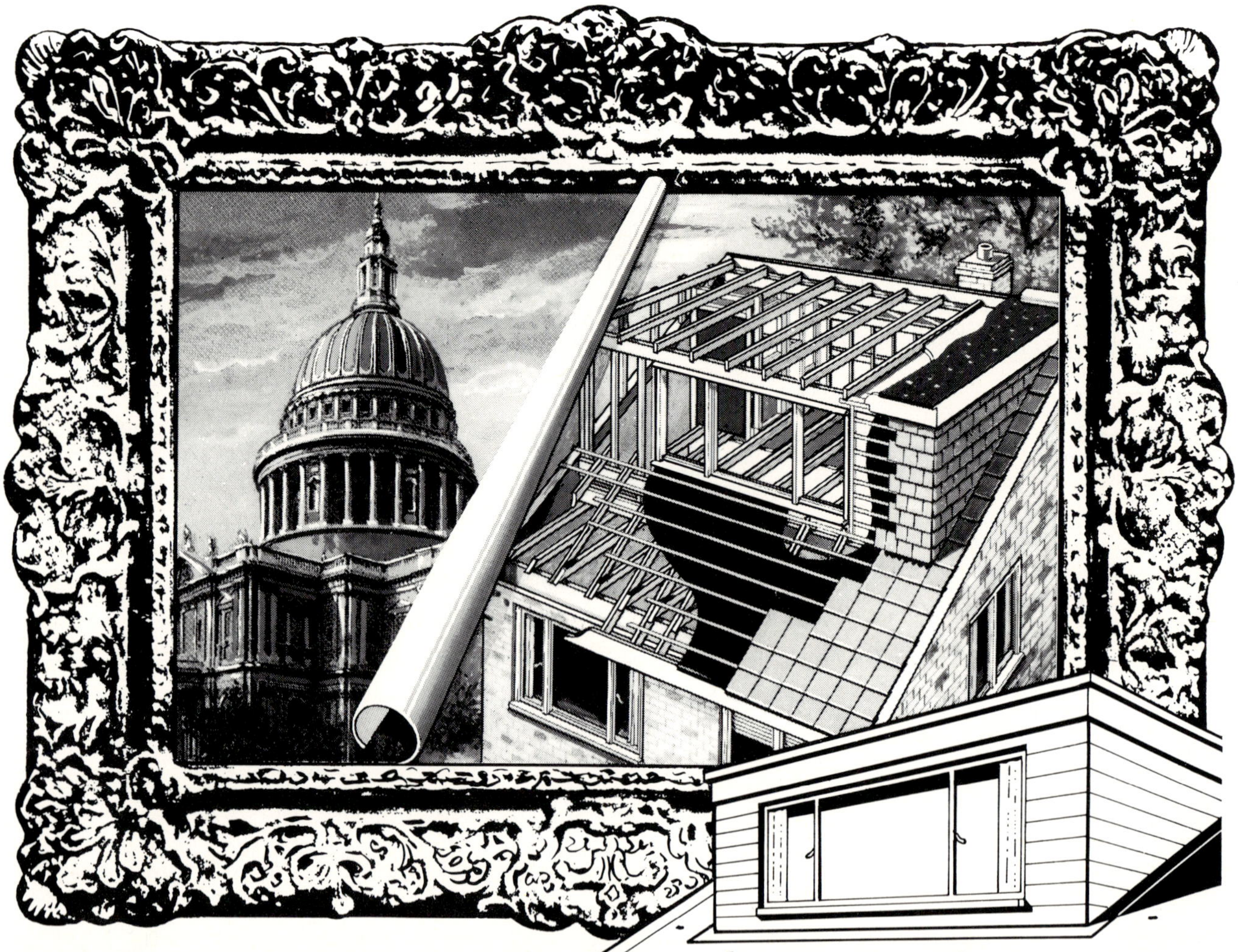

Behind every Masterpiece is a CRAFTSMAN BUILT FRAME

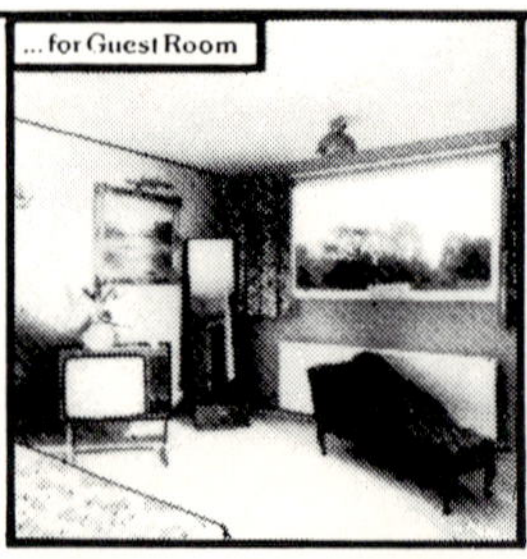

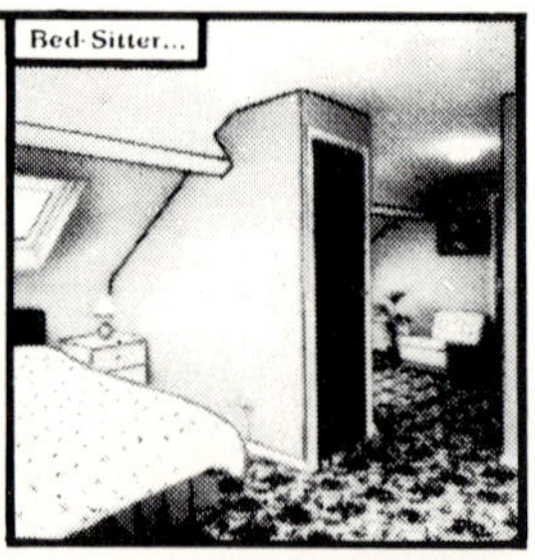

FOR LOFT CONVERSION

Today, with the Charles Grosvenor tradition of high quality craftsmanship, it is not necessary to move home in order to gain that invaluable extra room.

For with our professional 'touch' backed by over 30 years experience, we not only provide a rather superior addition to your existing living space, but skilfully blend a conversion to suit almost any individual property.

By increasing the value of your residence in this advantageous manner, plus our extremely favourable terms and guaranteed work, you would do well to take advantage of a Charles Grosvenor FREE Survey - Quotation today, without obligation.

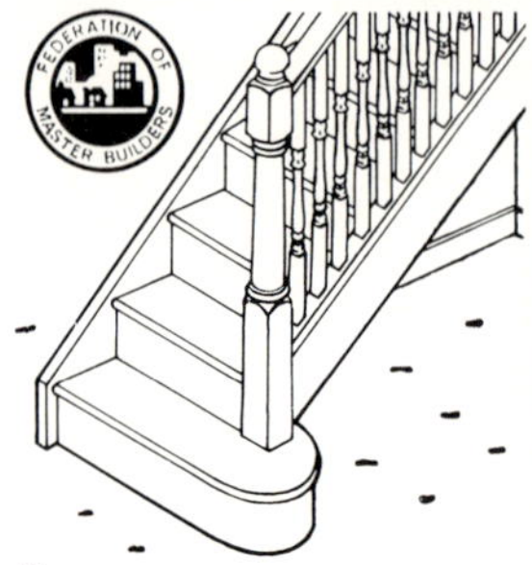

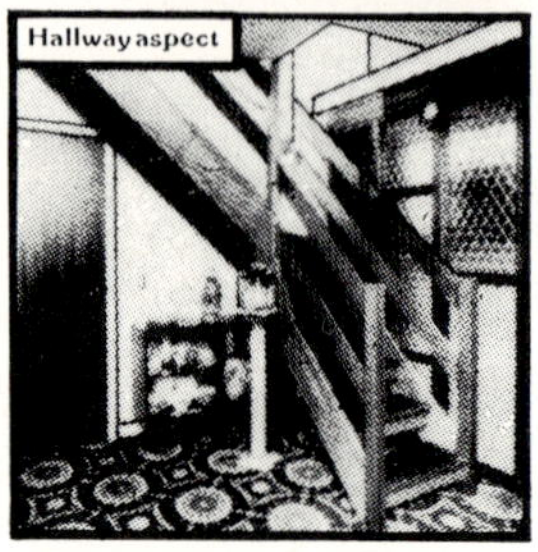

OR TIMBER STAIRWAYS

Being both elegant and impressive the practical beauty of a Charles Grosvenor Stairway can only enhance your home and its value.
Our renowned range of designs (including non-standard) are craftsman built by our Taylor-Made Division from the finest selected woods.
They can be fitted by us or simply supplied for D.I.Y. enthusiasts as a replacement or for adaptation to any proposed area.
Contact us for a FREE Estimate and make your 'home choice' the Masterpiece in Craftsmanship.

Free CONVERSION QUOTATION, STAIRWAY ESTIMATE & LITERATURE ON REQUEST

Contact today's Masters in Craftsmanship

LOFT CONVERSION

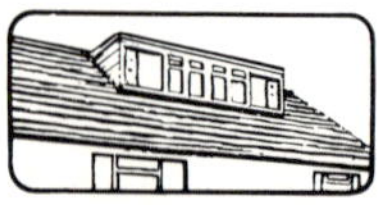

Charles Grosvenor Group of Companies
Incorporating
Charles Grosvenor Construction Ltd & Taylor-Made Constructions Ltd

TIMBER STAIRWAYS

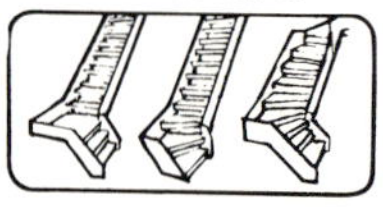

Head Office: 300, Birchfield Road, Redditch, Worcs. B97 4LZ · Tel: (0527) 43668 · Southern Area Office: Bracknell (0344) 421913

LADDERS 1

A fair proportion of outdoor jobs have to be carried out at a level too high to be reached from an ordinary step ladder. Long ladders are by far the most popular access equipment.

You can either buy a ladder, or hire when you need one. Which makes most sense will depend on how often you think you will use the ladder. Consider this carefully and compare local hire charges with prices before deciding.

SELECTION

Ladders are made of wood or aluminium; occasionally the rungs (the part you stand on) are aluminium, and the stiles (the upright sides) in timber.

Whether you hire or buy, opt for an aluminium model if possible. These are more expensive, but last longer and require no maintenance. They are much lighter to handle, and less likely to develop dangerous faults such as loose or broken rungs. Their only disadvantage is that they spring a little in use, which can be disconcerting at first. However, this is not dangerous provided you climb carefully.

If you buy a timber ladder, make sure that it is of the best quality. Both stiles and rungs should be of straight grained timber, and the rungs securely fixed to the stiles. A metal rod (or tie bolt), should be fixed under the rungs to reinforce them. Timber ladders must be well maintained to avoid rot.

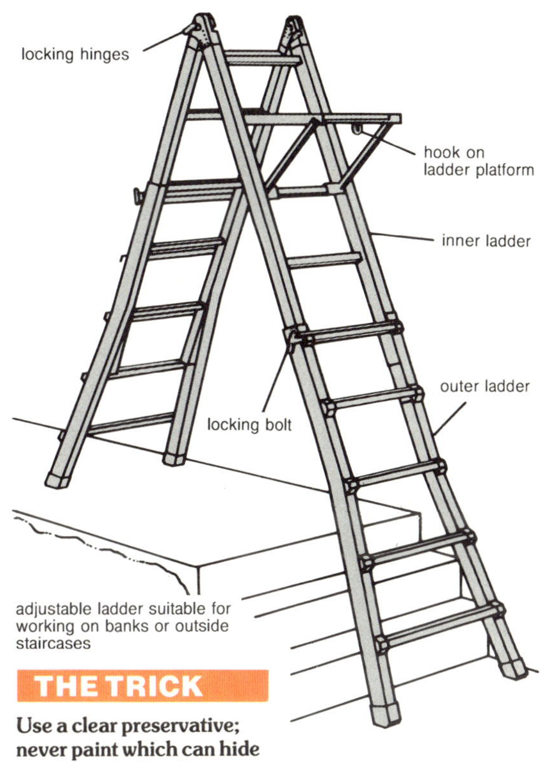

adjustable ladder suitable for working on banks or outside staircases

THE TRICK

Use a clear preservative; never paint which can hide cracks and other damage.

LENGTH

Unless your house is a bungalow, you will need an extending ladder. Up to a maximum of 9m. (30ft), you can get by with a two-section one; but if you want a longer one you would do better with a three-section version.

How do you discover the length required? The ladder must extend by at least three rungs beyond where you are standing – preferab y more – so that you have something to hold onto. There must also be a generous overlap between sections, and the ladder must stand away from the wall at its foot by about a quarter of its height.

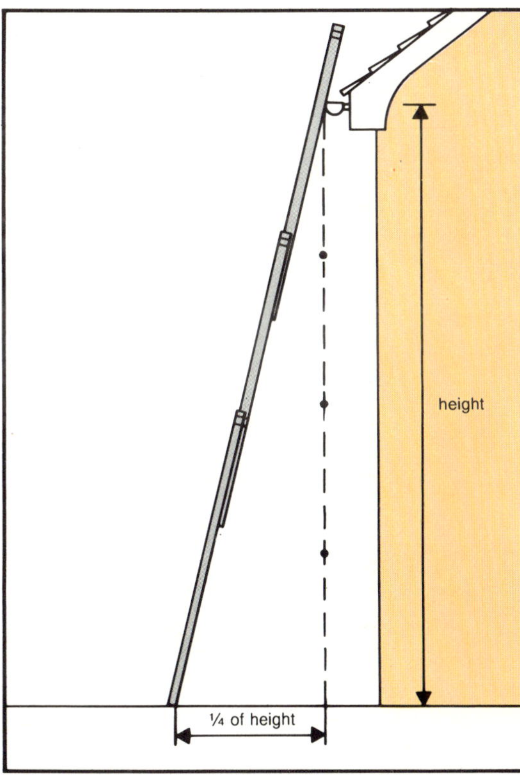

THE TRICK

One way is to measure to the eaves (by measuring the ceiling heights of the rooms inside), add 1.2m. (4ft), and that is the height you need.

Most people will find it works out at about 6.7m. (22ft).

Some ladders are manually extended; others are rope-operated – much easier. Wall wheels allow the top section to ride up more smoothly. You can also get non-slip feet, spikes for use on soil, rubber tops to protect the wall from abrasion, etc. Traditionally the rung shape was round, but square and D-shaped (flat on top) versions are available: the wider the surface, the more comfortable to stand on. Aluminium rungs should be non-slip.

USING THE LADDER

Once you have chosen your ladder, make sure you use it safely. A fall from a ladder could cripple you for life.

RAISING AND MOVING

Your first task is to raise it to the upright position. Get a helper, if possible, for this. He/she should stand at one end with a foot placed firmly on a rung. You take hold of the other end and raise it above your head. Now walk towards your helper raising the ladder as you go. If you cannot get a helper, try to jam the ladder against the base of a wall, or under the sill of patio doors.

THE TRICK

The ladder should be upright when you carry it alone. Raise one arm to hold the highest rung you can reach, then pass the other arm round the other side of the ladder to grip a rung low down, thus locking it against your body.

With a helper, carry the ladder horizontally, one at each end.

EXTENDING

Usually you lean a ladder against the wall to extend it. The top section of a manual one has hooks near the bottom, which hook on to a rung of the lower section. Grasp this top section and extend it as required in two or three steps. Make sure its hooks locate properly on a rung while you pause. If it needs to go higher than you can comfortably reach, extend it flat on the ground.

A rope-operated ladder has a locking bracket controlled by the rope. A tug clears the bracket from the rung on which it is located; a pull on the rope then takes the extending section upwards. Hold the rope with one hand and grasp a rung of the extending section with the other to take its weight.

When raising either type, check that the top does not foul guttering or other projections.

LADDERS 2

SAFETY

Make sure that, when fully extended, there is an overlap of at least three rungs between sections. The ladder should be 250mm (10in.) away from the wall for every 1m. (3ft) of height.

In use, the ladder must be secured both top and bottom. At the top it should be lashed to hooks screwed to the fascia board (leave them there for future use). A downpipe or the centre mullion of a window are not strong enough!

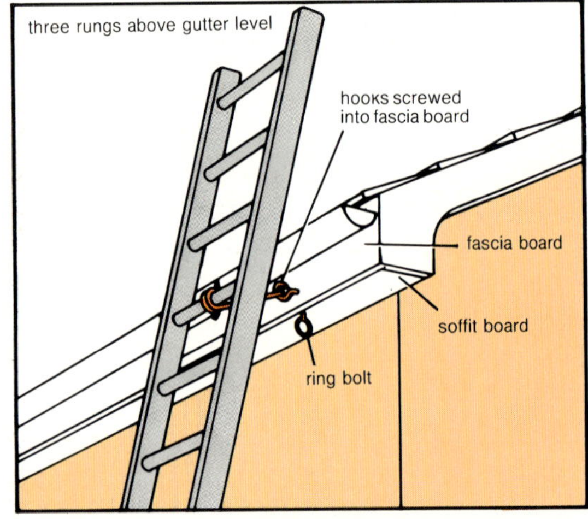

THE TRICK

Never lean the ladder against a window pane. Bridge a window by tying a length of wood to the top of the ladder.

At the bottom, you could tie it to a stake driven into the ground, or to a piece of wood inserted in the front door letter box, and positioned vertically across it. On soft ground place it on a board to stop unequal sinking, and nail a batten to the board to stop the feet from sliding off. Place sacking under the feet on concrete.

As you climb a ladder hold the stiles, not the rungs. Tools without sharp cutting edges, such as paint brushes, should be carried in a pocket. Suspend paint cans by a hook from a rung. Carry sharp tools in a bag or bucket. Never carry more than one handful of equipment at a time – the other must be free to allow you to hold on.

As you work, there is a temptation to lean out or stretch sideways just that little bit further to spare yourself the fag of having to move the ladder. It is very dangerous: resist it at all costs.

STORAGE

Store the ladder in some out-of-the-way place where burglars will not spot it.

THE TRICK

Make sure you lock it up: a cycle chain is ideal.

A ladder should not be suspended by its rungs. If you want it off the ground, hang it sideways.

ROOF LADDERS

If you ever need access to a pitched roof, you cannot just walk across it. Not only do you risk breaking slates or tiles in doing so; you might also easily slip and injure yourself. Instead you should use a roof ladder.

These ladders are also made in timber and aluminium, but even more than with ordinary ladders, the lightness of the aluminium version means that it is the kind you should go for. You can either buy or hire a roof ladder.

There are wheels on one side of the end of a roof ladder, and hooks on the other side. You carry it up to the top of your ordinary ladder, place it on the roof, and push it upwards on its wheels. When it reaches the ridge, turn it over so that the hooks can grip on the ridge. The ladder needs to be securely tied at the eaves: it can, for instance, be lashed to the top of the ordinary ladder once it, in turn, is properly fastened in place.

Manoeuvring a roof ladder up from the ground is not easy. Probably the best way is to take a length of rope up your ordinary ladder, drop one end down to the ground where a helper can tie it to the roof ladder, then, with the helper guiding things so that no damage is done, haul up on the rope.

Make sure that the roof ladder is really secure before you attempt to climb onto it.

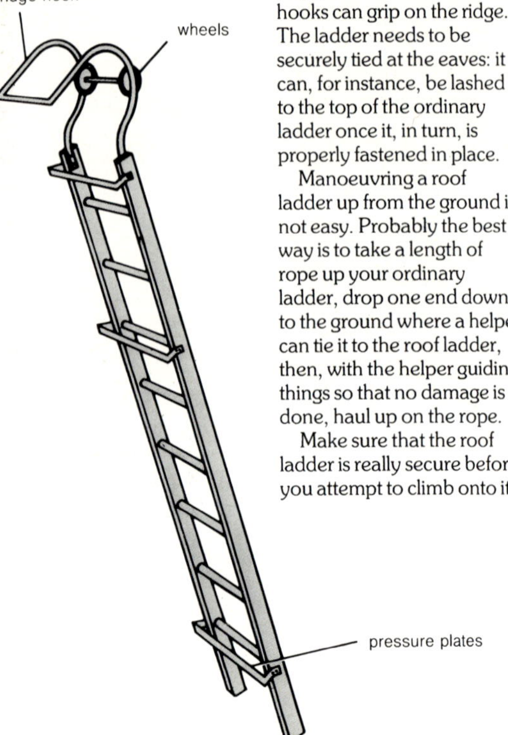

ACCESS TOWERS

The alternative to a ladder is the access tower, which consists of a series of metal frames that slot together to make a tower of the required height. A platform of boards is fitted, and you stand on this while you work.

It is more comfortable, less tiring and safer to work from such a tower than a ladder, except in instances where you will need to be aloft for only a very short time. In fact, by comparison the tower suffers from only two disadvantages – it takes longer to erect, and it is more expensive to hire or to buy.

Normally, these towers have a maximum height of 4.9m. (16ft) although that can be increased to 6.1m. (20ft) if outriggers are added. You can add about 1.8m. (6ft) to these figures to indicate maximum reach so you can see a tower will be suitable for most domestic situations. Furthermore, a ladder can be rested on the platform to allow you to climb onto the roof.

Just like ladders, a tower needs to be lashed at the top. If it has the normal 1.2m. (4ft) square base, lash it when it reaches a height of 3.7m. (12ft). Some towers, however, have a base that is 1.2m. × 600mm (4 × 2ft); these should be lashed at 2.4m. (8ft) or more.

There are one or two other safety points to observe. For instance, you should always fit a hand rail to the platform and a toe-board so that tools and materials cannot be kicked off. Make sure, too, that the tower is absolutely level. It has adjustable feet to allow you to do this.

THE TRICK

If you wish to site it on soft ground, place boards underneath the feet so that they will not sink in to different depths, thus throwing the tower out of true. If the feet have castors, lock them before you climb up.

Never move a tower on which there are people or objects.

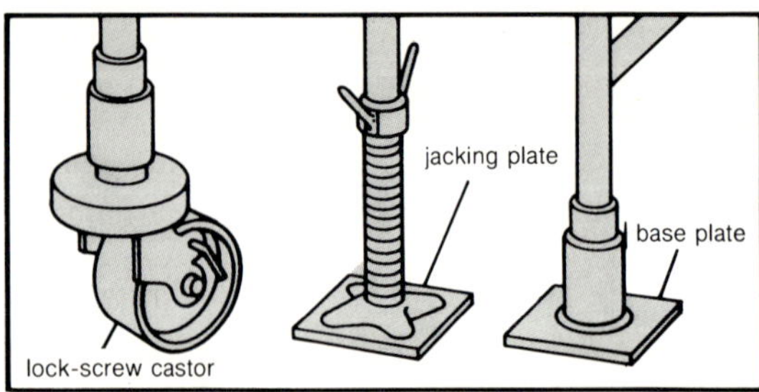

SCAFFOLDING

For some of the more ambitious jobs, proper scaffolding is required. Erecting this is a skilled job, however, and unless you really know what you are doing you should leave this to the professional.

ROOFS 1

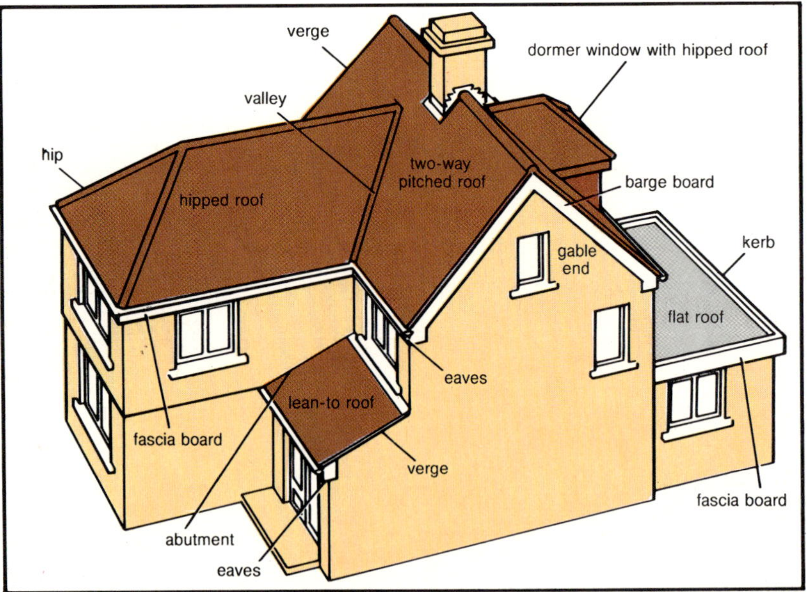

Most roofs are pitched (or sloping) because this is best for shedding rainwater efficiently. The most simple type is the mono-pitched, which has just a single slope. It is in general confined to single-storey lean-tos (garages, porches, extensions, etc) that join up to the main wall of the house.

Most houses usually have a two-way pitched roof, which is tent-shaped with two sloping sides meeting at the top (or ridge). The end wall on such houses is the gable wall, and is usually triangular at the top. The roof normally projects slightly beyond the gable wall to protect it and be supported by it, such a projection being known as the verge. The ends of the roof are concealed behind timber members (or barge boards).

Sometimes the gable wall is as high or slightly higher than, the ridge, and squared off with coping or rendering. A wall against which a roof joins up (see diagram), is known as an abutment wall.

A variant is the Mansard roof. This has a pitch at two angles – a steeper, almost vertical, one at the sides, with a shallower one on top. Such roofs usually have rooms in the loft.

The hipped roof has an extra slope, rising pyramid fashion from an end wall to the ridge. Sometimes, as when there are dormer windows or with an L- or T-shaped roof, both styles may combine. A hipped roof will create a series of angles – the internal ones are valleys, the external ones hips.

ROOF COVERINGS

Pitched roofs may be covered with slates or tiles. Slate roofs, however, will have tiles at the ridge and hips. The slates or tiles are held to a series of battens which are nailed across the main structural members (the rafters) which form the slope on both sides.

To make the roof really waterproof, it is lined with roofing felt. The felt goes under, and is held in place by, the tiling battens. It should sag slightly between the rafters to form a small channel in which any moisture can collect and run down. It should project beyond the slates/tiles so that excess water will be conducted safely into the gutter.

The wooden understructure of a roof consists of a series of triangles. The bottom member is the joist, which carries the ceiling of the top-floor room. This is fixed at each end to a length of timber (a wall plate) sitting on the external walls of the house. The sloping sides of the triangle are formed by the rafters. These are joined to the wall plate at their lower end and also fixed to the sides of the joists. At the top the rafters are fixed to a length of timber (the ridge board). Additional intermediate support is also given.

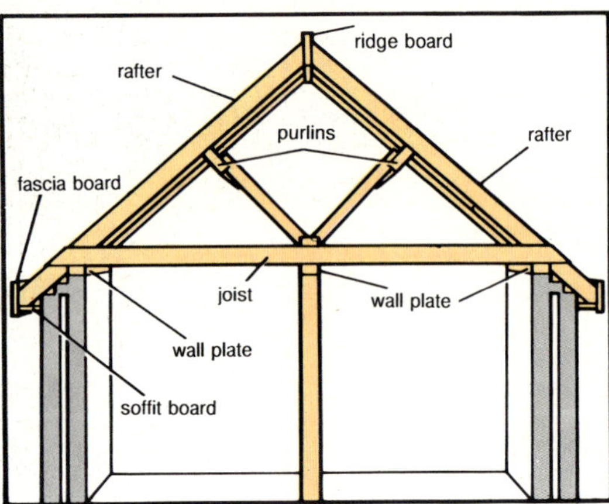

In modern houses, the triangles are prefabricated and delivered ready to be hoisted into place. Such roofs are of trussed rafter construction and the components are so inextricably linked that you cannot remove any of them without seriously weakening the whole structure. The rafters of a hipped roof, at the corners where it meets the pitched roof, are called hip rafters.

Usually the roof projects well beyond the eaves (the point at which it meets the walls) to give extra protection against the weather. Here are two other lengths of timber. The gutters are fixed to the 'fascia'; that underneath the rafters is the soffit board. The loft space needs to be well ventilated to keep moisture at bay (see page 130).

REPAIRS

Major roof repairs are beyond the skills of the do-it-yourselfer. If there is anything seriously wrong with your roof, you should call in a builder or specialist contractor. Re-roofing is a major expense, but it is possible to get a loan to pay for the work.

One or two minor maintenance jobs can be tackled, provided you have adequate means of access, are not affected by vertigo, and follow the safety rules (see pages 169–170). One of the most common tasks is the replacing of slates or tiles.

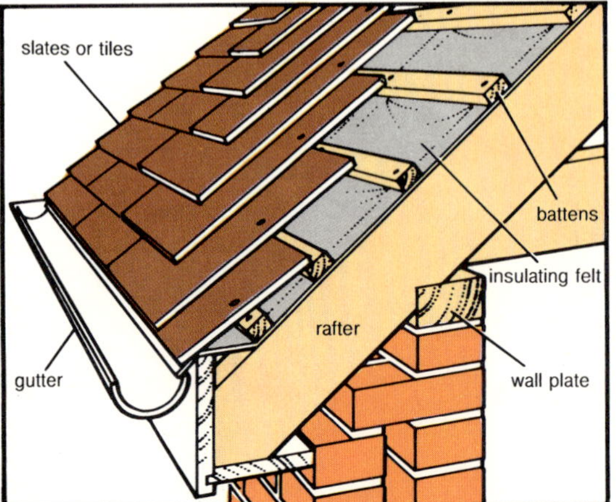

REPLACING SLATES

Slates are fixed to the battens by two nails per slate. The nails can be at the top or in the middle; the latter is the best position as the slates are less likely to be lifted up by high winds – a common cause of breakage. Either way, you will not be able to see the nail heads because they will be hidden under the overlap of surrounding slates. So, if the slate you wish to replace is damaged, as opposed to being missing, how do you free it?

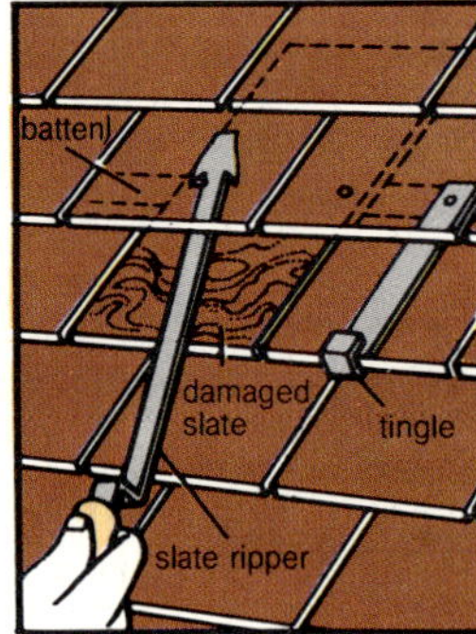

THE TRICK

You use a slater's ripper. This has a long flat blade with a hook on each edge at the end. Push the blade under the broken slate, and locate a hook on each nail in turn. A sharp jerk will break the nails and you can pull the slate clear.

Now fit the replacement slate. It is fairly easy to lever it into the correct position, but be sure to keep it flat to avoid breaking it. How can you fix it when the overlap will get in the way?

THE TRICK

Instead of nails use a small clip (or tingle), which you make from a 225mm (9in.) strip of lead, aluminium or copper, 25mm (1in.) wide. Bend over one end and push it under the slates above to locate it on the batten. Now ease the slate into place. When it is correctly lined up, bend up the other end of the clip so that it holds the slate securely.

REPLACING TILES

It is easier to replace a broken tile. Tiles have two nibs on their upper edge and these locate on the tiling battens. As a result, it is only necessary to nail every fifth or fourth row of tiles. You thus stand a good chance of having to deal with an un-nailed tile.

THE TRICK

To get the tile out, use a trowel. Push it under the tile, and gently lever upwards until the nibs are lifted clear.

A trowel will also help you to lift up surrounding tiles (be careful not to dislodge them) when pushing the replacement tile into position. You can also push it under the broken tile, to find out whether it is nailed or not. A tile that is nailed in place is dealt with just like a slate.

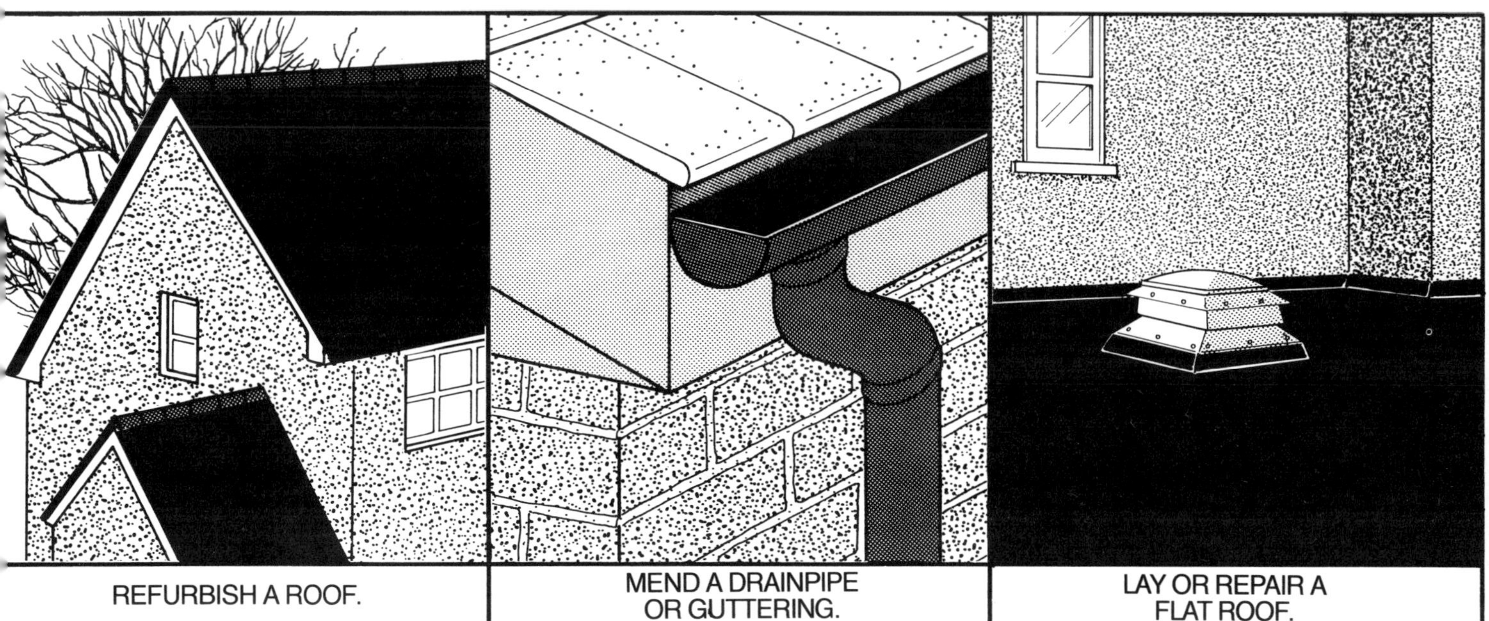

ROOFS 2

RIDGE TILES

The ridge tiles are held in place by mortar; if this cracks, perhaps because of slight settlement in the roof, rainwater can get under the tile and loosen it. A loose ridge tile is dangerous, so it should be re-fixed as soon as possible. The conditions that caused one to come loose are probably affecting the rest so tackle the lot while you are up there.

A missing or broken ridge tile will need to be replaced. Shop around to try to get one that matches exactly. If you cannot, buy an entirely new set. An odd ridge tile detracts from the appearance – and ultimately the value – of your house.

Remove the existing tiles by chipping away the mortar, with a hammer and cold chisel. The new ones are bedded in a mortar of 3:1 of sharp sand:cement.

The tiles tend to soak the moisture out of the cement too quickly so that it shrinks and cracks, and does not hold them securely in place. You can prevent this by soaking the tiles thoroughly in water first.

The mortar should be spread evenly along the ridge. The tiles are set in place, then tapped firmly into position with the handle of a small trowel. The joins are then pointed (see page 186). Some ridge tiles have a very deep cavity underneath. Don't attempt to fill this with mortar, for such a large amount would shrink and crack and thus not hold the tiles securely.

THE TRICK

Instead, fill the gap by mortaring-in bits of broken tile – if you have any. Otherwise 'slips' are sold specially for this purpose at builder's merchants.

Hip tiles are dealt with similarly. However, the bottom one must be cut to follow the angle where it meets the eaves. This bottom tile must be fitted first when you are replacing an entire row. Stretch a string line from it to the ridge so that all the tiles will be fixed at the same level.

The curled piece of metal at the bottom of the hip tiles is called a hip iron, and is screwed to the hip rafter to stop the newly laid tiles from slipping down before the mortar has set. Make sure that the hip iron is still in position before you start repairs to the tiles.

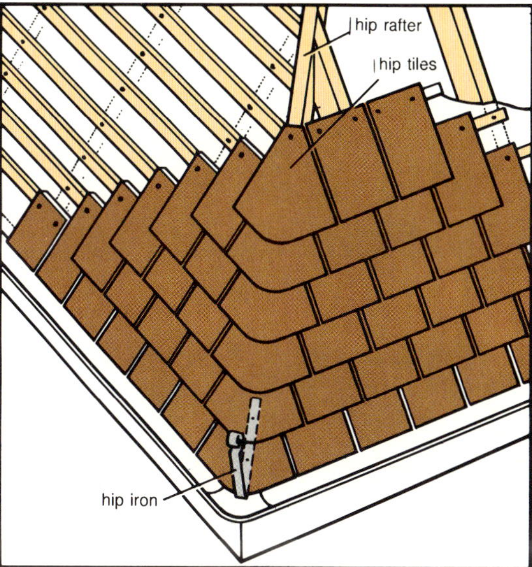

FLAT ROOFS

The flat roof is not, in fact, truly flat otherwise rainwater would not run off; there has to be a slight slope (or fall). Flat roofs do not shed moisture as effectively as pitched ones, so they tend to be installed on smaller, less important parts such as garages or extensions.

Like pitched roofs, flat roofs are supported on a network of rafters, spaced at intervals somewhere between 400–450mm (16–18in.), and supported at their ends on wall plates. These may rest on the top of the building's walls, or in single storey lean-to buildings, they could be fixed to the main walls. Lengths of small timber tapering towards their ends, known as firring pieces, are fixed on top of the rafters, to give the required slope.

The main covering is made up of some form of decking, such as lengths of natural timber (either tongued and grooved, or straight edged), exterior grade plywood or chip-board, compressed strawboard, or a concrete screed on top of some board. The whole thing is topped off, to ensure it will be waterproof, by two or three layers of roofing felt.

Where there are three layers of felt, the first one may run in the direction of the fall, the second across it, and the top one as the first. In other cases, all three may go in the direction of the fall.

THE TRICK

You ensure that the joins will not coincide by starting the first layer along one edge of the roof, the second at the other edge (the width of a roof never equals a set number of rolls of felt) and the last one as the first.

On a roof that has only two layers of felt, the first may go across the roof, with the second in the direction of the fall, or both may run along the length, starting off on different edges.

No matter how many layers, the final one should incorporate stone chippings, to reflect the sunlight, the ultra-violet rays of which can damage the felt. It is possible to buy felt with chippings already added. However, many people prefer to sprinkle the chippings as part of the installation, because the same felt can be used throughout.

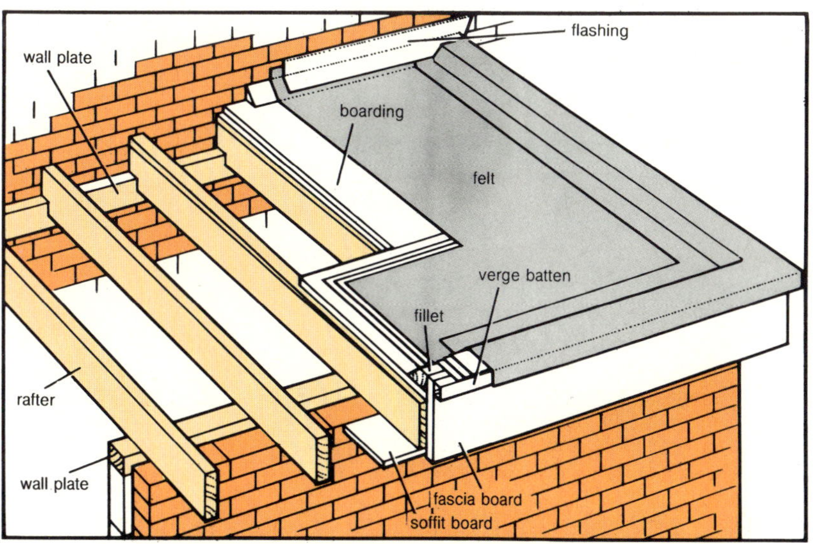

REPAIRS

Various repairs are needed from time to time on flat roofs. As with pitched roofs, probably the first sign that something is wrong will be a wet patch on the ceiling below, indicating a leak. Don't expect the trouble spot to be immediately above this patch. With any type of roof, penetrating moisture can travel some way on top of the ceiling before finding a way through. There is nothing for it but to get on the roof to carry out an inspection.

One of the most common faults is that a bubble develops in the top layer of felt, caused by moisture seeping beneath the material and swelling up under the heat of the sun. To correct the fault, make a cross-shaped cut in the middle, and peel back the pieces.

THE TRICK

Leave for a day or two to dry out properly, then bed the pieces back in a bitumastic compound sold at builder's merchants for flat-roof repairs. Press the pieces well down, apply more compound on top and replace any chippings you have disturbed.

You may discover a hole in the felt. If this takes the form of thin cracks, seal them with the bitumastic compound. A large hole can be repaired too – provided you can get hold of felt offcuts.

THE TRICK

As the material is sold by the roll, look for a builder doing similar work and ask if you can buy a small piece.

You need a piece about 50mm (2in.) bigger all round than the hole. Cover the area with bitumastic compound, bed the repair piece in it, making sure it is well stuck all round its edges, and press well down. Don't forget to add a few stone chippings.

ROOFS 3

REFELTING A FLAT ROOF

Eventually the time may come when the entire roof must be refelted. You will recognize the signs: there will be extensive cracking and crazing, perhaps several holes here and there, and the whole thing will look faded and tired. If it is a small roof – on a garage or single-storey extension, for instance – then it is possible for you to tackle the work, but it is doubtful whether refelting a house roof is work for the do-it-yourselfer.

Before you begin, you would do well to have a word with the Building Control Officer's Department of your local authority. They will advise you on the treatments of which they approve, and the type of felt they recommend: you ought to get one that is fire resistant as well as being waterproof.

THE TRICK

Buy the felt well in advance, cut it to size with a sharp knife, and let it lie flat for a day or two. It will uncurl, and be easier to handle.

The procedure is slightly different according to the type of decking you are working on. Most people will find that they are dealing with some form of timber: either natural in the form of planks, or plywood or chipboard.

FIXING THE NEW FELT

Now you are ready to fix the felt. In general, the do-it-yourselfer would do well to plump for three layers of felt, rather than two. However, your local authority may have views on this, and indeed, on whether the middle layer should go across the other two, or whether all should run in the same direction, plus other aspects of the fixing. Follow their advice.

This is a general method of laying felt. The first layer is fixed with nails: use 20mm (¾in.) extra-large-head galvanized clout nails. Lay the first length along one edge but begin nailing in the centre of the sheet and work outwards. Nails should be used at 150mm (6in.) centres.

THE TRICK

Make sure, as you drive them in, that the material is completely flat because any air pockets trapped underneath could cause bubbling later on.

Overlaps should be at least 50mm (2in.), and on the overlaps, the nails should be at 50mm (2in.) centres.

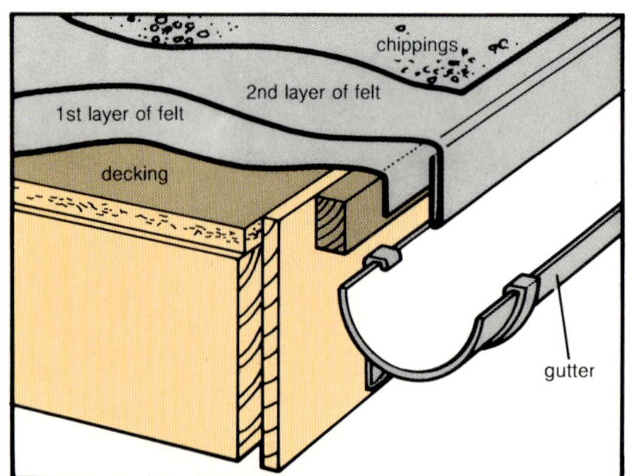

Subsequent sheets are bonded in position. Professionals use a hot bonding method but this is out of the question for do-it-yourselfers who would do better to use a cold mastic, available from builder's merchants.

This is the method. Lay the first length flat, then roll half of it back on itself. Apply mastic to the decking, then roll the felt back carefully bedding it down into position. Flatten it down from the centre outwards, making sure no air bubbles are trapped underneath. When you are satisfied that the felt is well fixed, roll the other half back, apply the mastic to the decking and roll this second half back into place, once again making sure it is well bedded down. All subsequent lengths should be fixed in the same way, allowing a 50mm (2in.) overlap. Use the same method for the cap sheet (as builders call the final layer). The roof edges are finished off with what are known as welted aprons.

50mm (2in.) overlap

Finally, bond 10mm (½in.) chippings in the mastic. They can be of gravel, calcinated flint, granite or limestone. They should be sprinkled at the rate of 100kg (220lb) per 5sq.m. (177sq.ft).

REMOVING THE OLD FELT

Your first job will be to remove the existing felt. At least the top layers of this will be stuck down.

THE TRICK

The best tool to use for removing these is an ordinary garden spade. Push the sharp edge of its blade under an overlap of the felt, and lever on the handle.

Soon you will be able to lift up the felt in large pieces. Any clumps that remain can be removed with an old carpentry chisel, or a long bladed knife.

The bottom layer will probably be fixed with clout nails. These need to be prised up.

You will probably find they have been driven too far in for the claw of a hammer to be inserted under their head, and you would do better to use a tack-lifter.

Once all the felt has been removed, it is a good idea to check whether there are any defects in the decking. These could be simple ones, easily dealt with. For instance, some of the nails might be missing. If so, drive in new ones, making sure that their heads, and those of any existing nails, are punched well home.

However there could be more severe problems. Water may have found its way through the defective felt and affected the timber, causing it to swell up; or even rot. You may be able to plane down a swollen board, but any that are subject to rot, or damaged in some way will need to be replaced. Woodworm attacks should be treated with a woodworm killer, or the board replaced if the infestation is very bad. Treat any new wood with preservative; do the old wood too, if it looks as though it is needed. Do not use creosote, because it reacts badly with the bitumen used in the manufacture, and the bonding, of the felt.

OTHER TYPES OF DECKING

There are one or two points to notice if you are dealing with other types of decking. For instance, joins between sheets of compressed strawboard are sealed by tape. If you damage or disturb the tape in removing the original felt, new tape, which is sold by builder's merchants, will have to be fixed. Sweep the surface of the board free of all dust and dirt, and make sure it is dry. Then seal it with a suitable primer. You must not use clout nails on this board.

THE TRICK

If you want to nail the first layer, use 45mm (1¾in.) × 8-gauge serrated aluminium nails. Alternatively you can bond it. All subsequent layers are bonded, too.

Concrete should be brushed thoroughly to get rid of dust and loose bits. It should also be truly level, so fill any depressions with either a sand/cement mix or an exterior grade filler. Seal with a primer, which will be sold where you buy the felt, then bond the layers of felt as already described.

ROOFS 4

CHIMNEYS

The flue that carries smoke and other combustion gases upwards from the fireplace cannot be allowed to terminate at roof level, otherwise the noxious fumes would be escaping too close to the house. Therefore it is carried upwards – to discharge at a better level – by means of the chimney stack.

The brickwork (or rendering) of the stack needs exactly the same sort of maintenance as the rest of the house walls. However, one or two specialized repairs are called for. Many do-it-yourselfers would hesitate to tackle these, put off not by their difficulty so much as the spot where they have to be carried out. Sometimes a chimney forms part of the gable wall: that is not too bad because you can reach it comfortably with an access tower. However, if it is in the middle of the ridge, then that is an entirely different matter. It is not merely a question of climbing up there yourself; you have also to take the necessary materials. Don't attempt this unless you are absolutely confident about working at heights.

REPLACING A DAMAGED POT

One of the most common things to go wrong is that a chimney pot may be damaged. The pots are bedded in a layer of cement known as 'flaunching', and you must first get rid of this.

THE TRICK

Cover the top of the flue so that no debris will fall down: it could carry soot down into a living room, or even block the flue.

Then chip off the flaunching with a hammer and cold chisel. You must get rid of all the flaunching, so finish off by rubbing the top of the stack with a wire brush. Place the debris in a bucket as you go and lower it to the ground with a rope. Tie the rope round the broken pot and lower this, too. You really need a helper to handle this bucket for you at ground level.

Haul up the new pot and stand it in position, then mix the flaunching: in fact, this is a good job for your ground-level helper to do. The mix should be a 1:3 of cement: sharp sand. Brush the top of the stack and the base of the pot with water so it will not absorb the moisture from the mortar, then apply the flaunching with a trowel.

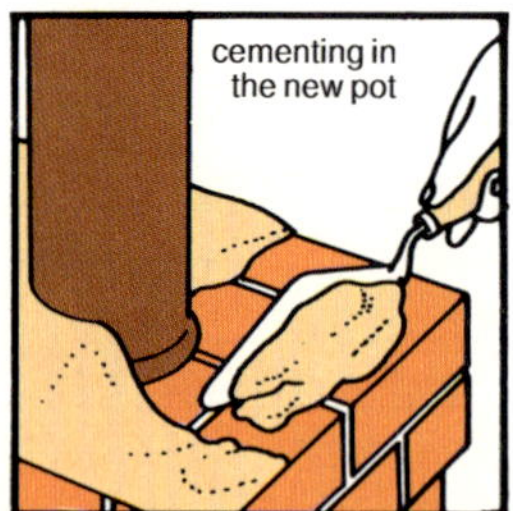

THE TRICK

The flaunching should be to a depth of 75mm (3in.) round the pot, but sloping at the edges so that rainwater is carried clear.

Brush off any mortar that has stuck to the pot.

Another possibility is that the flaunching itself might become cracked and loose. In that case it should be chipped off as above – take care not to damage the pot – and replaced.

BLOCKING OFF A FLUE

You might wish to block off the top of a flue: perhaps as a result of removing the fireplace in the room below. Begin by chipping off the flaunching round the pot and lifting the pot clear. Then get rid of the rest of the mortar, as already described.

There are now two possibilities. Special capping pots, to be bedded in mortar, are sold at builder's merchants. Alternatively, you can use a piece of slate, which must obviously be bigger than the flue mouth. Lay a 25mm (1in.) thick band of mortar round the top of the flue, and bed the slate in this. Now cover the whole top of the stack with a 75mm (3in.) bed of mortar, sloping to the sides so that rainwater will run clear.

THE TRICK

Remember that a flue capped off in this way needs to be ventilated with an airbrick otherwise it might become damp.

You must also incorporate a grille when blocking off a fireplace in a room (see page 159).

FLASHINGS

The joint where a roof meets a vertical surface such as a wall or chimney stack is obviously a vulnerable point. To make sure it is waterproof, it is dressed with a strip material which used to be of lead but, nowadays, is more likely to be in bituminous felt, or even plastic. Builders call such material 'flashing'.

Some flashings can be quite complicated: for instance where a pitched roof meets an end wall, stepped flashings are required. The arrangement round the base of a chimney stack is even more tricky. When you add to that the difficulties of access to such spots, you will perhaps feel that maintenance on these flashings is best left to the professionals. However, simpler flashings, such as where a single lean-to storey meets a house wall, can certainly be tackled by the do-it-yourselfer. Flashings of this type are fixed by being inserted into the horizontal mortar joint immediately above the roof line and bent down to meet the roof, on which they are bedded in mastic.

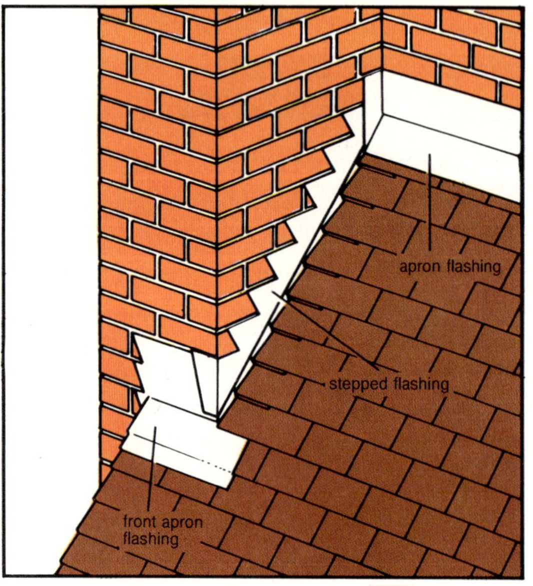

REPLACEMENT

Where the flashing is in really bad condition however, it will need to be replaced. Rake out the mortar joint and pull the old flashing clear. Carry out a further raking, if required, to clear out the mortar to a depth of about 25mm (1in.) and get rid of all loose material. Clean up the brickwork and roof, using a wire brush.

Take hold of the flashing, bending it as required, and push it into the joint. Wedge it there with small pieces of timber for instance. Then bend the flashing over the roof, and seal it with mastic to stop it from curling. Remove the timber wedges, and point the mortar joint.

Proprietary plastic flashings, specially designed for d-i-y use, are sold. Follow the instructions supplied with them.

MORTAR FLASHINGS

A mortar fillet is sometimes used. This can be either on its own – especially, for instance, where the party walls of a row of terraced houses extend beyond the roof line – or underneath flashing. The effect of the weather, and/or settlement of the building, can weaken this fillet. If there is just a small defect here and there, repoint with new mortar as needed. However, when the whole thing looks ready to crumble, chip it all away with a hammer and bolster chisel. Then form a new fillet, using a 1:3 mix of sand:cement.

THE TRICK

It is not easy to form a really neat fillet, but if you use a filler knife you stand a better chance than with a trowel.

A crack line above or below a fillet can be sealed with a mastic gun.

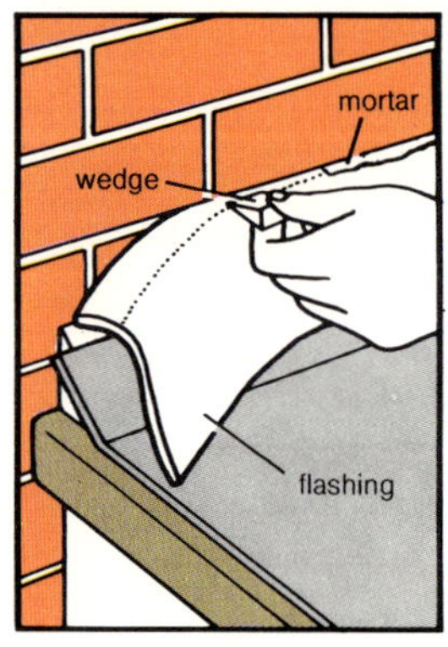

REPAIRS

The simplest fault may be that a crack or hole has developed in the flashing. In that case, coat it with a 1.5mm (1/24in.) layer of mastic, bed in a small piece of metal foil or roofing felt, then cover with a further layer of mastic. Porous flashing can be coated along its entire length with the mastic.

It may be that a perfectly sound flashing has fallen away from the wall because the mortar has deteriorated. You should then rake out the joint, push the flashing back, and repoint it.

RAINWATER DISPOSAL 1

The rainwater that falls on your home's roof is collected and conveyed to the drains by what builders call the 'rainwater disposal system'. This consists of a network of gutters and downpipes, known collectively as rainwater goods.

Rainwater goods have traditionally been made of cast iron, and most of the gutters and downpipes on our homes today are in this material. However, despite its strength and durability, cast iron suffers from one big drawback: it rusts, which is a very important defect in items designed to convey water! As a result, builders looked for an alternative material and for a time, before the last war, rainwater goods were made in asbestos. Even then it was realized that this was far from being the perfect material. True it is not affected by water, but gutters and downpipes made from it were bulky. Nowadays, of course, we know asbestos to be a health hazard. In any event, very few were installed. Finally it was realized that rainwater goods could be made in plastic, and this material has been used for them ever since 1945.

Plastic has many advantages. Provided it does not suffer physical damage, it is virtually everlasting, does not corrode, is weather-resistant, does not need to be painted unless you wish to change its colour, and is light to handle, easy to work. As a result, all new or replacement rainwater goods are now in plastic. Cast iron versions are virtually unobtainable, asbestos ones certainly so.

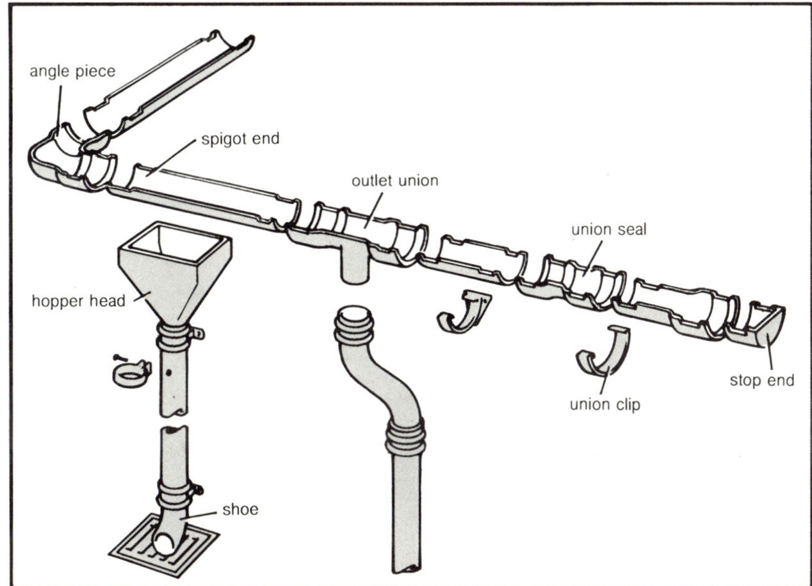

GUTTERS

MAINTENANCE

The most common fault with any type of gutter is an overflow. Usually the cause will be a blockage as the result of gathering dirt, falling leaves or a bird's nest. The remedy is obvious – clear it.

THE TRICK

First bung up with a rag the top of any nearby downpipes, so that you don't push the debris down them.

Then clear cast-iron gutters with a rounded garden trowel, plastic ones with a half-round scoop made from hardboard. Shovel the debris into a bucket hanging from a ladder rung.

cleaning out gutters

Finally flush out the system with buckets of cold water, scrubbing out the insides of the gutter with an old brush, or cloth if they are plastic.

THE TRICK

If there are a lot of deciduous trees near your roof, it might be worth fitting plastic netting to the top of the gutters.

The overflow may, however, have come about because the gutter has sagged. You can sometimes bend an iron bracket upwards to restore the gutter to the correct level. Another possibility is to push bits of wood between bracket and gutter, then fill the gap with a glass fibre repair kit. In both cases, take care that you do not break the seal where two lengths of gutter join up. With plastic, it is better to re-site the bracket slightly higher up.

REPLACEMENT

Leaks can develop in a gutter. In the case of cast-iron, it may be that rust has caused a hole to form. Small holes can be repaired with glass fibre or waterproof tape. If the damage is extensive, however, a whole section of gutter will have to be replaced. No matter whether the gutter is cast-iron or plastic, the new section can be in plastic – in fact, you will probably have no choice because cast-iron is no longer available.

Begin by removing the defective section. Lengths of cast-iron are fastened together with a nut and bolt, and the joint then sealed with waterproof mastic. The nut will be far too corroded for you to unfasten it. The best method is to saw through the bolt with a hacksaw. Next tap out the stub with a hammer (being careful not to strike the gutter with too much force for it can shatter dangerously) or drill it out. Then lever the sections apart with an old chisel or screwdriver.

You should not let the damaged gutter just drop to the ground, as it can shatter, causing injury with its fragments to children or pets. Better to carry it down the ladder, or tie a rope to it and lower it gently.

Plastic guttering comes in lengths usually of 2, 3 or 4m. (6ft 6in., 9ft 11in., or 13ft 2in.). Cut it to the dimension you require with a hacksaw or fine toothed carpentry saw. Fix it in place with the special adapter supplied for connecting plastic to metal. Paint the plastic the same colour as the metal and it will not be noticeable.

PAINTING

If you have cast iron rainwater goods, paint them regularly to keep rust at bay. Any rust already present should be removed with a wire brush, emery paper, or a chemical treatment. Get rid of loose and flaking paint as well. Bare metal should be treated with an appropriate primer – spot priming will be sufficient if there are only one or two bare bits. Follow with an undercoat and two of exterior-quality gloss.

THE TRICK

Don't neglect the inside of gutters or the backs of downpipes – use a piece of card or hardboard to protect the wall from splashes.

On asbestos, use a water soluble paint stripper to get rid of loose and flaking paint. Never use a blowlamp because its heat could cause the asbestos to crack and perhaps explode. Scrub down finally with a brush using lots of water.

Do not use glasspaper or other dry abrasive material on asbestos, as inhaling the dust of asbestos puts your health at risk.

As for the choice of paint, use an exterior-grade emulsion or cement paint, which is resistant to alkalis and moisture, but will allow the asbestos to breathe. Treat the inside of the gutters with bituminous sealer.

Plastic rainwater goods are usually light grey in colour, although white and black varieties can be bought. If you want to change these colours, apply first an all-purpose primer, followed by an undercoat, then one or two coats of gloss. If they are already painted, and the paint is in good condition, apply one or two coats of gloss. A chemical paint stripper, but never a blowlamp, can be used on plastic rainwater goods.

painting the inside of the gutter

RAINWATER DISPOSAL 2

BRACKETS

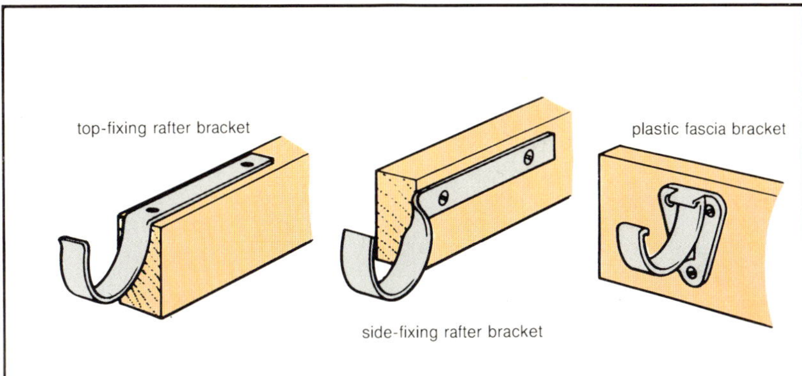

LEAKING JOINTS

A leak might develop where the two sections of gutter join up. If the gutter is in cast-iron, re-make the joint. Remove the bolt, scrape off the old sealant, and clean up with a wire brush. Spread a bed of sealant on the bottom of the two overlaps, bring them together, and fit a new nut and bolt with a washer to each side. Mop up any excess sealant. The inside of the joint should be treated with bituminous sealer: in fact, it might be worthwhile to treat the whole gutter.

Nothing should go wrong with the joins in plastic guttering, but there might be accidental damage. Some systems are joined by a self-locking seal, in other cases the joint is solvent welded. The method varies, but you can usually see which has been used. With self-locking seals you can make a damaged joint waterproof with non-setting mastic. Renew the solvent if that is the method used (see page 119).

The support brackets might be in bad shape, so inspect them. Withdrawing the fixing screws of old corroded brackets is not easy. There are, however, one or two dodges to force them.

THE TRICK

You can play a blowlamp flame on their heads for a short burst. The heat causes both screw and timber to expand slightly, and thus loosens them. Or you can place the blade of a plastic-handled screwdriver in the head of a screw and give the handle a sharp blow with a hammer. This can also free the bond between metal and timber.

If all this fails, you will have to wrench the brackets clear. Make good and paint any damage you cause.

The new brackets are best screwed to good timber, in a slightly new position.

THE TRICK

Run a length of string from between the brackets you will be retaining on each side of the new one to make sure this latter is at the right height to give a correct fall in the new gutter.

Some gutter brackets are screwed to the rafters under the slates or tiles. This means you will have to remove the slates or tiles concerned to reach it. If you want to replace such a bracket, unscrew it (see above) and take to a builder's merchant to obtain a matching replacement. You should either make new screwholes for it, or use slightly longer screws when installing the new bracket.

Paint it with rustproofing paint before replacing the slates or tiles.

DOWNPIPES

A blockage can occur in downpipes as well as gutters, it is usually caused by similar debris. You clear it by pushing it through with a plunger.

THE TRICK

A makeshift one, made from a wad of rags tied to the end of a stick, will do. Cover the gulley to stop the dirt from going down into the drains.

Such a task is a bit complicated on houses, because of the offset (or 'swan's neck') to carry the run under the eaves; you cannot push a stick round that. There may also be bends and curves elsewhere.

To unblock a house downpipe, you will have to lift it clear of the clips or brackets holding it and clear it out on the ground. That does not mean dismantling the whole run. The pipes sit loosely in place not only so that they can easily be pulled clear, but, more importantly, also so that you will see at a glance where the blockage lies. When you spot water bubbling out of a joint, you can be sure that the trouble lies in the section below.

REPLACEMENT

A leak might develop in a downpipe: caused by rust if it is cast iron, physical damage in the case of plastic. As with gutters, small cracks can be sealed with waterproof tape or a glass fibre repair kit. The damage may be so extensive that a new length of pipe will have to be fitted. This will be in plastic, no matter which type of system you have at present. Dropping a plastic length of pipe into an otherwise metal set-up presents no problems at all. Paint the plastic so that it merges with the metal.

SECURING LOOSE DOWNPIPES

Downpipes are usually secured to the wall of the building by means of brackets; if these fail, the downpipe will swing about and will be very likely to break. It is therefore important to check on these regularly. If one does come loose, this is what you do.

Start at the bottom of the downpipe and remove the lowest bracket by levering out the nails which hold it to the wall. Use a piece of wood to protect the bricks. Remove the section of downpipe thus released and lay it aside. Repeat this operation on each section until the loose bracket is reached.

THE TRICK

If the loose bracket is near the top of the pipe, and you are dealing with a cast-iron pipe, consider replacing it with a plastic one rather than re-installing the cast-iron sections.

If the problem was caused by the softwood plug coming away from the mortar, scrape out the hole left and cut a new plug from a softwood batten to fit it.

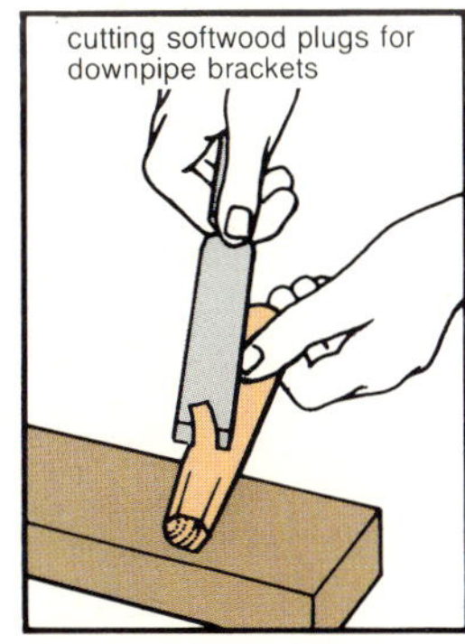

Hammer it home until flush with the wall's surface. If the mortar is in bad condition, repoint the wall around the bracket position and then recut a suitable hole – 15mm (½in.) across and 65mm (2½in.) deep is about right.

Reposition the downpipe and the bracket around it. Then nail the bracket into the softwood plug, using the proper stackpipe nails (see page 59). Continue down the wall replacing the downpipe sections and brackets as you go. Check the other plugs as you replace the brackets and renew any that seem loose.

Plastic downpipes are secured by a clip around the neck of the pipe which is then bolted to a wall bracket. The same sort of softwood plugs are also used as seating for the wall bracket screws and should be installed as described above. Make sure that the edges of any cuts in the pipes are clean and straight (see page 119 for cutting and soldering plastic pipes).

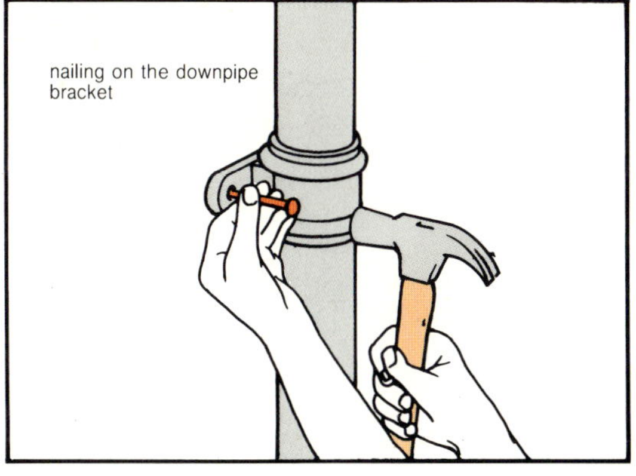

BRICKWORK 1

The exterior walls of your house may be of solid or cavity construction: i.e. consist of two separate walls (or 'leaves') with a gap between, but joined here and there by metal strips (known as wall ties, see page 139). If it was built before 1914, the walls will almost certainly be solid; if built after 1945, the walls will almost certainly be cavity. Between those two dates, either could have been used; so measure the thickness at a window or door opening. Solid walls will be 225 or 350mm (9 or 13½in.) thick, while cavity walls will be 280mm (11in.) plus. In both cases the plaster will be 10 or 20mm (½ or ¾in.) thick.

AIRBRICKS

The foundations of a house with a suspended ground floor need to be well ventilated in order to keep them dry, and thus clear of wet or dry rot. The normal way of ensuring such ventilation is to fit so-called airbricks in the external walls and leave gaps in the intermediate (or sleeper) walls.

We say 'so-called' airbricks because they can be in metal (usually galvanized cast iron) as well as terracotta. The metal is usually painted, but terracotta airbricks are sold in colours to match the brickwork of the house. They both come in two patterns: square hole and louvre. The sloping louvres offer more protection against driving rain in exposed situations, but otherwise there is little to choose between them.

The important thing about airbricks is to keep them clear of obstructions, otherwise they will not keep a good current of air flowing through. Blockages can arise accidentally. For instance, garden soil can become piled up against them, or a bulk delivery of builder's sand or fuel could cover them. Always include the airbricks in the periodic inspections you carry out on the outside of your house (see page 165).

More seriously, the brick is often blocked off deliberately – usually to stop draughts coming into ground floor rooms inside the house. This is something you should never do. Draughts are another word for ventilation, and they are essential below the floor to keep the foundations in good order. Any draught-proofing measures needed should be carried out inside the room (see page 136).

Another reason for blocking off an airbrick is to keep out vermin: mice, for instance, can squeeze through its holes.

THE TRICK

If that becomes a problem, cover the brick with fine-mesh netting, but never block it off completely.

Airbricks are often fitted to small rooms in the house – larders, small boxrooms, under-stairs cupboards – where the ventilation provided by the window, if any, is felt to be inadequate. They can also be specified in kitchens and bathrooms with condensation problems.

FITTING

You can buy airbricks in sizes to match those of house bricks. They are 220m (about 9in.) long, just like bricks, and come in heights of 70, 145 and 220mm (2¾, 5¾ and 8⅔in.): i.e. one, two or three courses of brickwork. Decide how big an airbrick you are going to fit, or have room for, and chop out as many bricks as necessary. Do this by hacking out with a club hammer and bolster chisel, the mortar holding them in place. You can make the job easier by first drilling round the bricks with a power tool and masonry bit. If working on a cavity wall, it is essential to avoid dropping debris into the gap, as this can cause a 'bridge' (see page 140).

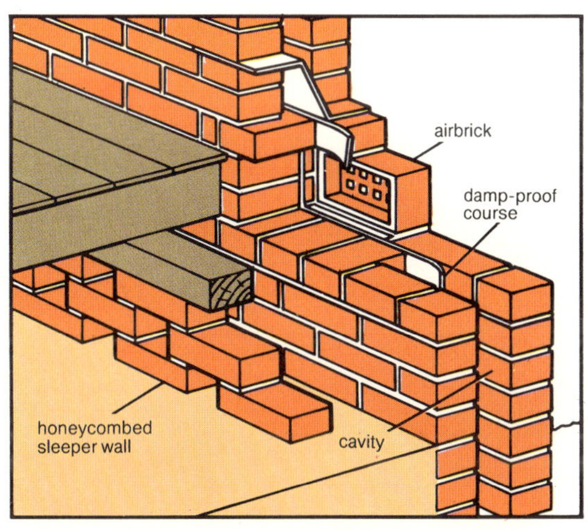

While you work, take care not to disturb surrounding masonry, but there is no need to give the wall any support whilst creating such a small hole. The airbrick is mortared in place. Aim to mix mortar of a colour that matches the old so the new work will not be apparent.

INTERIOR FINISHING

A hole cut to take an airbrick for a room will need to be neatened on the inside. Grills in various patterns and materials (e.g: aluminium, fibrous plaster and plastic) are sold for this. Choose whichever type appeals to you. Some incorporate a fly screen, and others have a control for regulating the size of the aperture.

On cavity walls you will also need a duct to ensure that the fresh air actually passes through to the inside and not down the cavity.

slates bridging cavity to ensure air reaches interior

THE TRICK

Such ducts can be bought, or you can make one by mortaring four roofing slates in place.

SUBSIDENCE

This is usually caused by movement of the underlying ground, rather than by the failure of the foundations, now that the Building Regulations lay down such strict standards (see page 166). It occurs after long periods of drought, which causes the clay subsoil to shrink away from, and cease to support, the foundations. It can also occur where a house has been built on 'made-up' ground – such as where a large hole has been filled – or over mine workings. The earth settles and so ceases to support the foundations. Houses built on railway embankments can suffer from the bank sliding down into the cutting.

THE TRICK

If you live in an area with a clay subsoil, check your insurance policy to see what it covers with regard to subsidence. Consult your surveyor, if buying a house in such an area, to see if he/she thinks special insurance would be necessary.

Subsidence can also be caused by floods, and by bad land drainage which causes water to lie around the building and soften the subsoil. Installing land drains will cure this.

Tree roots can also damage foundations by pushing against the concrete to crack it, or by drawing water from the subsoil and so shrinking it away. No tree should be planted within 5m. (16ft 6in.) of a building and particularly not those liable to grow to more than 6m. (20ft) in height. Willows and poplars, both of which require a lot of water, are especially to be avoided.

SYMPTOMS AND TESTS

If you see vertical cracks in the walls on either side of a corner, or a wall out of true, suspect the foundations. Diagonal cracks from the tops of doors and windows are another sign, while vertical cracks under windows or at other points, suggest the foundations may be being pushed upwards.

THE TRICK

To check if movement is still occurring, glue a glass microscope slide over the crack; if it breaks, you have problems.

Repairing foundations and replacing lost subsoil (or underpinning) is difficult and expensive: call in an expert builder, and let him do the necessary buttressing and excavation. Otherwise your house may literally collapse around you.

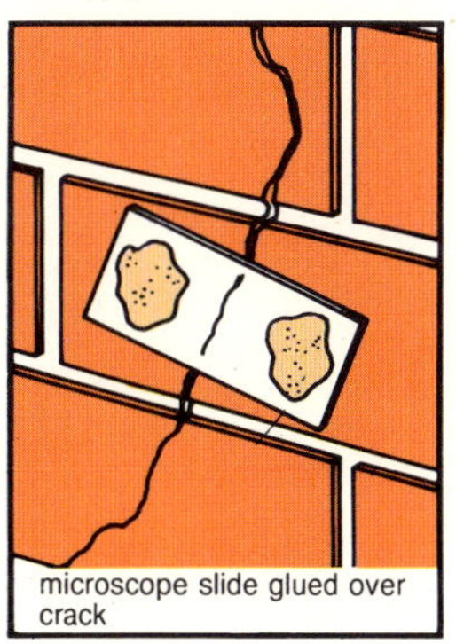

microscope slide glued over crack

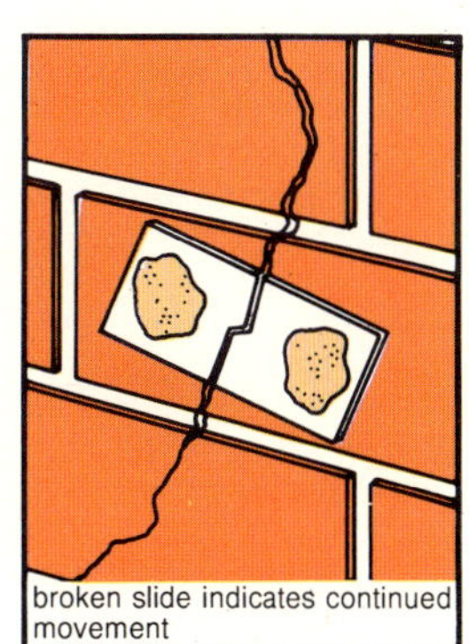

broken slide indicates continued movement

BRICKWORK 2

REPOINTING

When the mortar between the bricks starts to wear down (rain, wind, physical damage can all be the cause), it becomes necessary to add new mortar on top of the old to bring it to the correct level. This process is termed repointing. This is not a difficult job, and requires only the minimum of tools but if you are tackling a whole house, or even one wall, as opposed to a small garage or extension, you must have proper access equipment (see page 170).

The repointing is done with a 4:1 sand:cement mix. You can buy the ingredients separately and mix them yourself, or obtain them ready mixed and dry-packed, requiring only the addition of water.

Divide the wall into easily managed sections: a square metre (3sq.ft) is about the right size for most do-it-yourselfers. Begin by raking out, with an old chisel or screwdriver, any loose or crumbling material from the joints. The new mortar must be at least 12mm (½in.) thick, so you may have to chop out a bit of good mortar to create sufficient depth. Then mix your new mortar.

THE TRICK

Dry brickwork can take up the moisture from the new mortar, so first give it a good soaking with water applied from a bucket with an old wall brush.

To do the actual repointing you need a small trowel (special pointing trowels are sold) and a hawk: a piece of timber about 300mm (1ft) square with a handle underneath (see below). You can buy one, or make it yourself from an offcut of plywood or blockboard, and broom handle or dowel.

Place mortar on the hawk, and smooth it to a pat. Pick up some on the back of the trowel, hold the hawk close to the wall, and push the trowel forward. At the same time tilt the front of the hawk upwards, so that the mortar is lifted clear. Press the mortar well into the joints.

Begin with the vertical joins. You will find that a small surplus is left at the outside of each joint. Chop this off when the whole section of verticals is completed. Next repoint the horizontals using a similar technique, drawing the trowel along to form a smooth continuous band.

THE TRICK

Builders take an old knife, sharpen it to a point at the end and bend the point at right angles to the main blade (they call this a 'frenchman').

Then they draw this along a straight-edge to remove the thick surplus at the bottom. Finish off the joint in one of the ways shown. They are all so shaped that a ledge is not formed where water can gather.

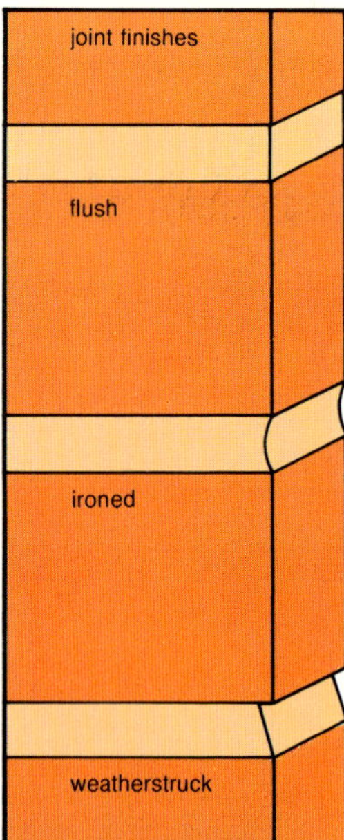

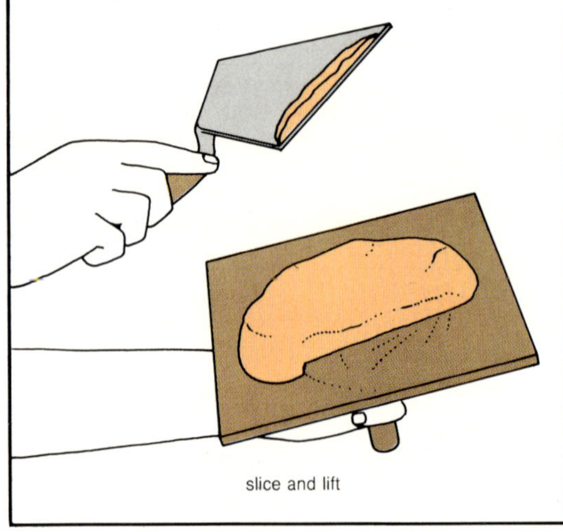

slice and lift

EFFLORESCENCE

You may see a white powdery substance forming on the walls of your home. This is efflorescence. Is it something to worry about? It depends. On a modern house almost certainly not, because it is caused by the salts in the brickwork drying out and crystallizing as they come to the surface.

In such cases, there is no need to get rid of it, but you can if you wish, do so with a stiff brush. You must not use water for this will make things worse by delaying the drying-out process.

On older houses, efflorescence might indicate that the walls have suddenly become damp, and you might check for a likely cause (see pages 140 and 142).

SPALLING

Spalling is the name given to a condition in which the face of one or more bricks on a house wall starts to crumble. It is caused by moisture, which has soaked into the brick, expanding as it freezes during very cold weather.

If the spalling is bad, and only one or two bricks are affected, you should replace them. First remove the damaged bricks by chopping out the mortar all round each of them. Use a thin cold chisel and club hammer for this. You can buy a new brick to replace the old, but you might well find it impossible to get hold of one that matches. Try turning the old brick round so that its inner face is now on the outside.

The new brick is mortared into place with a 3:1 of sand:cement mix. Small packs of suitable mortar to which you merely add water can also be bought. Mix the mortar, then spread it on the bottom and sides of the opening, then on top of the replacement brick. At all costs try to avoid dropping mortar in the gap of a cavity wall (see page 140). Lay the brick in place, cleaning up any mortar that oozes out.

tapping replacement for spalled brick into place

There is a tendency for the surrounding brickwork to soak moisture from the new mortar, causing it to set too soon with the result that it might crack.

THE TRICK

The way to avoid this is to wet the brickwork thoroughly first with water applied by brush.

Where the spalling is extensive, more drastic remedies may be called for. These might include the rendering of a complete wall (see page 187) which is not really a job for a do-it-yourselfer.

WALL FINISHES 1

BRICKWORK

Exterior brick walls, unless in bad condition, are probably best left alone. They require little maintenance, apart from repointing (see page 186), whereas once painted or rendered, they require regular maintenance. You can scrape off surface stains with a scraper or wire brush but, if you do, make sure you do the whole wall – otherwise it will look patchy. If in a very exposed position, or if it looks dampish, it might be worth painting on a coat of exterior water repellant. This is a colourless liquid which causes the surface to throw off water and will not colour the brickwork. Note that it will not cure rising damp.

THE TRICK

Sometimes rubbing a brick wall with another brick of a similar colour and texture, will improve its general appearance. Match the colour carefully otherwise you may get a streaky effect.

PAINTED BRICKWORK

If you have any painted brickwork, or intend to paint brickwork for the first time, be sure to brush off the brickwork first with a stiff (but not wire) brush. Replace any damaged bricks (see Spalling, page 186). Never paint a wall with efflorescence showing, as it will come through the paint and spoil it.

THE TRICK

If the brickwork is porous, thin the paint and give the wall two coats.

Always paint from the top downwards starting in the top right (or left if left-handed) corner.

You can use an emulsion or a cement paint or stone-based paint. Some ordinary emulsions can be used outdoors, providing the manufacturer states this is possible; but you would do better to use a specially-formulated outdoor emulsion which would contain a fungicide and reinforcing agents such as mica or nylon fibres. Stone-based paints usually contain an additive, such as crushed natural stone, silica or mica – which produces a textured finish.

These paints can generally be used on any outdoor wall surface, but you should always check the paint's limitations in the manufacturer's instructions and follow the application directions carefully. Never be tempted to do the next coat before the paint has had time to dry properly, otherwise the second coat will not adhere correctly.

TILE CLADDING

The best treatment for this is to scrub the tiles with clean water. Don't use a detergent, otherwise any immovable stains will show through when the tiles are dry. If the staining is very bad, consider using a tile paint to improve the overall appearance. However, this will mean another area which will require regular maintenance from now on. Replace broken tiles as described on page 171; obviously on a vertical wall, every row of tiles will be nailed on.

CEMENT RENDERINGS

This is a good way to cover a wall in bad or unattractive condition. To render an entire house is probably beyond the capabilities of all but the most enthusiastic and devoted do-it-yourselfer. It is extremely hard work which requires a lot of care and a fair amount of practice before you start on a large area. However, it is perfectly possible to do a small area – such as the back wall of a conservatory or a garage wall – without too much trouble. There are three main sorts of cement rendering.

1. Cement Rendering This can be finished in a variety of different ways (see below) and is the simplest to apply (see below). A mix of 1:4 parts of cement:sand is adequate for most surfaces; although on cement blocks a mixture of 1:2:9 parts of cement:lime:sand is better. On exposed walls, use 1:1:6 parts of cement:lime:sand.

You must allow enough time for the coat to dry before applying the final top coat – usually 1–2 days in summer, but up to a week in winter, is necessary.

2. Roughcast This is a mix of cement and specially graded sand usually in the proportions of 1:3 of cement:sand and gravel. It is usually applied by means of a Tyrolean Projector (which can be hired (see page 165)). This is generally only effective on brickwork, blockwork or previously undecorated rendering. Three coats are required: one face on to the wall, then one angled from the right and another from the left. This ensures an even coating overall.

3. Pebbledash and Spardash This is applied as a final coat on top of a straight cement rendering and involves casting pebbles or crushed stone onto the wet mortar from a shovel. You should use a wooden float trowel to press the pebbles into the mortar once the section is well covered.

roughcast sprayed on by Tyrolean projector

APPLICATION

You need some 10 × 10mm (½ × ½in.) battens to make a form work for the panels of mortar. Nail the first one on the corner of the wall, using a spirit level to get it upright. Nail other battens at about 1.5m. (5ft) intervals so as to form a series of panels.

Then mix your mortar, using one of the mixes given above. Don't mix more than you can handle in about 30 minutes (less if it is hot). Flick water onto the wall to dampen it if it is dry. This allows the mortar to dry properly. Scrape several floats of mortar onto your hawk (see page 234). Using a steel float, cut a section of mortar away from the mass on the hawk. Hold the hawk near the bottom of the first panel and tilt the mortar onto the float which will be almost upside down at this point. Push the mortar from the float onto the wall and spread it upwards. Continue filling until the mortar is just higher than the two battens; then use a straight-edge to skim off the excess.

push on mortar with steel float

THE TRICK

It is a good idea to lay a plank along the foot of the wall which you are rendering to catch any mortar drips – these can be used again, just scrape them up and spread it back.

Continue in this manner, mixing the mortar, spreading it on, and levelling off until all the panels are filled. Leave to dry for about four hours, then scratch a random pattern into the mortar to make a key for the second coat. Remove the battens, fill the gaps left with the mortar mix and level off. Leave for 24 hours to dry – 48 if an exposed wall using the stronger mortar (see left) – then damp the surface down and apply a second coat about 5mm (¼in.) thick.

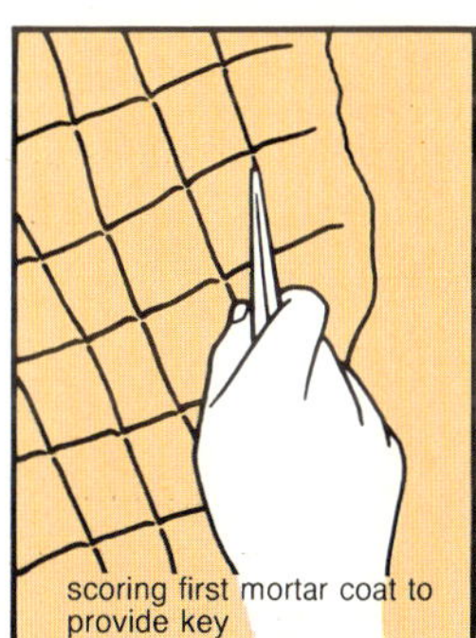
scoring first mortar coat to provide key

THE TRICK

If you are intending to pebbledash the wall, you will need a coat about 15mm (½in.) thick.

dampen and smooth second mortar coat with steel float

Finish the second coat with a steel float if you want a smooth finish; or use a wooden float for a matt finish. Don't work the surface too hard, otherwise you will bring the cement to the surface and it will not dry properly. You can also use a decorator's comb to make patterns (see page 188).

SYNTHETIC RESIN FINISHES

These are proprietary paints which are designed to go over cement renderings of various sorts, blockwork, brickwork, asbestos sheets and paint. They have high durability and good covering power; they can also be finished in a number of decorative ways – some of which are shown on page 188. They come in a range of colours – including some interesting darker shades – and are claimed to last well even in very exposed conditions.

WALL FINISHES 2

Many walls, usually solid ones, are treated with a mix based on sand and cement to give then extra weatherproofing. Such mixes are also used as a decorative feature on modern, sound cavity walls, as well as suspect ones. There are many different names for these treatments, according to the exact nature of the materials used, and the finish given to the surface – rendering, stucco, pebbledash, roughcast are some.

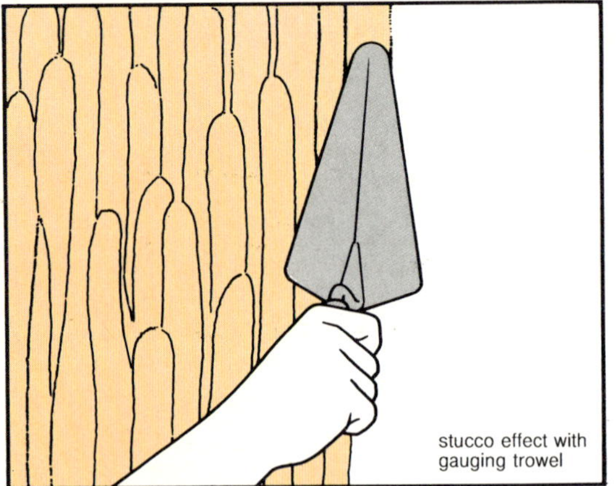
stucco effect with gauging trowel

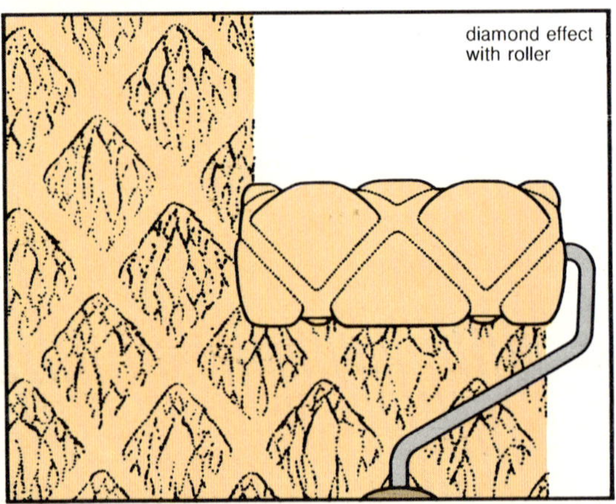
diamond effect with roller

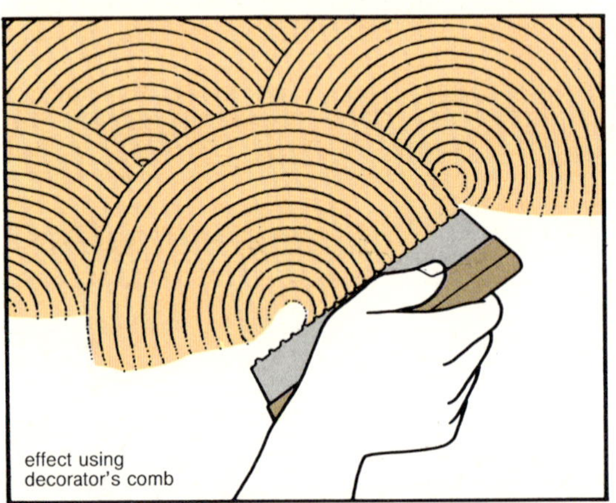
effect using decorator's comb

swirl effect using float

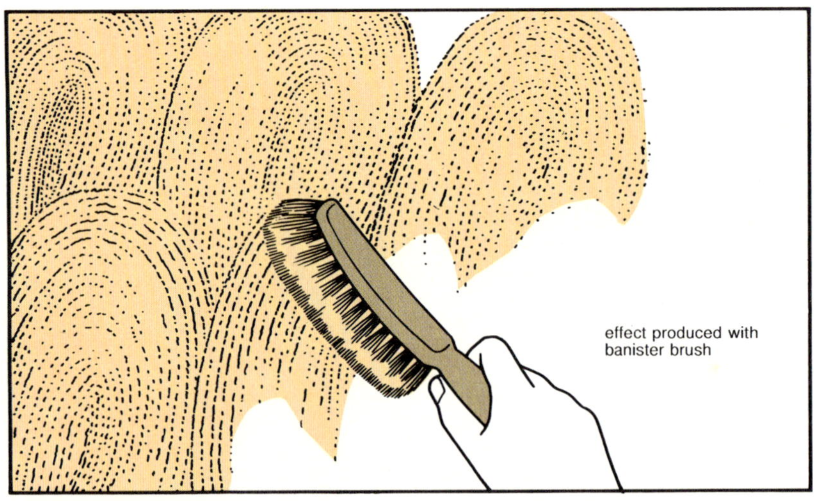
effect produced with banister brush

MAINTENANCE

Applying such a finish from scratch is a work beyond the capabilities of the do-it-yourselfer. However, you can carry out repairs to an existing finish, and unfortunately, these are all too often necessary. The reason is that these finishes, like all sand:cement mixes, tend to shrink with age. Furthermore, they have to withstand the movement to which all buildings are subjected. As a result, a network of tiny cracks may develop.

These cracks are not only unsightly; they can also let in water. The moisture then works under the surface of the mix and can loosen its bond to the underlying brickwork. This action is accentuated when water expands as it freezes. As a result, some of the surface may become loose, 'blisters' can form and whole sections fall away from the wall.

It should be the aim of your maintenance to ensure that such troubles never happen. Happily you have a powerful ally in the shape of modern masonry paints which will cover hairline cracks and make the surface waterproof. So regular repainting of the house is a priority to keep it safe and sound, as well as making it more attractive to look at.

FILLING CRACKS

These masonry paints will not bridge cracks bigger than, say, 1.5mm (1/24in.) so larger ones have to be filled. Exterior-grade fillers are sold but, if the cracks are large, a sand:cement mix is more economical. You can mix this yourself (use 1 part of cement to 3 of sand) or buy a small pack of ready-mixed mortar to which you merely add water.

Clean out the crack to get rid of all loose material, using the point of a small trowel, or filling knife. Then push home the filler.

THE TRICK

If the crack is very wide or deep, you should do the filling in two applications.

Smooth it off with the surrounding area. The filler will be visible afterwards, so if you have treated a lot of cracks you will probably need to repaint to conceal them. In fact, such filling is best regarded as preparation for repainting.

REPAIRS TO RENDERING

Any defects in rendering should be dealt with as soon as possible, in order to keep the weatherproofing of your home up to a high standard.

If a blister develops, you must first hack it off, right back to the brickwork, with a hammer and bolster chisel. Make sure you get rid of all loose material. Begin in the centre of the blister, and work outwards to the edges, until you come to sound material. Similarly, you must hack off all round a bare patch getting rid of doubtful material, until you come to a sound edge.

THE TRICK

You can identify a blister by tapping the rendering with the wooden handle of a tool. If it sounds hollow, there is not perfect adherence to the underlying brickwork.

The hole is filled in with mortar. Once again, you can buy this dry-mixed, or make your own. If you decide on the latter, you need 1 part of cement to 5 of sharp sand, with a proprietary plasticizer added. Do not add too much water, aim for a stiff consistency. Apply the mortar from a hawk, using a steel float (see page 187).

First, however, you should coat the bare bricks with a PVA building adhesive, used according to the manufacturer's instructions.

The mortar should be applied in two stages as described in Cement Renderings, page 187.

THE TRICK

With the finishing coat still soft you can apply textured finishes. To get a scraped finish, scrape with something like an old saw blade. For a textured finish, work the surface with a trowel, or banister brush; use this type of brush, too, to get a wavy effect, or dab with a fabric pad for a bold texture.

The patch will finally need to be painted to match the rest of the wall.

GLAZING 1

TYPES OF GLASS

Most of the glass in use for window glazing today is known as float glass, manufactured by a process in which molten glass is floated on top of liquid tin while it cools. The resultant product is smooth and free of distortion.

Previously there were two types – sheet glass, used for smaller areas, and plate glass for larger installations. Both have just about been phased out, although some low-grade sheet glass is still made for use in greenhouses and seed frames, and is known as horticultural glass. It is not good enough to be used in house windows.

SAFETY GLASS

There are three types of safety glass:

Toughened glass Strengthened by a special heat process (known as annealing); the glass crazes, instead of shattering, when broken. Toughened glass has to be ordered specially because it cannot be cut, drilled or smoothed at the edges.

Laminated glass Consists of separate thin panes with layers of plastic in between. If you break it, the glass merely sticks to the plastic. Laminated glass has the advantage over toughened glass that it can be cut (but only by a skilled operative) and offers a higher degree of security because it is extremely difficult to push anything throught it even when it has been broken.

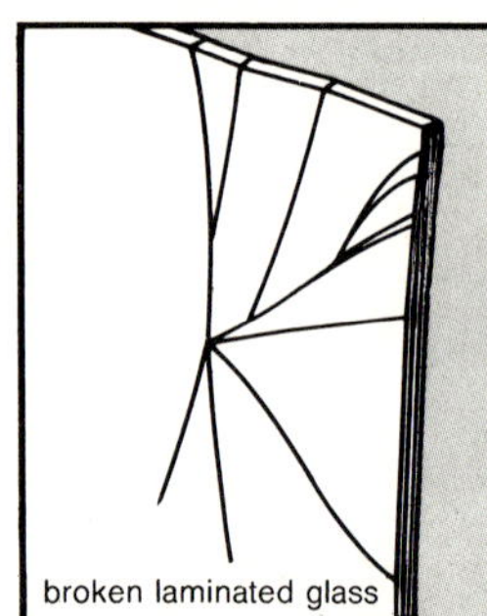

broken laminated glass

Wired glass Consists of welded wire mesh sandwiched between two layers of glass, the whole lot being fused together. The wire holds the bits in place should there be a breakage. The wire, of course, means that the glass is not so good for seeing through, but that is not the point. Wired glass has a one-hour fire rating – the wire once again holds it together longer under intense heat – and so it is used for roofing and skylight work, where other types might melt in a fire and fall on people below, and in other situations as a fire barrier.

SIZES OF GLASS SHEETS

Glass thicknesses have been metricated. They used to be expressed by its weight in ounces per square foot e.g. 18, 24, and 32oz (510, 680 and 910g) and by fractions of an inch for the more substantial sheets e.g. 3/16, 1/4 and 3/8in. (4, 6 and 10mm). Now millimetres are used.

What is the best size to use? The most common size for reglazing a window is 4mm (3/16in.), but you can get away with 3mm (1/8in.) for smaller, sheltered ones. Large picture windows and patio doors require 6mm (1/4in.) or even 10mm (3/8in.) glass. For patio doors and other windows in a vulnerable spot you should consider a safety glass.

SAFETY

Glass is a dangerous material which can cause very nasty cuts, especially when formed in a jagged edge, so it must be treated with respect. Protect your hands and, even more importantly, your wrists by wearing thick gauntlets. If you only have gloves you need wrist bands as well. Pieces of the material might drop on your feet, so make sure the shoes you are wearing are stout ones. Better still, put on strong boots.

THE TRICK

Most important of all your eyes might be at risk, particularly if you are drilling glass, so protective goggles are a must.

DRILLING GLASS

To drill a hole in glass it is best to use a special glass bit, which has a spear-shaped point. Some people get by with a masonry bit, but you risk breaking the glass if you do. The bit can be fitted to a hand drill, or even an electric one provided it is capable of a very slow speed (say about 900 rpm). An electric drill held in a stand ensures greater accuracy. The bit needs to be lubricated, with either paraffin or white spirit.

THE TRICK

Make a small well round the position of the hole using putty or modelling clay, and pour the lubricant in it.

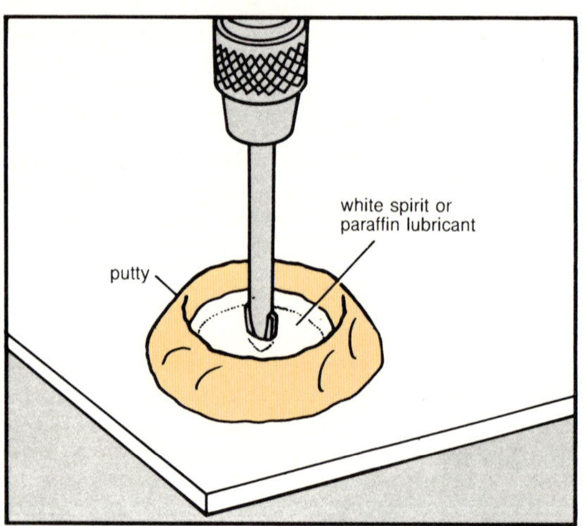

Begin by resting the bit on the surface and, without turning, apply just enough pressure to make a surface mark on the glass. Then you can turn a hand drill, or switch on an electric one with much less risk that the bit will skid. This dodge is not necessary with an electric drill in a stand, because the bit cannot move out of position anyway.

THE TRICK

You must make sure throughout the operation that the lubricant is reaching the tip of the bit. So rotate the drill slightly from time to time without switching off a power tool, or stopping turning a hand one.

CUTTING LARGE HOLES

If ever you want to install an extractor fan in a window, you will need to cut a circular hole in the middle of the pane. For this, you need a tool known either as a circle cutter or a beam compass. It consists of a beam (hence the name) at one end of which is a pivot with a rubber suction cup, and at the other a cutter.

Set the cutter to the radius of the circle you wish to cut, and position the pivot at its centre. Move the cutter round the circumference, applying firm but even pressure with one hand, and holding the centre still with the other. Now make a second circle, in the same way, just inside the first. Then in the inner circle, using your ordinary glass cutter, make a series of straight score marks in a mesh pattern – a process known as 'cross-hatching'. The lines in this should be 5–10mm (1/5–2/5in.) apart.

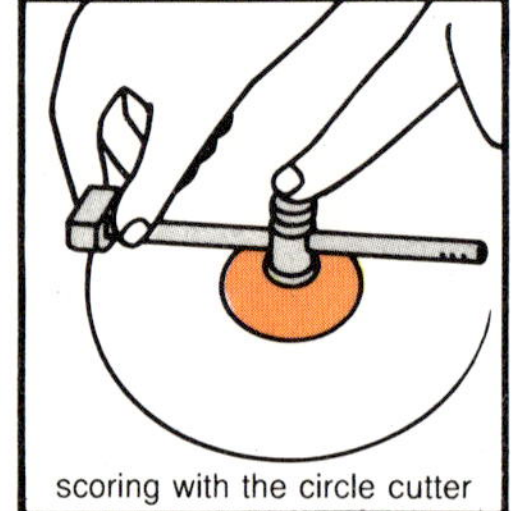

scoring with the circle cutter

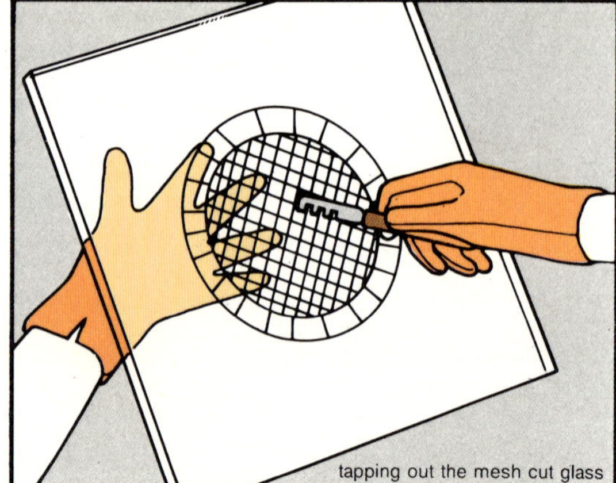

tapping out the mesh cut glass

Finally, make a series of score lines from the inner to the outer circle.

Working from the opposite side of the glass that you scored, tap it from the edge of the inner circle working inwards, increasing the strength of the taps as you approach the middle. Eventually, one piece formed by the mesh will fall out. This allows you to insert the breaker rack, to get rid of the rest. Alternatively you can continue tapping. Once the middle circle is out of the way, nibble out the glass towards the outer circle.

THE TRICK

The edge of the cut will need to be smoothed, so wrap fine glasspaper round a pencil.

Can this operation be carried out on a window in position? It is not easy, and there is a strong risk of failure. Professional glaziers tend not to try. The price of glass is but a small part of their total operating costs, so the usual practice is for them to cut the hole in a sheet on the bench back at their workshop, bring the sheet to you and fit it in the frame as a new pane. They find this much quicker and cheaper.

However, it is probably worth the do-it-yourselfer's while to try to cut the hole in the window. If you break the pane and have to install a new pane, you have lost nothing. Note that the glaziers make the hole in the glass before cutting the pane to size. For cutting glass in straight lines, see page 319.

GLAZING 2

Despite the success of the replacement-window industry, most windows are made up of panes of glass held in a timber frame by putty. From time to time a pane gets broken, and should be replaced immediately. It is not just a question of keeping the weather out. A cracked pane might fall out, and injure someone below.

The new glass should be 3mm (⅛in.) all round smaller than the opening for it, to give the glass room to expand during warm weather. When measuring, don't assume that the opening will be square; take the dimension on each side and at the top and bottom; then work to the smaller figure.

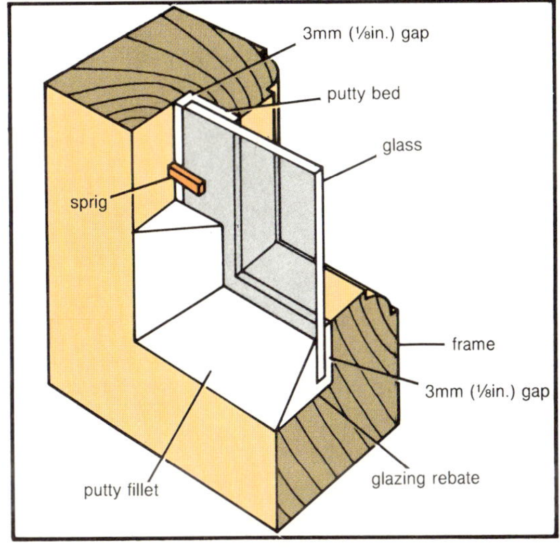

THE TRICK

If your window becomes damaged when the glaziers are closed, tack polythene over the opening for overnight protection.

REMOVING THE OLD GLASS

When a window needs reglazing, the first job is to remove the old glass. Take care over this: it can be a risky operation. Probably the best way is to score the pane all the way round about 25mm (1in.) away from its edge. Tap the glass out with a hammer, making sure it does not fall down to cause injury to anyone below.

The greatest care is needed when you are working on an upstairs window. If the window is a hinged opening one, you can best control the fall of glass by opening it fully, and working from the inside face. On other types work from the inside, and try to hold the glass so it cannot fall.

You will need to get rid of any putty remaining in the rebate: scrape it out with an old chisel. You should remove the old glazing sprigs with a pair of pincers. Dust the frame out, then coat it with a wood primer.

REGLAZING

You will need, as well as the glass, new glazing sprigs and putty. Take a handful of putty and knead it into a pliable ball. Press a layer 3–5mm (⅛–⅕in.) thick into the rebate all round.

THE TRICK

If the putty is too dry, add a little linseed oil.

Use your thumb to ensure it is pushed well into place.

Take hold of the new pane and lift it into position, leaving the 3mm (⅛in.) expansion gap at the bottom. Now push it gently into place against the rebate. Make sure in doing so that you apply the pressure at the edges and not in the centre. Some of the putty will be pushed out of the rebate, but you should be left with about 3mm (⅛in.) behind the glass.

Now you have to drive glazing sprigs, flat on, into the timber to hold the glass in place.

THE TRICK

Don't attempt to do this with a hammer, as you would break the glass. Use the edge of a firmer chisel instead.

Next run another layer of putty on the outside of the glass, and smooth this down with a putty knife, paying particular attention to a good mitre at the corners. The putty tends to stick to the knife, but you can prevent this by wetting the blade.

THE TRICK

A moistened paint brush, run over the putty when it has been neatened off, helps to ensure that it sticks to the glass.

Neaten off the putty inside too and get rid of any excess. It should fall slightly away from the glass so that condensation will run off.

STEEL FRAMES

These are tackled in pretty much the same way as timber frames, except that, because you cannot drive sprigs into the metal, you use instead wire clips which are inserted into holes formed in the frames during manufacture. There is no need to insert a clip into every hole – three or four on each edge are enough.

You must also use the correct type of putty. The traditional linseed oil putty works because it dries out as the oil is absorbed into the timber. Steel cannot absorb the oil, so you must use a self-hardening putty. Dual-purpose putty can be bought.

ALUMINIUM FRAMES

These are often used in a window modernization scheme, and in double glazing, and are glazed in a different manner. Inside the aluminium section there is a rubber or plastic insert that holds the glass, and makes a weathertight join. Each side of the frame is fitted to the glass separately, being hammered into place. It is a skilled job and probably best left to the professional.

CONCRETE 1

Concrete is a very strong building material made by adding certain ingredients (sand and aggregate), plus water, to cement. Aggregate normally consists of gravel or crushed stone. The type of sand to use in concrete mixing is known as 'sharp sand'. It is a coarse material containing lots of tiny pebble-like stones and therefore is sometimes called 'fine aggregate' with the crushed gravel types described as 'coarse aggregate'. For some purposes only sharp sand is added to the cement.

Another type of sand is available – soft sand, a very fine material. This is for use in such mixes as bricklaying mortar, not concrete. Many experts reckon you get the best job if you order the aggregate and sand separately, but it is possible to obtain them ready mixed. This mixture is generally termed 'all-in ballast' or sometimes just 'ballast'.

BUYING CONCRETE

There are three ways of buying concrete. Firstly, it can come ready-mixed, delivered to your home by one of the large lorries – or a mini version of them – that service the building sites. This is not necessarily a dear way of buying concrete; in fact, it can often work out the cheapest However, it is applicable only when you need a lot of the material. Remember, too, the concrete remains workable for only about four hours after delivery, less on a hot day. So you will need lots of energy – or helpers – to cope with a bulk delivery.

How little will such firms deliver? Some of the lorries hold up to 6cu.m. (212cu. ft), but many will sell you much less than that. It is something – along with the price – to discuss with suppliers. Look in the Yellow Pages under 'Concrete: ready-mixed'.

If you will not be using large quantities, you will have to carry out the mixing yourself. There are two ways of doing so: by hand or by machine (which you can hire).

In between ready- and self-mixes come the dry bags, which give you, in sacks of various sizes, concrete (or mortar) to which you merely add water. These are very handy for small jobs and repairs.

THE MIXES

In what proportion should the various ingredients be mixed? That depends on the work you are doing – you get a sort of recipe for the job in hand. However, do-it-yourselfers will probably find that four basic mixes will serve their purpose. These are the 'recipes' to follow when mixing the concrete yourself.

General purpose: (To be used for all jobs except where otherwise specified.) To 1 part of cement, add 2 of sand and 3 of aggregate, or 4 of all-in ballast. (Less all-in ballast is specified because the sand compacts in with the aggregate.)

Foundations: (Including bases for pre-cast pavings.) To 1 part of cement, add 2½ of sand and 3½ of aggregate, or 5 of all-in ballast.

Paving: (Including paths and drives.) To 1 part of cement, add 1½ of sand and 2½ of aggregate, or 3½ of all-in ballast.

Bricklaying mortar: There are three possible mixes: 1 part of masonry cement to 4½ of sand; 1 part of Portland cement to 5½ sand plus a proprietary mortar plasticizer; or (if you want a white mortar) 1 part of white Portland cement to 1 of hydrated builders' lime and 5½ of sand. In each case the sand must be soft.

Should you be buying ready-mixed or dry-packed material, tell your supplier exactly what you want the concrete for.

receiving a delivery of ready-mixed concrete

MIXING BY HAND

To mix mortar, you need a clean, dry, flat surface. If you have nothing suitable, buy a sheet of hardboard and work on that. You also need a couple of shovels and buckets – two of each because separate ones should be used for the cement otherwise it will dry and harden on them – plus a watering can.

If you are mixing everything from scratch, measure out the sand and gravel, making sure your bucket is full to the brim. Empty the buckets into a heap and make a crater in the centre. Now measure your cement in a bucket.

THE TRICK

Knock the bucket two or three times to make sure the cement packs well down, and that the bucket is full.

Pour the cement into the crater, and turn over the heap with a shovel to mix it thoroughly. You will know it is well and truly mixed when the entire heap is a uniform grey colour, without streaks.

mixing the dry ingredients

THE TRICK

A dry-pack mix should be turned over thoroughly in the same way because the constituents often separate during handling.

Make another crater in the centre of the mixed pile, and pour water into it from the can – many people like to remove the rose for this stage. Push material into the water from around the edge of the crater and mix. Now add extra water to the pile, this time with the rose on the spout, and keep turning over until the mix is of the correct consistency. The mistake many do-it-yourselfers make is to add too much water. The material should be workable, but not too sloppy.

THE TRICK

There is a simple test you can make: flatten the top of the pile with the back of your shovel. The mix surface should then be just moist and close-knit.

MIXING BY MACHINE

If you use a machine then, for the first mix of the day, put half the coarse aggregate and half the amount of water you think you will need, into the drum first. This helps to scour out the machine. Add cement and sand alternately, keeping the mix fairly wet, then finally the last batch of aggregate.

THE TRICK

Don't overdo the mixing – a couple of minutes or so should be enough.

If the mixer is too small to allow you to tilt the drum to pour the concrete directly into a barrow, empty it onto a sheet of hardboard ready to be shovelled as needed.

good layout for making concrete by machine

CONCRETE 2

BUILDING A SLAB

The wet concrete needs to be placed in some kind of mould (or formwork) to shape it as you want, then allowed to dry and set. For most do-it-yourselfers, the most usual shape will be as a level sheet (or slab), to form a path, patio, drive or base for a shed or sectional garages.

DEPTH

How deep is the slab to be? That depends on its intended use and the type of soil on which it will be constructed. For simple paths, patios and bases for small buildings, a concrete depth of 75mm (3in.) is recommended. Usually, the concrete can be laid directly on the earth.

THE TRICK

On clay or peaty soils, a sub-base 100mm (4in.) thick is required. This sub-base can be of hardcore, crushed stone or hoggin (sifted gravel).

Drives or hardstanding for vehicles need to be much thicker – at least 100mm (4in.) of concrete and as much as 150mm (6in.) on clay or other poor soils. In both cases the concrete should be laid on a sub-base 100mm (4in.) thick.

EXCAVATING

Having worked out the slab depth, begin to excavate using a spade. The excavation should be a good 150mm (6in.) beyond the size of the slab so that you have sufficient space to work in. To make sure of the correct size, drive a peg into the ground at each corner, and run brightly coloured string between the pegs.

Begin by stripping off all vegetable matter and getting rid of roots. The top soil can be used elsewhere in the garden. Aim to make the excavation a uniform depth; you can ensure this by driving pegs in here and there making sure they all protrude by the same height from the ground, then placing a straight-edge and spirit level across them to ensure the tops are level. Then dig throughout to the same height from the top of the peg.

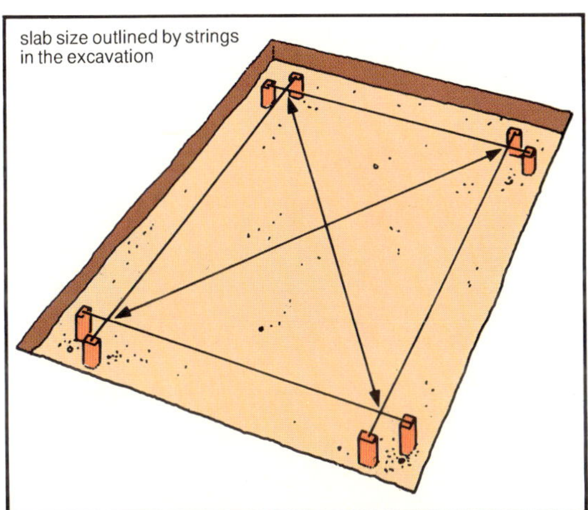
slab size outlined by strings in the excavation

FORMWORK

When excavated, make sure the base is well compacted. Then set up the formwork of timber at least 20mm (¾in.) thick, and as wide as the depth of the slab. It should be held in place by stout wooden pegs. Measure the diagonals (they should be of equal length) to make sure the corners of the formwork are square.

A slight fall should be arranged so that rainwater will run off the slab, away from the house if it adjoins it. The fall should be 1 in 50 (20mm per metre run) but 1 in 40 (25mm per metre) is better where the surface is not very smooth. You ensure such a fall by making the formwork that much lower on one edge.

THE TRICK

To measure this, run a length of clear hosepipe filled with coloured water. At the ends, the pipe should bend upwards, and be tied to a peg. The water will be the same level at each end. You can thus judge when the formwork is the correct amount lower.

Next lay the sub-base, then the concrete. To avoid cracking, you should not lay too large a slab in one go. It is best to regard the maximum dimensions in any direction as 40 times the slab thickness, or 3m. (10ft), whichever is least. Slabs bigger than this need joints between them. Form these by dividing the slab up into sections (or bays). Do not exceed the recommended maximum size, and make them roughly the same size and shape.

Few do-it-yourselfers will be called on to lay a slab greater than 3m. (10ft) wide but paths and drives could easily exceed that in length. Create a bay by fixing an extra piece of formwork across the path at the recommended spacing. Lay that bay, allow it to harden for a day or two, remove the timber, then lay the next bay, right up to the edge of the first one. The concrete will shrink slightly on drying out, leaving a gap for expansion and contraction as the temperature changes.

If you are using a large delivery of ready-mixed concrete, lay the whole slab at once, forming the joint with a strip of hardboard left in place.

tamping down the concrete in the formwork

LAYING CONCRETE

Pour the concrete into the formwork, and rake it level, finishing about 15mm (⅔in.) higher than the formwork. Make sure it goes right into the corners.

You tamp it down level by placing a 'tamping beam' across the formwork. A length of 100 × 50mm (4 × 2in.) timber resting at each end of the formwork will do for widths up to about 1m. (3ft). You can probably handle such a beam yourself. Tamping down slabs wider than this will require two people, and needs a stouter beam 150 × 50mm (6 × 2in.). Fix a small cross handle at each end.

THE TRICK

If you have formed a joint with hardboard, work towards the joint first from one side then the other, to make sure it does not get pushed flat.

CURING

The slab will be stronger if the concrete is allowed to dry out (cure) as slowly as possible. Cover it with a sheet of polythene, weigh down the sheet with bricks at the edges, and sprinkle sand on top.

Concrete also needs protection from frost, and if you are caught unawares, emergency steps are required.

THE TRICK

The best is a 'quilt' or sandwich of straw between two sheets of polythene, or you can just pile sand or soil on top of the curing sheet.

Leave the slab, ideally, for seven days, or longer. If necessary, you can begin building on it within two or three days taking care not to crumble the edges or corners. The curing sheet should be left on for three days if possible.

SURFACE FINISHES

The slab will now have a rippled, washboard-like surface and can be left to set like this. However, several finer finishing treatments are possible. You can trowel smooth with a steel float. A wood float gives a textured finish: use it in overlapping semicircles to produce the fish scale effect; or use the back of a shovel in the same way.

Draw a stiff or nylon broom across the concrete for a good non-skid effect. A soft broom will given an even finer finish. Let the surface harden a little, then give a gentle brushing along with sprayed water, and the coarse aggregate will be left slightly proud, for another distinctive effect. If you want this effect, exaggerate it by spreading extra coarse aggregate on top and tamping it down with a wooden float.

The edges need to be slightly rounded. Use an arrissing tool, or make one by bending a piece of sheet metal round a dowel, and nailing a piece of wood to it as a handle. This is run along the edge between concrete and timber.

TIMBER MAINTENANCE 1

TIMBER-FRAMED HOUSES

More and more of these houses are being built nowadays, because they are considerably easier to erect than the old-style cavity wall designs. Based on concrete foundations and ground slab, the wall frames and roof trusses are prefabricated and nailed together on site. The outer walls are usually clad in brickwork at ground level and tiles or timber boarding at first floor level.

The inner walls are formed by insulation of some description, a vapour barrier and plasterboard. It is vitally important that this vapour barrier is pierced as little as possible: all services are installed in the cavity before the walls are finally closed.

If you decide to install extra sockets, additional plumbing, or anything else which requires you to penetrate the cavity wall, you should seriously consider whether it could not be placed on one of the internal partition walls.

THE TRICK

If you do have to cut the vapour barrier, always be sure to reseal it as fully as possible, before closing the hole. Plastic insulating tape will close long cuts and should also be used around pipes and cables to minimize the break.

This does not mean that you cannot hang pictures or fix things to outside walls (see page 28). However, if your house is badly exposed on one side, you should consider before fixing a complicated shelving system, etc, to that wall.

If you have cause to cut into any part of the timber framing anywhere in the house, be sure to coat the cut with a preservative fluid before closing the hole.

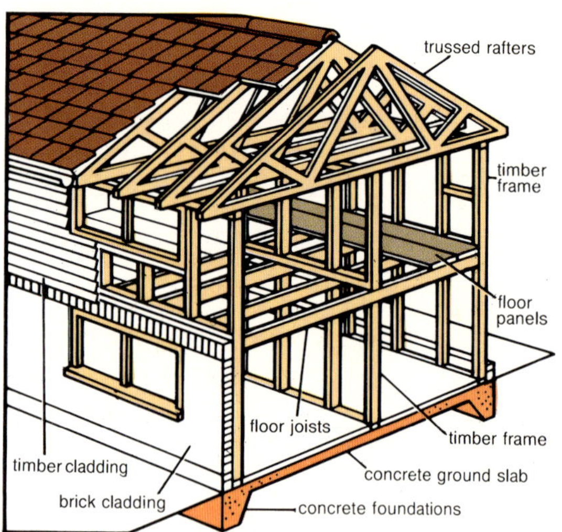

NEW TIMBER IN OLD HOUSES

If you have cause to replace any structural timber in a traditional style house, you should coat it with a suitable preservative fluid before fixing it in place – there are always bits you cannot reach once it is in position. This is a sensible precaution because, unless you are building an extension, rooftrap or something like that, you are replacing the timber because of rot or failure in some way – initial precautions will make the new piece less likely to fail in future. There are many different preservative fluids on the market, often specifically designed for one condition – ask your builder's merchant to recommend a suitable one for the condition in your house. It is very important that you should follow the manufacturer's instructions exactly. Many fluids are highly flammable. Some should not be allowed to touch the skin.

THE TRICK

If using them in a confined space, use a face mask, gloves and sufficient clothing that drips will not fall on your skin.

Dealing with a severe infestation of woodworm – or an attack of dry rot – is not a task for the do-it-yourselfer. Apart from requiring specialized equipment, many building societies will not give a mortgage on a house that has had such an infestation without a guarantee from a remedial company that they have treated the area.

The British Wood Preserving Association (BWPA)
150 Southampton Row,
London WC1B 5AL
(01–837 8217)

They vet specialist woodworm and rot treatment companies before granting membership and maintain a list of members for specific areas.

TIMBER MAINTENANCE 2

TIMBER CLADDING

Very many houses nowadays have timber cladding on the upper storey of the exterior – it is particularly favoured with timber-framed houses (see page 194). This cladding may be installed as either feather-edged boards or tongue-and-grooving. It may be finished with gloss paint, with varnish, or with a wood preservative.

GLOSS PAINT

Clean down the cladding with dry wire wool to remove flaking paint. If you wish to repaint it, see page 196.

THE TRICK

If you wish to apply a preservative, even if you are going to repaint later, you must strip right back to the bare wood.

VARNISH

Strip back to the bare wood, using a proprietary stripper or sandpaper. If the sun has bleached any patches of wood which were bared by peeling varnish, use a wood stain to restore the colour. Then use an exterior-grade polyurethane varnish in three or four coats.

PRESERVATIVES

Strip back to the bare wood as before. Preservatives can be colourless or include a stain. They give protection against rot and woodworm. Two coats is usually adequate and the wood should require no further maintenance except washing down and two new coats, next time you redecorate.

CEDAR SHINGLES

If these have been left untreated, and so weathered to an unattractive grey, restore them with a coloured wood restorer.

HARDWOOD DOORS

These are usually of oak or teak. They should not be fed with oil, which attracts dirt. Scrub them down thoroughly to remove as much dirt as possible; then strip off any varnish and sand smooth. Then treat with hardwood preservative or give three to four coats of exterior polyurethane varnish.

OUTSIDE DOOR BOTTOMS

Garage door stiles tend to rot. If they are caught in time the rail tenons will still be usable.

Mark out a line well above the rotten area, sloping downwards across the face of the stile. The angle could be set out using a 30° set square as a guide. The cut should be horizontal across the door thickness. When the cut reaches the panel or the match boarding, you should be able to pull away the lower (rotted) piece of the stile, working it off the rail tenons. Check the rail for rot and, if sound, coat all exposed tenon parts with primer.

Cut a new lower portion for the stile, groove or rebate it and cut the mortises. Prime it well and then knock it on to the tenons. Insert screws into pre-bored and counter-bored holes (second holes bored into the screw hole so that the screw head will be well into the wood), and screw the repair piece into position. Drive in newly cut wedges at each side of each tenon, and additionally, drive dowels into holes bored through the stile and on through each tenon.

The screwing is positioned through the long, wedge-shaped top of the repair piece.

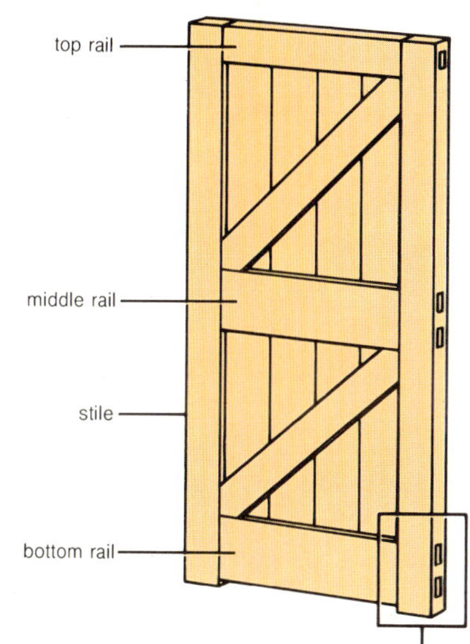

THE TRICK

If the rail tenons are poor but the rail is usable, cut mortises into the end of the rail and glue in new tenons. Dowel them through for strength.

The whole width of the bottom of a door can be replaced in this fashion.

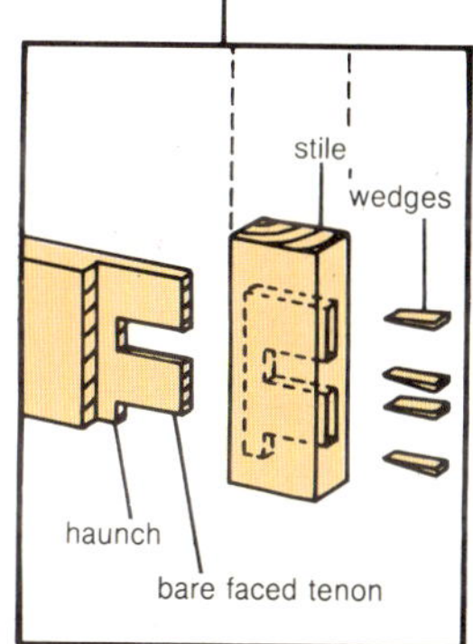

EAK OIL
eeps teak and ther hard woods peak condition, roperly protected om the elements.

WOOD DYES
Transforms the natural beauty of wood giving a high quality appearance.

POLYURETHANE VARNISHES
Varnishes wood, cork, chip-board and veneer. Gloss finish in a choice of wood-shades. Or clear varnish – in gloss, satin or matt.

SCRATCH COVER
In 5 woodshades. Revolutionary way to treat deep scratches, dents – even small nail holes.

PLASTIC WOOD FILLER
Fills cracks, gaps and nail holes, both inside and outside.

KNOTTING
Seals knots in wood before varnishing or painting, preventing knot resin bleeding through paint film.

EXTERIOR DECORATION

PREPARATION

Never start to redecorate your house outside before doing any repairs needed. If you have been checking out the building regularly (see page 165), you should either know where these are necessary, or have already completed them. When the building is in a decent state of repair, you can start on the painting. Always plan to paint during (hopefully) a spell of warm dry weather; damp will eventually cause the paint to blister (if trapped underneath), while frost makes gloss paint go dull.

The correct order of redecorating a house is as follows:

1. Gutters – inside and out
2. Soffits, fascia boards, eaves
3. Walls and gables
4. Timber cladding
5. Windows
6. Doors
7. Downpipes, airbricks (if metal), other metalwork

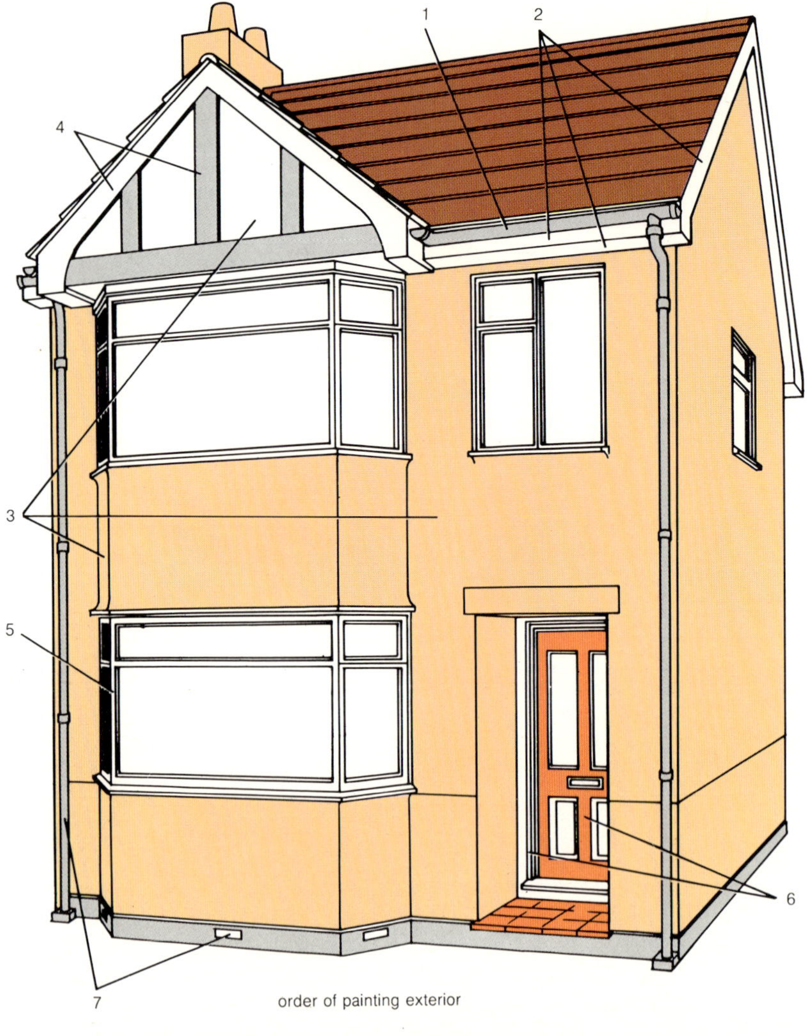

order of painting exterior

STRIPPING

If you have areas of poor paintwork, it is important that you should strip them right back to the original surface. It is not necessary to do the entire surface – take it back to a point where the old paint is sound and a join will not be too noticeable.

Before you start stripping, scrub down all external gloss with sugar soap or a decorator's detergent in solution with warm water.

THE TRICK

Protect the ground below – and any plants – by laying sheets of thick polythene over them.

Burn or use a chemical stripper to remove all loose and flaking paint. Be very careful if using a blowlamp out of doors: the flame is often invisible in strong sunlight. It is unwise to use one on the softwood fascia or soffit boards – if there is an old bird's nest inside, it could cause a nasty fire. Never use a blowlamp near thatch – the reeds can smoulder for hours before bursting into flames.

Rub down (see page 231) all sound paint to provide a key for the new paint. Then prime any bare surfaces.

THE TRICK

Unless you are planning to take a very long time to complete these decorations, you would be well advised to do all the preparatory work at once, to avoid getting dirt and paint flakes on newly completed work.

PAINTING

The techniques for painting outside are very similar to those for painting inside (see pages 237 to 246). Straining paint, the painting sequence, brush holding and the techniques to be used with gloss paints are all identical.

Always check that the paint you are proposing to use is suitable for an exterior application. This should always be stated on the tin, but if you are uncertain, ask.

Don't forget to rub down any gloss paint between undercoat and first gloss coat and between first and second gloss coats. The additional key provided by this may make all the difference between the work lasting two years or five years.

Always use a paint kettle when painting from a ladder and never fill it more than one third full. Then, if you have an accident, the damage should not be too great.

THE TRICK

Ask your butcher for a meat hook which is ideal for suspending the kettle from the ladder rung. Never hold the kettle – it means you have no spare hand to hold on with.

Always work from the top downwards, then any splashes will be covered up later.

SPECIFIC AREAS

For painting gutters (inside and out), see page 181.
For wood painting techniques, see page 244.
For painting walls, see page 187.
For dealing with timber cladding, see page 195.
For painting windows, see page 246.
For painting doors, see page 246.
For painting downpipes, see page 181.
For painting metalwork, see pages 241 and 244.

SECURITY AND SAFETY

Never be tempted to go on painting too long – especially if it is very hot. Pushing to get a job finished has caused more accidents than almost anything else. Also don't go on painting if you cannot see properly – painting in the twilight can result in bad coverage.

Don't let your children play underneath while you are working or climb a ladder while you are already on it. Pets – particularly large dogs – should be kept well away from any redecoration area.

Remember your home is particularly vulnerable to burglars while windows and doors are open to dry, and while long ladders and/or scaffolding towers assist entry. Try to ensure that someone is always around while decoration is going on.

THE TRICK

If you must leave a ladder up overnight, tie a plank to the bottom rungs to discourage children from playing on it and burglars using it.

CLEANING UP

If you get paint splashes on windows, use fine wire wool to remove them. This will not scratch the glass, whereas

scrapers or sandpaper will.

On brickwork, scrape off the paint; then use a wire brush over the whole brick to hide the marks.

If you get paint on quarry tiles (on a porch floor for instance), again scrape off the paint, then wipe over the tiles with a cloth soaked in white spirit. Finally wash down with warm soapy water and no sign should remain. Always wipe up paint splashes as soon as you notice them.

FENCES 1

There are two reasons why you should aim to keep the fences of your home in good order. Firstly, a well-kept fence acts as a barrier deterring children and, provided the gaps are not too big, even pets from entering your garden. Secondly, nothing makes a home look so shabby, and therefore detracts from its value, as a worn-out fence.

Before looking more closely at fences, let us sort out a bit of jargon. The parts of various types of fence have their own special terms, but there are a few general names. The main vertical members, sunk in the ground, are posts; the horizontal members are rails; and the vertical members fixed to the rails are boards. As the top of a post is end grain – into which rainwater can enter more easily – in the better installations, a shaped bit of timber (known as a capping piece) is fitted for extra protection. Both hardwood and softwood are used to make fencing: the former is obviously dearer.

STANDARD FENCING

Various styles of fence are fitted to British homes. Here are the most common:

Close-boarded fencing
This is the traditional type of garden fence, and it has the big advantages that it affords the greatest degree of privacy, and the most complete deterrent to wandering pets. It is also strong, and built to last. It has, however, one overwhelming disadvantage. It uses so much timber that it is very expensive. As a result a lot of cheaper alternatives have been devised.

The boards of these fences are often feather-edged: i.e. they are thinner along one edge so that they can overlap. The triangular-section rails to which they are fixed are known as arris rails, while the horizontal member fitted to the better-quality versions along at ground level is the gravel board.

Interwoven fencing This is an attempt to get the privacy and deterrence factors of the close-boarded kind at a lower cost. Because it uses less timber, it succeeds in this aim; but it is not so strong. Interwoven fencing consists of thin lengths of horizontal timber that interweave between vertical ones. It is sold in panels of varying heights and standard lengths.

Horizontal overlap fencing This does pretty much the same job, is about as strong, and costs more or less the same as interwoven fencing. It consists of horizontal lengths of thin timber that overlap slightly. Like interwoven it comes in various heights, and standard lengths.

OTHER FENCES

Although interwoven and horizontal overlap are cheaper than close-boarded, they still cost a fair amount of money. Therefore a variety of inexpensive fences, using less timber and therefore offering lower standards of privacy and deterrence, but nevertheless giving a visual demarcation of the limits of your property, have been introduced.

Post and rail This is one of the most popular of these: in suburban avenues it usually takes the form of so-called ranch-style fencing, in which both posts and rails are of planed timber, and painted, usually white. More rustic versions are available, however.

Picket fencing Sometimes known as palisade fencing, this is an attractive and traditional type of fencing that uses more timber, and is therefore a little pricier, than post and rail. It is still more economical than many other types, especially if a low-height variety is used. Picket fencing consists of pickets or palisades shaped in a pointed or rounded profile at the top, and nailed to rails that are slotted in tenons in the posts.

Split chestnut pale This consists of a series of rustic-like chestnut pales held together by two or three bands of wire, and fixed at the ends to posts, which will usually require to be braced. It is not the most attractive of fences, but it is economical, and perhaps more suited to back, than front, gardens.

Chain link fencing
Probably the type that allows you to fence off a garden with the minimum of fuss and expense, although in appearance it is not everyone's cup of tea. It consists of lengths of meshed wire of varying heights (you can use it for anything from a garden to a tennis court) stretched between posts, to which it is fixed by means of straining bolts.

Bare steel wire would, of course, soon rust, so it is usual to use either galvanized wire or plastic mesh. You can use timber posts for this fencing, but since they would rot long before the steel or plastic did, it is probably better to invest in concrete or steel posts.

close-boarded | interwoven | horizontal overlap | post and rails | palisade or picket fencing

GATES

If a timber gate will not close properly, it may be that the hinges have worked loose. The timber of the gate may have shrunk, enlarging the holes round the screws.

THE TRICK

Fit thicker, longer screws if possible; otherwise insert a plastic wall plug in the hole, and drive the screw into that.

If the posts are fixed to a wall, they may have come away from the brickwork. Normally, the fixing is by means of timber plugs set in the mortar. Take the post down, mortar in the new plugs, and refix with screws or nails.

Timber posts that are part of a fence may be out of true.

THE TRICK

One way of reinforcing the setting is to dig a trench across the opening, nail two thick boards to the feet of the posts, then fill the trench with concrete, topped with soil.

The fault may lie with the gate. The timber may have swollen, and will need planing down. Or perhaps its framework has sagged. In that case, drive wedges between it and the ground to brace it properly in position. Then fit steel repair plates to strengthen the weak points. As with fences, when a gate is really in bad trim, it is probably better to replace it.

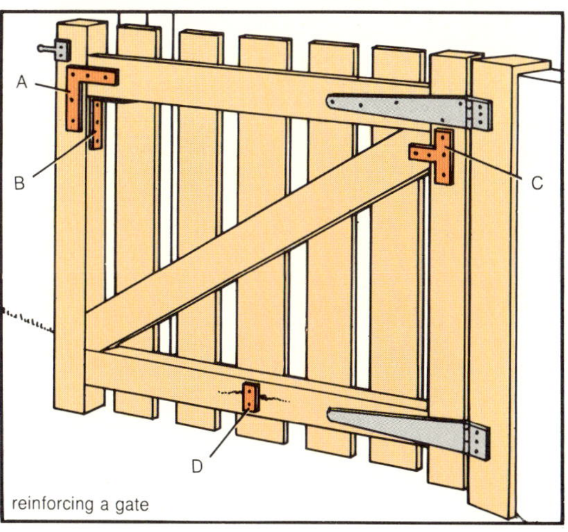

reinforcing a gate

FENCES 2

MAINTENANCE

All timber should be well protected. Post and rail and picket fences, and occasionally the close-boarded, are painted. Preservatives are less expensive and easier to apply. Creosote is the cheapest and best known. It penetrates better into the wood if you heat it first. Its main disadvantage is that it never really dries out properly, and may "bleed" in sticky patches.

THE TRICK

Types other than golden brown obliterate the natural grain, so always go for this.

It harms vegetation and irritates the skin, therefore handle carefully. It is a waste to use creosote on hardwood.

Proprietary preservatives, with no ill effects on plants or wild life, are available; although they are more expensive. When applying, remember that it is the part up to 150mm (6in.) above the ground and, in the case of posts, 150mm (6in.) below, that is most at risk. Never allow soil to pile up against the fence.

Metal also needs protecting, unless it is galvanized or plastic coated. Make sure you get rid of all rust first, prime bare areas with a metal primer, then undercoats and apply one or two top coats.

TIMBER FENCES

As for other maintenance, more faults will develop in close-boarded and similar fences because there is more timber to be erected, and they present a greater mass to the wind. Boards can be blown off, or pulled away from their rails. Nail them back, using galvanized nails.

THE TRICK

If the boards are old, drill a pilot hole first to stop splitting.

Rails might start to rot, where they slot into the posts. You can remedy this by nailing small blocks of wood around the hole.

THE TRICK

If the rail is badly affected, fit a galvanized bracket.

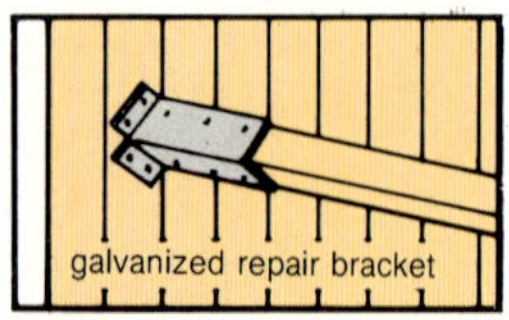

When a fence leans out of alignment, it is usually because of a fault in the post. This may have been affected by rot, or not set properly in the ground. If you see any signs of rot cut it off and douse the area liberally with preservative. If the rot is well advanced, reinforce the post with a spur, which should be bolted to sound timber at least 450mm (18in.) above ground. Usually concrete spurs are used. If obstacles present difficulties, an angle iron, fixed on at least two corners of the post, makes a good substitute

A post that is leaning badly should be re-set; one badly affected by rot must be replaced. Begin by digging out the existing post.

THE TRICK

If this proves difficult, drive a stout spike into one side of the post, then place a car jack under the spike and elevate it.

Make sure the new post is set far enough into the ground – the existing hole may not be deep enough. For low fences, the post should be sunk by one third the height of the fence. Between 1.2–1.8m. (4–6ft), there should be 750mm (2ft 6in.) below ground, standing on a layer of gravel or rubble to provide drainage.

Make sure that the post is vertical, then brace it in that position with a batten nailed to it and a stake in the ground. Fill the hole around with well rammed soil (gravel for light fences); heavier ones and tall interwoven panels, especially in exposed areas, require concrete. Use 1 part cement to 5½ all-in ballast, or 1 part cement to 4 sharp sand, to which you add small pieces of broken rubble.

Do the filling in stages, ramming each layer down well. You can fit the cross rails immediately (they help to keep the post true), but do not nail any panels or boards to them for a few days.

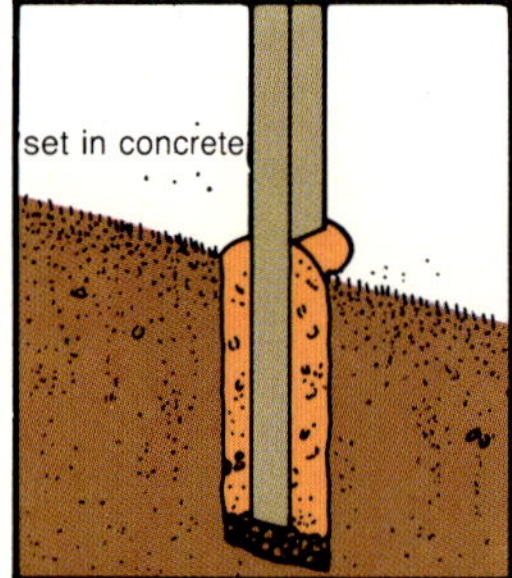

braced with batten and stake

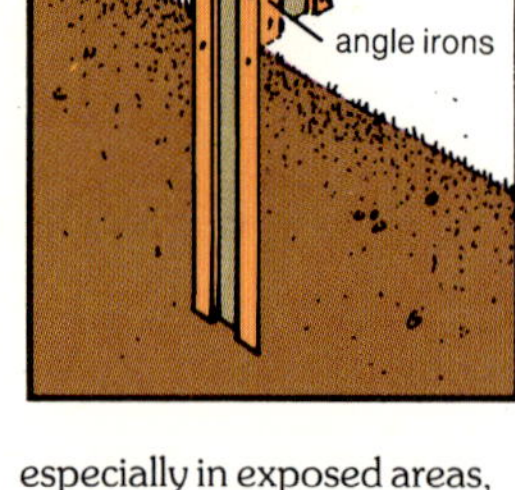

NEW FENCES

If your fence needs to be replaced, prise off any boards from the rails, or remove panels. Wrench the rails free, sawing through them if need be. Take up the posts.

Run a string along the length of the fence to indicate the position of the posts so that they will be in line. Mark on a spare batten the length of the rails or panels and use this as a measuring rod to get the correct post spacing.

Holes dug with a spade need to be of quite a diameter. If they interfere too much with flower beds or pavings, consider using a hole borer, which can be hired, and will make neat holes.

CHAIN LINK FENCES

The end posts must be set in concrete, and braced with struts set in concrete too, to withstand the tension of the wire, to which the mesh is attached. Intermediate posts are needed at maximum 2.75m. (9ft) intervals. These should be sunk about 450mm (18in.) below ground, and set in well-rammed soil. Let the concrete set before attaching the wires.

Insert a straining bolt in the end posts – concrete ones will have pre-drilled holes, but you usually have to bore them in timber. A wire is needed near the top and bottom of the post for a fence up to 1.2m. (4ft) high; a third should be specified for taller fences. Loop the end of the wire through the eye of the bolt, and twist it back on itself by about 150mm (6in.) Then tighten the bolt.

Now fix the mesh: staple it to timber posts, but, on concrete, use a spacer bar which is threaded through the mesh and bolted in place. The mesh is fixed to the wires with a small loop of wire at 150mm (6in.) intervals along the top wire, but 450mm (18in.) elsewhere. Tighten the wire with pliers. The mesh needs to be held very taut whilst this is done, so you will need a helper.

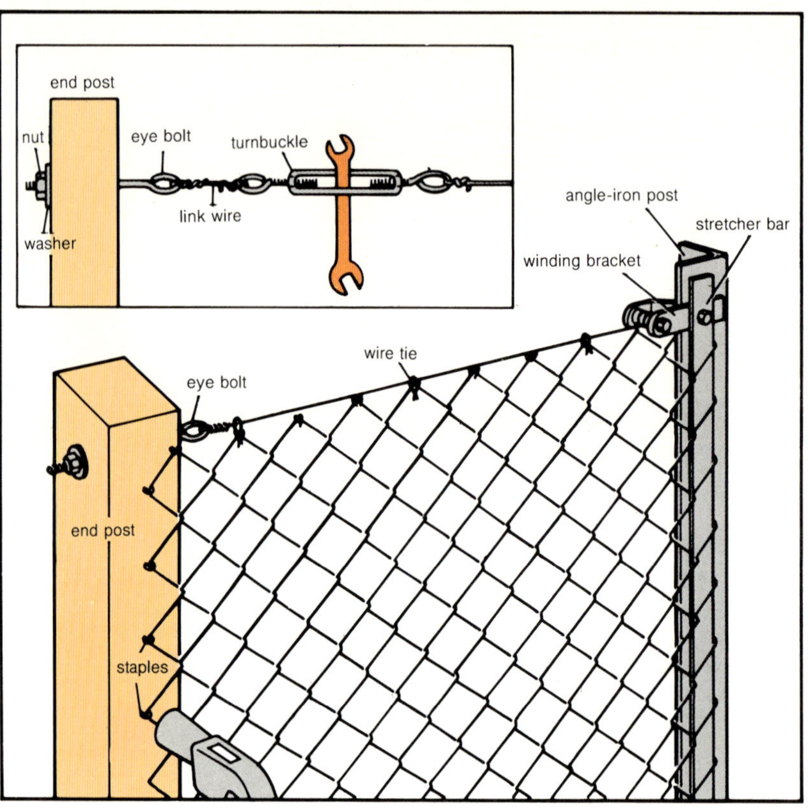

FLOORING

Beard
ROSETTA IN BROWN
...one of 16 superb designs/colourways in the new Linda Beard DOLLY MIXTURES collection of self adhesive vinyl floor tiles, from Halstead Flooring. Dolly Mixtures are easy to lay and easy to look after with a wipe-clean, high gloss finish.
Put fashion on YOUR floors with Linda Beard DOLLY MIXTURES.
Linda Beard
DOLLY MIXTURES
FROM
Halstead Flooring
James Halstead Ltd., PO Box 3, Radcliffe New Road, Whitefield, Manchester M25 7NR. Tel: 061-766 3781.
Stockists include branches of Asda, B & Q, Co-op, Debenhams, International DIY, Jupiter, Lewis's, Makro, Texas, Unit Sales, Woolworth, W.H.Smith Do-It-All.

PREPARATION 1

Before the floor is laid, the sub-floor must be clean, smooth, level, permanently dry, and of sound construction. The sub-floor must be clean because small bits of grit could rub against the back of the flooring, causing wear, and show through thin materials as small pimples. Grease could have an adverse effect on the adhesive holding the floor in place, if not the flooring material itself. The sub-floor must be smooth, because any high spots will get scuffed by passing feet, and the wear will not be even. It must be level because a series of ridges looks odd, and will be highlighted if the floor is to be polished later; again, you could get excessive wear. It must be permanently dry because damp will attack the flooring and any adhesive holding it in place. It must be sound because there is no point in merely covering up a sub-floor that needs to be repaired, also the defects might damage the floor covering.

There are two basic types of sub-floor – direct-to-earth and suspended. A direct-to-earth floor actually rests on the ground below, while a suspended one is fixed some way above it.

Modern direct-to-earth floors are made of concrete; in older houses they can be of flagstones, quarry tiles etc. Suspended concrete floors are usually found only in high-rise buildings: e.g. in a modern block of flats. The overwhelming majority of suspended floors are made of timber – floorboards, plywood or chipboard – fixed to a series of joists below.

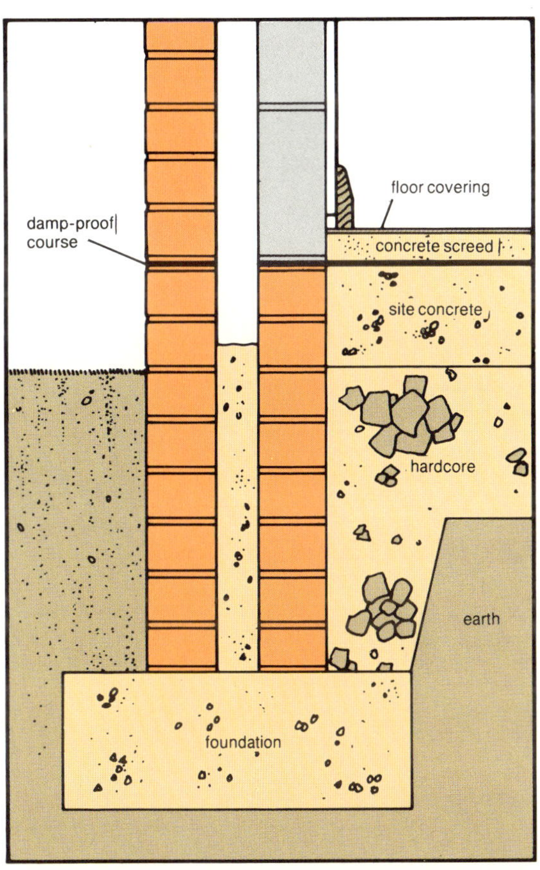

DIRECT-TO-EARTH SUB-FLOORS

Being laid directly on the ground, a direct-to-earth sub-floor raises one big question: is damp coming up from the ground? If it is, you should not lay any floor covering on it without first curing the condition as the moisture will attack any adhesive and cause the material itself to rot.

A modern sub-floor – one built since 1945 – should be all right, because it will incorporate a barrier against damp. It will probably consist of a layer of hardcore on the earth, topped by a bed of concrete known as the site concrete. Over this site concrete will be a damp-proof membrane, which will be covered by another thin screed of concrete, designed to give a smooth sub-floor on which your floor covering can be fixed. This kind of sub-floor should be perfectly sound.

TESTS FOR DAMP

To test for damp, take up the existing floor covering at one corner, and see if it has been affected by damp or not. If it has, then you know your floor needs treating. If it has not, then neither should the new floor covering. There are other rough and ready tests you can carry out.

THE TRICK

You can take a sheet of metal and heat it on a blowlamp or a gas ring, then lay it on the bare concrete. If damp is present, a patch will appear on the concrete, and moisture beads will gather on the underside of the plate.

THE TRICK

Another test is to lay a sheet of vinyl flooring or a piece of glass face down, and seal the edges with putty. A tell-tale patch will appear within a couple of days if there is any damp.

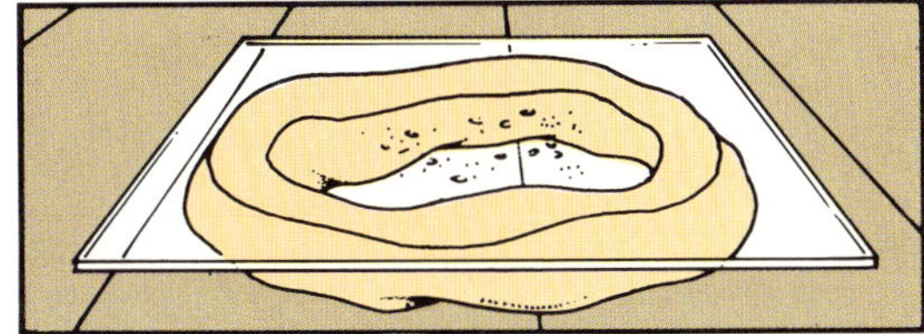

However the tests, if positive, go no further than to indicate whether moisture is present or not. To discover if it is there in harmful quantities experts have to take readings with scientific instruments. If you are in doubt about your sub-floor, contact a local flooring contractor and see if he will test it for you (for a fee).

Apart from damp, a direct-to-earth concrete floor might be uneven, and there might be dusting. Treat them as described for suspended concrete floors (see below).

ASPHALT FLOORS

Asphalt floors, and sub-floors built of other impervious materials, are rare in domestic situations. You should screed over them to a depth of about 3mm (⅛in.) with latex levelling compound, then treat them just like concrete.

QUARRY TILES

Old-fashioned floors, such as those covered with quarry tiles and other similar materials, present a problem because they are probably laid on top of a damp sub-floor. That may not be evident, but the minute you cover them up with a modern flooring material you will get 'sweating'. The best thing to do is to take up the tiles, then treat the floor to make sure it is dry. If tests carried out before you take up the tiles indicate that the floor is permanently dry, then you might get away with screeding them with a levelling compound.

But why cover up quarry tiles, anyway, especially if they are visually sound? Such tiles are becoming popular again, and you would do well to leave them as they are, unless you have a real damp problem.

SUSPENDED CONCRETE SUB-FLOORS

You will probably only have this kind of sub-floor if you live in a modern, high-rise block. It should give no trouble, and require little in the way of preparation. Shoddy workmanship may, however, cause two problems: the floors may not be smooth and level, and the concrete could be dusting.

The former fault is cured with a levelling compound. If there is excessive dust, the concrete should be treated with a sealer-primer which you can buy from a builder's merchant.

DAMP-PROOFING A SUB-FLOOR

A sub-floor that is badly affected by rising damp really needs to be lifted up and reconstructed – heavy work for a builder, rather than a job for a flooring contractor. However, there are one or two less drastic remedies that will work in certain cases. The companies which specialize in manufacturing damp-proofing materials, produce liquid damp barriers for applying to floors. You apply the liquids with a brush or a spreader.

These liquid damp-proofers can be covered with most of the usual flooring materials, and they are particularly suited to those that have to be stuck down. Be warned, however. The surface of these materials is impervious, to keep the damp at bay, and some glues will not dry out on them. Always check with your supplier before ordering.

Another damp-proof membrane that can be used is a sheet of polythene. Examples of the flooring that polythene can go under are dry-laid interlocking panels of parquet, and sheets of chipboard. One parquet supplier recommends 500-gauge polythene, while one of the biggest manufacturers of chipboard suggests 1000-gauge. It is best to check what type to use with the technical department of the company that makes the flooring material you have chosen.

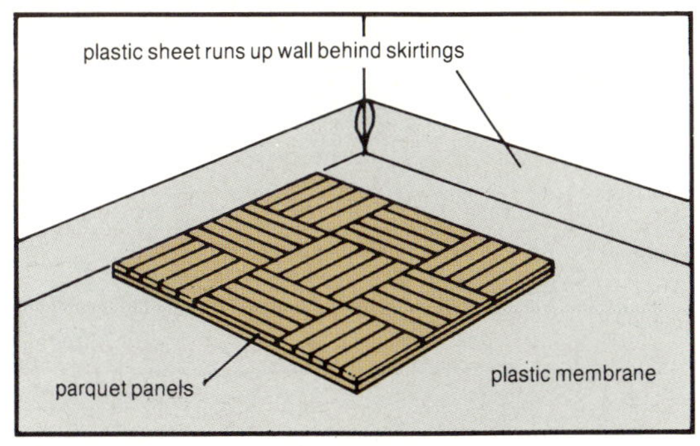

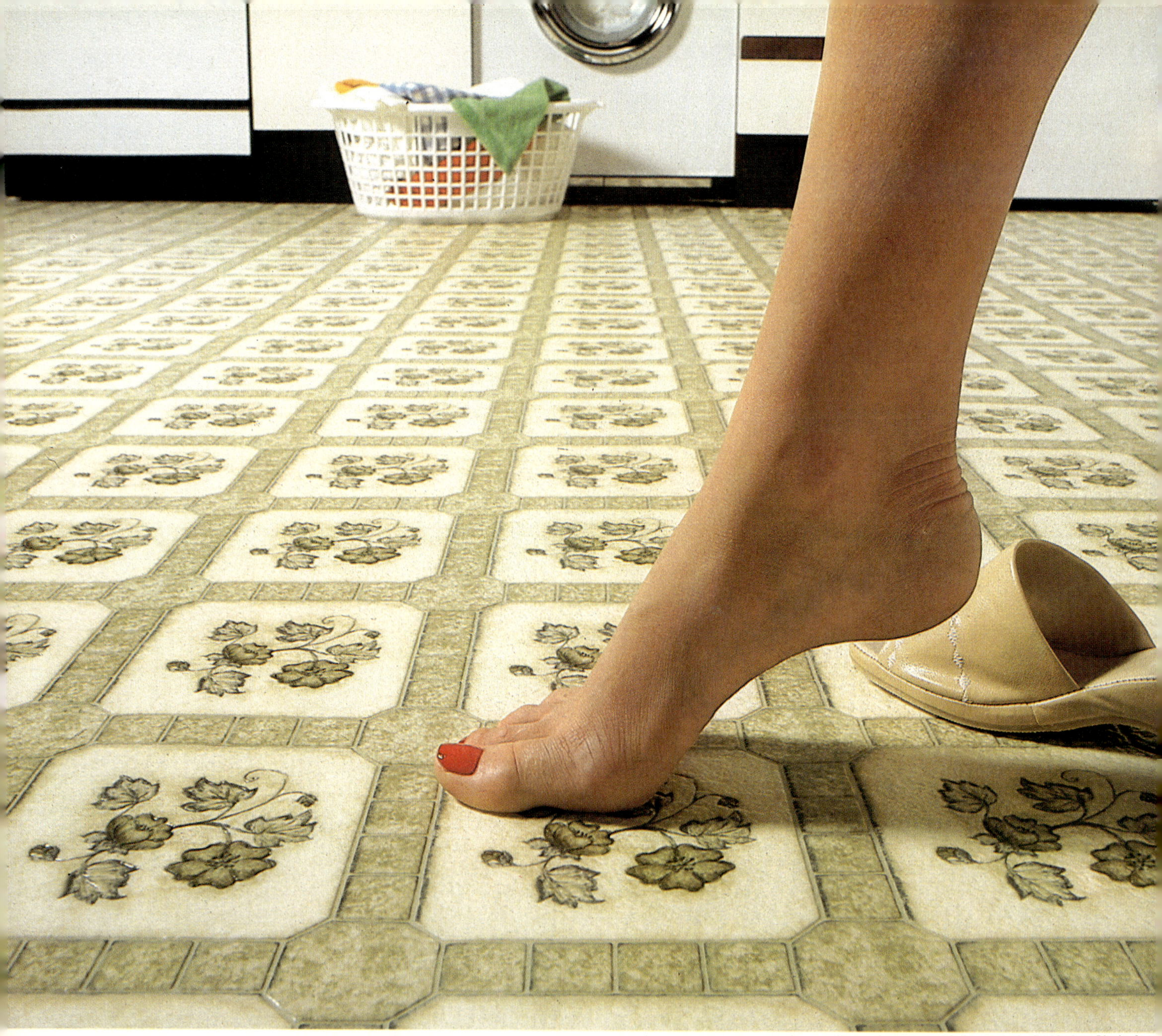

Kitchen appliances by Ariston. Kitchen units by Be Modern Limited.

Step deeper into vinyl comfort, with Marley SupaSoft.

Vinyl flooring has never been so soft, so comfortable to walk on. Marley SupaSoft has a supa-thick built-in foam underlay that means more warmth and comfort beneath your feet.

Luxurious vinyl flooring has never been so practical, so manageable.

Marley SupaSoft rolls out in a new 3-metre width — perfect for the kitchen — to give you all the beauty and benefit of one-piece seamless flooring. It's also available in a standard 2-metre width.

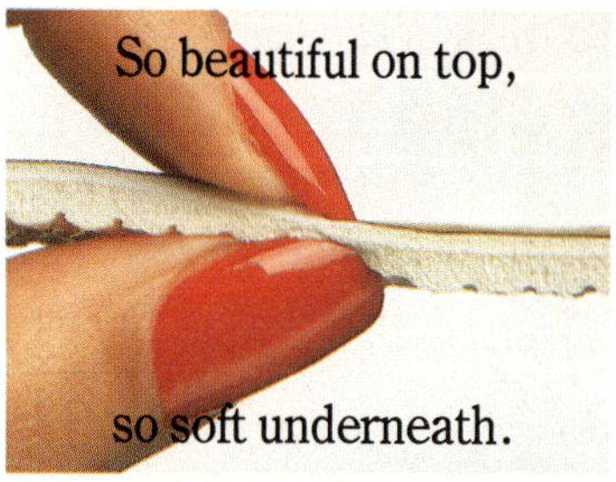

Marley SupaSoft is so beautifully hardwearing. A supa-tough, easy-care, anti-slip vinyl top layer keeps patterns and colours beautiful and protects SupaSoft's supple softness, year after year after year.

Marley SupaSoft. Beautiful vinyl flooring that's luxuriously soft, yet incredibly hard-wearing.

Step deeper into vinyl comfort, step deeper into Marley SupaSoft.

5 year guarantee

MARLEY Supasoft

MARLEY FLOORS LTD., LENHAM, MAIDSTONE, KENT, ME17 2DE. TEL: MAIDSTONE (0622) 858877. TELEX: 95234.

PREPARATION 2

SUSPENDED TIMBER SUB-FLOORS

Most British homes have suspended timber sub-floors at least on the upper storeys, and the majority of those built since the 1920s have them on the ground floor, too. This type is easy to recognize, as it consists of timber nailed to a network of joists underneath. Usually the timber will take the form of floorboards.

Floorboards can be attractive in their own right. If you want them as your final floor they are usually sanded and sealed (see page 222). Adequate preparation is even more important than when the boards will remain as a sub-floor.

The boards may have shrunk so that gaps have appeared between them. They may have warped and curled up at the edges. The nails holding them may have sprung loose. Some boards may be defective – cracked, split or broken. They may have woodworm. People's feet may have worn them badly in certain areas, especially near the door. Old nails and tacks may still be in them. There may also be grease on them – spillages, also stains and polishes applied over the years – which may have a detrimental effect.

Most of these faults will be cured if you first cover the boards with hardboard before carpeting. In fact, it is always a good thing to overlay a boarded floor before putting on a floor covering. The hardboard will cover small indentations and gaps between the boards, and give a level sub-floor. It will also act as a barrier against grease and give a smooth, stable surface on which to lay your decorative floor. However, you will still need to replace defective boards (see pages 14 and 26), to fix firmly any loose ones, punch home any nails sticking up, and take out old tacks (see page 205). A very old floor, where years of foot traffic have ploughed out deep grooves may also need levelling.

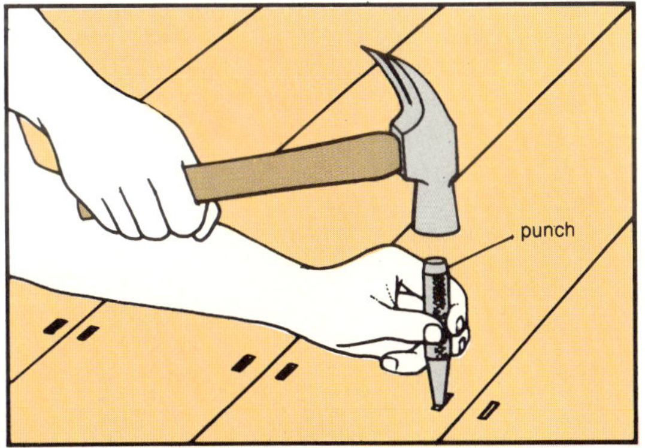

WOODWORM AND ROT

There is no point in covering up a timber sub-floor that is infested with woodworm or rot, and hoping that the attack will go away. It won't! You must get rid of the trouble. Dealing with extensive attacks of worm or rot is beyond the scope of this book – call in a professional firm. However, you can cope with minor outbreaks yourself.

Don't assume that, because the attack seems minor on the surface, it has not got a real grip underneath the floor. In fact, if you suspect an outbreak it is not a bad idea to lift a board here and there to see if it is worse underneath. Special liquids, which you can brush or spray on, are sold for killing woodworm.

LEVELLING A BOARDED FLOOR

A timber floor is levelled with a latex-based levelling compound which you can buy from builder's merchants. You should always follow closely the manufacturer's instructions. The compounds usually come as a powder that you add to water, and then trowel onto the surface. The sub-floor must first of all be free of dust and grit, and there should be no grease or polish on it. Some manufacturers supply a de-greasing agent for use with the compound. Begin at the far end, and work towards the door. Always let the compound dry and set properly before putting a floor on to of it.

THE TRICK

One simple test to decide whether your boarded floor needs levelling or not, is to put a sheet of hardboard on it, and press at a number of places. If the board feels soft and springy at various points, then the sub-floor does need levelling. If it is firm it can be left as it is.

OVERLAYING WITH HARDBOARD

Hardboard comes in a range of sheet sizes, and professionals tend to use the biggest – 2440 × 1220mm (8 × 4ft). However, you would probably do better with 1220mm (4ft) square, or even 900mm (3ft) square.

THE TRICK

Hardboard should always be 'conditioned' before it is used. Brush into the reverse side of the board ½l. (¾pint) of water per 1220mm (4ft) square sheet. The boards are then stacked flat for 48 hours, back to back, in the room they will occupy. It is important not to leave them any longer than this.

HARDBOARD TO BE COVERED OVER

Hardboard is fixed to a sub-floor by nailing. The conditioned board dries out once fixed, and tightens up on the nails to form a perfect sub-floor. You can use panel pins, but ring nails are best. Begin nailing in the centre of an edge of the board that butts up against a wall, and work forwards and outwards, so that the sheets will lie quite flat.

THE TRICK

Hardboard should be laid smooth face downwards, because the heads of the fixing pins will be lost in the mesh, and not harm the final covering. The mesh also presents a keyed surface that will exert a better grip on the final covering, especially if it has to be stuck down.

Begin laying in a corner of the room away from the door. Overlaid hardboard does not have to fit as closely to the wall as would a top covering, so even if the corner is not a perfect right angle you can normally just lay the board in position and fix it. Butt the next sheet up and fix that too. Carry on until you come to the end of the room, where you have to cut a board to fit. There will normally be no need to scribe this board (see page 206). Just measure at each end how wide it should be, and cut it to fit. Use the waste to start the next row. In this way, you will make sure that you stagger the joins, or 'break the bond'.

HARDBOARD AS A FINAL FLOORCOVERING

If hardboard is to be used as a top covering it is fixed in a slightly different way. The sheets still need to be conditioned, and the method of nailing is the same, but the board should be laid smooth side upwards.

CHIPBOARD SUB-FLOORS

Not all suspended timber floors are clad with floorboards. Flooring-grade chipboard, or sometimes plywood, has been used instead. These sub-floors normally require much less preparation than floorboards. There is no need to overlay them with hardboard; ensure that they are firmly fixed to the joists below and that all the nail heads are punched well home.

Ceramic, marble, cork or brick? Or beautifully real 'Peel & Stick'?

New Marquis Floor Tiles.

You can always count on Marley for beautiful designs and rich colours.

Now, you can step even closer to the look of luxury with Marley's new Marquis 'Peel & Stick' floor tiles.

Marquis floor tiles look beautifully real. Deep embossing adds the all-important dimension of natural light and shading, and means they beautifully reflect all the luxury of ceramic, marble, cork or brick.

Marquis floor tiles come in a range of superb designs and a wide spectrum of colours.

They are easy to lay and very easy to keep clean.

In the realm of 'Peel & Stick' floor tiles, you'll find Marquis are without peer.

'Easy to lay. Easy to clean'.

Marley Floors Limited, Lenham, Maidstone, Kent ME17 2DE. Telephone: Maidstone (0622) 858877. Telex 95231.

SHEET VINYLS 1

Today, if you are laying a sheet material in your home, it is almost certain to be a vinyl. People still refer to all sheet flooring as 'lino' (short for linoleum), although it was long ago passed in the popularity stakes by vinyl. You use the same basic method for laying all kinds of sheet flooring.

TYPES OF VINYL

Vinyl flooring is available in a wide range of qualities, thicknesses, patterns, colours and textures. Before deciding, have a good look round your local shops, and read magazine advertisements, to see what is available.

The word 'vinyl' is actually an abbreviation of polyvinyl chloride (it is often known by the initials PVC), which is a flexible plastic to which other materials are added to give it the special character that turns it into a flooring material. The ratio of PVC to other materials used can be as high as 85:15, or as little as 20:80. As PVC is an expensive material, the price you are asked to pay for the flooring will be a pretty good guide to how much vinyl it contains. However, that does not mean you should ignore the cheaper grades. There are many areas in your home for which they would be suitable.

Sheet vinyls have a clear vinyl 'wear' layer on the surface, and on some brands this layer has a really glossy appearance. Under it is the printed pattern, or solid colour if the vinyl is a plain one, which is welded to the felt backing. Cushioned vinyls have a layer of foam on top of the backing, which makes them softer to the touch, warmer, and more resilient. As a result, they are the most popular form of vinyl.

All types of sheet vinyl are bought from the roll, but the width will vary according to the brand, since some companies are manufacturing in metric sizes and others are sticking to the old imperial widths (even if they are giving them a metric equivalent). However, the most popular widths are around 2 and 4m – about 6 and 12ft. The bigger widths are trickier to handle but, in most cases, they allow you to cover the room with one continuous sheet, doing away with the need for joins. This means you are spared the trouble of matching up the patterns.

TAKING UP OLD FLOORINGS

It is not always absolutely necessary to take up the old floor before you lay a new one. You may have vinyl tiles that are perfectly satisfactory in every respect, except you don't like the colour. Provided that the existing tiles will form an adequate sub-floor you can stick new ones on top of them. Wood block, or parquet, can form a satisfactory sub-floor, too, if it is firmly fixed and dry. However you usually will achieve a far better result if you remove the existing floor before laying the new one.

If this floor is loose laid, or a carpet tacked in place, you merely roll it up and carry it outside. A flooring that has been stuck down is, however, rather more tricky, because it will have to be scraped up.

THE TRICK

One of the best tools is an ordinary garden spade: it has a sharp blade that you can shove under the edge of the flooring, and a long handle that gives you a lot of leverage for prising up the material.

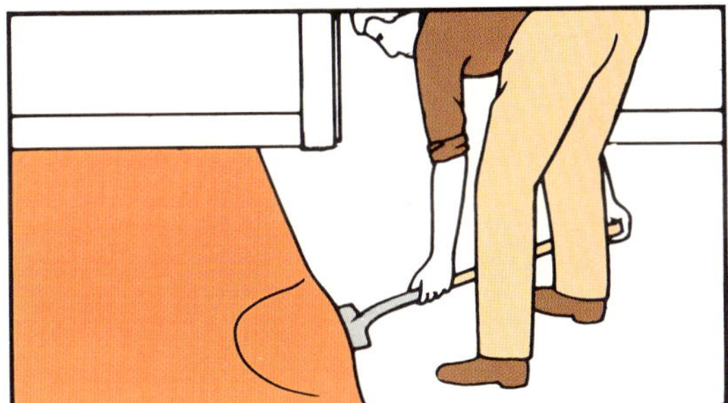

Also you can work standing up, which imposes less strain on your back.

TAKING UP OLD TACKS

You can use various tools for taking out old tacks. A claw hammer and a pair of pincers are probably the most obvious.

Many tradesmen use a tool known as a tack lifter for taking up old nails (see page 296). Push the V under the head of the nail, twist your wrist, and the nail should come out easily.

THE TRICK

Both of these tools can damage the floorboards; so if you intend to have the boards on view afterwards, protect them with a scrap of hardboard or card.

PLANNING THE WORK

Assuming you are dealing with a vinyl not wide enough to cover the whole room: i.e. that the material will have to be joined – and that the room is square or oblong – i.e. that it has no alcoves, or other features round which you will have to cut – your first job is to work out how much material you will need. To do that, you will have to decide which way the lengths are to run.

THE TRICK

Ideally, sheet material should be laid at right angles to the window, for then the seams will be less likely to show. However, if you will be laying the vinyl directly on to floorboards (although it is better to cover these with hardboard first) the vinyl should go at right angles to these. The most important thing to avoid is a seam in the middle of a doorway.

First measure the length of the room, adding 75mm (3in.) extra for trimming. The length that will go into the doorway should be measured to a halfway point under the closed door. Now measure across the width of the room to determine how many of these lengths you need. For instance, if the room is 3.35mm (11ft) across, and you are dealing with a 2m (6ft) wide vinyl, you will need two lengths – there will be a certain amount of wastage at the side. If it is 4m (13ft) across, you will need three lengths. The wastage will be much more, but perhaps you can make use of the excess somewhere else.

CONDITIONING VINYL

If you were getting a professional to lay the floor, the material should arrive one day and the fitter ought not to turn up for another two days or so. The reason for this is that vinyl tends to shrink slightly when first laid, unless it can be left standing upright for a day or two in the room where it will be laid.

THE TRICK

In winter the room should be heated to ensure that the flooring will be flexible, which makes it easier to lay – vinyl tends to be hard and brittle when cold.

When you are laying vinyl yourself make sure that you allow it to acclimatize. Resist the temptation to buy it and lay it all in the same day.

SHEET VINYLS 2

STRIKING THE BASE LINE

Unfortunately, no room in any house is perfectly square, and although in some rooms the discrepancy is so small as to be unnoticeable, in others it will be obvious once you start to lay a patterned flooring, particularly one with a strong pattern running in one direction. To guard against this, you need a base line from which to work. Measure the two opposite walls that will be at the ends of the lengths of vinyl, and mark the centre of each of them. Between these two points you must snap a chalk line (see page 14).

CUTTING AND MEASURING

If one end, as opposed to a side, of the lengths of vinyl is to lie against the wall containing the door, it is not a bad idea to make your first length the one that goes into the doorway. Measure the room, add 75mm (3in.) for trimming, and with sharp scissors or a Stanley knife cut a piece from the roll to that length. Place it on the floor so that it is about 25mm (1in.) from the wall against which the side of the vinyl will go, and 'lapping up' the wall at each end by half the trimming allowance. Make sure that it is parallel to the base line you have struck. At the doorway end, make it lap slightly higher up the wall – the length to which you have cut it allows it to finish halfway under the door.

THE TRICK

Now draw a pencil line at a couple of points across both the sub-floor and the vinyl. These 'check marks' (or cross checks) allow you always to bring the flooring accurately back to its original position.

SCRIBING THE EDGE

You now have to scribe the edge (or selvedge) of the flooring to fit against the side wall. Use a scriber if you own one, but you can make do with a block of wood and a pencil. Measure the gap between the selvedge of the vinyl and the side wall to discover where it is greatest, and cut a small piece of timber to that length. Now jam the block hard against the skirting board, and place the pencil up against the block. Run pencil and block the length of the wall, scribing its contours on the face of the vinyl and making sure you keep the wood at right angles to the wall.

Cut the vinyl with scissors or a sharp-bladed Stanley knife along the pencil line. Bring the vinyl back to the wall, using the check marks to position it accurately, and it will fit snugly against the wall.

FITTING

Now you can fit the vinyl against the end walls; it is better to begin at the doorway. Again, use your scriber if available, but you can make do with a small piece of timber about 100mm (4in.) long. With the scribed selvedge accurately in place against the side wall, draw a chalk line on the floor along its oppposite edge, and make a pencil check mark across this same edge. Now fold back (or buckle) the vinyl away from the door wall by a distance equal to the length of the piece of wood. Keep the outer edge of the buckled vinyl on the chalk line. Use the piece of wood to scribe a pencil line parallel to the end wall, following its irregularities closely. In the doorway use the timber to draw the contours of the door frame mouldings. Mark the other side of the door opening and the rest of the wall beyond. Be sure to keep the wood at right angles to the wall, etc. The vinyl should be cut so that it finishes halfway under the closed door. Cut the material to the line you have made, and push it into place to check that it fits properly. Now repeat at the other end. The flooring should fit snugly in place.

The doorway may, of course, be on the selvedge of the length of vinyl. It is trimmed in the same way, but when you position it 25mm (1in.) away from the wall ready to trace the guideline onto it, you will need a piece of wood long enough to reach to the centre point of the closed door. You will trim a wider strip from the selvedge, except for the stretch that goes into the doorway.

The next length is butted up against this first one on their meeting selvedge, but match the pattern carefully. Then scribe this length to fit the end walls as above.

Inevitably, the last length will have to be cut to width to fit the space available. If the piece is grossly oversize, cut it (along the edge that will fit against the side wall) so that the excess is less than 300mm (1ft). Place it on the floor overlapping the preceding length, with patterns matching. Butt it up against the far wall, lying as close as possible.

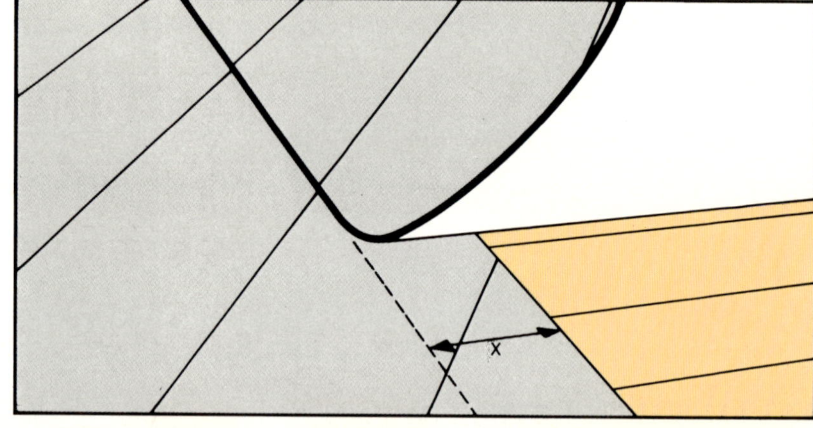

THE TRICK

Peel back the overlap to measure the distance marked X as shown. Now take a ruler and pencil and scribe on the vinyl a line parallel to the far wall and the distance X away from it.

Cut to this line. Finally, scribe to each end, and fit.

SHEET VINYLS 3

TRIMMING THE EDGES

Some sheet flooring materials have a special edge meant to be trimmed because, say the makers, the limitations of the manufacturing machinery mean that the factory edge cannot be absolutely true. In any case, the edges might get damaged at some point on their way from the factory to you. You should be able to tell if your material has a trimming edge, because it will not be a perfect match at the edges, and you will only be able to get a perfect match if you overlap two lengths. If in doubt you can always ask when you order your material whether it has a trimming edge or not. If it has, this is what you do.

Having laid the first length satisfactorily with one selvedge against the wall, you slip the second one underneath it at the selvedge away from the wall, and move it around until you have matched the pattern perfectly.

THE TRICK

It's a good idea first to place a length of scrap under the seam of the two overlapped sheets.

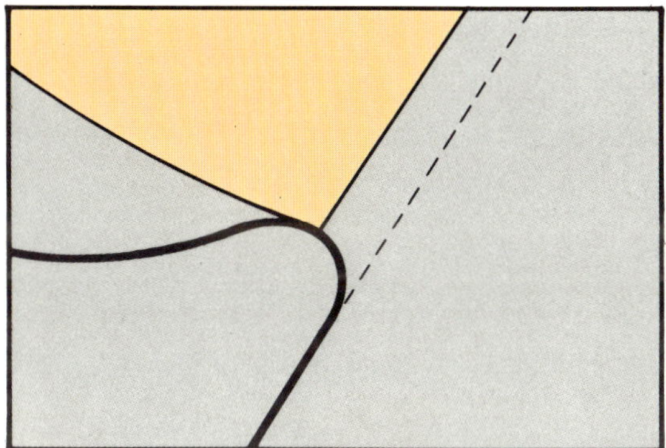

Using a straight-edge and a Stanley knife with a sharp blade, cut through both pieces at one go at a convenient point – about 10mm (½in.) from the edge. Peel away the two strips you will have cut – one from each edge – and the two main pieces will match up perfectly.

STICKING DOWN

Many people merely loose-lay sheet flooring materials, but it is better to stick them down to their sub-floor with an appropriate flooring adhesive. Otherwise the flooring might shrink in the warmth of the room, and unsightly gaps appear in their seams and round the edges. It must be stuck down on the day it is laid, for if you leave it overnight it may shrink and not be such a perfect fit. Some manufacturers offer their own adhesive, while others recommend which glue you should use. The adhesive should be applied with a corrugated spreader.

THE TRICK

Do not use any other kind of tool for this, or try to improvise a spreader by making it yourself from hardboard, because the depth of the corrugations is critical.

They are not put there to comb the adhesive into ridges; they are a gauge to ensure that the glue is spread to the right depth.

Ordinary vinyl should be stuck down all over. Apply the glue over the entire floor using your notched spreader. A cushioned vinyl need normally be stuck only at its edges and the seams.

Lift up the edges and spread a 50mm (2in.) wide band of adhesive on the floor, 25mm (1in.) each side of the join. Carefully replace the vinyl, then rub the seam with a clean rag, using plenty of pressure to ensure a good bond. Always follow the manufacturer's instructions on sticking down a vinyl.

All this raises the question: suppose you ever need to get at the sub-floor – to raise a floorboard, for instance, to gain access for electrical or plumbing work? Well, you have a problem, but the flooring manufacturers merely shrug their shoulders, and say that it is very seldom necessary in the average home to take up floorboards, and in the meantime their material must be stuck down to look good and wear well. Once sheet flooring has been stuck down, obviously you will ruin it if you attempt to take it up, and removing it should be regarded as a last desperate measure. If you feel that access below your floorboards is essential, you should choose a different flooring material altogether.

Material which is stuck down all over should be firmly pressed in place in doorways. Tradesmen use a roller for this, but when you are only an occasional floor-layer it is not worth your while buying – or even hiring – a roller, so just go all over it making sure it is sticking properly.

PROTECTING THE EDGE IN DOORWAYS. Various metal strips are sold for fixing in doorways to protect the edge of the vinyl from being scuffed. These strips come in the middle of the closed door, and if you are fitting one make allowance for it when scribing the vinyl to fit.

DEALING WITH ALCOVES

There are two ways you can cope with an alcove, such as at the side of a chimney breast:

The first is to make a 'release' cut parallel to the selvedge, to allow the material to lie down flat in the alcove and lap up against its wall, as well as the wall of the chimney breast. Then trim to both these walls in the usual way.

The other method, a useful one where there are a lot of projections, is to make a template (see page 210).

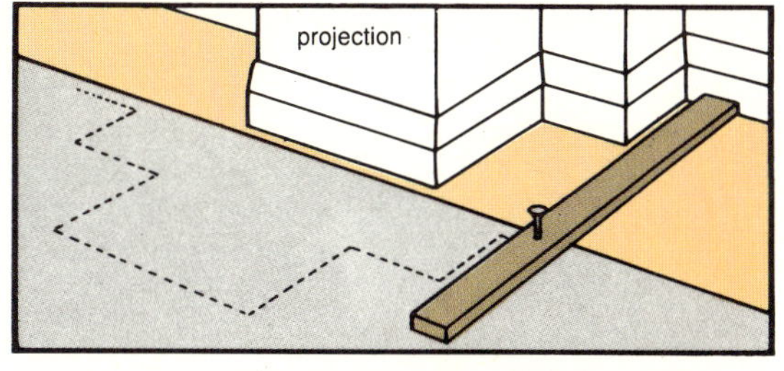

THE TRICK

You may well find it easier first to trim off the excess lapping up the chimney breast, so that you are left with just the normal trimming allowance.

FREE-HAND CUTTING

When dealing with a flexible sheet material, such as vinyl, some people prefer what is known as free-hand cutting. You let the vinyl ride up the wall by about 50mm (2in.), then crease it along the line where it meets the bottom of the skirting board. Draw a sharp knife along the line, and you will cut the material to a perfect fit. It is obviously a much quicker method, but there is quite a knack to it. You have to hold the knife perfectly upright all the time, and most do-it-yourselfers tend to let the knife slip from the vertical – the blade will wander away from the wall, with the handle pointing towards it. As a result, at these points you will cut away too much vinyl, and there will be a gap when you come to fit it against the wall. It takes quite a bit of practice to make an accurate cut each time, so probably the block of wood method is better. However, free-handing is necessary in fitting the wider vinyls (see page 211).

And for our next trick...

Nairn will help turn this

SHEET VINYLS 4

THE TEMPLATE METHOD

Very small rooms, such as bathrooms and lavatories, can be covered with one continuous sheet. The method used is known as the template method.

Cover the sub-floor of the room with a sheet of paper. Felt paper is best, but any stiff paper will do. If the paper curls, turn it over.

THE TRICK

If you cannot get a single sheet of paper big enough, use several, taping, stapling or gluing them together.

Then draw two pencil lines – the tradesman's cross checks – across both pieces of paper at two or more points so that you can glance at them from time to time to make sure the paper has not been disturbed. It is a good idea, too, to make cross checks from paper onto the sub-floor if there are any isolated projections round which you have to fit the vinyl.

When the paper is down on the floor trim it all round so that it stops about 15mm (½in.) short of the perimeter of the room, and any obstacles. Then fix it firmly in place, with drawing pins on a wooden floor, or weights on a concrete one.

You need a pair of compasses with a locking device, which you should set to a gap of about 25mm (1in.).

THE TRICK

While working you may disturb this setting, so it is a good idea to draw a few circles on the paper before starting, to give you a quick reference against which you can check the compass setting from time to time.

With the compasses' point on the skirting board and the pencil on the paper, run the compasses all the way round the room, making sure they are at right angles to the wall throughout. When you have marked out the perimeter of the room in this way, do the same round any obstacles in the middle of the room – such as a lavatory or pedestal washbasin. You now have on the paper template an outline of the room, and everything in it, that is just 25mm (1in.) – or whatever dimension you choose – smaller than the room.

MARKING UP THE VINYL

To make a perfectly accurate outline, place the paper on the vinyl that is intended for the room, and reverse the compasses: i.e. put the point on the line you have drawn, and the pencil on the vinyl, and trace on to the flooring material the outline you have drawn on the paper. Cut along the pencil line, and you will have a sheet that should fit the room perfectly. There are one or two points to watch here. Take the flooring somewhere convenient – a larger room, for instance. Position the template on it carefully so that the pattern will be well set out in the finished result. Fix the template to the flooring with pins or a weight. Throughout the tracing, keep the compasses at right angles to the traced line. Before you start and again when you have finished, check the setting of the compasses. If this has been disturbed at all, you will have to begin again.

If there are any pipes or similar small circular obstacles sticking up from the floor, the paper should be cut to a rough fit round these too. Place a ruler on top of the paper and jam it hard up against each of the four 'sides' of the pipe, so that you draw a rough square on the paper. When tracing back, you merely put your ruler on the lines of the square on the template, and draw on the flooring a smaller square, the sides of which would be touching the position of the pipe. It is then a simple matter, using your compasses, to determine the centre of this square and draw a circle, centred on that point, of the same diameter as the pipe. If the pipe is oval, or any other irregular shape, it will need a five or six-sided shape drawn round it.

To fit behind the lavatory, basin or pipe, or any other similar obstacle that stands clear of a wall, you will have to cut a line from the hole you have made for it to the back of the sheet. Then it will go down in place. On a plain flooring, or one with only a slight pattern, this line should be straight.

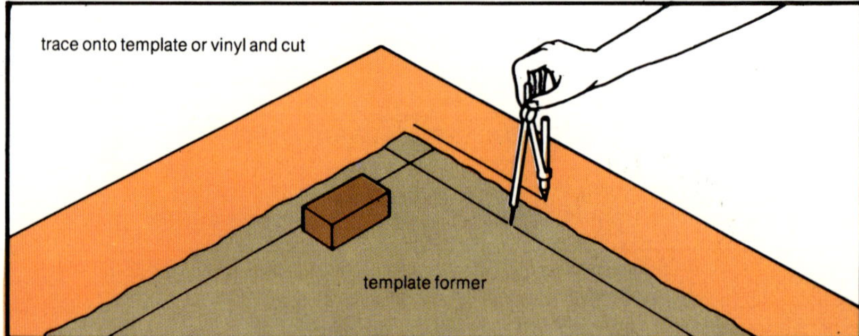

THE TRICK

However, wherever possible you should follow any natural lines in the pattern, which will make the cut less noticeable. The imitation grouting in a tiled pattern is probably the best example of the type of line you can follow, but there are many others. The more irregular this line is, the less obvious it will be.

(Believe it or not, but tradesmen refer to this method as 'Van Dycking', after the artist.)

STICKING DOWN

In sticking down a seamless material you work on half at a time. Roll back the flooring, apply the adhesive to the sub-floor, then smooth the flooring back in place. In the case of a room with a chimney breast, roll the material out of the alcoves, spread the adhesive, and glue the material in place. Then roll back the other half, glue that, and the job is done.

SHEET VINYLS 5

LAYING WIDE FLOORINGS

The introduction of wider-than-normal floorings – those that measure 4m (12ft), for instance – has meant that you can now cover much bigger rooms with continuous sheet, or put down a seamless floor, as they say in the trade. In theory you could use the template method here, too, but it would get very unwieldy. The trade uses the free-hand cutting method (see page 207). It is difficult, but it really is the best method for laying a seamless floor. You should proceed slowly and carefully until you gain confidence.

When laying a seamless floor, aim to buy a roll of vinyl that is about 75mm (3in.) larger all round than the size of the room. Obviously, there will be no trouble about having the roll cut to the length you want, and many retailers will also cut it to width. If yours won't, however, then you should try to do this yourself before taking the material into the room where it will be laid. Perhaps you have a larger room where it can be done. If not, try using the lawn, provided it is perfectly dry.

POSITIONING

Put the cut roll down in the room. Because of its size, you will find it better to lay it diagonally to two opposite corners. For these first few operations you will need a helper, although a good tradesman would manage it himself. Together you should unroll the material to its fullest extent. Measure the room and pick out the longest wall, which is the one to which you should work. Lay the longest edge of the vinyl against this wall to see if it can lie squarely alongside the skirting board. To test this you may have to move the material a fraction of an inch or so along the floor.

THE TRICK

The best way of doing this is to stand on it with your feet close together, then make a little forward jump, coming down with a slight thrust in the direction you want it to move.

If you are lucky enough to find that this wall is square, you will be spared the bother of having to scribe the material to it, and you can concentrate on trimming it to the other walls. Arrange it so that it laps up the foot of the other walls – remember you have cut it slightly oversize to allow it to do this. Crease it where it meets the foot of the skirting, running a block along the meeting line to emphasize the crease. Then cut along this line with a Stanley knife.

That is basically what happens, but there are a number of dodges that you will find useful. Let us first take a closer look at what is involved in lapping the sheet up the wall. You have to be careful not to crease the material until you are ready to cut it, so when you first have to fold it over make sure it lies loosely.

RELEASE CUTS

To enable the vinyl to lie snugly up the wall when you crease it, you must make a series of release cuts, one at each internal corner. Now snip off a triangular piece at the corner, to make a V shape as the flooring laps up the two adjacent walls.

THE TRICK

Even the professionals do not expect to cut off the piece accurately at one go. They snip off less than they think will be necessary, then gradually remove the rest a strip at a time until they have a perfect fit.

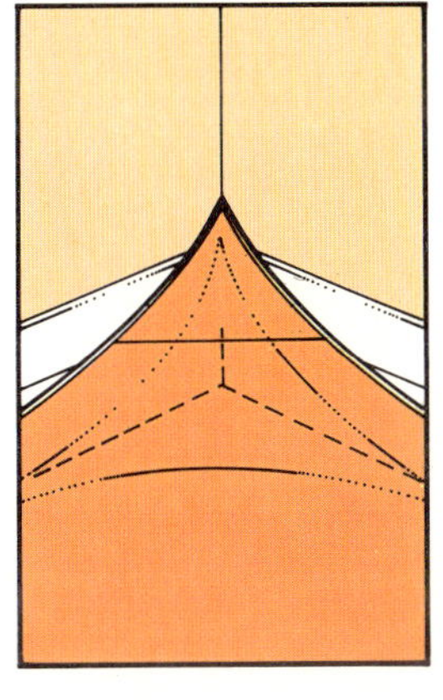

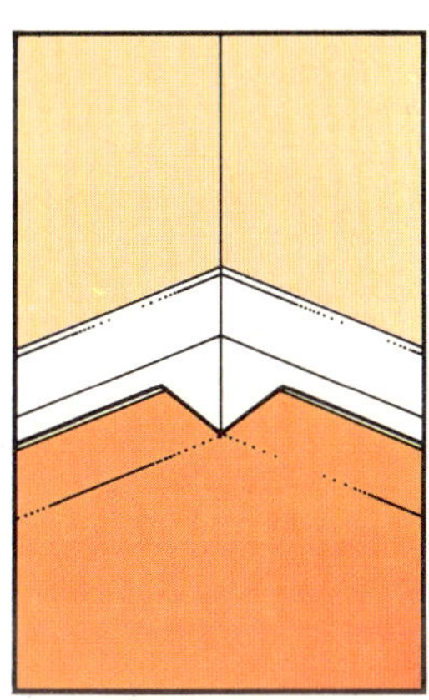

Release cuts will also be needed at external corners, where an obstruction such as a chimney breast juts out at an angle to the main line of the wall. Here, in front of the fireplace, you would have a lot of excess material, and in such instances it is essential to have a helper to hold the waste while you cut, so that it will not flop over and crease or tear. Then trim off all but about 75mm (3in.) of the waste.

THE TRICK

No matter how small the obstruction causing the external angle, a release cut is needed in every case. For instance, a cut would have to be made at every forward projection in a door architrave, or a fireplace surround.

Now go back for a moment to that long wall. Supposing it is not square, as we assumed. In that case, let the vinyl lap up it, and crease it in just the same way as for the other walls.

TRIMMING

With all the release cuts made, and the vinyl lapped on every wall, go all round the room making sure it lies snugly against the wall, creasing it as described earlier. Then cut the material in with an ordinary, sharp-bladed Stanley knife. Begin at one corner and work your way round the room tearing off the cut strip when it gets too unwieldy. As I have warned, be careful at first. The main thing is that the point of the blade should touch the vinyl right at the point where it meets the skirting board, and the top of the handle should be away from the wall, so that the knife is at an angle of 45°. If your knife slopes the opposite way, the cut would be made away from the wall and you would have a gap round the whole perimeter of your flooring.

FITTED CARPETS 1

Laying wall-to-wall carpet in a room is just about the most difficult flooring operation that the do-it-yourselfer can tackle. You need specialized equipment as well as specialized skills and knowledge. When you think how small the laying charges are, compared with the high cost of buying the carpet in the first place, you begin to wonder whether it is worth tackling the fitting yourself at all. In fact, many shops selling carpet offer to do the fitting at no extra cost.

So really there are only two instances when unskilled amateurs should lay their own carpet:

1. When you are taking up a carpet that has been in use for some time, to be re-laid in another room (e.g. when moving house); and
2. When the carpet is foam-backed.

The reason is this: most types of carpet need to be stretched if they are to look well and wear well. It is here that specialized equipment and skill are called for. Carpet that has been in use for some time will be much easier to stretch than new carpet, as it will have been stretched when it was originally fitted, and the passage of feet over the years will have helped it to stabilize its shape and size. The carpet will also be easier to cut and handle in general. Foam-backed carpet is one type that does not need to be stretched – in fact, you would damage it if you tried to stretch it.

Anyway, let us take a look at what is involved in fitting a carpet, and then it is up to you to decide if you want to tackle it.

CARPET GRADES

There are various grades of carpet available, according to whether the area in question has heavy, medium or light use. It is a waste of money to lay heavy-duty carpet in a bedroom, while a light-duty carpet in a heavy-duty area (like a staircase) will wear out in a matter of months rather than years. Consult the salesman for advice on which grade you require. There are many different ways of making carpets, but four of the most common are illustrated here.

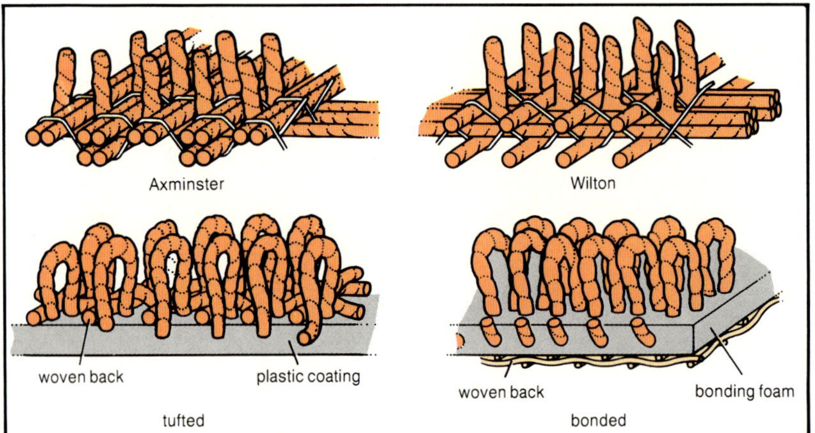

FITTING GRIPPER STRIP

There are two ways in which carpet that is not foam-backed can be fixed round the edges. You can tack it to the floor or the skirting board, with a turnback of about 50mm (2in.) to stop it fraying. However, that method has now been largely superseded by the gripper strip method. Gripper strips are lengths of battening about 6mm (¼in.) thick and 25mm (1in.) or so wide. Tacks stick up at an angle from the strip, and it is to these tacks that the carpet is fitted.

On timber sub-floors, the strip is nailed in place, and most carpet fitters use strip with pre-fixed nails, which stand proud of the timber, their heads the same side as the points of the gripper tacks. You just lay the strip down in place and drive home the nails. Having pre-fixed nails obviously saves a lot of time and trouble, and the nails are spaced at the correct distance.

For fixing on hard sub-floors (marble, tiles, concrete, etc.) you can buy strip that is not pre-nailed, which you fix with either special adhesive (the company that makes the strip will supply it) or with nails designed to penetrate concrete. However, it is also possible to buy pre-nailed strip suitable for fixing to concrete.

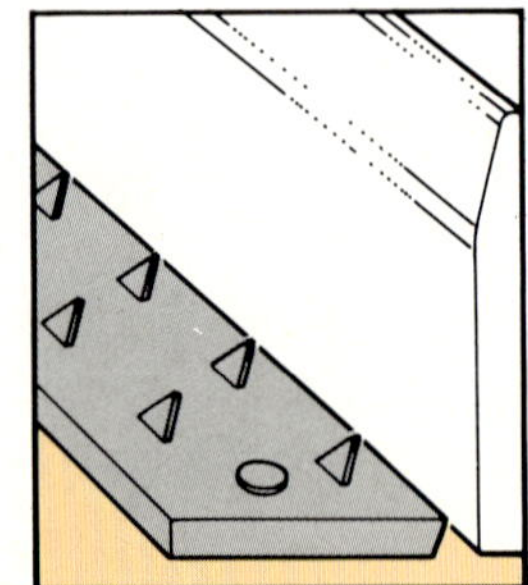

FIXING

For striking the fixing nails, a special carpet fitter's hammer is used. This tool has a small striking face so that it can hit the heads of the fixing nails without touching, and thus blunting, the points of the tacks that will grip the carpet, yet the head is heavy enough to drive home the nails effectively.

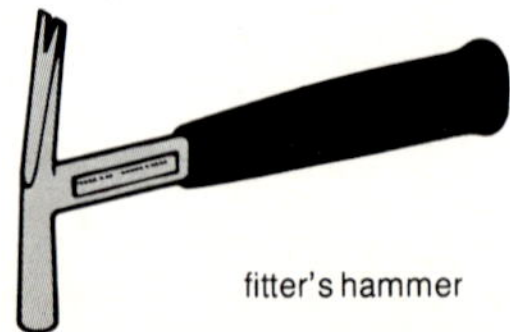

fitter's hammer

THE TRICK

You can use an ordinary hammer and, when the nail head gets down near the level of the points of the tacks, you can finish off with a heavy nail punch.

The strip should be fixed with the gripping pins pointing towards the wall, and you should leave a tiny space (or gully, as the professional calls it) between strip and wall. It is important to maintain the same gully all the way round the room, even in front of projections such as pillars or fireplaces. However, you will not be able to get so close to radiators, or built-in cupboards that have a toe space at the bottom. Here you will have to leave a bigger gully.

THE TRICK

The underlay should go as close to the base of the cupboard as possible, which means it will have to pass under the gripper rod, although normally it stops on the room side.

There is no need to mitre the strip at corners and if your room has a curve, you cut the strip into very short lengths to follow its line.

To cut the strip, the professional uses special shears but do-it-yourselfers use an ordinary saw.

DOORWAY STRIP

Special strip is sold for fitting in doorways. For the room doorway you use a metal threshold strip, which has gripping pins just like the timber strip, but also incorporates a metal moulding to cover the edge of the carpet.

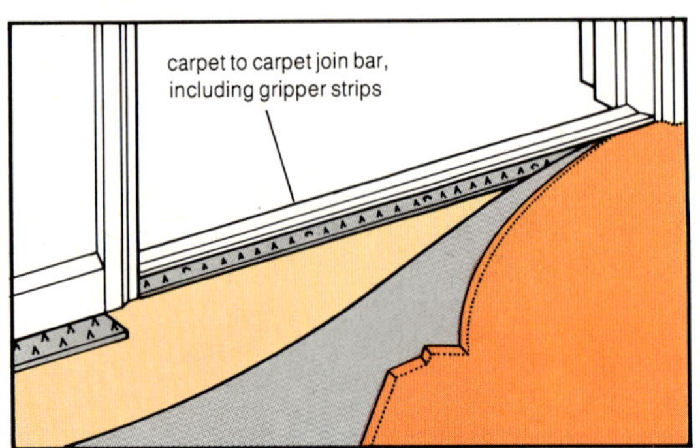

THE TRICK

This moulding is tapped down with a hammer (use a scrap piece of wood to protect the metal) to form a tight join with the carpet when the job is done.

Two-way thresholds are also available, to cover the ends of both carpets where different ones are used in the room and in the passageway outside.

There is also an edging strip for use in low traffic areas, such as in front of a cupboard, where it is not possible to form a gully.

FITTED CARPETS 2

THE UNDERLAY

Your carpet will wear better and last longer if it has an underlay, and this should be fitted next. Cut it roughly to length and fit it, starting in one corner of the room. Fasten it at the beginning just inside one edge of the gripper strip, then stretch it towards the opposite wall and fasten it. (The way to do the stretching is described below, under carpet fitting.)

To fasten down the underlay on wooden floors, the professional uses a stapling hammer, which operates when you tap the face of the work with it. The do-it-yourselfer usually makes do with a hammer and tacks.

Once the underlay has been fixed trim it to fit at the far end by running a sharp knife along the inside edge of the gripper strip, which will act as a guide. On a boarded sub-floor, unless you first line it with hardboard, it is good practice to lay felt paper under the underlay, because it covers any gaps in the floorboards though which dust and grit, which could damage the carpet, might be blown. This paper, too, is fitted inside the gripper strip border, and it is stapled or tacked in place just like the underlay. A stapling hammer or tacks will not work on concrete and similar sub-floors.

THE TRICK

Here you stick the underlay round the edges, and at any necessary joins, with double-sided carpet tape.

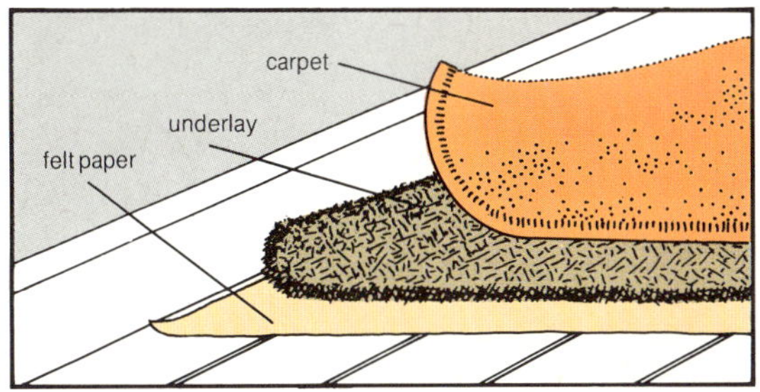

INSTALLING THE CARPET

To start off the carpet, you use what is known as the compressed edge technique, and you begin in a corner of the room. Let the carpet ride up the walls in this corner by about 10mm (½in.), then smooth it on to the gripping pins with your fingers (be careful that you do not hurt yourself). For the next step, the professional uses the fitter's hammer, although you might have to improvise with a bit of wood.

THE TRICK

Place the head of the hammer on the carpet and press the carpet down to form a sort of U shape in the gully. Keeping the hammer in this position, and maintaining downward pressure all the time, draw the hammer all the way along the wall in one direction from the corner, then along the wall in the other direction, forcing the carpet into the gulley as you move.

Now you have to stretch and hook the carpet on to the gripper strip on the two opposite walls. The principle is this. Carpet has natural elasticity, and after being stretched tends to spring back again. At the moment of maximum stretch, you hook it on to the gripping pins, it immediately contracts, and is firmly hooked in place.

Finally, you have to trim the carpet to fit the walls onto which it has been stretched. You will find it easier if you have first trimmed the carpet to its approximate correct size. Then you go round the two walls with a carpet knife, trimming off the excess and leaving a surplus of about 10mm (½in.). This excess edge must then be turned into the gully. To do this, the professional would use a carpet fitter's awl, but a thin stick will do instead for you. You run the awl, or stick, along the two walls, pushing the carpet neatly in place.

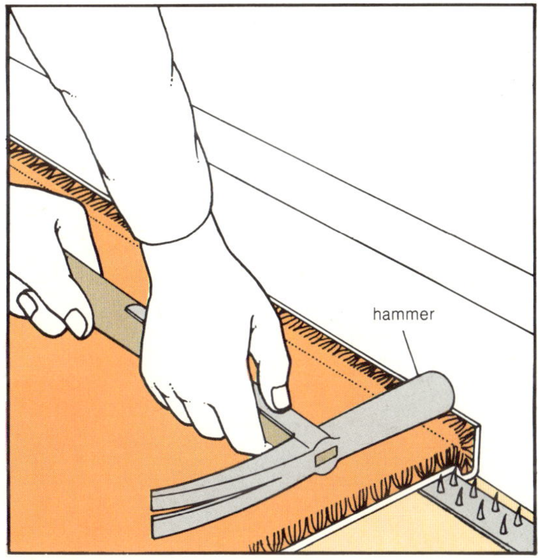

STRETCHING THE CARPET

The most important aspect of fitting a carpet is the stretching, and to do this, the tradesman uses a device known as a carpet stretcher, or knee kicker. At one end of this there is a large pad and at the other a sole with teeth. Kneeling down on the floor, he inserts the teeth into the carpet, then 'kicks' the pad with his knee. This stretches the carpet and pushes it towards the wall. When the carpet is at its maximum stretch, he hooks it on to the pins of the gripper strip. The carpet contracts immediately, and is firmly held in place.

It is not easy for the do-it-yourselfer to get hold of a carpet stretcher, in any event quite a lot of skill is called for in using a knee kicker. It is all too easy to damage the carpet and to inflict injury on your knee.

There is, however, a way of fitting carpet without this device, and that is to push the carpet along with your feet. It does not work all that well with new carpet, but can be used when re-laying old carpet. However do not expect to achieve a professional result.

Begin at the wall where you first used the compressed edge technique, and move gradually to the opposite side of the room, pushing the carpet along as far as you can.

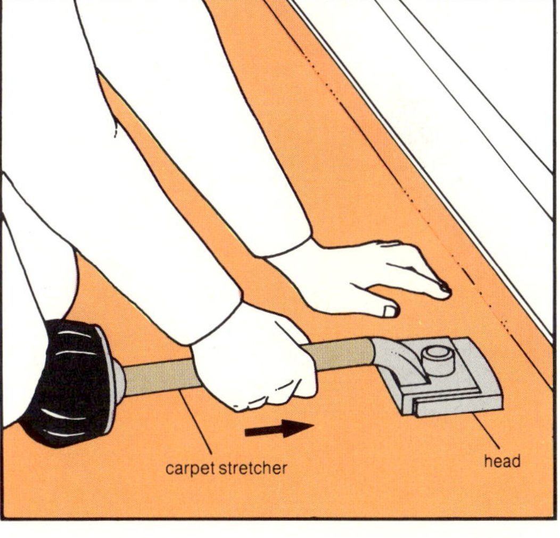

THE TRICK

Put all your weight on one foot, and push with the other. Alternatively stand with your feet close together and make little jumps, pushing forward as you land so that the carpet, too, is pushed forward.

THE TRICK

Sometimes it helps if you drive a tack in here and there so that the carpet will not spring back before you have hooked it on to the strip at the other wall.

Do not drive these tacks in too far, because you will want to take them out later.

FITTED CARPETS 3

CUTTING INTO ALCOVES

Rooms are not always square or rectangular. There is often some sort of alcove – at the side of a chimney breast, for instance. This is how you deal with it. Cut your carpet long enough to reach to the far end of the alcove, then lay it down in position, letting it ride up the wall at the front of the chimney breast, as needed. (You should not, of course, have the fire alight as you do this.)

Now make a cut in the carpet at right angles to the wall containing the chimney breast and alcoves. The cut should be long enough to create a tongue that just reaches the back wall of the alcove, and is slightly wider than the alcove. This cut, known as a release cut, will allow the tongue to drop neatly down into the alcove. You can then carry on fitting the carpet in the normal way.

Other alcoves, such as bays and doorways and so on, are dealt with in a similar manner.

JOINING CARPET

You can buy carpet wide enough to fit the rooms of the average-sized home, but in very large rooms two or sometimes more lengths of carpet have to be joined. This is highly skilled work, and is not to be recommended for the do-it-yourselfer. So if your room calls for carpet to be joined, you ought to call in a professional to do the work for you.

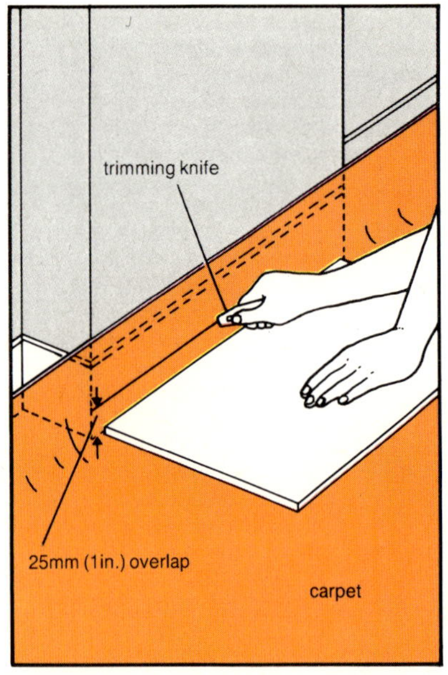

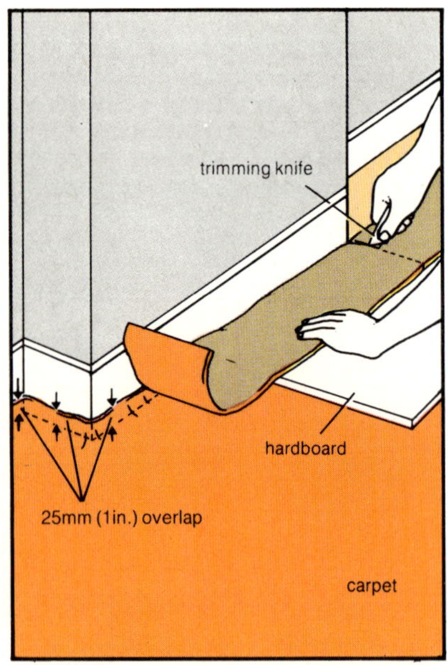

FOAM-BACKED CARPETS

Foam-backed carpet is much easier for the do-it-yourselfer to lay, because it does not need to be stretched. Nor does it require a separate underlay, for the foam backing acts as one, so you do not have to stretch an underlay either.

Begin be measuring the room very accurately. Cut the carpet to fit, with an allowance for trimming. The tradesman would work on a very small allowance indeed – perhaps just 10–25mm (½–1in.) leaving just 5–10mm (¼–½in.) to be turned up on each wall. That would not be enough for the do-it-yourselfer, who could well have made an error in the measuring. So you might do better to add at least 50mm (2in.): i.e. a 25mm (1in.) turn-up at each wall as a trimming allowance. In fact, you might aim for even more, provided that does not involve you in buying extra carpet.

Lay the carpet down on the floor, letting it ride up the wall by whatever allowance you have left, and make any release cuts necessary to allow the carpet to lie flat in doors and alcoves.

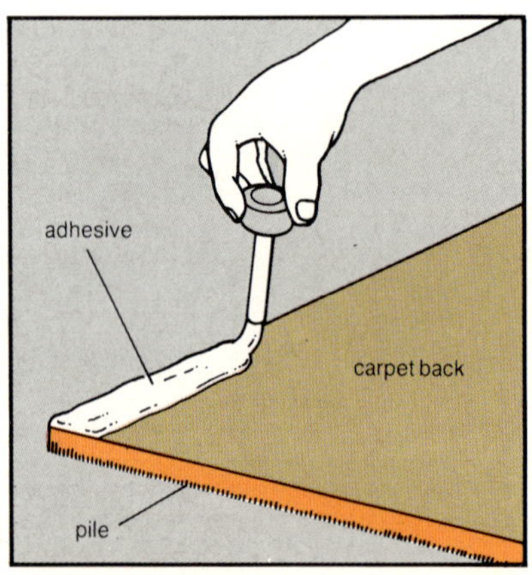

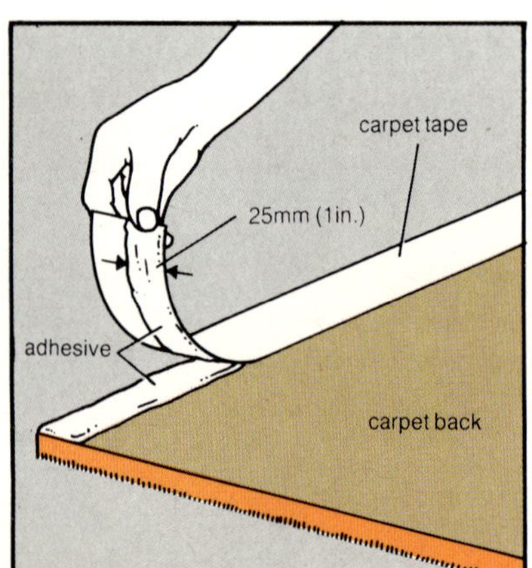

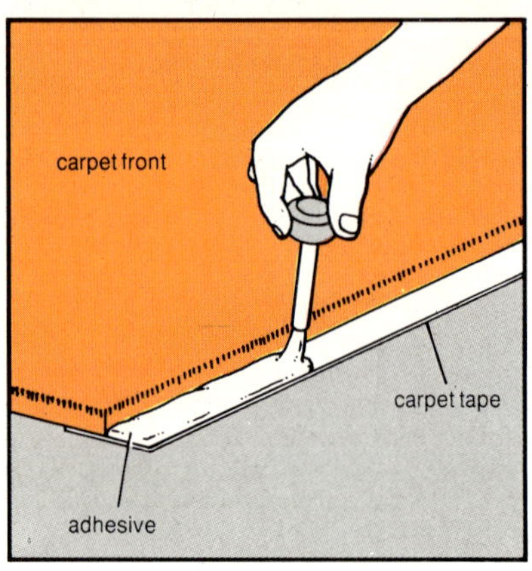

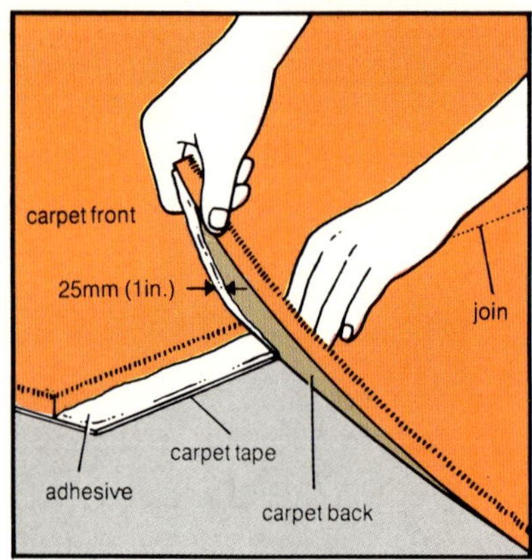

FIXING

One other thing that you will find much easier to do with foam-backed carpet than with other types is joining it. You begin to fit the carpet at any seam that is necessary in the centre of the room. To join foam-backed carpet you need carpet seaming tape 50mm (2in.) wide. Some types of tape are self-adhesive (on both sides); glue has to be spread on other tapes. Always follow the manufacturer's instructions, which should be read in conjunction with these general guidelines.

Many professional carpet layers snap a chalk line on the sub-floor (see page 14 for how to do this) along the line of the join; they find it is an aid to greater accuracy. Then they butt the two lengths of carpet together to see if the join is satisfactory. A factory edge is rarely good enough for a true butt joint, and it is usually necessary to trim both edges to get a good fit.

THE TRICK

Place one edge on the chalk line and, using a straight-edge and a carpet fitter's knife or Stanley knife, trim the carpet to get a good edge. Now place this good edge on the other length of carpet, and use it as a guide for trimming this second edge true.

When you are satisfied that the edges are a good match, stick the tape down on the floor, its middle coinciding with the position of the join. If you can only get hold of narrow tape, 25mm (1in.) wide, stick down two lengths side by side. Rub the tape down so that it is firmly stuck. If you are using self-adhesive tape, now peel off its protective backing; if you are using tape that needs gluing, spread the glue on.

THE TRICK

Lay the larger piece of carpet on the tape first, and smooth it down into place, then apply a small continuous bead of adhesive along the seam carpet edge.

Lay the other piece of carpet down in place, and press the entire seam firmly together. You will then get a good join between the two.

Now stick down the carpet all the way round the room with tape, in the way already described, and use a straight-edge to press it well into the join between sub-floor and skirting. Finally trim off the surplus using a sharp-bladed knife suitable for carpets.

THE TRICK

Hold your knife slightly at an angle so that the handle leans away from the wall, otherwise you might trim off too much.

Press the material firmly down on the tape once more, and the job is done.

STAIR CARPETS

There is no reason why you should not lay your own stair carpet, which does not require specialized equipment. However, a badly fitted stair carpet can be dangerous, particularly with very old people or children, so do make sure that you fix the carpet securely; if in doubt, call in a professional.

Stair carpet probably takes a bigger pounding than any other flooring, so it is vital to fit an underlay, so that you get maximum wear. You can use a continuous length, but it is more usual to use stair pads. The pads go on the tread, not the riser, but they should be big enough to fold over the nose of the stair, as this is highly vulnerable. The pads are held by the metal angle strip, which goes on top of them. Do not fit a pad onto the bottom tread (see below).

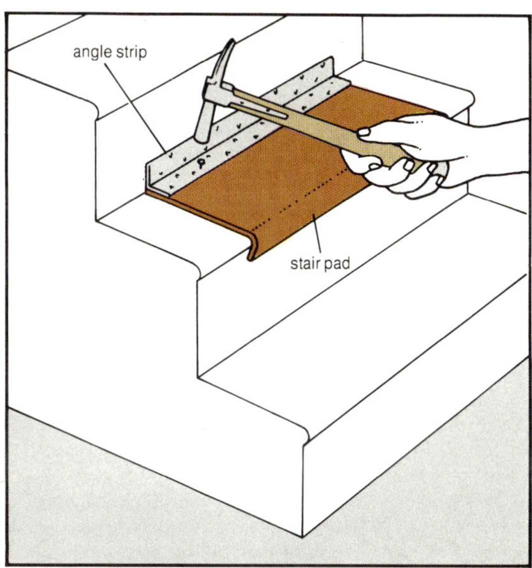

THE FIXING TECHNIQUE

At one time stair carpets were held on by rods or clips; nowadays, an invisible fixing method is usual, similar to that used for room carpet. You will probably use the invisible method; however, the principles are just the same if you decide to use clips or rods.

Invisible fixing is by means of metal angle strips with pressed-out teeth, similar to gripper rods. The angle goes in the join where the tread (the part you walk on) meets the riser (the vertical bit), known as the crotch. There are teeth on each side of the angle, pointing towards the crotch.

You can fix the angle in place with either screws or nails. If you do not have a carpet fitter's hammer, you will have to use a nail punch and, because this will slow you down, you might use screws. The metal angle is nailed or screwed to the tread first, then the riser.

FIXING TO STRAIGHT STAIRS

A stair carpet needs to be moved about 75mm (3in.) twice a year to distribute wear evenly, your carpet should have 450mm (18in.) reserve for this. Many people do not bother about moving their carpet, but it will not last as long.

THE TRICK

Carpet should be laid with its pile running down the stairs. The direction in which it feels smoothest should run from top to bottom.

You begin laying at the bottom. Put the carpet pile side down on the bottom tread, trapping it under the metal angle. It takes the place of underlay.

THE TRICK

Bring the carpet down over the nose and fasten it to the base of the bottom riser by nailing a strip of hardboard through its back.

Now run the carpet up the stairs, one tread at a time, and fix it to the metal angle. The tradesman uses a stair tool rather like a miniature spade. He pulls the carpet taut across the tread, and smooths it into the angle, pushing it onto both sets of teeth of the metal angle with the broad blade of the tool. A wooden spatula would do instead. Make absolutely sure that the carpet is tight and securely fixed. Carry on up the stairs, pushing the carpet securely onto the teeth of each angle, until you get to the top. Here you can tack the carpet in place, or buy a metal or plastic binder bar for fixing it.

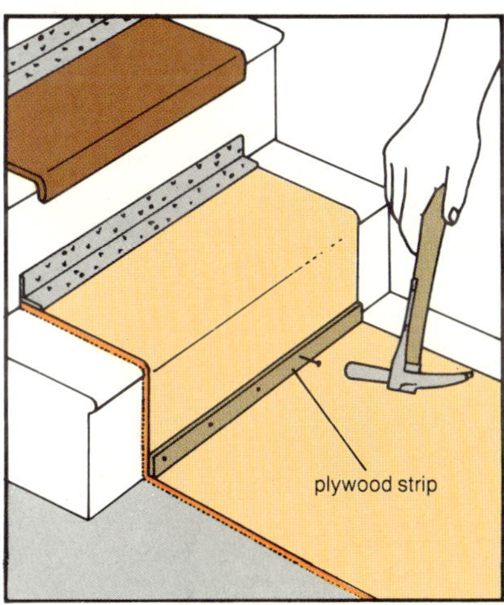

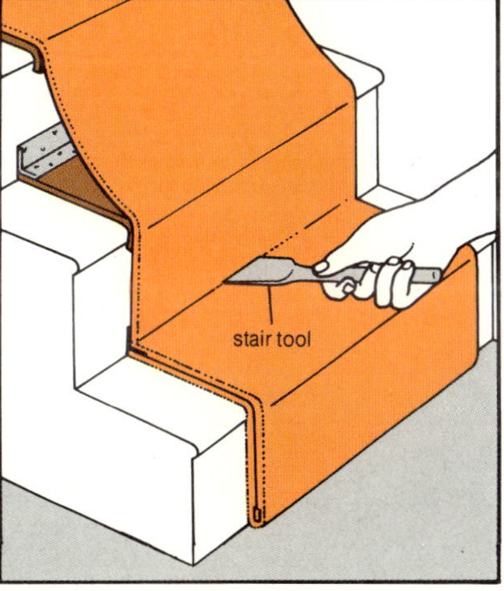

STAIRCASE TURNS

In many homes the staircase turns round a corner. To make this turn, the tread (known as a 'winder') is narrower at one end than at the other. When you have stretched the carpet across the winder, you will be left with an excess of carpet at the narrow end. You get rid of this by forming a pocket that is fixed to the riser above.

Do not fix any metal angle on the winder. Stretch the carpet taut across it, and form the pocket necessary to get rid of the extra.

THE TRICK

Hold the pocket on the riser above, and make a pencil mark on the back of the carpet at each side at the bottom of the fold. Turn the carpet back, keep the two marks you have made close into the crotch, and nail a strip of hardboard or thin plywood over the folded carpet and through into the riser.

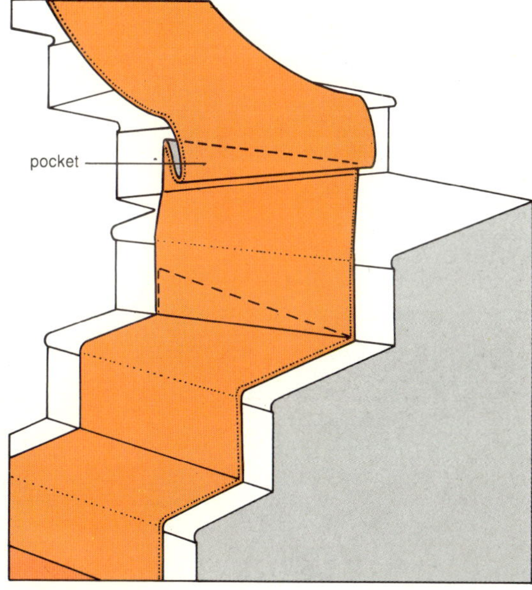

Sometimes a staircase may turn so sharply that you get an unusually deep fold that will stick up over the top of the riser. This should be folded back again, and tacked in place.

Fold the carpet back the right way, take it up the riser, and over on to the next tread. If this, too, is a winder then use the pocket method to hide the excess. Otherwise fit it in the normal manner.

A continuous length of underlay should never be taken round winders. The length should be cut into pads, and omitted from the riser, to go round the curve.

MOVING THE CARPET

To move the carpet, you will have to release it from its fixing at the top, then re-roll it, taking it away from the fixings as you go. It is important to detach the carpet correctly: roll it away from the top half of the angle, and lift it clear of the other.

Re-set the carpet on the bottom tread, this time about 75mm (3in.) from the riser, and tack it in position. Fix a 75mm (3in.) wide pad between the carpet end and the riser, trapping it under the metal angle. Now use the same hardboard strip to fix the carpet to the base of the bottom riser, and re-lay the carpet in the normal way. When you get to the top, you will have to fold under the excess 75mm (3in.) of carpet that you have gained. You can get rid of this by making a pocket on the top riser.

After another six months, the carpet should be moved again, positioning the bottom end a further 75mm (3in.) away from the stair crotch. Eventually, the excess will disappear altogether from the bottom.

CARPET TILES

Until quite recently carpet tiles were thought of by many people as being a gimmick, and not a serious contribution to solving flooring problems. In fact, they have many advantages over conventional fitted carpets.

The first big advantage of carpet tiles is the cost. If you casually compare the price per square metre, or square yard, of tiles and broadloom carpet you might think that, quality for quality, there is hardly anything in it. However a number of factors combine to make tiles cheaper in the long run. To begin with you do not need any underlay with carpet tiles (provided the sub-floor is even, and suitable) or any gripper strip round the edges.

There is less wastage. You buy tiles by the pack, and it is much easier to get closer to the exact area you require than when ordering body carpet from the roll. In cutting broadloom carpet to fit round a fireplace hearth, and into a bay and the chimney breast alcoves, for examples, the waste can be as high as 12 per cent of the total.

Tiles will last much longer than equivalent quality carpet, because you can move them around to equalize wear.

THE TRICK

To put off the day when threadbare patches first start to appear in areas of heavy traffic, about once a year you should take up tiles from near doorways and in front of the fire, etc., and exchange them for tiles in less-used parts of the room, such as under furniture.

It is not a catastrophe if you stain or damage a tile – even one in a conspicuous spot. You merely take it up and clean it (some tiles are actually washable), or exchange it for an undamaged one hidden under a piece of furniture.

You can take carpet tiles with you when you move house, and they are more certain than a broadloom carpet to fit your new rooms. You can use tiles in different colours to create patterns. When you decorate you can temporarily take up those round the edge of the room when you are painting the skirting board or door frames. Finally the advantage for the do-it-yourselfer must be that tiles are simple to lay.

LAYING THE TILES

When you buy carpet tiles you will usually find an instructional leaflet with them, giving tips on laying them, as well as hints on caring for and cleaning them. However, here is some general advice.

PREPARING THE SUB-FLOOR

The sub-floor requires that the usual preparation should be carried out (see pages 201 and 203). The backing of some makes of carpet tiles is affected by the bitumen present in many plastic floor tiles and solid composition floors. Ask about this when you buy your tiles, but if you are in any doubt you can solve the problem by putting down a paper felt underlay.

SETTING OUT THE TILES

Remember that, although you will have bought them because you wanted a carpet look and feel to your room, these are still tiles, and must be properly set out (see page 217–8). Some manufacturers recommend that the first few centre tiles are stuck down with carpet adhesive, but the others are merely butted up against them.

CUTTING

In the cutting, there are slight differences from other types of tiles. You still place the tile you want to cut on the last complete tile in the row, place a guide tile over it, and jam it up against the skirting board. However you cannot score and snap a carpet tile as you do vinyl and cork.

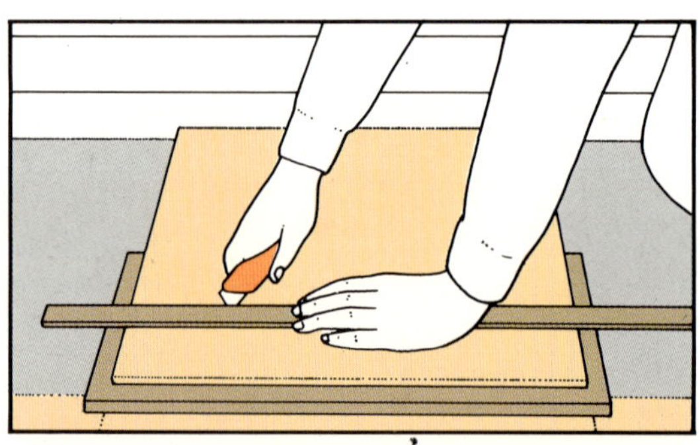

THE TRICK

Instead, mark on the face with chalk where the cut must come, then cut it with either a Stanlev knife or scissors.

FITTING THE TILES

You have to make sure that the tiles are well butted up against each other, otherwise they might start to move as people walk over them. Hand pressure is not really enough, and a lot of tradesmen use a knee kicker. For carpet tile laying, it is extremely simple to improvise a substitute. All you need is a piece of timber about the size of a float trowel. Give it a handle by fixing a short length of 25mm (1in.) diameter dowel, glued into a socket made by boring a hole in the top of the timber. The teeth of the tool can consist of two nails driven through the top so that they stick out on the underside. However the nails must not project by too much, 3mm (1/8in.) is enough.

To work the tool, place it on top of the tile so that the nails grip into the material, then push forward to butt the tile tightly against its neighbour.

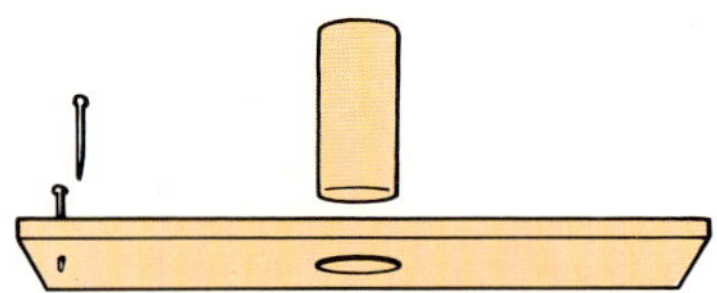

THE TRICK

If you find that the odd tile here and there moves during use; put a spot of adhesive or a length of double-sided sticky tape underneath it.

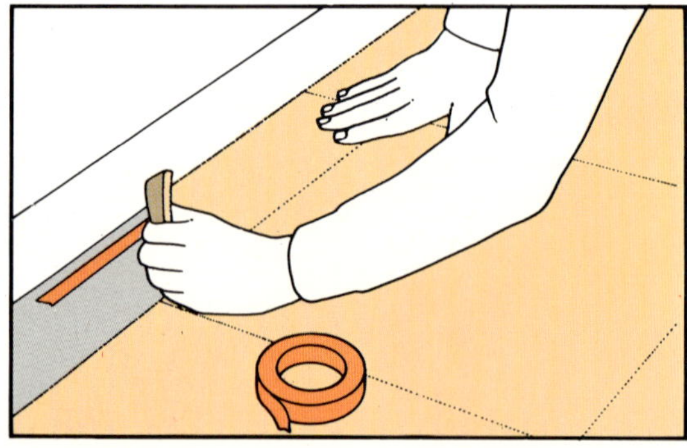

Just as with ordinary carpet, you should protect the edges of the tiles near the door with a length of aluminium carpet threshold, or a thin strip of timber.

TILES IN PATTERNS

As with any type of tile, your carpet tiles need not be in one colour. You can combine two or more to create attractive patterns. Don't forget, though, that with carpet tiles the pattern might not just be one that you are creating when the floor is first laid.

THE TRICK

If you ever transfer the tiles to a larger room – if, for instance, you move house – you will not have enough of them. It might be an idea to buy extras and use them to form a pattern.

One type of pattern can be created only with carpet tiles. If you choose a type with a distinct pile, you can lay tiles in opposite directions and create a two-tone effect, even though you have only one colour of tile.

TILED FLOORS 1

Tiles today are made from a wide variety of materials. There are vinyl tiles, cork tiles, carpet tiles (see page 216), and ceramic tiles (including quarry tiles) – all suitable for flooring use. The overwhelming majority of tiles laid in homes today are of vinyl, but the principles of laying are the same for all kinds of floor tiles. The only differences are the way you cut the tiles, and the adhesive you use for sticking them down.

THE TRICK

Always follow the recommendations of the manufacturer about glues.

Some tiles are self-adhesive – you merely peel off a backing strip before fixing them in position. Anyway, let's get down to examining the principles of tile laying.

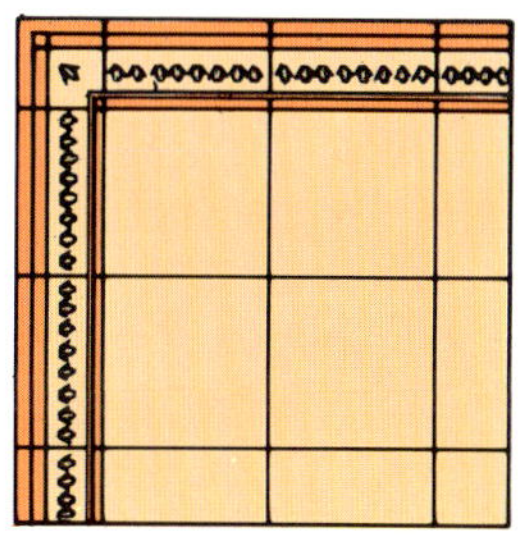

QUANTITIES

Tiles are sold in packs of nine, ten or a dozen, and it will say on the pack what area they cover – usually a square yard or a square metre.

THE TRICK

Measure your room, then multiply the width by the length to give the area. Divide this by the area the pack covers, and you will know how many packs to order.

Because tiles can be bought in such small quantities, the wastage is usually much less than with other floorings. It is vital that the tiles are arranged in a neat style – that the lines do not go off in an odd fashion, and that everything looks even and in order.

FINDING THE CENTRE OF THE ROOM

To ensure that your tiles are properly set out, you begin your tile laying not, as you might suppose, in one corner of the room, but in its centre. So you have to find that centre.

Let's begin by supposing that we are dealing with a room that is fairly true: i.e. it is more or less square or rectangular. Measure carefully two walls that face each other, determine the centre point of each, and mark it. Between these two points snap a chalk line (see page 14). Now measure the chalk line, find its centre point and mark it. Let us call this point A. You now need a line going at right angles to the chalk line, from A, and, as you probably will not have a set square that is big enough, this is how you mark it.

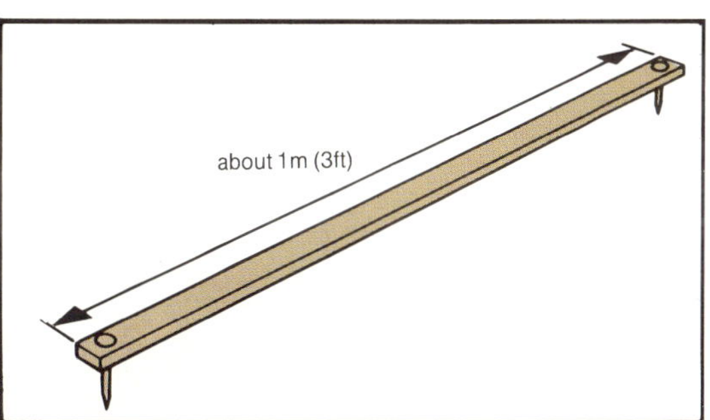

THE TRICK

You need a scriber which you can improvise from a thin length of battening about 1m (3ft) long (the length is not critical). Drive a nail through it at each end, so that the points stick out on the other side.

Put one of these nails on point A, and use the other nail to scribe another couple of marks on the chalk line, either side of A – B and C. Now, using B as centre for one of the nails, scribe an arc. Repeat this operation, using C as a centre. A chalk line struck between the meeting points of the two arcs (D and E) will give a straight line at right angles to the original chalk line.

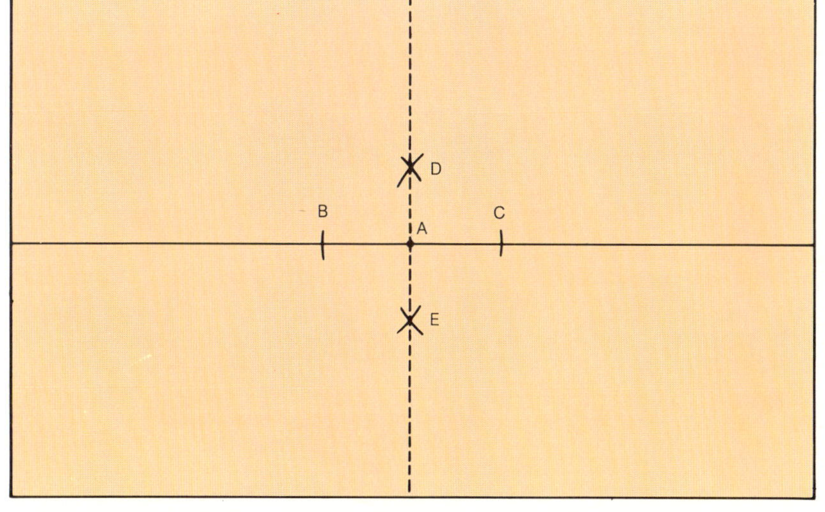

IRREGULAR-SHAPED ROOMS

Now let us move on to a room that is irregular in shape. You need a base wall from which to work, and the one that contains the doorway is as good as any. Begin by snapping a chalk line parallel to, but 75mm (3in.) away from it. Measure this line carefully, find its centre, and mark it (A as shown). Now make a scriber as described left. Place one nail on point A and use the scriber to mark points B and C on the chalk line. Use the batten again to scribe two arcs centred on B and C, meeting at D. Now snap a chalk line running through points A and D to the wall opposite – this line will be at right angles to the base wall. Find the centre point of this line (E), and use the method described above, for regular-shaped rooms, to mark a line that is at right angles to the line at E.

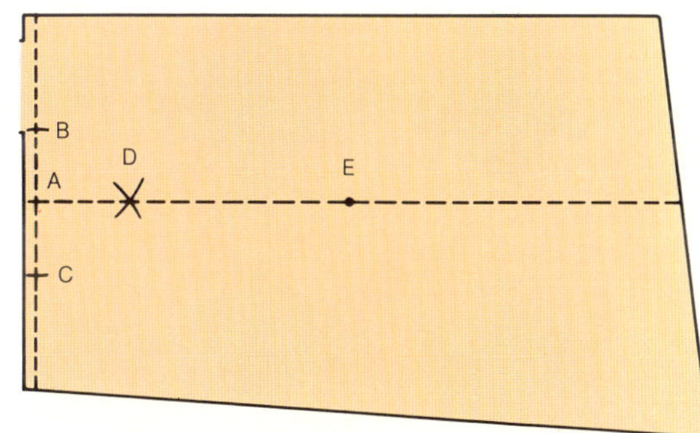

The irregularity of the room may be caused by bays and alcoves. In that case square it off as shown by snapping chalk lines that give what the tradesman calls false wall lines.

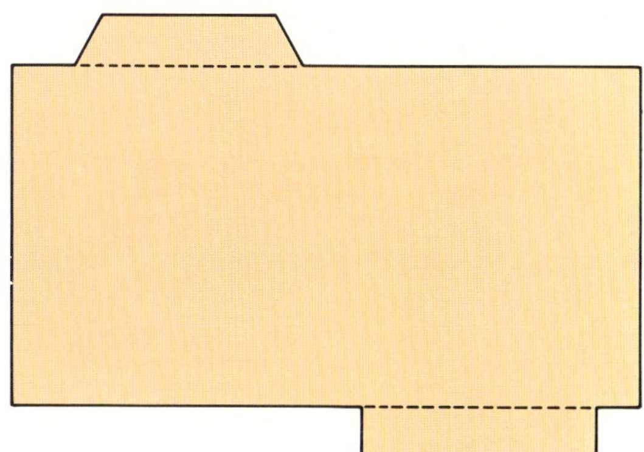

TILED FLOORS 2

SETTING OUT THE TILES

Having found the centre of the room, you can begin to set out from it. The first tile you lay is the all-important one, for you will then butt others up around it, and further tiles in turn will be butted up to these. So the positioning of this first one will determine the whole look of your floor. Normally there are four possible positions for it, as shown:

1. It can be placed centrally on line A, but just to the side of line B.
2. It can be central on line B, and just to the side of line A.
3. It can go into any corner formed by the intersection of the two lines.
4. It can go centrally on the room's middle point.

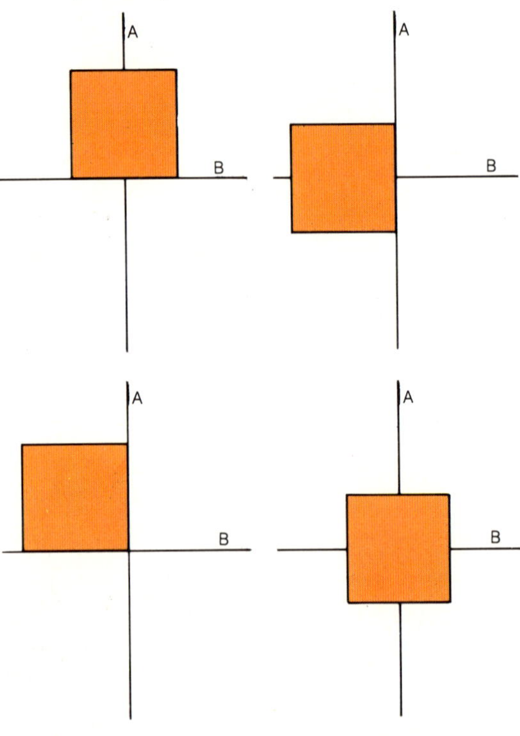

Which of these positions do you choose? The answer is simple – it is the one that gives you the largest cut tiles at the ends of the rows. It is bad practice to cut a tile so that it is less than half size, although you cannot always avoid doing so. If a tile is so small at this point, just think, with the walls running out of true, how minute it could be when you get in the corners. Small tiles not only look unattractive, but it is difficult to spread adhesive on the floor in such a small area, and the tiles might end up not properly stuck down. In fact, professional floorlayers often say that one way you can spot a do-it-yourselfer's work is by walking on the cut tiles round the border. You will feel them move, and hear them crackle under your feet, because they are not gripping the sub-floor all over.

If you are tiling a kitchen or a bathroom, then the border of cut tiles will come up to the base of the sink or bath or basin – the most likely places to have water spilt on them. The water could easily seep under the tiles, attacking adhesive, tile and sub-floor. It could do considerable damage, apart from loosening the tile. Of course, loose tiles are dangerous, as well as being unsightly. So for all these reasons your setting out must aim to give you tiles that are at least half size.

DRY SETTING

To find out which of the four positions described above is best for the first tile, unpack your tiles and set a selection of them out 'dry' as the tiler would put it: i.e. without any adhesive, or without peeling off the backing of self-adhesive tiles – and experiment. You could begin by placing a tile just to the side of line A, then setting out a row of them stretching to the wall. You will soon see whether that is the best position, or whether the tile should go centrally on the line. Now set out another dry from line B, and see what the correct placing ought to be. It will soon be obvious which of the four possible positions you should choose.

In a room that is unconventional in shape, like the one on page 217, you will have to experiment with a very thorough dry setting out to every wall and corner, to make sure that there will be no small and awkwardly shaped tiles anywhere.

DOMINANT FEATURES

Now let us go on to consider another type of room – one that has a dominant feature, for instance, a bay window and/or a fireplace hearth and chimney breast. You must take these features into account during your setting out, and centre your tiles on them as shown. However keep your tiles parallel to the original base lines. In a situation such as this, awkward or narrow cuts will have to be accepted – they are the lesser of two evils. In this diagram, incidentally, just two features are shown.

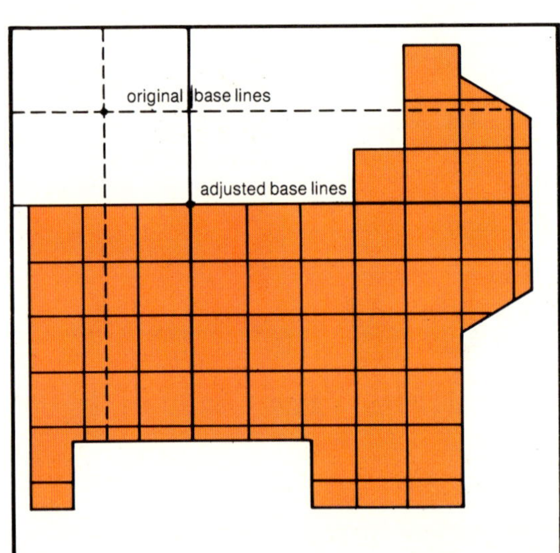

THE TRICK

It is impossible to centre the tiles on three or more features, except by chance. If you have this many to cope with, you will have to discover, by setting the tiles out dry, the two features to which you should relate the positioning of the tiles in order to get the most pleasing result.

Kitchens and bathrooms can give some awkward floor shapes. Here it would be quite impossible to find the centre of the room. All you can do if you are faced with this kind of thing is to strike a base line parallel to the doorway wall and, working from it, go in for every possible trial setting until you come up with the one that is the best compromise in offering the largest cut tiles all round the borders.

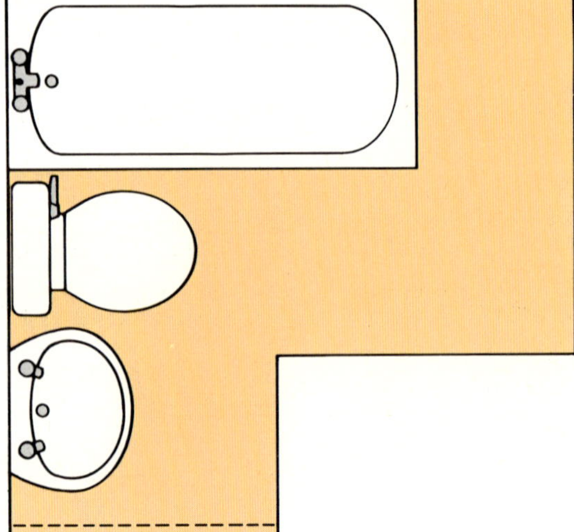

Setting out is a task that many do-it-yourselfers are inclined to skip. You probably want to get on with the job of sticking the tiles down, so that the work will be over and done with and you can admire the result, but try and resist this temptation. You will have to live with your tiled floor for a long time, and it is worth taking trouble over this initial stage, so that it will look attractive.

DIAGONAL PATTERNS

It is usual for tiles to be laid squarely, but some people prefer them in a diagonal pattern. The setting out for this is somewhat more complicated. Find the centre of the room, as explained – A (see page 217). Take a scriber, place one nail on A and mark points B, C and D and E on the base lines with the other nail. Place one pin of the batten on B, and scribe arcs at F and G. Move the batten to C and scribe arcs at F and H. Repeat this at D, marking arcs at H and I, and at E marking arcs at G and I. Now strike diagonal chalk lines through F and I and G and H. It is to these lines that you work. However carry out trial settings with the tiles dry, just as though it were a square floor, to see where your first tile should go to give the largest cut ones at the edges.

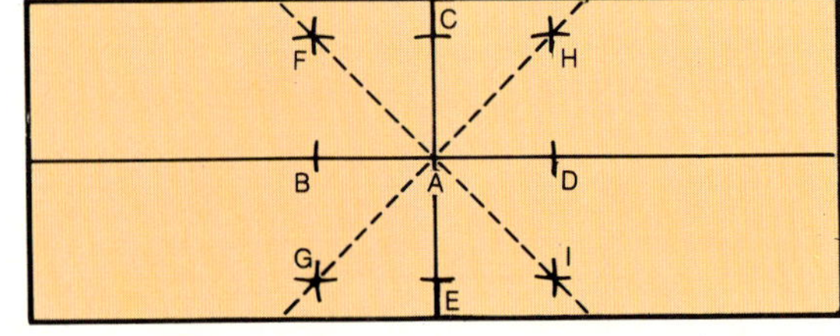

TILED FLOORS 3

FIXING THE TILES

Put the first tile in place, draw round it with a pencil, lift it, spread adhesive on the sub-floor and carefully fix the tile in the right place.

THE TRICK

Let the adhesive set, until the tile cannot be pushed out of true. Then you can go on to the rest.

First lay all the whole tiles (the field) leaving a border all round the room to be filled with cut tiles. In an average-sized room you might well divide the field into quarters, cover that section of the sub-floor with adhesive, and lay the tiles. Then go onto the second quarter, the third, and the fourth. The adhesive should be spread on the sub-floor with a proper corrugated spreader, as supplied. It acts as a depth gauge, ensuring that the correct amount of glue is applied. Take your second tile and butt it up against the first. Then go onto the others, taking care that they are all square, and the joins will make a network of straight lines.

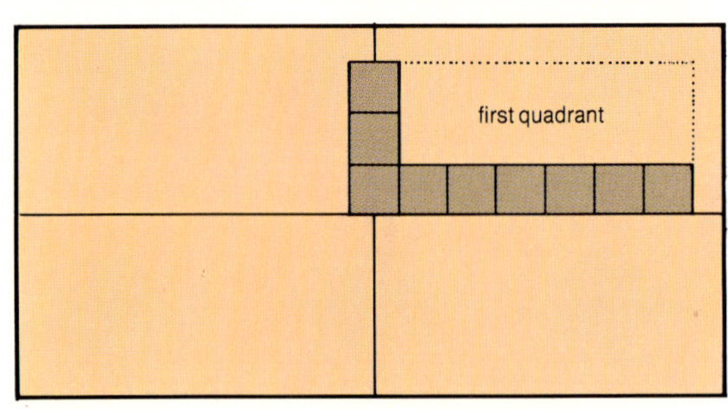

CUTTING THE TILES – METHOD 1

When the field has been laid, and the adhesive set, you can cut tiles to fill the border of the room. The principle is the same for all types of tile – it is only the implement you use that varies. The most straightforward example of tile cutting is a simple infill at the end of a row of vinyl tiles. You don't need a ruler as there are no measurements to be taken.

Take the tile to be cut (A) and place it on top of the last complete tile stuck down in the row (B). Now take a third tile (C); this is a guide, so it must be square and not damaged in any way. Place tile C on top of tile A, but jam it hard up against the skirting board. Make sure tile A is correctly positioned, and draw your knife across its face and along the edge of tile C. In the case of cork and vinyl you will then be able to snap the tile in two. The part of tile A not covered by tile C will fit the vacant space. The cut edge of the tile goes against the skirting board, and its factory edge butts up against tile B.

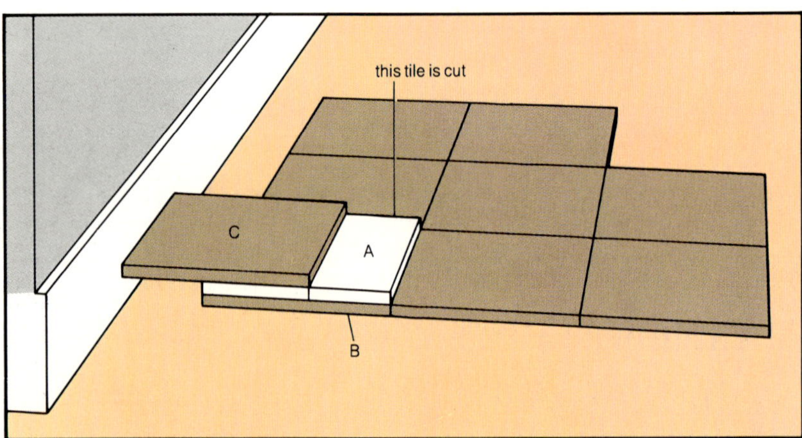

THE TRICK

Whenever you are fixing a cut tile, aim to get factory edge to factory edge for a neater finish.

In some instances, however, more than one cut will be called for. The simplest example is in the corner of a room, where the tile must first be cut to width, then to length. In all other instances it is better to mark the tile with a pencil and cut it to size later on, rather than try to cut it on the spot, because until the marking is fully completed you cannot see exactly where the cuts must start and finish.

You may have to cut a tile to fit round an irregular-shaped object such as a lavatory pan. In such instances you still place the tile to be cut on the last complete tile in the row, then mark it using a thin offcut of full-width tile. Jam the offcut against the lavatory base, then take both pencil and offcut round the pan, marking a pencil line on the tile that has to be cut. Then cut the tile with a knife or scissors. If inexperienced, make this cut tile slightly oversize, then finally trim it to a perfect fit with glasspaper or a file. Another way is to adapt the templating method described for one-piece fitting of sheet vinyl (see page 210).

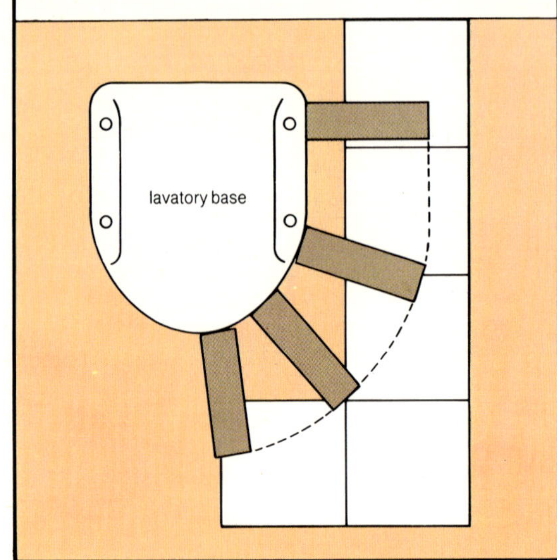

CUTTING – METHOD 2

Another method of cutting is to lay the field complete except for a border one and half tiles wide, instead of just half a tile.

THE TRICK

Place the tile to be cut (A) on the sub-floor against the last one in the row. Place guide tile B, half on top of tile A, and jam it hard against the skirting board. Draw your knife along the edge of tile B and across the face of tile A, and cut it.

Eventually tile B goes against the field, and the cut portion of tile A fills the space between it and the wall. In the meantime, place them dry one on top of the other on the field beside the space they will occupy, until you can fix the whole border at one go.

This method gives you a much wider area to work in when spreading the adhesive on the sub-floor, and it is easier to ensure you have covered the entire surface.

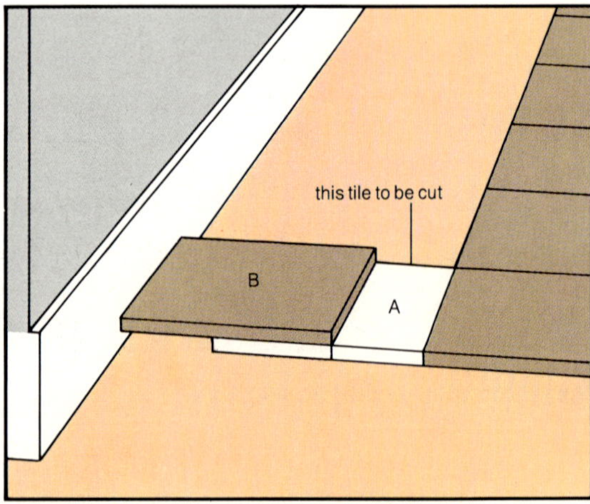

CENTRE HOLES

Sometimes you have to cut a hole in the middle of a tile, to take a pipe to a radiator or washbasin. Push the tile up against it on two sides, and mark on its edges the centre of the pipe. Using a set square, draw a line from these points towards the centre of the tile. The point where the two lines cross is the correct position for the centre of the pipe. Cut a hole here, either using a brace and bit, or by drawing round a coin of appropriate size and cutting with a knife. To fit the tile round the pipe you must make a cut from this hole back towards the wall.

THE TRICK

Try scoring the tile on the back (the position of the cut does not have to be accurate), then snapping the tile. An irregular break will be less obvious when the tile is stuck down on the floor.

It is much quicker to stick the entire border down at one go – it is less fiddly, and you are less likely to miss parts of the surface as you spread the adhesive on the sub-floor. So that you will know the correct position for the cut tile, place it dry on the last tile in the field, adjacent to the space it has to fill, until you are ready to stick the whole border.

CERAMIC TILES

The methods of laying ceramic floor tiles are exactly as for other tiles, but there are one or two additional points to watch.

In the first place, ceramic tiles are much heavier than any other form of floor covering, and they place quite a strain on a suspended wooden floor (with a direct-to-earth one, it obviously does not matter). A suspended timber floor in good condition is fully capable of supporting this extra weight, but the strain might be too much for one that is faulty. So, if you are thinking of laying ceramic floor tiles on a timber floor, walk across it and see whether it seems firm and strong. If it does – as it ought to in a house that is not very old – then you can go ahead. However, if you are in any doubt it might be better to settle for another kind of floor, or to call in a surveyor and ask his advice.

THE TRICK

No matter how firm it is, a timber floor should first be covered with hardboard.

Ceramic tiles need their own specific adhesive – a cement-like material – which is combed on like any other adhesive with a corrugated spreader.

CUTTING AND FIXING

The most difficult aspect of ceramic tiles is cutting them, because they are tough and thick and a knife and scissors would make no impression on them. The tradesman uses an implement known as a tiling spike. This is a short length of tough metal about 100–150mm (4–6in.) long, going to a point at the end, and with a rubber or plastic knob at the other end to protect his hands. When marking a tile with this tool, you use either methods already explained (see page 220).

When marking the tile, you must press quite firmly, for the aim is to cut though the glaze on the face of the tile. Then cut through the glaze overlapping down the sides of the tile. The professional then places the tile on a firm surface, with just the waste portion overhanging. He presses down with a short, sharp jerk on this waste, and the tile snaps cleanly along the line. It sounds easy and it is, but there is undoubtedly a knack to it, and the do-it-yourselfer might not have as much success in cutting thick, tough floor tiles in this way as he would in dealing with thin wall tiles.

You should buy, as well as the spike, one of those tile cutters that looks like a cross between tin shears and a pair of pliers. You grip the tile in the jaws of this cutter, the score line right on its cutting edges, then press, and the tile should split neatly in two. These cutters, do, in fact, have a cutting wheel for scoring the glaze of a tile, but it is not very convenient to use this when you are marking, so do the scoring with a tiler's spike.

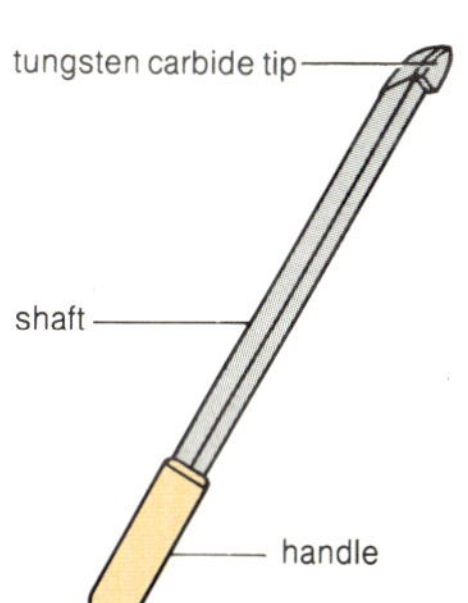

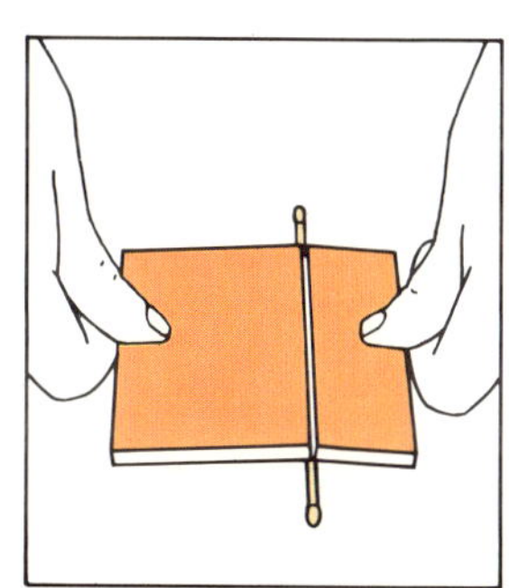

SPACING THE TILES

Most tiles are butted firmly up against each other, but you must leave a space between ceramic tiles because they expand and contract according to the weather. Most British tiles have two little lugs on each edge, which you match up to the lugs of the neighbouring tile to ensure correct spacing. Many imported from abroad do not have lugs, however.

To ensure correct spacing between these, take some thin timber – about 5mm (¼in.) wide – and cut it into very small lengths, which you stick between the tiles to act as spacers. Pull the timber out once the glue has begun to grip. Alternatively, use matchsticks.

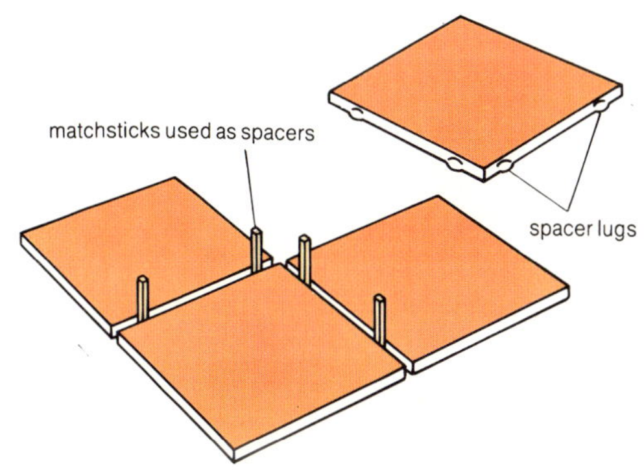

GROUTING

The space between the tiles has to be filled to stop dirt from collecting, and you do this with a material known as grout. Make sure the adhesive has fully set, however, before you walk across the tiles to apply the grout. Some grout comes ready mixed, but others are a powder to which you add water. A sponge or a squeegee mop are ideal for applying the grout. Dip your sponge into the grout, then wipe it across the face of the tiles, pushing it down into the gap wipe off the excess. Leave the grout to settle.

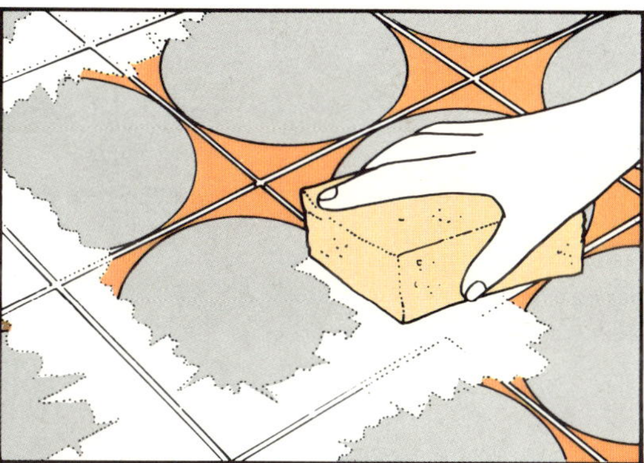

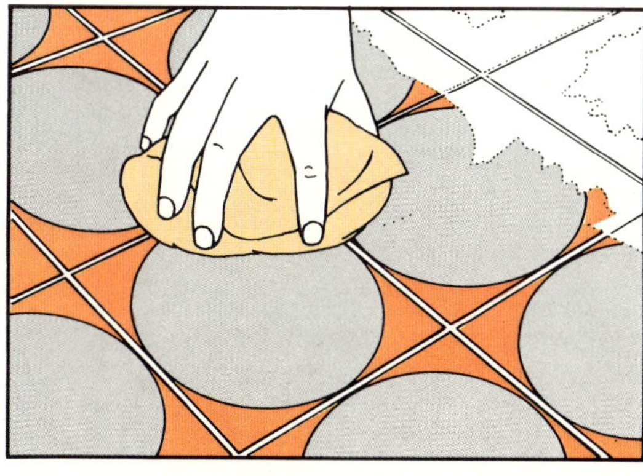

THE TRICK

Finally polish the face of the tiles with a clean cloth, buffing them up and at the same time getting rid of any grout that has hardened on the surface.

PATTERNED FLOORS

Tiles can easily be used to create patterns. The most obvious example is the draught-board pattern, which consists of alternate black and white (or dark and light) tiles, but there are many other possibilities.

PLANNING THE PATTERN

If you decide on a patterned floor, then you must work it out properly.

THE TRICK

Measure the room, and draw its plan on to a sheet of paper. Draw in small squares to represent the tiles. Now colour in the squares to create a design.

Then have your chosen plan in front of you when you come to lay the floor, and follow it closely.

A patterned floor complicates the business of ordering the right number of tiles for your room of course. First find out the quantities in which the tiles of your choice are sold, and work out a pattern that does not involve too much wastage – although they are sold in such small quantities that you should not have much of a problem.

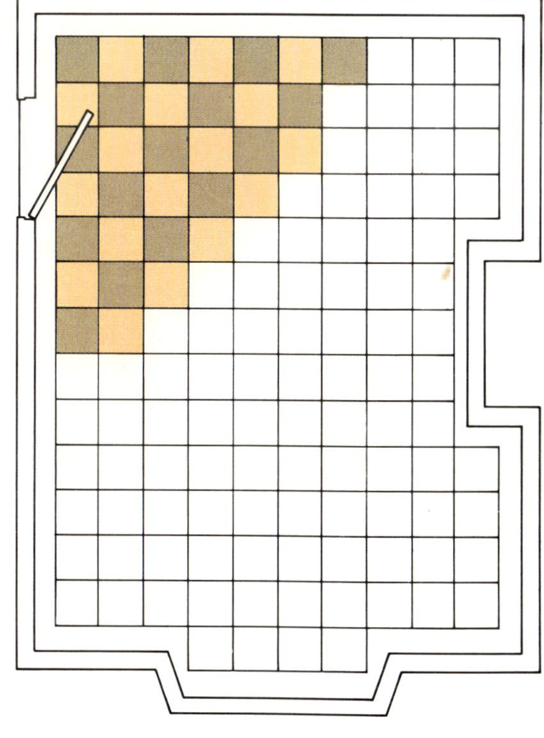

SANDING AND SEALING 1

PREPARATION

As your sanded floor is going to be fully on view, it is vital to replace any broken or damaged boards. Your new wood will probably not be the same colour, so try to put the new boards in inconspicuous spots.

THE TRICK

If a defective board is in an obvious spot, replace it with one take up from another part of the room. Your new wood can then take the place of this latter board.

Go over the floor, carefully punching down the nail heads well below the surface. You will need a hefty punch and hammer for this. For the best results, the nails should be covered up with matching stopping.

The reason for driving the nails home is that, if left proud, they might tear the sandpaper. It is infuriating to fit a new sanding belt only to have it torn seconds later by a nail. You should also make sure that no tacks are left either. Finally, any traces of floor polish could prevent the final treatment from drying out properly.

THE TRICK

Get rid of it by going over the floor with steel wool dipped in white spirit. Wear gloves to protect your hands.

SANDING MACHINES

You must hire a proper flooring sander. They look something like a heavy-duty lawn mower, and they sand by means of a belt of abrasive material. Don't be tempted to use the disc sanding attachment for your electric drill: its action is wrong. You need to work along the grain of the boards which a belt sander does, and a disc sander goes across it. As a result, a disc will cause slight scratching that will show up very clearly once the seal has been applied.

You also need an edging sander, to tackle the thin strip all round the room that the other sander cannot reach, because it is too near to the skirting board. This is a disc machine but your electric drill cannot substitute for this as the work is very heavy. The professional edging sander is a much more robust tool, and it is worth paying the small loan charge.

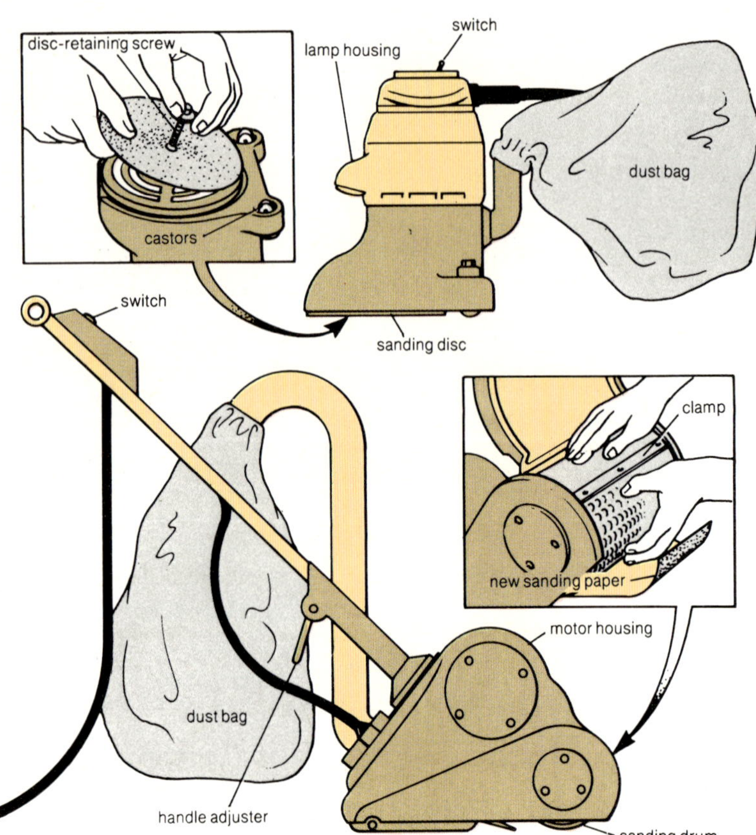

USING THE SANDER

When you first switch on the motor of your floor sander, the sanding belt will begin to rotate, but it will not immediately be in contact with the floor. You have to operate a lever which lowers it onto the floor. It is vital that the sander should never be stationary while the moving belt is touching the boards, because it will make permanent gouge marks.

Fit abrasive paper onto the machine, and tighten up the tension of the drive belt then set yourself up in position. It does not matter where you begin so long as you work along the length of the boards, not across them.

Switch on the motor, then operate the lowering mechanism. When the abrasive paper touches the floor, it will start to scream as it bites into the wood. Immediately let the machine move forwards. If you try to restrain it, this is when it will cause damage. However, it must not move forward too quickly – many have a belt that you strap round your back, to help you to control it.

On a floor where not too much stripping is needed, let the machine go forward to the far end of the room, then lift up the belt, before it cuts into the skirting board. Now lower it once more, and, with the belt still moving, pull the machine back to your starting point, where you must raise the belt once more. If the floor looks all right, go forwards and backwards over the next strip. You must raise the moving belt when you change direction, to prevent the sanding paper making unsightly score marks.

If your boards are in very bad shape, you may have to start off with the coarse paper going backwards and forwards over a small stretch, about 1m. (3ft), gradually extending this as you bring the boards into reasonable condition. Then, when you work with the finer grades of paper, you can cover the whole span at one go.

Your first passes over the boards will be with coarse paper. When you have got the worst off, go over them again with medium paper, before finally finishing off with fine.

You will have started the sanding about 1m. (3ft) from one wall – the length of the machine and the space you take up behind it. When you have finished sanding the room from one wall, turn the machine round and work in the other direction.

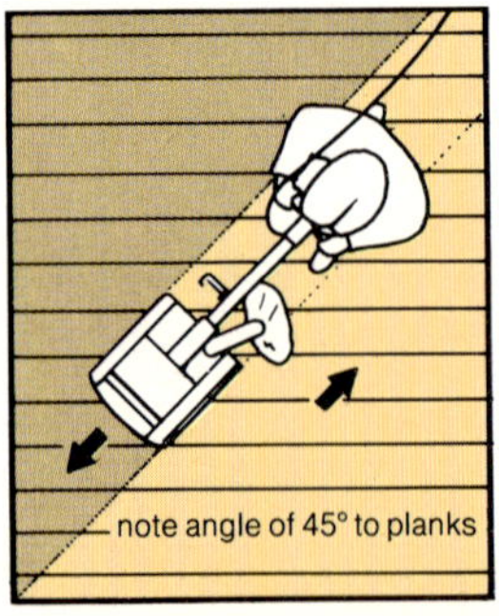

THE TRICK

Your boards may have warped so that they curl up at the edges. In that case, sand them with coarse paper at an angle of 45° until you bring them down flat. Then you can go along the grain with finer paper to finish off.

SANDING THE EDGES

The edge sanding is done with a portable, hand-held disc sander. Don't put the whole disc flat on the surface, but keep just one tip of it in contact with the work, otherwise the load will be too strong for the machine, which might stall.

THE TRICK

You must work along the length of the boards when working with the edge sander, because, if you go across them, you will make scratches that the finishing treatment will highlight.

This is easy enough along the long edges at the side of your main runs, but trickier at the ends. You can guard against any scratches showing by giving these ends a final hand sanding, or even using a powered orbital sander on them.

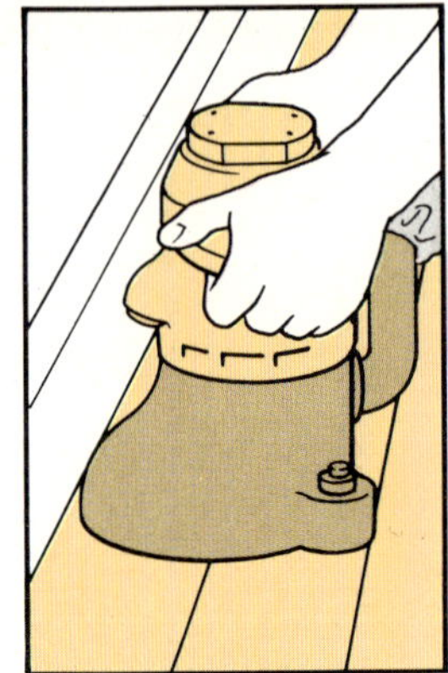

THE FINAL CLEAN-UP

The sanding will, inevitably, produce a lot of dust. You will cause dust when working with the edging sanders – tools that do not normally have a dust bag. You must remove all this dust before applying the finishing treatment. The bulk of it can be swept up, or removed with a vacuum cleaner, but there will still be some lying around. You must go over the floor thoroughly with a clean, dry cloth, which you should shake regularly outside.

Whatever the job in hand, use Pro-Techs.

The first-ever range of specially designed DIY gloves.

The trick of any successful DIY job, as any professional will tell you, is to use the right tools for the job.

Yet it's surprising how few DIY-ists use the right gloves for the job.

Particularly when you think of the hell hands can go through.

That's why they need protecting.

And that's why Marigold have designed Pro-Techs.

The first-ever range of specially designed DIY gloves for professionals and enthusiasts alike.

Whatever the job in hand, get your hands on a pair of Pro-Techs.

You'll find them at larger DIY stores everywhere.

We think you'll find them just the trick.

LRC Products Ltd., North Circular Rd., E4 8QA.

PVC Pro-Techs.
A chemically resistant glove that protects hands from harmful paint strippers, wood preservatives and the like.

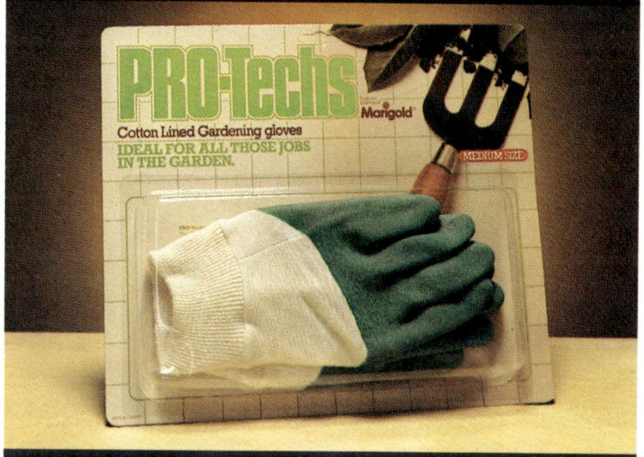

Gardening Pro-Techs.
A hard-wearing cotton lined latex glove that prevent green fingers from becoming grazed fingers.

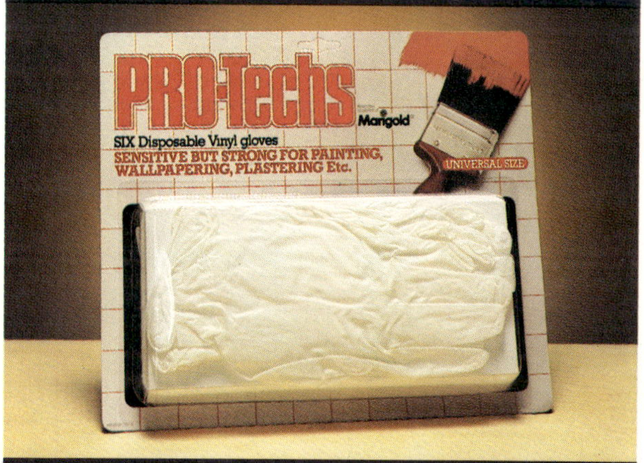

Disposable Pro-Techs.
A sensitive yet strong vinyl glove for those messy one-offs like painting and decorating.

Heavy-Duty Pro-Techs.
A super rugged leather and cotton glove that can tackle – and tame – the heaviest manual work.

SANDING AND SEALING 2

Many people do not really know why a floor is sanded before being treated with a seal. The main reason for sanding floorboards is to clean them. Over the years they will have been treated with a variety of stains and other treatments, and paint, etc may have been splashed on them. Apart from this, dirt will have become ingrained. Sanding gets rid of all this accumulation by removing a top layer of wood about 15mm (1/16in.) thick. It will also get rid of any small dents and make the surface smooth, but this is only secondary.

PREPARATION

If your boards have not been stained and polished, then sanding may not be necessary. If they are new, or even if old but have been protected under carpets or linoleum since they were laid, they are probably ready to receive the seal as they stand. They may have surface dirt, but that can be removed by less strenuous methods than sanding. Give them a good scrub with a solution of detergent in hot water. Detergent is best as the dirt is held suspended in the solution and can be mopped up. Make sure you wash thoroughly, as the finished result will depend on how clean the boards are. Pay particular attention to the nail holes, because dirt will almost certainly have lodged there and, if left, will cause 'black eyes' shining through the finished work. Finally, rinse down well, and leave everything to dry. It may seem bad practice to recommend wet treatment on bare timber, but there is nothing wrong with a single treatment like this.

Once you have scrubbed the boards you may find a few paint marks left by builders. You can get rid of these either by scraping or with a paint remover. However, if the boards have been stained, then they will have to be sanded (see page 222).

APPLYING THE SEAL

A floor that has been stripped needs protection, and modern wood seals are ideal for this. They have a transparent finish that highlights the wood, and they bond its fibres together. The seal is also flexible. You can get seals with high gloss, matt or satin finishes. Make one final test before you start the finishing treatment. Apply a little seal in an inconspicuous spot, and leave it to dry overnight. Next morning rub the seal with the edge of a coin. If the finish is unaffected, you can go ahead. If it produces a white powder, there is something on the surface incompatible with the seal, and your preparation has not been thorough enough. You must therefore carry on with further sanding.

Your first coat of seal should be applied with a cloth pad, and rubbed well into the wood to ensure the maximum bond. If the room is well ventilated, the floor should be dry enough to take the second coat in six hours. Use a brush for this second coat, which should be a thin one, and well brushed out with no puddles of liquid lying around – thin coats dry out more quickly, and reach a tough, durable state more rapidly.

In some cases an extra coat may be needed – it depends on the material and on the standard of finish you require – and this can be applied, again by brush, once the second one has dried. For a really superb finish, rub the last coat but one with very fine steel wool, to get rid of any specks of dust that might have settled on it, before you apply the final coat.

When the last coat has dried you can walk over it in soft-soled shoes, but do so with care, since the seal goes on curing for about 48 hours, and the floor will not be at its toughest until then.

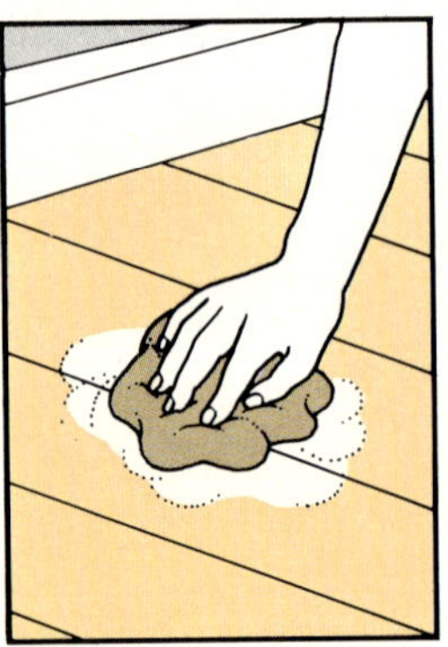

DYEING THE FLOOR

You may not like the colour of the boards once you have stripped them. Use a wood dye on them, before the seal. Apply this dye with a cloth pad, liberally and evenly. If you apply the dye sparingly, it will look patchy.

These dyes can only darken timber – you cannot change the wood to a lighter colour – and you must choose right at the start the shade you want, for you cannot darken the colour with extra applications. Leave the dye to dry for 24 hours, then seal as above.

CARING FOR THE FLOOR

A floor that has been sealed will last longer if you give it a good polishing annually. You can lengthen its life by giving it an extra light polishing once a month. Dust it regularly, for dust can scratch the surface. Spills should be wiped up with a damp cloth.

When the film of seal starts to wear away, re-seal it before it gets worn right through to the timber. You need to treat only the affected area, not the whole floor. Lightly sand it by hand, using fine paper, dust off, then apply one coat of seal.

SANDING PARQUET

A parquet or woodblock floor can be treated in a similar manner to boards. Because of the patterns in which parquet floors are laid, the grain will be going in opposite directions. Therefore the floor should be sanded twice, in directions at right angles to each other. Make sure that the final sanding, with fine paper, is very thorough, to remove all scratch marks.

PAINTING THE FLOOR

Treating timber floors with paint is a fairly recent fashion. Paint has no special advantages over timber seals (in fact, it won't wear so well) but it does come in a wide range of colours, and you can make your floor all one colour, or paint patterns on it.

Several patterns suggest themselves. You could treat separate boards in a range of different colours, for instance. Alternatively, you might find the centre of the floor, improvise compasses from a nail, a piece of string and a pencil, and draw a series of concentric circles. Paint these in different colours for a target effect. A large draught-board pattern is another possibility, or you could draw diagonals from each corner of the room, and paint in contrasting colours the triangles you have made. As you can see, the possibilities are endless.

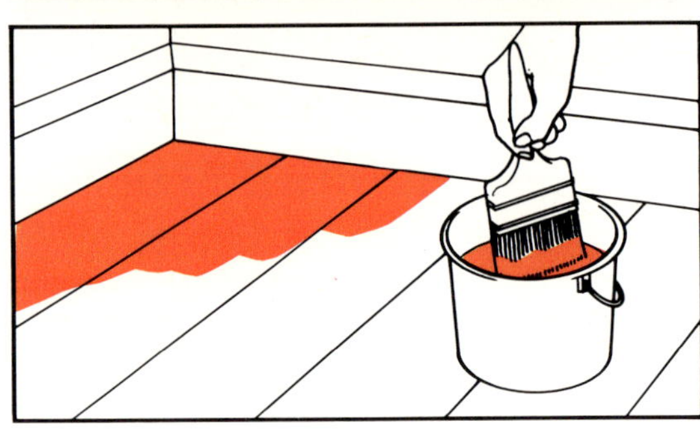

But how practical are they? A painted floor will not stand up to a lot of wear and tear, especially downstairs where people will walk across it in outdoor shoes. Upstairs however – in a bedroom, for instance – where it is more likely that you will be wearing slippers, the floor might remain unscathed for two or three years, more if you touched it up occasionally.

The paint to use is a top-quality liquid gloss, and you should start off with clean, bare timber, which you first prime, then undercoat. Finish off with two top coats of gloss. Your preparation could consist of sanding (see page 222) but because of the cost of hiring the machines and buying the paper, it might work out cheaper to line the floor with hardboard. Compare prices locally before you start work.

CHIPBOARD FLOORS

Many people regard chipboard, like hardboard, as just a material for lining a poor sub-floor. In many modern houses chipboard is used instead of floorboards. It can also be an attractive material in its own right and, when given two or three coats of seal, it forms a good and economical floor. Warmth and added interest can be created if you scatter rugs here and there, especially in areas of heavy traffic.

If you wonder whether rugs on such a floor would be dangerous, don't worry. Floor seals do not have a slippery finish and, in any case, the surface of the chipboard would tend to grip the rug.

THE TRICK

However you could, if you wish, hold the rug in place with double-sided carpet tape.

INSTALLING A CHIPBOARD FLOOR

You must use flooring-grade chipboard, which usually comes in panels 2.44 × 0.60m (8 × 2ft). The panels are tongued and grooved on the edges and all you need to fix them is a little glue smeared on the tongues. You partly slot the tongue into the groove, run a bead of woodworking adhesive into the trough, and tap the panel home with a hammer. Protect the edge of the board with an offcut of timber – waste chipboard with a groove that can locate on the tongue of the panel is best of all.

REMOVING THE SKIRTING BOARD

You need space at the ends of the room to carry out this operation, and to create this you must take off the skirting board. This is not a difficult job. Skirting boards are merely nailed in place, and you prise them away by driving an old chisel behind them – you will probably need a hammer to drive it home – and levering. As you do, you will see where the nails are, and it is at this point that you apply pressure. When the job is finished, re-fix the skirting in the same way, by nailing it. Before you start laying the chipboard, make good with cellulose filler or plaster any damage you have caused to the wall which will be visible when the job is finished.

LAYING

As you hammer the panels home when fixing them, you will probably find that glue oozes up from the gap. Wipe this up with a damp cloth immediately, or it will spoil the result. No matter how quickly you act, however, some glue might soak into the board and, as a result, once you have applied the seal the boards will be a little lighter at the edges.

THE TRICK

To avoid this, many people give the sheets the first coat of seal before they start work.

The sequence for laying the chipboard is just as for hardboard. You begin in one corner of the room, leaving a gap between the board and the wall. It is not necessary to scribe the chipboard to fit the wall.

To make sure you do not close the gap round the edge of the first boards as you hammer neighbouring ones on to them, drive wedges of waste timber between board and wall. Just as with hardboard, when you come to the end of the first run you will have to saw a panel to length to fit the available space, and you break the bond: i.e. ensure that the joins do not coincide, by using the offcut to start off the next row of panels.

The panels will also have to be cut to width, when you come to the far end of the room, in order to fit the space available. None of this cutting, however, need be very accurate, because you have to leave a gap which will be covered by the skirting. At the end of the runs, there will not be enough room for you to wield a hammer.

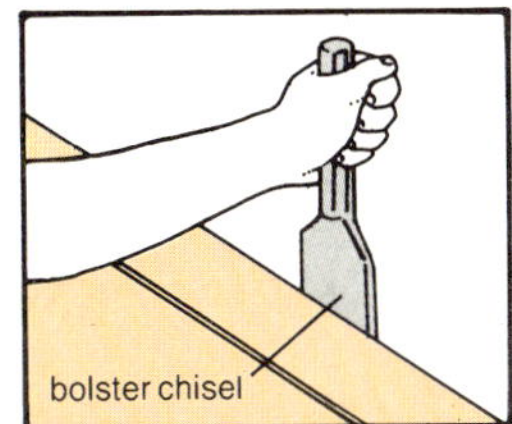

THE TRICK

There you should use a bolster chisel. Jam the bolster down the side of the board and lever the board home.

When the chipboard has been laid, you can finish it. A seal is the ideal finish and this is applied as on floorboards (see page 224). This finish is very durable, and is not out of place even in kitchens and bathrooms. Where a lot of water is likely to get spilt, however, it is better to cover the chipboard with vinyl in sheet or tile form.

FLOATING FLOORS

Chipboard is also a very handy material for topping off what is known as a floating floor. This is a name given to a floor which covers-up crudely laid concrete, or a concrete floor which has deteriorated over the years. Cover the concrete with sheets of polystyrene – 12mm (½in.) is the minimum recommended thickness – which smooths out slight hollows and humps in the concrete and acts as a cushion against sharp ridges. The polystyrene is then covered with sheets of 1000-gauge polythene to keep damp at bay, if necessary. Both polystyrene and polythene are available from builder's merchants.

The polystyrene is merely loose-laid on the sub-floor, the sheets being butted together. Cutting it to fit – it comes in sheets 2.44 × 1.22m (8 × 4ft) – is easy; use a Stanley knife. The polythene is then loose-laid on top. The joints of this material should, however, overlap by 150mm (6in.), and the overlap should be taped down with a vapour-resistant tape about 35mm (1½in.) wide. This again you can get from a builder's merchant.

THE TRICK

At the edges of the room, the polythene is turned up the wall by 100mm (4in.) and then held in place by the skirting when this is re-fixed.

You then lay the chipboard just as though you were dealing with an ordinary sub-floor, and it can be sealed or covered with whatever flooring material you like.

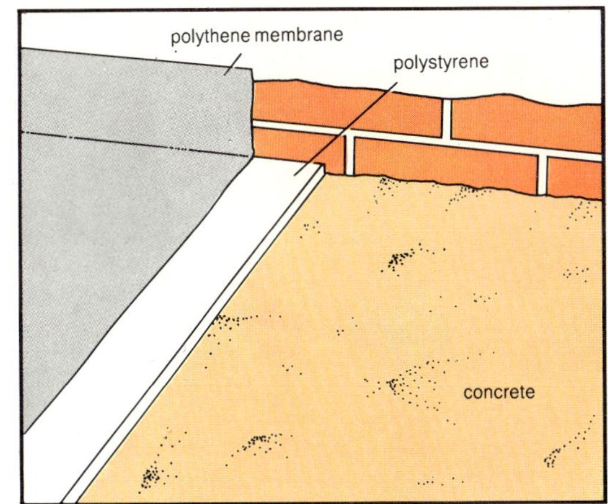

ALISTAIR
MACKINTOSH LTD
ALISTAIR MACKINTOSH LTD
BALLERLY ROAD
GARRETS GREEN
BIRMINGHAM B33 OSL
TELEPHONE: 021-784 6800

DECORATING

PREPARATION 1

The preparation is the most tiresome and tiring part of any decoration job, but you ignore it at your peril.

In essence, the preparation consists of ensuring that the surfaces you are going to decorate will be stable, clean, dry and suitably primed for the decorative finish.

CLEARING THE ROOM

Clear as completely as you can before you begin. If you can take all the furniture out into another room, then do so. Otherwise, arrange it all together in the centre of the room, and throw dust sheets over it. Leave enough room to place access equipment over or round it. Pictures and ornaments must be taken down. The curtains must be unhooked and the curtain track unscrewed, so that you can deal with the window frames properly. Lampshades need to be temporarily removed, also door furniture.

You should dust all surfaces, and vacuum clean everywhere.

Ideally, too, you ought to take up your floor coverings but, if you have fitted carpets, here's a dodge.

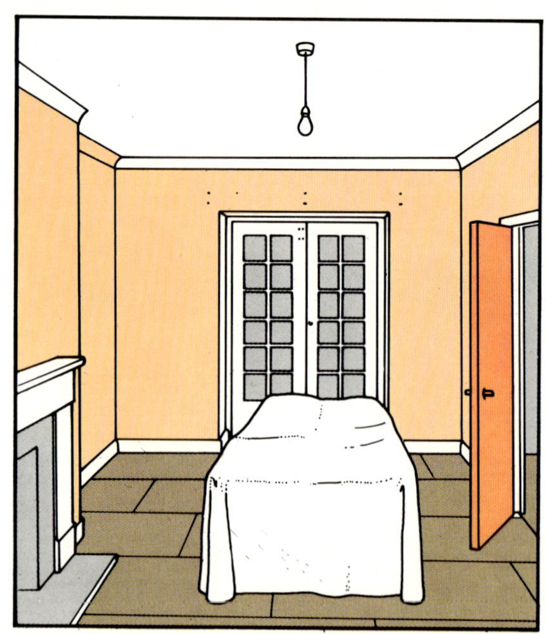

THE TRICK

Place dust sheets on the floor – which you ought to do whether you have a fitted carpet or not – and fasten them all round the edges with masking tape. Position this masking tape carefully so that it just covers the edge of the carpet, but allows you to work on the skirting board.

STRIPPING OFF WALLPAPER

To strip wallpaper, you need a bucket, a large (100 or 125mm (4 or 5in.)) brush and a 75mm (3in.) scraper.

Pour some water into your bucket, then brush it on to the walls, taking care that you do not get any on the floor. The water gets through to the glue behind and breaks down the old paste. Stripping powders added to the water make it cling to the surface, and not run off down the wall uselessly.

THE TRICK

The professional will squeeze a few drops of washing-up liquid into the stripping water, as this seems to have the same effect.

Work on one wall at a time, or begin on the ceiling (if it is papered). Soak it thoroughly once, then give it another dousing. You must let the water do the work. If you try to remove the paper too soon, you will dig into the plaster below, gouging out holes that you will then have to fill. Paper should peel away from the wall in long strips.

When all the paper is off, go over the wall again with water and the scraper, getting rid of any old lumps of paste and paper. Then move on.

WASHABLE AND PAINTED-OVER PAPERS

Score the surface in some way, to make holes through which the water can pass. You can make holes with a scraper or a wire brush, but you might be better off using coarse glasspaper. Papers that have been painted over should be treated in the same way.

ANAGLYPTAS

Use a sharp-pointed putty knife, held with the flat of the blade at an acute angle to the wall, to dig into the material and strip off the top layer of paper. The bottom one can then be treated just like ordinary wallpaper. A Supaglypta (see page 252) is more difficult to deal with; you should rake its surface with a wire brush.

VINYLS

Vinyls are easiest of all papers to strip as they consist of a top layer of plastic bonded to paper underneath. Take hold of one corner of the plastic surface, and peel it away in one length. You can strip off the whole length while standing on the floor. The backing paper then stays on the wall to act as a lining, and the new surface goes directly on top of it. When you have two layers of backing paper left on, then you should strip them off just like ordinary wallpapers.

TOOLS

You cannot decorate a room and stand on the floor the whole time; you must have some means of access at all stages during decorating. An ordinary pair of household steps simply will not do for many operations.

SCAFFOLD BOARDS

Go to your local timber yard and buy some unplaned timber at least 230mm (9in.) wide and 40mm (1½in.) thick and long enough to suit the size of your room. Professional scaffold boards are shaped at the ends and strengthened with metal strips.

The professional usually suspends his board between two pairs of steps. You can borrow an additional pair. Otherwise, you will have to improvise, by using anything strong enough to take your weight. Be sure that everything is stable before you risk clambering up because you can have a very nasty fall indeed. When you come to tackle the hall and landing, a more complicated set-up will be called for (see page 261).

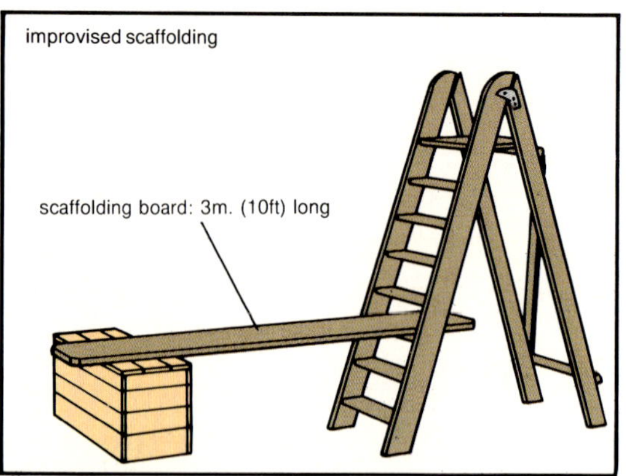
improvised scaffolding

SCRAPERS

Scrapers look exactly like the filling knives you use for stopping up holes, but they are in fact totally different. A scraper needs a rigid blade to work properly, whereas the filling knive must be flexible. You need both.

Scrapers come in a range of sizes. For stripping off wallpaper, use a 75mm (3in.) blade; while for paintwork you should go for a 50mm (2in.) blade. Scrapers with a 25mm (1in.) wide blade are available. A good-quality scraper will be 'tanged': i.e. its blade will run right through the handle.

SHAVE HOOKS

For scraping off narrow strips, the professional would use a shave hook. There are three types of shave hook: triangular for flat surfaces, heart-shaped for curved mouldings, and the combination hook, so called because it combines the shapes of the other two.

To use a scraper, place the blade on the surface and push it upwards, or away from you on a horizontal surface. To use a shave hook you pull downwards, or towards you. You can use much stronger pressure with a shave hook. Decorators prefer them, when burning off window frames, as the paintwork does not have to be so soft. Thus there is less risk of cracking the glass.

shave hooks and how to use them

PREPARATION 2

WASHING DOWN

Walls and ceilings which have been painted must be washed down to get rid of all dirt and grease. When washing down, begin at the bottom of the wall and work upwards. The reason is that, if you worked the other way about, the dirt you loosened would cause a build-up of grime lower down the wall which would be very difficult to remove.

You need a bucket, plus a rag or sponge and (preferably decorator's) detergent. Mix the detergent with water according to the instructions, soak your rag in it, then wring it out. Rub it over the surface in a circular motion to loosen the dirt. Rinse out your rag in the detergent, and with top-to-bottom vertical strokes get rid of the loosened dirt. You might have to repeat this two or three times. When satisfied, tackle a similar patch next to it, until you have completed a whole band along the bottom of the wall. Next tackle another band on top of it, and finally one on top of that

When you have completed the top band, rinse the whole wall immediately with clean water before going on. When rinsing, work from the top downwards. Use plenty of water, changing it frequently.

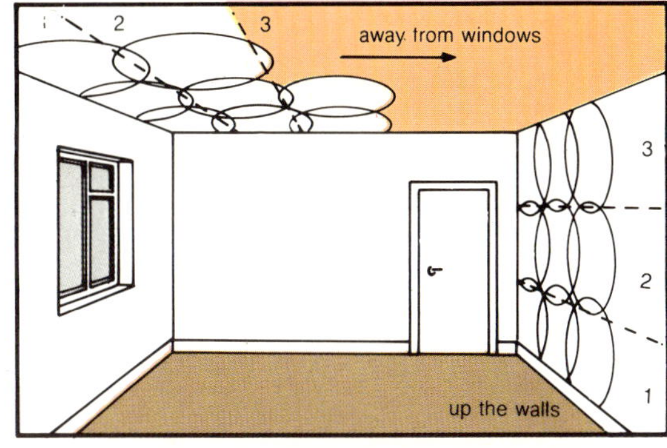

THE TRICK

If there is any mould growth on the walls, wash down with a solution of 1 part of ordinary domestic bleach to 16 of water. Leave for about two hours, then wash down with detergent, finally rinsing off with the bleach solution once more.

You must let the paintwork dry out thoroughly before you apply paint or wallpaper to it.

PAINT STRIPPING BY BLOWLAMPS

Most blowlamps nowadays work off liquid gas, which is a safe and highly convenient fuel. Although gas-operated lamps are not dangerous, there is one safety point you should observe. When you screw on a new canister, there is bound to be a slight escape of gas when the cylinder is first punctured. This operation is best done well away from a naked flame.

When you are burning off, your aim should be to scorch the timber as little as possible. Remember that the flame can only scorch bare wood.

THE TRICK

Start burning off by tackling any small, fiddly bits such as the moulding on a panelled door. If you left these until last, the flame would be playing on nearby bare wood, and would scorch it.

First, let your blowlamp flame play on the paintwork to warm it. Then go over it again, this time scraping off. On large areas and vertical strips, the scraper should always be below the flame; on horizontal ones it should follow behind it. That way you will not get burned.

THE TRICK

Always keep the scraper at an angle – i.e. its scraping edge not horizontal – so that your hand will not be directly under hot paint as it drops to the floor, and if the scraper slips forward into the path of the lamp, your hand will not move into the flame.

The paint that drops off will be hot and can burn. If you want to protect the floor covering, put down a sheet of hardboard. Don't use any combustible material.

If you are working in an old house with many coats of old paint you will probably find that your scrapers get clogged very quickly.

THE TRICK

Before you start to burn off, make up a strong solution of garden lime in water and brush it on the paint. That will stop the clogging.

The competent professional uses a blowlamp even on window frames, although you probably know how easy it is to crack the glass with the heat of the flame. He turns the flame down low, keeps it continually on the move and he uses a shave hook for removing the paint. He is particularly careful in the corners of the frame, where there is often a large build-up of paint, not to leave the flame playing on one spot for too long.

CHEMICAL PAINT STRIPPERS

If you find that you are breaking the glass, change to a chemical paint stripper. It is as well to use these on metal too, which can be distorted by heat.

The mistake many people make with chemical strippers is that they do not allow them enough time to do their work. You have to leave it there for some time – follow the manufacturer's instructions – before you can begin to remove the paint. It is a good idea to brush on one application, leave it for about 10 minutes, then brush on more stripper and leave this for the same time. The first application causes an initial bubbling up of the paint, and the second will then stay in place and be less liable to run down the surface while getting at the layers of paint underneath.

If you have to remove flaking emulsion paint from a plaster wall, this can usually be done with a scraper.

THE TRICK

For stubborn surfaces, use a diluted chemical stripper – three parts of stripper to one part of water.

A chemical stripper needs to be neutralized when you have finished, otherwise it might affect the new paint you put on. Usually you neutralize with either water or white spirit – follow the manufacturer's instructions. As a general guide, use water on indoor woodwork, but white spirit is better out of doors because water is more likely to introduce damp into exterior woodwork.

Always wear rubber gloves when you are using a chemical stripper, because these materials are caustic. Avoid inhaling the fumes; always make sure that the room in which you are working is well ventilated. In particular don't smoke; because you inhale much more strongly when smoking and there is a greater risk of your drawing in the fumes.

When you have finished, you should give the timber a thorough sanding to get rid of any small flecks of paint still left, and generally smooth down the work.

RUBBING DOWN PAINTWORK

Large flat areas of paintwork, such as a flush door, should always be rubbed down before you paint them. Even if the existing coat was superbly applied and is still in good condition, there will be a few specks of dust that settled on the old paint before it dried out. You may well find imperfections in the paintwork – the odd run, for instance.

The best material for rubbing down paintwork (as opposed to bare surfaces) is wet-and-dry, which is an abrasive paper that you can use wet or dry. It is far better used wet; dunk it in a bucket of water, then use it to rub down the surface.

One advantage of wet-and-dry is that, when used wet, it does not cause dust. This is especially important when dealing with old paint which might contain lead (modern paints are non-toxic). If you rub down with ordinary glasspaper, you will raise a possible harmful dust.

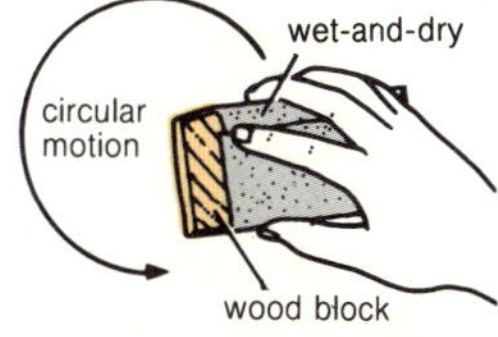

THE TRICK

Rub round in all directions, and not just in one straight line, otherwise you might wear out a groove in the surface.

THE TRICK

Wet-and-dry is an expensive material, and you can make it last longer if you smear it with ordinary household soap first.

When you have finished rubbing down with wet-and-dry, rinse the surface well with clean water and a sponge. Then leather off with a wash leather.

PREPARATION 3

METALWORK

Metal is treated pretty much like woodwork, but there are two big differences. You cannot use a blowlamp on metal because the heat will damage it; if any paint needs to be stripped from metal you must scrape it off or use a chemical stripper.

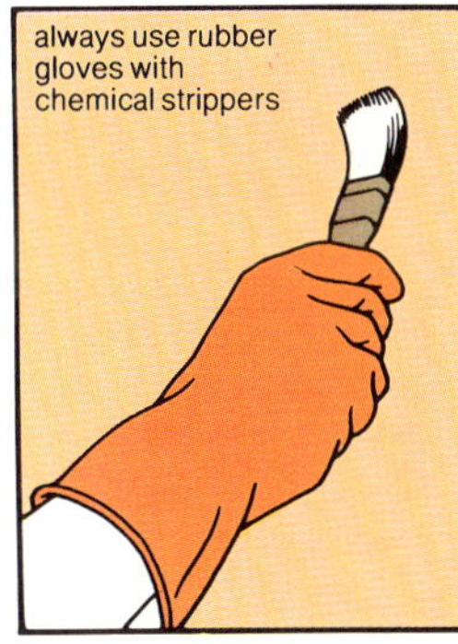

Fortunately, paint does not cling so well to metal as to wood, so this does not pose too much of a problem. The other difference is that ferrous metals produce rust, which is a big enemy of paint. If you apply paint on top of rust, it will lift off in no time.

Fortunately, almost the only place where you will find metal inside the average British home is in the window frames, and most of those installed since the war have been treated during manufacture to make them rust-resistant. However, the earliest metal window frames were not made rust-resistant, and most of these are now suffering from some degree of attack by rust. Where the frames are seriously pitted, or rust has caused them to warp, the only answer is to have the old frames replaced with new ones. If the attack is not too bad, you can try scraping the rust off.

Some of these old frames have been so well cared for that they are in perfect condition. These and the post-war ones are treated as though they were wood. If the paint on them is in good condition, just wash it down; but if it is defective it will have to be stripped. Take care when scraping that you do not dig too deeply into any protective coat of galvanizing, and that you do not leave the bare surfaces wet as this would cause rust.

In an old house you might come across iron and steel in other parts of your room. The fireplace could be made of iron, for instance, or you could find the odd bracket or similar fixture. Fortunately these will not be so exposed to moisture as window frames, so rust should not be as much of a problem. But any rust will have to be got rid of – use a wire brush or emery cloth, depending on the nature of the surface and how bad the pitting is.

Other metals you might find in your home are aluminium and copper – the former on window frames, especially if you have had double glazing installed recently, and the latter on pipes for domestic water and central heating.

Aluminium has a smooth and rather greasy surface. If you want to paint it, wash it down with white spirit and, while it is still wet, rub it with wet-and-dry abrasive paper. Clean off with a clean rag soaked in white spirit, and then wipe it down with a clean dry cloth. Prime it (see page 241) without delay.

Copper is a metal that does not take paint well, and as a result is best left unpainted, though if you want to hide ugly old pipes treat them as described for aluminium.

THE TRICK

When you rub down, make sure no particles of copper that fall off are left on adjacent areas; when you paint these later, green copper stains could show through.

THE TRICK

A wire brush in an electric drill is a good tool, but wear goggles to protect your eyes.

GETTING RID OF WHITEWASH

Whitewash and non-washable distempers have not been used for years, but you still come across them when renovating old houses. You cannot put paint on top of them, and they have to be removed. For this you need plenty of water, and an old short-haired brush or rag. Dip the brush or rag into the water, and attack the surface vigorously with a circular motion, working the whitewash up into a scum. Then rinse it off with a rag and lots of clean water. This is a very unpleasant job, especially as whitewash was often put on ceilings, but it has to be done.

If you are in any doubt as to whether a surface is whitewashed or not, try washing it. Whitewash will come off; emulsion paint (and washable distemper, which can be treated like emulsion paint) will stay in place.

WALLPAPER SURFACES

Like every other decorative material, wallcoverings must go on a suitable surface if they are to give their best. The ideal surface is a plaster wall that has always been wallpapered in the past; then all you need do is strip off the old paper (see page 228) and hang your new paper. Here are a few recommendations for coping with some of the surfaces you might meet in your home.

1. Emulsion-painted surfaces These need to be washed down, then sealed with a multi-purpose primer, thinned down according to the manufacturer's instructions. Size before hanging the paper (see page 254). An emulsion with a high sheen needs to be stripped off with a chemical paint stripper, which is such a chore that it might deter you from choosing paper for that wall. A silk finish emulsion should be treated like gloss paint.

2. Gloss-painted surfaces The surface must be well washed to get rid of grease, rinsed, allowed to dry, then sized. Hang lining paper first. A very smooth, hard oil paint needs rubbing down to provide a key.

3. Distempered surface Non-washable distemper and old whitewash must be removed. With washable distempers, just scrape the surface to get rid of loose and flaking material, then apply a multi-purpose primer, which needs to be sized once it has dried. If the surface of a washable distemper is sound, it needs merely to be sized before you start hanging the paper.

4. Wallboards Coat any screw or nail heads with a zinc chromate primer, then treat the board with wallboard primer. Size once the primer is dry. On very absorbent surfaces, such as medium-density hardboards, you can apply size before the primer.

5. Concrete This must be thoroughly washed down with detergent first, allowed to dry, then sized.

6. Polystyrene wall linings These are often stuck to a wall to make it warmer, and thus less condensation-prone. The polystyrene should be treated with a lining paper. Use a thick paste – preferably one containing a fungicide like those for use under vinyl – to inhibit mould growth.

FILLING

When all the surfaces have been stripped and/or rubbed down, you can tackle the filling. When should you fill? Before, or after, you have put on the priming coat? The professionals disagree on that point. Some say that you should apply the primer first, because it will impart a coating to which the filler can stick; others say that the priming coat should go on last because the filler needs priming like any other bare surface. However, one very experienced professional said that he would always prime before filling exterior woodwork, but fill first indoors.

TOOLS

Small holes and cracks are best stopped up with a cellulose filler. There are two tools you use for applying this: the filling knife and the putty knife. The filling knife is usually used on cracks, especially long ones, in the middle of a flat surface. A filling knife looks just like a scraper, but has a flexible blade.

You also need a container for your filling material. An old plate or saucer is often used, but this is inadequate if you have a big job that will require a lot of filler. Professionals use what they call a 'hawk', and it is very easy for you to improvise one. Take a small sheet of plywood, about 300mm (12in.) square, and in the middle and at right angles to the board, screw or nail a short length of wood as a handle.

SMALL CRACKS AND HOLES

If it is a long, thin crack you are dealing with, begin by raking it along its length with the pointed edge of the filling knife. The idea of this is to enlarge the crack enough to take the filler, and to get rid of any loose material. Load your knife with filler, then draw it across the crack at right angles to its length, flexing the blade as you do so, to push the filler well in. Next draw the knife down the length of the crack, with the blade flat on the surface, to remove any surplus filler.

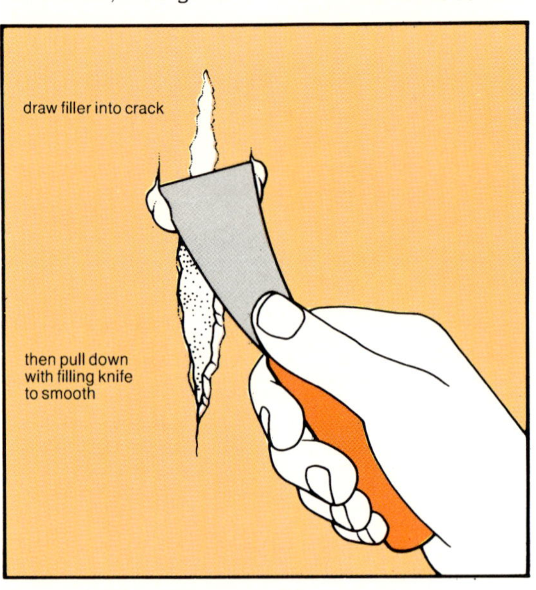

The putty knife is spear-shaped, and is the tool with which a glazier applies putty when fixing a pane of glass in a window. The decorator uses it, however, to fill small holes. You hold the handle in the palm of your hand, and extend your forefinger along the blade to steady it. The straight edge of the blade is used to apply the filler, and the curved one to remove any surplus. The straight edge of the putty knife blade is very useful, too, for applying filler in an angle: e.g. between a door frame and the wall.

THE TRICK

Whatever type of hole or crack you are filling, try to leave the filler slightly proud of the surface. Then when it has dried you can rub it over with glasspaper to sand it down flush.

PLASTERING

If you have extensive areas of bad wall surface – large holes or big stretches of crumbling plaster – then cellulose filler will be too expensive, and you should use plaster instead. This is available in small packs.

Hack away, with a trowel or scraper, at the defective area until you have got rid of all the loose and crumbling plaster, and you come to a firm edge. If the base coat of the plaster (either plaster or sand and cement rendering) is suspect, hack this off as well until the wall behind is exposed. On lath and plaster walls it does not matter if you have to expose the wall back to the laths.

Apply the plaster to the wall using either a trowel or a filling knife – even a float trowel where the hole is big enough – putting on enough to allow it to stand slightly proud of the surrounding wall. Then go over with a short length of timber which is straight and true, to remove surplus plaster, and finish the repair flush with the surface. Lightly stroke the new plaster with a trowel or knife moistened in water to make the surface smooth.

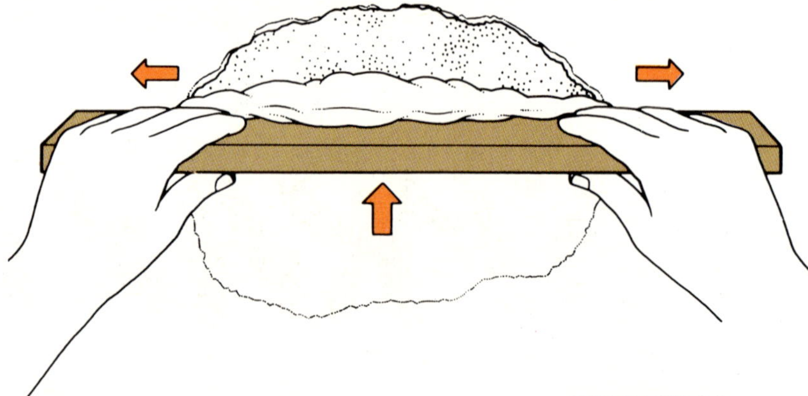
use a straight and true piece of timber to level large holes

scrape back to sound plaster

THE TRICK

Finally, feather out the edges with a damp brush or sponge, and the repair will be hardly detectable. Then leave it to dry out thoroughly.

If the hole or crack is a deep one, it should be filled in two operations. The surface of the first application of filler should be scratched with the trowel or knife, to key it. When it is really dry, the top coat can be added.

A wall that you intend to paint needs much more attention from the filling point of view than one that will be covered with paper, for a paper can hide cracks that will show through the paint. In fact, if your wall is covered in small cracks it will be a never-ending job trying to fill them, and a better treatment would be lining paper, followed by thick wallpaper. If you insist on a painted finish, then you should apply a lining paper suitable for receiving paint (see page 263).

A fine surface filler is available for use where you want to ensure a really superb painted finish, which will usually be on woodwork. The fine surface filler is not for deep holes or cracks, but for covering up small defects. You apply it with a broad filling knife, which you flex as you draw the filler across the surface, spreading it well out.

REPAIRING A CEILING IN BAD CONDITION

Ceilings are often in a worse state of repair than walls. If the one you are tackling is bulging and falling away, first go over it nailing it back to the joists, using galvanized clout nails. Clout nails are advisable because they have a big head, and would hold the ceiling more firmly in place; use galvanized ones so that they will not rust as they are dampened by the paste of the paper. You should always cross line such ceilings (see page 263). Therefore, your first ceiling lining paper should go at right angles to the window wall: i.e. in the opposite direction to that recommended for the ceiling paper (see page 264).

WAGNER SPRAYTECH (UK)

Wagner Spraytech (UK) Ltd
Unit 3
Haslemere Way
Tramway Industrial Estate
Banbury
Oxon OX16 8TY
Telephone: 0295 65353/4

PAINT

Paint is the most versatile and the most popular decorating material available today. You can get a paint to cover just about every material you are likely to meet in the modern home, indoors or out. Not only will the paint look attractive but it will also offer maximum protection to your home. Furthermore, paints are easily the cheapest form of decorating you can choose.

Before you can start to paint, you have to decide what type of finish you want for the various surfaces in your home. A bewildering array of new paints has been introduced in recent years, so here is a quick guide to what's what on the paint shelf. Incidentally, all paints made by reputable manufacturers are durable and easily washed.

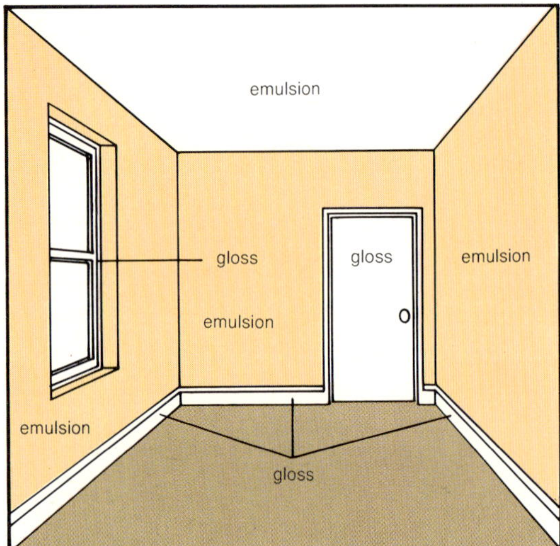

OIL PAINTS – GLOSS

For the maximum protection of woodwork and metal you should use an oil paint, which comes in two types: the liquid form, and the thixotropic (sometimes known as a gel or non-drip). A liquid gloss gives the best, toughest and longest lasting finish of any type of paint. It is, however, the trickiest paint of all to apply, because you have to judge exactly how much to put on the surface. If you put too little, you do not get a sufficiently protective film; put too much and it tends to run (see pages 244,246). Brushes used for liquid gloss are the most difficult to clean, because generally you must use a proper solvent such as paraffin, white spirit (often called turps substitute) or a proprietary brush cleaner (see page 240).

OIL PAINTS – EGGSHELL

Eggshell paints are oil paints without a shiny surface. They have now diminished in popularity because of competition from the newer types of paint. Many professional decorators like the eggshell paints.

darker paint on ceiling and upper walls makes a tall room appear lower

open up a long narrow corridor with a bright colour at the far end

EMULSION PAINTS

Plaster surfaces do not need the same protection as wood and metal. They also have more imperfections and these would tend to be highlighted by the sheen of a gloss. So it is better to use an emulsion paint, which is cheaper, easier to apply, quick drying, does not have the same lingering smell, and you clean your brush afterwards in water.

Emulsions also come in liquid and gel form. Once again, the manufacturers tend to think of the liquid variety as a trade product because it is slightly more difficult to apply, and the gel as being for do-it-yourselfers. Once again, they are not entirely correct, because, as with gloss paints, a gel emulsion can be applied more thickly, and therefore requires fewer coats – a fact by no means entirely without appeal to the tradesman.

Although emulsion paints do not offer the same protection as gloss, they are nevertheless very tough. The modern varieties, when made by reputable manufacturers, are fully able to stand up to any conditions they will meet in the home, even in the areas of the hardest wear, such as kitchens and bathrooms.

GLOSS EMULSION

There is also an in-between paint known as gloss emulsion, which combines the advantages of both types of paint. Just like an emulsion paint, it is easy to apply, there is no lingering smell, it dries quickly, and you wash your brushes out in water afterwards. Yet it does have a shiny surface, and you can apply it as a top coat on wood and metal, as well as using it on walls. It is a highly versatile product. However, it is not so tough or shiny as the true gloss, and many brands of this type of paint cannot be used out of doors. The trade tends to regard it as a convenience product for the not-so-skilled amateur.

SILK FINISH – EMULSION

Many emulsions have a silk finish, which represents quite an advance in paint technology. Achieving the finish was not the problem; the trouble was that at one time silk finishes tended to go shiny when you washed them. However, that has been overcome, and emulsions with a silky sheen are now among the most popular paints on the market, and some manufacturers recommend them for woodwork, too.

SILK FINISH – GLOSS

In recent years, a series of gloss paints with a silky finish has been introduced. These are – to date – the ultimate in convenience, for they are all-surface paints (you can use them on walls and woodwork in any part of the house), thixotropic, almost as easy to apply as emulsions, and it is easy to clean your brushes afterwards. However, they are expensive to buy.

BRUSHES

In just about every book on home decorating you are advised to buy the best paintbrushes you can afford. However, this is not always so. We do not suggest that you buy really cheap brushes, because a bad brush is a waste of time. The paint will not flow from it properly, and it keeps shedding its hairs as you work. However, there is no need to go to the other extreme and buy top-quality tradesmen's tools.

The best material to use for the hairs of a paintbrush is bristle, which grows on the wild pig. Some of the large brushes (and the cheaper small ones) substitute such materials as horsehair and vegetable fibre. They do not make such a good-quality brush.

WALL AND CEILING BRUSHES

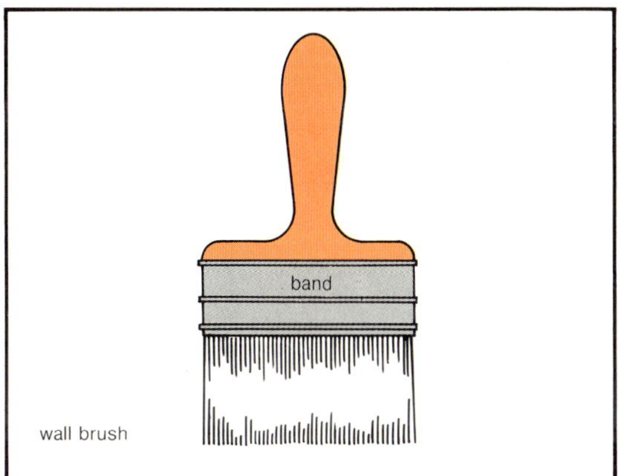

The brush for applying water-based paints (emulsions) is known as a wall brush. You can buy wall brushes in 100, 125 and 150mm (4, 5 and 6in.) sizes. Paint-holding capacity is the principal consideration here. The bigger the brush, the less time you have to spend recharging it; but it will be heavier and consequently more tiring to wield.

The wall brush has a big brother, known as the distemper or ceiling brush. The distemper brush is 175mm (7in.) wide, and is extremely heavy when fully charged with paint.

The best-quality wall brushes are of pure bristle, the visible length of which is about 100mm (4in.). The metal band holding the bristles in place should be copper. Nails or pins of phosphor bronze will be driven through the band to hold the bristles in and the band joint will be soldered. Some wall brushes have hairs which include cheaper materials as well as bristle. This is known as a mixture brush. In the cheapest brushes, the band is often made of nickle-plated steel with an interlocked joint. The pins could be of stainless steel, or even omitted altogether.

THE TRICK

Before you use a wall brush, flick and pull the bristles gently so that any loose ones will be dislodged. Then rinse the brush thoroughly in clean water. This gets rid of dust and loose particles, it also helps to stop the paint from drying on the bristles.

FLAT VARNISH BRUSHES

The brush used for applying gloss paint is known as a flat varnish brush. Two types of handle are found: the beaver tail and the American pattern.

A good flat varnish brush should always be made of pure bristle – do not compromise here – and the best have a nickel-plated ferrule. The bristles should be full and strong with a soft tip suitable for spreading and laying off gloss finishes. The outside bristles should be slightly shorter than those in the centre so that the brush tapers slightly towards its tip. However, the tip itself should be full and straight.

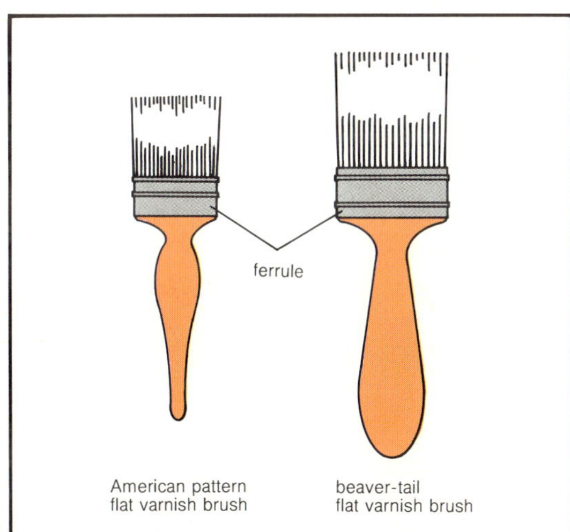

THE TRICK

When you are buying a varnish brush, examine it carefully, and open up its bristles. Look how much hair and how much wood are visible.

On very poor-quality varnish brushes, wedges are driven into the stock to thicken out the apparent amount of bristle. Look, too, at the hairs in the centre, for it is here that the cheaper materials are placed.

THE TRICK

Do not condemn a wall brush because it has a wedge: here the wedge brings the tip of the bristle to a knife-like edge, and allows you to get into the stock of the brush to clean out the emulsion.

For interior work you will probably get away with two sizes: 50mm and 25mm (2 and 1in.). The 50mm would be used for large areas, such as doors; and the 25mm for door and window frames, etc. If you have Georgian-style windows with many small glazing bars, it might be a good idea to get a 20mm (¾in.) brush.

You should pick the best from a do-it-yourself shop's range, but go for middle quality in a trade outlet. The same kit would do for woodwork out of doors unless you have large areas to deal with, such as garage doors. In that case it would be as well to buy a 75mm (3in.) brush, but it could be of lower quality.

THE TRICK

A professional uses a brand new brush only on primers and undercoats, which runs it in properly for use with top coats, smoothing down the bristles to a firm soft tip. Before starting work he always flexes the bristles through his hands to get rid of loose ones.

HOW TO HOLD THE BRUSH

The two types of paintbrush are held in entirely different ways. To grip the flat varnish brush, you do not use the handle at all. Instead you hold it by the ferrule, your four fingers on one side and your thumb on the other. That way you are able to flex your wrist and stroke the paint properly in both directions. If the handle is not used, why bother to have one at all? The fact is that a handle is absolutely necessary for the balance of the tool. Without one you cannot grip and control the brush properly.

On the other hand, you do use the handle to wield the wall brush. In fact, if you grip it just as though it were a ping-pong bat, you will not go far wrong. The reason for this is that when applying wall paints to large areas, you use the brush in a sort of back- and fore-hand style.

THE DOOR JAMB DUSTER

One other brush that top tradesmen consider indispensable is the door jamb duster, which they use for dusting off woodwork.

When you've made a
natural decision..
Timbercare keeps the ideas alive

Brings out the best in natural wood

Exterior Satin Finish

This finish is designed to preserve and protect smooth finished, exterior wood surfaces. It is the durable, microporous system which is resistant to water and does not peel or flake.

Can be maintained (when required) by simply cleaning down before applying one or two coats.

Exterior Preservative

Does not peel or flake but is a deeply penetrating microporous preservative for the long term protection of rough sawn exterior timber such as gates, fencing, sheds and trellis work. Gives excellent protection against the effects of sunlight, rot and mould growth. When required, refurbishment is easy, simply brush down and apply one or two coats.

Timbercare Interior Varnish (Gloss or Eggshell)

Polyurethane based varnishes for interior use on smooth interior wood surfaces such as floors, stairs, furniture and doors.

Exterior Gloss Finish

The durable, lead-free microporous finish which dries to a hard brilliant gloss with exceptional resistance to weathering. Possesses excellent obliterating power and retains its gloss and colour for many years.

Can be maintained when required by cleaning and rubbing down before applying one or two coats.

Timbercare Wood Primer

The microporous, lead-free primer for all types of soft woods and hard woods providing a sound key for the application of Timbercare Gloss Finish.

Covers up to 15 square metres per litre. Touch dry in 2 to 3 hours, hard dry 5 to 6 hours and recoatable overnight.

Timbercare Wood Primer is Off White in colour and supplied in 1 and 2½ litre tins.

A range of paints and finishes for the professional

Manders Paints Limited

PO Box 9, Mander House, Wolverhampton WV1 3NH

Telephone: (0902) 711511. Telex: 335491 Mander G

BEFORE AND AFTER PAINTING

OPENING THE TIN

Whether newly bought or not, you should dust the tin thoroughly, or any dust might get into the paint and spoil the result.

Before opening, you should always read the instructions on the tin. If you delay doing that paint might run down the sides, and obliterate them.

THE TRICK

A good idea for opening is the small tool that is sold for piercing cans of orange juice and the like; you can buy them at ironmongers. Place it on the edge of the can with the point upwards and under the rim of the lid, then lever.

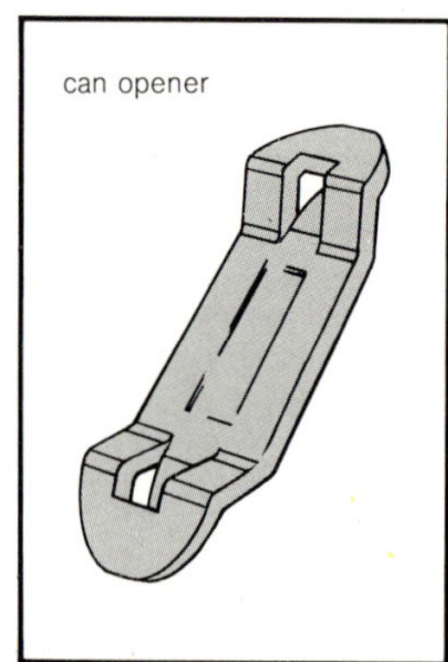
can opener

STRAINING THE PAINT

If the can of paint you are about to use has never been opened before, it will not need straining. If it has been used, then almost certainly there will be hard paint and skin that you must get rid of. Always store your paint with the tin the right way up, and the lid fixed firmly in place, so that no air can enter.

When you open a can of paint, stir it thoroughly, making sure you mix in all the sediment at the bottom. If the tin is fairly empty, and has been standing for some time, you may find a thick layer of skin all over the top of the paint. Try to cut this off intact with a knife, keeping as close to the sides of the tin as possible. Then stir the rest.

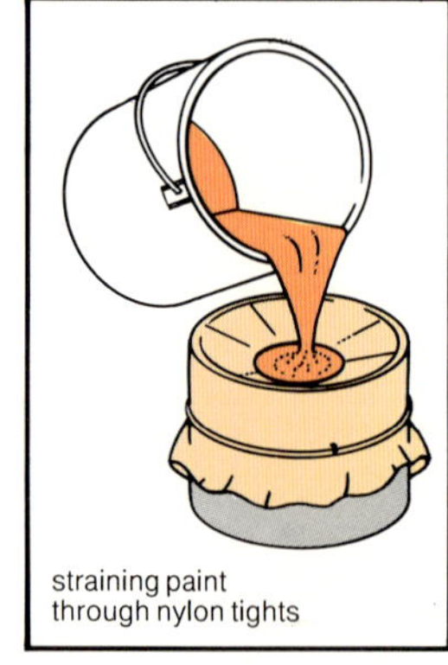
straining paint through nylon tights

THE TRICK

An old pair of nylon tights is still the best thing to strain paint through.

The strained paint should be free of all sediment, and you can start to use it immediately.

If you are using a thixotropic paint, you will see a notice on the tin warning you not to stir it, and in general you should follow this advice. If there is any liquid on top of the paint in a previously opened can, pour it away. If the paint seems in very bad condition you can stir it after removing whatever layer of skin lies on the top. Strain the liquid, then put it on one side to stand for a day. It will then re-solidify.

PAINT KETTLES

Even with brand-new paint, you will find a build-up of hard paint forming on the rim. You can pick up small flecks of this as you load your brush and these will be transferred on to your work. You know what a problem it is wiping them off. You will avoid this by using a paint kettle.

When using paint from a can that has been opened previously, you have to strain it to get rid of old skin, that means pouring it into another receptacle. You might as well use the proper thing.

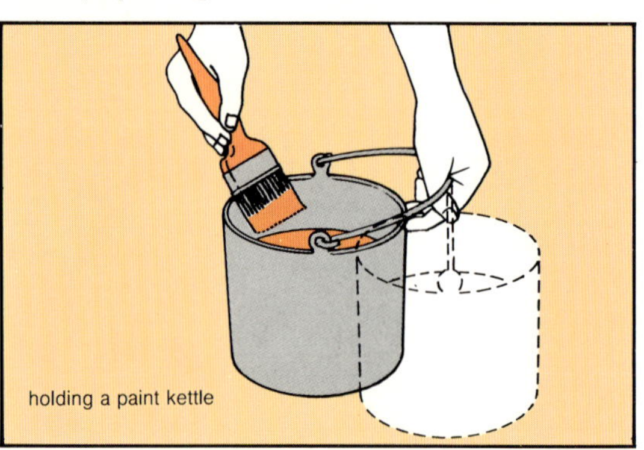
holding a paint kettle

THE TRICK

The correct way to hold a paint kettle is that its handle should lie in the fingers of your hand, but your forefinger should extend along and under it. When you want to charge your brush, stretch out this forefinger, which will pivot the kettle out of the way of your hand, giving you access to the paint.

Paint kettles were traditionally metal, but plastic ones are much cheaper, and are easier to scrape clean afterwards. You can flex them so that the paint film cracks and falls away from the surface.

THE TRICK

To clean a metal kettle, professionals take it out of doors, soak a rag in paraffin, place the rag in the kettle and set fire to it. Any remaining paint can be scraped off, and the kettle cleaned with abrasive paper.

CLEANING BRUSHES

At the end comes the job that most people hate, however it should not be skipped. Paintbrushes are expensive and a good one is worth taking care of.

GLOSS

The most difficult paint to clean out is gloss, and a wide range of proprietary products is sold to make things easier. Most professionals, however, prefer to use paraffin. Stand your brush in an old jar,

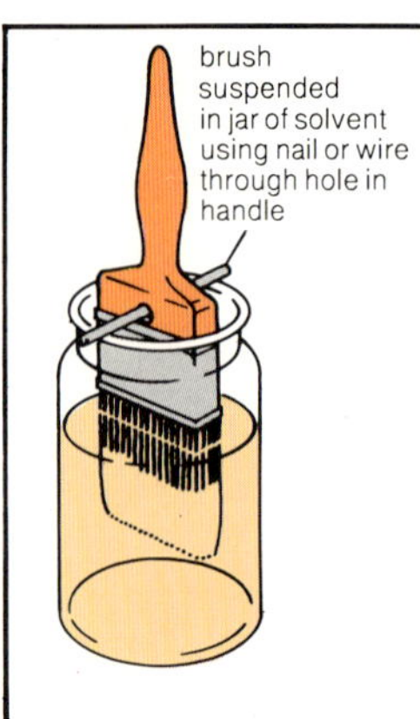
brush suspended in jar of solvent using nail or wire through hole in handle

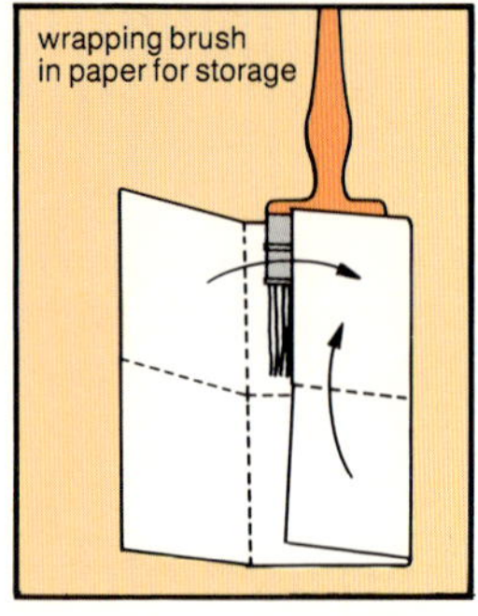
wrapping brush in paper for storage

making sure it sits squarely on its bristles (if it is a good one there is no need to suspend it by means of a hole bored in its handle, for its bristles will be firm enough). Pour in just enough paraffin to come to the top of the bristles. When you want to start work again, wash it out in clean paraffin, shake it thoroughly, then work it dry on a clean rag.

When you have finished decorating, wash your brush out first in two changes of paraffin, then in soapy water, finally rinsing it out in clean water. Shake thoroughly, or spin the handle between your hands, then dry on a clean rag.

The brush should be stored wrapped in paper – kitchen paper is ideal. Smooth the bristles neatly into place as you wrap, then store it flat on a shelf. Never store a brush wrapped in impervious materials, such as polythene, they stop the bristles drying out properly.

With some modern gloss paints, brush cleaning is much less trouble than that, and you clean them with a solution of detergent in water. Always follow the instructions on the tin. Varnish brushes should never be soaked in water.

EMULSION

Emulsion paint is cleaned out of a brush with water. Make sure that you wash the brush even when you knock off work for a short break, as emulsion paint can harden in the stock while you work, and be very difficult to remove. Shake the water out of the brush thoroughly before you start work again.

PRIMERS AND UNDERCOATS

THE PAINTING SEQUENCE

If you will be painting every surface in your room – the walls and ceiling, as well as the woodwork – then you should start with the ceiling, go on to the walls, and do the woodwork last. If you get splashes of emulsion paint on the woodwork, you should remove them before applying your gloss paint. Wipe them off immediately with a rag, or flick them off with a scraper if you do not notice them until they have dried.

If you intend to have a mixture of paint and paper, you should do all the painting first. That way you do not have to worry about splashing newly hung paper with paint, and you need not bother to 'cut in' properly (see page 246). You can let the paint stray as it will, and get a neat join by trimming the paper accurately.

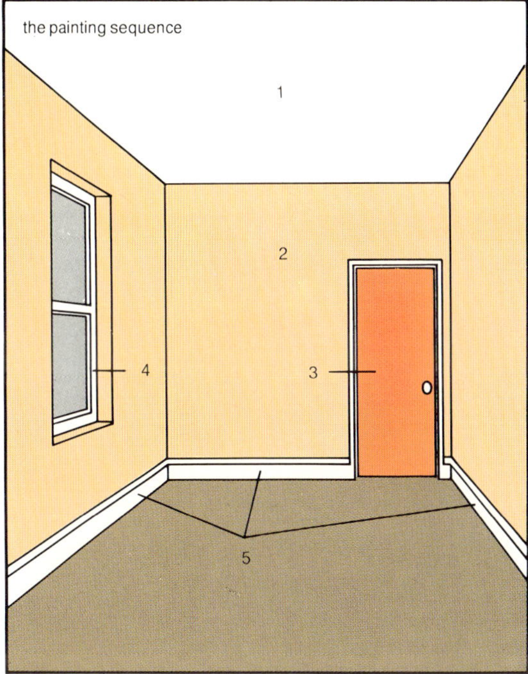

WOODWORK

Although woodwork is painted last, we deal with it first, as it is the most complicated.

KNOTTING

If the surfaces are bare, examine them to see if there are any knots or resinous areas. Unless these are sealed they will 'weep' through the finished work, and discolour the surface. You seal them with a liquid, appropriately called knotting, which is brushed on.

THE TRICK

If your existing paintwork suffers from discoloration caused by the oozing of resin from knots, this does not mean that the paint must be stripped off – provided that it is otherwise in good condition. Knotting can be applied on top of the existing finish, and it will protect subsequent coats.

PRIMERS

A primer provides an essential base for the rest of your paintwork. On wood, it fills the grainy surface of the timber and seals it, provides a key for subsequent coats and helps to cushion them against movement in the timber and, finally, plays an important part in protecting the timber against damp and moisture. You should use the conventional white or pink oil-based wood primers. In general these are non-toxic: i.e. they do not contain lead. Brands that contain lead are available

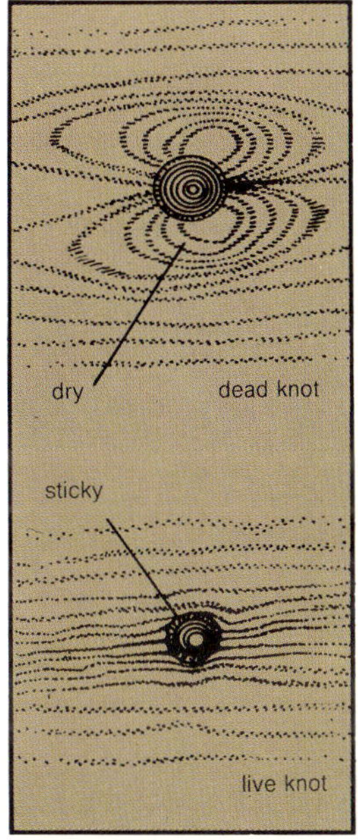

and you might like to use them out of doors, where they will offer stronger protection (see page 246).

The new multi-purpose primers are also suitable for timber, and on interior work so are the primer undercoats. The latter are acrylic, water-based products so they dry very quickly. Their obvious advantage is that they speed up redecoration.

Some softwoods are resinous. You can recognize them for they will feel very sticky to the touch, and you will see orange resin streaks oozing out. These need an aluminium primer, and it is not a bad idea to treat very resinous areas with knotting first.

Plywood, blockboard and chipboard should be treated just like timber. Use an all-purpose primer, or a primer-undercoat on hardboard. Insulation boards, however, tend to be very porous, so use a primer sealer. If you come across any asbestos, this should be treated with a primer sealer before you paint.

THE TRICK

Never rub asbestos with glasspaper, don't even dust it off, for you might release dangerous particles into the air. Wash it down with clean water, then wrap the rag you have used in a polythene bag and throw it away.

UNDERCOATS

If you will be applying a liquid gloss as the finish, then you should apply an undercoat on top of the primer. At one time undercoats were considered essential with gloss paint, but recently they have fallen out of favour. However, you get a better finish if you use one; in many instances one undercoat and one coat of gloss will be better than two coats of gloss.

The instructions on a tin of gloss used to say that it was advisable to use it only with the same brand of undercoat. There may well have been a large element of sales talk in this. However, now that so many paints are formulated in different ways, it is important to use the same brand of undercoat and finishing paint, for only then can you be sure that they will be compatible.

The undercoat always used to be a close match in colour to the top coat, and in many cases this is still true today. However, this colour matching is no longer necessary because the pigments in modern top coats have much more obliterative power.

If you are using a thixotropic gloss, undercoats do not apply, and you can brush on your top paint coat upon coat, until you get a finish that suits you.

PAINTING ON PAINTED WOODWORK

If you are decorating on top of an existing finish and have decided on a liquid gloss, it is a good idea to specify an undercoat first. Undercoats have a lot of body which will help to fill in small surface defects and leave a slightly textured surface, providing a good key for the top coat. Once again, an undercoat is not necessary with gel paints.

METALS

The traditional metal primers tend to be toxic, so you might prefer a multi-purpose primer, especially as in most homes there will be only small areas of metal in among a lot of woodwork. Aluminium is now to be found in increasing quantities in homes. If you wish to paint it, do not use a lead-pigmented metal primer, but settle for an all-purpose primer instead.

One problem metal you will come across is copper, usually as pipes. Copper is best left unpainted, but you may well want to cover up old and ugly pipes. In such cases, no primer is recommended. Just make sure the metal is clean and free from grease, then apply gloss paint directly to it.

APPLYING UNDERCOATS AND PRIMERS

These paints are applied in a fairly similar manner to brushing on gloss (see page 244). However, they are not so free flowing, so there is less risk of runs. This is particularly true of primer going on a bare surface, therefore laying off is not so important. However, it is vital that these paints are applied evenly, to give a good base for the top coats. Brush wood primers hard against the bare surface, almost forcing it into the timber.

RUBBING DOWN BETWEEN COATS

When applying gloss paints, you should always give a light rub down with wet-and-dry paper between coats: primers, undercoats, the lot. This is not so much to apply a key – modern gloss paints do not really need one – but to get rid of any imperfections in your previous coat. At the very least, specks of dust will have settled on your work; sanding will get rid of these.

A Good Workman
Never Blames His Tools
At Briton we think our paint brushes are the best. To prove it we painted one red stripe with our Super Bounty 2″ Brush and another red stripe with the top selling imported brush.
As you can see, the results speak for themselves.
The Briton Super Bounty 2″ Brush has 5,000 more bristles than the other brush — longer, thicker bristles. So it picks up more paint and spreads it more evenly. And there's less work because you don't have to dip into the paint pot so often.
Next time you are looking for a paint brush ask for a Briton.
Briton Chadwick
Attleborough, Norfolk NR17 2HZ, England.
Telephone: Attleborough (0953) 453201.

2"
BRITISH MADE
2"
Briton
SUPER BOUNTY

GLOSS TECHNIQUE 1

A liquid gloss, although it gives the best finish, is the most difficult of all the paints to apply. Having mastered the art of applying this with a brush, you will be better able to understand the principles of painting.

PREPARATION

Dust is the big enemy of a good gloss finish, so at the beginning you should make sure there is none lying around on the floor – sweep it well, or better still vacuum clean it first. Avoid wearing woollen clothing from which loose fibres could fall on to the work. Finally, just before you begin, rub your palms over the surface – 'palm the work off' in the jargon of the trade. The slight dampness of your skin will pick up any loose bits of dirt.

You start the actual painting by loading your brush, and to do so you should dip its bristles to about a third of their depth into the liquid. Aim to submerge them each time to the same depth so that you always get an equal amount of paint on them. Then press the bristles first against one side of the container, then against the other, to squeeze out surplus paint. You will find it easier to do this in a kettle than in a paint can – yet another reason in favour of using the proper receptacle.

APPLYING LIQUID GLOSS

Let us imagine for a start that you are painting a largish flat area – a flush door would be the most obvious example, and that you are right-handed; you will work the opposite way around if you are left-handed. Begin at the left-hand side of the door, but bring your brush into contact with the work 25–50mm (1–2in.) short of the top.

THE TRICK

If you begin right at the top, paint will bubble over on to the top, then flow back and you will get an unsightly build-up of paint; in the words of the tradesman, you will 'pick up a thick edge'.

Apply the paint from the top of the door down to about waist height, using upward and downward strokes. Hold the brush as explained on page 237 and flex it against the work which will cause the paint held in the bristles to flow down to the narrow tip of the brush. Remember that a gloss paint needs to be applied liberally in a full-flowing coat. Don't dab your brush at the work as though you were trying to stab someone. It should approach the work gently in an arc, like an aeroplane coming in to land.

When you have covered about 200–300mm (9–12in.) of the width of the door, then, without reloading the brush, spread the paint out evenly with a series of horizontal strokes across the original vertical ones. This process is known as cross brushing. This guards against the possibility of unsightly 'tears' and runs. Finally, without further charging your brush with paint, make a series of light-as-a-feather strokes in the original vertical direction. This process is called laying off and should be done very gently and delicately. Your brush should be at an angle to the work, and its bristles should just touch the paint. Take great care over laying off. It is the finishing touch that stamps the final seal of quality on your work.

Having dealt with this first section of the door, you can go on to the next one immediately to the right of it. This you will deal with in exactly the same way, but make sure during your cross brushing that you carry your strokes right into the paint on the first section. Continue in this way until you have finished the entire width of the door.

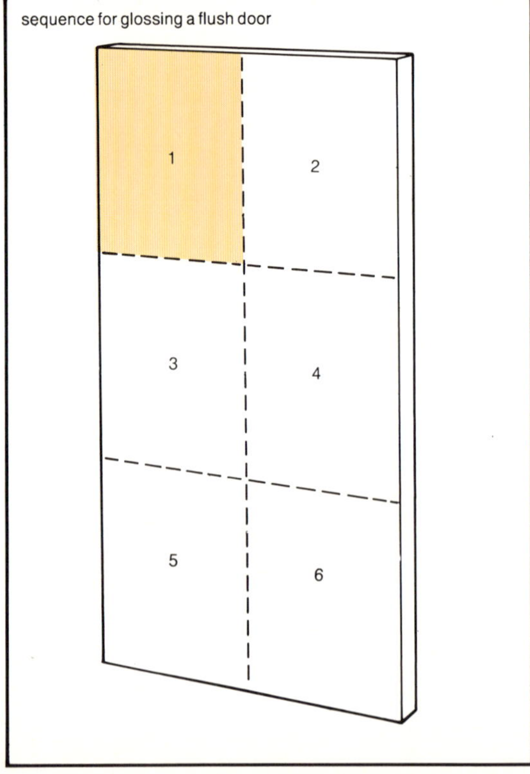

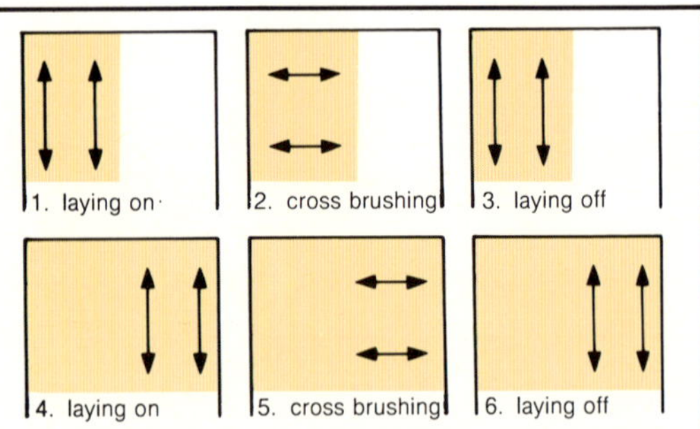

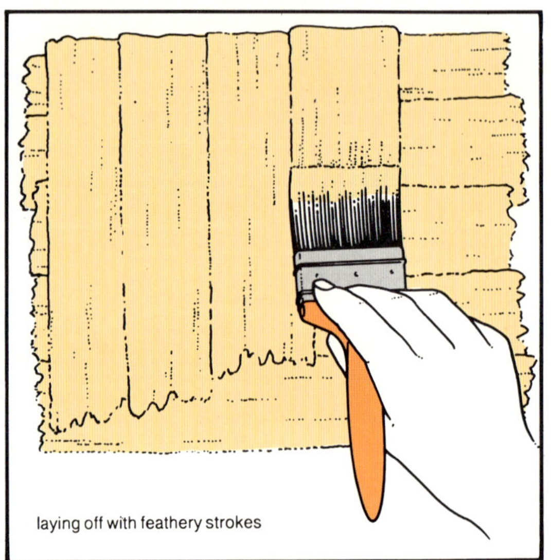
laying off with feathery strokes

THE TRICK

You should then carry out a final cross brushing of all the paint you have applied.

With the top band completed, you can now go on to the one underneath – most people would split the average door into three horizontal bands, but you might make do with two. However many you decide on, treat them all in the same way that I have described for the top one, but carry your vertical strokes – both those for the original application of paint and the laying-off ones – into the top band of paint, otherwise you will get a hard, visible edge where the various sections meet. Similarly, the horizontal strokes of your cross brushing should go into the neighbouring paint. When the whole panel is finished, give a final laying off. Then stand back and examine your work to make sure the entire surface is covered, and that there are no runs.

On long narrow stretches of wood such as skirting boards and door frames, this technique is obviously not called for. All you have to do is make sure the paint is well spread, so that there will be no runs. Each time you reload your brush after it has run dry, carry your first strokes well into the paint already there, so that you will not get a hard join line showing.

APPLYING GEL GLOSS

You treat a gel gloss very like a liquid one, but when you charge your brush there is no need to press it on the sides of the kettle to get rid of surplus paint.

You apply the gel in pretty much the same way, too, except that you have to be aware of over-brushing. A gel paint spreads because pressure from your brush causes it to turn liquid. When you first dip your brush into the kettle, the paint that it touches turns liquid, and clings to its bristles. As you withdraw the brush, the paint solidifies again (which is why there are fewer drips with this type of paint). When you brush the paint on to the wood, it will again turn liquid, allowing you to spread it out, and it will turn solid once more as your brush leaves it. If you overdo the brushing out, then the gel will be too liquid, and you will lose the big advantage of a gel gloss (which is, of course, that it is less likely to run than a liquid one, and so you can apply it more thickly). So with a gel gloss you must aim for less cross brushing and laying off.

For over a decade, the Ronson has remained one of the world's best selling blowtorches.

Safe, simple and easy to use, it is an essential part of the tool kit of home handymen and professionals.

The versatility of the flame, from a roaring 1,000°C to a fierce 1,900°C pinpoint, allows 101 different jobs to be done in the home, garage, workshop and garden.

Powered by a disposable butane gas cartridge which gives you up to 15 hours' burning time, the Ronson Blowtorch has a self-sealing valve for safety and convenience.

IN THE HOME

IN THE GARDEN

IN THE GARAGE

IN THE WORKSHOP

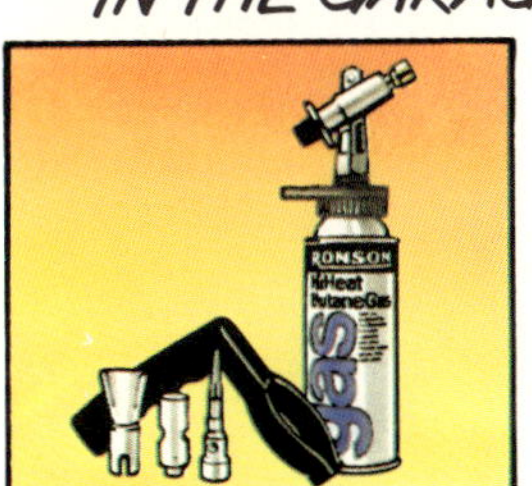

Available at leading Hardware and DIY Stores.

The name on the flame

Alfred Preedy & Sons, p.l.c. Ronson Division, Burnt Tree House, Burnt Tree, Tipton, West Midlands DY4 7UG. Tel: 021-520 6201.

GLOSS TECHNIQUE 2

HOW TO 'CUT IN'

'Cutting in' is the term the tradesman applies to getting a neat join where paints of a different colour meet: i.e. the angle between a coloured wall and a white ceiling, or where the paint meets a different decorative material, such as at the join between paint on a kitchen cabinet and the plastic worktop.

Where there is a definite angle at the point where the colours or materials meet, as in the examples given above, then cutting in is easy to achieve. Load your brush lightly, place it on the work about 3mm (1/8in.) away from the edge, then slowly and gradually push it along to meet the joint. Now press lightly on the brush, so that it will not wander about, and firmly draw it along, to make a straight line. It sounds easy, and it is easy, once you have a little practice.

Some cutting in, is however, more complicated than this – where, for instance, there is an abrupt colour change in the middle of a wall, as in some modern designs where a wall might be decorated in several bands of different colour. The only way to achieve a good break here is with masking tape. Decorator's masking tape is self-adhesive, and you stick it down in place where you want your neat join to be.

Apply your paint, making sure you come right up to the edge of the tape, and straying on to it if necessary. Let the paint nearly dry before tearing off the tape. You will then see a very neat join. Incidentally, don't try to make do with ordinary sticky tape; it simply won't work.

THE TRICK

It is a good idea to go over it with a seam roller (see page 254) so that you can be sure it is firmly stuck down, and paint will not be able to creep under the edges.

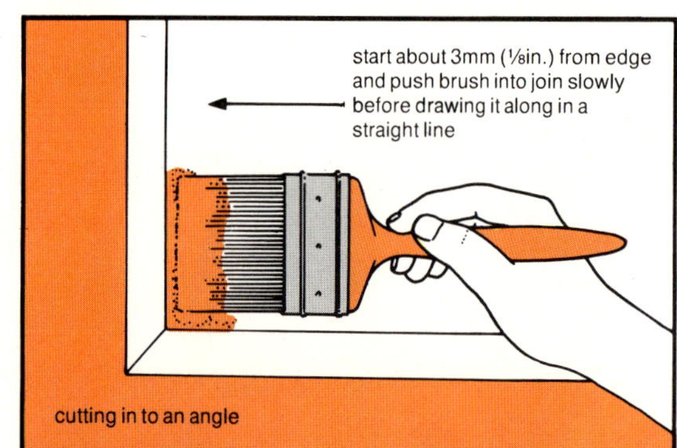

PAINTING PANELLED DOORS

Before you start to paint, you should first remove all the 'furniture' – handles, catches, etc. – that you do not want to be coated with paint. It is definitely quicker to remove the furniture and replace it when you have finished than try to paint round it. Some professionals replace the handle straightaway after painting – if you take great care over this, you can manage it without disturbing the paint – so that they can open and close the door immediately. Some, however, prefer to wait for the paint to dry before refixing everything.

THE TRICK

Then it is a good idea to drive a wooden peg into the hole for the handle so that you can operate the door without touching the paint.

Incidentally, do you know which colour the edges of a door should be painted? The rule is quite simple: the edge nearest to the handle should be painted the same colour, and at the same time, as the side that opens into the room. The hinge edge should be treated as part of the other side of the door, which may well be a different colour.

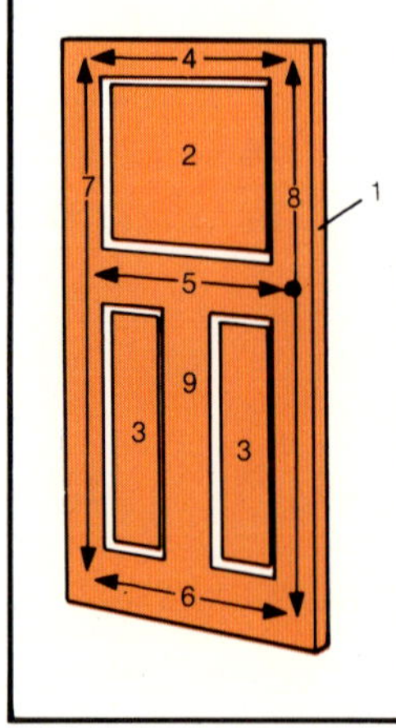

PAINTING WINDOW FRAMES

One obvious instance of cutting in occurs when you paint window frames. There are several dodges designed to make it easier for the amateur to paint window frames – from masking tape to shields of various kinds. The professional knows that proper cutting in is the quickest and easiest method of dealing with window frames. You adopt the same course. A few practice runs, and you will find it very easy to cut in properly.

The window frames are the part of the interior woodwork that has to stand up to the most exacting conditions, for you get a lot of condensation on them, and, if there is no radiator under the window, they are in the coldest part of the room. So take great care of the frames and do the job properly. They need to be well prepared in the first place, and you must carry out your painting thoroughly.

Do not cut in right to the edge of the glass, but allow a thin strip of paint (about 3mm (1/8in.) wide) on the pane as protection for the putty.

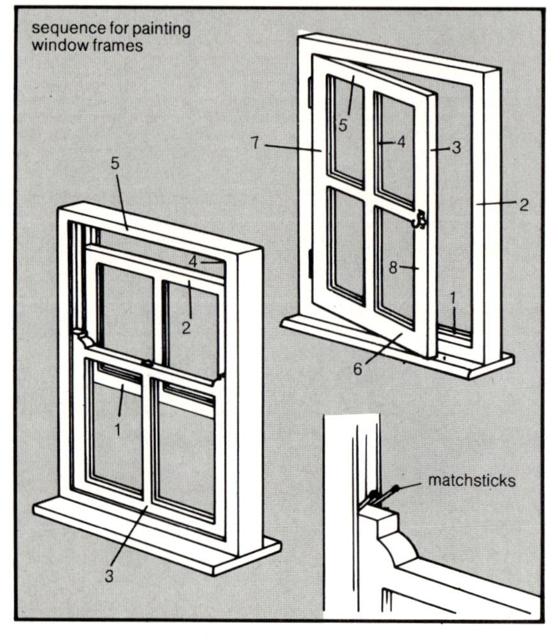

PAINTS THAT ARE DANGEROUS

At one time most paints contained lead, which is a poison and, if taken internally, can have dangerous, not to say fatal, consequences. The danger is not only to the decorator who is applying the paint: think of a child biting at the bars of a cot or a toy that has been treated with lead-based paints, or a pet gnawing at woodwork. However, there is no need to worry. Practically all modern paints, especially those that are available over the retail counter, are non-toxic and you can use them anywhere in your home with complete safety.

Some paints with dangerous quantities of lead are available to the trade, and many decorators will tell you that they offer the best protection for woodwork, particularly out of doors. This is especially true of some primers. There is no reason why you should not apply these paints, provided you are fully aware of the sort of material you are handling.

THE TRICK

Keep the paints well away from children and pets, and confine them to areas of your home well out of harm's way. While you are painting keep your hands away from your mouth – a warning that applies particularly to smokers.

However, most do-it-yourselfers will feel that the safe non-toxic paints offer all the protection that is needed, and will stick to these.

Whatever the job in hand, use Pro-Techs.

The first-ever range of specially designed DIY gloves.

The trick of any successful DIY job, as any professional will tell you, is to use the right tools for the job.

Yet it's surprising how few DIY-ists use the right gloves for the job.

Particularly when you think of the hell hands can go through.

That's why they need protecting.

And that's why Marigold have designed Pro-Techs.

The first-ever range of specially designed DIY gloves for professionals and enthusiasts alike.

Whatever the job in hand, get your hands on a pair of Pro-Techs.

You'll find them at larger DIY stores everywhere.

We think you'll find them just the trick.

PRO-Techs

Marigold®

LRC Products Ltd., North Circular Rd., E4 8QA.

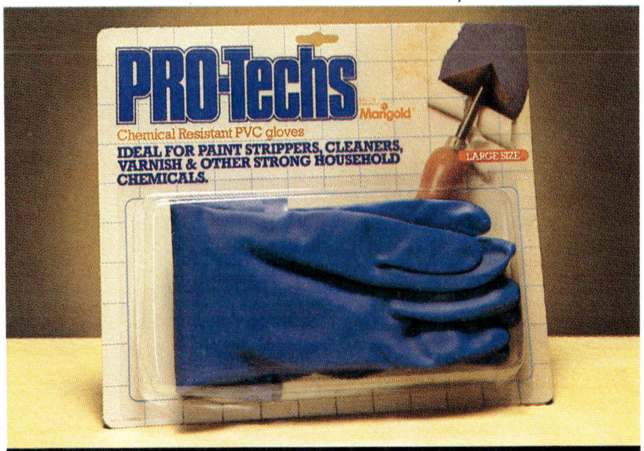

PVC Pro-Techs.
A chemically resistant glove that protects hands from harmful paint strippers, wood preservatives and the like.

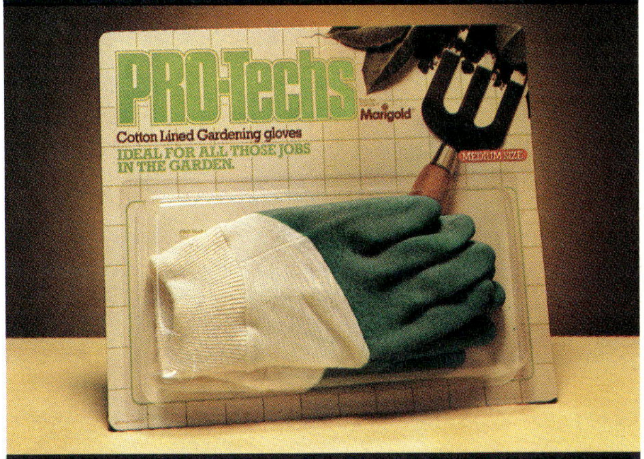

Gardening Pro-Techs.
A hard-wearing cotton lined latex glove that prevent green fingers from becoming grazed fingers.

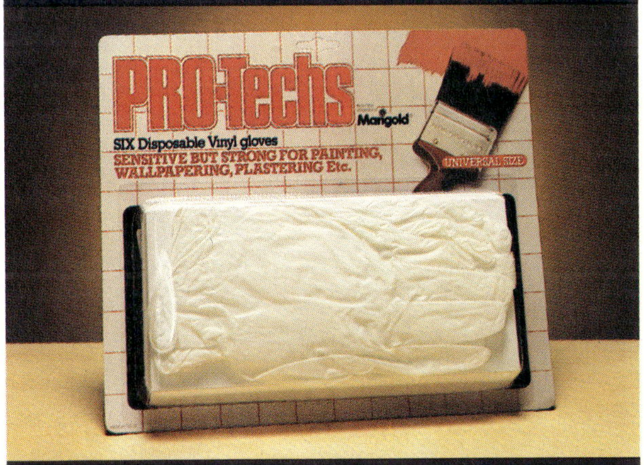

Disposable Pro-Techs.
A sensitive yet strong vinyl glove for those messy one-offs like painting and decorating.

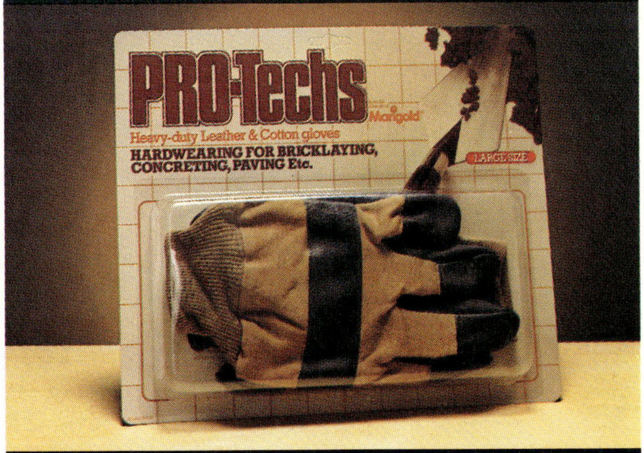

Heavy-Duty Pro-Techs.
A super rugged leather and cotton glove that can tackle – and tame – the heaviest manual work.

Do you still turn pale at the thought of using colours?

Every year, people spend ages trying to choose the right colours for their home.

And every year, some of them end up wishing they'd spent a bit longer.

To make it easier to choose a colour scheme, Dulux have created the Colour Collections. There are six in all, each of

which contain seven or eight shades that tone with each other perfectly.

Here, for example, we've used Muffin on the walls and ceiling, with Barley White picking out the skirting board, cornice and fireplace.

Then, for contrast, we painted the door in rich Spice.

All you need to do is choose a collection and then toy with a couple of variations of your own. (The mistake people often

make is to rely on just one colour to decorate a whole room).

To help you along, we've prepared a brochure about the Collections which you can pick up at your local paint shop or Dulux Colour Centre.

Once you've selected two or three shades that appeal, you can start to decorate. Without ending up having to redecorate.

ICI **Dulux** ***THE COLOUR COLLECTIONS.***

EMULSION PAINTS 1

Emulsions are the easiest of all paints to work with, which is why they are so popular. All you do is load your brush, bring it to the work, then spread the paint out in all directions, making sure you cover the area evenly and thoroughly. An emulsion paint can run, just like gloss, so you have to take care that it is well brushed out.

DEALING WITH NEW PLASTER

Not often as a do-it-yourselfer will you be called upon to tackle new plaster. However, you may well have had a lot of renovation work done in an old house, that will leave you new plaster to deal with. This must be left to dry out thoroughly before you put a decorative surface on it. That means waiting for at least six weeks, and preferably three months. If you ignore this warning, you risk the paint losing its opacity, starting to discolour, and even flaking off.

As the plaster dries out, you may get a white powdery deposit on the surface, the technical name for which is efflorescence.

brushing off efflorescence on plaster with a stiff brush

THE TRICK

Do not try to wash this off, because it is dampness that caused it. If you wet the plaster again you will only make things worse. Wipe or brush it off with a stiff brush, then wait. The condition should eventually cure itself as the plaster dries out.

If it does not, then you have a damp problem and you should call in a builder.

Another occasion would be in a room whose walls have always been papered, and which you are deciding for the first time to paint. In this case just ordinary preparation would be called for.

PRIMERS

Primers are not necessary on bare plaster, nor do emulsions have an undercoat. On bare surfaces or one that is highly absorbent, you can thin the first coat of emulsion with water. The instructions on the tin usually give you details of quantities to use when thinning. The same goes for cement, concrete, brickwork, etc., and when you are applying emulsion paint on top of lining papers and Anaglypta. Use a primer-sealer after you have removed whitewash or non-washable distemper. In the case of new plaster, however, it is a good idea to leave the first coat to dry overnight.

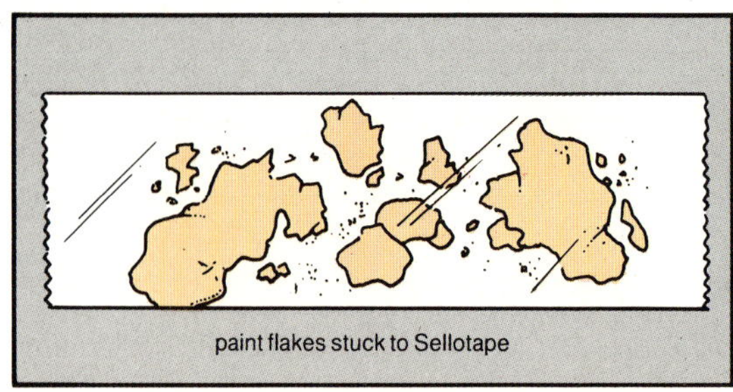
paint flakes stuck to Sellotape

THE TRICK

When you are dealing with walls that have already been treated with emulsion paint, rub your palm over the surface to see if a powder deposit is left. Otherwise stick a short length of Sellotape on the surface and see if any of the paint comes away when you peel the tape off.

Should these tests reveal a powdery surface, after washing treat it with a coat of stabilizing solution. When this has dried you can go on to paint in the normal way. In general you will find that two coats will be all that are required.

PAINTING WITH A ROLLER

Although you can never achieve as good a surface as with a brush, especially when applying gloss, a roller is an extremely useful device for covering large areas quickly, where it will give you a finish that is perfectly adequate.

The covering of the roller, which actually applies the paint, is known as the sleeve and this is now generally removable so that you can clean it more easily, and also buy replacements when it has worn out. Sleeves are made of plastic foam (the cheapest of all) or from synthetic or natural fibres. Paint with foam, mohair, short woolpile or short synthetics on plaster, lining paper, wood, boards such as plywood and hardboard, metal etc.; but with a sheepskin or a long synthetic pile on embossed wallpapers, Anaglyptas, brick, concrete and cement rendering. Synthetic fibres are impervious to water, so you should use these with emulsion paints and water-based paints for outside walls. Natural fibre sleeves are for gloss paints (including eggshells and undercoats) and out of doors for oil-based masonry paint. Rollers come in a range of widths, commonly from 150mm (6in.) to 250mm (10in.).

Rollers are loaded with paint from a tray. Both can be bought separately, but it is usual to get them as kits.

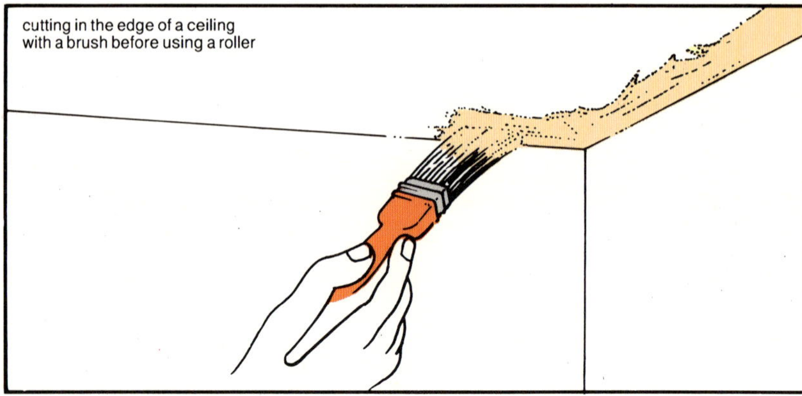
cutting in the edge of a ceiling with a brush before using a roller

Strain your paint from the can into the tray: some have a line indicating how much can go in, but otherwise leave about half of the sloping part uncovered. Push the roller into the deepest part of the tray, then roll it backwards and forwards on the slope to distribute the paint evenly and squeeze out all the excess. Your aim should be to load the roller enough for it not to dry out too quickly, yet not so much that paint drips everywhere.

Make your first run upwards on a wall, and away from you on a horizontal surface. Roll it steadily and slowly, making sure the entire surface is covered. When the paint starts to run out, recharge the roller immediately. Resist the temptation to make your paint go further by trying to squeeze that little bit extra from the roller; you will get a worse finish. Rollers cannot get too near an angle, and your cutting in here must be done with a small brush. Use your 25mm (1in.) varnish brush.

When you come to clean the sleeve, first roll out as much excess paint as you can on sheets of old newspaper. Then remove the sleeve, and wash it. Unless there are instructions to the contrary on the paint tin, you should clean oil paint out in paraffin, then wash the sleeve in detergent, finally giving it a good rinse. Emulsion paint can be cleaned from the sleeve with water.

loading a roller

THE TRICK

You can fit a broom handle to your roller so that you can tackle the ceiling while standing on the floor. Another advantage is that, with the handle held at an angle, the sleeve will not be directly overhead, so there is less risk of being splashed.

EMULSION PAINTS 2

PAINTING A CEILING

Many do-it-yourselfers attempt to paint a ceiling from just a pair of ordinary household steps, and in so doing they make a very big mistake. The area of ceiling you can reach from the top of the steps is very limited, and you have to get down continually from them to move them on to the next spot. To paint a ceiling properly, safely and without undue exertion you must have a scaffold board (see page 228).

In most normal-sized rooms you will be able to cover a ceiling completely from just three positions of your scaffold board, you will have finished the job in a small fraction of the time it takes from a pair of steps, and will feel much fresher into the bargain.

You should paint a ceiling in strips parallel to the wall containing the largest window. So set up your scaffold parallel to this wall, and just far enough away from it to be able to reach the end of the ceiling. Paint from this position a strip as wide as you can comfortably reach, then move your scaffold and go on to tackle the next strip.

THE TRICK

In no circumstances try to make the far edges of the strips a neat straight line, because the joins between the strips will show. You should aim for a ragged effect, and carry the paint from one patch well into the next.

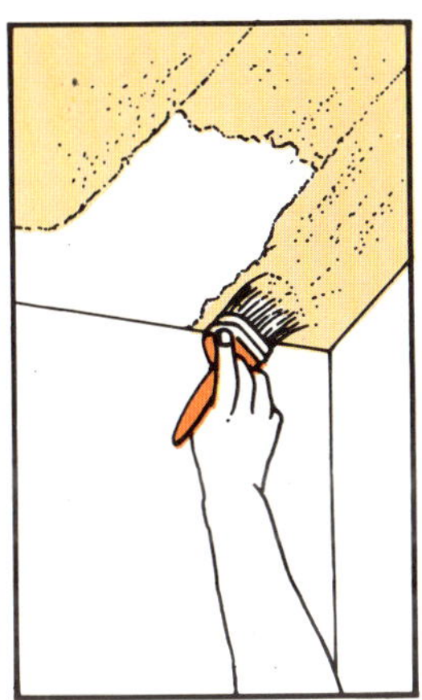

Working from a scaffold you will find that the edge of the first strip will still be wet when you come to paint alongside it. You will therefore be able to carry the new paint well into it. If you were working from steps, the first strip might well have hardened when you came back to it. So you would get a hard line between the various strips, which could be visible as what the professionals call a 'lap' mark in the finished result.

When painting the ceiling, there is no need to attempt any cutting in where the ceiling meets the top of the walls. Just make sure the ceiling itself is properly covered, and if the walls are to be a different colour, then you can go for your neat join when painting them.

Painting a ceiling is a hard, demanding job – like any work where you have to keep your hands stretched up high – but try to keep at it to finish it in one go, so that you always have a live, wet edge to pick up. Have a rest when the job is finished. If you are elderly or have a weak heart it might be better for you not to paint the ceiling. You could ask a friend or relative to do it for you, or call in a professional. You can decorate the rest of the room yourself, but if you are in any doubt on this point ask your doctor's advice.

how to paint a ceiling avoiding lap marks

PAINTING THE WALLS

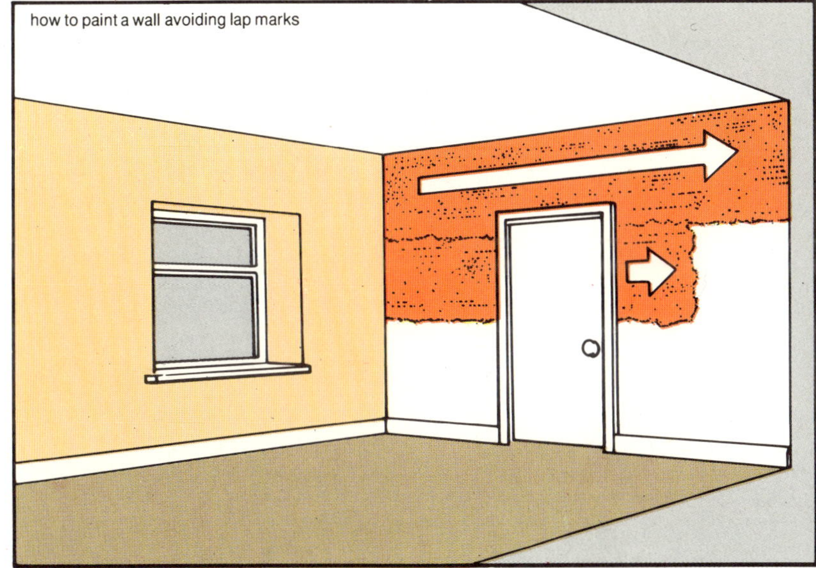

how to paint a wall avoiding lap marks

Walls should be painted in a series of horizontal strips, and you should begin each strip at the source of light, which means the window end in the case of walls at right angles to the window wall, and near a subsidiary source of light, such as a door or secondary window, for other walls. You should aim to work on each wall fairly quickly, for emulsion paint (which is what you will nearly always be applying on a wall) dries much more quickly than other paints, and it is important to keep the wet edge live in order to avoid lap marks. If you find yourself getting tired, you would do better to keep going and have your rest when each individual wall is complete. Painting a wall is not so demanding as tackling a ceiling. As with a ceiling, don't let the bottom of the strip end in a rigid, straight line. Make it a ragged one as an insurance against lap marks showing through.

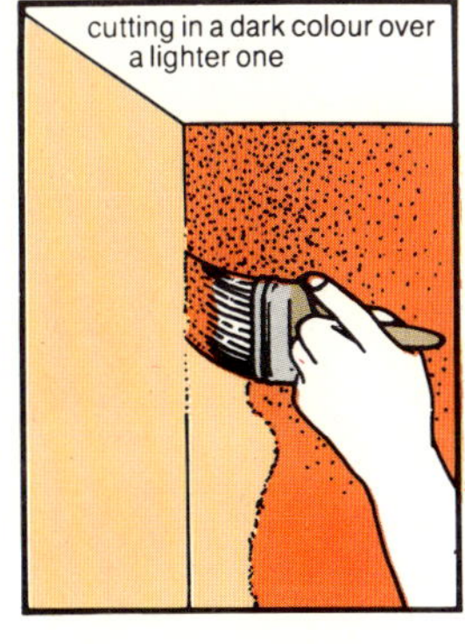

cutting in a dark colour over a lighter one

You will work more quickly if you tackle the top of the wall from a scaffold board rather than a pair of steps. Set your board at a height that allows you just comfortably to reach the top of the wall. If the ceiling is of a different colour, then do your cutting in first of all. Using a fairly narrow brush (25mm (1in.)) is fine, but some decorators think they get along better with a 50mm (2in.) one. Next paint the top horizontal strip, making it of a depth you can conveniently manage without stooping, which would be tiring. Then remove your scaffold board, tackle the next strip, and finally the one or two others that will be necessary to complete the average-sized wall. At the top of each strip, carry the vertical strokes of your brushwork well into the paint above – you will be able to do this if the wet edge is still live – to avoid a rigid dividing line showing between them. It was fashionable to have the walls of a room in different colours.

THE TRICK

If you intend using more than one colour always put the lighter one on first and don't bother about cutting in neatly. Just make sure you cover the entire area fully and allow the paint to stray as it will. Then do your cutting in when you come to apply the darker colour, which will obliterate more easily.

I have stressed the importance of a live, wet edge when painting with emulsion much more than I have with gloss paint. There are two reasons for this. In the first place emulsion paint dries much more quickly than gloss. In most ways this is a big advantage, for it means that you can finish off decorating a room much more quickly. Nevertheless, you have to get a move on when using it to make sure there will always be a wet edge to pick up. Secondly, you are normally dealing with much larger areas, so the edge could have dried when you come to pick it up again.

The consequences of the wet edge going off would be more serious with gloss as the lap mark would be harder and more visible. However it is not so likely to happen, because the paint takes longer to dry, and you are coating a much smaller area.

TYPES OF WALLCOVERING

Many of the so-called 'wallpapers' that are used in our homes do not, in fact, consist of paper at all, so the trade tends to use the all-embracing term 'wallcovering' to cover the full range of decorative materials (other than, of course, paint) that are used on a wall.

BASIC WALLPAPERS

Ordinary wallpapers are, in fact, the most common type of wallcovering, and offer the widest range of pattern. While some exclusive papers, particularly the hand-printed ones, carry price tags that put them in the luxury class, wallpapers are by and large the cheapest form of wallcovering. At the lower end of the scale, they do not cost all that much more than emulsion paint.

The big snag with ordinary papers is that you cannot really clean them. True, some of them are described as waterfast, but that means little more than that you can wipe off any paste that gets on the pattern during hanging.

THE TRICK

If you do have any accidents with an ordinary paper you can often remove spots of grease, etc. by rubbing them gently with small lumps of bread. But washing is right out.

You can use these papers widely in homes where they are not likely to be subjected to the ravages of young children or pets.

WASHABLE PAPERS

This is an ordinary printed wallpaper that has been coated with a thin film of plastic, so it is still in order to refer to it as a 'paper'. The amount of washing that washables will stand is, however, limited. You can wipe dirt from them with a soapy cloth, but beware of using too much force. Washables can be used on any surface that is likely to suffer from stains and splashes, but are not suitable for really heavy-duty areas.

VINYLS

These are not really papers, for the colour, design and any surface texturing of a vinyl are all contained in a PVC film. This is bonded to a paper backing only so that it can be handled more easily. You can actually scrub vinyls without any fear of damaging or wearing away the surface of the design, so obviously they are ideal for kitchens, bathrooms, children's bedrooms and staircase walls. However, they are expensive. Bear this in mind when deciding whether to choose one or not.

RELIEF DECORATIONS

Another group of widely used wallcoverings are known as relief decorations, because they have a design that is deeply embossed in them. This makes them highly suitable for covering up bad wall surfaces, and they are extensively used in the renovation of older properties. Most of them are manufactured by the Crown company, and the names given are all Crown trade marks. However, similar products come from other companies, and some relief decorations are sold under store brand names.

These decorations usually have a white surface meant to be painted, so that the design possibilities are endless. You choose a pattern that appeals to you and give it whatever colour you wish.

The cheapest of the Crown relief decorations is Anaglypta, which consists of two layers of paper bonded together. Supaglypta looks similar but is made from cotton fibres rather than wood pulp, so it is stronger and the pattern can be more deeply embossed. Vinaglypta is a relief decoration with a vinyl surface – in other words you get the hard-wearing qualities of a vinyl in addition to all the advantages of an embossed pattern. This, again, is more expensive.

WOODCHIP PAPER

This consists of small chips of real wood sandwiched between two layers of paper in a random pattern. This is ideal as a cover-up for bad walls, and has a surface that is meant to be painted. It is relatively cheap.

FLOCK

Real flock papers, as well as being expensive, are very delicate, and almost impossible for the do-it-yourselfer to handle successfully. Vinyl flocks, however, are just as tough, and can be washed just as easily as ordinary vinyl.

PAPERLESS 'PAPER'

The latest form of wallcovering, made by ICI and known as Novamura, is made from lightly foamed polythene. The big difference about it is that you paste the wall, not the material, and hang the Novamura from the roll. Novamura is easy to clean, to hang, and to strip off when you want to redecorate.

LUXURY PAPERS

After this, we are getting into very specialist – and expensive – fields. Foils and metallic papers conduct electricity, so they should not be hung in bathrooms, or tucked behind light switches and socket outlets.

HOW MUCH WILL YOU NEED?

You should always buy at the start as much paper as you will need to finish the room. If you don't, and have to go back for an extra roll, you may find that it has come from a different printing batch, and a slight colour variation will show up when the paper is on the wall.

Wallpaper shops have printed tables to estimate the quantities required. They ask you to measure the height of your room, and its perimeter, and the table tells them how much you need. They ask you to include doors and windows in your perimeter measurements on the basis that this ensures an extra allowance for trimming. This is a bit rough and ready.

THE TRICK

The decorator measures the height of the wall to be papered – from skirting board to ceiling, or picture rail. Wallcoverings in Britain come in standard rolls that are 10.05m (33ft) long, so he can work out how many drops he will get out of a roll. In deciding on the number of drops, he will take into account the size of the pattern, for you can get a lot of wastage in matching up a large repeat. To find how many widths of paper will go round the room, use a spare roll of paper – 520mm (20½in.) wide – as a measuring stick. Work out how many you will need by walking round the room and placing it on the wall. Ignore doors and windows in this measuring. Divide the number of widths by the number of drops per roll, and you have the number of rolls required. Add a little extra for areas over doors, and around windows.

Some continental and specialist papers can vary in size from the dimensions given above, so it is always wise to check.

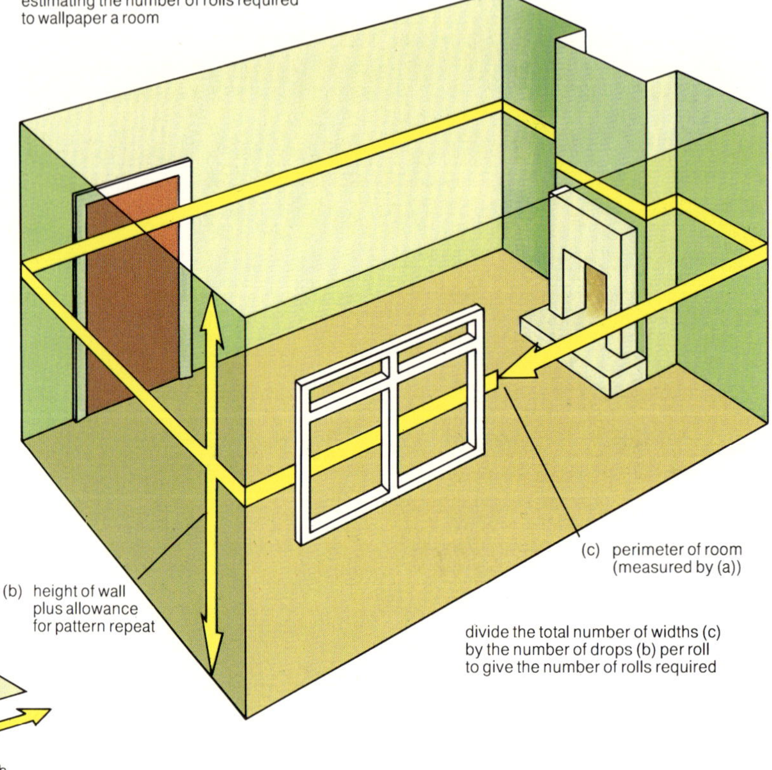

EQUIPMENT FOR WALLPAPERING

THE TOOLS

Your first requirements are an ordinary plastic bucket in which to mix your paste, and a clean stick to stir the mix as you add the paste powder to water.

RULE AND PENCIL

The paper must be cut to the correct length (and sometimes width, too) and for this some measuring device is needed. When you are wallpapering, many of the measurements you need will be horizontal ones, and these can be taken much more quickly if you have a rule that can be held rigid in one hand. The professional decorator tends to prefer a folding, boxwood rule. After you have measured the paper, you need to mark it, and for that you should use a pencil only.

SCISSORS

The paper will need cutting to size, and many people use a pair of dressmaking scissors. But remember, the longer the scissor blades, the straighter will be your cut. The scissors the tradesman uses are about 300mm (12in.) long, but these are unwieldy; 255mm (10in.) is the maximum size of blade to go for, but you might even plump for blades as short as 175mm (7in.). However, you would find it difficult to cut wallpaper accurately with anything shorter than that.

THE TRICK

Since a lot of the cutting is done while the paper is wet, scissors used in decorating pick up a lot of moisture. Buy a pair that are non-rusting such as stainless steel ones. These are not easy to find but, if you hunt around, you should come across some.

When you are working with vinyls, a retractable-bladed knife, such as the Stanley knife, can be used for the trimming.

BRUSH

The brush which you use for emulsion paint is perfectly satisfactory for pasting the paper, and it is very easy to clean the old paste out of it when you have finished.

Don't choose too big a brush – one with bristles about 75mm (3in.) long would be ideal. Anything bigger you would find too heavy to wield.

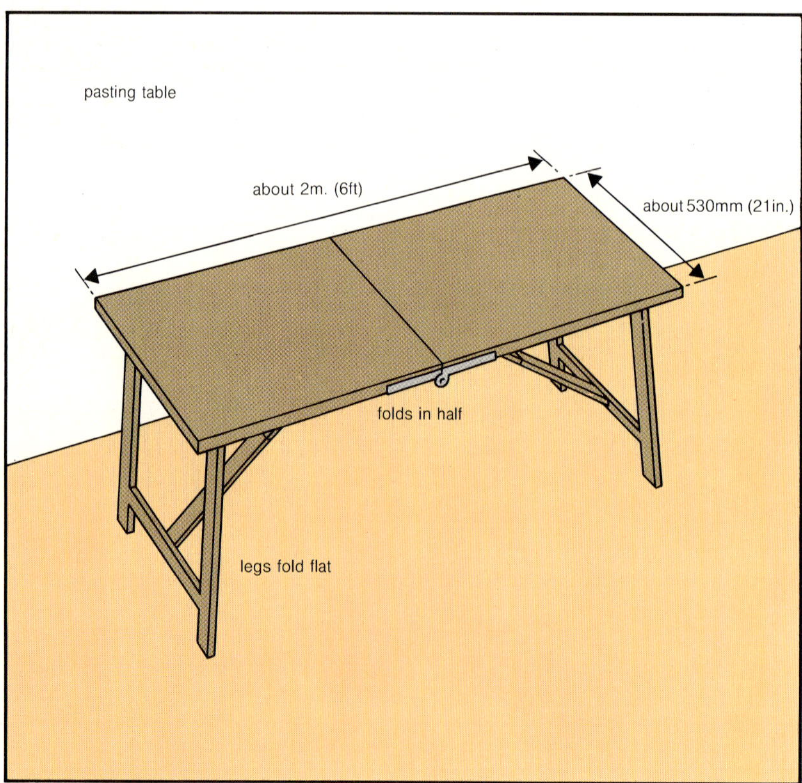

pasting table

PASTING TABLE

The pasting has to be carried out somewhere, and the professional uses a proper pasting table. This is a lightweight one that folds up, so that it can be easily carried around. Because they think they will not use it all that often, many do-it-yourself decorators try to skip buying a pasting table and use some substitute: taking a flush door from its hinges and using that on the kitchen table is a popular dodge.

STEPS

Most walls are higher than the average person can reach, and you need a means of getting to the top of them. A pair of ordinary household steps is all you need for this. A scaffold board is no use when you are hanging paper on a wall.

PLUMBLINE AND BOB

The paper must be hung truly vertical, and to ensure this you will need a plumbline and bob. Purpose-built versions are available but this could be improvized – by tying a small weight (a nut for instance) on to a length of thin string.

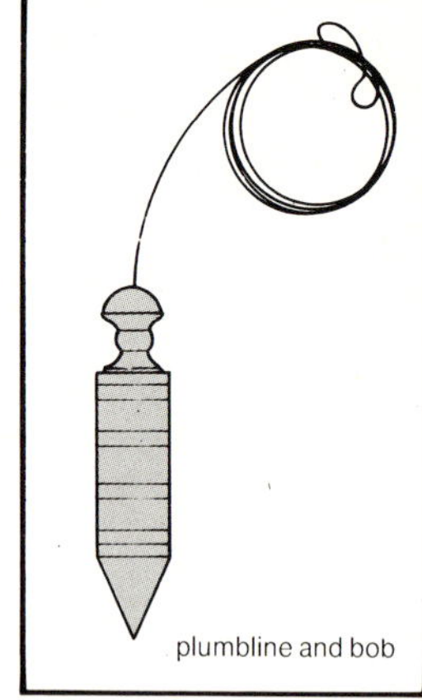
plumbline and bob

THE TRICK

An old typewriter ribbon spool is a good thing to keep your makeshift plumbline on, and it helps you to use the line properly by holding it a little proud of the wall.

PAPERHANGING BRUSH

To smooth the paper to the wall, you brush it in place, using a proper paperhanger's brush. You cannot make do with a paintbrush instead. One possible makeshift is a clothesbrush, but you cannot work so quickly or effectively with this. Your paperhanging brush must have soft bristles, especially if you are hanging embossed papers, because you use a dabbing motion to press the paper in place, and hard bristles might damage it.

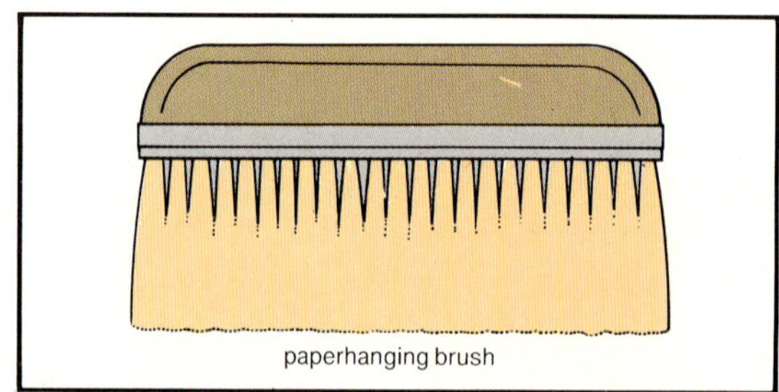
paperhanging brush

SEAM ROLLER

This is a small wooden or plastic roller with a small handle which flattens down the join between two lengths of paper. There are two basic designs of seam roller. One has a fork-like handle that holds the roller between two prongs. In the other type, the roller is fixed to a single arm. This type is the most versatile, as you can get into corners with it.

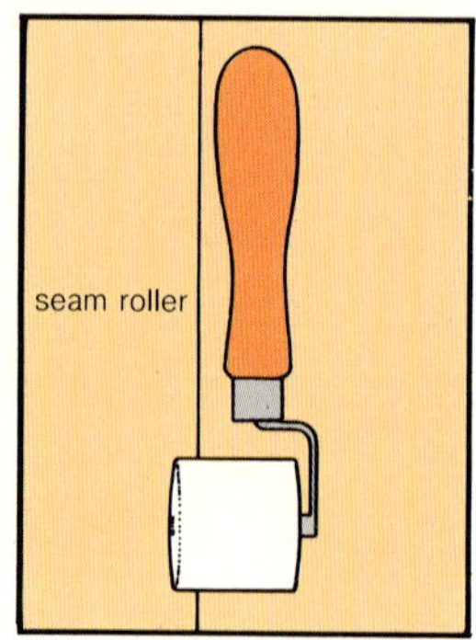
seam roller

SPONGE OR RAG

Lastly a sponge or old rag is always a handy thing to have around when you are hanging wallpaper, so that you can mop up splashes and the like.

SIZING

The walls need to be sized before you can hang paper on them, because they would otherwise be too absorbent and would dry up the adhesive on the back of the paper too quickly. This means that the paper would not stick so well and you would not get so much 'slip' as you tried to slide it into position.

You can buy special size, but the adhesive you are using on the paper will do. There should be instructions on the back of the packet telling you how to mix the powder to use it as size. Apply the size to the wall with your pasting brush. Take care that you spread the size out evenly, and that you cover the entire surface.

PREPARING TO WALLPAPER

ORDER OF WORK

If you are going to paper the walls of a room, then any painting of woodwork, etc. should be done first. If you are papering the ceiling, this should be done before the walls (see page 264).

Where should you start your wallpapering? A paper with a small, unobtrusive pattern, a plain texture, or a vertical stripe is the easiest thing to hang. With this kind you begin in a corner near the window and work towards the door. When you get to the door, go back to the other window corner, and work towards the door. There are two reasons for this. Firstly, if you are working away from the light, joins will be less likely to show. Secondly, the perimeter of your room will not be equivalent to an exact number of rolls, and you have to lose a fraction of a width somewhere. A favourite place for this is over the door.

Much harder to handle are papers with a large, dominant pattern, as they have to be 'set out' properly, otherwise they look ridiculous. With them you should begin on a dominant architectural feature, such as the chimney breast. Find the centre of the chimney breast and work outwards. Some patterns will look better with the first roll centred on this line, others with a length hung both sides of it.

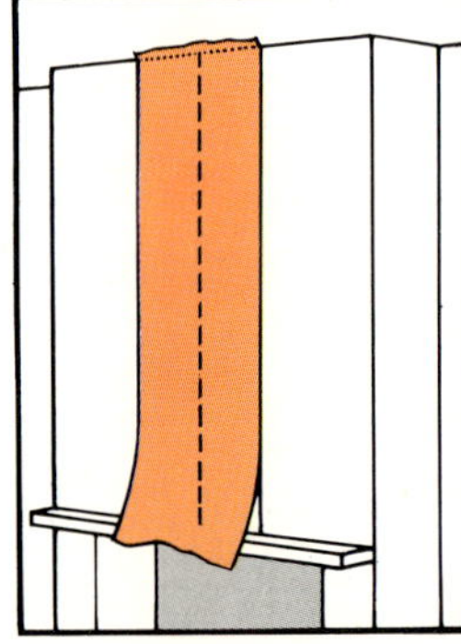

THE TRICK

The easy way to find out is to stick three or four shallow strips of the paper actually in position, and decide which looks best.

Having finished the face of the chimney breast, turn your attention to the fireplace alcoves if you have them; once again set the paper out centrally, leaving half rolls, if need be, on the sides of the chimney breast.

In a room without a chimney breast you would probably take, as the dominant architectural feature, the wall at which everyone looks.

As you work around the room, bear in mind the importance of balancing a paper of this sort, and set it out properly. Considerable craftsmanship is called for in coping with a large pattern, and you should start with a simple pattern.

MIXING THE PASTE

First mix your paste. Get on with cutting up the rolls into the correct lengths while you wait the requisite fifteen minutes or so for the glue to stand. Be sure to specify the right glue. In general you must use a cellulose adhesive for ordinary lightweight papers, a starch-based one for heavier-duty papers, and one with a fungicide for vinyls because the glue cannot 'breathe' through the plastic facing of these coverings, and mould would grow underneath. Always check whenever you buy a paper what type of glue the manufacturer recommends. If you follow his instructions, and things go wrong, you have a sound basis for complaint.

THE TRICK

Many professionals tie strings to the handle holders across their bucket to form a brush rest. If you leave the brush standing up in the paste, it will flop down and paste will get the handle. If you rest it on any surface it might pick up dust and dirt, so this is well worth adopting.

Follow closely the instructions on the packet when mixing the glue. Normally you pour into the bucket the correct amount of water (you should use a measuring jug), then sprinkle in the paste slowly and gradually, stirring it with a clean stick as you do so. Be careful not to pour the powder too quickly, otherwise lumps tend to form.

Mix right at the start enough paste to do the whole job. It will not go off, even overnight.

If in doubt, always mix your paste too thick, rather than too thin. It is easy to thin down by adding extra water, but you can't add extra powder to thin paste, because it will go lumpy.

THE TRICK

If you are worried about the paste, make a simple test. Load your brush with paste, and dab it on the back of a length of paper you are to hang. Now lift the brush; if the paper comes with it, the paste is all right.

When tackling a small job you will want only a half, or a quarter, of the packet. Divide it up by weight, using the kitchen scales. Then write on the packet what proportion is left.

MEASURING UP

Measure the height of the wall to be covered from the top of the skirting board to the picture rail or to the ceiling. Then add 75mm (3in.) as a trimming allowance (i.e. 40mm (1½in.) top and bottom) and that is the length to which you should cut each drop. The measurement obviously has to be transferred to the paper. You can do this by placing your rule on an unrolled length, and marking it.

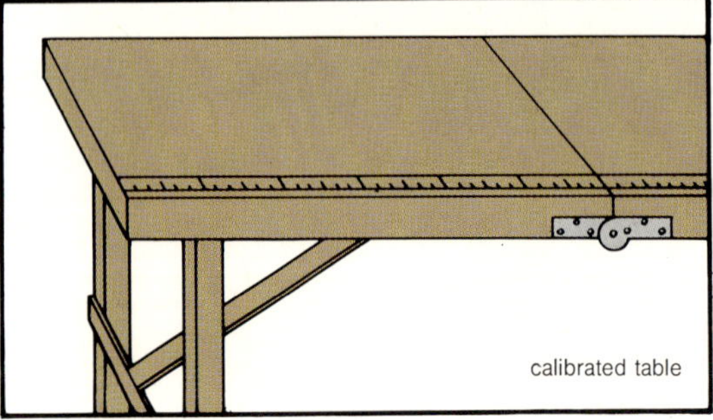
calibrated table

THE TRICK

Far better and quicker, however, to have a calibrated pasting table, so that you see at a glance where you must cut. Calibrating a table is easy enough. Get a 2m (6ft plus) dressmaker's tape, cut it to length and glue it to the top. You will find it easier if the rule is on the near side of the table.

It is necessary, incidentally, to measure only the first drop you cut for each wall. All subsequent ones are cut to the same length, using this first drop as a guide.

SHADING THE ROLLS

Look on the back of the roll, where you will find a number. Check that all the roll numbers are the same. These are batch numbers; papers that have ostensibly the same pattern in an identical colourway can show slight variations in shades if they are not part of the same batch. These variations will not be very marked, and you will notice them only if lengths from different batches are hung side by side. If you find rolls from different batches make sure they do not go on the same wall. If doing so would leave you with a lot of waste paper, go back to the shop – before you have cut the rolls up – and explain what has happened. The shop ought to change them for you.

Finally, partly unwind all the rolls of paper you have bought, and place them one on top of each other on your table to check visually that they all match up properly. Professionals call this 'shading before hanging'.

CUTTING AND PASTING

CUTTING TO LENGTH

Don't just unwind the paper and cut it to length haphazardly. First determine which is the top of the pattern, so that you do not hang it upside down. Nothing looks so ridiculous and amateurish as that, yet it can easily happen if you don't watch out. You cannot assume that the bit that comes off the roll first is the top.

Remember that it is the pattern at the top of the wall that will be noticed by people entering, so it has to start at a sensible place where it will look attractive and not comical. Find such a spot as near to the beginning of the roll as possible, where 'the pattern is full', then add your 40mm (1½in.) trimming allowance and cut the paper. There will be a small amount of waste at the start of the roll.

Having cut the paper at the top, cut it to its proper length, plus another trimming allowance of 40mm (1½in.). Take great care over this first drop, for you use it as a guide for cutting the rest. All subsequent drops should start at the same point in the pattern repeat, so that they will match up exactly on the wall.

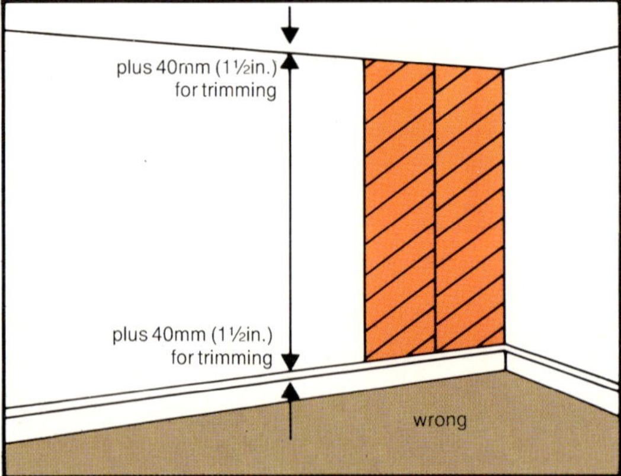

SQUARING UP

Make sure that your first length of paper is hung truly vertical, for its position will determine that of all the others on the wall.

Let us assume that you are starting at the left-hand end of a wall, and working towards the right. Reverse all the instructions if you are working from right to left. Place your steps there, climb them and at the top of the wall, at ceiling level, make a pencil mark – the width of a roll of wallpaper less 13mm (½in.) from the left-hand end. Place a spare roll of paper on the wall to act as a gauge. Hold the top of your plumbline on this pencil mark. When the line is steady, make a mark down it on the wall with a pencil held in the other hand. Start this line fairly near to the top of the wall (within 150mm (6in.) and continue it downwards for as long as you comfortably can. There is no need for you to draw from top to bottom of the wall.

THE TRICK

Make sure that your pencil line is directly behind the line, don't draw on the line's shadow.

PASTING THE PAPER

Place your paper on the table. If it will not lie flat, back-roll it to ensure that it does so. When you start to paste, the top of the paper should be positioned to line up with the right-hand end, the bottom portion overhanging at the left. Next push the paper away from you so that its far edge slightly overhangs the back edge of the table.

Dip the brush into the paste so that its bristles are about two-thirds submerged, then press it against each side of the bucket in turn to make sure that the paste is evenly distributed and all excess has been squeezed out.

Mentally divide that part of the paper on the table-top into quarters, and paste them as shown. Apply the paste with your right hand and hold the paper steady with the left. Thus you will be able to ensure that your left hand is always on a dry bit of paper. If you put your left hand on a pasted portion of paper you will be drying off the paper at that point. It is not unknown for five little blobs to show through when a paper has been hung and finally dried out – especially on a ceiling.

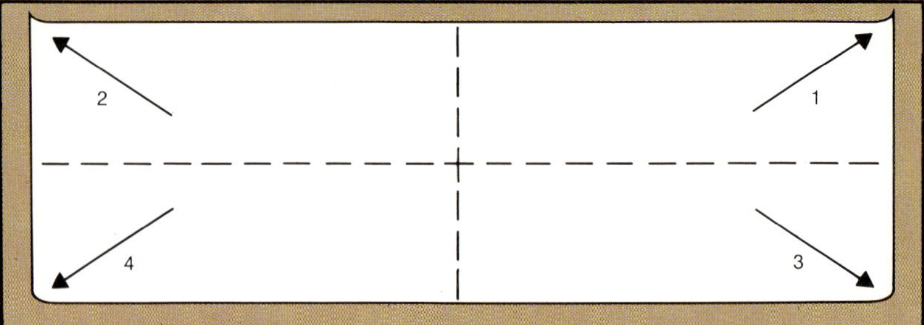

Paste with a series of zigzag strokes from the centre of the paper towards the edge. If you do the opposite – i.e. paste from the edge of the paper inwards – you would undoubtedly get paste on the face of the paper.

After you have pasted the two far quarters, drag the paper towards you (make sure you don't get hold of a pasted portion), allowing it this time to overhang slightly the nearside edge. Now finish pasting the last two quarters.

With all four quarters pasted, take hold of the right-hand edge of the paper, each corner between a thumb and middle finger. Raise it and move it to the far end of the table, letting it drop gently so that the paper is neatly and squarely folded in two, the edges parallel, top to bottom. To make sure that you will not get any paste on the ceiling when you come to hang the paper, fold over the top 20mm (¾in.) i.e about half the extra bit that you allowed for trimming.

Move the folded paper along to the right, and you should be able to accommodate the rest on your table. Again, this will need back-rolling if it starts to curl up. Paste as already described, then take hold of it at the left-hand end and fold inwards until its edge meets that of the previous fold.

THE TRICK

If any paste gets on to the table-top during this, sponge it off immediately, cleanliness is all-important when you are hanging wallpaper.

Your paper has now been properly pasted and folded. It should have one large fold (the top one) and a smaller one at the bottom – the proportions will probably be about two-thirds to one-third.

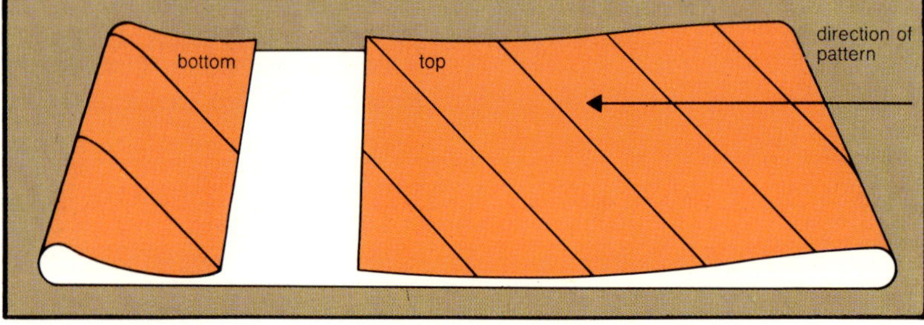

SOAKING

If you are dealing with an embossed or duplex paper (i.e. one that consists of two layers of paper bonded together) it needs to be left to soak. Simplex (single-layer) papers do not need soaking. One of the snags of soaking wallpaper, however, is that if you leave it saturated it will stretch. To match up the patterns you have to make sure that each length of paper stretches by exactly the same amount. There is only one way to ensure that – leave each of them to soak for exactly the same length of time. Somewhere between 10 and 15 minutes is ideal.

THE TRICK

Write in pencil on the back of the paper, at the top where it will get trimmed off, the time at which you finished pasting. Then you will know when you can start to hang the paper.

At first you will sit around waiting for 10 minutes to pass between pasting and hanging, but as you become more experienced you will paste two, hang two, as the tradesman does.

WALLPAPER HANGING 1

Take your pasted paper neatly over one arm and climb your steps. Take hold of each corner edge of the top between the thumb and finger. The small portion that you folded over at the top will, as well as keeping paste off the ceiling, ensure that your fingers stay dry. Let the paper fall out of its top fold.

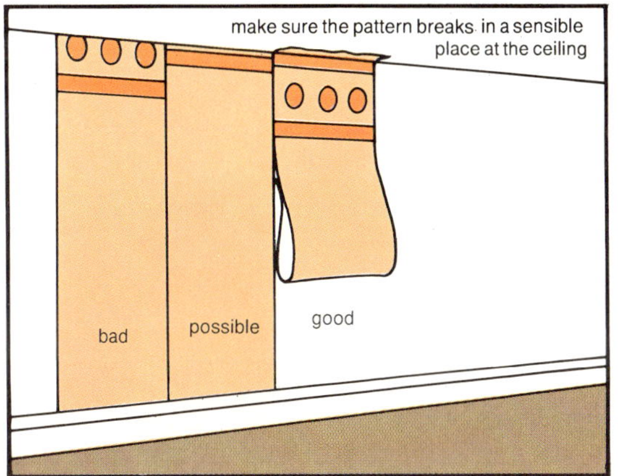

THE TRICK

So that it will not go crashing down too much, stretch out one foot, balancing on the other, and hold the bottom fold on the outstretched instep.

THE FIRST DROP

Bring the paper to the wall, place the top right-hand edge on the plaster and, with your hand flat on top, slide this edge so that it just 'kisses' the pencil line. It is important not to place the whole width of the paper flat on the wall as you do this sliding; just one small portion is sufficient. You want to ensure that the break in the pattern where the top meets the ceiling comes in an attractive and logical position. Take great care over this with the first drop. Its position will determine that of all the others.

When you are satisfied, let the paper lie flat on the wall, and use your paperhanging brush to smooth it into place. Work from the centre of the paper outwards, using not-too-heavy strokes, so that you do not alter the positioning of the paper. Be sure not to move it from the vertical. Brush it well into the angle where it meets the ceiling, using a dabbing motion.

Note that the paper goes 13mm (½in.) or so on the adjacent wall, all the way down. This 'turn' will be covered when you come to paper that wall.

TRIMMING

Take your closed scissors and score along the meeting line between wall and ceiling. Peel the paper away and, working from the reverse side, cut along the score line neatly and cleanly. Sponge off any paste that has got on to the ceiling, then brush the paper back into place. Now pull the paper out of its bottom fold and smooth it in place. Hold your pencil upright, and almost flat against the wall, then draw it along the paper where it touches the skirting board. The line will be slightly away from the wall. Peel the paper away and, working from its face side, cut the paper just above the line. Brush the paper back in place. If any paste gets on to the skirting board, wipe it off. You cannot use this method at the top because you have to cut on the face side of the paper. At the top that would involve almost standing on your head, or pulling too much of the paper away to allow you to see the decorative side.

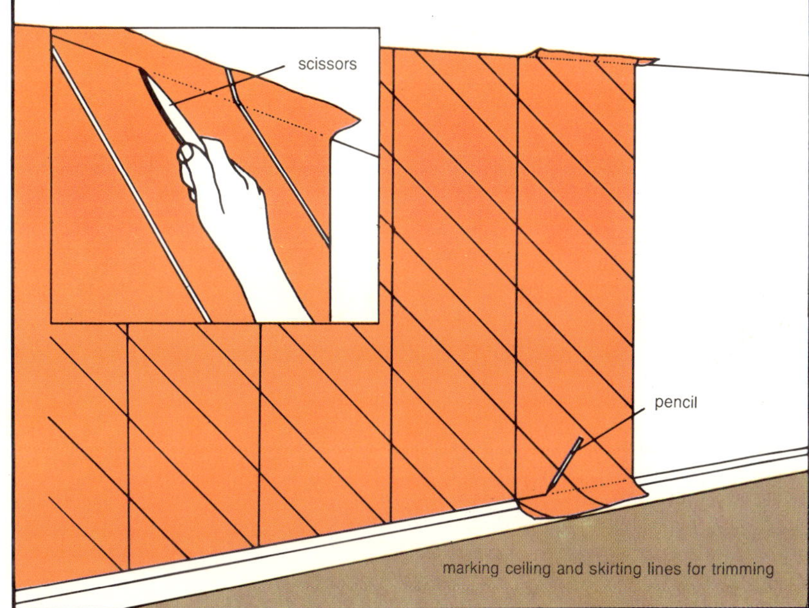

marking ceiling and skirting lines for trimming

FURTHER DROPS

Subsequent lengths are hung in much the same way. However, you bring the top left-hand edge to the wall first, and slide it so that you get a good pattern match with the first drop, then smooth this into place. Top and bottom trimming is done as before.

USING THE SEAM ROLLER

It is essential to use the seam roller on vinyl. The purpose is to flatten the join between the two lengths and stick it down firmly, but you must be careful. The seam roller tapers slightly at the end furthest from the single arm, and it is this tapered tip that comes into contact with the paper.

THE TRICK

The taper means that you cannot bring the roller accurately right down the join in one long movement. Instead you must make a series of strokes in a zigzag motion. Don't make too many strokes, otherwise you will get a polished effect on either side of the join.

Carry on hanging the third and subsequent drops. Never use a seam roller on embossed papers.

THE END OF THE WALL

Inevitably, the last drop will need to be narrower than the roll of paper. Measure it at its widest point – you will normally be able to see this, but if you cannot, take measurements at random points to find it.

To the widest measurement add 13mm (½in.) and cut your roll to this width.

THE TRICK

Place it pattern-upwards on your pasting table, lay your rule on the paper and mark the required width at intervals of 300mm (12in.) or so all along the paper. Stand at one end of the table, sight along the marks and cut to them with your scissors. There is no need to join up the marks with a pencil line.

You will now have two lengths of paper: one cut to width, which we will call piece A, and the other portion, which we will call B. Do not throw B away. Paste, hang and trim A in the normal way, turning it round the corner by its small surplus width as needed.

On the return wall drop and mark a plumbline the width of B from the corner. Paste B and hang it to this plumbline. It will overlap A by varying amounts, according to how far out of true the walls are. It is impossible to get a good pattern match down the whole drop, so you should aim to do your perfect matching at the eye level of a person standing up, because that will be the one that people will notice most when they enter the room. The top and bottom matching will have to work out as it comes.

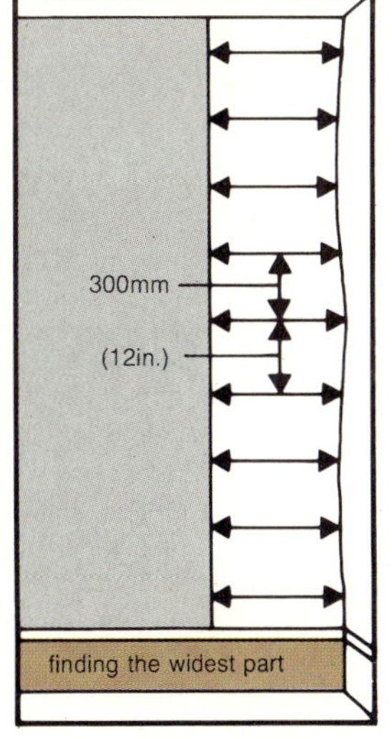

finding the widest part

Now complete the rest of the wall in the normal way, butting up the first complete length against B, and following on with subsequent drops as before.

This is for dealing with an internal angle – i.e. the return wall comes towards you. External angles are much easier because normally you can take the paper right round. However, where the angle is a long way from being truly upright, there can be problems. It is then better to turn the corner with two drops, in a similar manner to internal corners.

Piece A should be hung first, leaving the excess width sticking out. Hang B on the return wall to a plumbline, trying to match up the pattern. Brush the excess of A round the corner and on top of B so that B's raw edge will not be visible. You might have to smear a little extra paste underneath the edge of A.

WALLPAPER HANGING 2

LIGHT SWITCHES

There are two basic types of light switch: the modern kind, which are rectangular and fit fairly flush to the wall; and the old-fashioned types that are circular and stand proud of the wall.

The former is by now probably the more common, so let us deal with it first. Hang your length of paper, making sure that its pattern matches up with that of the adjacent drop, and allowing it to lie on top of the switch. Spear the paper at the centre of the switch with the point of your closed scissors, and from this hole make a scissor-cut to each of the four corners of the switch. You will be left with four flaps. Fold these back, mark with a pencil where they touch tne edge of the switch just as you would when trimming the paper to the skirting board, and cut along this line. It is permissible to hide any 'tails' under the cover of the switch (always providing that you are not dealing with a metallic paper). Pull the switch cover away from the wall by withdrawing the screws you see on its face, having first turned off the electricity at the mains, and push the 'tails' underneath. Then screw the cover down again and restore the power.

The principle of dealing with a round switch is similar, in that you spear the paper at the centre of the switch in just the same way. However, you make many more cuts from the centre outwards, until you are left with a lot of little tails. Brush these well into the base of the switch, and mark them where they touch it. Then you can trim them to fit neatly, and brush them well back into place.

In both cases you will need to lift the paper away from the wall to do the cutting.

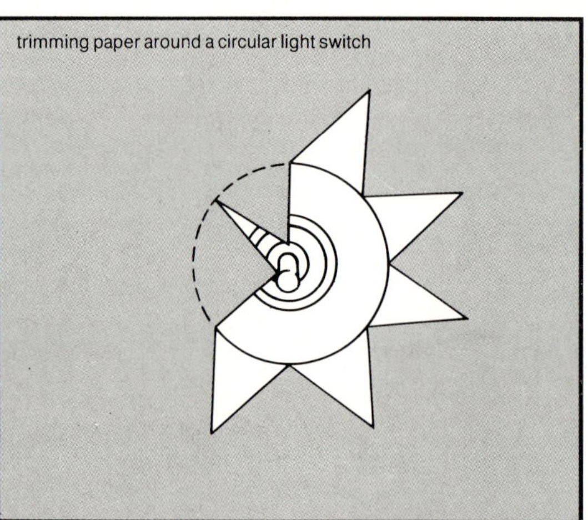
trimming paper around a circular light switch

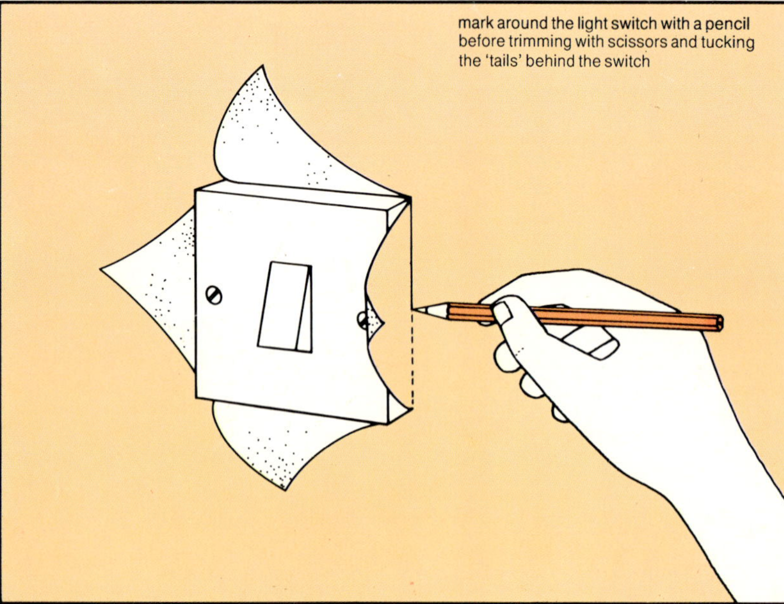
mark around the light switch with a pencil before trimming with scissors and tucking the 'tails' behind the switch

DOORWAYS

At least one wall of the room will have a doorway, and one drop of paper will need to be cut to a sort of L-shape to fit round it. Hang the drop in the normal way, matching it up to the adjacent drop at one side, and letting it lie over the face of the door frame, with the door closed, at the other. Make a diagonal scissor-cut from the outer edge of the paper to the top outside point of the door frame. It will now be possible to brush the paper down flat, with waste sticking up all round the door frame. Trim the paper first to meet the ceiling, in the normal way. Then trim it to fit the top and side of the door opening, using the pencil-marking method described for cutting to the skirting board (see page 259). Finally, cut it to fit the skirting.

In modern small homes, doorways are usually right at the end of a wall, so all you now have to do to complete that particular wall is hang a short, narrow piece over the opening. This is a good place to 'lose' a half-width drop (see page 259). However, it may be that you will need a second L-shaped piece, cut in just the same way, at the other side of the door. This second L-shaped piece could be narrow, to allow you to 'lose' the half width. In the case of very wide door openings – french windows, for instance, or intercommunicating doors between a living and dining room – you will need an L-shaped piece at each end, as well as several short drops between.

papering around a doorway

FIREPLACES

A simple uncomplicated modern fireplace is dealt with just like a wide door opening; you will need an L-shaped piece at each end, and shorter drops in the middle. However, as a chimney breast is the most instantly obvious part of the room, you must not try to 'lose' narrow drops here.

In Victorian or older houses, however, you may have a fireplace with a lot of ornate moulding at each end. The way of dealing with this is similar to the method for tackling a round light switch: i.e. you make a lot of short cuts away from the moulding, then brush the paper back in place, leaving a lot of tails sticking up. Mark these with a pencil where they meet the moulding, pull them back and cut them to fit. The more complicated the moulding, the more cuts (and tails) you will have to make to fit. Finally, brush the tails back in place, and they will not be noticeable.

THE WASTE BITS

The result of all the trimming will be a lot of left-over bits and pieces of paper. What are you to do with them? One thing you must not do is simply throw them on the ground to lie around anywhere, for wet paste is slippery and you could have a nasty accident as a result of skidding on a piece of paper. So you must carefully put them somewhere out of harm's way. The traditional place for this was the fireplace (with the fire unlit, of course) because that is somewhere you would not want to walk, and yet the paper would not be piled up against a wall needing to be decorated.

THE TRICK

Today, of course, many rooms do not have a fireplace. The best alternative is a plastic sack or other receptacle. Then when the job is done you simply dispose of the sackful of paper.

WALLPAPER HANGING 3

THE WINDOW WALL

Since you start papering a room in the angles at each end of the window wall and work towards the door (see page 256), the window wall itself is something that has to be tackled in isolation. It is best if you make it the last job in the room. Some older houses have a complete wooden frame round the window opening, and you deal with this as though it were a doorway, cutting in under the bottom of the frame in the same way as you did at the top. More tricky, however, is the arrangement found in most modern homes where there is an opening – known as a reveal – in which the window is set. This is the procedure for dealing with a wall in which there is a reveal.

First find the centre point of the wall over the window, and drop and mark a plumbline there. Begin hanging short drops of paper from the ceiling, carrying them under the top of the reveal – or soffit, as this top is known – to meet the timber of the window frame itself.

Your first of these short drops can be centred on the plumbline or just to the side of it; work out which arrangement will give you the best turn into the side of the window – you will see what this means as we carry on with the instructions.

Trim the short drops in the usual way to the ceiling and frame. Normally, you can go straight from ceiling to frame with one length, but if the angle is badly out of true it might be better to do this with two pieces – i.e. first cover the soffit with a small piece of paper, then paper the wall over the opening from ceiling to soffit. This top piece would overlap that on the soffit – since the overlap would be pointing away from the room, it would not be visible.

Carry on hanging short drops on one side of the first – you can work to the left or right just as you wish, but for the rest of these instructions I will assume that you are working to the left. Eventually, you will come to the point where you have to deal with your first floor-to-ceiling drop – this is labelled piece B in the diagram.

THE TRICK

It will, of course, butt up to the short drop on its right, but even so it is an aid to greater accuracy if you also drop a plumbline on its left, and hang it to this.

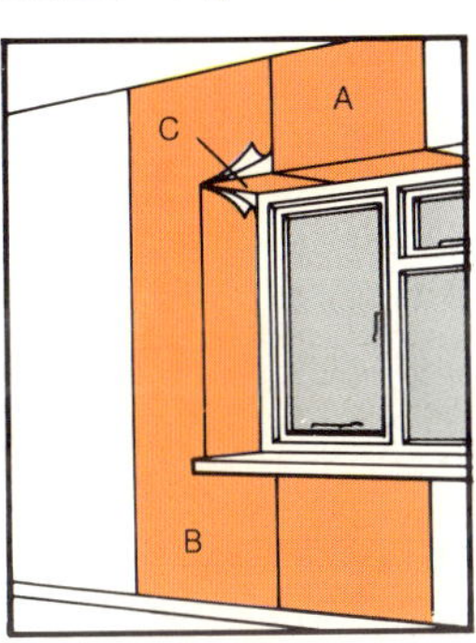

Brush the paper in place until it lies over the window opening. Now make two horizontal cuts – one along the line of the soffit, the other along the line of the window ledge. You will be left with a sort of 'hinge' that you can turn down the side of the opening. It is better if this 'hinge' stretches to the frame; you can usually arrange this according to the positioning of the first short drop over the top of the window, in relation to the plumbline. Otherwise, you will have to fill in with a narrow strip. Brush the 'hinge' against the side of the reveal, mark with a pencil its meeting line with the frame, peel it back and cut it, then smooth it down. The drop should now be trimmed round any projecting window ledge and in the normal way to the ceiling and skirting.

There will still be a small part of the soffit, at its far left end, to be covered. Do this with a small, separate piece of paper (piece C in the diagram), which you match up to the rest of the paper on the soffit. Piece C must pass over the edge of the soffit, and pass up and under B at this point – you will have to peel B away from the wall to allow it to do this, then brush it back in place.

Now go back to the top of the window and work to the right in just the same way. Finish off by hanging short drops under the window ledge.

Some windows go right up to the ceiling, in which case you begin your papering with a full-length drop on each side of it, cutting the drops just at sill level to turn into the reveal. You might then be left with a half-width drop under the window, but this would not matter too much, especially if the wall there is not very high, and you intend to put furniture in front of it. Your problems are least of all where there is a floor-to-ceiling window with no wall underneath to be papered.

With the area around the window completed, you can now carry on hanging drops in the normal way right to the ends of the wall. At each end you are certain to need a drop that is less than full width, and you measure for this and cut it as described in the section on completing the end of a wall (see page 259).

Do you remember how when you started out from these corners you allowed a small overlap to go on the window wall (see page 259)? Your last drops here will overlap this to ensure a very neat job. Once again aim to get your best pattern match at the eye level of a person standing.

THE TRICK

Papering a window wall is not all that difficult. However, if you still think it is too much for you, just paper up to the edge of the opening, and paint the walls of the reveal in the same paint as that on the window frames and ledge. No one will notice what you have done.

PAPERING A STAIRWELL

There are two problems about papering a stairwell. The first is actually getting up to those high spots, which involves complicated scaffolding. The second is that you will be hanging side by side widely differing lengths of paper. That means they will also vary in weight when wet, and the longer lengths of paper will stretch more than their neighbouring short ones. That is going to cause real problems in matching up the patterns which takes real craftsmanship to overcome.

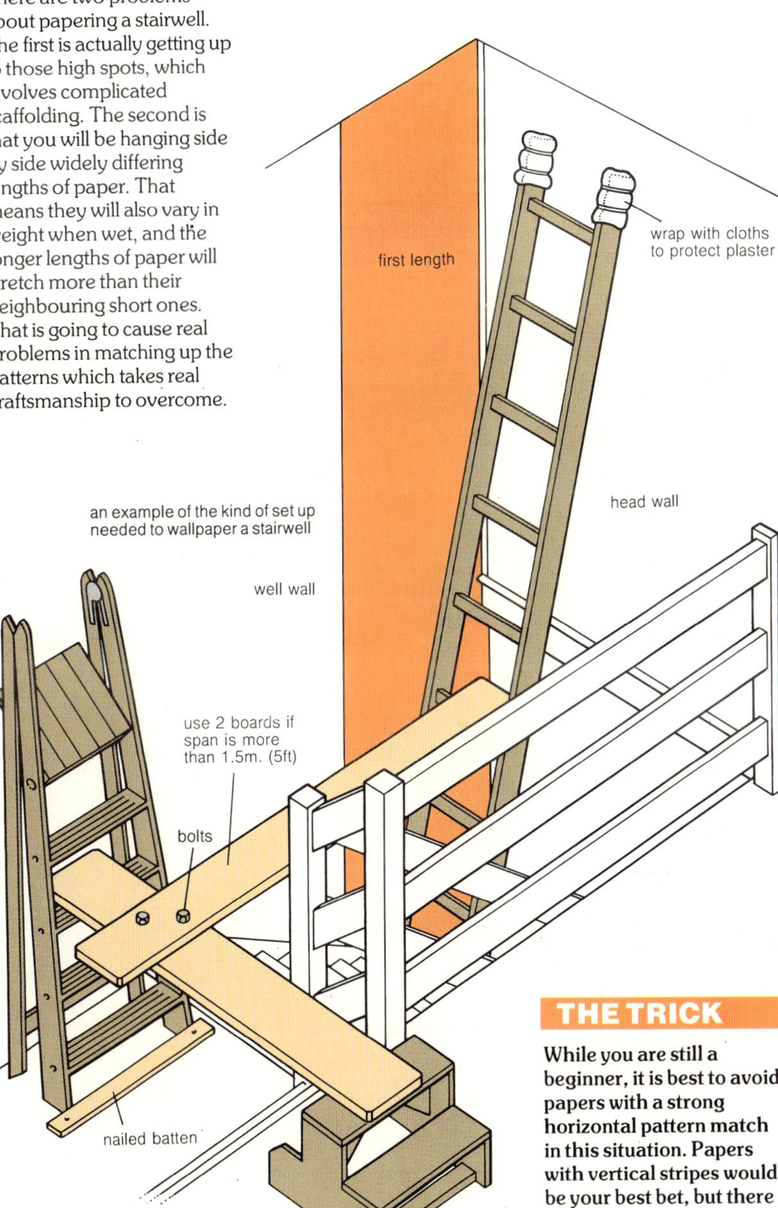

THE TRICK

While you are still a beginner, it is best to avoid papers with a strong horizontal pattern match in this situation. Papers with vertical stripes would be your best bet, but there are other patterns where the matching is not all that important.

HANGING VINYL WALLCOVERINGS

You hang a vinyl wallcovering in much the same way you deal with ordinary wallcoverings, but there are one or two differences. You must, of course, use a suitable adhesive (see page 256). Vinyls need one that has a fungicide, as explained earlier. The only size that you can use is one made from this special adhesive. There is no need to allow vinyl to soak once you have pasted it.

You can use a Stanley knife with a sharp blade to trim a vinyl at skirting level. Place a straight edge on the paper where it meets the skirting, then run your knife along it to cut it to fit; it is much quicker than the pencil and scissors method needed for trimming wallpaper (see page 259). This will not, however, work with ordinary wallpaper, as wet wallpaper tears and you get a ragged line. Where the angle between ceiling and wall is true you can use the knife and straight edge method on vinyl here, too. More often than not, however, the line will wiggle all over the place, and you will have to use the scissors method described for cutting wallpaper at ceiling level (see page 259).

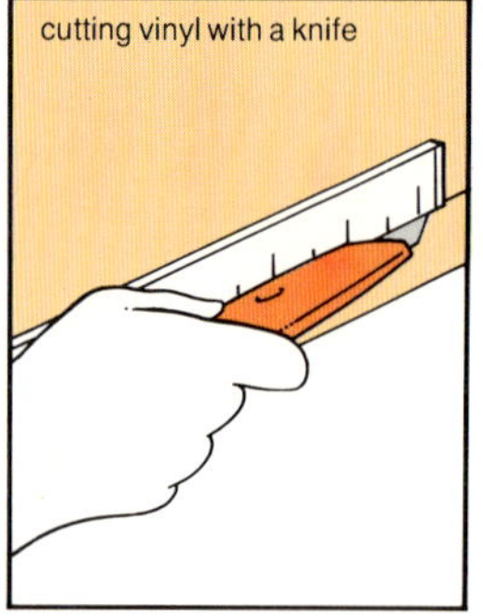
cutting vinyl with a knife

Another big problem with vinyls is that, using the normal vinyl paste, you cannot stick vinyl on top of vinyl which is necessary at corners, for instance (see page 259). You may get away with a small overlap, and one thing you can do is leave it in position for a day or two in the hope that it will stick.

THE TRICK

If it does not, you can always re-stick the join neatly, using a latex adhesive such as Copydex.

THE TRICK

Where you get a large overlap, you should smooth the second length down in place so that it overlaps the first. Now make a vertical knife cut through the centre of the overlap, using a straight edge or the pattern of the paper as a guide. The blade of the knife must be really sharp, otherwise it will tear the paper instead of cutting it. Open up the joint and you will be left with two long, thin, separated strips of vinyl. Peel these off and throw them away. Smooth the remaining vinyl in place, go over the join with a seam roller, and you will get a perfect join and very neat finish.

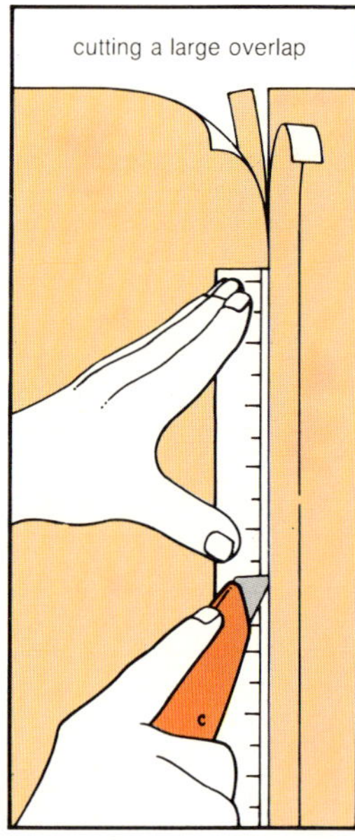
cutting a large overlap

READY-PASTEDS

Ready-pasted paper is treated on the back with a coating of adhesive, but this adhesive needs to be soaked in water to become activated. When you buy a ready-pasted paper, you are given a cardboard trough which you fill with water up to the recommended level. Watch this level as you work, by the way, for the water will need topping up from time to time. Place the tray on the floor under the length of wall that the first drop will cover.

Cut the first drop to length, allowing the normal trimming allowance top and bottom, then roll it up and soak it in the trough for the time the manufacturer recommends. It is important that you follow this recommendation exactly. Too much immersion in water, and you might wash the glue off, and anyway the paper will become too soft and tear easily. Too little, and the glue will not work properly. However, it is better to be, say, half a minute over rather than half a minute under time. If it is paper you are dealing with, you must roll it with the pattern inside; with a vinyl you can have the pattern inside or out. In both cases it is vital for the roll to be only loosely wound so that water can get at every part of the adhesive. The other important point is that you should start rolling the paper from the bottom, so that the top of the pattern will be on the outside of the finished roll, and it will be the top that you first draw out of the trough.

After the recommended soaking period draw the roll out, unwinding it as you do so, and immediately hang it on the wall. The normal rules about sliding it into position, matching up the pattern, and trimming it to fit all apply.

THE TRICK

While you are working on the top part of the paper, leave the bottom hanging over the trough, so that any excess water will run over the surface of the wallcovering – especially if it is a vinyl – and go safely into the trough, instead of on your floor.

Even so, you might want to place a small sheet of polythene or something similar under the trough to guard against splashes.

When you come to work on the bottom of the length, move the tray along so that it is in the correct position for the next drop, and put this in to soak now so that it will be ready when you come to work on it.

When smoothing the wallcovering down in place, it is best to use a sponge for vinyls and flat unembossed papers, but for heavy embossed papers use a paperhanging brush.

drawing ready pasted paper from the trough

VERY LONG DROPS

Where you have a very long drop (the most usual place is the staircase) the technique of soaking needs to be slightly different, because with the normal method the moisture would not get at the heart of the roll.

This is what you must do. Roll the paper loosely with the pattern inside, but this time starting from the top of the drop so that the bottom of the pattern will be at the end of the roll when you have finished. Dunk the roll in the trough. Now, with the paper still submerged in the trough, rewind it, but this time as tightly as possible.

THE TRICK

To avoid any strain on your back when you bend down to do this, place the trough on a table at a convenient height for working.

However, on no account must you try to minimize the discomfort of the cold water by using hot, because this will soften the paper too quickly, making it difficult to hang, and will cause lack of adhesion.

Your winding will mean that the pattern is now on the outside, and the top of the drop is at the end – all very convenient for when you begin hanging. Pull the paper, still in a roll, out of the trough, gripping it lightly in the middle of the roll with the palm of one hand. Hold it vertically, first one way then the other, so that all the excess water drains out and into the trough. Now you can hang it, holding the roll in one hand, matching the pattern with the other, and feeding it from the roll as you move down the wall.

You can see that such a roll of paper will be very rigid, and because of that ready-pasteds are much easier for the do-it-yourselfer to hang on a ceiling – as you will see (page 264) it is the way that folded ceiling paper flops about that makes it difficult for the do-it-yourselfer to control.

LINING PAPERS

Many people seem to shun lining papers – you have only to ask at your local shops about these papers to discover that. Professionals, however, make extensive use of them – as a preliminary cover-up for walls that are in bad condition, and also to ensure a really tip-top finish for heavyweight and hand-printed papers. Indeed, some of the really top-class professionals would never dream of hanging any sort of paper on any kind of surface without lining first. If you want your work to look professional, you should do the same. In fact, the only time when you can really dispense with a lining paper is when you are hanging a lightweight paper on a perfect surface. In addition, hanging lining papers is excellent practice for coping with a ceiling (see page 264).

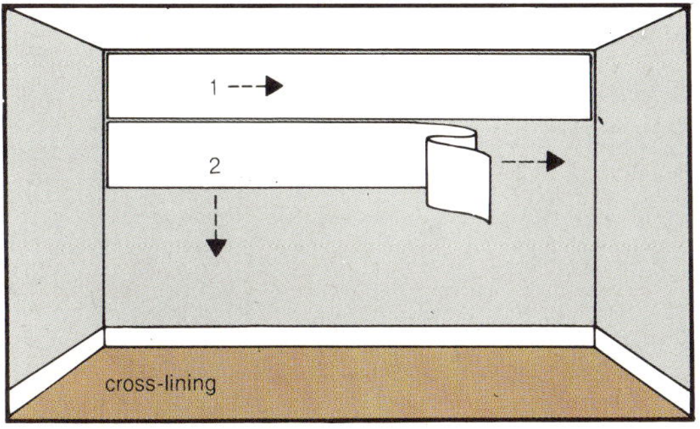

There are various grades of lining paper. The worse the condition of your wall, the thicker the lining you need. Linings are available, too, in light and dark shades. Always hang a dark lining under a dark top paper and vice versa, so that if your paper does open up a little at the joins, it will not be quite so noticeable. There are also lining papers suitable for taking paint.

Lining papers are always hung in the opposite direction to the paper that will cover them – hence the phrase 'cross lining' which the professional uses. On a wall, therefore, this means that the lining is hung horizontally. Some walls are in such a bad condition that it is a good idea to hang two lining papers on them. In such cases the first paper will be hung vertically just like wallpaper, and the second one horizontally in the normal lining paper manner. For a painted finish the lining is hung vertically, like ordinary paper. If you decide on two linings before painting, the first one should be horizontal.

The reason why the various layers go at right angles to each other is that paper which has been moistened by paste shrinks as it dries out, and this shrinkage is mainly across the width. The combined effect of the shrinkage of two papers hung in the same direction would tend to pull them apart at the joins, and that would look very unsightly indeed. In any event, even without such shrinkage, the fact that the two joins coincided would tend to produce an untidy effect.

EQUIPMENT

The equipment you need is exactly as for wallpapering, with one addition. Where the lining is to be hung horizontally, in most rooms a pair of steps will not be enough on their own when you are hanging the top length, as you need to walk at the right level all along the length of the wall. That means you need a scaffold board (see page 228).

The lining paper should be cut to the same length as the wall, plus an allowance of about 40mm (1½in.) at each end for trimming.

Use an ordinary cellulose paste for lining papers, mixed according to the manufacturer's instructions. The lining is pasted in much the same way as ordinary wallpaper, but the folding is different. You need to fold the lining concertina-like with 230mm (9in.) pleats.

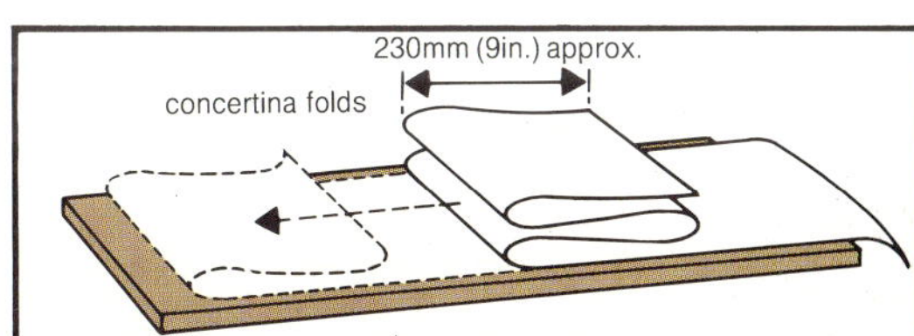

CROSS LINING

When you hang lining paper there is no need for any pencilled guideline. If you are cross lining, aim to follow the line of the ceiling with the first length, leaving a 6mm (¼in.) gap all the way round: i.e. between the top of the paper and the ceiling, and at each end. Pull out the first fold of paper and position it accurately on the wall, then brush it in place. Then let the next fold come out, position it accurately, and brush it in place. Walk along letting the paper unfurl from its folds; brush it accurately into place as you go. When the whole length has been hung, walk along it smoothing it out with your brush, from the centre of the paper outwards to the edges, to make sure there are no air bubbles trapped in the middle. Then trim it to length at the ends.

Now you can hang the second length in the same way, although in most rooms you will not have to stand on a scaffold board to do this. Once again, it is better to leave a 6mm (¼in.) gap all round: i.e. between the two lengths of paper, as well as the ends. You can butt the two lengths up to each other, but under no circumstances should you allow them to overlap. If you find your second roll straying on to the first, then pull it down, re-position it accurately, and begin again.

Carry on with subsequent lengths in this way, until you have to cut one to width to fit the space available. Do this exactly as you cut the wallpaper to turn round a corner (see page 259): i.e. measure the gap to be filled every 300mm (12in.) or so, remembering to leave a 6mm (¼in.) gap between the bottom of the paper and the skirting board. Transfer your reading to the paper, making a mark with a pencil. Then cut along the length of paper, to join up the marks. Paste and hang it in the normal way.

HANGING LINING PAPER VERTICALLY

Lining paper that is to be hung vertically can be treated just like wallpaper. The job is, however, much easier. There is no need to bother about a plumbline and you can follow the angle of the wall, leaving a gap of 6mm (¼in.) between the first length and the corner. A similar gap should be left between the rolls and at the top and bottom. There is, of course, no pattern to match up, so there is no need to slide the paper around, and you do not need to leave so much trimming allowance at top and bottom.

Vertical lining paper that is to receive a painted finish should be butt jointed, otherwise the gap would show, and it should overlap at the corners of the room just like wallpaper.

If, by some chance, you do have to hang one wallpaper over another, try to offset the joints so that they do not coincide.

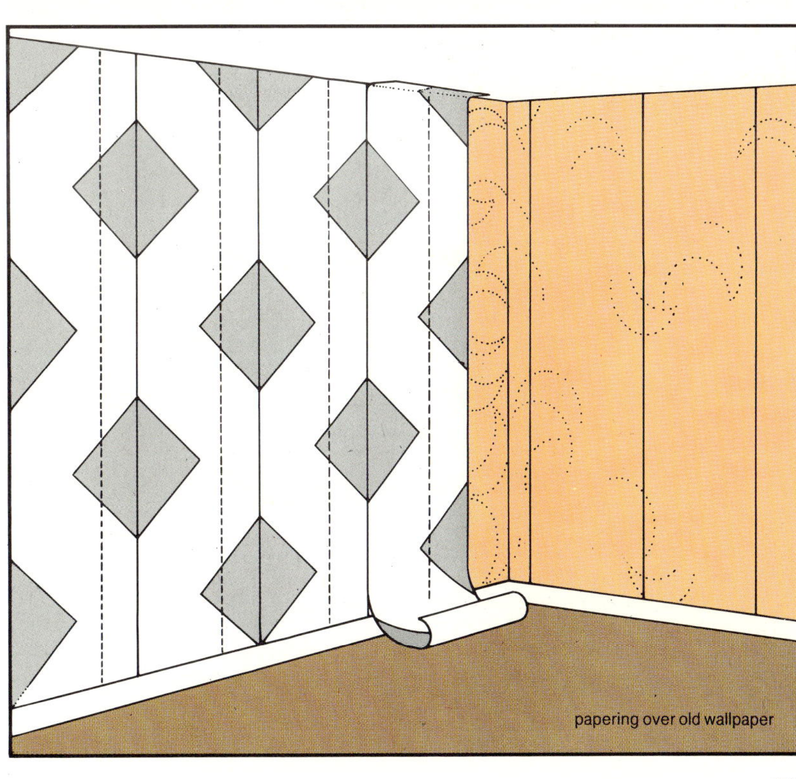
papering over old wallpaper

PAPERING A CEILING

HANGING THE PAPER

Except that you also need a piece of chalk, you need the same as for hanging lining paper (see page 263). Your paper should be cut to the same length as the ceiling, plus an allowance at each end of about 50mm (2in.) for trimming.

Ceiling paper should be hung parallel to the wall containing the main window. Begin at this wall and work away from it. You need a guideline on the ceiling to which to hang your first length, so you must 'snap a chalk line' (see page 14).

The correct position for this line is the width of a roll of paper from the window wall, less 13mm (½in.). The paper should overlap on to the walls by that allowance on every edge. This overlap will eventually be covered up by the paper on the wall, and you will get a perfect join.

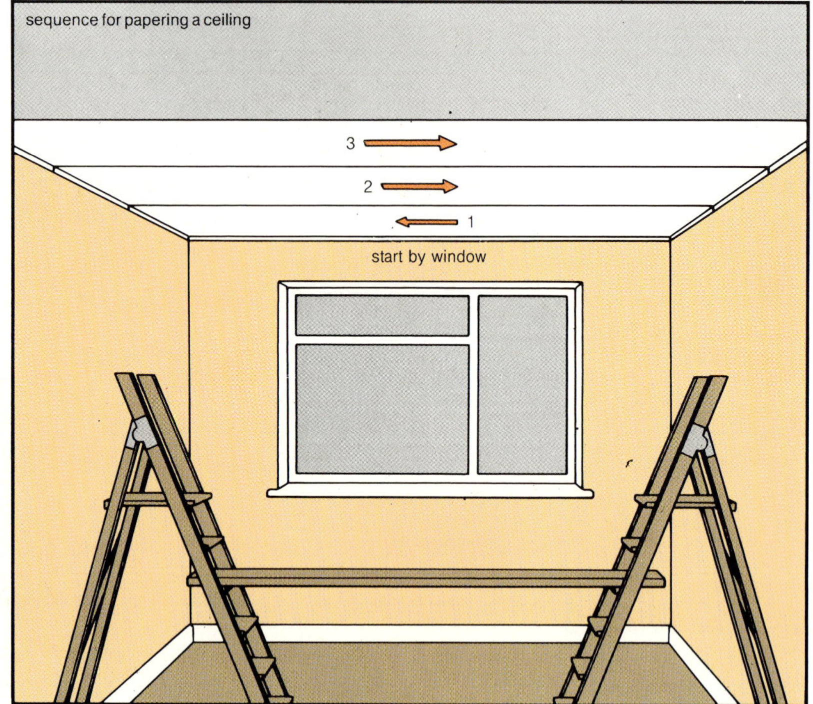

It is vital that you stand directly underneath the chalk line in the case of the first length, and underneath the joins between the various lengths for subsequent ones. You cannot hang ceiling paper accurately unless you are right beneath the line to which you are working. So position your scaffold board safely and securely directly under the chalk line.

For this first length, you must stand facing the window, and a right-handed person would work from right to left. For all the remaining lengths you stand with your back to the window, as that is the only way you can work directly under the joins. As you will still be working from right to left, this means that you will be papering from the opposite side of the room to where you started the first length. Bear this in mind when pasting and folding the paper. For the first length, begin pasting and folding at the end opposite to that you start at for the rest; otherwise it will be 'upside down', if you can use such a phrase. A wide variety of papers can be used on a ceiling nowadays. Until recently only the traditional ceiling papers were used. Some, which are still available, do not seem to have a pattern as such. Nevertheless they have a texture, and if this is the wrong way round it will be noticeable in the finished result. It is quite common to put an ordinary wallpaper on the ceiling – sometimes the same one that is going on the walls – here it is vital to get the patterns the same way round.

THE TRICK

To avoid any embarrassingly obvious mistake, always mark the paper when you cut it to indicate the top, so that you can paste and fold it the right way round.

Ceiling papers are pasted just like wallpapers (see page 258) but they are folded concertina-like, as for lining papers (see page 263) but in 380–450mm (15–18in.) pleats.

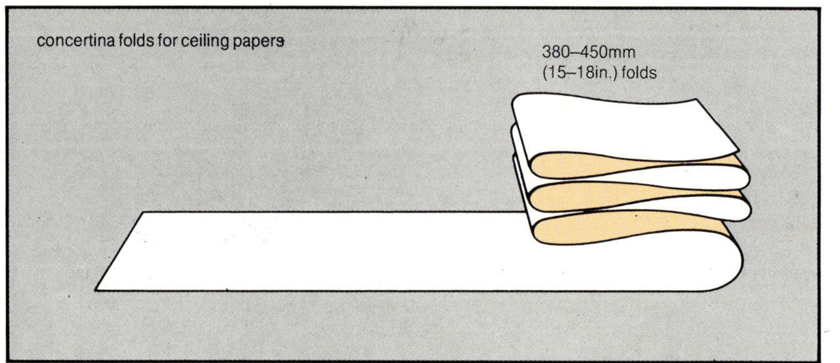

THE TRICK

If you take hold of a length of pasted and folded ceiling paper you will find that it flops at each end. The way to stop that is to place a spare roll of paper underneath it as a support and hold it with your left hand.

FIRST LENGTH

Climb up on your scaffold board, holding the roll of paper in your left hand. Unfold the first section of paper, place one edge on the ceiling, and slide it along with your right hand to position it accurately on the guideline. Then take the paper-hanging brush in your right hand and brush the paper on, smoothing it out and getting rid of any air bubbles. Move along, allowing the next fold to open up, position that accurately on the guideline, and brush this in place. Carry on until the whole length has been hung.

You must keep your left hand (holding the folded and pasted paper) high up near the ceiling. Because this is tiring, you will tend to let your arm drop down. If you do, you will impose too great a strain on the paste, which will simply be unable to hold the paper on the ceiling. So you will go on brushing and brushing at paper that, infuriatingly, keeps falling down.

When the complete length has been hung, walk along your scaffold board giving the paper a final smooth, and checking that no air bubbles have been trapped, then trim it at the ends. Remember that it must overlap down the end walls, as well as at the sides, by about 13mm (½in.).

THE TRICK

There is no need to measure this, however. Use your forefinger as a guide.

FURTHER LENGTHS

Now paste and hang the next length. For this second length, your scaffold board will remain in the same position. As it is directly under the chalk line, it will also be under the far edge of the first length, which is the guide to hanging the second length. Position this so that it butts up against the first, matching the pattern if there is one, then smooth it in place with your brush. Hang the length all the way along, just as you did the first, then trim it at the ends.

For the third roll, move your scaffold board along until it is under the far edge of the second roll. Then hang this third length in the same way that you dealt with the second. Carry on in this way until you have to cut a width to fit the space remaining. This you do just as when cutting for the end of a wall (see page 259), although you do not need the offcut. The cut edge will overlap the wall by 13mm (½in.) so it does not matter if your cutting is a little ragged, as it will be hidden by the paper on the wall.

LIGHT ROSES

One good thing about ceilings is that there are not so many obstructions as on a wall, so there is less fiddly cutting and trimming. However, in just about every room there is the rose for a ceiling light flex. If this comes in the middle of a length, tackle it as an old-fashioned round light switch (see page 260). If the rose comes at the edge of a length, cut the tails from that edge inwards, then smooth them down and trim them.

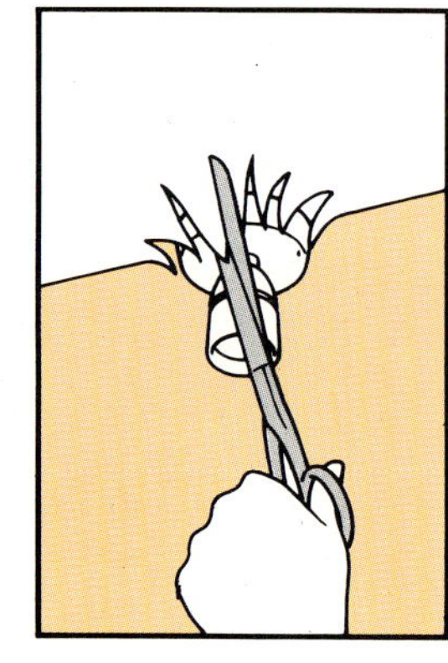

Cristal takes the bother out of tiling.

ORDINARY TILES CAN CAUSE FIXING PROBLEMS... CRISTAL UNIVERSAL SOLVES THEM.

Use Cristal Universal ceramic tiles and make light work of tiling.

For one thing, you don't have to bother about how many corner and edging tiles you need.

Because in every box of Cristal Universal you'll find some of the tiles already glazed along one or two edges (unlike ordinary tiles which generally come with lugs and raw edges).

All of course tremendous help at the planning stage.

Spacing them is easy and accurate too, thanks to the fact that we've angled the tile edges. Just place them edge to edge.

No more bother about spacer lugs, or raw edges.

CRISTAL'S ANGLED EDGE ENSURES EVEN SPACING.

Okay, but what about cutting?

Again, no bother. With Cristal Universal–the DIY tile–it's easy. (Our 4¼" tiles make it really easy since they're especially thin.)

To help you even further we've produced our special Cristal tile cutter.

Even finding the style that's right for you is no bother, for Cristal offer the biggest choice of designs in the land.

Send for our free booklet, 'DIY Ceramic Wall Tile Planning and Fixing', and see for yourself how easy it all is.

cristal

Britain's biggest choice of ceramic wall tiles.

H & R Johnson Tiles Ltd, Tunstall, Stoke-on-Trent ST6 4JX.

TILING WALLS 1

For many years now applying ceramic tiles to a wall has been one of the easiest of home improvement jobs. The introduction of very thin tiles, which are easy to cut, and the replacement of the old sand-and-cement fixing methods by simple-to-use adhesives made this so. They changed tiling from a task that, only a generation or so ago, was regarded as among the most skilled in the building industry to one that is now no more difficult than hanging wallpaper.

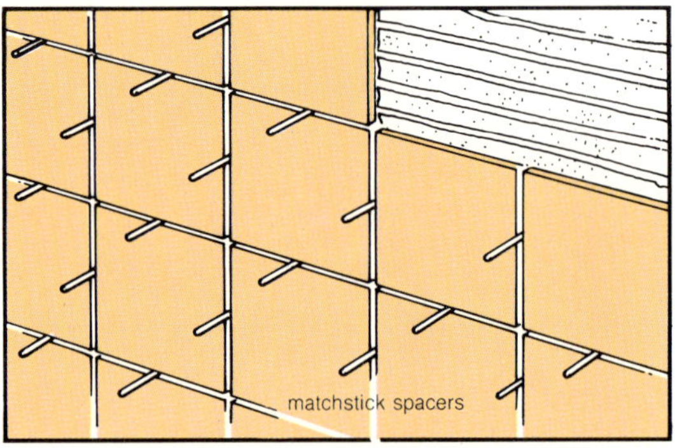
matchstick spacers

UNIVERSAL TILES

In fact, wall tiling has now been made easier than ever by the invention of the Universal tile. What is different about this tile? Well, all its edges, instead of being at right angles to the face, are bevelled off at an angle. This solves one of the most difficult aspects of wall tiling: i.e. ensuring the correct spacing.

Ceramic tiles expand and contract slightly with changes in temperature, and room has to be left all round them to allow for this. Obviously, for the sake of neatness, the spacing must be even. Various dodges have been suggested from time to time to ensure accuracy. One of the first was that you should insert matchsticks, thin dowels, even bits of the carton in which the tiles were delivered between the tiles; and then pull them out once the adhesive had set. Later on tiles were manufactured with small spacer lugs on all edges. However, with Universal tiles it is even simpler. All you do is butt each one hard up against its neighbours, because the bevel will leave a sufficient expansion gap. If you are dealing with old stock, or imported tiles, you will still have to use the matchstick or spacer-lug method.

So that dirt and germs cannot collect there, the spacing between tiles is filled with a material called 'grout', which is sold specifically for this purpose. (In some cases, the same material is used both as adhesive and grout.) Grout is still used on Universal tiles to fill the gap over the bevels.

The other point about Universal tiles is that, in each pack, there is a selection with glaze on one or two edges. These can be used at the ends of rows and the two top corners of a panel.

Formerly it was necessary to get special tiles for these positions, which were known as RE (for round edge) at the end of a row, and REX for corner positions. This may still be the case with certain imported tiles.

A SIMPLE TILE PANEL

Because of these advances, creating a simple tile panel on a wall, such as a splashback over a washbasin or a bath, or a kitchen worktop, is child's play. This is especially so if you can make the panel from whole tiles, with no cutting involved. The tiles can go on most wall surfaces, but not on timber because this moves as it absorbs moisture, and such movement will cause cracking in the tiles. The surface must, of course, be clean, dry, level and in sound condition. So carry out any preparation necessary.

Draw the shape of the panel in pencil on the wall. Tiles tend to slide down the wall when first fixed in place, until the adhesive starts to grab. The top edge of the washbasin will stop them from doing this. However, where the panel extends beyond the basin, fix laths to the wall on each side to perform the same function. The adhesive is applied to the wall with a trowel, and then spread with a special adhesive comb that forms ridges over the wall.

Now fix the tiles in place, one at a time, starting at one end of the bottom row. Make sure that each tile is well positioned, and butts firmly up against its neighbour (except where spacers are needed). When the panel is complete, leave it for at least 12 hours, then apply the grout. This is done with a sponge or squeegee. You merely load the sponge with grout, and draw it across the face of the tiles, pushing the grout well into the gaps. Remove any excess from the face of the tiles with a clean dry sponge and finally polish with a clean dry cloth.

fixing laths to stop the tiles sliding down before adhesive dries

THE TRICK

It is not a bad idea to draw round each tile with a short pointed stick (a lollipop stick is ideal) to get a really neat join.

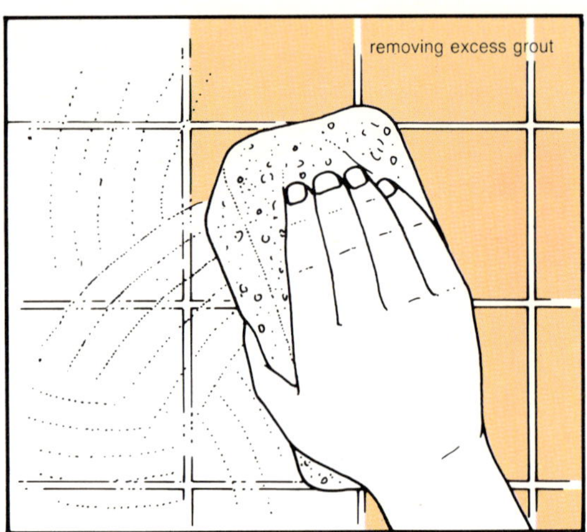
removing excess grout

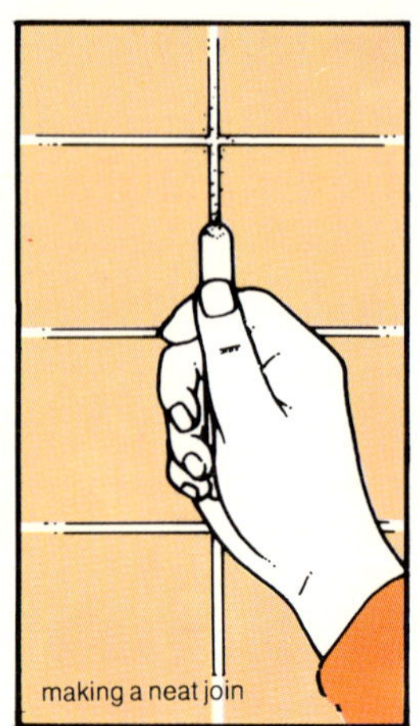
making a neat join

Basically that is all there is to it. It is not really much more complicated when cutting is involved. For this you need a tiler's spike and a straight edge: you can use a metal rule or piece of small true timber. Place the straight edge on the face of the tile where you want to cut it, and draw the spike along it in a clean, firm stroke which cuts through the glaze. Score also the glaze on the tile edges. Now place the scored tile over a matchstick, or on the edge of a bench with just the waste portion overhanging. Press down hard, and the tile will snap cleanly along the line. If, at the first attempt/attempts you break a tile, don't worry. You will very soon get the knack.

THE TRICK

It is well worth buying a reasonable number of extra tiles to allow for mishaps when cutting and for later repairs. If you want to install an extra socket in your kitchen for instance (See page 85). you may be very glad of seven or eight spares.

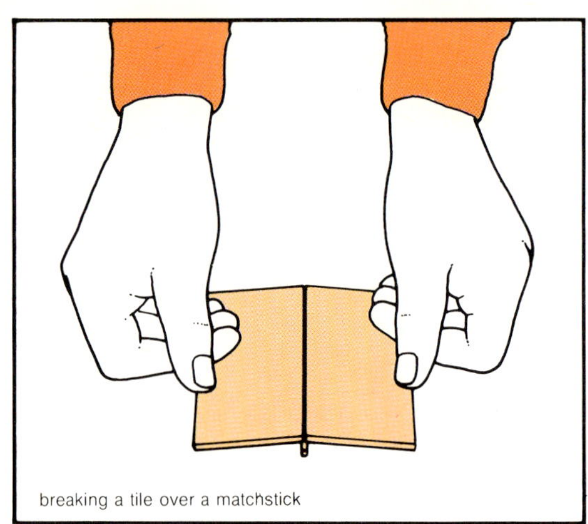
breaking a tile over a matchstick

TILING WALLS 2

LARGER AREAS

When you want to undertake more ambitious jobs, such as tiling a whole wall or even an entire room, there is a little more involved. Your first problem will be the floor. You cannot use this as the base for your first row of tiles because it is very unlikely that it will be truly level. So you need to find its lowest point.

THE TRICK

To do this take a long, true lath, cut it to the same length as the wall, and lightly tack it to the wall, approximately one tile's height from the floor. Use a spirit level to ensure it is horizontal. Now at various intervals measure the distance from the lath to the floor until you establish the lowest point. Repeat this process on all the other walls if you will be tiling them, to determine which will be the lowest point in the room.

Once you have found this, make a pencil mark on the wall exactly one tile's height up from it. Here you firmly fix in place a lath, its top edge on the pencil mark – on one wall if that is all you will be tiling, but otherwise all the way round the room, once again using a spirit level. Your first row of tiles will rest on this lath.

TILING TECHNIQUES

You are now ready to tile. Begin in the angle formed by the two vertical and horizontal laths. Your aim should be to fix all the field (the whole tiles) in place; then to cut and fix the half tiles individually later. Work on about 1 sq.m (3.3 sq.ft) at a time.

THE TRICK

Use adhesive tape to hold soffit reveal tiles in place until adhesive starts to grip.

When the adhesive has set you can remove the laths, and cut tiles to fit the spaces on each side all round. Measure each tile individually, and remember to leave space at the cut end for grout. Where small bits have to be removed from the bottom row of tiles to fit the floor, you will do better to use a tile file rather than try to snip them off.

There are two methods for cutting awkwardly shaped tiles. You can score the tile, then nibble out the waste with pincers; or you can buy a special tile saw-blade to fit a hacksaw.

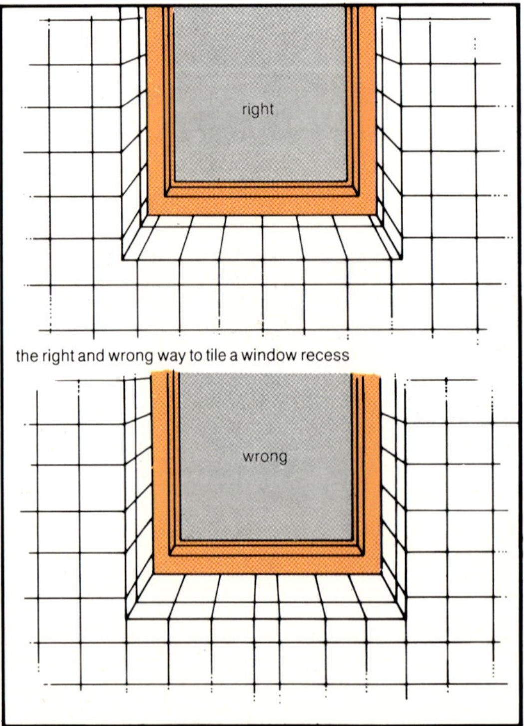

the right and wrong way to tile a window recess

THE TRICK

Where a hole must be cut in the middle of a tile (to fit round a water pipe for instance), snap a tile in half, and cut a semicircle out of each piece. The snap line will hardly be noticeable when the two pieces are glued to the wall and pushed together.

Leave the wall for another 12 hours or so after fixing the cut tiles, then you can apply the grout.

SETTING OUT

The other problem is that the tiles must be arranged very neatly, and to ensure this the tiler undertakes what he calls the 'setting-out'. If the wall you are tiling has no features or obstructions, the setting-out can be quite simple. What you must realise is that you cannot begin tiling at one end of the wall because the corners will not be true. If you did make a corner your starting point, you would not get a neat grid of grout lines. Therefore you must have a cut tile trimmed to fit the space available at each end of every row. Because it is not easy to snip off less than about 25mm (1in.) from a ceramic tile – either as waste or to use on the wall – you should set out the tiles so that the cut ones are as near to half width as possible. Here is how you do that.

THE TRICK

Measure the length of the wall, and mark its centre. Place a tile on the floor centrally on this point, then add others to form a row along the wall until you reach its end. Now set another row of tiles out, but this time with the first tile just to one side of the centre point. You will then be able to see at a glance which arrangement would give the best cut tile.

Make a pencil line on the wall showing where your first whole tile in from the corner should go. At this point tack a vertical batten to the wall, using a plumbline to ensure that it is truly upright. You can place a tile loosely in the angle as a final check that everything is all right. It is here that you begin tiling.

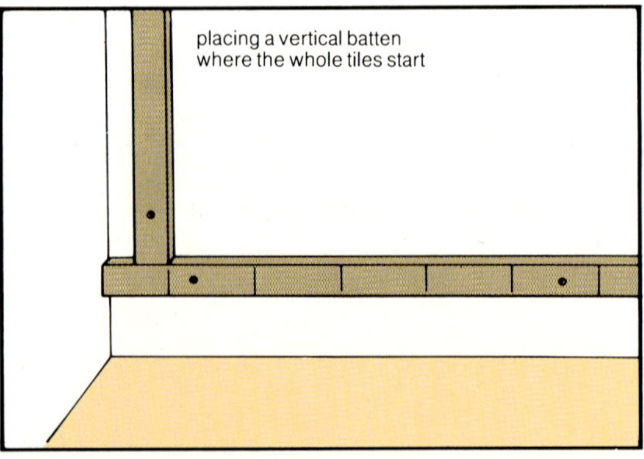

placing a vertical batten where the whole tiles start

WINDOWS

The setting-out becomes more complicated when the wall has a feature, such as a window. You should have cut tiles of equal width each side of the window and also, ideally, at each end of the wall. Such an ideal will usually be unattainable, so base your setting-out on the window as that will be the main focal point. Do try to avoid any 'horrors' elsewhere.

making a measuring staff

THE TRICK

This more complicated setting out cannot be accomplished with the aid of tiles placed on the floor, and you need what the tiler calls a 'measuring staff' or 'measuring rod'. To make one of these take a length of timber and on it mark a series of tile widths. By placing this rod on the wall here and there – preferably using it in conjunction with a spirit level to ensure greater accuracy – you will be able to ascertain where cut tiles at the ends should be positioned.

Once again, fix a vertical lath here.

Plastering is a very difficult job. Where practice won't make perfect. Even for a DIY expert. No wonder it has always been best left to the professionals.

But Polycell now introduce a system that brings repair plastering within the reach of any handyman (or woman).

Perfect plastering without special skills, special tools, or even plaster.

The system consists of two products, Polyplasta and Polyskim.

Polyplasta is perfect for deep repairs.

Polyskim is ideal for smoothing over uneven surfaces, or going over Polyplasta for a fine finish.

As they are not plaster, you can forget all the old worries.

"Preparation is hard." Wrong.

Preparation is easy; it doesn't take long.

Remove old loose plaster with a chisel or something similar.

Brush off any surface dust.

Don't bother to wet or soak the surface itself, as you would have to with plaster.

"It's hard to mix them properly." Wrong.

Polyplasta and Polyskim are ready-mixed. The right consistency is guaranteed, so there's no risk of sagging, even when you're applying Polyplasta up to two inches deep.

"You'll have to be quick." Wrong.

As both stay workable for up to four hours you get plenty of time to get a really smooth finish.

"They're messy." Wrong.

There's no dust or splashing because both are ready-mixed. They will stick to almost any kind of surface. Firmly. So there is no risk of them falling on to the floor.

"There's a lot of waste." Wrong.

The tubs are resealable. You just use what you need and keep the rest. There's no wastage and no "left-overs" to dispose of.

"You need special tools." Wrong.

All you need for Polyplasta is a filling knife, trowel or float.

Polyskim is applied with a paint brush and smoothed over with a spreader that comes free in every tub.

"You can't decorate for a long time." Wrong.

You shouldn't paper or paint over traditional plaster for at least three months, except with emulsion paint.

Polyskim and Polyplasta can be painted or papered over as soon as they are fully dry, usually within a few days.

"It's so easy you can't go wrong." Right.

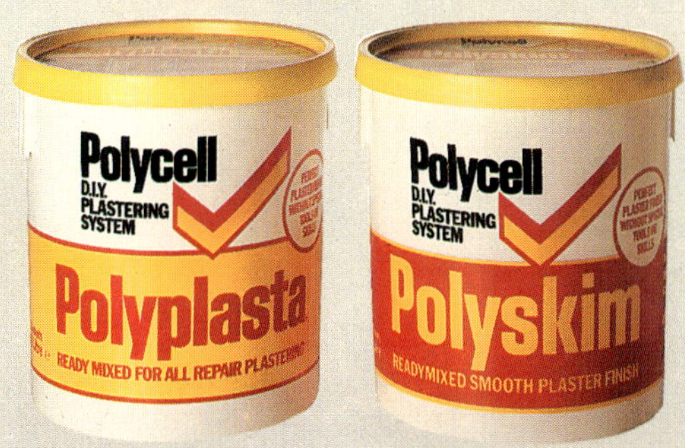

Polycell. Do it right.

THE LEISURE 2000 SERIES.

IT'S LIKE HAVING A BUILT-IN COOKER WITHOUT HAVING TO REBUILD YOUR KITCHEN.

Although there are hundreds of cookers from which to choose, there are only two options.

Either an inexpensive free-standing cooker without all the time saving gadgets you really need.

Or a sophisticated built-in cooker that demands an expensive kitchen refit.

Fortunately, now there's the Leisure 2000 series. A range of beautiful freestanding gas cookers, that give you all the features of a built-in cooker without the cost.

The Leisure 2001, for instance, has a grill centre that includes not only a rotisserie, but also the unique Leisure Rotoaster (a built-in sandwich maker and kebab turner).

There's also an electronic clock plus automatic controls programmed by microchip.

If you would like the advantages of a quality built-in cooker without having to rebuild your kitchen, why not call in to your local gas showroom today?

Or fill in the coupon at the back of this book.

From all the cookers available there may be two options, but there's only one choice.

LEISURE

Advanced Kitcheneering.

Leisure
A member of the Glynwed International plc group of companies.

OTHER WALLCOVERINGS

A variety of other wallcoverings is available from specialist outlets, such as silks, woven grasses, suedes etc. In general, they are not recommended to the do-it-yourselfer. They are usually difficult to hang, and cost a lot. If you ruin one or two drops, that becomes very expensive indeed; moreover, many of them are easily soiled if you get paste on the front.

If you do wish to hang a fabric-like covering on a wall, then the best advice is to go for a paper-backed one. Hessian is available in two basic forms: you can buy ordinary furnishing hessian, which can be hung on the wall with wallpaper adhesive, and has the advantage of being inexpensive. However, the big drawback is that, as the adhesive dries out, the material shrinks; and unsightly gaps will develop between joins. Paper-backed hessian is, however, one of the easiest coverings to hang. It is as simple as wallpaper, with the added bonus that there is no pattern to match.

arrangement to assist hanging a wide wall covering

Any kind of fabric can also be fixed to special track or battens to cover a wall; it is like having flat curtains. This is another expensive treatment, especially if you use a track system, but it does make a good cover-up for walls in bad condition. It can work out cheaper than having them replastered, for instance, and you can incorporate insulation material behind on a wall in an exposed position.

THE TRICK

You can fix the fabrics by stapling them to vertical battens screwed to the wall. Lengths of braid attached to the material with a fabric adhesive will cover up the staples. If you adopt this method, however, you must make sure you get an even tension throughout the fabric.

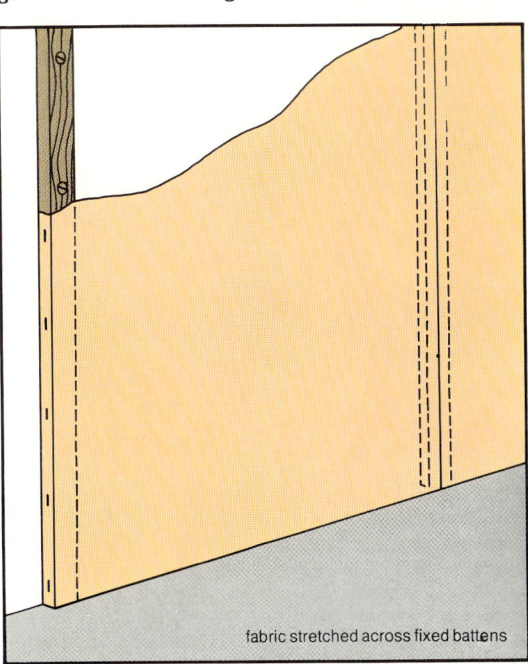
fabric stretched across fixed battens

FRIEZES

Friezes (or borders) have been popular at various times. The Victorians made extensive use of them, and they were a feature of interior decoration during the 1930s. Not surprisingly, they're coming back into fashion.

The traditional way of using friezes was to place them at picture-rail level where they acted as a break between the paper on the wall and that on the ceiling. However, you can also surround a small insignificant window with a frieze, and install a roller blind to use for privacy – a much cheaper treatment than fitting curtains. You can run them as a border along skirting boards, or round a bedhead and they will help to make insignificant features seem more interesting and important. In a bathroom, where you get such fittings as bath, basin and lavatory all at different heights, run a frieze all round the room at dado level and it will help to unify everything by tying it together in one neat package.

You can also use friezes to change the appearance of awkwardly-shaped rooms: an over-tall one can be brought down to a human scale by friezes – perhaps even two or three bands of them between doorway and ceiling where the room is really high. They are an inexpensive way of introducing a pattern into a room; you can treat the walls of a room with emulsion paint, then create panels – perhaps coloured in a contrasting tone – by forming squares or rectangles with borders. You will thus get a feel of pattern for a much smaller outlay than with wallpaper.

HANGING

There are no special pastes or pasting brushes for friezes. You use an ordinary wallpaper adhesive, which you apply with a flat varnish brush: 75mm (3in.) or 25mm (1in.) according to the width of the frieze. The adhesive is applied on a pasting table, and you will straightaway notice a snag. The frieze is so small in relation to the table that you will tend to brush paste on to the table itself.

THE TRICK

Cover the table with spare lengths of lining paper or old clean newspaper. Cut your first length of frieze, place it on the far edge of the table, and paste it. Bring the next length just far enough forward to clear any remnants of old glue on the paper, and paste this one. Continue until you have covered all the paper, then throw it away and start off with a new piece.

Friezes will be used in varying lengths. If you are creating panels with them on a painted wall, the runs will be comparatively short. However, if a frieze is to be applied horizontally all the way round a room, the lengths will be very long.

pasting a frieze

THE TRICK

So that they do not become unwieldy, fold the lengths concertina-fashion, just like ceiling paper.

Hang them too, in the same way. Unfold the first section of frieze, place it in position on the wall, and smooth it down with your paperhanging brush. Allow the next fold to open up and brush this into place. Carry on in this manner.

hanging a frieze

LEVELLING

You will need a line to which you can work if your frieze is not to look out of alignment. Where it is to border on an architectural feature or part of the joinery, there is no problem. You just smooth it out close to the edge of the skirting board, door architrave or whatever. However, it is a different matter if the border is to be in the middle of a wall. How can you ensure it is attractively set out?

Should it be a horizontal run, snap a chalk line where you want to position the top edge of the frieze. You can use a spirit level to ensure that such a line in truly horizontal.

THE TRICK

It is really more important that the line be parallel to some feature of the room – a picture rail or the ceiling – should this be out of true. Where a picture rail slopes slightly, decide how much below it you wish to hang the frieze, then measure that distance down from the rail at each end of the chalk line.

Where dealing with a vertical run, drop a plumbline and bob, and make pencil marks along its length (see page 258). Once again, to have the frieze in line with a nearby prominent feature is more important than to make it truly vertical.

CURTAINS & BLINDS

WINDOW SHAPES

Few things affect the appearance of a room more than curtains. Windows are the most important fixture in any room, yet frequently are the most neglected. Too many people hang up a pair of curtains, regardless of the shape and size of the window, and think no more about them. Here are five essential points to help set your priorities and plan successfully:

1. Appearance Remember that the use of texture and colour contribute to the overall design of a room.

2. View Do you want to see out or not? Your 'view', particularly in an inner-city area, may be a brick wall!

3. Privacy Bedrooms and bathrooms obviously need to be 'peeper-proof'.

4. Noise Fabric can not only help soak up sound from outside but also prevent the spread of sound from room to room inside. Do you or your family play musical instruments?

5. Light control Too much light can damage carpets and furniture, while in dark rooms the little light available needs to be maximized.

VERTICAL WINDOWS

How you treat this type of window depends to a large extent on the architectural style of your home. Tall, narrow windows, often sashed, in a period house with high ceilings, present no problem. Choose formal fabrics, furnish each window with floor-to-ceiling curtains and accentuate their slender, graceful proportions. If you feel ambitious, make pelmets or swags and tails (see pages 285, 286), providing they do not clash with a particularly ornate ceiling or cornice. Otherwise select a neat interesting heading, e.g. pinch pleats (see page 280), and suspend the curtains from a brass or wooden pole.

Vertical windows in a modern home with low ceilings are more complicated to dress. You need to minimize the height by extending the curtain rail beyond the window frame on either side so that the open curtains lie flat against the wall. Where such a scheme is impractical, shorten the total effect by making sill-length curtains in a patterned fabric with a horizontal theme.

HORIZONTAL WINDOWS

Deep picture windows or patio doors across a wall are a familiar feature in many modern homes. Clever curtain designers continue this horizontal theme with carefully chosen fabric, a neat pleated heading, and important floor-to-ceiling curtains which sweep away to one side during the day.

Where there are several small windows across a wall, often quite high up, use matching patterned wallpaper and fabric to minimize any unevenness, and fit the curtains to the actual height and width of the window.

THE TRICK

Use a simple gathered or pleated heading and stick a piece of fabric over the front of the track so that, when the curtains are drawn back, no ugly aluminium or white strips break up the patterned surface.

DORMER WINDOWS

Usually these are small windows with no wall space at the sides. Although attractive, they do tend to tunnel both light and air. This means that normal window treatments will usually restrict both even more. The answer in most cases is to make roller blinds instead of curtains. Alternatively, you could use light filmy fabrics, assuming they provide the necessary feeling of privacy at night.

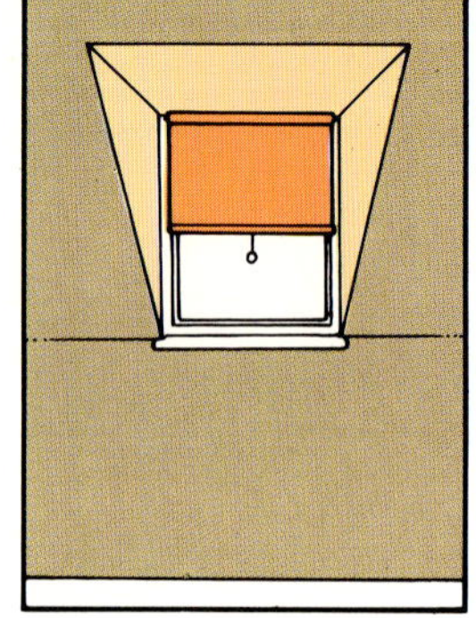

BOW AND BAY WINDOWS

Both these types of window enhance and enlarge a room. The unimaginative home decorator will simply run curtains right across the front. This type of treatment does provide maximum light during the day and saves fabric. But, when drawn, the curtains cut off the bay, ruining the proportions of the room and changing its character completely.

A much better way to dress both bow or bay windows is to hang curtains from a flexible aluminium track fixed to follow the sweep of the curve. Whether you choose several small curtains or two large ones, depends on the width of the frame between each window section. The small type of bow window, frequently installed in the 1970s, will obviously only sustain one pair of curtains. The need for unity is paramount, so do link the effect together with a pelmet or valance (see pages 285, 286).

THE TRICK

Anchor the full height (i.e. from track to floor) of the outside edges of the curtain flat against the wall to avoid unsightly gaps.

ARCHED WINDOWS

Arched windows are architecturally expensive to install, and invariably an attractive feature of any room or hallway which it would be a pity to disregard. You could:

1. Frame the window: hang panels of fabric high, well above the top of the window and wide enough apart to leave the entire window exposed when the curtains are open.
2. Confine the curtaining to the rectangular section of the window below the arch. This is particularly suitable for a window on the stairs where large quantities of fabric are unnecessary and may present a hazard.
3. Make cafe curtains (see page 282). Use sheer fabric for the top arched part of the window and suspend separate curtains from a rod for the lower part which will draw well back.

4. For a really stunning look, fix two curtains permanently round the arch (use flexible track) and loop back the sides with cords or tie-backs (see page 284).

Undoubtedly your budget will be the most important single factor to influence any decision on:

1. Your choice of heading.
2. The overall size of the curtains.

Short sill-length curtains require less fabric and are thus more economical than their glamorous floor-length counterparts. On the other hand, full-length elegance need not cost a fortune if you suspend the curtains from rods or tracks hidden by a pelmet or valance, since the required fabric width for this type of treatment is only one and a half times the length of the track.

However, if you prefer the prestigious look of an elaborate, deep-pleated heading, be prepared to pay for your pleasure; some headings of this type require a fabric width of two and a half or even three times the length of the track.

Whatever style of curtain you choose, never skimp on fullness. Lots of cheap cotton fabric looks much better than too little expensive velvet.

FABRICS AND FITMENTS

TOOLS

Long lengths of material, which need to be cut out, make the work different from that of home dressmaking. Thus the most important thing you need is a really large table (a table-tennis table suitably covered is ideal) or, better still, a clean carpeted floor on which to cut fabric.

Pins Use good-quality dressmaker's steel pins which do not rust.
Needles These must be sharp and rust-free. Keep a selection to use with various types of fabric.
Thread Match thread to your chosen fabric. Thus always use synthetic thread for nylons, polyesters and man-made fibres. Use Sylko 40 or 50 for general purposes on medium-weight fabrics.

THE TRICK

If you prick your finger and accidentally bleed on to the fabric, chew a length of cotton thread and dab it on to the material to remove the stain without leaving a water mark.

Scissors You will need two pairs. Scissors with extra long blades speed up the cutting process. A smaller pair are useful for thread, etc. Always buy scissors of quality and keep them sharp.
Metre measuring stick An inexpensive aid to accurate measurement sold in most d-i-y shops. No self-respecting curtain maker would be without one!
Linen tape measure The cotton sort shrinks.
Steel rule Good for measuring windows before you put up tracks or poles.
A 'Quick Unpick' Invaluable little tool for unpicking stitches swiftly, obtainable from the haberdashery counter in department stores.
Ironing board and iron You will need both constantly. Watch out for, and clean away, man-made fibre deposits on the base of the iron when using synthetic materials.
Sewing machine Because so many long seams have to be worked when you make curtains and drapes, a good sewing machine is almost essential. When and if you do invest in one, remember that it is one of the few items which can be purchased with a view to lasting a good long time. Choose a model to suit your individual needs. Treat whichever type of machine you buy with care and consideration. Always read the instruction manual thoroughly before you begin to sew with a new or unfamiliar machine. Better still, ask the dealer (or the owner if you are buying secondhand) for a demonstration.

CURTAIN TRACKS AND RAILS

There are numerous types of track, rail and pole currently available in a wide variety of materials: e.g. brass, plastic and aluminium. Spend a little time exploring the full range. When you do make a decision, remember that the type of track you choose must depend on the following points:
1. Your proposed window treatment. Keep a rough sketch of your plan in your pocket for easy reference.
2. The style of heading you wish to use. If your design includes a pelmet, both the heading and track will be out of sight and can therefore be of the simplest kind. Sophisticated pinch pleats, on the other hand, look best suspended from a smart, transverse cord-operated rod.
3. The weight of your chosen fabric. Inexpensive extruded-plastic track is fine for filmy sheers or light cotton fabrics. But strong aluminium track or sturdy wooden poles are the best answer for long, heavy curtains.

Whichever type of track or pole you choose, however, do make sure you buy all the necessary attachments and fittings at the same time. It can be very frustrating searching for obsolete accessories.

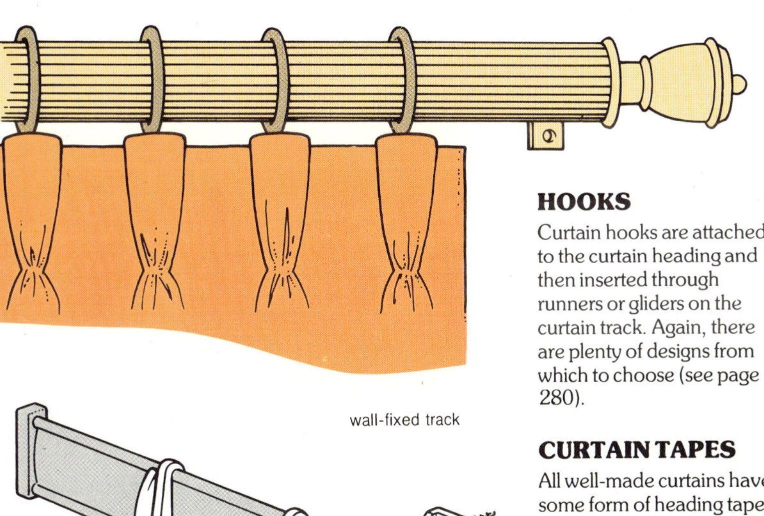

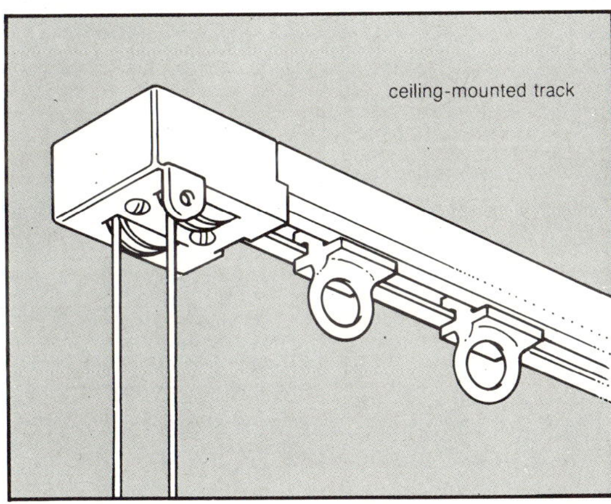

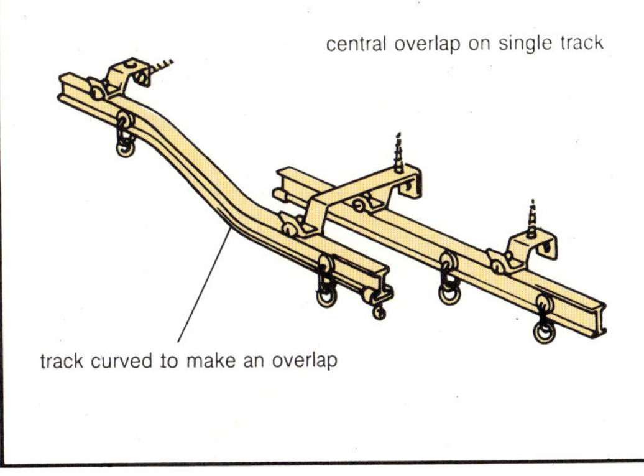

HOOKS

Curtain hooks are attached to the curtain heading and then inserted through runners or gliders on the curtain track. Again, there are plenty of designs from which to choose (see page 280).

CURTAIN TAPES

All well-made curtains have some form of heading tape to provide a firm base for the hooks. There are many different types of drawing tapes which, when applied to the curtain, are then drawn up to produce gathers, pleats or a smocking effect (see pages 280, 281).

FABRIC CHOICE

Choosing your fabric for curtains should be fun, but buy in haste and you will certainly regret at leisure. So take time to visit several different types of fabric supplier before you make your final selection. The furnishing fabric hall in a large department store is a good place to make a start. Check out any local discount houses, which frequently offer the keenest prices, particularly for linings. Finally, remember the small interior design shops; these are often a source for the more unusual designs and fabrics, sometimes at surprisingly modest prices. Remember to:
1. Consider suitability for the room, function and wearability. In America furnishing fabrics carry labels concerning the care, durability, and stain and soil resistance of the material. Here we are not so lucky, but some curtainings have a fadeproof guarantee. Watch out for this if you are proposing to sew unlined curtains.
2. Buy only curtain fabric. Material marked as suitable for upholstery often has a higher cotton content which will induce creasing.
3. Take care when choosing patterned fabrics. Large pattern repeats can involve you in a considerable amount of extra expenditure. Smaller patterns require less fabric and are thus more economical.
4. Before reaching a final conclusion, ask to see fabric draped. Patterns and texture look very different lying flat on a counter.
5. Even if you know sewing curtains will take you for ever, do buy sufficient material to complete the task. Colour and patterns are often difficult to match exactly at a later date.
6. Take a sketch of your proposed window treatment to the shop, together with the exact measurements. Discuss your plans with the salesman/woman and let them check your fabric requirements. They are usually very experienced at estimating materials.

PREPARATION

MEASURING UP

Once your plans are finalized, the next step is to measure accurately the actual area the curtain is to cover. For successful curtains you must start with the correct measurements.

THE TRICK

Professional curtain makers always place the pole or track in position before they measure for fabric. So buy and fix your track first; and then measure with a steel rule or wooden metre stick.

LENGTH

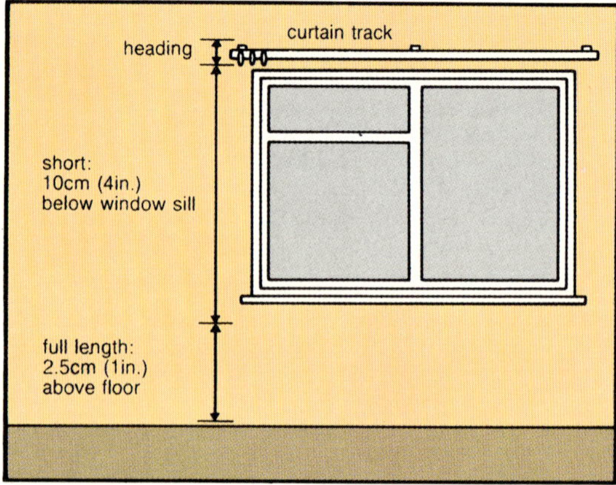

Measure the drop from the base of the glider or ring on the track to the required length. Allow for an extra 10cm (4 in.) below the sill for short curtains and make full-length curtains fall to within 2- 2.5cm (¾-1in.) of the floor. Make velvet or other heavy curtains very slightly shorter to allow for them to drop slightly when hung.

Measure from the base of the glider or ring on the track upwards for the required heading. Allow approximately 2.5cm (1in.) for a simple gathering tape and between 5 and 15cm (2-6in.) for the more elaborate varieties. Allow 7.5cm (3in.) for turning at the top of the curtain. Allow 15cm (6in.) for the lower hem.

With the above measurements, use the standard curtain makers' formula:

Length or drop = hook drop + heading + turning + hem.

WIDTH

Begin by measuring the width of the track not the window. Then multiply the figure by that of your chosen heading (e.g. 1½ for a simple gathered heading), add 30cm (12in.) for side turnings plus overlap, and this gives you the total width of fabric required. Divide this figure by 2 if you are making a pair of curtains.

The curtain makers' standard equation is:

Track length × 1½ (simple gathered heading) + 30cm/12in. ÷ 2 = the width of each curtain.

If you plan a return to the wall at the outer edge of the curtains, add that depth to the length of the curtain track.

ESTIMATING THE TOTAL AMOUNT OF FABRIC REQUIRED

To find out the total length of fabric you need, multiply the required length by the number of widths needed to cover the window. In order to do this easy sum, you need to know how many widths of fabric are needed in each curtain. This example will help you calculate correctly:

To make one curtain measuring 193cm (6ft 4in.) wide, you need to join together one and a half widths of fabric 122cm (4ft) wide. Thus, to make curtains measuring 193cm (6ft 4in.) each, you need three widths of fabric 122cm (4ft) wide.

THE TRICK

Where it is necessary to join together an odd number of widths of fabric (three is the usual number of widths for a pair of curtains), always place complete panels at the centre of the curtains with the two half-width sections down each outer edge.

If your chosen fabric is patterned, allow one pattern repeat per width of curtain required.

Because of their diverse countries of origin, curtain fabrics are sold in varying widths ranging from 122cm (4ft) to 137cm (4ft 6in.). To be safe, always assume for the purposes of your calculations that all fabrics are 122cm (4ft) wide.

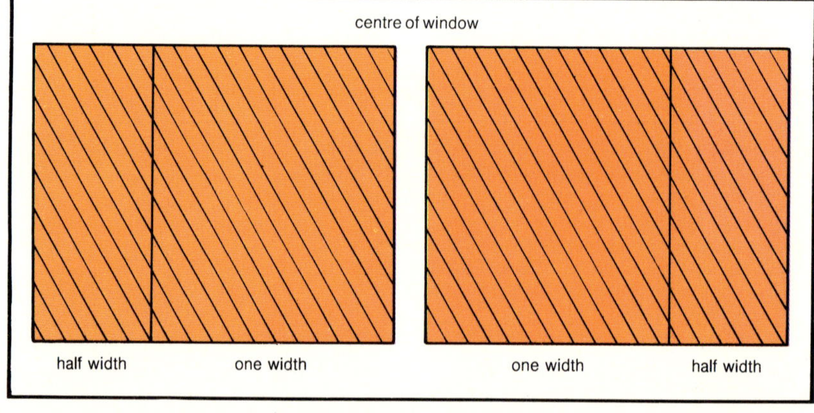

CUTTING OUT

It is absolutely essential that curtain lengths are cut straight across the fabric. Even a small mistake at this stage can make your curtains hang unevenly.

THE TRICK

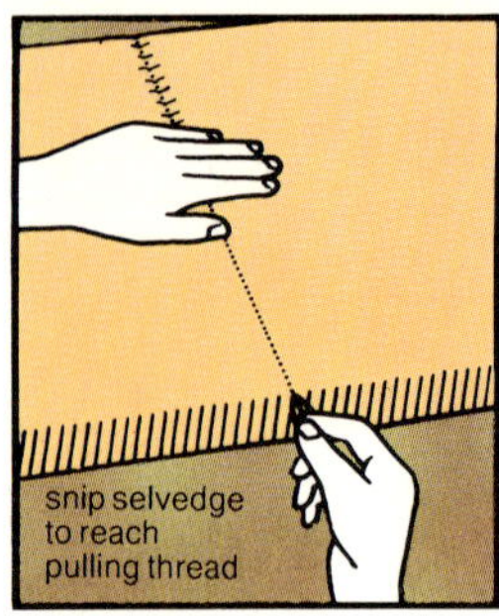

Wherever possible professional curtain makers draw a couple of threads across the width of the fabric to use as a cutting guide.

So follow their example when you use straight-woven fabrics.

Linens, chintz and cotton-printed fabrics present more of a problem: the grain of the fabric is frequently unstable due to the looseness of the weave; while the pattern is sometimes stretched out of line during the printing process. The way to overcome these difficulties is to place a metre stick at right angles to the selvedge of the fabric and chalk on a cutting line. Or try this excellent tip:

THE TRICK

Place your fabric on a rectangular table with the selvedge running down the length of the long side. Then use the end of the table to square up the fabric and mark in a cutting line.

straighten selvedge on long side; trim end square

Besides being straight, panels of patterned fabric must match. Mentally rearranging an unmatched pattern on a pair of curtains can be very irritating. Some fabrics do match equally at the selvedge; others, in fact the majority of patterned fabrics, do not. These have what the trade terms 'a pattern drop'. When you buy this type of material, remember to allow extra metreage to cover the drop.

THE TRICK

A quick way to work out the extra fabric requirement is to allow for one pattern repeat on each length of curtain you cut out. Plan to finish at the same position of the pattern on each panel.

Finally, here are a few hints to help you cut out with confidence:

1. Before you take up the scissors:

a. Measure and mark, with pins or chalk, the position of your cutting line.

b. Re-check that you have allowed sufficient fabric for turnings and pattern repeats or drops.

2. Mark the top of each panel of fabric as you cut it from the roll. This is essential when you use velours or velvets, where the pile should run down the curtains.

3. Cut away the selvedge to prevent puckering. Some people prefer merely to clip the selvedge at 5cm (2in.) intervals, but I have always found it best to remove them completely.

4. Remember to cut away and discard any wastage immediately on a patterned fabric to avoid confusion at a later stage.

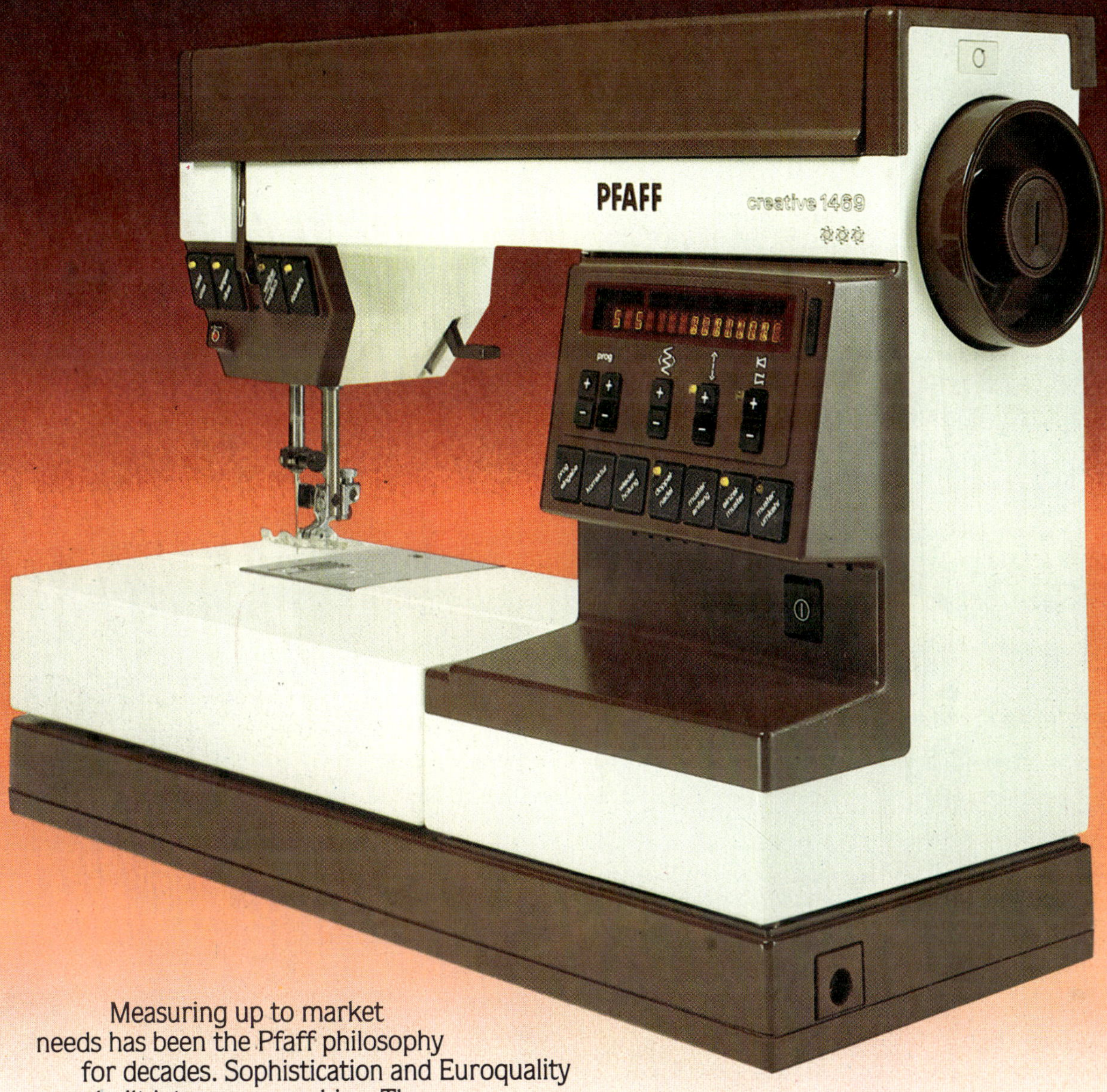

MAKING UP

MAKING UP CURTAINS

Any professional curtain maker, when asked for advice, will almost certainly reply, 'Make your curtains from the bottom up.' To the novice, such a statement seems at first impossible. Friends given the above tip nearly always go on to ask, 'How can I get the hems exactly right without hanging the curtains first?' Let me assure you that if you do hang your curtains before completing the bottom hems, the chances are that you will never get those hems straight!

THE TRICK

The secret of success lies in taking exact measurements in the first place, plus constantly checking those measurements every 10cm (4in.) as you apply the heading tape.

Then, in the unlikely event of the curtains needing a slight adjustment at the hanging stage, this can be quickly made – either by changing the position of the hooks (on a hand-pleated heading) or re-applying the heading tape. With a 'Quick Unpick', commercial tape can be ripped off, then machined back into place at the adjusted level. The whole operation can be completed in less than half an hour. Correcting the bottom hem is much more time-consuming as it includes re-mitring the corners and adjusting the lining and interlining; unpicking a carefully hand-worked hem can be heartbreaking. Worse, the difficulty of laying the completed curtain out flat once the heading pleats have been made means the end result is unlikely to prove satisfactory. So please, when making up your curtains, start at the bottom and finish at the top.

The next step is to learn the basic method for making curtains and, since this is much the same whether or not the curtains are to be lined, it is advisable to master the technique for making unlined curtains first, before you attempt the lined or inter-lined variety.

The main differences in the construction of lined and unlined curtains are that in the former widths need only a plain open seam and simple turned-in hems down each side, while in the latter widths must be joined by a run and fell seam; they have double hems down each long side and across the bottom edge.

MAKING UNLINED CURTAINS

1. Cut out the curtains carefully. Remove the selvedges. If using more than one width of fabric in each curtain, seam the panels together. Make sure the pattern matches at the seam line. Use a run and fell seam for both strength and appearance.

If you prefer to retain the selvedges, clip them every 5cm (2in.) along the length of the curtain and apply a flat seam. Press the seam open.

2. Place the completed panels right side down on a table or on the floor and, working on the wrong side of the fabric, pin a 3cm double hem down each side of the curtain. Slipstitch the hems into place.

3. Turn up, pin and tack a double hem 7.5cm (3in.) deep at the bottom edge of the curtain. Mitre the corners, inserting weights if desired. Small lead weights can be bought strung on tapes or encased in cord ready to insert into hems to make curtains hang straight and smooth. Weights also provide ballast for corners.

4. Turn the top of the curtain down 7.5cm (3in.) to the wrong side of the fabric.

5. Apply the chosen heading tape (see pages 280/281) with machine stitching. Remove the tacking. Apply hooks or split rings. Draw the curtain up to the required width.

6. Hang the curtains and set the folds, a favourite professional dodge to ensure crisp pleats.

MITRES

A truly perfect mitre can only be produced when the two hems are the same width. However, many curtain makers disregard this piece of theory, preferring to make the bottom hems slightly deeper (7.5cm/3in.) than the side hems.

a. Fold down the two hems so that they are of exactly equal width and press.

b. Open the hems out flat and make sure the press marks are clearly visible.

c. Fold the right side of the fabric over the wrong side, i.e., fold the corner inward on the inner fold lines. Press.

d. Cut off the corners, leaving a small seam allowance. Refold the hem to complete the mitre and slipstitch the two folds together.

THE RUN AND FELL SEAM

Place the wrong sides of the fabric together with the raw edges even. Pin, tack and then machine approximately 1.5cm (½in.) from the edge. Press the seam open. Trim one edge to within about 0.5cm (⅛in.) of the sewing line. Turn in the other edge and fold this over the trimmed edge. Pin and then machine close to the fold or slipstitch by hand. Press.

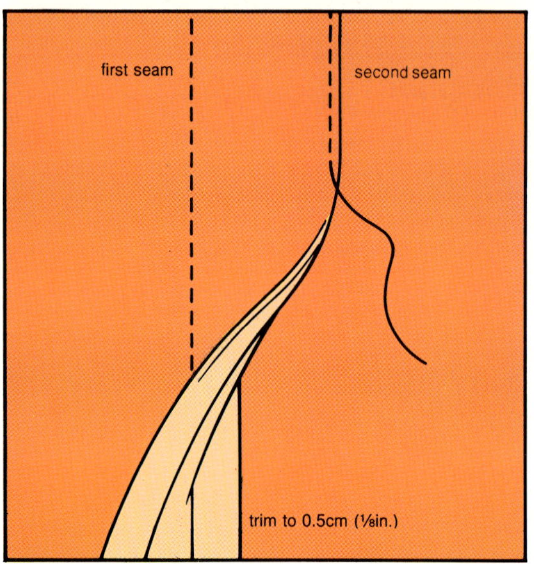

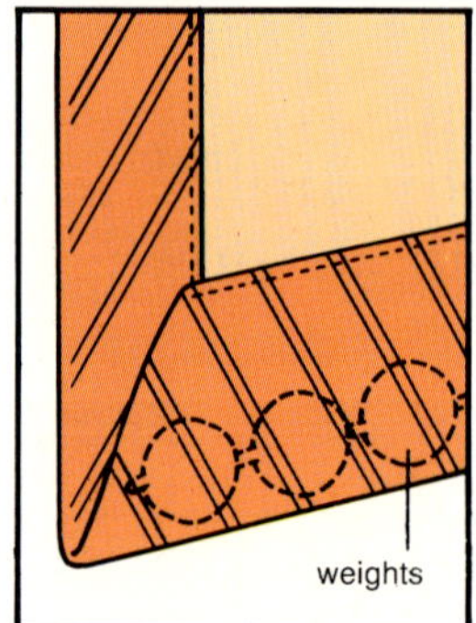

THE TRICK

Open the curtain fully and from the top form neat folds by finger-pressing down each pleat or fold for 30cm (12in.) or so. Tie loosely with a scrap of material. For full-length curtains repeat the process, making two or three ties down the length of the curtain. Leave the ties in position for two to three days for the fabric to develop a 'memory'.

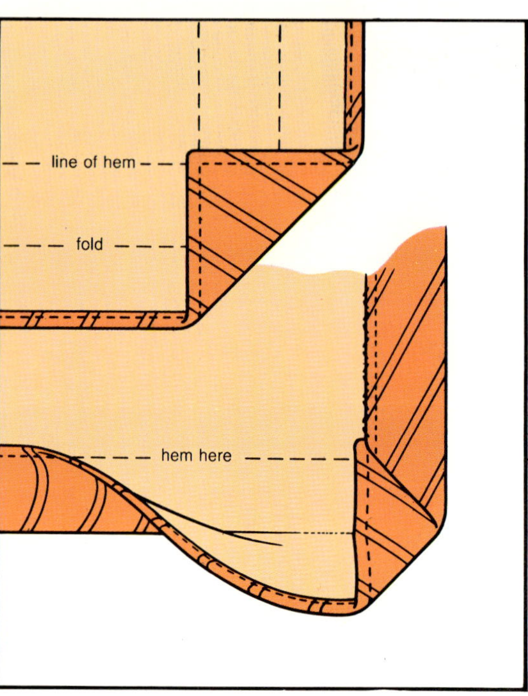

PULL-CORDS

Constant handling of curtains soils and spoils the fabric. Pull-cords are a practical way to deal with curtains where a cording set is not an integral part of the curtain track.

LINED CURTAINS 1

LINING FABRICS

Apart from those for kitchen or bathroom, all curtains look best lined. A good lining not only protects the main fabric from dirt, dust and sunlight but also gives a uniform look to the outside of your home. In addition, some linings provide an extra source of insulation: e.g. the metallic variety, popular since the 1960s, or the newer, less expensive thermal lining – a plain white bonded cotton fabric.

Cotton sateen is the fabric most generally used to line curtains. It can be bought in a wide range of colours and in many different qualities. Colour depends upon your personal preference but on no account attempt to economize on quality. Loosely woven, cheaper varieties of sateen, often imported, can cause your carefully sewn curtains to drop after only a few weeks. It will almost certainly shrink with cleaning; and has even been known to rot after relatively little wear.

Sateen lining is sold in 122cm (4ft) widths, but do check at the time of purchase. Some can be as wide as 183cm (6ft); while some 'bargains' are very narrow indeed, which is often why they are being sold cheaply.

INTERLINING

This is a soft, loosely woven fabric used to give body to curtains and provide insulation. (Silk or cotton curtains made up with interlining look sumptuous.) The materials used are bump or domette. Bump is a thick, fluffy fabric made from cotton waste usually 122cm wide. Domette, although similar, is not quite so thick and fluffy. Neither fabric is washable, thus all interlined curtains must be dry-cleaned only.

THE BAG METHOD

Many busy people favour this way of making lined curtains principally because the entire operation can be performed with a minimum of fuss on a simple sewing machine. No particular skill is required and there are no tricks of the trade to divulge. Because no chapter on curtains would be complete without mentioning the method, here is a brief explanation:

1. Measure the track and drop of your window and calculate the amount of fabric required, bearing in mind your chosen heading. (see pages 280, 281).
2. Cut out the main fabric and seam together any necessary widths.
3. Cut out the lining 2.5cm (1in.) smaller than the main fabric all round. If you fail to do this, the lining will curl round to the front of the curtain no matter how much it is pressed.
4. Pin the right side of the lining to the right side of the main fabric. Machine stitch side seams, equalise turn back and sew foot seams. Turn the curtain right side out. Hem the mitres in. Tuck in the top.
5. Apply the heading tape and insert the hooks.

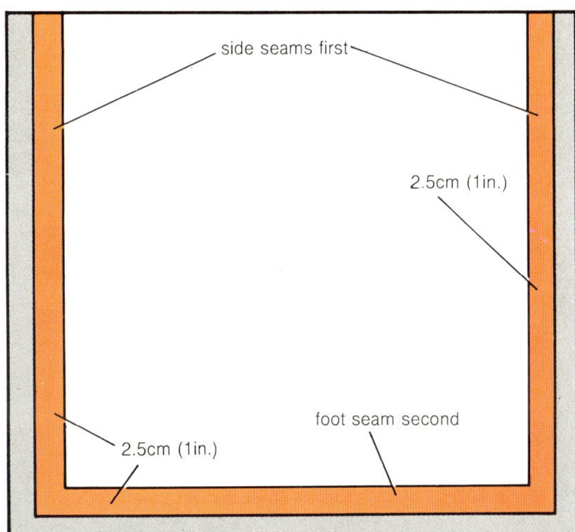

DETACHABLE LOOSE LININGS

At first glance, detachable loose linings seem the answer to a prayer. They are quick and easy to make, and they can be removed for cleaning or changed from one set of curtains to another in a matter of moments. Their practicality depends on the fact that they are made with their own special lining tape and are therefore quite separate from the main curtains. They simply share the same hooks as the curtain.

However, in spite of their many advantages, curtains with detachable linings somehow miss the smooth professional look gained from locked-in linings. To overcome this, some curtain makers slipstitch or tack the linings to the curtain down each long side to unite the two fabrics and prevent the lining from showing at the outer edges. This course of action seems to defeat the object of the exercise!

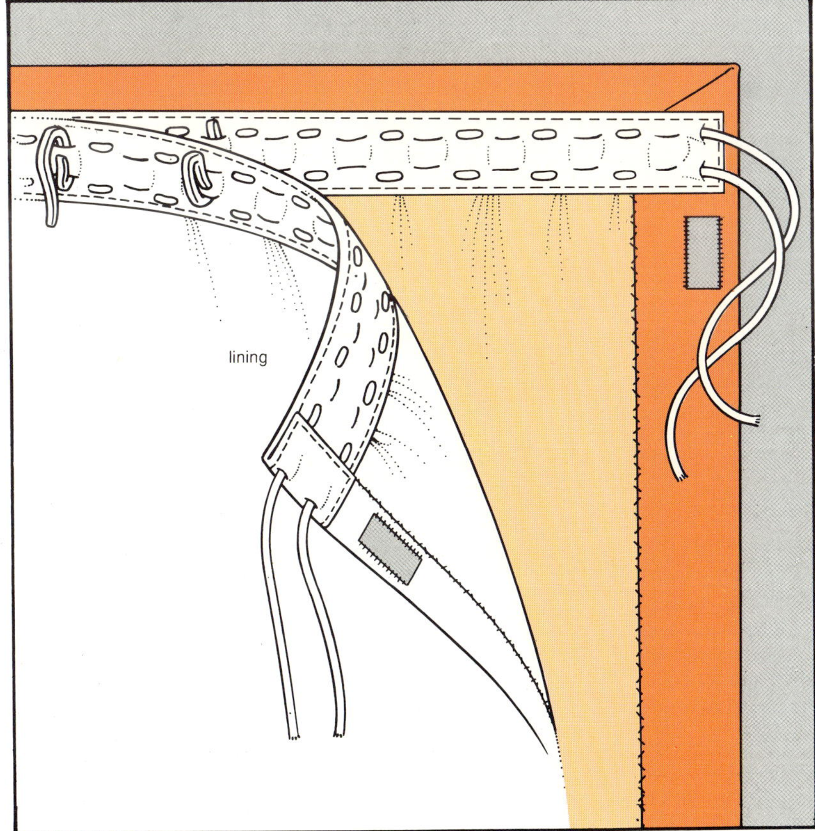

THE TRICK

Professional curtain makers prefer to stick strips of touch-and-close fastening (Velcro is the best-known) to both lining and main fabric at intervals down the long sides and thus avoid any chance of the lining and curtain parting company, while at the same time retaining the practical aspect of detachable linings.

The method when making detachable linings is as follows:

1. Make up the curtains in the main fabric as for unlined curtains.
2. Cut out the linings to the same dimensions, but make the length 2.5cm (1in.) shorter than that of the main fabric, measuring from the heading tape to the base of the hem.
3. Apply the lining tape in the following way:
a. Cut the lining heading tape to the required width plus 7.5cm (3in.) for turnings.
b. Pull the cords free from each end of the tape for 4cm (1½in.).
c. At one end knot the cords together, and leave the other end free.
d. Fold the knotted cord under the tape and stitch into position.
e. Lay the tape right side up on a table.
f. Feed the lining right side up between the two layers of the tape and pin and tack into position, extending the tape 3.5cm (1¼in.) at either end of the lining fabric.
g. Tuck surplus tape under at each end to lie level with the lining tape.
h. Machine along the lower edge of the tape through all three thicknesses i.e. through tape/lining/tape.
4. Pull up the cord ends to make the lining 5cm (2in.) narrower than your curtain. Knot off the cords.
5. Slip the hooks first into the slits in the lining tape, then into the pockets of the curtain heading tape, and turn into their final position. Your curtains are now ready to hang.

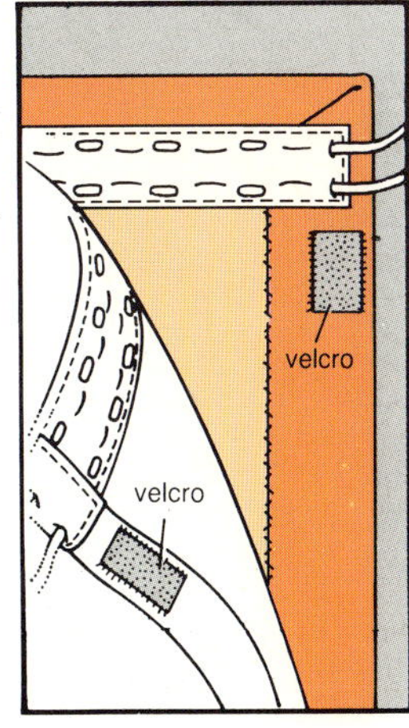

LINED CURTAINS 2

LOCKED-IN LININGS

The best way to approach making this type of lined curtains, particularly if you are a complete novice, is to break the job down into three stages. The following three short sets of instructions should help you feel confident to tackle the task and at the same time make the work seem easy.

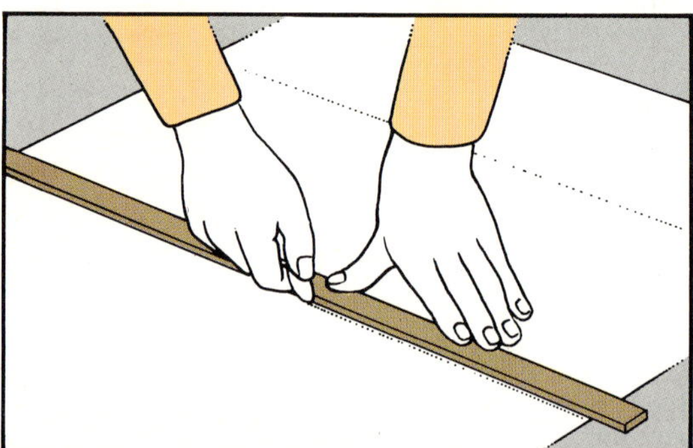

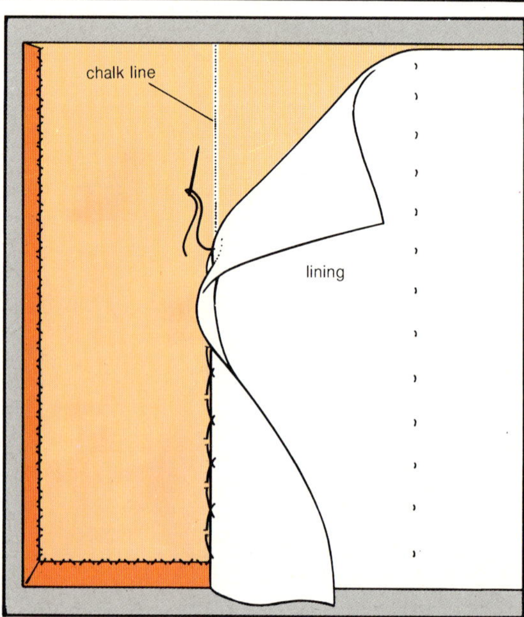

MAIN FABRIC

1. Measure and cut out the material carefully. Remember to match up any pattern repeats. Remove selvedge.
2. Plain seam the widths or half-widths together to form complete curtain panels. Press open the seams.
3. Turn the fabric in 6cm (2½in.) down each of the long sides, and make a 7.5cm (3in.) double hem across the bottom edge. Pin, tack and then use a large hem stitch for all three sides.
4. Mitre the corners (see page 276).

LINING

1. Cut out the lining to the same measurements as the main fabric. Remove all selvedges.
2. Plain seam the widths or half-widths together to form complete panels. Press open the seams.
3. Spread the main fabric out on a flat surface, wrong side uppermost.

THE TRICK

To keep your stitches, and incidentally the fabric, straight: measure and draw vertical lines, 30cm (1ft) apart, down the wrong side of the fabric. Use tailor's chalk for this.

4. Place the lining over the curtain fabric, wrong side down (i.e. with the two wrong sides together). Position the lining approximately 2cm (¾in.) from the top of the curtain.
5. Carefully fold back the lining from the left to the first chalk guide line on the right side. Lockstitch the lining into position (see box). Begin your stitches 15cm (6in.) from the top of the curtain and make them 10cm (4in.) apart. Be careful not to pull the thread too tightly or the main fabric may pucker. Pick up only one thread of the main fabric at each stitch. Once the line is completed, bring the lining forward to the next and repeat the locking process. Continue across the curtain as necessary.

THE TRICK

Always use thread for locking which matches the main fabric, not the lining.

6. Once the lines of locking are completed, trim away any excess lining fabric extending beyond the curtain edge. (To recap, this means that the lining should lie flush with the main fabric down both the long sides and across the bottom edge.)
7. Fold the lining in 2.5cm (1in.) and pin in position down both long sides and across the bottom edge. Make sure the corner of the lining meets the mitre on the main fabric.
8. To hold the fabrics securely in position for further stitching, make a line of tacking 5cm (2in.) from the top right across the curtain.
9. Slipstitch the lining to the main fabric down both the long sides and across the bottom edge. Begin the stitching 15cm (6in.) from the top of the curtain to allow for the heading.
10. Remove the line of tacking across the top of the curtain. Turn in both the main fabric and the lining. Press. Apply your chosen commercial heading tape. Add the hooks and hang the curtain.

INTERLINING

Interlining gives curtains extra body and the luxury look. It also provides a certain amount of insulation. However, interlining adds considerably to the overall cost of curtaining. Remember that most interior designers working to a small budget prefer to recommend their client to install curtains made from generous amounts of inexpensive fabric: e.g. cotton, lined and interlined, rather than use a more expensive fabric with a simple lining.

You need exactly the same amount of interlining fabric as for the finished flat curtain. This is what you do:

1. Cut out the main fabric and lining for the curtain. Join together widths where necessary.
2. Cut the interlining to the exact size of the final finished flat curtain. Join together widths where necessary by overlapping the raw edge of the wrong side of one length with the edge of the right side of another length.

THE TRICK

Join with two rows of machine stitching. Bump and domette stretch, hence the double row of stitching to provide extra strength.

3. Spread out the main fabric on a table or floor, wrong side uppermost. Position the interlining over the wrong side of the curtain 7.5cm (3in.) from the top, leaving 6cm (2½in.) borders down both sides of the main fabric.
4. Fold back the interlining from the left to within 12cm

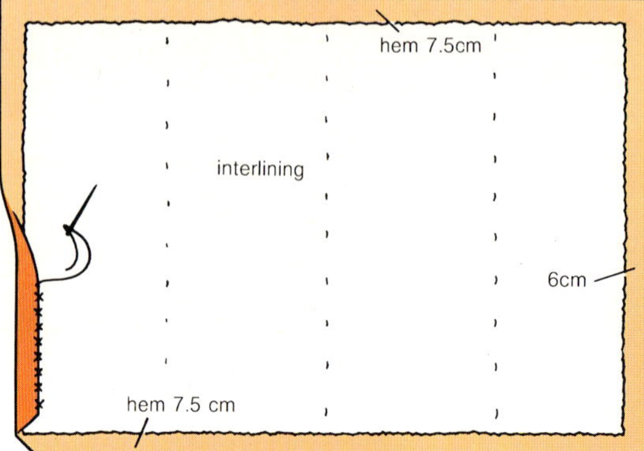

(4¾in.) from the right and lockstitch (see right) into position. You need to stitch approximately three rows of locking every 120cm. Detailed instructions are given above.
5. Turn the edges of the main fabric down the long sides and across the hem over on to the interlining. Herringbone/catchstitch into position and mitre the corners (see page 276).
6. Place the lining over the interlining, fold in 2.5cm (1in.) at the sides and along the bottom edge. Match mitres and slipstitch into position.
7. Fold down the top of the main fabric over the interlining. Insert any additional stiffening. Turn in the top of the lining and slipstitch into place.
8. Apply the chosen heading.

LOCKSTITCH

A loose stitch, approximately 1.2cm (½in.) long and worked from left to right down the length of a curtain. Lockstitch is used exclusively to secure linings and interlinings.

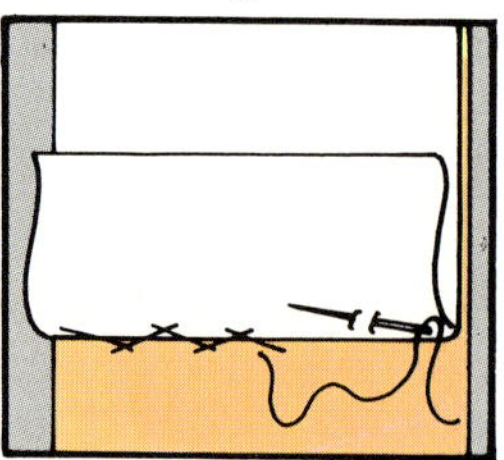

CHOOSING VELVET CURTAINS-BY A WOMAN WHO'S NO SOFT TOUCH

"Draperite use only the best 100% cotton pile velvet. And the traditional skills of experienced cutters plus the high-technology precision of blind-stitched base hems promise absolutely consistent quality. I know–I went and saw for myself!"

Judith Chalmers

Satisfaction made to measure

Whatever length of curtains you want, Draperite will make them beautifully for you.

You'll find a choice of 28 superb patterns and shades–and superior quality sewn-in linings add the luxury of genuine insulation. Delivery is free, and Draperite's unconditional "replacement or-refund" guarantee gives you absolute peace of mind.

Telephone or write today for your FREE sample pack

– featuring the whole Draperite range with full price list. It also contains addresses of 30 W.H. Smith Do-It-All stores with Draperite showrooms–where you can see Draperite velvet curtains for yourself on full-length display (state reference: TT 3/84).

Draperite Ltd., FREEPOST, (no stamp needed), Eccles, Manchester M30 7JZ.

Draperite

Luxury velvet curtains.
See them on display in the Draperite showrooms at

DO IT ALL

Branch address details in your free sample pack.

CURTAIN HEADINGS 1

Commercial tapes are available in a wide variety of styles and colours and are the quickest and easiest way to head curtains. There are no pleats to plot and pin into place, and they are suitable for easy-care laundering or dry-cleaning. Individually designed hand-made headings give a more professional finish to curtains, but are time-consuming. However, the task of sewing headings yourself can be enormously satisfying, and provide curtains with an extra touch of elegance at a fraction of the cost of professional work.

Commercial heading tapes are available in two basic styles: drawing tape, which is used for simple gathered headings, pencil pleats and some types of pinch pleats; and slotted tape, used with long-pronged hooks to produce a variety of single, double or triple pinch pleats. All types of drawing tape, whatever the make or width, are applied in precisely the same way.

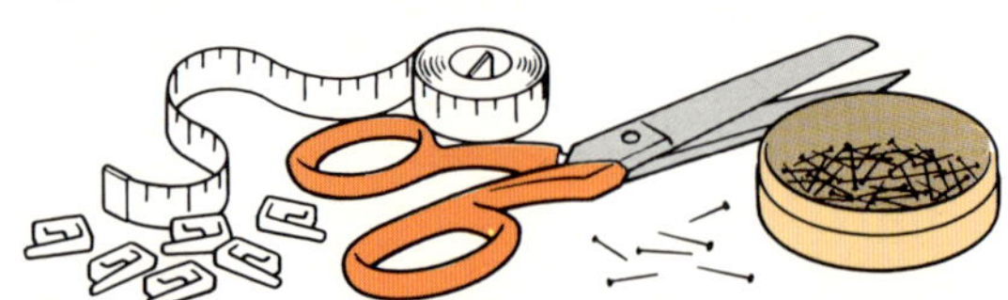

HOW TO APPLY DRAWING TAPE

1. Measure the width of the curtain, and cut the tape to this width, adding 3cm (1½in.) for turnings.
2. Measure the curtains from the bottom up to ensure correct placing of the tape (see individual instructions for positioning specific tapes).
3. Pin the tape across the curtain. Check your measurements from the bottom up, every 10–12cm (4–5in.), for a really accurate result. A crooked tape means curtains of uneven length.
4. Tack the tape to the curtain, slip in a hook or two and check against your window.
5. Ease the cords from the last 1.5cm (¾in.) of tape at each end. Tie one pair of ends in a reef knot. Tuck in the ends. Leave the other pair of cords free.
6. Machine stitch the tape into place, carefully avoiding the two loose ends of cord.

THE TRICK

Stitch along the top edge of the tape first. Remove from the machine and stitch the bottom edge in the same direction. This prevents puckering.

7. Draw the free part of the cords up to make the curtain the required width. Distribute the fullness, then tie the cords firmly, but do not cut them off. Instead wind them round a 'cord tidy' and tuck it into the last pocket of the tape.

THE TRICK

Drawing up bulky curtains can be quite hard on the hands. Knot one set of cords at one end and loop them round a door handle; then, holding the other pair of cords, work the curtain up towards the door.

COMMERCIAL HEADING TAPES

SIMPLE GATHERED HEADING

Suitable for use under a pelmet or valance, or where only a small frill is required. Use a standard cotton or man-made mixture tape 2.5cm (1in.) wide, with woven pockets at intervals to accommodate hooks or split rings. The fabric width required is at least one and a half times the length of the track.

Position the tape across the width of the curtain, 2cm (¾in.) from the top when a pelmet or valance will be used, or to 3–5cm (1½–2in.) from the top for frilled curtains.

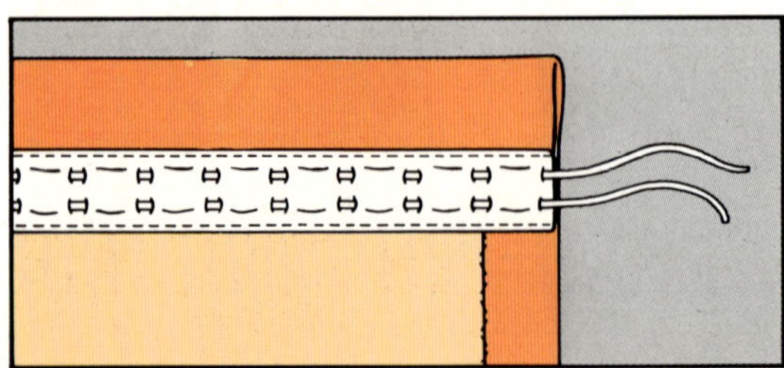

THE TRICK

As this type is not stiffened, stiffen the top 5cm (2in.) of the curtain with iron-on dress interfacing or buckram for a neat crisp frill (see page 286).

BOX-PLEATED HEADING

Produced with another style of commercial drawing tape, the box-pleated heading is useful for pelmets and valances as well as curtains. Fabric requirement is two and a half times the length of the track. Apply the tape exactly as for any other drawing tape, but watch out for any special instructions from the manufacturers. (See also page 286).

PENCIL-PLEATED HEADING

All commercial tapes for this heading are drawing tapes. They are available in a variety of widths from approximately 6.5 to 15cm (2¾–6in.) and in two basic styles: those requiring long-pronged hooks for the heading to stand straight; and those stiffened with woven nylon thread which require no extra support or stiffening. Ordinary curtain hooks or split rings may be used with the second type. It is also possible to buy pencil-pleating tapes with three alternative suspension points, useful for fabrics you fear may shrink.

Position the tape with the top approximately 2cm (¾in.) below the top edge of the curtain and proceed as before.

If using the type of tape which requires long-pronged hooks, check the manufacturer's instructions to make sure you apply the tape with the pockets accessible.

PINCH-PLEATED HEADING

For this heading there are drawing tapes which form three pleats, followed by a flat section repeated along the curtain when the strings are pulled up; and slotted tapes with woven pockets, into which pleater hooks are inserted at regular intervals. However these latter are not much in use nowadays.

The fabric width required when using these headings will depend on your design. Drawing tape and slotted triple pleats require two and a half times the length of the track; single slotted pleats only one and three-quarter times the length of the track.

Apply as for simple gathered tape, but be sure to arrange the pleats symmetrically.

To produce single pleats, push the two centre prongs into two separate pockets; for double pleats use three prongs; and for triple pleats push all four prongs into separate pockets.

For those who like to change styles, there are tapes with a dual set of drawing cords (one white, one coloured) available which produce two styles of heading with just one tape. Pull up one set of cords and you get French pleating; the other produces pencil pleats. This dual purpose tape has three pocket positions which allow curtain lengths to be adjusted.

THE TRICK

If the window frame has a return at the outer edge, do not gather the curtain at this point. Instead, arrange the tape so that there is a single hook at the outer edge and allow the first pleat to fall at the corner of the return.

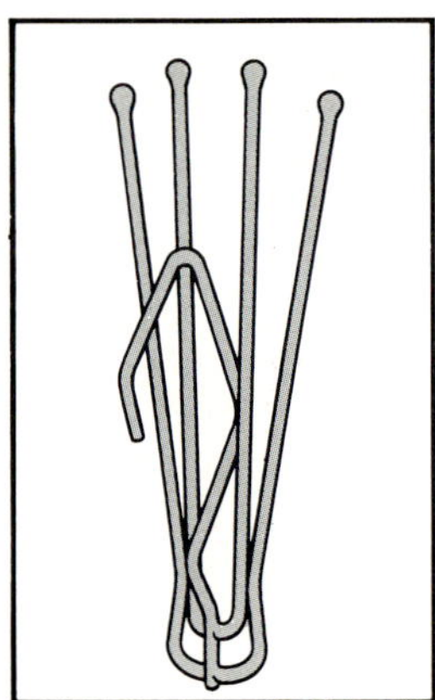

CURTAIN HEADINGS 2

SMOCKED HEADING

Another attractive commercial tape treatment is the smocked heading, which is made with a special variety of drawing tape. Popular with interior decorators, this requires only twice the width of the track in each curtain. If you are pushed for funds, it can be made up with only 80 per cent fullness. It is an exceptionally pretty heading which gives a professional finish to both main curtains and nets. Apply the tape as described on page 280, placing it 3–5cm (1½–2in.) below the top of the curtain.

SCALLOPED HEADINGS

This type of heading is generally used for unlined cafe curtains at windows or to conceal shelves or doors. However, it can also look very attractive used on full-length curtains suspended from wooden poles. It is not difficult to make; the secret of success lies in selecting a sufficiently firm fabric to show the scallops off to their full advantage. A scalloped heading requires only one and a half times the length of the track. Scalloped headings are made in the following way:

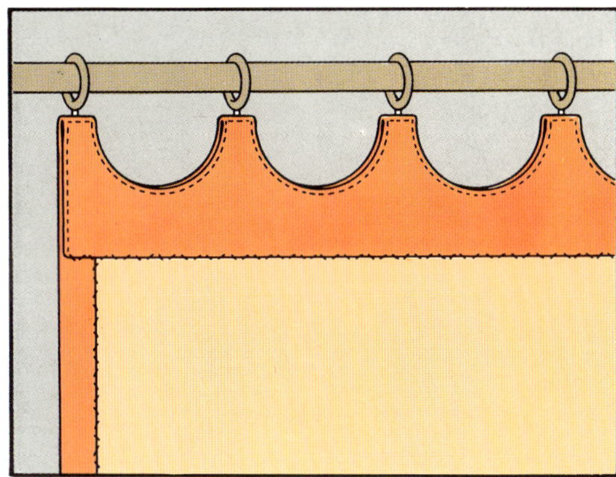

1. Make up a stiff card template for the scallops first. (A scallop is really just a circle squared off at one end.) Draw round a saucer, tin lid or other circular object if you do not own a pair of compasses.
2. Next, make a paper pattern of scallops to fit the finished curtain. The quickest way to do this is to cut out a sheet of paper the width of the curtain. Fold it in equal sections, and then draw on it the shape of your desired scallop using the previously prepared template. Cut through all thicknesses of the paper and open out.
3. Cut out and make up an unlined curtain (see page 276). Do not hem the top edge or apply a heading tape.
4. To make the scallops on the main fabric, fold over the top hem to the right side of the material. Pin and then tack the paper pattern to the turned-over hem. Be sure to tack in between each scallop. Machine stitch round the outline of each scallop.
5. Tear away the paper pattern and cut away any unwanted fabric to make the scallops. Leave 1cm (½in.) edges. Snip the turnings at the curved parts and clip the corners. Turn right side out. Tuck in the raw edges and hem stitch to the wrong side of the curtain.
6. Attach curtain rings to the top of the straps of the scallops.

HAND-PLEATED HEADINGS

Most beginners are afraid to tackle hand-pleated headings for curtains, yet the techniques required are not particularly arduous to learn; although finding sufficient time for the sewing might be another matter! However, once you see your first finished hand-headed curtains hanging, you will be so pleased with their appearance that you will probably never want to use commercial tapes again; at least, not for any special window treatments.

The secret for all types of hand-pleated heading lies in stiffening the top 10–12cm (4–5in.) of the curtain first. Do this with buckram or any other type of heavyweight dressmaking stiffening, either iron-on or sew-in. Both are equally satisfactory.

To stiffen any type of heading, cut the buckram, 10cm (4in.) wide, to the width of the finished flat curtain. Tack the stiffening to the wrong side of the main fabric approximately 7.5cm (3in.) below the top of the curtain. Make sure that you get it straight. Iron or catchstitch the stiffener into final position. Cover with the lining and continue to complete the curtain in the usual way. Lastly, stitch in your chosen style of pleats.

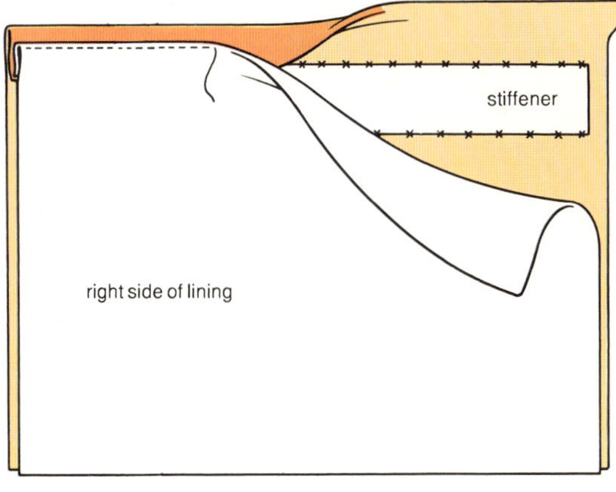

BOX PLEATS

Box pleats make an attractive heading which can be used for lined or unlined valances as well as curtains. Once you master marking out the fabric, the rest is easy.

Your fabric width requirement in this case is three times the length of the track. For ease of calculation, make your final width of fabric divisible by 10, 20 or 30cm (4, 8 or 12in.): i.e. the amount of fabric each pleat will require. The procedure is:

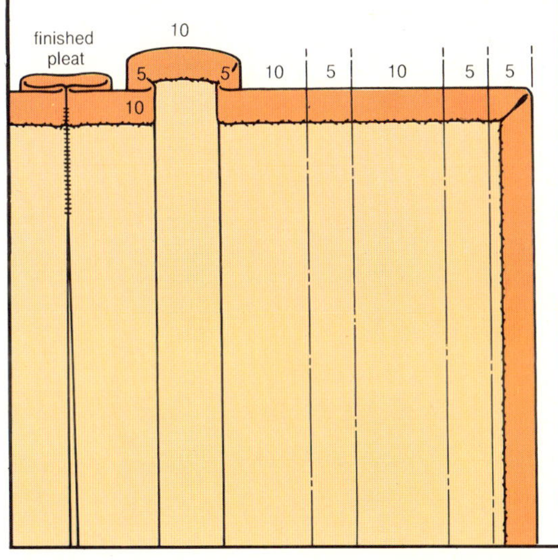

1. Make up the curtain in the usual way. Add the stiffener, fold in the lining at the top and hem into position.
2. Lay the curtain out flat and measure and plot the pleats. To do this, make your first mark 5cm (2in.) in from the edge of the curtain, follow it with a further 5cm (2in.), then mark 10cm (4in.) and 5cm (2in.) points alternately across the rest of the curtain, ending with two 5cm (2in.) spaces. This will allow you 10cm (4in.) pleats with 10cm (4in.) spaces between each.
3. Then fold the pleats, begin at a point 20cm (8in.) in from the edge of the curtain and join this to the next point 20cm (8in.) further on. Pin and tack the pleat into position. Leave a space of 10cm (4in.) and then join the next two 20cm (8in.) points together. Repeat the pattern across the curtain, finishing with the two 5cm (4in.) spaces. Finally, machine stitch the pleats on the right side of the fabric to a depth of 8cm (3½in.).
4. Form and flatten pleats on the right side of the fabric and secure with a few stitches. Press.
5. On the wrong side of the curtain, slipstitch the pleats together, taking the thread right through from the lining to the main fabric to prevent sagging.
6. Apply non-drawing tape to the wrong side of the curtain to help stabilize the pleats. (The tape must be hemmed into position all round.)
7. Sew ordinary brass curtain hooks on to the tape in the usual way, 2cm (¾in.) in from each edge and behind each pleat across the curtain.

OTHER CURTAINS

SHOWER CURTAINS

Shower curtains can be made in two ways. The first and by far the more effective is to make up an unlined curtain to match the window curtains and add a detachable showerproof lining (see pages 276, 277). Simple plastic fabric shower curtains, on the other hand, require a minimum of stitching, are relatively inexpensive and can be made up in under an hour.

When estimating the amount of fabric required, remember that shower curtains can be up to one and a half times the width of the rail but fullness is not particularly necessary. Allow 5cm (2in.) of extra material for each side hem, 5cm (2in.) for the bottom hem and 10cm (4in.) for the heading. Do not forget to calculate for any pattern repeats if necessary.

From your local soft-furnishing specialist buy some dual-purpose shower-curtain hooks which act both as hooks and runners. Next, beg, borrow or buy a special eyelet hole punch.

THE TRICK

Use nylon or other synthetic thread for sewing and adhesive tape or paper clips instead of pins for tacking.

When you machine stitch a plastic fabric, always use a long, loose stitch to avoid any excess tension.

THE TRICK

A tiny drop of sewing machine lubricant applied to the tip of the needle will make stitching easier.

The method to follow is:

1. Join together any necessary widths of material. Use a French seam (see box) to keep the curtain water-tight.
2. Turn in and machine stitch double hems 2.5cm (1in.) deep down each long side and the bottom edge of the curtain.
3. Turn over a 5cm (2in.) double hem at the top, but do not stitch down. Instead use the hole punch to make metal-trimmed eyelet holes 5cm (2in.) apart along the top of the curtain.
4. Insert the dual-purpose hooks into the eyelet holes and hang the curtain from the shower rail.

If you are unable to obtain an eyelet hole punch, stitch a nylon heading tape along the top of the curtain. It will work perfectly well, although the extra stitching must eventually weaken the plastic fabric.

FRENCH SEAM

The French seam is the most suitable for joining together widths of net curtains. It is very hard-wearing and has the advantage that no lines of stitching show through on to the right side of the fabric.

Place the wrong sides of the fabric together with the raw edges even. Tack and stitch approximately 1–1.5cm (½–¾in.) from the edge. Fabrics with a tendency to fray need the extra width.

Trim and remove the tacking. Turn the seam back on itself and stitch another seam 1cm (½in.) from the first, this time with the right sides together. Make sure you enclose the raw edges.

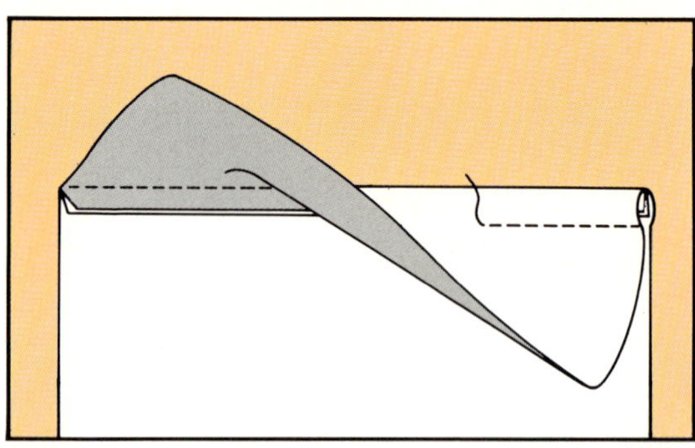

CAFE CURTAINS

The charm of cafe curtains lies in their versatility. They provide a casual, relaxed look; they can be made in multiple tiers of varying lengths, any of which can be opened or closed independently; and they lend themselves to almost any type of heading that suits your mood and room.

Basic cafe curtains usually comprise two small pairs of curtains, one each for the lower and upper parts of the window. Thus two tracks or poles are needed, one at the top of the window and one half-way up. Scalloped headings are frequently chosen for both curtains. Single-tier cafe curtains are simply half-length curtains, often with a scalloped heading, used to screen an ugly view or provide privacy for the occupants of a room.

Cafe curtains are constructed in the same way as lined or unlined curtains, except on occasions where a scalloped heading is used. Remember to fix both poles or tracks before you measure for fabric. Then let your imagination and natural flair have a chance to shine.

The length of cafe curtains naturally varies according to style. When estimating fabric requirements remember that for single-tier curtains – or for the lower panel of two-tier curtains – you should measure from the lower edge of the track to the lower edge of the window sill and add 15cm (6in.) for the hem, plus the depth of the chosen heading.

For the top panels of two-tier curtains, measure from the lower edge of the top track to the lower edge of the lower track and add 15cm (6in.) for the hem, plus an allowance for your chosen heading.

Fabric width will depend on your chosen heading; scalloped headings need only one to one and a half times the length of the track.

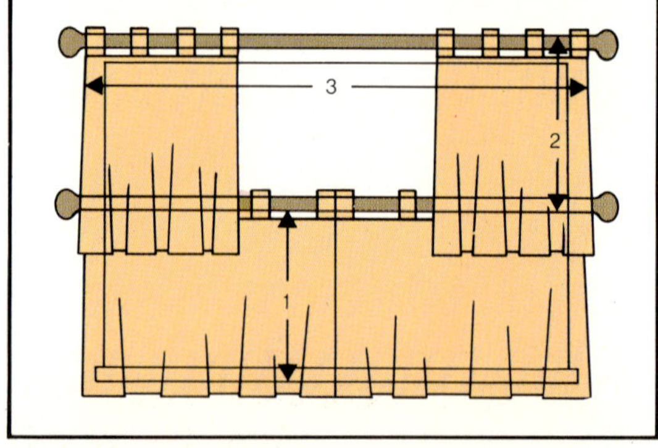

CARE OF CURTAINS

Being good to your curtains can extend their life span. Fabrics vary in the care they need, but they all need your help. Monthly brushing by hand or vacuum cleaning will remove surface dust, but more radical cleaning is needed at least once a year. However, because of their size or construction, many curtains are impossible to launder at home, so choose the best dry-cleaner in the district. On the other hand, even if the curtains are washable, remember that stiffeners and trims may not take to water as happily as the curtain fabric.

The following fabrics must be dry-cleaned: all velvets, velours, chenilles, tapestries and brocades, together with all fabrics containing wool or silk, plus all pelmets, curtains or valances into which buckram has been inserted.

Fabrics which may be carefully washed are: colourfast cottons, linens, polyester mixtures, nets and sheers made from man-made fibres. In all cases check the washing instructions; some fabrics must not be put in the tumble drier or ironed.

Glass fibre fabrics, although not much in use now, should be mentioned because they must be washed by hand and drip-dried. Iron or dry-clean them at your peril.

THE TRICK

Window condensation may cause staining no cleaner can remove. Be sure to suspend curtains so that your expensive fabric does not touch the glass.

Ena Shaw

Fine Furnishings for over 50 years

SPECIAL LIMITED OFFER!

WASHABLE VELVET CURTAINS

FREE THERMAL LININGS!

Including the famous Ena Shaw
Made-to-measure service

Panache

Washable Velvet Curtains

The special ENA SHAW offer of FREE THERMAL LININGS now gives Panache, fully washable 100% cotton pile velvet curtains, even more value. You will appreciate how thermal linings can make a significant reduction of heat loss from your windows – giving extra comfort and reduced fuel bills.

This special offer is still fully inclusive of our superb made-to-measure tailoring service. When you buy luxury velvet curtains you want a perfect fit to furnish your windows beautifully. We will ensure just that. And you have the choice of standard pleated headings at no extra cost, or if you prefer, pencil and pinch pleats at a small extra charge. Remember Panache velvet curtains retain their lustre and style, even after repeated washings and are now available with FREE thermal linings. But hurry, this is a strictly limited offer. To dress window 3′ deep x 4′6″ wide

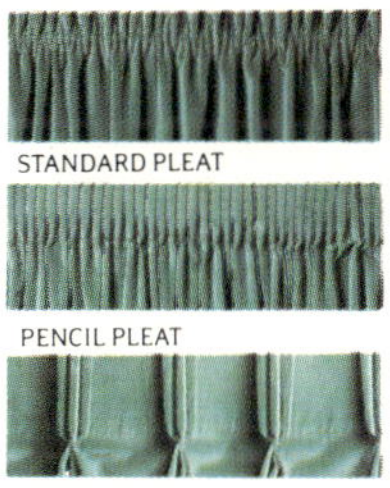

STANDARD PLEAT

PENCIL PLEAT

PINCH PLEAT

£26.95 PER PAIR

Remember all Ena Shaw prices are per pair
It's always best to check. Then you'll see how much value we give.

PRICES PER PAIR OF LISTER CURTAINS

drop	2 curtains each 1 width each approx 46″ wide	2 curtains each 1½ widths each approx 69″ wide	2 curtains each 2 widths each approx 92″ wide	2 curtains each 2½ widths each approx 115″ wide	2 curtains each 3 widths each approx 138″ wide	2 curtains each 3½ widths each approx 161″ wide
3′0″	25.50	38.25	51.00	63.75	76.50	89.25
5′0″	34.80	52.20	69.60	87.00	104.40	121.80
7′0″	43.70	65.55	87.40	109.25	131.10	152.95
9′0″	52.65	78.98	105.30	131.63	157.95	184.28

Lister

Traditional Cotton Velvet Curtains

Beautifully tailored to your measurements and fully lined at no extra cost.

World famous cotton velvet, woven by Britain's most famous manufacturer, LISTER is now, due to the rising cost of imported velvets, even BETTER VALUE. It's the ENA SHAW tailoring service that makes all the difference and gives that special feeling of luxury. Every Lister curtain is made to hang beautifully and fit perfectly. The 100% cotton linings, permanently sewn in, and standard pleated headings are available at no extra cost. We are also able to give you a choice of pencil pleats, pinch pleats and thermal linings for a small extra charge. To dress window 3′ deep x 4′6″ wide

£25.50 PER PAIR

THE ENA SHAW CHARGE ACCOUNT

As a reputable longstanding company, we are able to offer all our customers the advantage of our easy purchase scheme. Written details on request.

FREE!

SAMPLE PACK AND ACCESSORIES BROCHURE ·
Decide how to dress your window – actual pieces of velvet plus brochure showing full range of curtain accessories.

PHONE FOR YOUR FREE PACK (0744) 50103 – 24 HOURS

New showrooms now open (Details in the pack)

24 hour dial a pack FREE service 0744 50103

Including details of Free thermal linings offer!

Free actual velvet samples and complete Lister and Panache price lists. Free comprehensive package illustrating exciting ideas for home decor – phone NOW!

Or simply fill in the coupon on the inside back cover

TRIMMINGS

TIE-BACKS

Many types of commercially made cords, tassels and gilded metal tie-backs are available. Yet simple unshaped or shaped tie-backs, made from matching fabric, are far cheaper, much prettier and easily made at home.

UNSHAPED TIE-BACKS

1. To calculate its length, measure round the open curtain, taking in as much fullness as necessary, and add an extra 2cm (1in.) to provide sufficient fabric for the hooks. The finished depth is usually about 10cm (4in.), but this can be varied to suit the window proportions.
2. Cut a strip of interlining to the exact finished size of your tie-back.
3. Cut out the main fabric and lining. Use the above measurements plus 1.5cm (¾in.) all round.
4. Shape the ends of the tie-back fabric into points or curves.
5. Tack the interlining to the wrong side of the main fabric. Turn the main fabric over the interlining 1.5cm (¾in.) all round. Press and herringbone into position.
6. Place the lining over the interlining, right side up. Turn the edges of the lining in so that they finish 0.5cm (¼in.) in from edge of the tie-back. Pin, press and slipstitch into position. Attach rings or hooks at each end and screw a hook into the wall or window reveal.

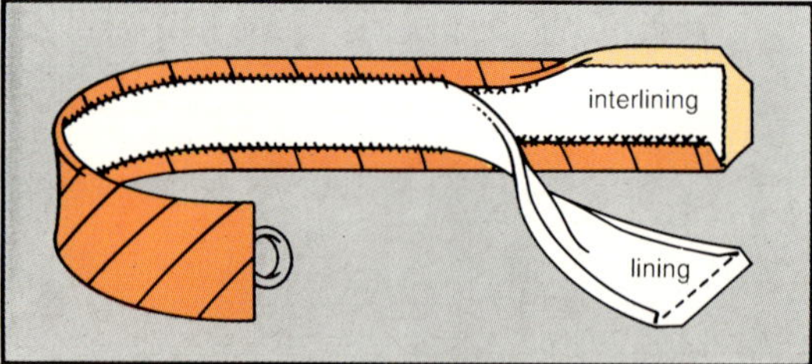

THE TRICK

For a crisp, neat finish with lightweight or sheer fabrics, attach a strip of buckram, cut to the same size, to the interlining to provide extra stiffening.

SHAPED TIE-BACKS

Traditional crescent-shaped tie-backs can look particularly attractive. Their lower edges can be scalloped or decorated with braid or piping.

This type of tie-back is not difficult to make.

THE TRICK

The trick is to experiment with a paper pattern. Draw one half of your shape on a folded sheet of paper. Make the centre of the tie-back at the fold of the paper. Cut out the paper pattern and try it round the curtain.

If you are not satisfied, start again. Remember all tie-backs must be sufficiently loose to allow the curtains to appear to their full advantage. Once a satisfactory design has been produced, the procedure is:

1. Place the folded pattern on double fabric and cut out both sides of the tie-back at one time. Allow 1.5cm (¾in.) for turnings all round.
2. Cut out the lining in exactly the same way.
3. Cut out the interlining and any stiffener to the same size as the finished tie-back. Do not allow for turnings.
4. Finish as for unshaped tie-backs (see above).

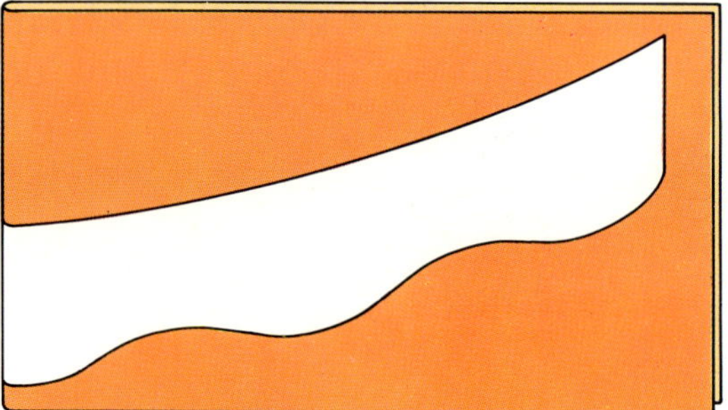

TRIMMINGS

The range of trimmings available is extensive. Measure carefully and buy only sufficient for your needs.

Remember that the trimming must be in keeping with the purpose of your curtains. If your curtains are washable, make sure the trimming is too. The weight of the trimming should be in unison with that of the fabric.

Always choose trimming by daylight and match it with a sample of your curtain material. An inspired guess in artificial light will almost certainly lead to an expensive mistake. Check that the heading on your chosen trimming has a firm finish and that the yarns of the fringe are even.

Finally, hand sew on all trimming. Wavy deviations will be very obvious once the curtains are hung.

THE TRICK

Whichever method you choose, chalk a guide line on the main fabric before you begin to apply any trimming.

Below is a list of nine common types of trimming and where to use them:

Silk ribbon An expensive but deliciously extravagant, way to trim a plain silk fabric.
Rayon or polyester ribbon Less expensive but acceptable substitute for silk ribbon.
Chenille bobble fringe Woolly textured but made from cotton. It looks great on cotton drapes and swags, or even a pelmet.
Cotton or silk cord Excellent trimming for tie-backs, or can be used equally effectively as a border.
Lightweight nylon fringe Excellent for edging washable curtains, etc. because it dries very quickly.
Rayon or other synthetic braid This looks good on glossy, glazed cottons. Some types can be bought in a natural colour and then dyed.
Silk tassel fringe For really sumptuous looks on very grand fabrics like velvet, brocade, etc.
Cotton ruching A fresh finish for cottons and linens. Ideal for kitchens and bathrooms.
Heavy cotton fringe Comes in any width. Use very broad widths to trim heavy curtains at long windows.

HOW TO APPLY BRAID

1. Mark in a guide line.
2. Centre the braid on the line, pin and then tack it into place.
3. Machine stitch the braid into position. If you are using a narrow braid, machine down the centre along its length. Wider braid must be machine stitched, or slipstitched by hand, along both edges.

THE TRICK

Check the tension on your machine before starting to ensure that the stitches are not pulled too tightly or the braid will pucker.

HOW TO APPLY DECORATIVE CORD

Cord has the great advantage of being much cheaper than braid and can be applied in exactly the same way.

Cord can also be stitched to the edge of the curtain:

1. Bind the end of the cord with thread to prevent it unravelling.
2. As it is impossible to pin cord in position before you stitch, hold the cord on the edge of the right side of the curtain with your left hand to control and guide the cord as you sew.
3. Use a matching button thread. Stitch strands from the back of the cord into the folded edge of the curtain.

Be sure the cord is firmly but not too tightly attached.

4. When you reach a corner, twist the cord slightly to make a neat turn.

THE TRICK

When you finish off, allow 2–3cm (1–1½in.) extra, knot the cord in two places and cut in between them – a precaution against unravelling.

Take the cord to the wrong side of the curtain, slip it under the lining and stitch down.

THE CONTRAST MITRE

This sounds more complicated than it is:

1. Cut two lengths of decorative border of equal width and overlap them at right angles.
2. Fold under both ends of the border at an angle of 45 degrees. Press and tack into position.
3. Machine stitch along the tacked line on the wrong side. Trim away excess fabric and press.

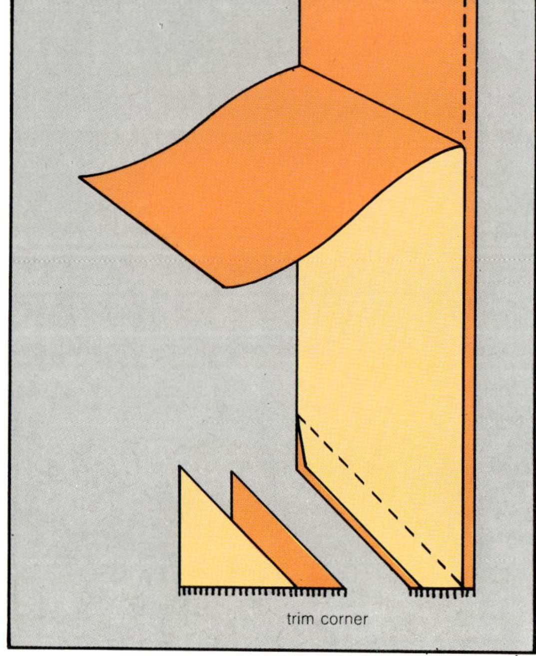

PELMETS

What is the difference between a pelmet and a valance? Very little: a stiffened pelmet is made from a straight piece of shaped fabric attached to a pelmet board. A valance is usually ruched, frilled or pleated and hung from a rod or track projecting above the window.

MAKING A PELMET BOARD

Before you can begin to make a stiffened-fabric pelmet, you must have a pelmet board. Here's how to make one:

1. Consider the position of your proposed pelmet and window treatment. Pelmets can be either recessed into the window frame or made to project away from the frame.
2. Measure up and make the pelmet board exactly like a shelf. Use 1cm (½in.) thick plywood or hardwood and buy angle irons for fixing. Pelmet boards are normally made 10cm (4in.) deep and extend 5–7cm (2–3in.) beyond the length of the track: i.e. 2.5cm (1in.) each end to allow for turning the pelmet fabric and for access to fit runners and hang curtains.
3. Fix the pelmet board as follows:

a. For recessed curtains: position the angle irons so that the pelmet board will lie flush with the inner edge of the beading of the window frame. Screw the angle irons into the back of the board and to the upper surface of the reveal.
b. For a projecting pelmet: attach the angle irons to the wall above the window. Position and fix the pelmet board as you would a shelf.

Remember that the board must project 10cm (4in.) away from the wall to allow clearance for both the track and the pulled-back curtains. It is easy to forget how very bulky curtains can be when drawn back.

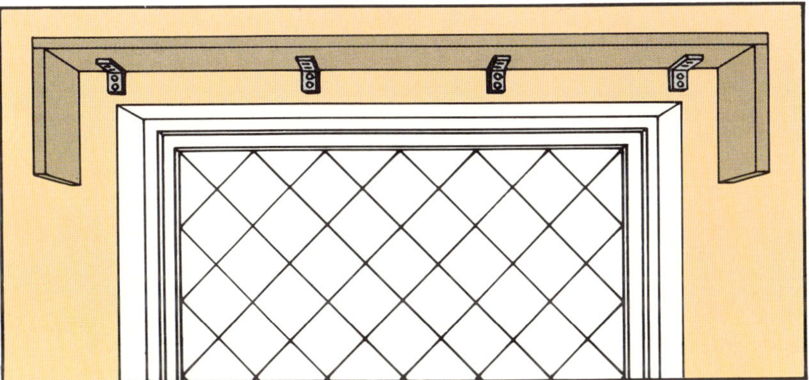

DESIGNING THE PELMET

Stiffened-fabric pelmets are usually made from the same type of material as the curtains, mounted onto stiff buckram and trimmed with braid or a fringe.

First, choose a shape for your pelmet: straight, curved, scalloped, what you will. Draw a rough sketch, bearing in mind that the depth of your pelmet must be in proportion to the curtains – allow approximately 4cm (1¾in.) for every 30cm (12in.) of curtain drop.

THE TRICK

The professional rule of thumb is to allow one-sixth of the total depth for floor-length curtains.

Next, look carefully at the design and ask yourself the following questions:

1. Does the point at which the curtains will hang, when drawn back, form the start of the end sections in your design? It must, because the end sections and returns must be made to the same depth.
2. Does the shallowest part of the pelmet cover the track or rail?
3. If the design is for a scalloped edge, will it fit in with your design? If your fabric is difficult to match, perhaps a less complicated design would be better.

Once you are satisfied it is sensible to make a template. Find a newspaper larger than the desired size of the pelmet. Fold it in half widthwise and draw out your design, starting from the centre and using readily available objects (e.g. household plates) as guides to draw round where necessary. Cut out the paper pattern, centre and then pin on the pelmet board to see how it looks. It is a good idea to leave your pattern in place for two or three days to make quite sure it is exactly right.

MAKING THE PELMET

When the design is finalized, you are in a position to estimate fabric requirements. First, measure the length of the pelmet board, including the two 10cm (4in.) returns at each end and adding on 5cm (2in.) for turnings. This measurement will give you the overall width of the fabric required. Next, measure the depth of your paper pattern and add 10cm (4in.) for turnings.

Remember most windows are more than 122cm (4ft) wide, the usual fabric width; a pelmet with a centre seam is to be avoided at all costs.

THE TRICK

To overcome the problem, centre one width of fabric with the middle of the pelmet pattern and add the necessary extra fabric to each side of this width.

You also need: lining and interlining, a piece of buckram (cut to the design of the pelmet), braid, cords, piping and possibly a tube of fabric glue.

There are two ways to construct a pelmet. You can either stick or sew a pelmet – both techniques are equally satisfactory and easy to use. Here's the 'stick' method because it's the quickest and is usually considered the best:

1. Cut out the materials as follows: the buckram exactly to your paper pattern; the lining and main fabric 10cm (4in.) larger and wider than the paper; the interlining to only 5cm (2in.) wider than the paper pattern.
2. Centre the shaped buckram over the interlining. Dampen the edges of the buckram slightly for about 2cm (¾in.) all round. Fold the interlining over the buckram and then steam press into position. (The damp heat releases the glue which provides stiffening. If this proves inadequate, add a dab of glue.) Start at the top, continue on round the pelmet, slash all concave curves, and cut away any surplus fabric on the convex curves.
3. Lay the main fabric on a table, wrong side up. Cover with the interlining and buckram. Lay the interlining against the main fabric. Fold the main fabric over the buckram. Dampen as before and steam press into position – slipstitch the corners.

If your fabric is particularly sheer, or you prefer to use the stitch method, attach the interlining/buckram/lining as for tie-backs (see page 284).
4. Apply any decorative trimming to the right side of the main fabric at this stage. Do this with stab-stitches from the front of the pelmet through the buckram to the wrong side.
5. Place the lining in position over the buckram. Fold in the turnings and slipstitch all round.

FIXING THE PELMET

A pelmet may be fixed to the pelmet board in various ways. The simplest method is to tack it in place with gimp pins and then, if necessary, cover the line of gimp pins with braid.

THE TRICK

Alternatively, use Velcro – one strip is stitched to the pelmet and the other stapled (with a staple gun) to the pelmet board.

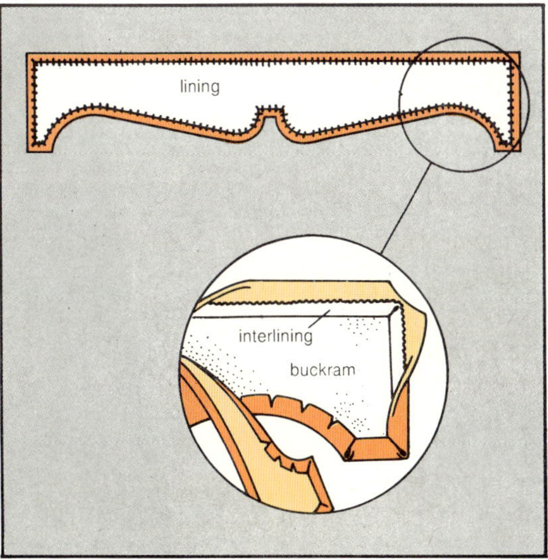

VALANCES, SWAGS AND TAILS

MAKING A VALANCE

A valance is a small, very short curtain and is made in almost exactly the same way. It gives a soft, informal look to curtains and may be simply gathered or pleated. While a gathered valance needs no stiffening, it is usually lined and finished with plain heading tape.

THE TRICK

More elaborate pleated headings, best made with the aid of a commercial heading tape, must be stiffened with interlining.

The tape should be positioned 5cm (2in.) from the top of the strip of fabric to prevent it sagging.

When estimating fabric requirements, remember that the depth of the completed valance is calculated in exactly the same way as that of a pelmet (see page 285). The width of the fabric is estimated in the same way as for curtains: i.e. depending on the chosen heading. The length of the fabric required is equal to the depth of the finished valance, plus allowances for hem and heading.

You also need: the same amount of lining as main fabric, interlining for stiffening, curtain tape to choice, and hooks.

THE TRICK

One professional advocates the use of 'smocking' heading tapes for valances, and very effective they look.

The procedure to follow when making a valance is:

1. Cut out and join together any necessary widths of the main fabric, lining and interlining. Place the main fabric wrong side up. Position the interlining over the main fabric and lock into position (see page 278).
2. Lock the lining to the interfacing. Leave 14cm (5½in.) unstitched at the top of the valance and 15cm (6in.) at the bottom for turnings.
3. Turn in the hem allowances all round the valance and slipstitch the lining to the main fabric as described for lined curtains (see page 278).
4. Apply your chosen heading tape; insert hooks and draw up to the required width.

To mount the valance, suspend it from either a valance rail – if you have one – or from screw eyes screwed into a pelmet board.

For an extra-simple unlined valance – suitable for a kitchen or bathroom – make a deep hem at the top of the valance and thread through a rod or wire.

SWAGS AND TAILS

These are formal headings for curtains which depend for their grace and elegance upon clever draping. They are not particularly difficult to tackle. The key to success lies in choosing the right sort of soft, supple material and in carrying out some careful preparation before you begin work on the main fabric.

It is also important to realize that both swags and tails, because of their many folds, use a great deal of material. Budget accordingly!

THE TRICK

Because draping is a skilled business, invest in some butter muslin or another inexpensive fabric with which to practise before you attempt the exercise in earnest.

HOW TO MAKE A TAIL

You need two tails for each window, one on each side of the centrally placed swag. The procedure is as follows:

1. Decide on a design or adapt the one shown to suit your windows. Then measure the width, the long side and the short side. Make a paper pattern with the measurements.
2. Cut out the fabric and lining to match the paper pattern. Allow 2.5cm (1in.) turnings all round.
3. Lay the main fabric, right side down, on a table and position the lining on top. Tuck in the turnings all round. Pin, press and slipstitch the fabric and the lining together.
4. If using the measurements shown pleat up the tail vertically to give a pleated width of 15cm (4in.). Leave a 10cm (6in.) return at the long side. Stitch in the pleats across the top of the tail only. You want them to fan out a little when hung.
5. Place the tail into position over the swag and fold the outer edge just over the pelmet board. Remember to place the return round the far side of the pelmet board. Fix into position with gimp pins or tacks.

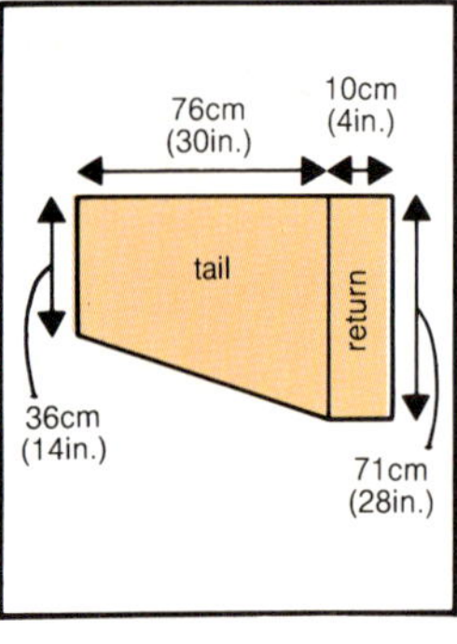

HOW TO MAKE A SWAG

Swags have a definite shape and form and must be pleated up individually. Shapes vary according to the size and effect required and sadly there are no ready-made pleating tapes to aid the making process. However, the average pattern can be adapted to suit most window treatments.

To make a swag, the method is as follows:

1. Measure, rule and cut out a paper pattern.
2. Cut out the 'practice fabric' to match the paper pattern.
3. Fold and press in 2.5cm (1in.) turnings on all sides of the fabric.
4. Tack and pleat up sides, the two shortest sides, opposite each other, to form a pretty curve. Do not worry if you fail to get both even on the first attempt. Draping swags is a knack which requires practice.
5. Once you obtain a satisfactory prototype and feel confident, cut out and pleat up the main fabric. Stitch the pleats securely into position.

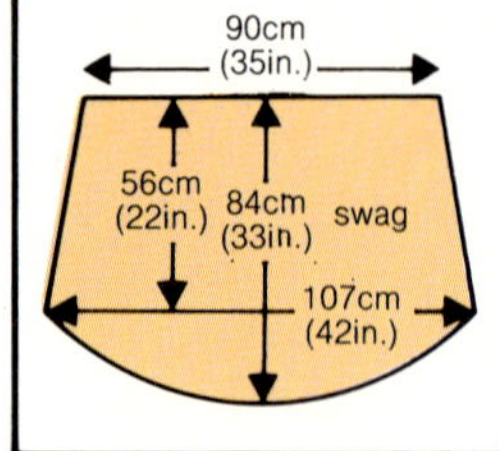

THE TRICK

6. Cut the lining to the same size as the now completed swag, plus 2.5cm (1in.) for turnings. Do not cut the lining to match the original pattern.

7. Seam the lining to the top edge of the swag. Fold in the lining turnings and slipstitch the remaining sides of the swag together.
8. Centre and fix the swag to a pelmet board with tacks or gimp pins.

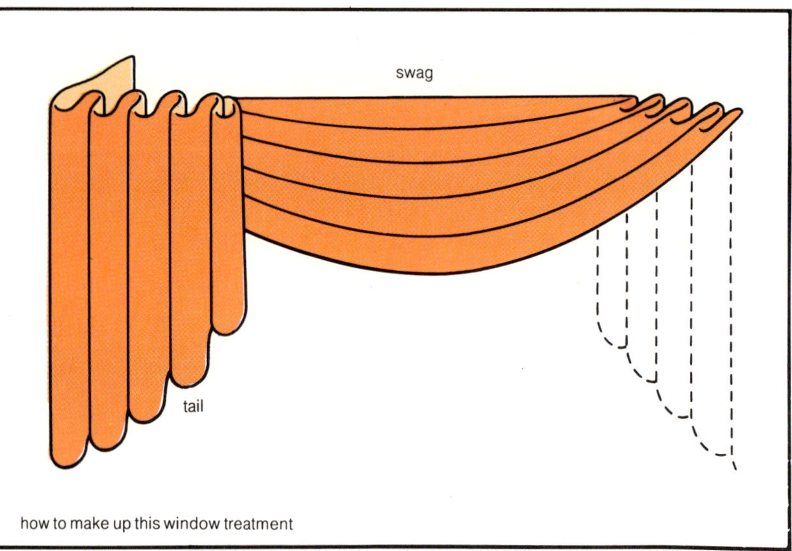

how to make up this window treatment

ROLLER BLINDS

Today there are so many kits available in the shops that making and fitting your own roller blinds at home in an evening is a relatively easy and inexpensive task.

What makes roller blinds so practical? To begin with, they can be trimmed to fit almost any awkwardly shaped window such as a dormer.

THE TRICK

They can be backed with black fabric to shut out unwelcome morning light.

Finally they can be decorated, trimmed or edged to suit your decor. Used in conjunction with dress curtains (which do not draw – the blind covers the naked window) they help cut the cost of curtaining. They are also extremely easy to keep clean.

MATERIALS

Consider first your choice of fabric. Roller blinds must be made from light, fairly stiff, closely woven material. Fabric with a loose weave may stretch with time and make your blind 'wavy'; while thick fabrics, will not roll satisfactorily from the start.

Specially prepared roller blind fabrics, which are sold in various widths up to 183cm (6ft), are the best bet for the novice blind-maker. They are available in a variety of colours and patterns from most department stores and provide an almost instant professional finish. They require no stiffening treatment. There is no danger of fraying edges – thus no need for side hems. In addition, they repel both dust and dirt, have a fade-resistant finish, and can be easily sponged clean.

However it is perfectly possible to use other types of furnishing fabric providing the material undergoes a stiffening process and, of course, that it is of a suitable weave. Special fabric stiffeners to strengthen cloth can be bought in aerosol cans or a liquid form.

THE TRICK

When you use stiffener from an aerosol can, be sure to spray both sides of the fabric. If you choose a liquid stiffener, either paint it over the material or dip the fabric into the liquid.

PVC or plastic-backed fabrics, which need no stiffening, may also be used for roller blinds and make a practical choice for kitchens and bathrooms where condensation may be a problem and frequent cleaning a necessity.

MEASURING UP

Your next step is to decide whether the blind is to be fixed inside or outside the window recess. Take exact measurements and do use a metal metre rule, not a cloth tape, because even the smallest slip can prevent a smooth fit.

To estimate the amount of fabric required, make the width of the fabric equal to the measurement of the trimmed roller. The length of the blind should be 30cm (12in.) longer than your required drop. This extra 30cm (12in.) is sufficient for the roller to remain covered when the blind is pulled down, and for the bottom hem.

Besides the fabric, you also need a roller blind kit. This consists of:

1. One wooden roller to be trimmed to an exact fit. The roller has a spring and metal cap with rectangular pin at one end. A second metal cap with a rounded end is also provided to fit on to the bare end of the roller once it has been trimmed to your requirements.
2. Two brackets for fixing the roller blind to the window frame.
3. Tacks to attach the blind fabric to the roller.
4. A wooden batten or lath to slip through the hem to keep the blind straight.
5. Cord holder and acorn, or half-handle for drawing.

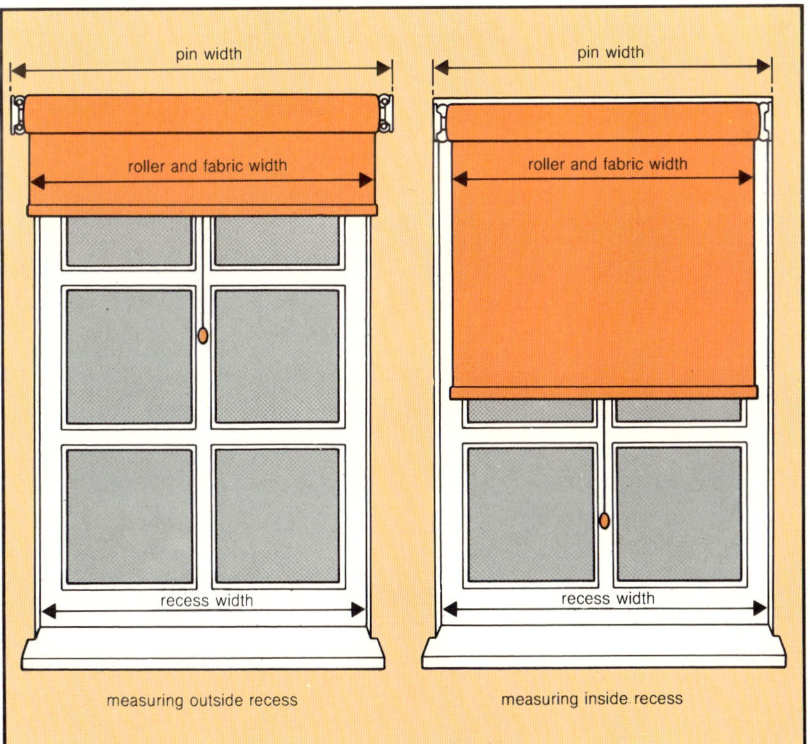

MAKING UP

To make up a roller blind, proceed as follows:

1. Fix the brackets, following the manufacturer's instructions.

THE TRICK

Double-check that you mount the bracket for the square pin on the left-hand side of the window and that for the round pin on the right.

2. Trim the roller to fit exactly between the two brackets. Fit the metal cap and round pin provided to the bare, trimmed end of the roller and hammer home.
3. Cut the fabric to the exact size of the prepared roller. Use a T-square or table edge to ensure an accurate result. Before you launch out with the scissors, look over the fabric and position any pattern or designs with care.
3. At the lower edge of the blind, turn up the fabric 1cm (½in.). Press. Turn up a further 4cm (1¾in.) and machine stitch the hem into position. Slide the batten or lath into the pocket thus formed.

For blinds with a decorative edge, make the lath tuck further up the blind.

4. Attach the fabric to the roller – more easily said than done!

THE TRICK

The trick here is to stop the fabric slipping about while you apply the tacks. To do this, place the fabric on a table, right side up. Lay the roller across the top of the fabric with the square pin on the left-hand side. Turn the fabric over 1cm (½in.) and stick it to the roller along the guide line with self-adhesive tape. With the fabric firmly in place, it is an easy matter to hammer home the pins provided.

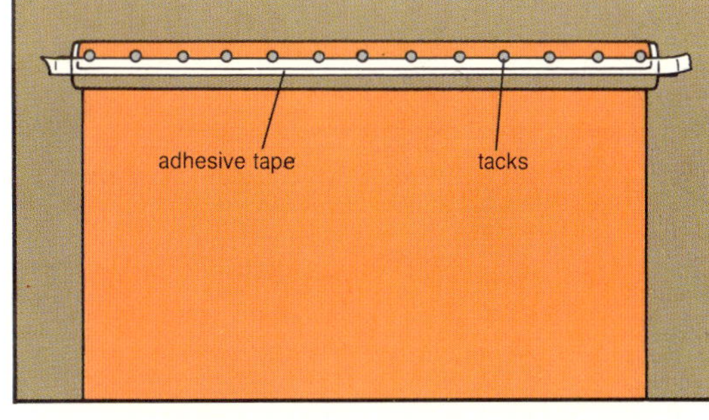

5. Insert the cord into the cord holder. Screw the holder into place on the wrong side of the blind. Slot the loose end of the cord through the acorn and knot.
6. Roll up the blind carefully by hand and slot into the brackets – square pin into the left-hand bracket, round pin into the right.
7. Adjust the tension by pulling the blind down as far as it will go. If further tension is required, remove the blind from the brackets, roll up again by hand, reinsert between the brackets and pull down. Be careful not to over-tension.

Remember also these tips: be certain your blind is assembled the correct way round; never put oil on the spring roller; and always use the cord to pull the blind up and down.

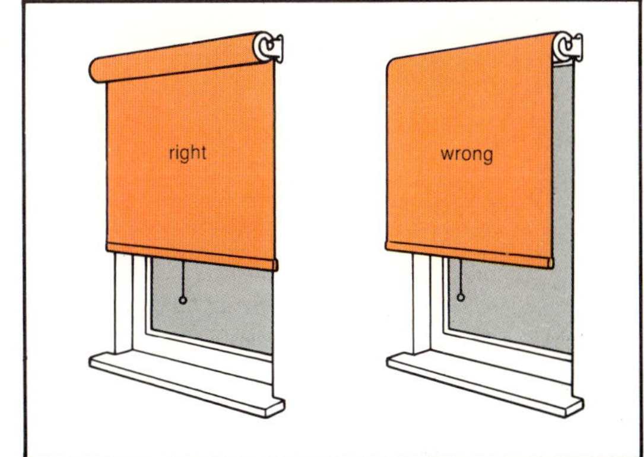

DECORATION AND TRIMMING

There are many interesting ways to trim a roller blind easily and with little extra cost. Some fabrics lend themselves to a cut-out design with a brass rod pushed through the bottom instead of a wooden batten. Another idea is to shape the bottom edge beneath the batten into scallops. Or you can simply add a fringe or braid.

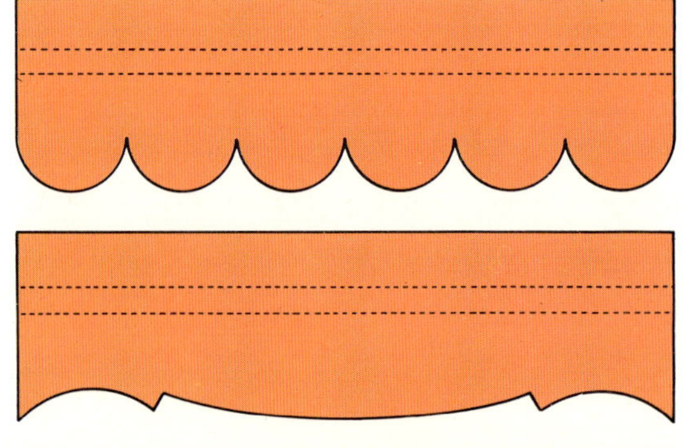

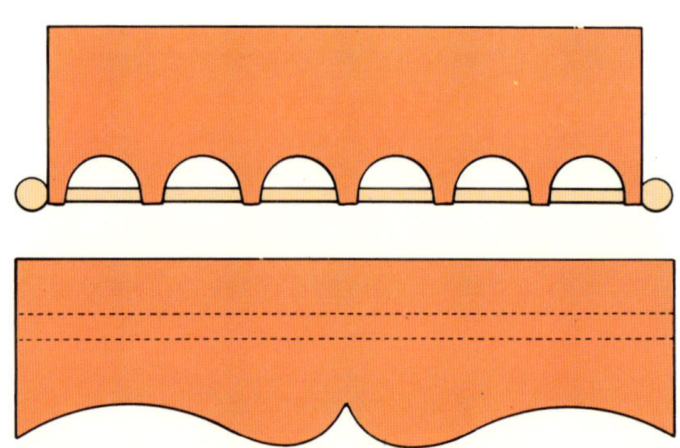

TO MAKE A SCALLOPED OR OTHER CUT-OUT EDGE

In addition to the regular roller blind kit you need:
1. Extra fabric to accommodate the scallops (add to the usual drop measurement twice the amount of the required scallop depth).
2. A strip of buckram.
3. Clear glue.
4. Stiff cardboard.

This is what you do:
1. Begin to make up the blind as usual. Fit to the roller, but do not make the pocket for the lath.
2. Make up a template from the cardboard. Use a pair of compasses, a saucer or round tin as a guide. Be sure that the design fits evenly on the width of the blind so that the scallops or points are equal on each side of the blind.
3. Fold back approximately 13–15cm (5–6in.) of fabric at the bottom to the back of the blind. Crease and press along the fold. Open out the flap made by the crease and cut a piece of buckram the same width as the blind but 4cm (1¾in.) shorter than the flap.

THE TRICK

Apply clear glue to both sides of the buckram and place into the pressed crease. Fold over the flap on to the buckram and press the three layers together firmly. Allow to dry. On no account allow glue to slip on to the 4cm (1¾in.) of fabric not covered by buckram.

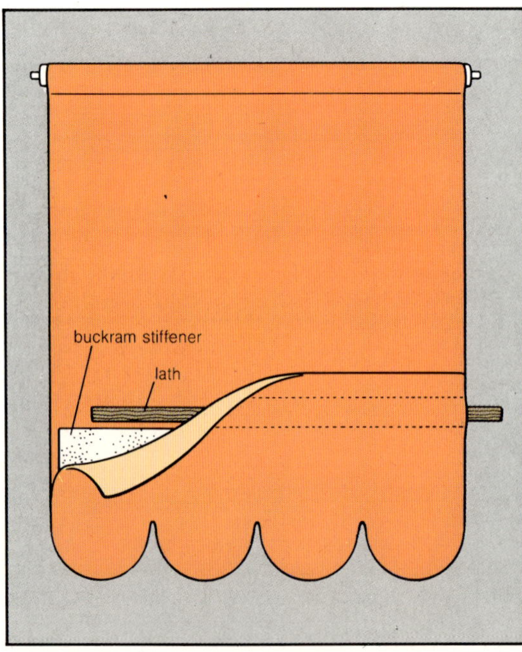

4. Once the glue is quite dry, make the pocket for the lath from the remaining 4cm (1¾in.) overlap by sewing two rows of machine stitching.
5. Lay the template on the front, folded, glued fabric with the lower bottom scalloped edge exactly on the crease. Mark round the curves and then cut out. The scalloped edge may be overlocked by machine stitching if you feel industrious, but it is not really necessary if the fabric has been satisfactorily glued together.
6. Place the lath in the prepared pocket. Apply the cord holder.
7. Trim the edges with plain braid, tassel, fringing or bobble fringe – all can be glued into position. Add a fringed or tassel pull instead of an acorn to complete the picture.

CUT-OUT EDGES WITH A BRASS BATTEN

Proceed as before and make a paper pattern. Remember to allow extra blind fabric for the edging. Mark a 4cm (1¾in.) allowance for the batten casing at the bottom of the fold. Add the buckram and glue the fabric together from the top. Be sure to leave the bottom batten allowance free from glue. Cut out the reversed tabs or scallops. Machine stitch the batten casing top and bottom. Slot in the brass rod and hang.

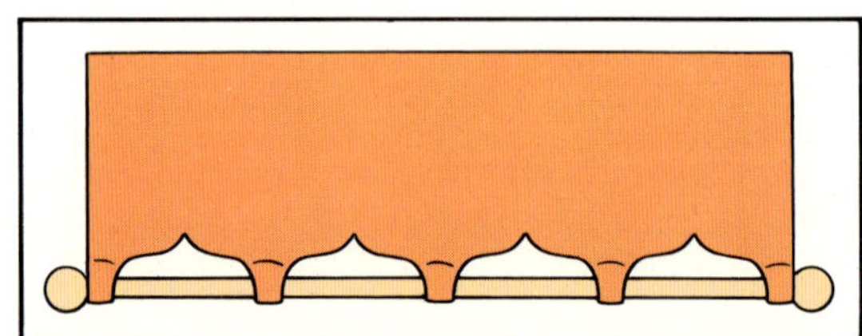

PIPING

Piping is made by covering plain white cord with a chosen fabric. It gives a simple, distinguished look and can easily be made at home, providing you own a sewing machine.

The type of cord used to make piping is available in various sizes and materials. Selection and choice depend upon where and how the piping is to be used. Small, short curtains are best decorated with a fine piping. Large pelmets over full-length curtains can accommodate a more substantial style of piping. Try to buy shrink-resistant cord if possible. Shrinkage in the wash or at the dry-cleaners will make your once-perfect piping pucker.

THE TRICK

If you cannot find shrink-resistant cord, shrink the ordinary sort yourself. Here's how: place the cord in a pan of boiling water and allow to simmer for three or four minutes. Drain and dry well before use.

HOW TO MAKE AND APPLY PIPING

1. Cut strips of bias from the main fabric. The best way to find a bias grain (i.e. 'on the cross') is to fold the raw edge of the fabric across the grain of the fabric parallel to the selvedge. This line is the bias line; so for bias strips, cut parallel to the folded line. Your strips need to be approximately 4cm (1¾in.) wide.
2. Join the bias strips together on the straight grain of the fabric. To do this, place the strips together with the right sides facing upwards and machine stitch the seam, making sure that the strips form a 'V'.
3. Place the bias strips, wrong side up, on a table and lay the cord down the centre. Draw the two edges of the fabric together to enclose the cord. Pin and tack the cord into place. Machine stitch down the strip of piping as close to the cord as possible. Use the piping foot attachment on your machine.

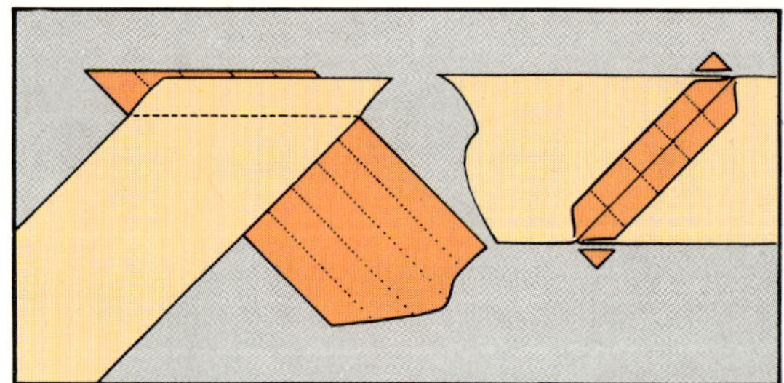

4. Apply the cord by stitching the raw edges of the piping seam into the main seam of the fabric: i.e. stitch two pieces of main fabric together with the piping sandwiched in between them.

THE TRICK

If the cord should need to be joined, unravel the two ends for 2cm (¾in.). Trim each of the three strands, making the cord different lengths, then retwist the two sets together and stitch into position. This way you avoid any ugly lumps or bumps in your finished piping.

FESTOON BLINDS

This type of blind is best made with lightweight fabric which will ruche gracefully and fall into soft, puffy folds – it will give a luxurious appearance to a bedroom or bathroom. The operational mechanism lies in the rows of rings attached to the back of the blind through which cords are threaded to pull the blind up or let it down. It is the raising of the blind, together with the vertical application of gathering tape, which produces the deep, ballooning folds.

MEASURING UP AND MATERIALS

First decide how many scallops are to be included in the blind. Next, consider the function of the blind. Will it be left down permanently or partially drawn up to show off the luxurious swags? Do you wish to ruche the blind all over? This will, of course, involve using more fabric. Finally, do you want to add a frill around the edges or along the lower hem? Once the above points have been settled, use the following guide to help you sort out the fabric requirements.

1. **Width** You need double the width of the window, plus 3cm (1¼in.) extra for side hems. If widths of fabric have to be joined together to achieve the correct blind width, allow a further 3cm (1¼in.) for French seams (see page 282).
2. **Length** For a straightforward festoon blind which will be raised to some extent over the window, you need one and a half times the length of the window plus 20cm (7¾in.) for hems. For an extravagantly full ruched blind, allow two and a half times the length of the window plus 20cm (7¾in.) for turnings.

You also need: a plywood heading board approximately 2.5–5cm (1–2in.) wide, cut to the width of the blind; a curtain track cut to the same length; two or three angle irons for fixing the heading board to the window frame; several screw eyes; non-stretch cord and a brass cleat to hold the blind cords in place; heading tape; simple gathering tape; small plastic split curtain rings; and standard curtain hooks.

MAKING UP

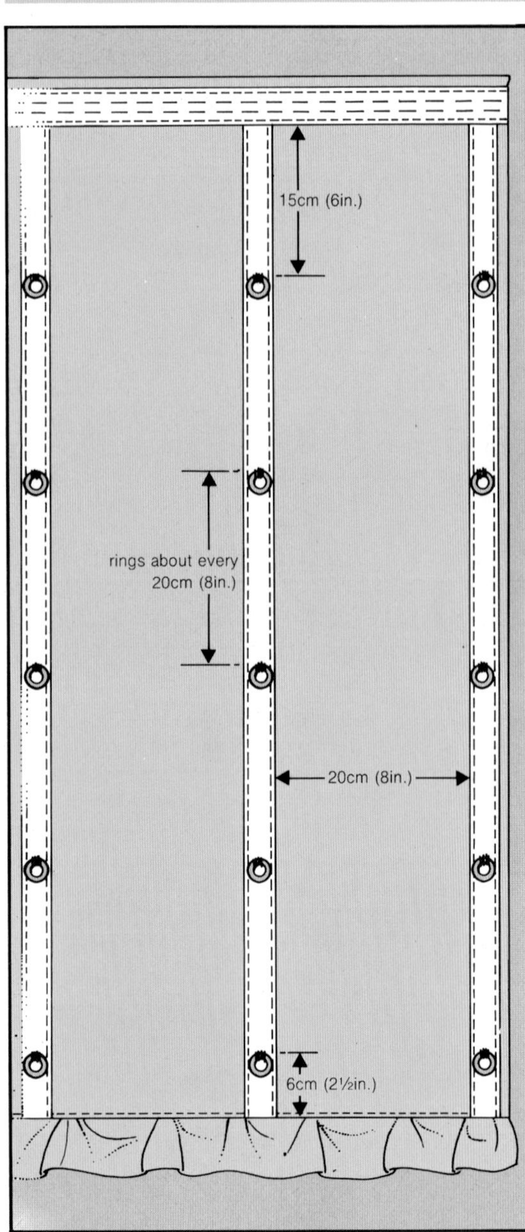

1. Cut out the fabric. Join together any necessary widths. Hem the sides and lower edge. Make and attach the frill if required.
2. Lay the blind out flat, wrong side up.

THE TRICK

Mark in with chalk the positions for the vertical tapes. These should be placed down each side and at regular intervals across the body of the blind – approximately 20cm (8in.) apart. Do not worry if the intervals between the tapes appear huge. Remember the distance between the tapes is at least double that of the finished swag, because at this point the blind is twice the width of the window!

3. Cut, pin and machine stitch simple drawing tapes into position down the vertical guide lines. Insert split rings at regular intervals approximately 20cm (8in.) apart along each tape. Place the first split ring 15cm (6in.) from the top of the blind and the last 7cm (2¾in.) up from the bottom hem. Make sure all the rings are parallel.
4. Apply the heading tape, draw up the blind to fit the width of the window and knot the cords. Draw the vertical tapes up to the required length of the blind and knot the cords. Distribute the gathered fabric evenly in both cases.
5. Cut lengths of cord (one for each vertical row of split rings) to measure twice the length of the blind and once the width. Lay the blind out flat, tie one cord to the first ring at the bottom of each and then thread up vertically through the lines of rings.
6. Mount the curtain track in the front of the heading board. Position and insert the screw eyes into the under side of the board, parallel to the vertical rows of tape and rings.
7. Hang the completed blind on the curtain track. Then, working from the left edge of the blind, thread the first cord through the screw eye on the board immediately above the tape and continue to thread the cord on to the right through each screw eye. Repeat the stringing for each tape. Knot all the cords together approximately 3cm (1¼in.) from the right outside edge of the blind.

THE TRICK

Use a larger screw eye on the far right of the blind to accommodate all the cords.

8. Fix the heading board, complete with track and blind, to the window frame with angle irons. Fix a cleat to the window reveal.
9. Cut the cords at the lower edge of the blind, then plait and knot them together. To raise the blind, pull the cords and wind the slack round the brass cleat.

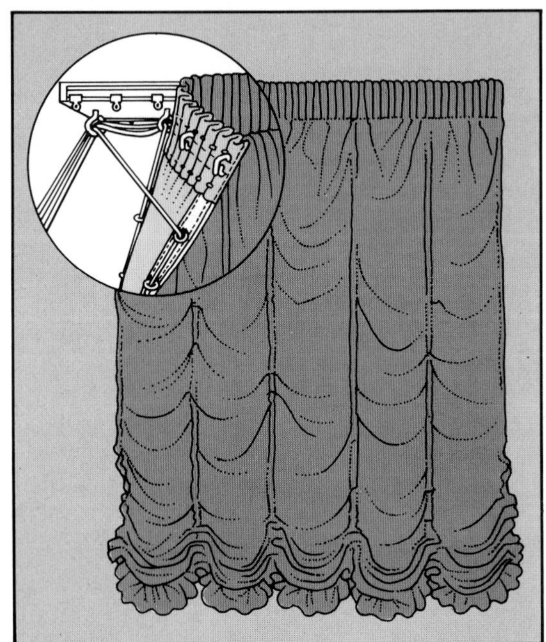

For windows there's no brighter range under the sun

Faber has always been the number one name in bright ideas for windows.

In venetian blinds there's nothing to compare with our top quality aluminium construction, choice of 25, 35 and 50mm slat widths and our huge range of either single or multi colour blinds.

The same is true about our vertical blinds, with either our standard or super mechanism and our simply enormous range of fabrics.

When it comes to roller blinds we stand out both in terms of quality and design choice too.

Not to mention our superb awnings, folk poles and out-standing Faber 66 curtain track.

The Faber range is made locally by British craftsmen, and widely available through leading high street retailers. If you have any difficulty finding Faber products, contact us at the address below.

Faber Blinds (GB) Ltd.,
Viking House, Kangley Bridge Road,
London SE26 5AQ. Tel: 01 659 2126.

OTHER BLINDS

ROMAN BLINDS

Roman blinds draw up to the top of a window in neat pleats. They are incredibly easy to make and work by being drawn up on cords threaded through rings and suspended from a wooden heading board.

The important differences between a festoon blind and a Roman blind are: a Roman blind is lined while a festoon blind is left unlined; and in Roman blinds the vertical tapes are not gathered up; thus, when down, the blind fits smoothly to the window.

For best results choose a sturdy fabric and good-quality lining, which is the most suitable combination to provide sufficient body for the blind to fold easily and hang plumb.

MEASURING UP AND MATERIALS

Measure the width and length of the window and calculate the fabric requirement as follows. You need the measured width of the window plus 3cm (1¼in.) for side turnings. For length, to the length of the window add 15cm (6in.) for top and bottom hems: i.e. 7.5cm (3in.) each.

You also need: a plywood heading board approximately 2.5–5cm (1–2in.) wide cut to the width of the blind; two or three angle irons for fixing the board to the window frame; screw eyes; non-stretch cord; simple drawing tape; split curtain rings; a metal rod the width of the blind; and a cleat to hold the cords in place.

MAKING UP

1. Cut out the main fabric and lining. The lining should measure 2.5cm (1in.) less all round. Seam together any necessary widths.
2. Place the right side of the main fabric against the right side of the lining. Pin into position and machine stitch down both sides and along the lower edge, just as when making a bag curtain (see page 277). Turn fabrics right sides out and press.
3. Mark in two parallel guide lines across the lower edge of the blind for the metal rod. Make the first line 10cm (4in.) up from the bottom of the blind and the second 5cm (2in.) up from that.
4. Mark in guide lines for the vertical tapes 15cm (6in.) from each outer edge and every 15cm (6in.) across the body of the blind. Pin simple drawing tapes on each vertical guide line and machine stitch into position.

THE TRICK

Begin each line from the metal rod guide line. Stitch through both the main fabric and the lining.

5. At the top of the blind turn in the raw edges of the lining and main fabric, tuck in the ends of tape and machine stitch across the blind.
6. Machine stitch along the metal rod casing guide lines. Unpick the necessary side hem at one end and insert the metal rod. Slipstitch the two sides together again.

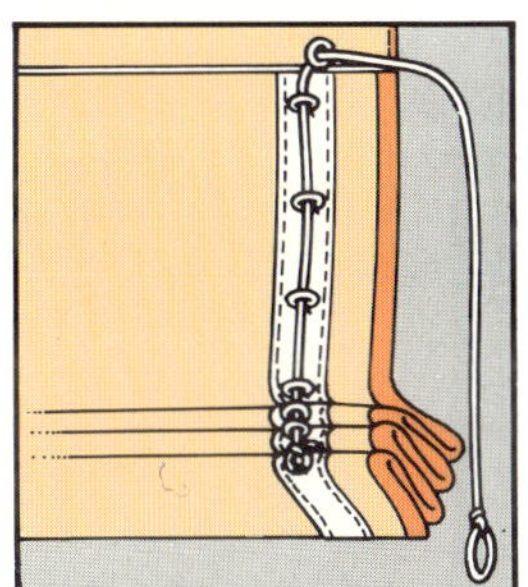

7. Insert the split rings into the vertical tapes. Make the first ring 15cm (6in.) from the top of the metal batten. It is essential that you place the rings at regular intervals and that they are evenly spaced and parallel.
8. Arrange the screw eyes on the underside of the heading board. Make sure each screw eye is placed exactly opposite each vertical row of rings on the blind.

THE TRICK

Use a slightly larger screw eye on the far right side of the board to help bear the weight of all the drawing cords.

Tack the blind to the heading board.

9. Cut lengths of cord twice the length of the blind plus once the width. Lay the blind flat out and tie one cord to each bottom ring. Thread the cords up through the rings to the screw eyes and on through each screw eye from left to right. Knot all the cords together 3cm (1¼in.) from the outer edge of the blind.
10. Fix the heading board with the attached blind to the top of the window with two angle irons. Position the cleat on the window frame to hold the cords when the blind is drawn up.
11. Cut the cords to make them level. Plait and knot together and add a decorative tassel for a fully finished effect.

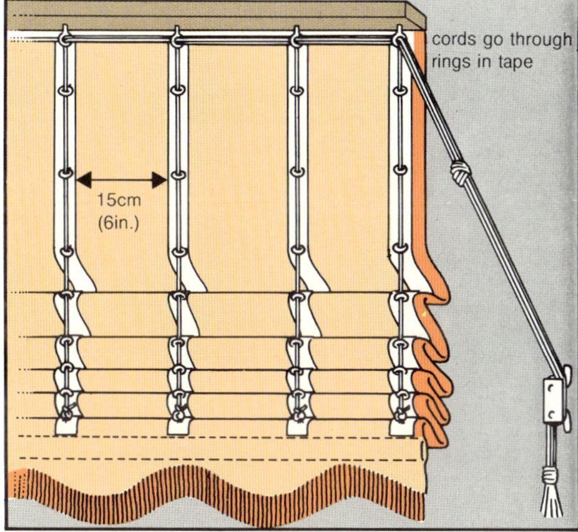

VENETIAN BLINDS AND VERTICAL LATTICE BLINDS

The main difference between these two sorts of blinds is that the slats run vertically in the vertical lattice blinds and horizontally in Venetian blinds. The slats in vertical lattice blinds are often about 15cm (6in.) wide and made of glass fibre cloth or a similar material. They usually have to be made specially for the window in question and are not installed except by the makers.

However, you will need to clean Venetian blinds on a regular basis, particularly if you have one installed in your kitchen. Be sure to dust it regularly; there is a tool available which does 3–4 slats at a time. If it looks grubby, let the blind right down and wash each slat with a soft cloth using plenty of soapy water. Don't forget to wash the cords at the side and the tapes and cords which raise and lower the slats. Do not raise the blind until everything is quite dry. If the blind is particularly dirty, you can soak it in the bath using a strong solution of detergent.

THE TRICK

The trick is to cover the bottom of the bath with an old sheet (doubled) or towel to prevent the slats from scratching the enamel. Be sure to wear gloves whenever cleaning blinds, the edges are very sharp.

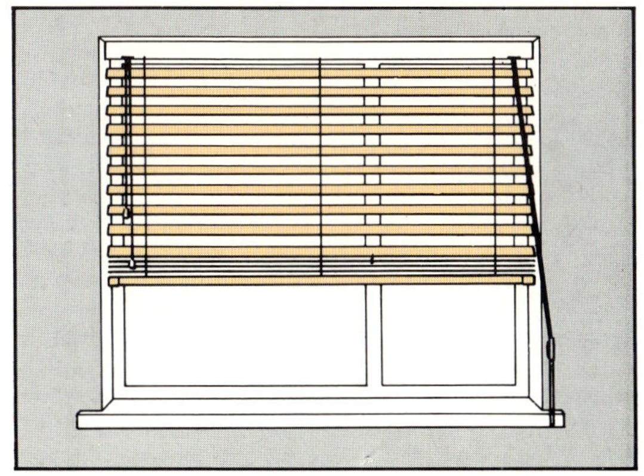

NETS AND SHEERS

Inner curtains of lace or muslin were first introduced in the nineteenth century. Today nets and sheers are an essential part of modern decor. Gleaming glass in a bare window may delight the modern architect, but it can be too much of a good thing in a home, particularly if you live in a town. Nets provide the necessary privacy in bedrooms and bathrooms, while full-length sheers help disguise ill-proportioned rooms, ungainly windows or depressing views.

Both net curtains and sheers are suited to home sewing. Straight machine stitching is quick and easy to do, while enthusiastic do-it-yourselfers' attention to detail ensures a professional finish which expensive shop-bought factory-made nets lack. Sewing your own nets means you can make allowances for uneven floors or oddly constructed windows and still save money.

MEASURING UP

If the golden rule for perfect window treatments is to use plenty of fabric, it is even more applicable when making nets and sheers. Both require at least three times the length of the track to look good, plus 2cm (¾in.) hems on either side. However, there are some very open weave sheers now available which do not require side hems, and thus save time for the home curtain maker. Moreover, many nets and sheers, particularly those with patterned or lead-weighted hems, can be purchased in any width, again saving considerable time and temper, for there are no panels to stitch together and no patterns to match.

For sewing you will need: 100 per cent synthetic thread, synthetic heading tape, a continental size 80 machine needle and some tissue paper.

THE TRICK

Layers of fine fabric tend to slip while being seamed together. Avoid this by stitching the seam with a strip of tissue paper between the two layers of fabric. Once the seam is completed, the paper can be torn away.

MAKING UP

The standard procedure for making up nets and sheers is very straightforward. Measure, cut out and hem up the sides and lower edge as for unlined curtains (see page 276).

THE TRICK

Make sure when you cut nets and sheers that you cut between a strong down thread so that small pieces of thread remain protruding horizontally. This helps the edge stay firm and free from fraying and allows a single hem in some cases.

Apply your chosen heading tape: a smocked heading looks good on nets; or perhaps your preference is for a simple cased heading which slots over a rod or wire.

CASED HEADING

Allow 12cm (4¾in.) above the rod or wire when you measure for fabric. Make up the curtain as usual, but at the top turn over and tack a double 6cm (2½in.) hem. Machine stitch in place with two lines of stitching 2.5cm (1in.) apart. Measure your first line of stitching 2.5cm (1in.) from the top of the curtain to provide sufficient heading above the rod.

CROSS-OVER CURTAINS

This style of curtaining is often made from net or other transparent Terylene fabric sold by the metre with a ready-made frill down each side. However, there is a snag about using this type of fabric: when you come to cut out the curtains, there will be no frill along the lower sloping edge! It is advisable, therefore, to buy plain, less expensive fabric and make your own frill. Each panel should be two to three times the width of the track, and you must remember to purchase sufficient additional fabric to make the frill.

To make up cross-over curtains, proceed as follows:

1. Cut out the fabric as shown and make a narrow hem along the sloping edge.
2. Make up a narrow frill, long enough to fit to three sides of each curtain.

THE TRICK

The simplest way to gather a frill is to stitch a simple drawing tape along the wrong side of a narrow strip of fabric and draw up to the required length. Knot the ends and arrange the gathers evenly.

3. Fit the frill to the curtains and pin in position. Machine stitch the frill into position.
4. Apply a simple heading tape to each curtain. Draw up and insert hooks.

THE TRICK

Arrange with an overlap on a double-rod curtain set specifically made for this type of window treatment.

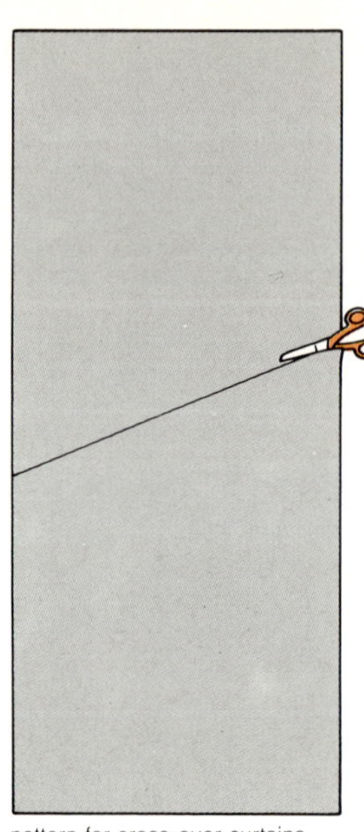
pattern for cross-over curtains

CENTRE-RISE CURTAINS

The same remarks as for cross-over curtains (left) apply to purchasing materials for this type of curtain. You will need two to three times the width of the track for the curtain and remember the extra material to make the frill.

To make up centre-rise curtains, proceed as follows:

1. Cut out the fabric as shown and make a narrow hem along the bottom edge, including round the cut-out.
2. Make up a narrow frill, long enough to run along the bottom of the curtain, including round the cut-out (see cross-over curtains for the trick).
3. Fit the frill to the curtains and pin on. Machine stitch the frill into position.
4. Apply a simple heading tape to the curtain. Draw up the tape cords, insert the hooks and hang. You could use a cased heading, but the tape looks prettier if the whole curtain is visible.

pattern for centre-rise curtains

UPHOLSTERY & CANEWORK

TOOLS AND MATERIALS

A magnetic hammer, with or without a claw end, is indispensable; it can pick up a tack, direct it to the exact spot on the frame and make the first impression without hitting your thumb in the process.

using a magnetic hammer

You will also need tacks, which come in various sizes – 6, 10, 13, 16, 20, 25 and 31mm (¼, ⅜, ½, ⅝, ¾, 1 and 1¼in.). You can get 'fine' tacks (i.e. with small heads) or 'improved' tacks (with larger heads). For fixing braid, you will need 13 or 10mm (½ or ⅜in.) gimp pins. For temporarily fixing material like hessian, scrim and top covers, use 40mm (1½in.) plated pins and some 100mm (4in.) upholstery skewers.

Scissors should be sharp-bladed and sturdy; a sharp knife will be useful for slashing old twine, dispensable covering, etc. You will also need a mallet, for knocking out old tacks; small and large pincers, for straining webbing where you cannot use a proper strainer; side-cutting pliers for prising out stubborn tacks; and a steel regulator for rearranging stuffing. Straight steel needles 255 and 360mm (10 and 14in.) long are for blindstitching, topstitching, putting in stuffing ties and buttoning; a semi-circular spring needle 125mm (5in.) long for sewing hessian or scrim around springs; and a fine curved needle 50–75mm (2–3in.) long for slipstitching the top cover. Normally you would use waxed or plain thread in a matching shade.

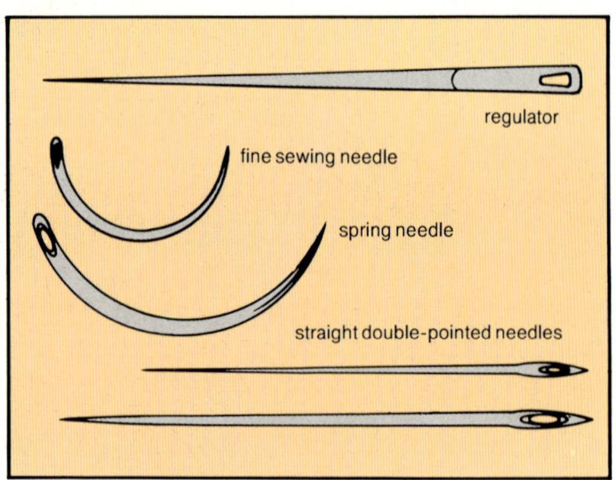

TACK-LIFTERS

You can buy a tack-lifter for prising out old tacks, or improvise one by grinding out a 'V' from the end of an old screwdriver.

Slip the lifter between the layer to be removed and the rail, set the 'V' under the rim of the tack head and gently tap the tack-lifter with the mallet. As the tack head lifts, lower the mallet until the tack is finally removed. Work gently, following the grain of wood; if the tack head breaks off or proves too stubborn, don't use force and risk chipping the wood. Either lift the tack with pincers or pliers, or just hammer flat.

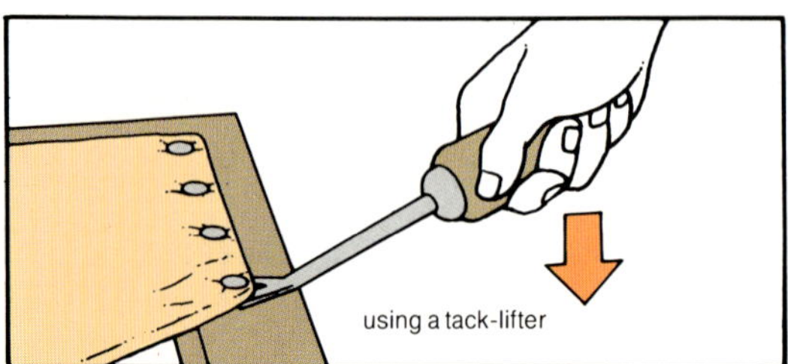
using a tack-lifter

WEBBING

A webbing stretcher or strainer literally takes the strain out of fixing webs with the correct degree of tautness. You can make your own from a block of wood about 150mm (6in.) long and 50mm (2in.) square.

Natural webbing is sold in 50 and 65mm (2 and 2½in.) widths and various qualities. The best is English black and white twill, made of pure flax. Other black and white webbing, made of jute and cotton, or hemp, will be satisfactory for most chairs though not quite so durable. Brown Indian jute webbing is best used only on arms and back. PVC webbing comes in 40 and 50mm (1½ and 2in.) widths and can be fixed with clips of suitable width.

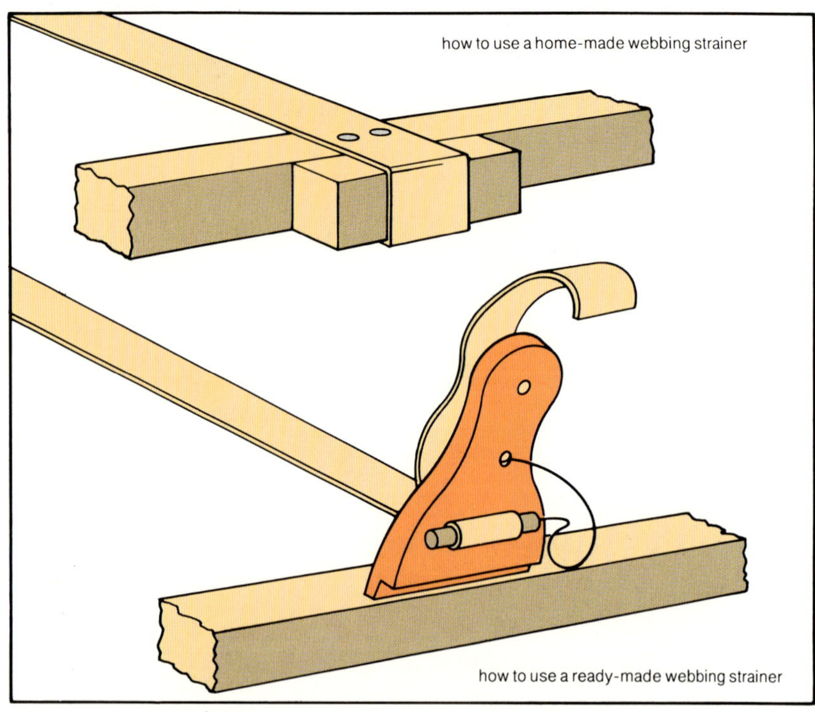
how to use a home-made webbing strainer

how to use a ready-made webbing strainer

OTHER MATERIALS

For supporting and covering springs, or for lining areas such as outside back and arm panels, you need both hessian and scrim. Hessian is a coarsely woven jute or hemp, 1830 or 1020mm (72 or 40in.) wide; the 475g (17oz) weight is used for springing and the 350g (12oz) for lining.

Scrim – normally 1830mm (72in.) wide, and in only one weight – is used for making things like stuffed and stitched pads.

Twines are usually sold by number, according to their thickness: No.1 for tying short, small-gauge springs; No.2 for tying larger springs and for buttoning and stitching; and No.3 for stuffing ties. You can, however, use just a No.2 for all these tasks. Springs are lashed with laid cord or 3-ply sisal.

Finally, have plenty of polyester wadding – this comes in 50m (54½yd) rolls, 690mm (27in.) wide – and calico or curtain lining fabric.

FOAM

Latex or polyether foam is a versatile substitute for fibre but can be hazardous in a fire because it gives off toxic fumes. Using flame-retardant foam, together with a top covering of natural fibres – such as cotton, wool or linen – should reduce the chances of flammability, but the safest option is to keep furniture well away from the fire and careless smokers. The secret of a perfect finish lies in the choice of density, hardness and thickness of the foam. Never buy the cheapest at the expense of quality.

Latex (a mixture of natural and synthetic rubber) is more resilient, more expensive, will last longer and remain more comfortable, but is hard to obtain. Polyether (plastic) is widely available and easier to handle; it comes in various densities and degrees of hardness; the two should not be confused. The density varies according to the amount of air in the foam; the range is 14 – 51kg per cubic metre (1 – 3lb per cubic foot). Manufacturers use various forms of numerical grading – normally the higher the number, the greater the density. Choose lower grades for back cushions, etc, higher grades for seats.

The choice of hardness (usually graded by number) will depend on you. The only way to decide is actually to sit on the foam before buying, or describe to the supplier your exact needs.

The thickness will depend on the style and look of the chair or stool, and on whether the foam is going onto a rigid wooden or webbed base, or on a 'suspended' platform of wire springs or rubber webbing. Generally, hard grades should be 90mm (3½in.) thick on a rigid base, and softer grades about 100mm (4in.). For drop-ins or fixed stuffed-overs, you can get away with 25–50mm (1– 2in.) foam, provided you bulk up the actual sitting area (see page 301).

When gluing foam, use the correct adhesive. Some petrol-based adhesives will melt the foam; others may never dry. Thixofix or L107 by Dunlop are ideal, but if in doubt ask the advice of upholstery suppliers or sales staff in hardware shops. If putting foam on tension-sprung or PVC-webbed bases, you can reduce the thickness by 13mm (½in.).

STRIPPING SEATS

THE SPRUNG CHAIR

A great deal of stuffing, stitches and layers has gone into the fully upholstered chair, all in the cause of comfort and appearance. Identify them and remember in which order they are removed because, generally, you'll be replacing them in reverse order.

Taking a typically sprung armchair, first untack the bottom hessian or linen, noting how it's been cut to shape around the uprights. Then remove the top covers in the following order: outside back; outside arms; any facing or scrolls on the front of the arms; seat, together with the front border; inside back; inside arms.

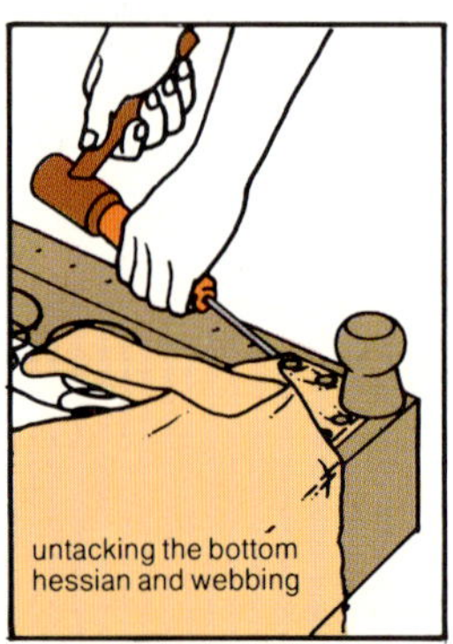

THE TRICK

Untack each piece carefully and label with tailor's chalk. They will serve as useful reminders when cutting your top cover.

Beneath the top cover, you will find some wadding – probably a little dilapidated – then a calico lining keeping the lower layers in place. Next may come a layer of polyether foam, placed on top of some scrim that has small pockets of fibre inserted in twine ties. This is followed by some foam chips, coconut fibre, Algerian grass or even horsehair, which is very fine, very scarce and worth re-using if you can.

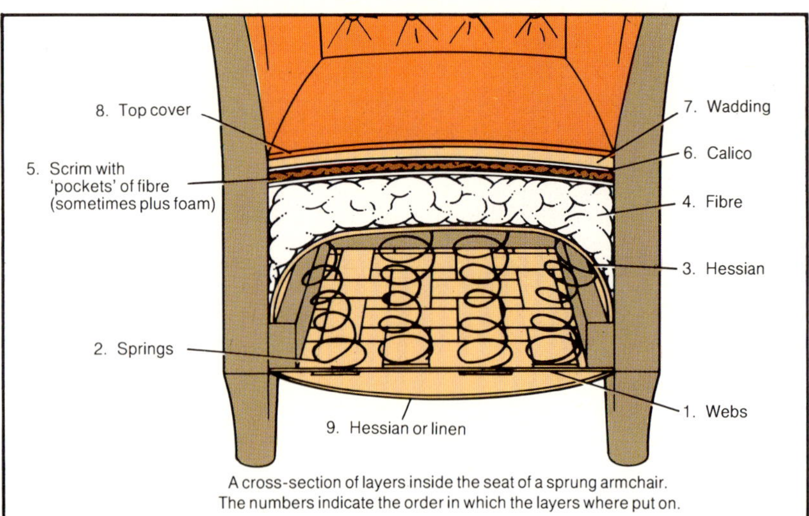

A cross-section of layers inside the seat of a sprung armchair. The numbers indicate the order in which the layers where put on.

THE TRICK

To clean horsehair gently lift it on to an old sheet, carry it out into the garden, if possible, and tease or 'card' it through you fingers, discarding any short, hard lengths and all the dust.

Now remove the next layer of hessian, cutting any ties, and look at the springs. See how they are tied or lashed to each other in such a way that, when pressed (or sat on) in the centre, each springs back to a vertical position – that is, unless the twines have broken or the springs are suffering from fatigue.

If you are very lucky, the webs holding the springs may be slack and not broken, and the springs may need just relashing to restore their original bounce. If so, follow the 'tucking' instructions (see page 307) and lash the springs (see page 300).

Otherwise, slash the twines and remove the springs, and also the webs. You may find springs on the back and even on the arms of a chair, but if not, the rest of the layers will be apparent. Never throw anything away until you are sure you cannot reuse it.

As you get closer to the bare frame, you may feel a joint begin to 'give' through weakness. To save further damage, wedge a block of wood under the part of the frame you are hammering, to take the pressure off the joint.

Finally, note the type of springs used. If they are the old variety, they will probably have nine coils, bound top and bottom with a length of wire, and may still have their bounce – test by pressing the top and bottom of each spring with your hands and observe whether it retains its shape when released. The modern, six-coil spring, self-bound top and bottom with a single twist of wire, usually suffers from fatigue more quickly and has to be replaced. You can obtain springs from an upholstery supplier (track down firms through the Yellow Pages), and choose from 100–300mm (4–12in.) in height, each of wire in 12, 11, 10, 9 or 8½ gauge. As a guide, you'd probably need 100mm (4in.) high springs in 10 or 12 gauge for some dining chairs, shallow arm pads or backs; 230mm (9in.) in 9 gauge for deeper, armchair seats; and 300mm (12in.) in 8½ gauge for very deep seats.

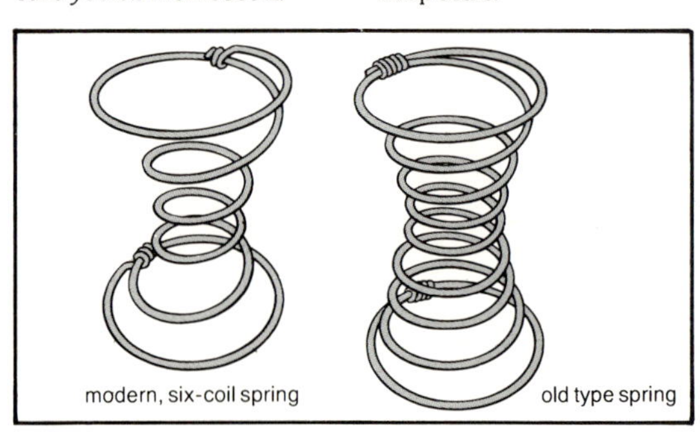

THE MODERN FIRESIDE CHAIR

Many modern fireside chairs have a loose cushion – sprung or stuffed – sitting on a platform or strips of PVC webbing, or on coils of tension springs. The back may be similarly cushioned, or stuffed straight on to the frame.

To dismantle, untack the outside back cover, beginning at the lower edge. Note how it's been cut to shape; label and put on one side. Similarly, untack the inside back cover, then any covering on the seat frame. You may find that the front edge of the seat cover has been seamed to a lining and stitched to form a 'sleeve' that covers the first few coiled springs. Make a rough sketch of how such pieces have been assembled.

Some of these chairs have a kind of 'bag' of wadding or kapok tacked to the back frame. Slash any ties that have been put through the stuffing, and see how the bag is formed; usually with a front piece of calico machined to a backing of hessian, and the whole thing tacked to the frame. Untack and unseam, and beneath the bag you may again find coiled tension springs, PVC webs or jute webs.

You can give a slack coiled spring a new lease of life, provided it is not the heavy 10mm (⅜in.) diameter type that is usually stretched across the 'lumbar' area.

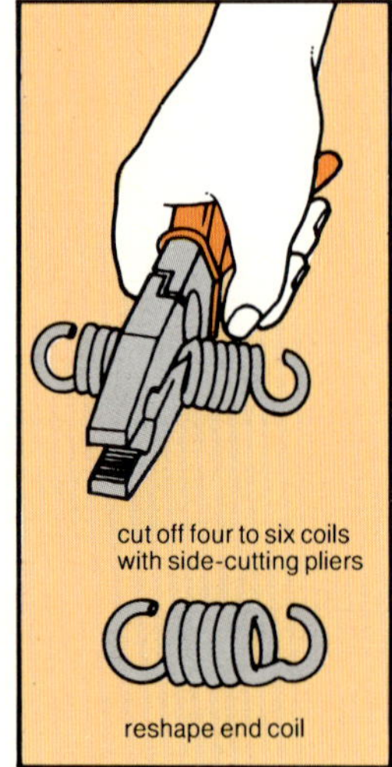

THE TRICK

Unhook the spring from the staple in the rail, cut off about four to six coils with side-cutting pliers, then shape the end coil into a new hook with pliers, to rehook to the staple.

If this method fails, you will have to replace them with springs of suitable width; they tend to come in widths from 376 to 526mm (14¾ to 20¾in.) in 14 gauge.

Now to the cushion. Snip away any piping around the edges, then slash the seams, keeping all the pieces as a guide. Inside you may find stuffing, foam and/or springs (see page 305). If replacing foam, which inevitably breaks down, choose the flame-retardant variety (see page 296).

THE STUFFED-OVER CHAIR

Dining chairs, ancient or modern, often come into this category. They are similar to sprung chairs except that they have no springs, relying for comfort on a stuffed and stitched pad tied directly to the webs. If the top cover is in fairly good condition, and only the webs and bottom hessian have split, you may be able to push up some springs from the bottom and reweb (see page 307). Otherwise, or if in doubt, strip the chair as you would a sprung seat.

The stitched roll round the edge of the pad is very important, because it alone must provide the firm edge to the seat, in the absence of any springs. If this roll is still quite firm but the scrim is torn, patch and restitch it (see page 308). If it has broken down, untack it, salvage any fibre from inside the pad, then strip off the webs.

WEBBING

The webs and springs are the foundation of your chair; it is essential to choose the right quality and apply them correctly.

PREPARING FOR WEBBING

If possible, use black and white webbing of the 65mm (2½in.) width, rather than the 50mm (2in.). This will reduce the number of webs needed and the work and time involved, plus the number of tack holes and wear and tear on the frame.

On a smallish, stuffed dining chair with a seat frame of, say, 430mm wide by 410mm deep (17 x 16in.), you require three webs from the back of the frame to the front and three from side to side. The middle webs are fixed centrally, with the outer two equidistant from the corner joints and the centre webs.

On the seat of a large, fully stuffed armchair, mark the centre point of each rail length with chalk, then fix a web about 13mm (½in.) either side, the two outer webs about 50mm (2in.) from each corner, and the remainder in between, separated by spaces of equal size. On a giant 760 x 760mm (30 x 30in.) seat, you will need six webs either way.

webbing the seat of a large armchair

WEBBING A CHAIR SEAT

Normally, a stuffed-over seat will have webs tacked to the top face of the seat frame. A sprung seat has the webs tacked to the bottom face and, in both cases, the bottom hessian or linen is tacked to the bottom face after the rest of the chair has been upholstered.

Working with the inside back of the chair facing you, fix the back-to-front webs first, then weave in the side-to-side ones. In this way, you have more room at the front for leverage and straining. On a wide settee, fix the side-to-side webs first then, working from the centre to either side, weave in the back-to-front webs. This prevents your having to strain the webs at one side of the frame and so risk these side webs breaking down.

To web, first turn back one end of a strip of webbing about 25mm (1in.) and, with the raw edge uppermost, fix to the seat rail about 6mm (¼in.) from the edge, with improved tacks in two staggered rows, using your magnetic hammer. On a firm, hardwood rail, use 16mm (⅝in.) tacks — three in a row along the fold and two more between these but about 13mm (½in.) further in. If the rail is softwood and inclined to chip, use smaller tacks and more of them.

THE TRICK

Hammer the tack heads flat. A bent head is likely to tear the web when any strain is put on it.

Thread the other end of the web through your strainer or wind it round your home-made strainer (see page 296) and take it across the frame to the opposite rail.

tacking the stretched web in position

THE TRICK

Keep the web absolutely straight; never pull it out of true to follow the shape of the frame or it will not provide the support needed.

Do not pull it so taut that you feel the frame 'give' or see the web begin to tear away from the back tacks. Hook the strainer over the edge of the rail, press down until the web is flat against the rail, and hammer in three tacks across the width, again about 6mm (¼in.) from the rail edge. Cut the web about 25mm (1in.) from the tacks, fold it back on itself, and secure with two more tacks placed between those beneath.

TYING THE SEAT SPRINGS TO THE WEBS

The seat of an average dining chair will probably take five springs; a large armchair as many as 16. If the armchair has a separately sprung firm-edge, you will need an extra four or six smaller springs along the front rail.

Place the springs in position on the webs, drawing round the bottom of each with chalk. On a smallish dining chair, place one spring dead centre and the four others to form a square around it, positioning each midway between it and the frame. On a larger seat, place the springs in rows of three or four across the width, keeping the spaces equal between each row.

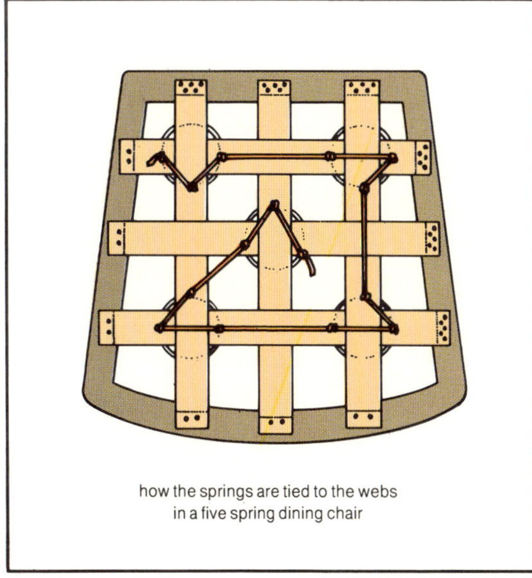
how the springs are tied to the webs in a five spring dining chair

THE TRICK

Ensure that the top knuckle (where the spring is finished off and joined to the first coil) is positioned diagonally and not running in line with the webs.

(Any front firm-edge springs are stapled to the front rail, the staples covering the bottom coils, and a length of webbing is tacked along the rail, covering the bottom stapled coils.)

Working from the bottom of the chair and using a spring needle and No.2 twine, tie each spring to the webs, starting with a slip-knot and tying at three points on each spring with a half-hitch. Finish with a double-hitch. If there are only five springs, tie the centre one first, then the outer four in the form of a square. If you have several rows, start with the back row and work from left to right, right to left, etc.

Work each row with one continuous length of twine. If you have to join halfway, with a reef-knot, there's always a risk of weakness.

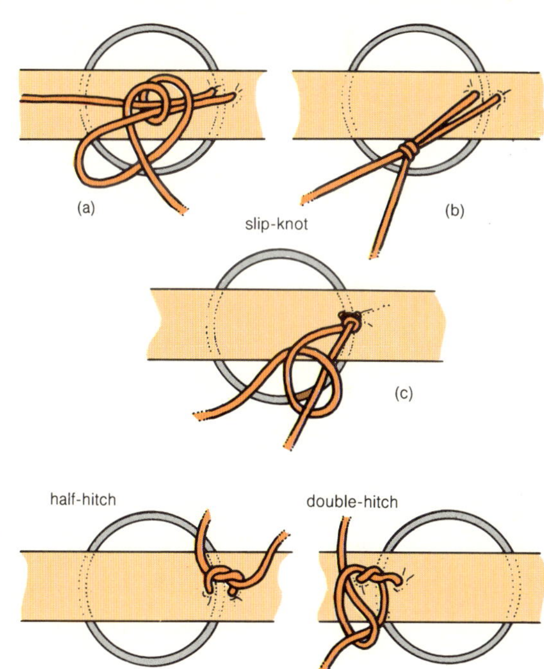

THE TRICK

To estimate how much twine you need, measure the length of each row and multiply by three.

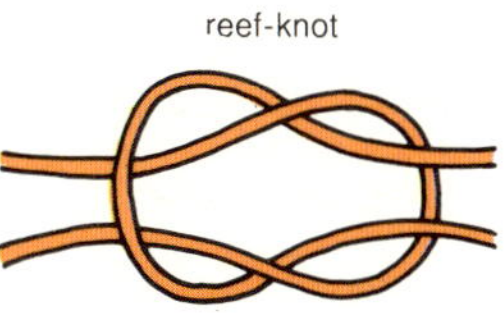

SPRINGING

LASHING THE SPRINGS ON TO THE SEAT

The way the springs are lashed ensures that, when the chair is used, the centre springs remain vertical and the surrounding springs are forced back into an upright position. The centre springs should be reduced by about 13mm (½in.) and all springs should finish the same height.

Generally, lashing is done back to front first, then across. For a large armchair, with 4 x 4 rows of springs, insert pairs of 16mm (⅝in.) tacks along the back rail, each pair in line with a row of springs, but tacked only halfway in. Using 3-ply sisal, tie the end round the 'waist' of the left-hand back spring with a slip-knot. Press the spring down and backwards diagonally towards the corner joint until the top coil is about 13mm (½in.) back from the bottom coil. Keeping the spring in position with one hand, pull the twine round one of the nearest tacks with the other. When the twine is taut, but not so that it pulls the spring out of position, hammer the tack home.

Bring the twine back to the top coil of the same spring, restore the spring's original back-slanting position and, keeping your thumb over the twine on the back of the top coil, secure the twine to the spring with a locked-loop. Pull it tight but do not let it slip. Bring the twine across to the front of the top coil and secure with a clove-hitch.

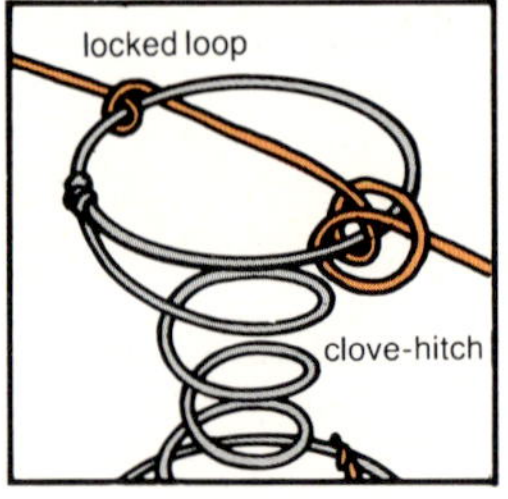

Continue down the row, tying each spring with a clove-hitch on each side of its top coil. Position the next two springs so that they are perfectly upright when depressed. (They will be sloped when the 'cross' springs are lashed.) Position the front spring towards you but diagonally into the left corner, with its top coil slanting about 13mm (½in.) away from its base. Lash the back of the top coil with a clove-hitch, then bring the twine down inside the coils and out through the front between the second and third coils down. When happy with its position, half-hammer a pair of tacks in the front rail, in line with your lashing. Wind the twine round both tacks, still keeping it taut, and hammer them home. Take the twine back up to the top coil of the same spring, and tie to the front of the coil with a clove-hitch.

Work back along the same row, securing the springs with clove-hitches over your original knots and always keeping the springs in position. At the back spring, after tying the twine to the front of the top coil, take it down inside the coils and out towards the back rail between the second and third coils. Tie it to the second back tack, with a half-hitch, and drive the tack home.

Lash the next two rows similarly, slanting back and front springs directly towards their nearest rails. The right-hand row will be similar to the left, except that the back and front springs will fan out to the right.

Lash the cross rows similarly – left to right, and back again, right to left – always maintaining the correct positions and slanting the left and right springs towards their nearest rails. Make an additional clove-hitch knot back-to-front over the lashings. Dining chairs are lashed in a similar way.

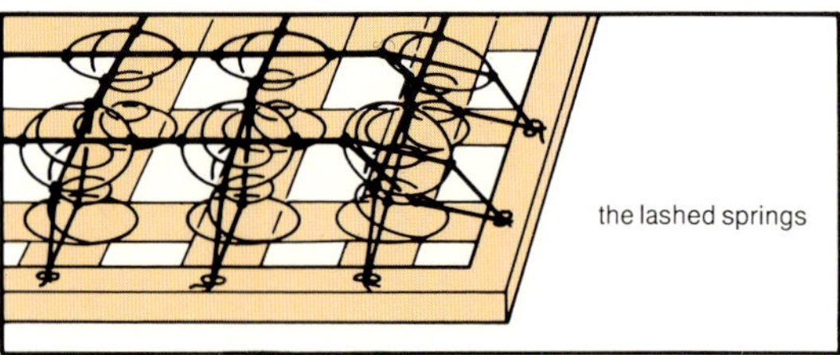

LASHING FIRM-EDGE SPRINGS

If your chair has smaller springs stapled to the front rail, these should be lashed independently so that they are level with the main springs. Secure some twine to the back of the right-hand spring's bottom coil with a slip-knot, bring the twine up to the top coil and, after depressing the spring, secure with a single half-hitch. Take the twine across to the front of the top coil, tie another half-hitch, then fix the twine round a tack in the front rail, with a half-hitch, having first pulled the spring down to the right height.

Tie the left-hand spring, making sure it is the same height as the right-hand one; finally lash the centre springs in the same way.

These front springs must be bound with cane or wire to give a smooth edge to the seat front.

THE TRICK

If the original cane is undamaged, reuse this; otherwise stretch an old spring by fixing one end in a vice and unwinding.

'Whip' the wire or cane to the springs using locked-loop knots and finishing with a reef knot, making sure the side pieces are firmly secured.

To bring these springs slightly forward, lace each with a strip of web, halved lengthways; loop the strip over the second or third coil, brace the spring slightly forward, then tack each end to the front rail.

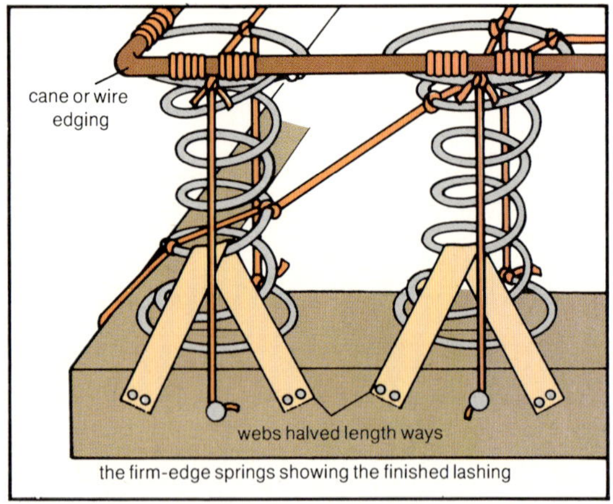

the firm-edge springs showing the finished lashing

Lash the front springs from side to side, beginning at the left. Fix the twine round a tack, take it up to the second coil of the first spring; through the fourth coil of the next spring, to the top coil of the same spring; to the top coils of the centre springs and down through the third and second coils of the right-hand spring. Tie each side of the coils with a clove-hitch; finally fix the twine securely to a tack.

COVERING ARMCHAIR SEAT SPRINGS

All springs are covered with hessian. For the seat of a large armchair, cut the hessian about 300mm (12in.) larger all round than the seat. Be sure to keep both warp and weft straight and never pull it out of true. Ease the hessian down the back and temporarily secure with 16mm (⅝in.) tacks. Snip diagonally into each back corner and ease it down either side.

THE TRICK

Don't pull the hessian too tightly or it will cause the springs to buckle.

Secure to each side rail with temporary tacks.

With firm-edge springs, ease the front of the hessian over these, but leave a 'gutter' between them and the main springs, so that they sit independently.

Thread a length of 3-ply sisal or laid cord along this gutter, securing the cord at each side rail round a tack. Lift the front of the hessian to secure the gutter. Fix the twine to a tack in the front rail at one side; then, using your regulator, thread it through the back of the hessian, loop it round the cord in the gutter, bring it back and fix to another tack on the front rail, on the other side of the first spring. Continue to the opposite side.

Bring the hessian back over the front springs and temporarily tack to the front rail. 'Box' it neatly at each corner, and blanketstitch each pleat down. Tack the lower side pieces of the hessian to the rails. Neatly blanketstitch all round the boxed top, using No.2 twine and a spring needle; loop the twine under the wire or cane edge.

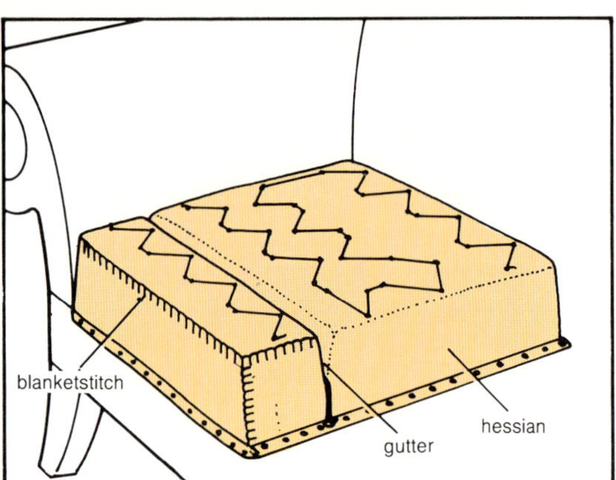

Tie the hessian to all the springs (see page 299), using No.2 twine and a spring needle. Start and finish with a double-hitch, and tie each spring with a half-hitch. Finally, lift the temporary tacks all round the seat rails, pull the hessian taut and retack. Trim the hessian about 50mm (2in.) from the tacks, double back and secure with more tacks.

THE DROP-IN SEAT

The drop-in seat has all its layers tacked to one frame. Its bottom always seems to sag more quickly than other types because there is no extra support from attached uprights.

STRIPPING

Support the frame in a vice, if possible. Cut away the bottom linen or hessian rather than knock out each tack, because the less hammering you give this one-piece frame, the better. Then loosen the bottom tacks, together with those holding the top cover, finally removing them with pliers or pincers.

Carefully turn the seat, lift off the top cover, wadding, and fibre or hair; then rip off the scrim and the webs. It is unlikely you can salvage more than the horsehair because of wear and tear, but make a note of order and fixing. When reupholstering more than one drop-in, number each frame according to the chair it fits; it is surprising how these frames differ within a set.

Once stripped, you can see the weaknesses: too many tack holes, splitting at the edges, possibly weakness at the corner joints. Strengthen the joints; then produce a 'new' firm edge.

THE TRICK

Sand down or chamfer any rough edges, then glue long strips of strong linen each side of the frame, using an impact adhesive.

Leave the corners bare. These will have to take several thicknesses of fabric and still fit.

UPHOLSTERING

You can upholster a drop-in frame with 25mm (1in.) thick foam instead of fibre and wadding, placing it directly on hessian-covered webs (or on hardboard – see page 307). Because of the thickness at the corners, slightly plane the frame with a wood chisel 50mm (2in.) from each corner. Cut the foam 13–20mm (½ – ¾in.) larger than the frame and chamfer the edge at an angle of 45°, but leave a 6mm (¼in.) 'lip' to tack to the frame.

The chamfered edge is pressed down onto the seat so that the foam domes.

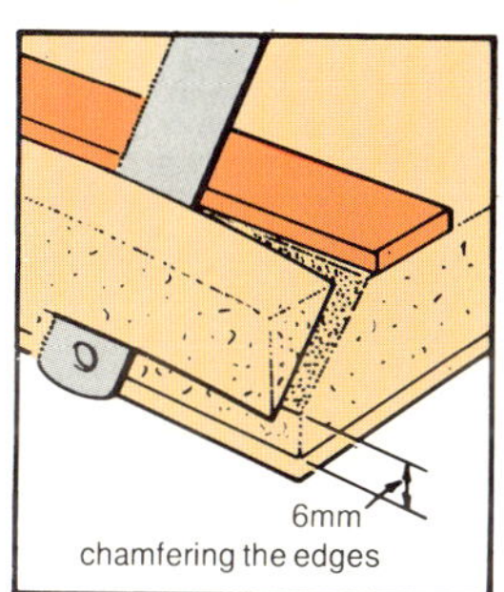

chamfering the edges

THE TRICK

To give an even better dome, glue a layer of 13mm (½in.) thick, hard-grade, dense foam to the centre of the seat foam, on the bottom, leaving about 50mm (2in.) margin all round.

Mark the centre of each rail down its side and underneath, and the centre of each side of the foam. Matching these, tack the foam 'lip' onto the rail edges using 10mm (⅜in.) tacks, about 13mm (½in.) apart.

Start tacking from the centre. About 50mm (2in.) from the corners, trim any excess foam. Fix the foam at each corner with one tack, then finish tacking. Make sure that no heads are left sticking up, to penetrate the lining or top cover. Tack a lining of calico over the foam onto the underside of the frame, then cut the top cover – sufficiently wide and long enough to reach under and cover the bottom rails. Notch the centre of each side with a small 'V'.

Place a layer of wadding over the lined seat, but don't let it stray down the edges or it may not fit. Temporarily tack the top cover to the frame with one 13mm (½in.) tack at the centre of each side rail. Then put three temporary tacks on the underside of the rail, centrally. At the corners, make a three-point pleat.

making three-point pleated corners

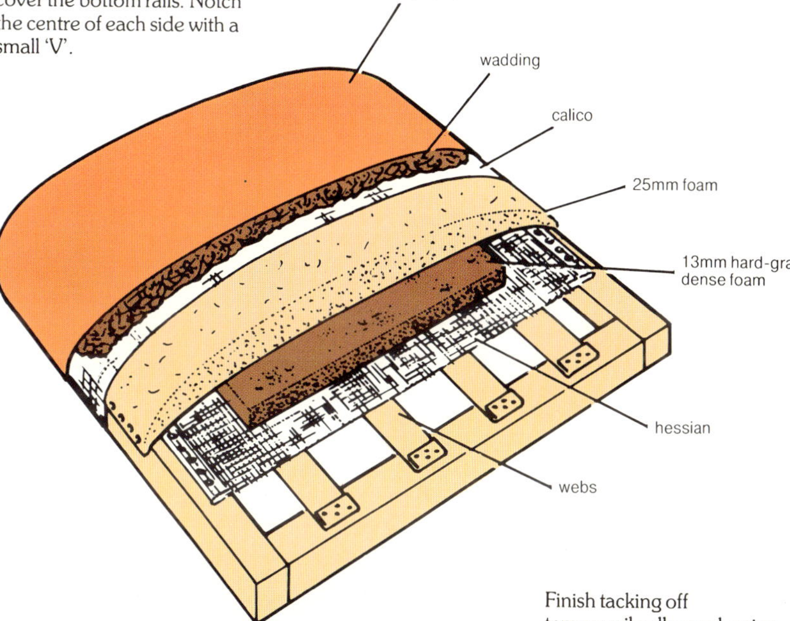

cut-away and cross-section view of foam upholstered drop-in seat

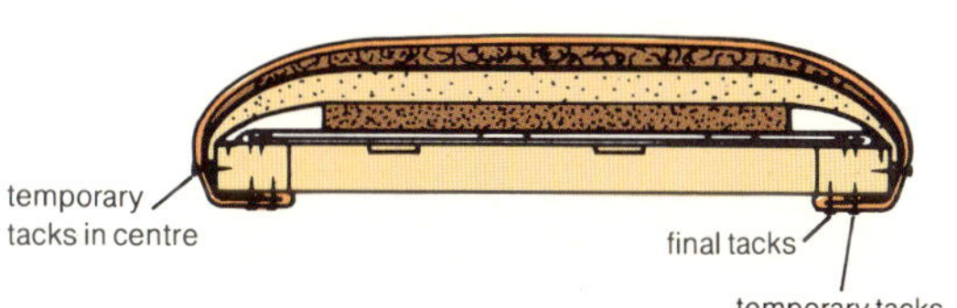

Finish tacking off temporarily all round, using tacks of the right size for the thickness of fabric, about 13mm (½in.) from the edge.

Turn the raw edge under, permanently tack all round just within the edge of the rail underside, and remove the temporary tacks. This way, you need not cover the bottom with hessian or strong linen.

CHOOSING HIDE

The great virtue of real leather is that it will last for years (provided you don't dry out its natural oils), and will give a luxurious look that fabric never can. It's also much easier to care for.

THE TRICK

Just give it an occasional wipe with a cloth wrung out in a good-quality leather soap solution. Never flood the leather. Allow it to dry completely before polishing with a soft cloth.

Alternatively you can use a proprietary cleanser. Every three months, 'feed' the leather to keep it soft and supple.

Cow hides, measuring about 4.5sq.m. (48sq.ft), are most frequently used. Several skins are peeled off one hide; the average armchair will take one and a half skins. Order from a reputable firm and store in a warm – not hot – place.

Take extra care in preparing the chair frame, strengthening if necessary, because more force is needed when pulling and straining into position. The stuffing must be much more rigid than on a fabric-covered chair.

When cutting, it is possible to save on skin by substituting toning fabric on unseen parts, as on the bottom of the seat cushion and on the corresponding platform which allows it to 'breathe'.

Using templates as pattern guides will also save wastage and produce a better effect. Ideally, cut hide from either side of the backbone area, using the thicker, inner edge for the front of the chair – the skin tends to thin out towards the legs and belly and is difficult to shape around sharp angles. If the backbone is nicely defined and you need to economise, cut so that the bone line runs down the centre of the back and seat. Avoid using the neck end; this normally has abrasions.

Smaller blemished pieces (used for borders, piping, etc) can be cut and rejoined by 'skiving'. Cut the pieces using a sharp knife. Thin the inside of one and the outer side of the other by cutting about one half the thickness of the leather. Hold the knife flat against the leather at a slight angle and taper off towards the edge. Glue the two bevelled edges together.

Hide cannot be easily manipulated around curves. Pull it over a curve, temporarily tack, then distribute the fullness evenly into temporarily tacked pleats. Make sure that the pleats are not pressed too flat and the tops lie below the flat surface of the arm or back. Readjust and retack as necessary, then tack off permanently.

THE TRICK

You can sometimes make a thick skin more flexible by damping it down on the wrong side, but don't overwet.

Because leather is much thicker, allow only 6mm (¼in.) seam allowance, especially on piped seams or cushions. Use a special bayonet needle in your machine. To finish off, turn under the raw edge and tack with brass or antique-finished upholstery nails.

THE FIXED STUFFED-OVER SEAT 1

The stuffed-over seat is a springless upholstered seat permanently fixed to the frame. Having tacked on the webs (see page 299), cut a piece of hessian about 300mm (12in.) larger all round than the seat and, keeping the warp and weft 'true', temporarily tack it to the top of the seat rail over the webs. As usual, start at the centre of each rail, and work outwards – if you start at one end, you may run out of material at the other. Keep the tacks about 50mm (2in.) apart. After tacking-off permanently, trim the hessian to the shape of the seat, leaving about 50mm (2in.) for turning. Cut diagonally into the corners, so that the turning lies flat, then turn all the edges back and secure by tacking in the spaces between the first tacks.

STUFFING

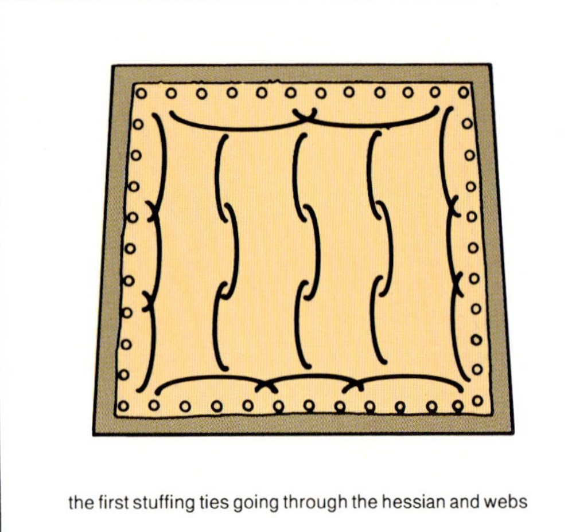
the first stuffing ties going through the hessian and webs

Put in the stuffing ties through the hessian and webs – about three rows, from back to front, starting at the back in each case; plus a row all round the edges – about three on each side and the front, and two along the back. These should be about 20mm (¾in.) in, to take the rolled edges. Ties are long, overlapping loops that hold the stuffing in place, each loose enough to take a large handful of fibre without snapping. To insert the ties, use a spring needle and one continuous length of twine. If you have to join with a knot, it will reduce the movement of the ties. Start with a slip-knot and finish with a double-hitch.

Tuck the fibre under the outer ties first so that it extends over the edge and stands well above it to give a nice firm base for your rolled edge.

THE TRICK

Take the trouble to insert the correct amount of fibre – as a rough guide, stuffing will compress to about one-third of its height when covered and stitched in. First tease it out, insert it under the complete loop, including the overlap, then pick at it again until it completely covers the ties.

Fill in the centre ties so that when pushed down the stuffing will assume the same final thickness as the edge roll.

THE SCRIM

Use scrim to cover the stuffing (not hessian, because its weave is too tight and its tarpaulin construction too rigid to mould and 'give' to your later blind- and topstitching). Cut the scrim about 300mm (12in.) larger all round than the seat to allow for 'rise' and turnings, then begin to tack temporarily to the seat rail, as you did the hessian, but over the stuffing. This time, however, tack right on the chamfered edge of the rail. Cut off the surplus scrim to within about 25mm (1in.) of the tacking line.

At the back, cut the scrim to shape round the uprights. The principle of shaping is the same for all layers of the upholstering, right through to the top cover where, of course, it is more crucial. Fold the scrim back on itself and cut diagonally from the corner of the fabric towards the upright, to within about 13mm (½in.) of it. Turn under the surplus with a regulator, fold the scrim back around the upright and temporarily tack it to the rail. At the front corners, pleat the scrim neatly before tacking down. Don't get the scrim too tight; if you do, you will not be able to make the roll properly.

Next, through-stuffing ties are put in to keep everything in place. These are similar to the first ties, except that they have no overlaps; they are just like close-up giant running stitches that go through scrim, fibre, hessian and webs. Put in four rows, running from side to side and starting at the back left-hand corner. Start and finish with a slip-knot.

Adjust the scrim, easing it down firmly over the stuffing, and checking that the threads are still running parallel with the centre of the rails. You may have to take up the threads at the corners to follow the shape of the seat. Tack permanently with 16mm (⅝in.) tacks through a single thickness, turn up the raw edges and secure with more 16mm (⅝in.) tacks. Now tease up the fibre beneath the scrim with a regulator until your edges are proud and buoyant.

how to tease-up stuffing through the scrim with a regulator

STITCHING

The edgestitching normally comprises two rows of blindstitching and one of topstitching all round, including the back. Use a smaller 255mm (10in.) straight needle, thread with twine and start at the back left-hand upright in each case. Blindstitch as shown, working a second row 20mm (¾in.) above the first, and extending just 75mm (3in.) in from the edge. Tease up the rolled edge once more, with a regulator, easing out any lumps of stuffing.

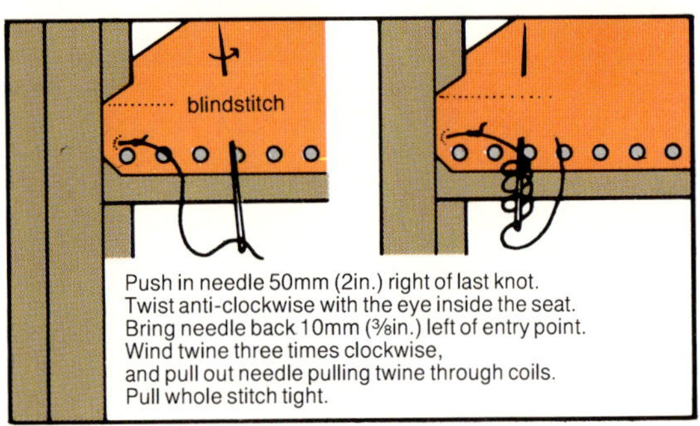

Push in needle 50mm (2in.) right of last knot.
Twist anti-clockwise with the eye inside the seat.
Bring needle back 10mm (⅜in.) left of entry point.
Wind twine three times clockwise,
and pull out needle pulling twine through coils.
Pull whole stitch tight.

THE TRICK

With chalk or pencil, draw a line all round the top of the pad, about 23mm (⅞in.) from the edge, and draw another all round the side about the same distance down.

Topstitching is similar to blindstitching, except that you pull the needle and twine free of the seat at each point. Tie off the first stitch with a slip-knot, as in blindstitching. Start your row by pushing in the needle 25mm (1in.) to the right of the first stitch, taking it out through the top line then back 25mm (1in.) so that it emerges where the first stitch ended. Wind the twine clockwise three times around the needle; pull the needle out towards you and, at the same time, pull the stitch up very tightly with your finger and thumb. Carry on all round the edge, finishing at the back upright by locking off as before; then do another row along the back.

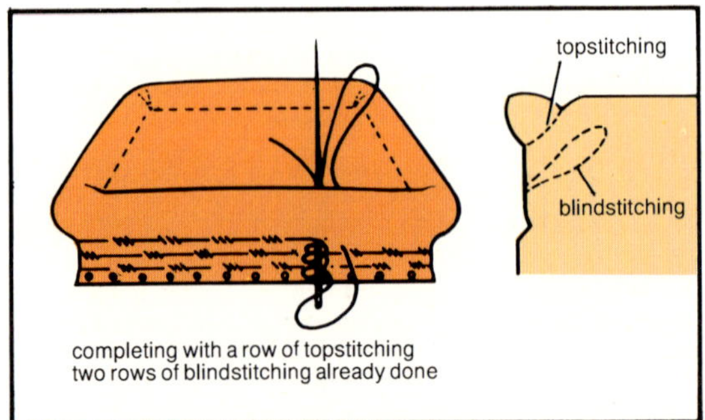

completing with a row of topstitching
two rows of blindstitching already done

THE TRICK

If the seat has rounded corners, make a slight tuck when backstitching to take up the surplus scrim.

Put in another set of through-stuffing ties – the same number and in the same direction as those put through the hessian and webs – but omit the outer ties round the edge. Push a little fibre under these, and some in the depressions between; then put a layer of wadding over the whole seat.

CALICO

Measure sufficient calico to go from the under-side of one rail to the same point on the opposite one. Tear rather than cut your piece of calico: just snip the first few inches, then tear along the thread to get a more accurate rectangle or square. Temporarily tack, with 13mm (½in.) tacks, along the centre of each rail.

At the back, push the calico right down beside the upright until you feel the point where the seat rail meets the corner of the upright. Make your diagonal cut (see page 303), leaving 6 – 13mm (¼ – ½in.) uncut, so that the calico can be gently torn to the correct point when adjusting. Finish your temporary tacking up to the corners. Finally, regulate the fibre beneath the calico and tack off permanently.

THE FIXED STUFFED-OVER SEAT 2

TOP COVER

Before buying a top cover, measure up the seat – never the old cover, as this will have stretched and broken down through wear – and draw up a cutting plan. For an ordinary stuffed-over dining chair, the process is simple.

Use a fibreglass measuring tape and write down the measures as you go. On a stripped frame, take the back-to-front measure from under the back tacking rail, across the top of the seat, to under the front tacking rail. This allows for the fullness of the finally stuffed seat, when the cover will be tacked off around the sides. Take a similar measure from under one side rail to the other. If measuring an old, upholstered chair, measure from and to the points where the old cover is tacked off, but add about 40mm (1½in.) to allow for flattening through use. If measuring your newly stuffed-and-stitched seat (see page 302) add 25mm (1in.) for tacking off and turnings. Finally, add 500mm (18in.) for wastage.

Buy the correct length of fabric: i.e. the length of seat, from back to front, plus allowances. Noting the width of the fabric, draw up a cutting plan. Even if cutting a single seat, it is useful to plan it, especially if you have chosen a patterned fabric. Cut a paper pattern in a square or rectangle the full length and width of the seat; any shaping will be done on the chair itself. Lay the pattern on the right side of the fabric so that any prominent motif is dead centre; if it is a plain fabric, you may be able to cut from one side of the width, and leave a 'spare' seat on the other side for another chair. In any case never cut across the full width of fabric when cutting out any pattern piece. It is surprising how you can manipulate other pieces to get the maximum yardage out of one length of fabric. Now chalk round the pattern and cut out.

THE TRICK

If using a piled fabric, make sure the pile runs from the back of the seat to the front to avoid shading (light and dark patches). To check, run your hand over the fabric, as you would stroke a cat. If the pile stands up, you are stroking against the run.

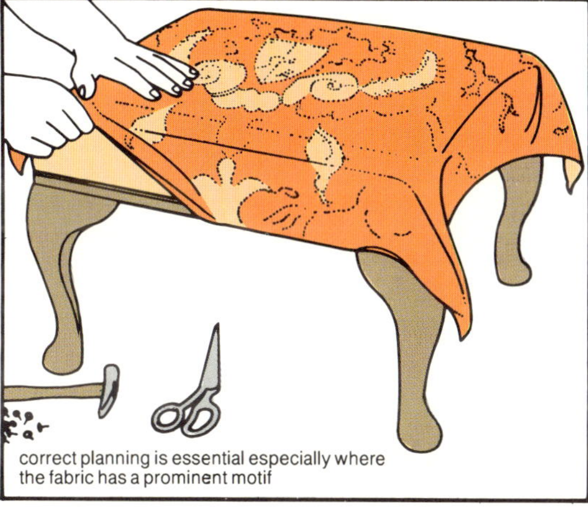

correct planning is essential especially where the fabric has a prominent motif

FIXING

Place a layer of wadding over your newly stuffed seat, and lay your cover in position. Keeping warp and weft straight, ease the cover towards the back of the chair with one hand, while using the other to keep the centre area in position. Tack centrally to the back tacking rail. Similarly, ease the front forward to the tacking rail and tack centrally; then temporarily tack either side. Continue tacking temporarily towards each corner to within about 100–125mm (4–5in.) of the front legs or back uprights.

According to whether you have square or rounded front corners, pleat and temporarily tack as shown. Then fold the fabric back at each upright and cut to within 5mm (3/16in.) of the corner of the upright. Fold the fabric back into the upright and judge how much surplus fabric you can cut off; trim, tuck under the raw edges and tack the lower edges to the rail. Shaping around the centre back rail of a settee is slightly different. Continue tacking temporarily up to each corner or upright.

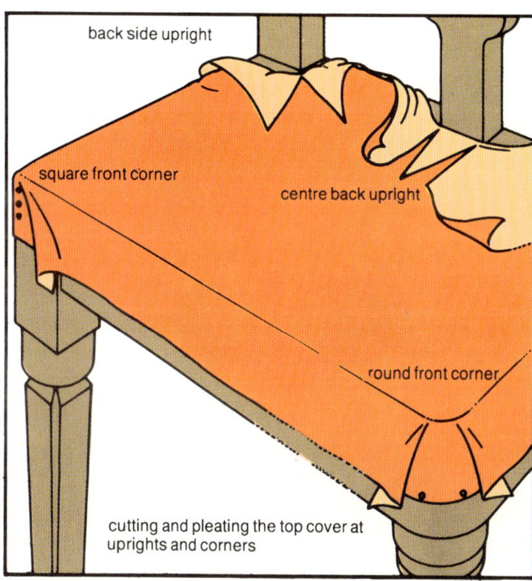

cutting and pleating the top cover at uprights and corners

Now stretch, tighten and retack the top cover all round, close to the show-wood, using 13mm (½in.) tacks and firming up and tacking off the corner pleats. Finally, cut away any surplus fabric along the line where the rail meets the show-wood.

Finish off by gluing a length of matching upholstery braid all round the sides to cover the tacks. Use a natural latex glue (e.g. Copydex or Clam 5) to coat the braid, then press in position. Fix it at each corner with a matching-coloured gimp pin that, when hammered gently into the rail, will virtually disappear among the threads of the braid.

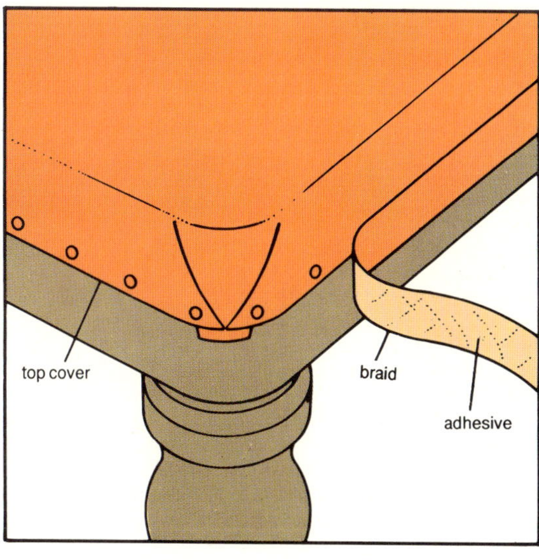

FOAM FIXED SEATS

When 'stuffing' a fixed chair seat with foam, you need to buy or make a tack-roll that goes round the edge. This replaces the edgestitching you would put on a traditionally stuffed-over seat.

Having webbed the frame (see page 299), buy sufficient 50mm (2in.), high-density, medium-grade foam to cover the full size of the frame, plus 13mm (½in.) all round. Chamfer the edge at an angle of 45° towards the bottom, leaving a 13mm (½in.) 'lip' (see page 301). If making your own tack-roll, cut a piece of hessian 75mm (3in.) larger than the seat all round. If you have bought a tack-roll from an upholstery supplier, the hessian need be only 13mm (½in.) larger for turnings. Temporarily tack the hessian to the frame with one tack centrally on each rail and one in each corner, leaving the 75mm (3in.) overhang, if needed.

To make a tack-roll, cut strips of cardboard about 13mm (½in.) wide from discarded cereal or other cardboard packets and tack these to the seat frame on top of the hessian, about 6mm (¼in.) from the edge. At the same time, keep the hessian taut but not out of true, and remove the temporary tacks as you go. Round this edge, on top of the cardboard strip, put wodges of fibre, then roll the excess hessian back over the fibre to make a 20mm (¾in.) tight roll. Fix the other side of the roll by tacking the hessian close to the fibre with 16mm (⅝in.) tacks, straight into the rail, keeping the tacks close together. Trim off the excess hessian all round.

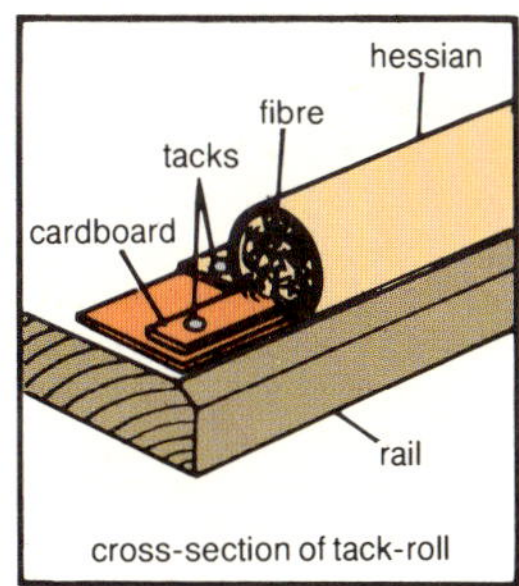

cross-section of tack-roll

Fixing a bought tack-roll cuts down a lot of work. Simply tack the flat felt strip all round the frame so that the roll sits just on the edge.

THE TRICK

Alternatively you can make a simple roll from strips of carpet felt underlay, each strip folded over on itself once or twice. Leave a 13mm (½in.) wide single thickness for tacking to the frame.

So that the foam will dome, put in three rows of stuffing ties through the hessian, from the back of the chair to the front in the centre of the seat (see page 302), and insert a couple of handfuls of fibre under each tie. Place the foam on top and start tacking, centrally, to the outer chamfered edge of the frame, covering the tack-roll. Finish tacking off in the usual way, then cover with calico (see page 302). Place a layer of wadding over the seat then top-cover as above.

OTHER SEATS

CIRCULAR SEATS

When scrim is pulled over a circular seat its threads slant out of true, making accurate blindstitching and topstitching impossible. Cut a border of scrim 100mm (4in.) deep plus a circular scrim top 50mm (2in.) larger than the frame diameter.

Machine the short ends of the border together, then machine top to border all round, clipping and trimming the seam allowance so that you get a good circle. Web and stuff the frame (see page 302), then tack and stitch the top in place, aiming for that final 75mm (3in.) deep 'wall'. Any deeper than 75mm (3in.) really needs springs.

BACKS

If your chair has a very curved shapely back, as some of the Victorian spoonbacks do, you need to blindstitch with a spring needle to get into the curve of the frame. Instead of foam, use a layer of rubberized hair which is thinner and more pliable and so accentuates the more delicate shaping of the back.

Modern fireside chairs with backs stuffed straight on to the frame, do not normally need any edgestitching. Simply tie and stuff as usual, making sure that the stuffing ties follow the shape of the back: i.e. run a row round the outer edges and across the lower back to form a square or oblong, then fill in with straight rows from side to side, and up and down. Always put extra stuffing in the lumbar region, as well as round the sides and top.

When you have filled in the depressions on the top scrim with more fibre, cover with a layer of wadding, then line with calico. The scrim and calico are tacked round to the back face of the side and top rails, with cut-outs at either side so that the fabric fits snugly round the arm rails.

BAG STUFFING

If your chair has the 'bag' of kapok tacked to the frame, resting on tension springs or PVC webs, you can either tack a layer of 25mm (1in.) foam to the rails and bulk it up with wadding, or make a new bag of calico or waxed cambric and tack that in its place.

THE TRICK

In either case, you need to place a layer of hessian against the springs or webs as protection against friction.

Cut the hessian 13mm (½in.) larger all round than the frame and tack with 16mm (⅝in.) tacks, doubling back the raw edges and retacking in the spaces between the original tacks.

Use high-density and fairly firm foam which should be cut 13mm (½in.) larger all round so that the sides can be tacked off and 'rounded' on to the frame.

For a new bag, cut calico or cambric 40mm (1½in.) larger than the frame. Machine the sides and top edge, allowing 13mm (½in.) seams, then turn through. Stuff with new kapok or, if you are allergic to that kind of filling, with cotton wadding or cotton felt. Machine the raw edges to close. Tack the corners to the frame. Then fold all edges round to meet the frame and tack, creating a soft rolled edge.

Put in stuffing ties, cover with a layer of wadding, fastened to the bag with more through-stuffing ties. Then add a final layer of wadding before fixing some calico lining.

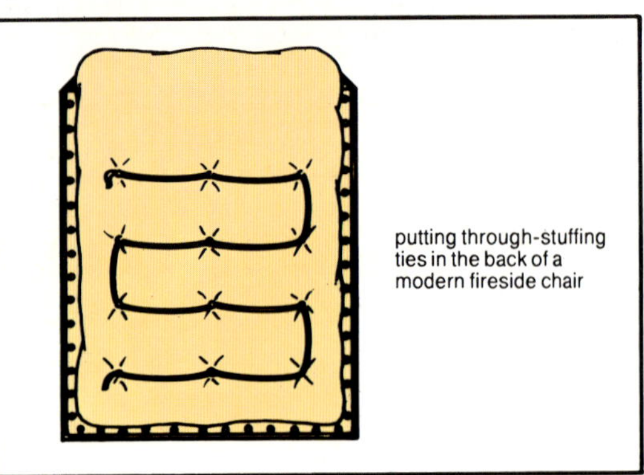

putting through-stuffing ties in the back of a modern fireside chair

THE SPRUNG SEAT

The method of top-stuffing a sprung seat is similar to the stuffed-over chair, except that the through-stuffing ties do not go right through to the webs.

On the monster armchair, arrange the first stuffing ties in the form of a square on the main seat, with a couple of rows running from front to back within the square. Along the front independent edge (see page 302), put one row of ties centrally, from right to left. As well as inserting fibre under all the ties, push a good amount into the gutter until it rises level with the rest of the stuffing.

Before temporarily tacking on the scrim, do some shaping snips at each side of the gutter so that the scrim fits the seat rails neatly. In addition to your through-stuffing ties on the main seat, insert another row along the front.

Cut off the excess scrim along the front edge, then make pleats at the four corners of the front independent edge or 'return'. Roll the scrim under the sprung edge and secure temporarily with skewers. Use a regulator to push the fibre forward at the front edge, and blanketstitch all round, using a spring needle and twine. Just catch the scrim to the hessian below the front length of wire or cane, and get the stitches straight to use as a guide later for piping or braiding.

Insert one row of blindstitching all round the front edge, just above the wire; then topstitch a fraction above the blindstitching. This gives a firm, almost rigid sitting edge. Use the regulator between each stitch to push the fibre forward. Neaten off the scrim all round as usual, nicking more into the corners where necessary, doubling over the raw edge and tacking off permanently.

CHAIRS WITH 'RETURNS'

It is best to cover a giant seat with 50mm (2in.) high-density polyether foam to give extra bulk. Cut the foam 205mm (8in.) wider than the width of the front edge and 100mm (4in.) deeper than the whole seat so that you have extra to push down the sides and back. At the front, cut the foam to fit the side indents.

Glue the foam to the seat using the correct adhesive (see page 296).

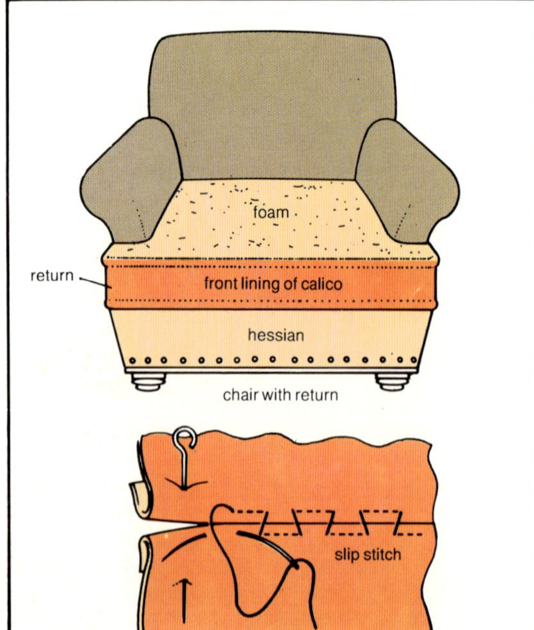

chair with return

THE TRICK

Cover the underside of the foam and the outer seat area of scrim with glue, but leave the tie area free. While waiting for the glue to 'take', slip handfuls of fibre under the ties to even up the seat.

Also cut a piece of calico to line the return. This should be as wide as the return by about 255mm (10in.) deep. Press the glued foam into position on the seat and push the surplus down the back and sides. Coat one side of the lining and the foamed return with more glue and, when it has taken, press in position, folding lining-plus-foam firmly round the front and side return edges to give a neat roll. Then slipstitch the lining to the chair under the roll using a fine plain thread and fine curved needle.

CHAIRS WITHOUT 'RETURNS'

On an armchair without a return edge, do two rows of blindstitching and then two rows of topstitching, aiming for a 75–100mm (3–4in.) 'wall'. This means that the first blindstitch will extend about 50mm (2in.) inside the stuffing; the second about 25mm (1in.). The first topstitch will end up about 31mm (1¼in.) in; the second about 13–20mm (½–¾in.).

Then come the through-stuffing ties, with fibre inserted under them, a layer of wadding and the final cover of calico.

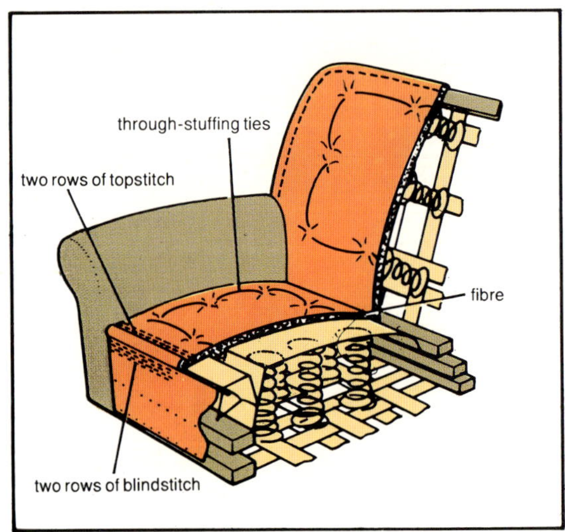

SEAT CUSHIONS

FOAM SEATS

Seat cushions often wear out before the rest of the chair. Choose a cover that complements the existing fabric, in the same weight and in a matching, toning or contrasting colour. A natural fabric, like wool, will allow the foam to 'breathe'. Leather cushions can be replaced with toning moquette, tweed or strong linen.

THE TRICK

Buy your foam before you buy your top cover, so that you can see exactly how much material you need for the borders.

Measure the exact area, add 6mm (¼in.) all round and either order the correct size of foam, or cut it to size yourself. Mark your cutting line with a ballpoint pen on both sides of the foam and down its thickness for extra guidance.

Cut the top and bottom panels from your chosen fabric to the exact area of your seat, plus 13mm (½in.) all round for seam allowance. Use a template for extra accuracy. Cut your border 6mm (¼in.) less than the depth of the foam, plus 25mm (1in.) to allow for the 13mm (½in.) seams at the top and bottom. As a result, the border will finish 6mm (¼in.) less in depth than the inside foam, and make a nicely compressed, wrinkle-free cushion.

THE TRICK

To prevent the foam disintegrating, line the foam with calico, gluing all round the sides (though not the seat area) with special foam adhesive and cutting to shape neatly at the corners.

The border should be in four lengths equalling each side of the foam cushion, plus 25mm (1in.) for seam allowance. Join them to make one continuous border. Make piping to go round the top and bottom panels by cutting sufficient lengths of 40mm (1½in.) wide fabric on the bias and joining – across the straight weave – to make two long strips each the length of the border.

THE TRICK

Choose 10mm (⅜in.) piping cord; if it is not pre-shrunk, wash first to prevent possible shrinkage when the cover is removed for cleaning or washing.

Lay the cord along the centre of each strip, on the wrong side. Fold the strip to enclose, and pin and tack as close to the cord as possible. Pin one strip of piping to one edge of the border, right sides facing, raw edges level and leaving the corded ends overlapping free. Machine with a zipper foot, close to the cord. Join the piped ends by opening the fabric, cutting the cord so that the ends butt up and seaming the covering on the wrong side. Fold the cover back and oversew to close. Join the piping to the other edge of the border in the same way.

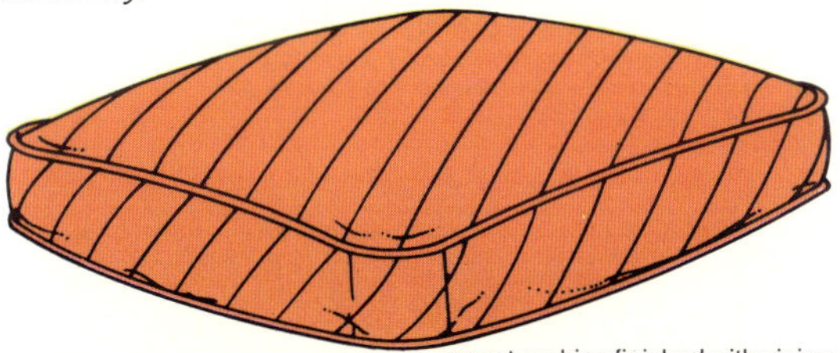

a seat cushion finished with piping

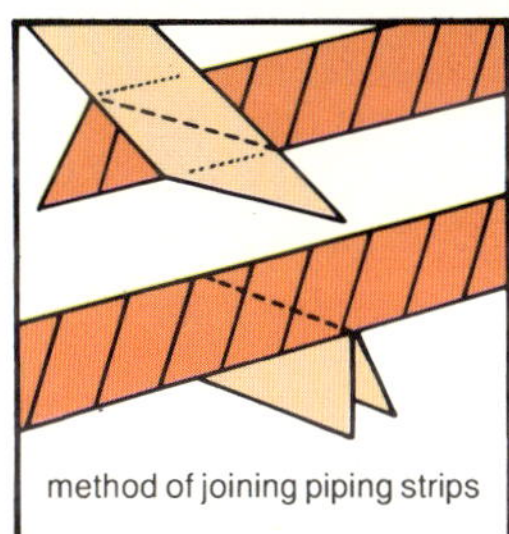

method of joining piping strips

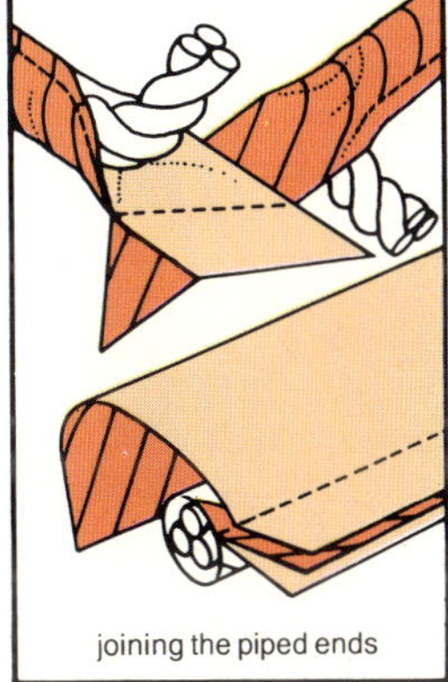

joining the piped ends

Place the border on the top panel, right sides facing, raw edges level, so that the piping is between the two (facing towards the centre) and the border seams match the corners of the panel. Tack and machine all round, close to the piping. At the corners machine in a curve; this will produce a pointed corner. Place the other edge of the border on the lower panel in the same way, but machine round the sides and front edge only. Nick away the seaming on the border at the corners so that piping lies flat. Turn the cover to the right side, and sew press studs, hooks and bars or a zip to the open end at the back. Insert the foam and close.

To add a little interest to a foam cushion, you can give it a rounded front, the exact shape depending on how you cut and glue the foam. The covers for such cushions require a little imaginative shaping, and you should always allow 13mm (½in.) for seams and make sure that the finished border panels are 6mm (¼in.) less than the depth of the foam.

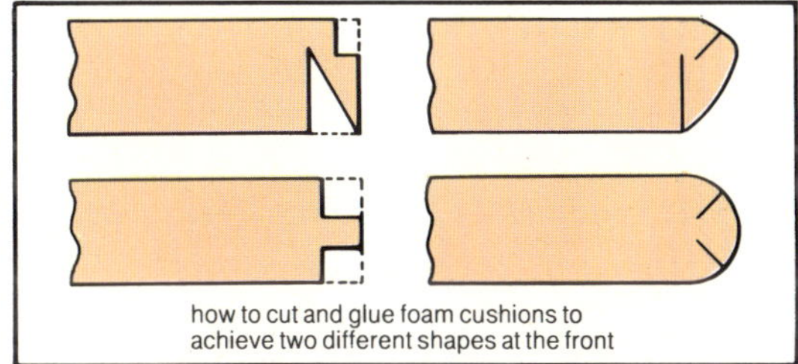

how to cut and glue foam cushions to achieve two different shapes at the front

FOAM-CHIP CUSHIONS

Foam chips in a calico pad make an effective cushion-filler. They are washable, provide a firm but pliable base and are easy to use. Make the cushion pad the same size as the finished cushion, but the cover 25mm (1in.) smaller all round. Machine two pieces of calico together, allowing 13mm (½in.) for the seams, round three sides. Trim the seams to 6mm (¼in.), turn the right side through and fill with sufficient chips to make a firm pad. To close, slipstitch the open end neatly.

THE TRICK

As chips have a tendency to fly all over the place, fill your pad over the bath.

FEATHER AND DOWN CUSHIONS

The crème de la crème of fillings is feather or down from goose, duck or even chicken. Down is the most expensive, the softest and lightest and, at the same time, the bulkiest of fillings. Feather-and-down mixtures are less expensive but heavier, and produce harder cushions. Feathers (of which chicken are the cheapest) are heavier still, because more are needed to give the required bulk.

It is not worth the trouble or expense of making a smallish cushion, as there is a variety on sale. For a large armchair or settee cushion, you can shop around for a supplier who will fill a pad for you. Contact upholstery suppliers listed in the Yellow Pages. Give them the exact size of the finished cushion and they will make the pad suitably larger.

Preserve any old feather cushion you may have with care.

THE TRICK

Don't attempt to wash the pad, since the drying process is long and sometimes unsuccessful. Put it in an airing cupboard for a few days, so that the feathers bulk up, then make a new inner cover of waxed cambric if the feathers are beginning to leak.

Make a removable top cover of washable fabric, 25mm (1in.) smaller all round than the pad. Curve out each side to a maximum of 6mm (¼in.) in the centre. This way the sides will straighten out nicely after filling.

'INVISIBLE' MENDING

Upholstery has many enemies, including smokers, pets and small inquisitive fingers, but there is often a simple solution to the odd tear or cigarette burn.

Moquettes and similar fabrics with looped weaves are very vulnerable. If just a few threads have been pulled, carefully pull a few new ones from the turn-under at the bottom of the chair, first removing the lower hessian or linen. Use a fine semi-circular needle to weave the new threads in place of the old, beginning and finishing with a tiny backstitch around the crossthreads.

THE TRICK

Cut away the old threads only after the new ones are fixed, and tie the ends firmly, once again around the crossthreads.

TEARS

To cope with a tear near a piped edge, fold under the raw edge furthest from the piping, pull it towards the piping and secure temporarily with one or two 40mm (1½in.) plated pins or the longer skewers, right up against the piped seam. With a fine semi-circular needle and plain thread, carefully slipstitch the fold of the tear to the panel on the other side of the piped seam, catching the fabric on both sides and drawing it close to the piping itself. Take your needle under the piping with each stitch as you catch one fold to the other.

A tear which is too far from a seam to catch up without ugly creasing, needs a 'hidden' patch. For this, you do not necessarily need a matching piece of top cover; just one that's a similar weight and a little larger all round than the tear. Snip off any stray threads along the edges of the tear, slip your patch beneath it and position it firmly and flat with the eye of a regulator or a small spatula. Lift the torn edges gently and fix the patch with a little natural latex adhesive, such as Copydex.

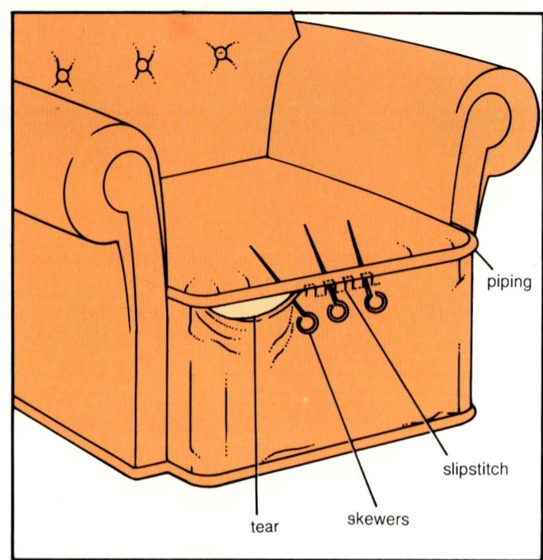

LARGER HOLES

A larger hole, for example, a cigarette burn, obviously needs a patch of matching fabric. For such emergencies it is always advisable to save any spare pieces of material when reupholstering. Otherwise, remove the lower hessian and see if you can take some surplus from the turn-under. If the hole is in the centre of a pattern motif such as a leaf or flower, carefully cut round the hole 13mm (½in.) inside the complete motif. Cut your patch to match, leaving a margin of 13mm (½in.) around the outside. On a plain fabric, cut away a square or rectangle, following the line of the warp and weft, and cut your patch similarly, again leaving 13mm (½in.) inner or outer margin.

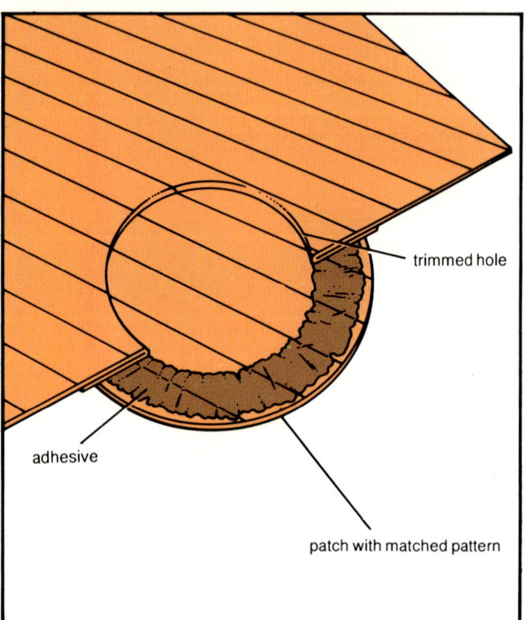

THE TRICK

Make sure the pile is running in the same direction as that of the fabric under repair so that you do not get any shading (see page 303).

Spread fabric adhesive on the margin of the patch, slip it in position, tuck under the margin around the hole and press flat, leaving a heavy object on top until the glue has dried.

THE TRICK

Alternatively, try cutting the hole and patch exactly around the same lines, slip a piece of iron-on interfacing (such as Wondaweb) into the hole with its edges extending under the raw edges and press the patch directly on top, using a damp cloth and a cool iron.

ARMS

Unfortunately, an upholstered chair arm holds an unfailing attraction for unruly cats, and often the front or top of the arm becomes a favourite scratching post. The front is fairly easy to re-cover. Snip away any piping or fringing that has been sewn up and around the scroll, and replace later. If the facing is trimmed with self-piping leave it intact. Push back any wadding or stuffing hanging outside the arm, put a new layer of wadding on top, pinning it temporarily in position, then cut a new cover the same shape, plus 13mm (½in.) all round.

If you have no matching fabric, introduce a contrasting or toning piece, but match up on the other arm. Turn under the 13mm (½in.) allowance and pin in position, close up to the seam or piping all round. At the bottom, where the facing joins the top of the front border, snip away the seaming on the border, slip new facing down behind it, and pin in place. Slipstitch all round, pulling the new fabric as taut as possible so that it lies perfectly flat, and replace any fringing with new, again slipstitching in position.

The inside arm is a little more tricky because it will have been the first part of the cover to go on the chair and therefore will be firmly encased by all the others.

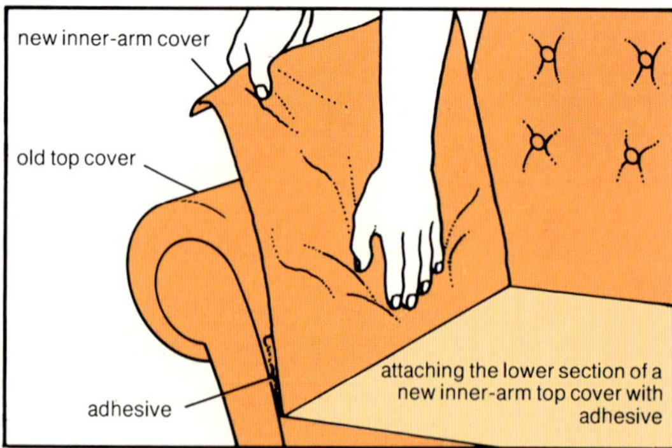

THE TRICK

Before pushing the lower section of a new inside arm top cover down between the seat and the arm, coat it with fabric adhesive and push down flat against the old arm immediately.

Place a layer of wadding over the top of the arm, and pull the new cover up and over, straining it across the width and along the length until you can pin it tightly in position over the old. When you are sure that it is as taut and true as possible, turn under and slipstitch the remaining raw edges to the seams or joins on the inside back, the front facing and the outside arm.

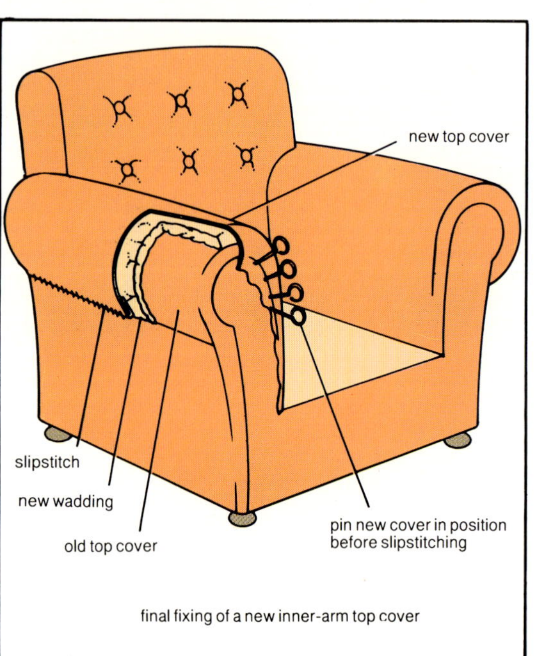

final fixing of a new inner-arm top cover

QUICK REPAIRS 1

REPLACING THE WEBS IN A SPRUNG SEAT

Sometimes you can get away with a short-cut, without stripping a chair down to its bare frame. Although the first sign of a saggy seat is a crinkled top cover, most of the actual wear and tear starts at the bottom, which is where you must tackle the problem.

If, after untacking the bottom linen or hessian, you find that only the webs have split, and the springs and stuffing still feel buoyant, replace the split webs with new ones. First, snip away all the ties from the worn webs; if you try to wrench any still-tied webs from the seat, you could pull the springs out of true. Rip off the old webbing, discard, then weave through new pieces, straining and tacking in place (see page 299).

THE TRICK

Don't hammer the tacks into the old holes, or they will simply fall out.

Reposition the springs on the new webs correctly by pressing them down from the top, in the centre of the seat. The centre spring or springs should end up centrally on the new webs; the outer ones placed equidistant between them and the frame. Now retie all the springs (see page 299) replace the bottom covering, or tack on a new one if there is any sign of wear.

If the webbing is just slack but not broken, snip the ties, tack new webbing over the old and then retie.

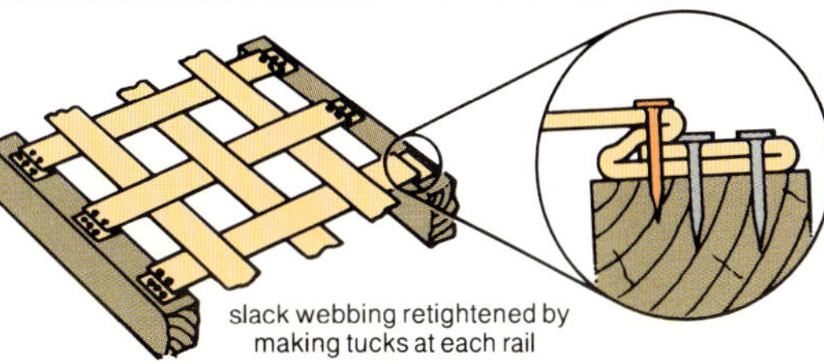
slack webbing retightened by making tucks at each rail

THE TRICK

Sometimes you can get away with putting tucks into slack webs, provided the slackness can be taken up at either edge without displacing the springs or stuffing. Fold the webbing back on itself at each rail to an equal depth. Don't make more than a 13mm (½in.) tuck at each side or the resultant strain may be too much for the web to take. Retack in the spaces between the old tacks.

SPRINGING THE UNSPRUNG CHAIR

A saggy stuffed-over seat can often be boosted by the insertion of small springs from below. However, first feel round the top edge to check that the stitched rolled edge has not collapsed. If it has, reupholster in the more conventional way – from the top.

Invert the seat, resting it on a bench if possible with the back hanging down before you, and remove the bottom linen or hessian.

Because the webs – and the hessian covering them – are normally tacked to the top face of the seat frame, leave them intact, together with the ties. Buy the correct number of 75–100mm (3–4in.) springs in No. 10 or 11 gauge – not too tall, or you will push up the centre of the seat and the edges will slope off. Place them in the correct position with the top spirals against the hessian (or webs, if these are the first 'layer' you come to).

chair with stuffed over seat

THE TRICK

Chalk round the spirals to mark the position of the springs, placing at least one spring centrally to take the most weight.

Tie the springs to the hessian (or webs) (see page 299), but tying from below rather than through the top of the hessian. Tack new webs to the bottom face of the seat and, making sure that the springs are sitting on an intersection of two webs and at the correct height and angle when depressed, tie these lower spirals to the webs, through from the bottom of the chair. Finally, cover the webs with a new piece of tacked hessian.

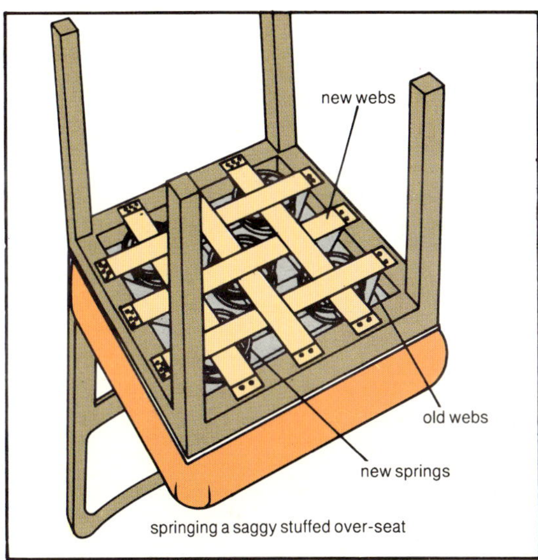

springing a saggy stuffed over-seat

MAKING A FIXED DROP-IN SEAT

Recalling how much wear and tear a drop-in seat frame takes, you may have to substitute it with a piece of 3-ply hardboard. Either cut out any corner struts and nail the board to the bottom face of the seat, cutting the corners to fit round the uprights; or make a new drop-in, cutting the board 10mm (⅜in.) smaller all round than the seat so that it sits on the inner ledge but leaves sufficient room all round for the top covering. Drill holes in the board at about 150mm (6in.) apart.

For the removable drop-in, cut a piece of foam 13–20mm (½–¾in.) larger all round than the board. Because you have no frame and will be 'stuffing' straight on to the board, choose 50mm (2in.), high-density polyether foam to allow for the extra depth. Chamfer the edges (see page 301). Glue an inner section of 13mm (½in.), hard-grade high-density foam to the centre of the seat foam, on the bottom, so that the top 'domes', then glue all to the board, remembering to use an adhesive specially made for foam. Fix your lining over the whole lot, pleating at each corner, and gluing to the underside of the board. After placing a layer of wadding on top, glue the top cover in position on to the board as you did the lining, under the board.

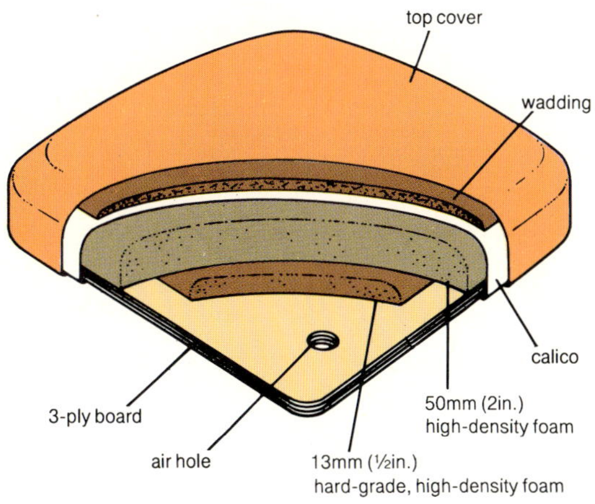

cut-away view of foam drop-in seat

NAILED-DOWN DROP-INS

If you have nailed the board to the bottom of the chair, buy 100–125mm (4–5in.) high-density foam to allow for the full depth of the frame plus 'top-stuffing' allowance. Cut this 20mm (¾in.) larger all round than the inner area of the seat. Chamfer the edges as before, but leave a 'lip' the depth of the frame from the bottom to the inner ledge, and if the front legs intrude into the seat area, cut out corner wedges from the foam to accommodate these, but cut only from the lipped section, not from the top, chamfered edge.

After gluing your inner section of foam to the bottom, glue the lining and top cover (with wadding between) to the sides and bottom of the foam seat, making the usual three-point pleat at each corner, but keeping the lipped sides and any cut-out corners as rigid as possible. Alternatively, if there are no cut-out corners, make a new cover to encase the foam. Slip the new seat into the chair so that it rests on the board.

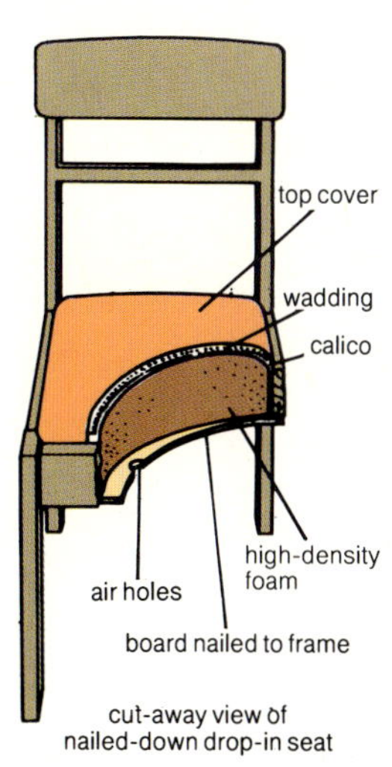

cut-away view of nailed-down drop-in seat

QUICK REPAIRS 2

BULKING UP

Should the top cover become flattened and worn all over, while the webs and springs are still in good shape, you will have to remove all the sections, bulking up the stuffing and putting on new covering. Remember to remove the pieces of the cover in reverse order of fixing: lower hessian, outside back, outside arms, front facings, seat and front border, inside back and, finally, inside arms. Leave a few holding tacks to keep the stuffing in place: e.g. at the top of the inside back and at the bottom of the front border.

Discard the old wadding on the inside back. If the stuffing is only slightly flattened, bulk up to an even surface by fixing layers of 13 or 20mm (½ or ¾in.) polyether foam over the arms, seat and inside back, tacking it to the relevant rails. If there are any deep hollows, remove the calico lining, lift the fibre and insert handfuls of extra fibre beneath to bring the surface up to the right level. Tease up the fibre with a regulator, replace the lining and lay new wadding over the top before fixing the top cover.

Where the existing foam on the inside back and seat has collapsed, discard and replace with high-density polyether foam of suitable thickness – 25mm (1in.) for the back, 50mm (2in.) for the seat (see page 296).

An example of how to measure and make a cutting plan for the top cover of an armchair

THE TRICK

When preparing to cut the new top cover, you can use the sections of the old cover as patterns for the new, provided they are still a good fit and not too old.

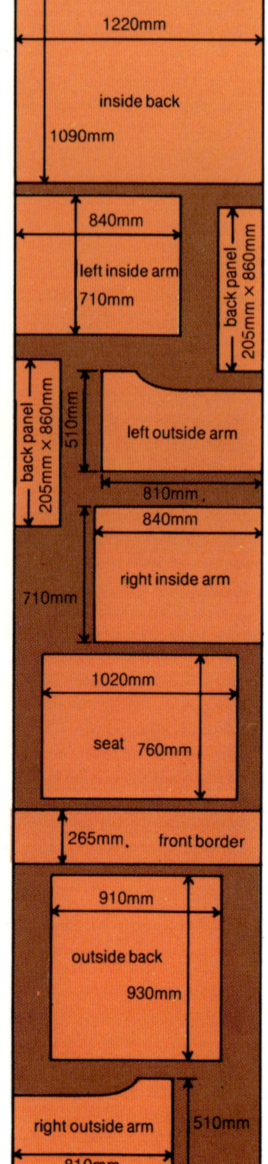

TIME SAVERS

If you start to strip off an unsprung dining chair and find that its stitched edge roll is still firm but the scrim covering it – and the seat – are torn, patch it with new pieces of scrim.

To patch the centre of the seat, cut scrim the correct size, plus 13mm (½in.) all round. Snip away and remove stuffing ties, then tease up the fibre inside the pad with a regulator. Position the new scrim on the seat, turn under the allowance along all the edges where the edge roll begins, and pin temporarily at each corner with skewers or long pins. Now blanket-stitch all round and insert new through-stuffing ties (see page 302).

If the covering on the rolled edge is torn, knock out the old tacks and retack, to secure, on the chamfered edge. Cut a piece of scrim the length of the rail and wide enough to reach from the side of the rail over to the inner edge of the roll, plus 25mm (1in.). Turn under 13mm (½in.) along one

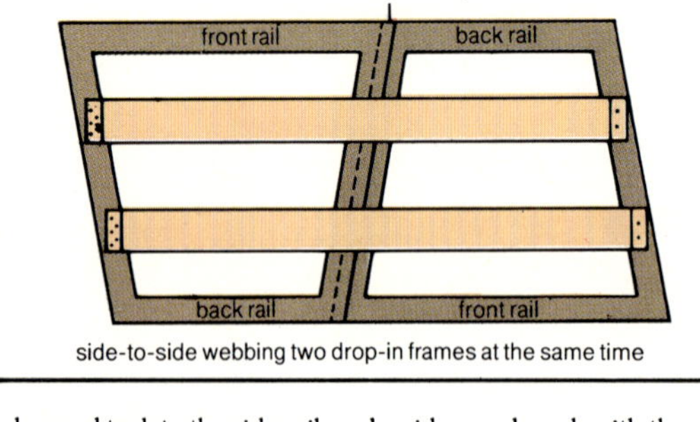

side-to-side webbing two drop-in frames at the same time

edge and tack to the side rail with 13mm (½in.) tacks, just below the original row of tacks securing the pad. Pull the scrim over the roll, turn under the raw edge, and temporarily fix the patch in place by pushing skewers or long pins through the edge diagonally from just inside the rolled edge through to the lower outside edge, close the the rail. Blanketstitch the folded edge of the scrim to the pad close to the inner edge of the roll. Remove the pins and insert a row of blindstitching along the patched roll (see page 302).

THE TRICK

Try to avoid the original blind- and topstitching or the inner fibre will bind.

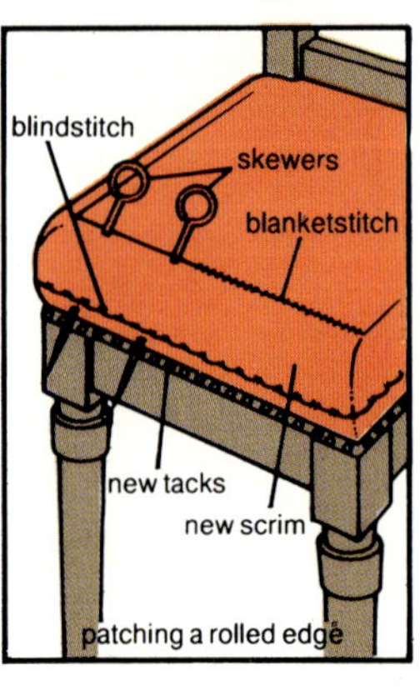

patching a rolled edge

DOUBLE WEBBING

Doing two jobs in the time it takes to do one is always worthwhile, and this you can do when webbing a pair of drop-in seats. This is also a good way of straining the webs where it would otherwise be difficult to get a purchase. Having ripped off all the covering, stuffing and webs, lay the two frames side by side on a bench with the front edge of one and the back of the other facing you, and the two slanting side rails overlapping each other by about 13–20mm (½–¾in.).

On the two outer rails of the pair, mark where the cross webs will go; they will line up automatically on the inner rails, once tacked in place. Normally, you'll have two webs going either way on each seat. Tack one doubled end of the first web to one of the outer side rails and, keeping the frames in the overlapped position, pull it over to the opposite outer rail. Secure with three tacks across the width of the web, cut off, double-back and tack off in the usual way. Secure the remainder of the cross webs in the same way.

Now, using the overlapped frame as a giant strainer, ease it off the lower frame, level it flush and, at the same time, strain and tauten the webs across both frames. Tack the webs in position on both inner rails, with the usual three tacks across the width. Cut the webs between the two frames, double-back each raw edge and secure with the usual two tacks to each web.

To interweave the back-to-front webs, reposition the frames so that the two front broad rails are overlapping – again by about 13–20mm (½–¾in.) – so that one of the shorter back rails is facing you. Again, mark the position of the webs on each back rail, and tack and interweave them, tacking off on the far back rail. Once more, level off the centre rails, straining the webs at the same time, and tack to each of those rails. Cut and tack off as before.

back-to-front webbing two drop-in frames at the same time

CANEWORK 1

MATERIALS

Caned seats come in almost as many variations as the upholstered kind – square, oblong, round, bow-fronted, narrow-backed, 'saddle', even egg-shaped – but the Standard Sixway pattern of weaving suits most of them. When starting, don't be discouraged if progress is slow and the effect not quite up to standard. The secret is not to attempt more than a couple of hours' work at a time.

You need very few tools and materials for canework and can use some you may have already obtained for upholstering, such as the regulator for final weaving, mallet for knocking pegs in and out of holes, and the sharp knife (for cutting any short lengths of cane or sharpening pegs). You can cut out the old seat with a keyhole saw; or use secateurs. Holes can be cleared ready for caning with a bradawl, or a long slim screwdriver (with shaft no wider than 3mm (1/16in.) in diameter) or, in stubborn cases, a fine drill. Use real cane, or rattan, for seating; plastic cane is really only satisfactory for stools or basketware.

Rattan is a sort of palm and, if of good quality, will be smooth and glossy on the right side, and tough and pliable. The 'eye' or lump where the stem of the leaf grew out should be smooth and unbroken. It is sold either in ¼kg (9oz) hanks, or in woven lengths of various widths. Woven cane comes by the foot, and widths available include 360, 410, 460, 510, 560 and 610mm (14, 16, 18, 20, 22 and 24in.). Wider lengths from 760mm (30in.) are also sold. Loose cane comes in numbered sizes – 1 to 6 for the seating variety – the higher the number, the thicker the cane. Centre cane (the milled core, again numbered according to thickness) is used for the pegs. You need a length of No. 10 or 12 centre cane for any permanent pegs; No. 14 or 15 for temporary pegs that will hold the cane in place while working.

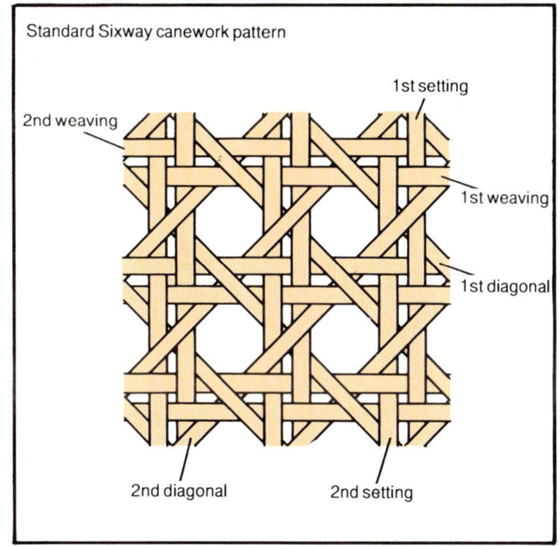

The size of caning will depend on the number and size of the holes in the pattern, and on the nature of the pattern itself. You will notice either single or double rows of caning running from back to front of the frame (called 'settings'); side-to-side rows (known as 'weavings'); and crossings ('diagonals'). There are many variations on this theme, but the most common in this country is the Standard Sixway – two settings, close together; two similarly close weavings, and two opposing diagonals.

Generally, two different sizes of cane are used on a Sixway caned seat: use thicker cane for the diagonals than for the settings and weavings.

THE TRICK

If recaning a single seat, you can economise by buying just one hank of the same (thicker) size.

When using No. 3 or 4 on its own, though, make sure that the distance between holes is wide enough to take it, or you get a thick, ugly pattern. If in doubt, choose one size down.

Measure the number of holes in 150mm (6in.) of the old caned seat, and use the following table to gauge the size of cane:

Holes per 15cm (6in.)	Size of cane
10	4
11	3 & 4 (or all 4)
12	3
13	2 & 3 (or all 3)
14	2
15	1 & 2 (or all 2)

Your ¼kg (9oz) hank should be ample for one seat. To finish off, you can either cover the edge with beading – from No. 4, 5 or 6 cane, depending on which thickness covers the holes – or simply glue final pegs in all the holes. A length or two of No. 2 cane will be needed for securing or 'couching' the beading.

Before clearing the seat of old cane, note the holes that take two parallel diagonals instead of one (known as 'doublers'), those that just have one setting or weaving, or neither setting nor weaving (known as 'misses'). Mark these holes accordingly on the frame or ink them in on a sketch of the seat.

Cut away the old seat and knock out the old pegs from below the frame. Every hole must be clean and completely free of any cane or plugs, so clear stubborn pieces with your drill, fitted with a bit the same diameter as the hole – usually 5mm (3/16in.). Use the same method to drill out any 'blind' holes (they don't go all the way through).

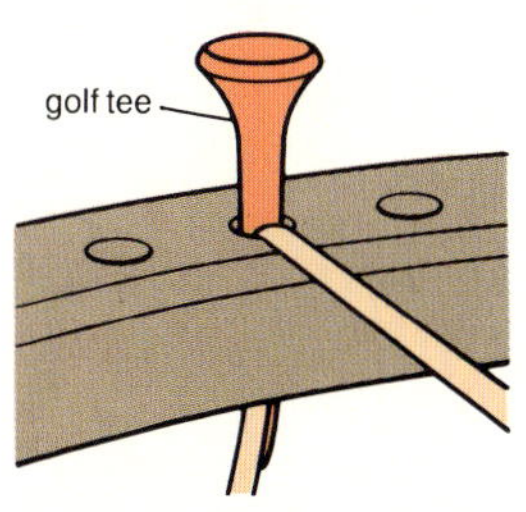

THE TRICK

Plastic golf tees make excellent, inexpensive temporary pegs.

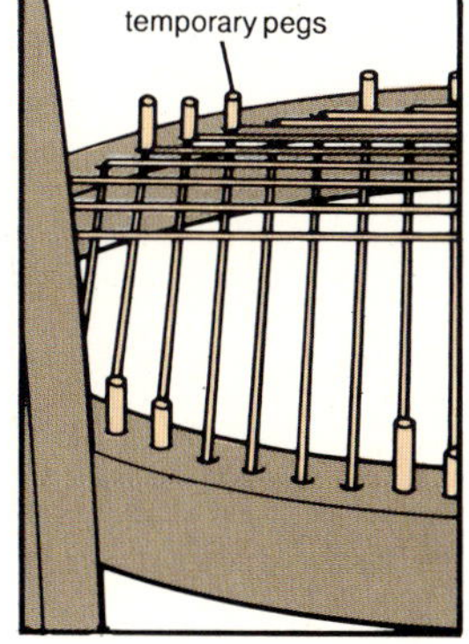

PREPARING THE CANE

Take your ¼kg (9oz) hank of cane and select four strands. Leave these in cold water for at least 10 minutes until pliable for working. When you are down to the last strand, add another four to the water.

THE TRICK

Don't leave the strands in the bath overnight, though: they may discolour.

Hang up the unused strands to dry, then pack in polythene bags and resoak when needed. It is a good idea to keep the floor free from dust, because cane picks up everything, especially when damp.

While waiting for the cane to soak, prepare your pegs. For temporary plugging, cut about 30 pegs from No. 14 or 15 centre cane, each long enough to stick up when plugged in. Use these to plug the holes in which you start and finish, 'double' or miss altogether (see above). Dip the heads of the 'misses' in blue ink, those of the 'doublers' in black, the starters and finishers in red, and leave to dry. When starting, you can either plug every hole as you go, or use a 'travelling' peg, lifting it and replugging as necessary. The 'traveller' or 'resident' pegs can be left natural. If using golf tees, sort them into appropriate colours.

Final pegs are cut from No. 10 or 12 centre cane, 3mm (1/16in.) shorter than the holes and pointed at one end. You need one for each hole.

THE TRICK

If you have stained your frame, leave these final pegs in a jar of the same stain till they take the colour; then scoop out with a draining spoon and leave on newspaper to dry.

While working, have a basin of water and rag standing by to redampen the cane as it dries out. Wipe the flat, non-shiny side to get maximum penetration of water.

CANEWORK 2

WEAVING A SQUARE SEAT

A square frame is the easiest, because you have no 'doublers' or 'misses' to worry about. However, instructions are given on how to double in the corners (see page 311).

FIRST SETTING

Start the first setting in the centre, working first to the right, then to the left. That way there will be less chance of missing any holes. If the pattern does happen to work out unevenly (as it could do on different shaped frames) you can double or miss at either side to restore the balance.

Insert your length of cane in the centre-back hole, leaving about 75–100mm (3 – 4in.) hanging beneath, and plug with a red peg from the top. If there are two centre-back holes, start from either, but be sure to link it with the corresponding hole in the front. Bring the cane straight across to the front and down the opposite hole, plugging it in position with your 'traveller' peg or a natural-coloured peg.

Throughout, keep the shiny side of cane uppermost on the seat and outwards on the under-rails as it goes from hole to hole.

Take your cane under the front rail and up the next hole on the right. Keep it in position with your forefinger while you take your traveller from the previous hole and plug this one. Finish this setting at the last hole on the right, leaving the corner holes free, and plug with a red peg.

Restart at the centre-back hole and work the left half. Plug a new length of cane in the hole to the left of the 'starter' hole. Otherwise join the new cane to the old: bring the straggling end of the old length up through the next hole on the left; push the new end down the same hole. Twist the new around the loop of the old cane two or three times, covering the old as well as the new loop. Thread the old cane back to the underside and pull both ends together gently but firmly.

If the cane is not too wide, you can knot off the ends for extra security. After the first 'looping', pass the new end through and above the single loop made by this end's first circle. Then pull the ends together, forming a knot.

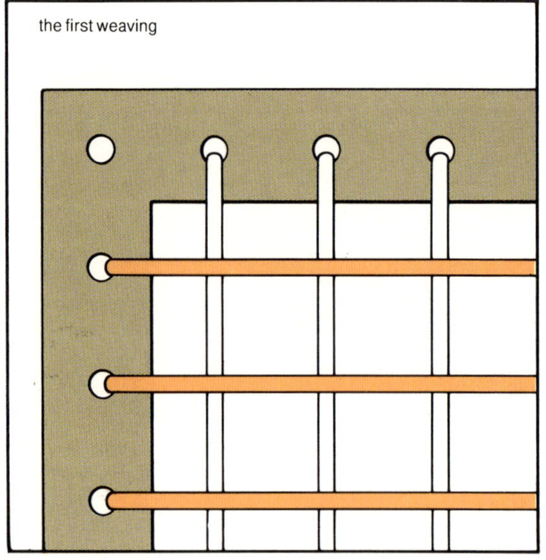
the first weaving

Finish your first setting, plugging in the last hole on the left and again leaving the corners free.

FIRST WEAVING

The first weaving is, in fact, taken straight across the frame, on top of the setting. Unplug your last hole on the left, take the cane left from the first setting across the corner under the frame and up through the first hole on the left side. Take the cane from side to side across the seat, joining and plugging where necessary, and finishing on the last hole on the right, leaving the corner free. Plug with one of your 'finisher' pegs.

SECOND SETTING

The second setting is worked like the first setting, except that it is slightly tighter and must lie to the left to ease the working of the next weaving stage. Each stroke goes over the first weaving. Start in the hole immediately to the left or right of the starter hole used for first setting. Then, the underloops will lie in the spaces left by the loops of the first setting. This makes for less bulk. Plug each hole as you go.

THE TRICK

To position the strokes, as you pull the cane up through each hole, press it flat with your middle finger and at the same time ease it to the left of the first setting.

SECOND WEAVING

The second weaving must be woven so that the cane goes in the 'right' direction and does not catch on the strands already set.

THE TRICK

To discover the 'right' way of cane, lay it flat on the table, shiny side up, and run your fingernail along it in the direction in which it will be woven. If your nail catches on the 'thorns', the cane is running the 'right' way; if it doesn't, turn the cane around and weave it in the other direction.

Start the second weaving at any end hole so as to alternate the underloops. Use one of the leftover strands from the second setting, take it under the frame across the corner and up the first hole on the side. Weave the cane over each left-hand (second) setting, and under each right-hand (first) setting, positioning it to the rear of the first weaving.

When you reach the other side, take the cane down the corresponding hole and up the next, then weave back, still keeping the corner holes free. Again, go under the first setting and over the second setting.

THE TRICK

Use a couple of pegs or a regulator to straighten the rows and force the pairs closer together, so leaving nice hollow squares between.

Pull the strand through after two or three pairs of settings in case you have to right a twisted cane. Don't worry if the pattern looks disappointing; the diagonals will pull it into shape. When you have plugged the final strand, loop all the straggling ends beneath the frame and generally tidy up.

MAKING DOUBLES AND MISSES

If you were doing an oblong, round, oval or bow-shaped seat, this is when you mark the holes where your 'doublers' or 'misses' go. On a square seat, you need only double in the corners, which are easily remembered. If using two sizes of cane, change to the thicker size for the diagonals.

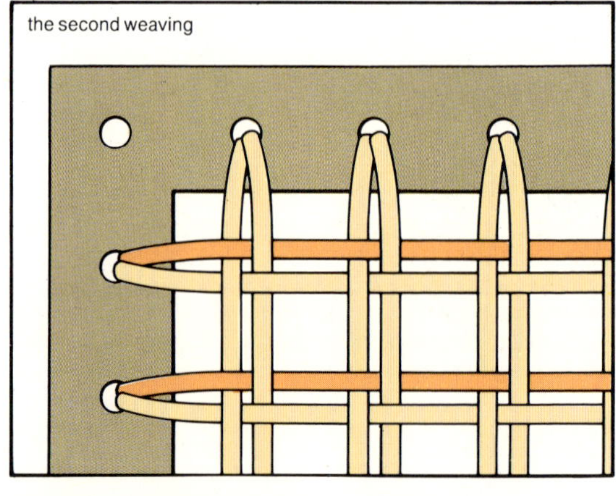
the second weaving

joining lengths of cane

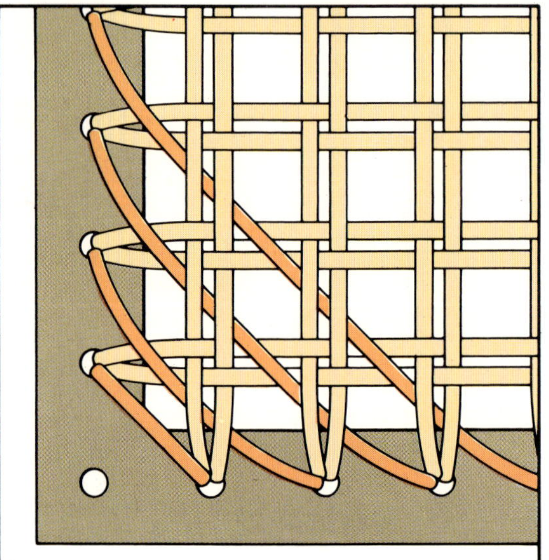
the first diagonal

FIRST DIAGONAL

To start the first diagonal peg the cane in the first hole at the left of the front rail leaving the usual 75–100mm (3 – 4in.) hanging. Take the cane diagonally across to the first hole on the left rail, leaving the corner hole vacant. Bring it up the second hole on the left rail, then weave it back to the second hole on the front, taking it over the weavings coming from the first hole on the left and under the settings coming from the first hole on the front. Gently pull the cane straight and plug it in this second hole. Take it under to the third hole on the front, up and back to the third hole on the left, again going under the settings and over the weavings.

CANEWORK 3

FIRST DIAGONAL

Continue weaving the first diagonal until you reach the top left-hand corner, where you double. Bring the cane out of the corner hole, over the weavings coming from the last hole on the left, under the settings, and over the weavings, across the opposite corner and down. Now bring the cane back under the frame and up the last hole in the front; across the top of the seat (over your corner stroke) and down the first hole on the right side. Then bring it back to the bottom right corner and up this hole.

When bringing this diagonal back to the top left corner, first take it over your short, opposing, diagonal stroke, over the weavings from the first hole on the right side, under the settings, and so on, up to the top left corner. There it will go under the settings coming from the first hole on the back, down the corner hole, then under and along to the first hole on the back and up through it. Continue working the first diagonal up to the top right, leaving the corner hole free and finishing at the last hole on the right side.

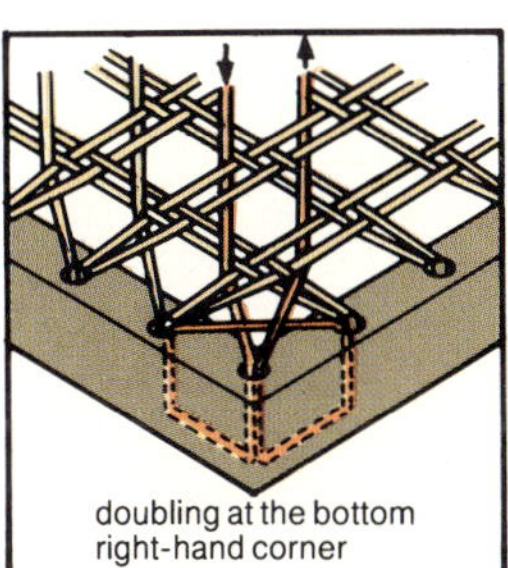

doubling at the bottom right-hand corner

SECOND DIAGONAL

Start the second diagonal at the last hole on the right front, working it in a similar way to the first diagonal except that you go under the weavings and over the settings. Still go over the weavings at either side and under the settings at the back and front of the seat. Work a double in the back-right and front-left corners, as before, and your finished seat will show two matching short diagonals at each front corner and singles at the back.

Loop off and trim the ends beneath the frame. Although the four thicknesses of cane in most holes will be enough to plug themselves, keep any temporary pegs in position, plus your starters and finishers, until you have decided how to finish the edge.

FINAL PLUGGING

Plugging is thought by many professionals to be a neater finish than beading. Remove all temporary pegs and plug with your prepared final pegs, hammering them in so that the tops are level with the seat.

THE TRICK

If a cane has not sufficiently tightened in any of the holes, put a drop of woodworking glue into the hole and, before it sets, hammer the peg home.

BEADING

As well as your No.4, 5 or 6 beading cane, you need some No.2 cane to 'couch' the beading around the edge. With all temporary pegs removed, and leaving the corner holes free, plug every other hole with pegs 20mm (¾in.) long cut from a centre cane. Tap each one down just below the surface. Take your length of dampened beading, push it up through one corner hole, leaving about 75mm (3in.) hanging below, take it down the corner hole at the end of the rail and draw it firm.

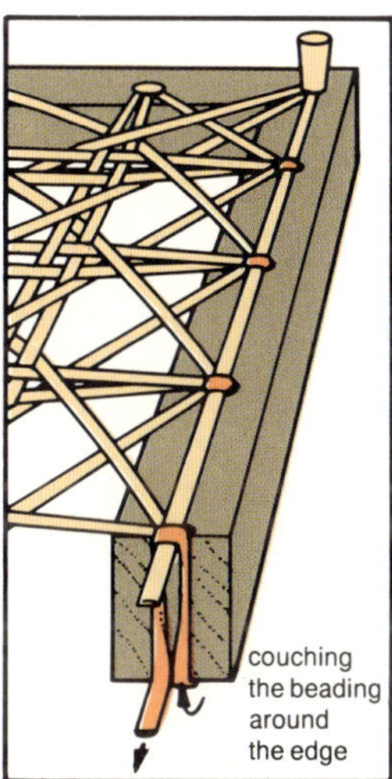

couching the beading around the edge

Now push the length of No. 2 cane up through the first unplugged hole, over the top of the beading and down its other side, through the same hole. Keeping the shiny side of both beading and 'couching' cane uppermost, and all the cane flat, continue couching along the under-rail to the next unplugged hole and repeat the up-and-over process. Complete all round the frame, pulling the No.2 cane firmly over the beading at each point. Turn the frame upside down and plug all the unplugged holes, including the corner ones, from below. Cut away any loose strands.

WEAVING OTHER SHAPES

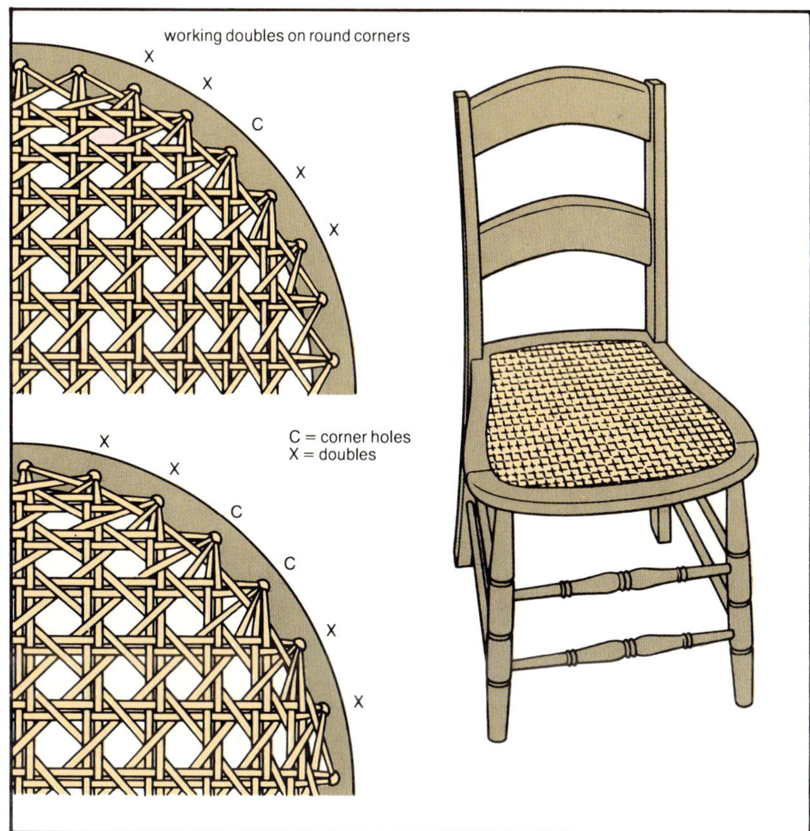

In seats other than square-shaped ones, you must work out where the doubles and misses come. This is not as difficult as it at first seems: it is simply a matter of seeing how the pattern best works. The most reliable way of discovering this is to work your way around the seat and not be afraid to undo the pieces if necessary and start again.

Keep the settings and weavings straight and parallel, and always weave the diagonals in the correct way – under the settings and over the weavings for the first strokes; vice versa for the second. Then you can hardly fail to meet up with the correct holes, missing the ones that do not line up, and compensating the pattern by doubling in some of the remainder.

On the majority of shapes, all the front holes will be filled with the settings, while some of the side holes may need to be missed. Similarly, the weavings sometimes have to miss holes on, for example, ovals and rounds. However, corners are always left free until the start of the diagonals, and no holes are left without any cane.

Diagonals always double in the corners. Discovering the 'corners' on a round, oval or bow-fronted seat must be left until the settings and weavings are inserted. On a bow-front, the corners are where the shortest settings meet the front frame, so the diagonals will double in these as well as in the hole above and below where the short weavings enter.

Oval and round seats have to be divided into quarters, the 'corner' hole or holes being midway between each section. Doubles will come in a variety of clusters either side of these 'corners'. Their position will depend on where the short settings and short weavings lie and whether the frame is evenly bored. Again, 'feel' your way through the pattern.

THE TRICK

To make things easier, use a separate strand for each diagonal, pegging at each hole. This means you can easily unpeg and re-do when you have gone wrong, and when doubling, you do not need to doubleback on yourself along the edge and produce a bulky, untidy effect.

THE TRICK

On a seat with a curved edge, start your diagonals at the centre front or back. That will ensure that your crossings don't drift from the correct 45°.

If you come across a chair with a 'saddle' seat or back (i.e. one that curves down in the centre), work the first two settings together, one immediately after the other. Then work the first and second weavings, so keeping the shape of the frame. Help the weavings through these pairs of settings with a regulator or a narrow plastic spatula.

You can stain the cane to match the frame. The polyurethane colouring used for wood can be fairly successful. Apply it to the underside of the cane first with a soft cloth or brush, wipe off the surplus, then apply a coat to the top side. For a darker shade, apply a second coat once the first is completely dry. If you want to leave the cane natural, use the clear polyurethane varnish as a sealant. This helps to prevent the cane from drying out and cracking.

To preserve the cane's supple nature, wipe with liquid detergent or soft soap in warm water once a month. Rinse off with warm water and, when dry, rub with a soft duster until it shines like new.

OUT NOW!
BRAND NEW WOODFIT HANDBOOK
Woodfit
Woodfit Limited
First for fittings
FURNITURE FITTINGS HANDBOOK 8th Edition
New extended 8th edition of Woodfit's Famous Catalogue/Handbook. An Absolute Must. Over 180 pages.
ORDER NOW! And nail your D.I.Y. problems for good.
Woodfit Ltd.
CATCHES AND HINGES
NEW
DRAWER FITTINGS
KITCHENS
Browse through over 180 illustrated pages – many in stunning full colour. Jam-packed with probably Britain's largest range of specialised D.I.Y. furniture fittings & fixtures, many exclusive to Woodfit, and not available in shops or stores.
For your exclusive copy send 50p (cheque/P.O.) payable to Woodfit Ltd. TODAY.
Exclusively yours for only 50p (inc. p&p)
Woodfit Ltd.
First for fittings
70 Kem Mill, Chorley PR6 7EA.

PICTURE FRAMING

WAYS OF MOUNTING 1

THE 'CLASSIC' FRAME

The most common frame, used for water colours, prints and many other types of pictures, comprises many more components than is usually assumed. Anyone who has tried to frame at home will know that, unless the picture itself is made of stiff card or board, it will start to buckle after a few days.

The professional framer overcomes this problem by 'hot-bonding' the picture to the backing board. The hot-bonding process uses a special double-sided adhesive sheet, a piece of which is cut to the size of the picture and laid under it. The picture, adhesive sheet and backing board are then placed in a powerful, heated press, which applies a pressure of about 1 ton per square foot at a temperature of about 100°C (212°F), for 20 to 30 seconds. When the press is opened, the picture is flat and rigid, and will stay that way forever.

Despite the apparently disagreeable conditions inside the press, the hot-bonding process causes no harm to any type of picture, be it a photograph, drawing, water colour or print. Furthermore, the hot-bond sheet does not stain the picture, which can happen with wet adhesives.

The mount is cut to the same size as the picture, and its centre is then cut out, using a machine in which the cutting blade is angled at 45°, to provide what is called a 'mitred mount' The angled sides present a more pleasing appearance than those of a 'straight-cut' mount, in which the cutting is done with a vertical blade.

The glass is cut to the size of the backing board and the parts are now ready for assembly into the frame. The frame may be made from any of the hundreds of wood mouldings and metal sections that are widely available.

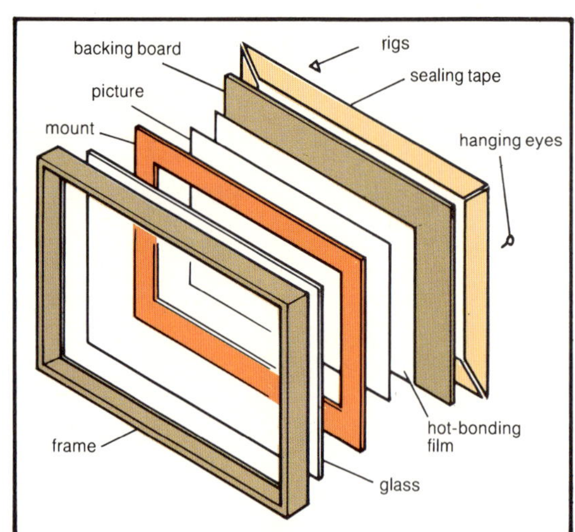

OTHER TYPES OF FRAME

DOUBLE FRAMING

In double framing, the picture (which may be mounted or unmounted) is placed in a relatively simple frame, which is then fixed to a larger, heavier board, usually with screws from the rear. This board is mounted in a heavier, more complex frame. The gap between the two frames can be filled with any colour or material, such as hessian, carpet or even wallpaper, to suit both the picture and the decor of the room.

In an alternative form of double framing (sometimes known as reversed or embossed double framing), the weights of the two frames are reversed, the inner one being the heavier of the two. Again, the gap between the frames can be filled with any colour or material.

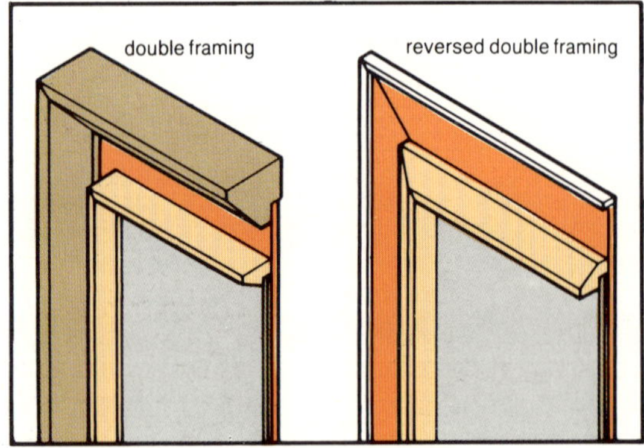

BOX FRAMING

To mount three-dimensional pictures, such as collages, dried flowers or plaster mouldings, it is necessary to use a box frame in which the front glass is mounted at a suitable distance from the backing board. As with slips (see page 315), this requires an additional rear frame, finished to match the main frame.

THE TRICK

Box frames can be doubled and used as display cases for items such as coins.

NON-RECTANGULAR FRAMES

It is possible to obtain non-rectangular frames to suit special pictures. Most power cropping machines can be set to accept the different corner angles required for six- or eight-sided shapes, but other polygons with odd numbers of sides need to be cut by hand, which always involves extra cost.

Circular frames can also be obtained, but usually in standard diameters and with a more restricted range of mouldings. Special circular frames can be made to order, as can elliptical frames made from parts of circles, but these need to be specially turned on a lathe and can be expensive.

EXHIBITION AND DISPLAY FRAMES

For temporary display purposes, pictures can be trapped behind a sheet of glass, which is clipped to a matching-sized sheet of blockboard, chipboard or plywood.

For lighter display purposes, the backing board may be reduced to a sheet of hardboard, with the assembly held together by spring clips, sometimes known as Emo clips. These clips provide a neat, unobtrusive mounting and are quite suitable for use in the home, but the picture itself must be stiffened to prevent buckling if it is to be displayed in this way for any length of time.

The small peg at the bottom of each clip is used to lock the clip in position. Hardboard backs can be supplied with shallow-sawn slots to accept these pegs, but small holes, drilled through the hardboard at the correct distance in from the edge, are equally good.

THE TRICK

As the edges of the glass are unprotected, they must be ground and chamfered before assembly.

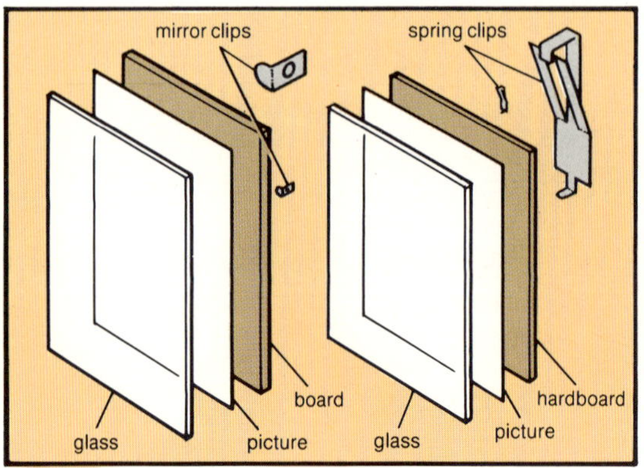

METAL FRAMES

Attractive frames can be made relatively cheaply by using one of the several metal framing sections that are available. The sections are made of rolled or extruded aluminium, usually with a bright, chemically applied finish that gives a silver or golden colour to the frame. The framing sections are machine-mitred to length and then slipped on to the glass/picture/backing board sandwich, which is retained in place by internal spring clips. The corners of the frame are held together by metal corner clamps, which are pulled tightly into the inside of the rear flanges of the frame by clamping screws which push against an internal face.

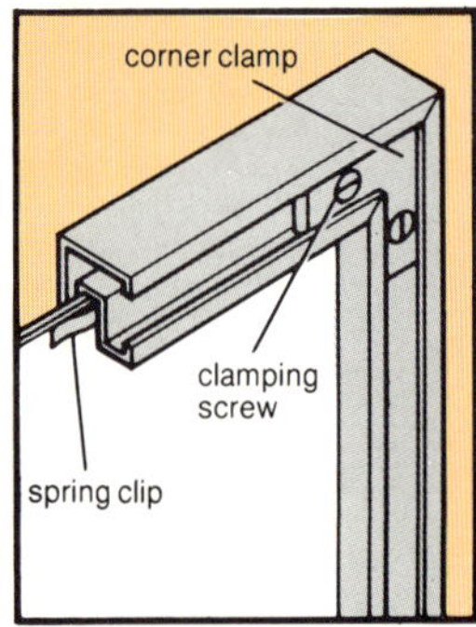

BLOCK MOUNTING

One of the cheapest ways of protecting and presenting a picture attractively is to use block mounting. Here a sandwich of heat-sealing film, the picture and hot-bonding film is placed on a sheet of chipboard and the whole is subjected to a heated press. The edges of the chipboard are usually chamfered to the size of the picture and painted matt black, although other colours can be specified. The front film, which provides permanent protection for the picture, is washable.

WAYS OF MOUNTING 2

MOUNT VARIATIONS

Except in the case of water colours, mounts are a matter of personal choice. For water colours they are essential, because no water colour should be allowed to rest directly behind the picture glass. Room-temperature variations, coupled with trapped moisture, can cause minute quantities of condensation on the back of the glass, which is enough to ruin a water colour. The thickness of the mount card is sufficient to protect the painting against this hazard.

Reverse mounts can be used when the picture or material to be displayed cannot or must not be hot-bonded to a backing board. This would apply in the case of a picture with archival value, which might need to be removed later, intact and unaltered, or to a piece of fine lace or old parchment. The picture or material is simply laid on to coloured mount card and is trapped in place behind the glass. While material will lie satisfactorily flat, buckling of paper cannot be avoided.

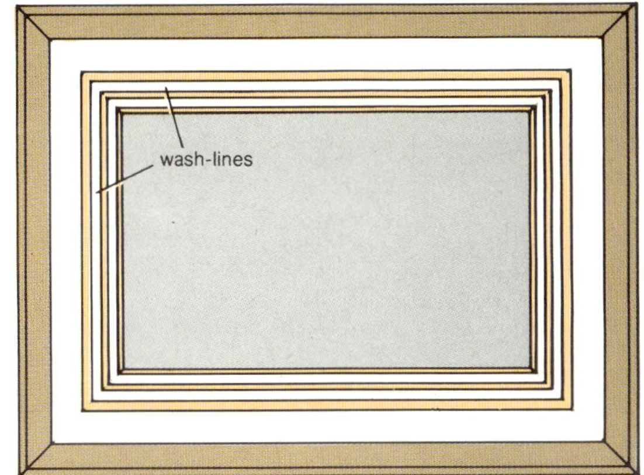

Mounts can themselves be decorated by 'wash-line', in which the mount, after cutting, has fine single or double lines drawn around the aperture. The lines may be black or coloured, and often the space between double lines is filled in with a light colour wash.

SLIPS

Slips are 'add-on' framing sections to augment the shape and appearance of the main frame. They are usually simpler in shape than main frames, often tapered, and sometimes have a very light additional moulding, in another colour, on their inside edges. They can be in plain wood, or can carry different finishes in paint and in materials such as hessian and velvet. Most professional framers carry stocks of such materials, in ranges of colours, that can be cut and stuck to any of the slips that are available, providing a totally custom-made frame for a special picture.

The extra thickness of a slip may call for an additional back frame, which is coloured and finished to match the main frame, but mouldings with extra-deep rebates, often used for oil paintings, may be used instead.

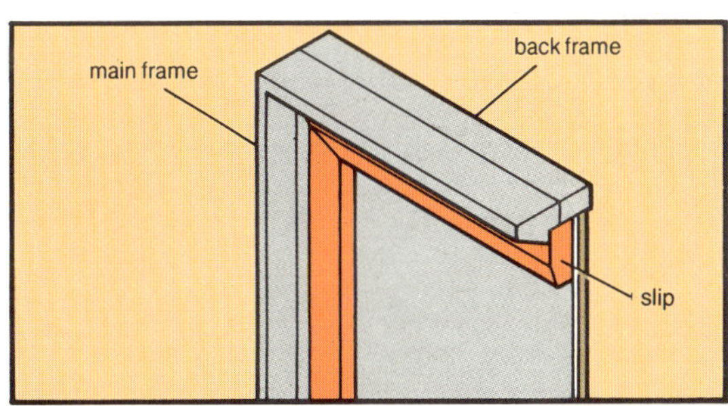

FRAME AND MOUNT SIZES

The appearance of a picture can be spoilt if the sizes of the chosen frame and mount are out of proportion with the picture. The width of the frame moulding, when viewed from the front, should be about one-twentieth of the longest dimension of the overall picture. If a mount is to be fitted, its nominal width should be not less than twice that of the moulding: i.e. about one-tenth of the longest dimension. If the complete picture is to be 500mm (20in.) long, the moulding should be 25mm (1in.) wide, and the mount 50mm (2in.) wide.

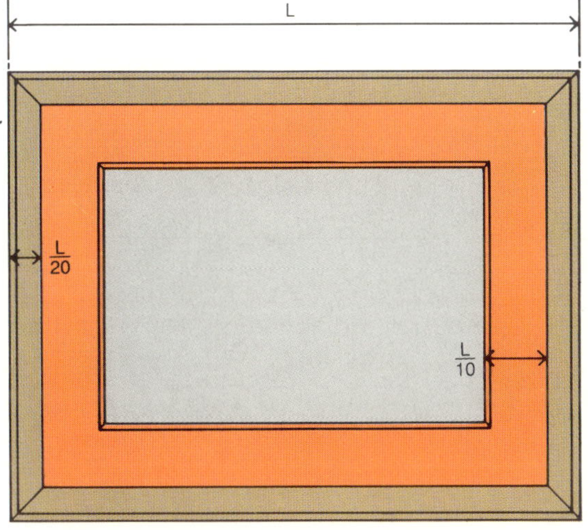

This proportioning is not only a matter of aesthetics. It concerns structural strength and safety too, because the width of the moulding determines its capacity to carry the weight of the picture glass and controls the size of the hanging eyes.

COLOURS AND TEXTURES

Choosing the colour and the texture of a frame and mount to suit a particular picture can be made a little easier by following some general guide lines that will help to ensure the most attractive presentation.

The colours of the frame and the mount should either contrast or blend with each other, the colour of the wall on which the picture is to be hung, and the general tone of the picture itself. Here 'tone' refers not only to the tints in the picture but to its content as well.

The frame acts as a transfer colour between the mount and the wall, blending in with both but with sufficient contrast to delineate it clearly. If the wall is white, a white frame would be lost against it, but at the same time a dark-coloured frame must not clash with the chosen colour of the mount. This is where multi-coloured frames, with fine stripes of colour or gold on a background colour, or with inserts of hessian, become useful. So does double framing, in which the gap between the two frames can be used as a transfer colour. Some examples follow.

Wall colour	Picture tone	Mount colour	Frame colour
white	blue – soft	medium blue	dark blue stripe
white	white/red – harsh	red/orange	aluminium/black
pale blue	blue – soft	dark blue	white/gold
pale blue	white/red – harsh	dark grey	black/gold
dark brown	blue – soft	grey-blue	striped oak
dark brown	white/red – harsh	dark brown	white

MOUNT PROPORTIONS: THE 'GOLDEN RATIO'

Modern practice calls for cutting mount apertures at a constant width from the edge of the mount because it is easier, quicker, and more economical to set the machine for constant-width cutting.

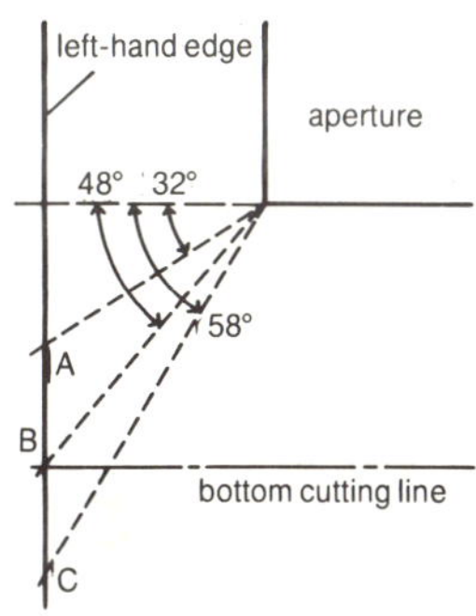

Many older pictures, and some modern ones too, use a deeper base for the mount, particularly for vertical pictures, and sometimes for horizontal pictures where the increase in width at the base is subtle but perceptible. The use of such extra depth is a matter of personal taste, but without it the constant-width mounted picture appears to be 'sunk' in its frame.

The amount of extra depth of the base is founded on the 'golden ratio', familiar to the ancient Greeks and to medieval and Renaissance mathematicians. The ratio is related to a series of numbers in which each number is the sum of the preceding two, i.e. 1, 2, 3, 5, 8, 13, 21, 34, etc. If such numbers are applied to any object's height and width, the resulting rectangle is said to be particularly attractive to the eye. The higher the numbers, the more closely they approach the golden ratio of 1.62:1. One of the peculiar properties of the golden rectangle is that cutting a square off it leaves another golden rectangle, and cutting a square off that leaves another, and so on.

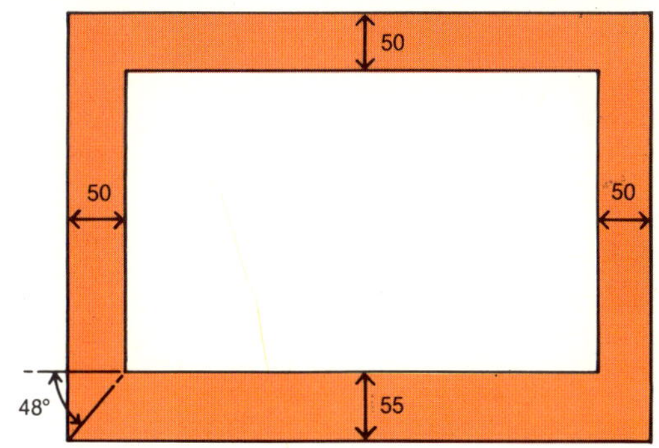

FRAMING 1

MOULDINGS

The most complex job in home picture framing is making the frame. Before embarking on the job consider the availability of tools, because what is available determines the type of frame moulding that should be chosen.

If you own a bench saw or bandsaw with tilting tables, a bench sander and planer and a drill press, you can choose practically any moulding because you can achieve the perfect 45° mitres required at each frame corner. Without that perfection, badly-made mitres can never be corrected on finished mouldings (i.e. already coloured when purchased) without damaging the finish or showing ugly fillings in the frame corners.

You should therefore buy unfinished raw-timber moulding, which can be subsequently filled with plastic wood if errors appear. It is coloured and finished after frame assembly.

Make your choice of moulding. Check that the rebate depth is adequate for your glass, picture and backing board.

THE TRICK

Make sure that you can cut all four frame members out of one piece of moulding, even if this means buying a longer piece. While two shorter pieces might appear to be identical, they will probably differ by a fraction of a millimetre; with this difference, the mitres will never match.

Finally, check the entire length of the moulding for damage or blemishes. If any are apparent, reject it.

MEASURING

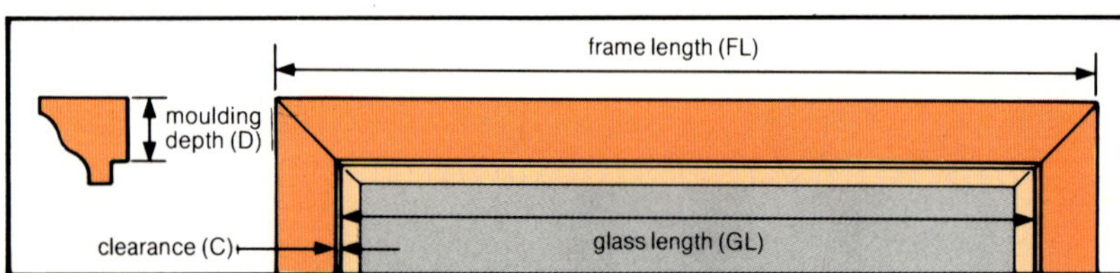

Determine the overall length and width of a frame as follows:

1. Measure the moulding depth D. (This does not include the depth of the moulding rebate.)
2. Measure the length of the glass GL. It is best to cut the glass before making the frame because it is easier to adjust the frame size to a piece of glass than vice versa.
3. Decide frame-to-glass clearance C. Up to 500mm (20in.) length, this should be taken as 1mm (1/32in.). For larger pictures, take 2mm (1/16in.). Then the overall length of the moulding to be cut is:

$FL = GL + 2D + 2C$ or, in non-mathematical terms:

Frame length = Glass length plus twice moulding depth plus twice the clearance.

The same formula applies to the height of the picture, based on glass height. If the glass is 500mm (20in.) long and the moulding depth is 20mm (3/4in.), then the frame length is:

$500 + (2 \times 20) + (2 \times 1) = 542$mm.

MARKING OFF

The moulding now needs to be marked off to the dimensions calculated above. Two tools are required: the first is a 90° carpenter's try-square. Draw two lines across the outside of the moulding, spaced at the correct distance apart to give the calculated frame length. Use a hard-grade carpenter's pencil to draw the lines: a properly sharpened carpenter's pencil (sanded flat to a chisel point) will draw the line right up against the edge of the square without blunting, which a round pencil cannot do.

The second tool is a 45° try-square with which 45° lines are drawn across the back of the moulding, starting from where the 90° lines touch the back face. These should be drawn clearly and sharply because they will be used later when bringing the moulding exactly to length.

Make sure that the 45° lines are pointing the right way! It is all too easy to find that the mitres are suited only to an inside-out frame.

THE TRICK

Remember that the outside edge of the frame is the longest dimension, and that the 45° lines must point inwards from the ends of the frame.

CUTTING

Cutting the moulding to length can be done by machine or by hand. The exact point of cutting is determined by what finishing tools are available.

If your workshop does not have a bench sander or planer or a planing jig, the moulding must be cut exactly on the 45° lines drawn on the back of the moulding; no further finishing can be applied to the mitred ends. Any attempt to sand or plane them to length by hand, will wreck the accuracy of the mitres, and expose open joints, at the front of the frame and round its edges, when assembled. In this situation, it is best to use unfinished raw-timber moulding.

Unless you own a tilting table bandsaw, the moulding must be hand-sawn to length using a mitring jig. Many makes are available in d-i-y shops; the best have adjustable saw guides, which can be set to fit the blade thickness of the saw to be used. A fine-tooth (24 teeth to the inch) tenon saw is the best tool for the job, reserved exclusively for cutting mouldings. The height of the blade (from the teeth to the blade stiffener) must ensure that the stiffener does not foul the tops of the blade guides. They should be set so that the blade just slides freely within them.

The moulding is placed in the mitring jig with the clamping vice run up lightly against it so that it can be slid into the correct position for cutting. The arrow shows how the 45° drawn line should be offset from the cutting line to allow for machine finishing later.

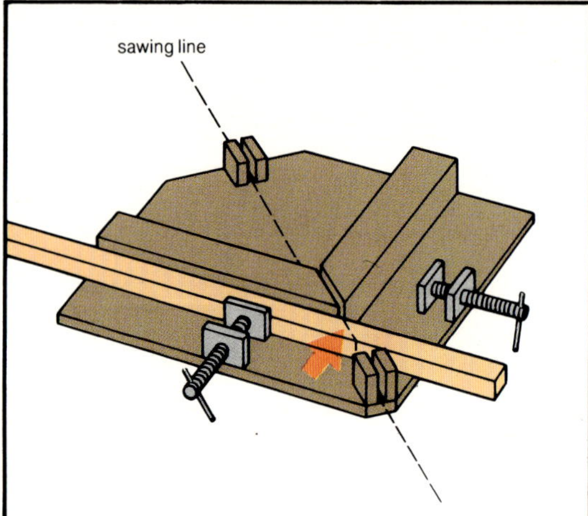

THE TRICK

With machinery or jigs available for finishing mitres, the cutting line should be offset by about 1mm (1/32in.).

If these are absent the line must be brought exactly to the edge of the saw.

It is easiest to have this line visible when lining up, with the moulding clamped backface-up in the jig; this is quite acceptable if the mitre is to be machine- or jig-finished later. However, if the sawing has to take place exactly on the line, then the moulding must be placed backface-down so that the saw cuts cleanly into the front of the moulding and leaves the furry edge at the back; this can be sanded off later. As the 45° line is no longer visible, position the moulding so that the first 90° measurement line, drawn on its outer edge, falls just below the edge of the saw.

With the moulding correctly positioned, the clamping vice is tightened up, ensuring that the moulding is lying flat and snug against its wall. Use very little pressure – hardly more than the weight of the saw – to saw gently through the moulding. Then reset the jig for the next cut.

FRAMING 2

MITRE SANDING

A rotary sanding machine, with a tilting table, will provide the perfect 45° mitre corner after rough cutting.

THE TRICK

Check the accuracy of the 45° table-tilt marker by sanding up two pieces of scrap hardwood or moulding in it and placing them together inside a 90° try-square.

It will often be found that the '45°' is way out, and the mitre will exhibit a yawning gap at one extremity. Correct the table marker accordingly.

Without a tilting table, a 45° sanding jig must be made from scrap pieces of hardwood. Its accuracy can be checked as above. It is essential that the front edge of the sanding table, on which the jig slides, must be exactly parallel to the face of the rotary sander. If the sander has to be set up each time as an accessory to a power drill, its accuracy must also be checked each time.

MITRE PLANING

The accomplished do-it-yourselfer can construct his own planing jig, sized to suit his largest plane. The steel runner plate must be thin enough to clear the plane blade as it slides by, and the bottom of the brass shoe must be exactly level with the bottom of the runner. All other dimensions are to choice. Note that the plane blade must be really sharp. The rough-cut moulding is clamped to the jig with a G-cramp, using a wood 'spreader'. The moulding is passed forward over the inverted plane blade, which is set to minimum cut. At each pass, a light planing cut is taken off the moulding, initially at a slight angle. When the brass shoe touches the base of the plane, the mitre is smoothly finished exactly square, at 45°.

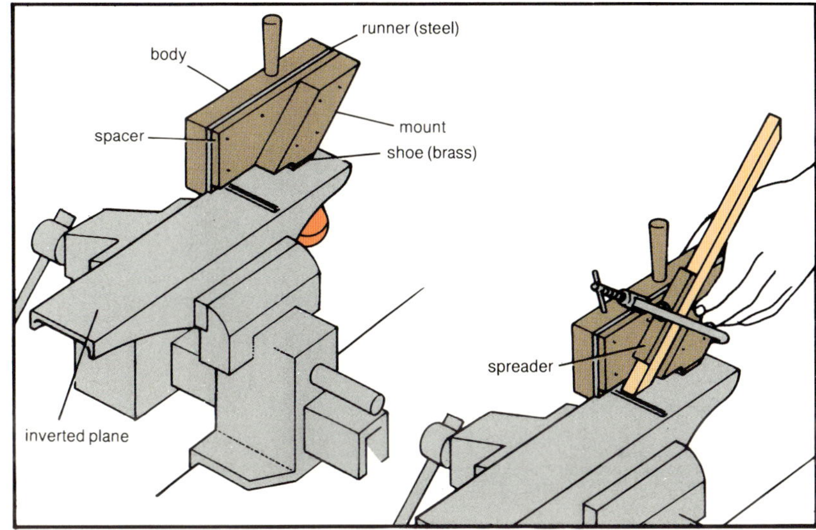

FRAME JOINTING

The joints are held together by adhesive, not pins. The pins are simply to hold the mitred corners together while the adhesive sets. If a belt corner cramp is available and sufficient care is taken that the whole assembly is dead square, there is no need for pins at all.

The operation is called 'pinning' because it uses moulding pins, not panel pins or nails. Only moulding pins are fine enough to drive into hardwood mouldings so near to the cut end of the wood without splitting it. Even then their position must be carefully controlled.

As the moulding sections get larger, they require bigger pins. The bigger the pin the more liable it is to split the timber unless a pilot hole is drilled first. This should be a fraction under the size of the pin.

THE TRICK

The correct drill is selected by placing the pin in the jaws of a sliding caliper and closing the jaws tightly on it. Lock them and remove the pin. Now select a drill that just slides loosely into the jaws. This means having available drills in $\frac{1}{2}$mm or $\frac{1}{64}$in. steps.

If the mitres have been finished to an exact and smooth 45°, square to the moulding, there is no need to use an assembly jig because they will pull the frame square and flat as they are joined.

Clamp the first piece of moulding, face up, to the front edge of the worktable, using one or two G-cramps and a spreader to protect the moulding face. Brush a smear of PVA woodworking adhesive onto the right-hand mitred end and bring the next piece of moulding in contact with it. Place the first pin in position, and lightly tap it into the moulding until it is rigid but has not yet broken through.

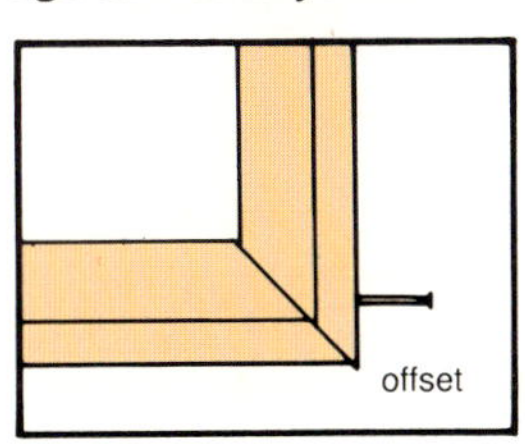

Now position the second piece of moulding so that it is offset from the clamped piece to overcome the subsequent slip when driving the pin home. How much offset to apply becomes a matter of habit after some practice. Guiding the left piece with your left hand, drive the pin in further, ensuring that, as it bites in, the two mouldings are absolutely flush at the front and the two mitres are exactly matched. If satisfied, drive the pin home, and put in the second pin.

If not satisfied, pull out the half-driven pin with a pair of pliers, taking care not to damage the moulding, and try again.

Now deal with excess glue in the joint. If the right amount of adhesive has been applied and the joint is good and tight after pinning, a slight 'weep' of adhesive should appear all round the joint. If you are using finished moulding, wipe it off.

THE TRICK

If using unfinished moulding, leave it to dry a little, then cut it away with a sharp craft knife. If you attempt to wipe it away while wet, it will smear into the grain and prevent the wood from accepting stain or other finishes later.

Repeat the process for the second joint, with the second piece of moulding clamped to the table, and for the third. At the final joint, the first piece of moulding will be hovering around, waiting to be joined. It will have to be lifted slightly to get the glue brush onto the final mitre.

Remove the assembled frame from the table, check it for flatness and squareness and leave to dry. If the mitres are perfect, it should be flat and square. If not, you may have to twist or 'lozenge' it very slightly; whereupon a gap will appear in one corner.

If the mitres are not perfect, assemble the frame in a mitring jig. The first two pieces are laid into the jig, again with a smear of woodworking adhesive on one mitre face, and are pushed tightly together. When the joint appears flush and square, the two pieces are clamped up tightly with the jig vice jaws, and the corner pins are driven in. The process is repeated for the other three corners.

Pilot holes for bigger pins can be drilled with the pieces clamped into a mitring jig, using a drill, but extra-long drills may be required.

THE TRICK

If the holes are pre-drilled before assembly, a vertical drill press should be used to ensure that the holes are exactly square to the moulding.

If they are not, driving pins into angled holes will cause uncontrollable slip during assembly, and no amount of offset will overcome it. Accurate, square-drilled pilot holes overcome slip automatically, because the pin begins to bite immediately driving starts, and no offsetting is necessary.

MOUNTS AND BACKING BOARDS

MARKING OFF MOUNTS

Lay the mount card face down on a clean flat surface, and mark off its overall length and depth along two adjacent edges. From these marks, draw the two opposing edges, making sure that the drawn lines are exactly at right angles to the card edges. A large set-square is best, with one edge laid along the card edge and the other used to draw the first part of the lines. Continue the lines until they form the complete rectangle, and check it again for accuracy and squareness.

Cut the card to size, using a Stanley knife with a new sharp blade. Use a steel straight-edge to guide it. The best surface to cut on is thick glass but, if this is not available, use thick cardboard or hardboard. Now mark out the aperture (see page 315).

MOUNT CUTTING

If the mount card is very thin (less than 1mm (1/32in.)), mitre-cutting is not worth the effort, because the mitre will be practically invisible. If the card is the thicker '6-sheet' or '10-sheet', then mitring is worth while.

A successful mitre cut can be made with no more than a good straight-edge and a steady hand. It is best to adopt a cutting angle of 60°, because it is very difficult to hold a steady 45° while cutting, whereas a constant 60° can be achieved after a little practice.

With the aperture marked out on the back of the card, place down the straight-edge a little distance away from the first line to be cut so that the angled knife will enter the card exactly on the line as shown.

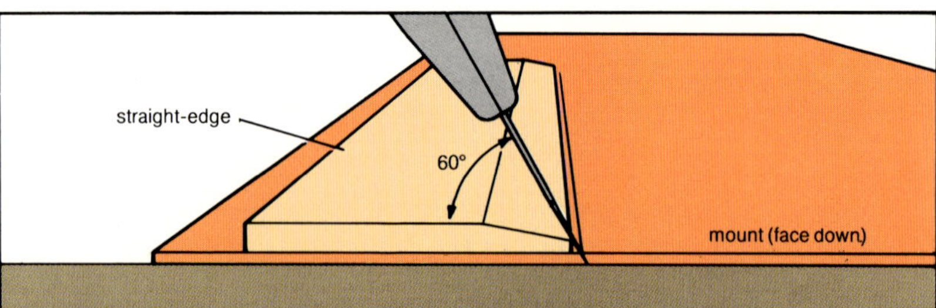

THE TRICK

Holding the straight-edge very firmly, start the cut a little way beyond the end of the line, and make a first shallow cut along the line, continuing a little beyond its marked end.

The small over-runs at the beginning and end are necessary to ensure a full cut-out, but they must not be taken so deep that the excess cutting appears on the front. A little practice on a scrap piece of mount card will quickly show the amount needed. For mount cards 1.5mm (1/16in.) thick, an over-run of 3mm (1/8in.) at each end will usually provide a perfect mitred corner with no evidence of over-cutting on the front.

If you find it difficult to hold the straight-edge firmly enough, clamp it down with G-cramps, so positioned that they do not interfere with the cut.

Continue cutting lightly from end to end of the line, including the over-runs, maintaining the cutting angle as closely as possible, until the blade is felt to cut through the card.

THE TRICK

Cut on glass if possible, because the blade will suddenly slip cleanly through without more effort, and glass prevents a slight 'burr' being raised on the front face.

Repeat on the other three sides, then turn the card over to examine on the front face. If completed fully, a full rectangle will appear, and the centre can be simply pushed out from behind. If incomplete, check where the edges have to be cut further, turn the card face down again, and gently complete the missing cuts, maintaining the original cutting angle and avoiding cutting beyond the original over-run limits.

BACKING BOARDS

Backing boards should be as stiff as possible, but thin enough that the frame moulding rebate will accept the sandwich of glass, mount, picture and board.

If sufficient rebate depth is available, the best material is 3mm (1/8in.) hardboard, machine-sawn to size and sanded on all edges. Most hardware shops will cut hardboard to the size required. If there is insufficient rebate depth, 2mm (1/16in.) cardboard may be used, cut to size with a Stanley knife, but this is the minimum thickness for pictures up to 500mm (20in.) in length. If the sandwich, with a 2mm (1/16in.) backing board, cannot be accommodated, a larger frame moulding, with a deeper rebate, must be used.

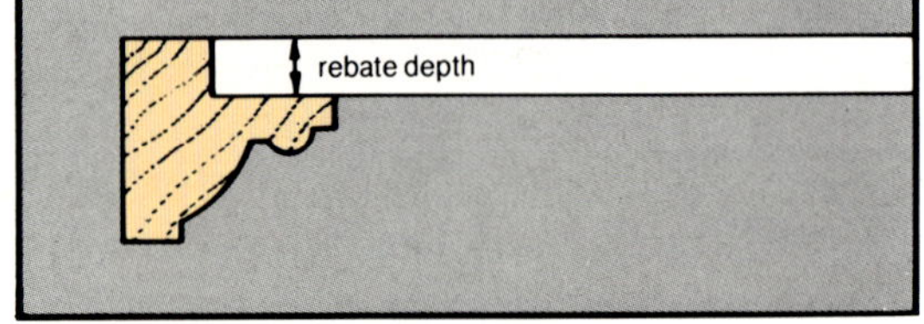

THE TRICK

Between 500mm (20in.) and 1m. (3ft 3in.), 3mm (1/8in.) or thicker hardboard must be used. Over 1m. (3ft 3in.), the backing board must be of plywood at least 6mm (1/4in.) thick.

FABRICATED MITRE MOUNTS

Very attractive two-colour mitred mounts can be made without resorting to angled cutting of mount boards. The mitres are made of folded paper strips stuck to a thick board and covered with a 'cover sheet' of another colour.

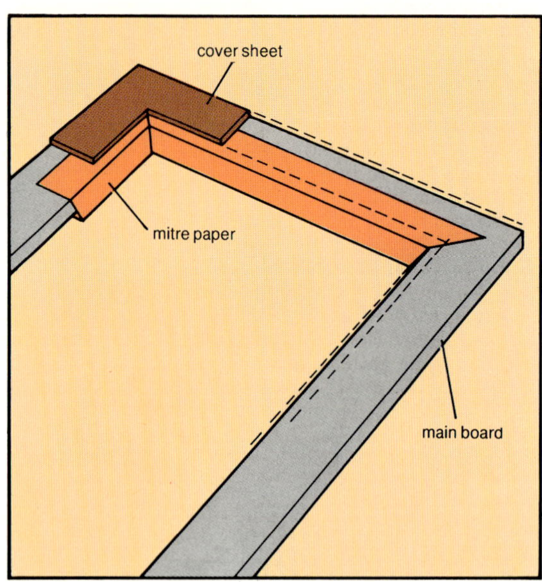

The main mount board can be made of thick cardboard, hardboard or wood. With cardboard, cut the mount as one piece, using a Stanley knife and a steel straight-edge. Do not worry about over-runs at the corners, as they will not be seen again. With hardboard, it is best to use strips cut to the main board width, with the rough faces glued together. Each butt joint (see page 35) is supported by the pieces of the opposing half. With wood, glued butt joints are adequate.

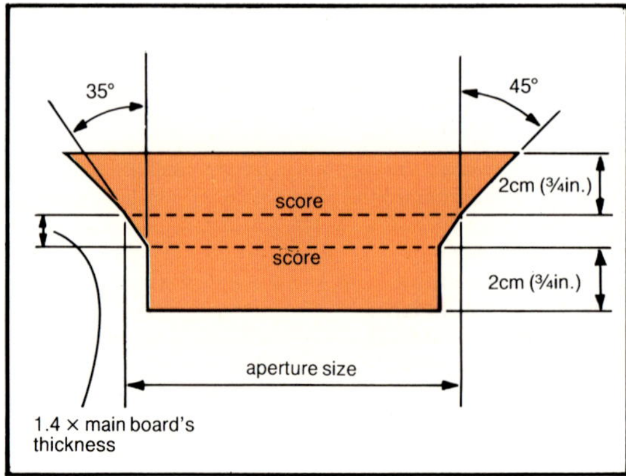

The mitres can be made from any good-quality white or coloured paper. After cutting out, the strips are folded along the score lines and are glued to the mount board as shown with the central section of each strip sloping down at 45°. The width of the central section (1.4 times the board thickness) ensures that this angle is achieved automatically when the two outer sections are glued flat to the board without bending the paper. The 35° angles cut at the ends of the strips also ensure that the mitre ends match properly.

THE TRICK

These ends may be touched with a little glue from behind.

Finally the cover sheet, also made from good-quality paper in a contrasting or matching colour, is cut and glued to the front. Its aperture is cut a fraction larger than the main board (say 1–2mm (1/32–1/16in.) all round) so that a thin stripe of the mitre paper can be seen inside it.

When deciding the size of the main board aperture, remember that the paper mitres will reduce the final aperture by the thickness of the main board all round; the main board aperture should be enlarged accordingly.

GLASS

The thinnest glass readily available from most suppliers is about 2mm (1/16in.) thick. It is suitable for pictures up to 500mm (20in.) in length. For larger pictures, 3mm (1/8in.) glass should be used. 2mm (1/16in.) glass is unnecessarily thick for smaller pictures (below 250mm (10in.) in length) where 1mm (1/32in.) is adequate, but these thinner glasses are very difficult to obtain now.

CUTTING

For framing one or two pictures, the quickest, easiest and cheapest way is to have it cut by a local glass supplier. When ordering the glass, specify the thickness needed, and remember the clearance required between glass and frame (see page 316) if the frame has already been made. The supplier will normally cut to an accuracy of 1mm (1/32in.). If many pictures are to be framed, and particularly if stocks of glass from old frames are available, then it becomes more economic to cut your own.

Cutting glass can be a frustrating, disappointing (and expensive) process unless you have the right equipment. You need: a flat table, large enough to accommodate the uncut sheet; a thick steel straight-edge, longer than the longest dimension of the uncut glass; a measuring rule; a glass-marking pencil or felt-tipped pen; a piece of old blanket to cover the table; and a glass-cutting tool.

The last item will make or, literally, break the job: it must be sharp. Throw away any old glass-cutting tools whose history you do not know; they will cost more in broken glass than a new one.

THE TRICK

The best type to buy is one with five or six numbered cutting wheels set into a rotating head. Start with No.1 wheel, and use it for not more than 10m. (30ft) of cutting, keeping a record of the length of cuts. Then change to No.2 wheel, and so on until all six wheels are used up. That will cover a lot of pictures.

To cut the glass, proceed as follows. Lay the uncut glass on the blanket-covered table. Check that two adjacent edges are dead square by laying a 90° try-square at the corner.

THE TRICK

If they are not, draw a line at right angles to one of the edges, using the try-square and the glass marker, at least 50mm (2in.) from the un-square edge, because this will be one of the cuts.

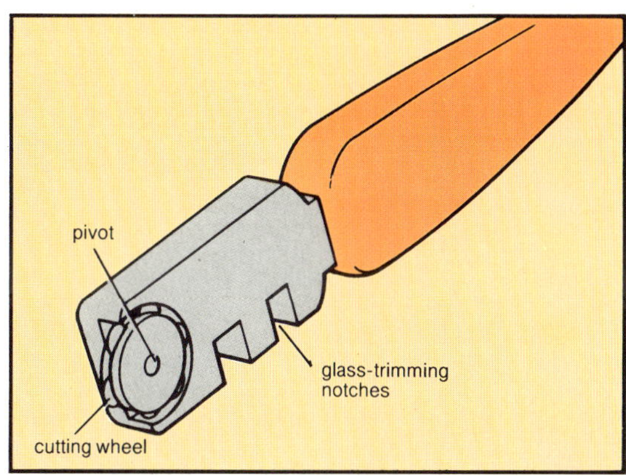

Using either the ready-squared edges, or one edge and the newly drawn line, lay out the rectangular shape to be cut, measuring as carefully as possible. Check for squareness with a draftsman's set-square. When satisfied that the dimensions are correct, and that no cutting line falls less than 50mm (2in.) from an uncut edge (to ensure a clean snap) you are ready to begin.

Lay the straight-edge near the first line to be cut so that the larger of the two pieces, after cutting, will be on your left (if you are right-handed). Bring the straight-edge up to the line, from the left, leaving a clearance so that the cutting wheel will fall on the line itself. With most glass-cutting tools, this clearance is about 3mm (1/8in.).

Hold the straight-edge very firmly with your left hand and lay the cutting wheel onto the glass.

THE TRICK

Draw it down the straight-edge using no more pressure than with a ball-point pen on a sheet of paper. If you have the right pressure, there should be no more than the faintest 'hiss' as the wheel runs down the glass, leaving behind it a faint grey line.

Crackling noises reveal excessive pressure, or a blunt wheel, either of which will ruin the cut.

Lift up the glass, and slide the straight-edge under it, lining up the straight-edge so that its right-hand edge lies directly under the line, with the piece to be broken off sticking up in the air a little. Holding the main (left) piece firmly with your left hand, place the palm of your right hand half-way along the right-hand piece and push gently. It will snap off instantly and cleanly. Repeat for the other edges.

Sometimes the break line will run away from the drawn line towards the end of the cut. If the run-off is into the final rectangle, the piece must be discarded and used for a smaller picture. If the run-off is outwards, it can be corrected by gently bending the excess piece downwards, either with pliers or with the slots found in most glass-cutting tools. It will break away, still leaving a small excess pinnacle of glass. This may be small enough to fall within the glass-frame clearance already allowed. If not, it may be gently broken away with a pair of pliers, until there is simply an uneven section of line left.

THE TRICK

In all such attempts at correction, glass fragments will fly, so wear goggles or spectacles.

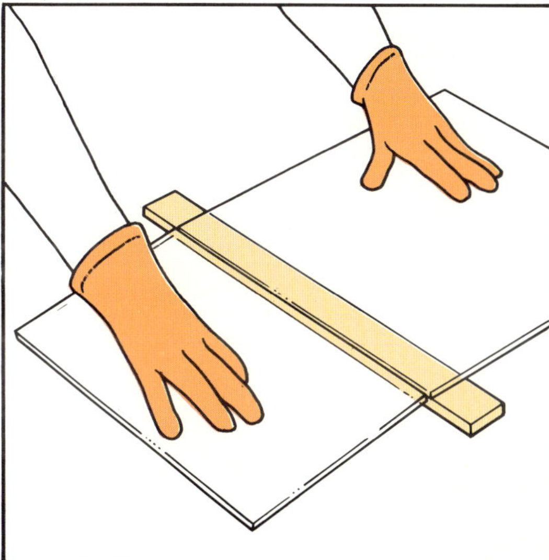

GLASS CLEANING

The glass is cleaned in two stages: first wet, before picture assembly; and then dry, during and after assembly (see page 321).

The sheet of glass is held in a sink, or washing-up bowl, filled with warm soapy water. Rub the warm water over both surfaces of the glass, using a dish cloth, turning the glass when necessary to get all of it under water. When it is free of dirt and greasy marks, take it out and stand it up to drain. When nearly dry, lay it on a clean tea towel, and buff the upper surface lightly with another. Using the second towel to prevent your fingers touching the glass, turn it over and buff the other side. Still using a towel, lift it up and lightly dust off bits of lint until it is gleamingly clean. Wrap in a sheet of newspaper, ready for assembly.

PICTURE PREPARATION

All the work described so far is for the benefit of the picture itself. It must now be prepared for framing. The preparation consists of two processes: trimming it to size, and bonding it or preparing it for hanging within the frame.

TRIMMING

Trimming might be required because the finished frame is slightly undersized. The picture must be cut down to the size of the glass, to give the same clearance. Again, the picture, particularly if it is a print, may have an excessively wide border which does not suit the mount or frame.

In either case, trimming is accomplished by drawing light pencil lines at the required distances from the picture edges, and cutting with a sharp Stanley knife and a steel straight-edge. Again, a sheet of glass is the best material to cut on (see page 36).

THE TRICK

The straight-edge should be laid on a clean piece of paper to ensure that it does not mark the picture.

BONDING

There are two ways of overcoming the buckling problem. The first is to 'hang' the picture within the frame, if it appears adequately stiff in itself. The second is to use bonding techniques that can be accomplished in the home.

'HANGING'

'Hanging' the picture consists simply of attaching it to the back of the mount with two short pieces of clear adhesive tape near the top corners. A long strip must not be used, nor should any other pieces be placed at the sides or at the bottom, because differential expansion and contraction between mount and the picture will inevitably lead to ugly buckling gaps.

THE TRICK

This can only work if the picture is already mounted or painted on thin card, or on very heavyweight water-colour paper.

If it is thinner, and particularly if it is a paper print or a photograph, one of the two bonding processes must be used – dry or wet.

DRY BONDING

Dry bonding is the better process, but the more expensive. It uses double-sided adhesive sheet, available from well-stocked artists' and drawing-office suppliers. It comes in rolls or large sheets that can be cut to size. The protective paper on one side is pulled off, and the sheet is carefully smoothed down onto the backing board and trimmed to size. Then the front protective paper is peeled off, and the picture is carefully smoothed down onto the sheet. Great care must be taken to ensure that the picture is lined up properly, because once it is down it can never be lifted again.

Being a dry process, this cannot cause staining of any type of picture. The bonding sheet effectively protects the picture from staining chemicals from the backing board.

WET BONDING

Wet bonding can be achieved satisfactorily only with spray adhesive. Glues in bottles or tubes cannot be controlled sufficiently to achieve a perfectly flat finish. Many of them can 'weep' chemicals through the picture, staining it permanently.

Unless the backing board is known to be of picture-framing quality, the picture must not be bonded down to it with spray adhesive.

THE TRICK

The picture must be bonded down to a stiffening sheet known to be free of staining chemicals, such as Bristol board or very heavy-quality white cartridge paper of at least 200g per square metre weight. For small pictures, white poster card or folders is satisfactory.

The white stiffening sheet should be left over-size before bonding, so that the picture can be laid on without worrying about exact positioning. The picture is held vertically, preferably by a pair of large tweezers, and the spray adhesive is applied to the back, following instructions. When the surface is totally covered with a thin, almost invisible layer of adhesive, lay it on the stiffener and smooth flat. The stiffener is then trimmed to the size of the picture.

THE TRICK

Spray adhesives are dangerous. They are inflammable and contain chemicals that must not be inhaled. Use them only in a well-ventilated room.

FINISHING

A frame made of finished, coloured moulding with accurate mitres needs no finishing except for the touching-up of pin heads and any tiny chips on the outer edges of the mitres. Touching up is best done with a small brush and model paints. A collection of basic colours in matt finish, plus black, white and brown, can be mixed together in tiny quantities to give almost any colour.

Unfinished raw-timber frames need further treatment. First, excess adhesive must be cut away with a sharp blade (see page 317). Second, if the mitres are not perfect, the gaps must be filled with plastic wood, preferably in a colour matching that of the raw timber. The plastic wood should protrude from the gaps, and be cut flush with the wood surface just before it goes hard. Attempts to sand it away after hardening will only damage the nearby timber, but a very fine (400 grit) paper can be used to smooth its surface after cutting.

The easiest and quickest finish for a raw-timber frame is stain and polish. Wood stain can be bought in a variety of colours and applied by brush or cloth. It runs into the wood quickly and smoothly, leaving no brush marks, and can be deepened in tone by successive applications. When a satisfactory tone is attained, it is finished by wiping on a good-quality wax polish with a soft, lint-free cloth. Then rub down until a soft gleam appears. Second and third coats of polish, after the previous coats have dried, provide more attractive depth to the finish, which is permanent.

A heavier-duty finish is stain and varnish.

THE TRICK

Varnish should always be applied from an aerosol, or thinned down with white spirit so that it flows onto the frame almost as freely as water, with repeat coats after each has dried.

Thick varnish, applied by brush, gives an unappealing, non-professional look to a finished frame.

Paint must be applied by aerosol or spray-gun, after the timber has been sealed by varnish. Once the timber is sealed, any spray-paint will adhere satisfactorily, including matt, semi-gloss or gloss automobile paints. With sufficient patience and care, striped effects can be obtained by laying down a base colour and then using masking tape to leave strips onto which other colours can be sprayed. After such spray-painting, no further finishing is needed.

ASSEMBLY AND FINISHING

INSERTION

Place the frame, front down, on a piece of old blanket, unwrap the clean glass, and lay it into the frame.

THE TRICK

If there are any signs of dirt or grease on the glass, clean its inside face by rubbing lightly over the face with a very fine (400 grit) piece of glasspaper, wrapped around a small block of wood. This effectively removes the last traces of dirt without leaving moisture in the frame.

Lay down the stiffened picture, or the stiffened picture stuck to its mount with adhesive tape, followed by the backing board.

Holding the whole assembly together, turn it face up and look very carefully for specks of dust, etc that might be lying under the glass. If any are visible, turn the picture over, take out the backing board and picture, and remove the specks. Don't rub the glass as it becomes electrostatically charged and attracts more dust, and you will be cleaning for ever. Put back the picture and backing board, and check once more for dust. If all is clear, you are ready to stake. If not, clean again, because this is your last chance to get in between the glass and the picture.

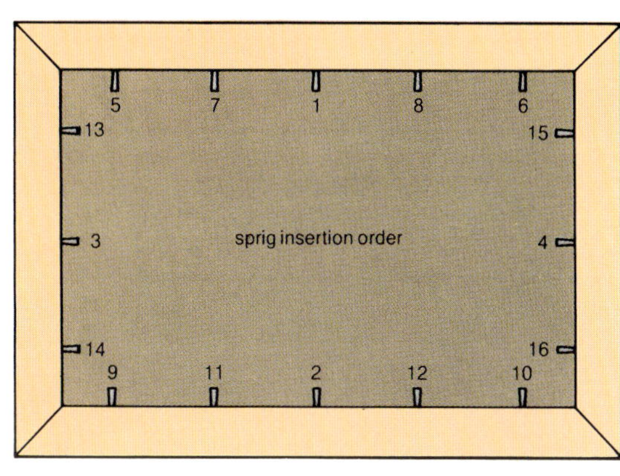

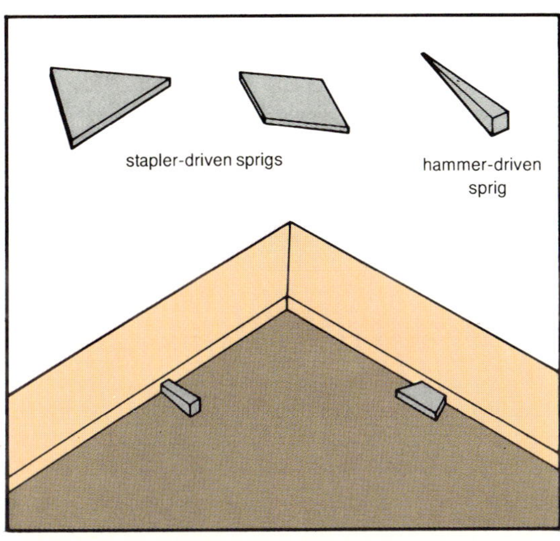

STAKING

Staking is accomplished by driving small steel 'sprigs' into the inside edges of the rebate (see page 318). The home framer must use traditional sprigs, driven in with a pin hammer. Do not use moulding or panel pins because, not being tapered like the sprig, they do not align themselves when driving in to bite down into the backing board.

THE TRICK

With the picture face-down on a piece of protective blanket, push the frame side up against a block of wood clamped to the work-bench, so that the shock of sprig-driving is taken out in the block.

Starting at the centre of one long side, place a sprig against the inside of the moulding as shown, press down on the glass/picture sandwich, and gently tap the sprig into the moulding, using a pin hammer sliding across the surface of the backing board. The sprig should be driven in to about one-third of its length. The spacing and number of sprigs depends on the size of the picture. A typical spacing is every 50mm (2in.).

SEALING

The back of the frame must be sealed, to prevent dust, mites and moisture entering, by laying down strips of adhesive tape. The tape should be pressed firmly onto the backing board and the frame, and should be trimmed so that it lies clear of the frame edge all round.

HANGING EYES

Hanging eyes should generally be placed one-third of the way down the vertical sides of the picture. Pilot holes, drilled with a hand or power drill, or bored with a bradawl, need to be made at these positions. The size of the holes depends on the size of the hanging eyes, which in turn depend on the size of the frame moulding itself. Eye sizes are always dimensioned by their overall length.

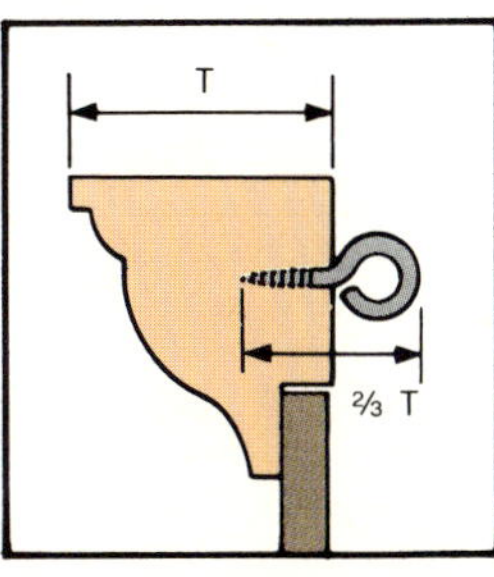

THE TRICK

The length should be two-thirds of the thickness of the frame moulding, with the eye screwed in until the circular part touches the wood.

Eyes are available in a range of sizes, and the nearest standard size should be chosen to meet the length criterion shown. Thus, for a frame moulding of 30mm (1¼in.) thickness, a 20mm (¾in.) eye should be chosen. For 20mm (¾in.) thickness, a 15mm (⅔in.) eye should be used; it is better to aim on the high side.

Length and screw size are generally related to each other. Thus a 15mm (⅔in.) eye normally has a size 4 screw, while a 35mm (1½in.) eye has a size 8 screw. These are the same sizes as those used for standard woodworking screws, and use the same pilot hole size, when working in hardwood.

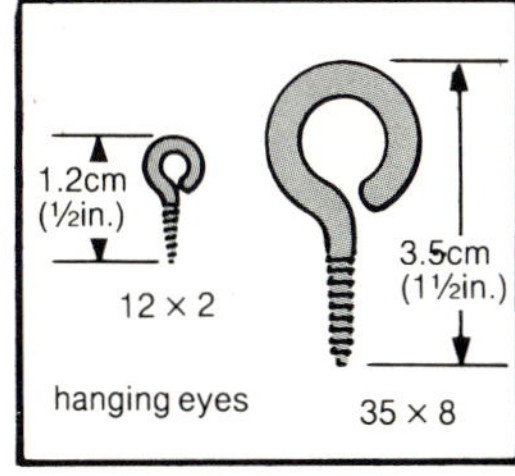

THE TRICK

It is far better to drill a pilot hole than to bore it with a bradawl, because a drilled hole gives a clean, straight and safe start to the screw thread. From size 6 upwards, boring can split the moulding, and a drill must be used.

HANGERS FOR THIN FRAMES

Thin frames fitted to large pictures cannot accept the recommended sizes of hanging eyes, so a different hanging system has to be adopted. The hanging points are transferred to the backing board, using a different form of hanger known as a 'D-ring'.

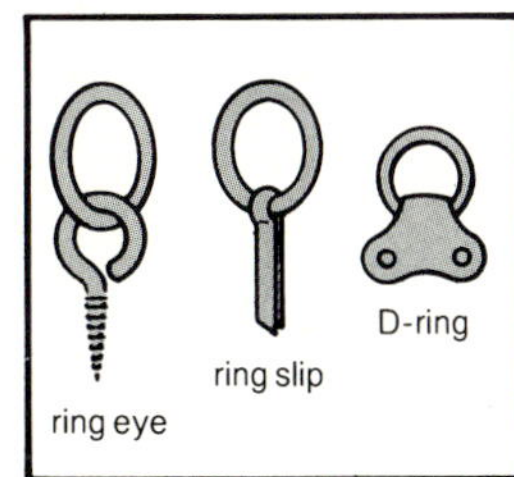

For this method, for pictures up to 2kg (5lb) in weight, 3mm (⅛in.) hardboard is the thinnest backing board which should be used. Above that weight, 6mm (¼in.) plywood must be used. D-rings cannot be fitted satisfactorily to cardboard.

Up to the 2kg (5lb) limit, one D-ring, centred near the top of the picture, is adequate. Beyond that, two should be fitted, angled inwards to line up with the hanging cord when it is fitted later.

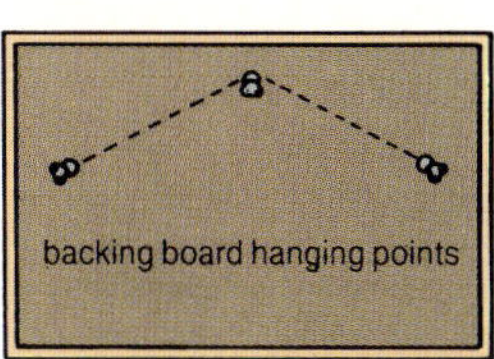

D-rings should be fitted to the backing board with bifurcated rivets. These can be hammered flat, as shown, after they have been passed through the metal hanger and the backing board, so that they do not produce bumps under the picture. It is important to ensure that the glass/picture/board sandwich is pressed tightly into the frame while staking and that an extra number of sprigs is used, so that it forms a tight assembly. If not, the weight of the glass will push the frame forwards, away from the backing board which is taking the load.

For very small and light pictures with thin frames, D-rings can be replaced by lightweight ring clips. A ring eye can be used for single-eye hanging of a small picture by inserting it at the centre of the top member of the frame, but this is rather unsightly.

THE TRICK

Ring eyes can also be used instead of normal eyes, having the advantage of hiding the hanging cord completely, because the rings pull inwards behind the frame.

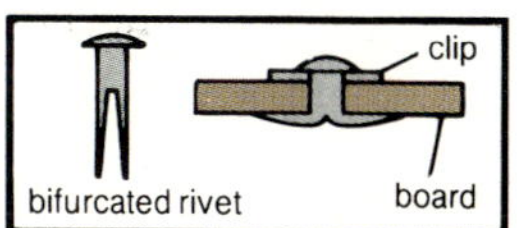

REPAIRS

DAMAGED FRAMES

The most common damage that is seen in old frames is the opening of one or more of the mitred corners.

If only one joint is damaged, the mitres can be cleaned and re-joined by glueing or fixing with a repair plate. If the other three joints are affected, the only thing to do is to dismantle it and rebuild.

To dismantle, pull and twist gently at each joint until the frame members part, taking care not to damage the sharp ends of the mitres. As the locking pins appear, insert the tips of a pair of needle-nose pliers into the

joint and push the pins out of the mouldings. As their heads come clear of the surface, pull them out with a larger pair of pliers.

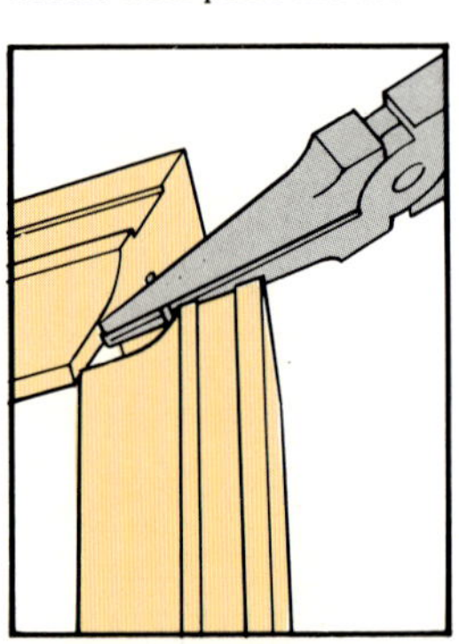

You now have four mitred pieces of frame moulding; the next stage depends on their condition. If the wood is undamaged and the finish is satisfactory, you need only prepare the mitre ends for re-jointing, which means sanding them back.

This is essential to ensure effective glueing of the new joints. Hand sanding should not be attempted because it invariably results in slightly curved surfaces, which will wreck the mitres. Jig sanding or planing will remove a fraction of a millimetre at each mitre. You must check that newly sanded opposing sides are exactly the same length. The frame is then re-assembled (see page 321). However, new moulding pins must be driven into new locations at each corner; the original pin holes are filled with plastic wood for subsequent touching-up.

If the wood itself and the paintwork are damaged, the dismembered frame provides an excellent opportunity to repair and to clean up each of the frame members. Strip the finish off with a chemical paint stripper (see page 231), or with a soft-mounted rotary sander if the shape is simple and flat. Wetting should be kept to a minimum, after which the member should be left to dry completely.

Fill chips and holes with plastic wood or Polyfilla, and sand back when dry. Sand the mitres and re-assemble the frame as above. Then re-finish the complete frame (see page 320).

PLASTER-COVERED FRAMES

Plaster-covered frames present a more daunting repair job, because damaged plaster must be replaced with new castings taken from other parts of the frame. Normally, these frames are symmetrical so that if the bottom right-hand corner is damaged, a replacement casting may be taken from the top left corner.

Castings are made by covering the area to be copied with oil (cooking oil will do) and then pressing on to it, firmly and carefully, a large lump of worked and warmed Plasticine. When the Plasticine is cool, it is carefully lifted off; the oil prevents it sticking. This mould is filled with a fine, runny, plaster mix. As the mix dries, it sinks in the middle. This depression is filled with more mix until the surface is flat when dry. The Plasticine is then peeled away from the moulding.

The damaged area on the frame is rasped and sanded away until a flat, level surface is obtained, and the sides of this surface are squared off. The back of the new moulding is also rasped and sanded flat, and its edges cut away, until it mates accurately with the surrounding plaster. A little more wet plaster is made up to act as an adhesive and a filler for the joints, the new moulding is set in place, the joints are filled, and the whole frame is left to dry.

After drying, the oil and old paint are removed with chemical stripper, the frame is washed and dried again, and the whole surface is re-finished.

PASSE-PARTOUT

Passe-partout framing tape is no longer available, but this does not prevent the home framer from producing an attractive frame using carpet tape instead. If the hardboard back and the glass have been cut to size, the only tools needed are a steel rule, a Stanley knife and a bradawl. Its limitations are that the maximum picture size is 250mm (10in.) square. Above this size, the glass may slip in the tape. The picture must be bonded down on to suitable stiff card (see page 320) to prevent it buckling.

Cut, or have cut, the glass and the 3mm (1/8in.) hardboard backing board to the dimensions of the picture or its larger mount. Mark a central point near the top of the hardboard and drill or bore a hole big enough (about 3mm (1/8in.)) to take a ring clip.

Assemble the parts as shown, with the rough side of the hardboard facing up. Push the arms of the ring clip through the hole from below, open them up and press them flat. Press the glass, picture and hardboard together to make a thin

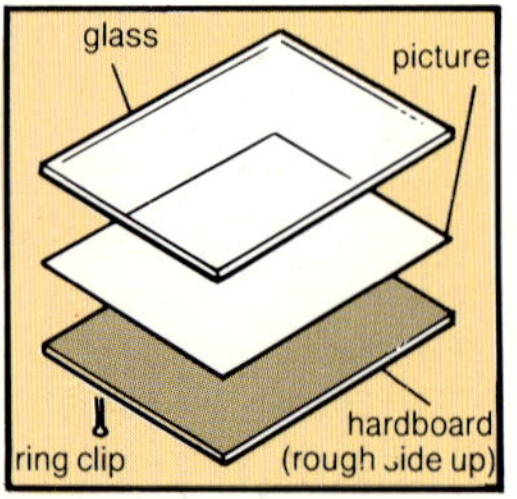

sandwich.

The best tape to use is carpet tape with a slightly stippled finish. A width of 50mm (2in.) is adequate, but wider tape may be used.

Cut a piece of tape slightly longer than the top of the picture, and peel off the protective backing sheet. Lay it over the top edge so that about 10mm (1/2in.) is covering the glass and press this firmly onto the glass. Accuracy is not necessary, because you are going to trim it straight later. Fold the tape over the edge, pressing it flat, and then again onto the smooth hardboard face at the rear, smoothing and pressing all along and making sure that the bent corners are tight and square. With a sharp blade, trim off the excess tape.

Depending on the 'straightness' of your eye, you can either trim off directly or mark off for trimming. Lay the rule at 6mm (1/4in.), parallel with the edge. Draw the blade along the rule, then peel the excess tape away. Repeat on the opposite side.

Next lay, fold and press down another piece of tape along one of the other sides, again not bothering with accuracy in laying, and trim off the excess at each end. Take care, this time, not to cut into the pieces of tape that are already there. Simply trimming off the excess width is not good enough, because the tape joints must be mitred. Draw a line at 6mm (1/4in.) from the edge, but at the ends draw two small lines at 45° (which can be estimated by eye) running to the corners of the picture. Cut these two lines first, from the face of the picture towards the corners.

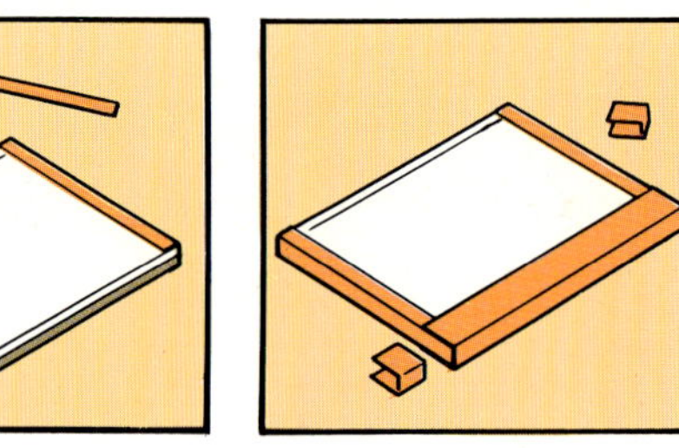

Now, with the steel rule laid firmly down at 6mm (1/4in.) from the edge, cut along the tape between the two 45° cuts, and peel away the piece as shown.

Repeat on the other side and the picture is ready to hang.

HOME SECURITY

GENERAL PREVENTION

An estimated 803,000 homes were burgled last year, and in most cases the thieves took things which were easy to remove, and which could be quickly turned into cash. There are precautions you can take to minimise the risk of it happening to you.

For completely confidential and reliable advice, go to the Crime Prevention Officer of your local police. He will be a specially trained and experienced police officer, who spends most of his time helping the public to prevent crime. Ring your local police station and ask for an appointment. When he visits you, do take them into your confidence. Tell them what you have to protect and what you most fear. They will advise you on what type of locks or alarms to use, and on reputable installers. There is no charge for the service.

He will almost certainly go round your property looking at all the possible entry points and advising methods of protection. You can do this for yourself (see diagram), but don't forget that a window you think inaccessible or too small to enter, may be easily breached by an athletic burglar.

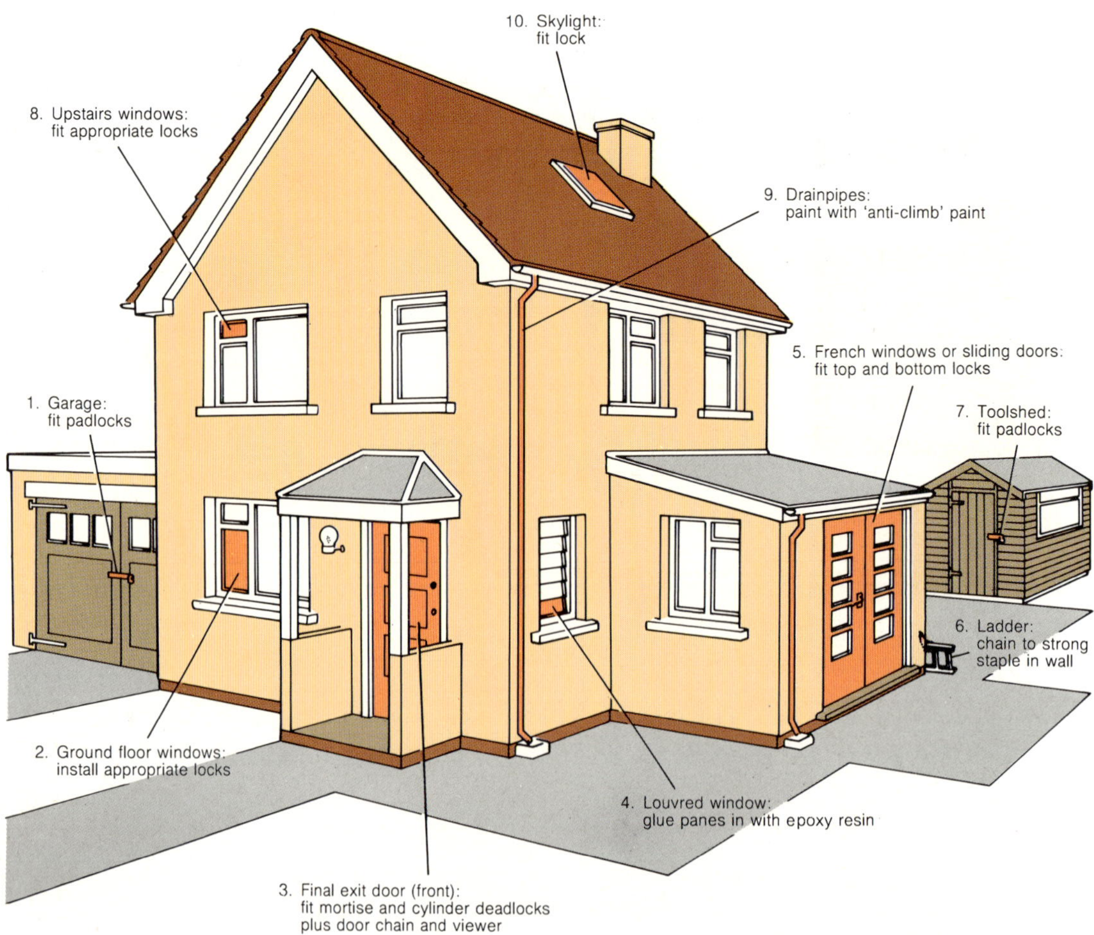

BURGLED?

If you have been burgled, ring the police immediately.

THE TRICK

Touch as little as possible before the police arrive as they will want to fingerprint all the rooms. Don't tidy up or move anything more than you have to as the pattern may link the crime to others in the area.

If keys have been used to enter, or stolen, get the locks changed as soon as possible. Contact the bank, credit card companies or travel companies if chequebooks, credit cards, traveller's cheques or tickets have been stolen.

THE TRICK

Make sure you lodge a claim with your insurance company as soon as you can. If you delay unduely, you may be in breach of the policy conditions.

Do ensure that your insurance is adequate and up-to-date at all times (see page 334). If you haven't any insurance, arrange some immediately.

LEAVING THE HOUSE

The best system of locks and alarms is useless if you don't use them. More houses have been burgled while the owner 'just nipped round to the corner shop' and left the back door unlocked than the police would care to count. Ten minutes is quite long enough for someone to search the house roughly and load goods to an appreciable value into a car boot. If you get into the habit of locking up every time you leave the house empty, even for five minutes, the better your chances of repelling a burglar. Even if you are going down the far end of a largish garden, it might be worth locking up if you cannot see the whole of the back of the house.

THE TRICK

Also remember that if you live in a high-risk burglary area, your insurance policy may include a condition that a pay-out will only be made if the premises were correctly locked.

If you are going out for the evening, draw the curtains downstairs and leave a light on and a radio playing. The important thing is not to advertise that the property is empty.

Never leave a key on a string inside the letter box or 'concealed' outside the house. Burglars know all the places people use thinking the key will be safe.

PRECAUTIONS WHEN GOING AWAY

Many homes are burgled while the owners are away because they have failed to work through the following checklist, and have made it quite obvious that the house is uninhabited.

CHECKLIST

1. Cancel newspaper deliveries.
2. Cancel milk deliveries.
3. Check your insurance is in order.
4. Inform the local police.
5. Deposit all really valuable articles in the bank. Move less portable things, like the video, out of sight.
6. Ask a reliable neighbour to keep an eye on the place, collect any parcels or circulars left obviously in the front door. Give them a key and the name of someone to contact in the event of a robbery.
7. Close and lock all sheds, garages, etc. Padlock your long ladder to a strong shed or garage wall.
8. Leave a light on a time switch (see page 88) set to come on at an appropriate time and go off at your normal bedtime.
9. Close and lock all windows, however small.
10. Close, but don't lock, all internal doors.
11. Lock and bolt all outside doors except the final exit door.
12. Set the burglar alarm if you have one and double-lock the final exit door.

MARKING PROPERTY

All types of property, from TVs and videos to the most delicate china and glass, can be marked either covertly with ultra-violet marking pens which will neither detract from its beauty nor devalue it, or overtly by stamping or engraving. Postcoding your property is an effective deterrent, as marked property is difficult to sell. It can also help the police return stolen property to its rightful owners should they recover it after a burglary.

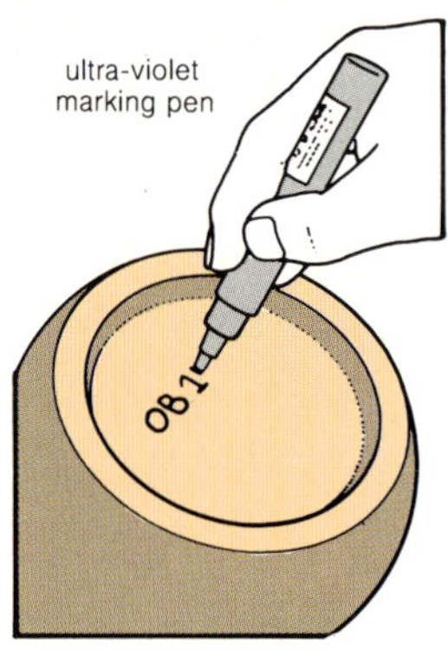

YOUR WEAKNESSES..

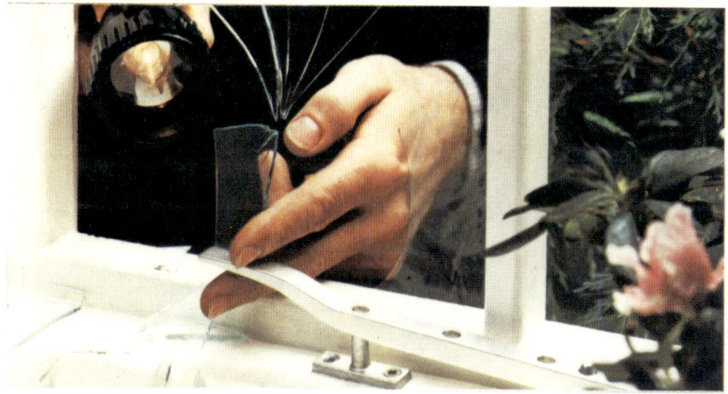

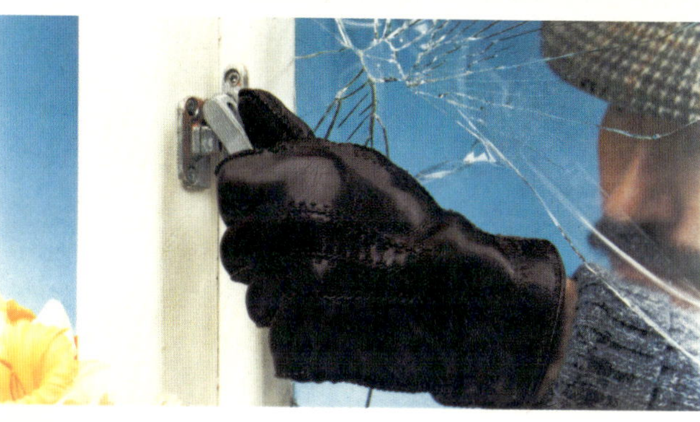

..ARE OUR STRENGTHS

Look at **YOUR** doors and windows. They may be vulnerable to attack!

Union Locks range of superbly engineered locks and door fittings enables you to greatly improve your home security.

Recognised as the leading name for locks, you can find Union products at all good DIY, hardware and ironmongery stores.

Take the first step to strengthen your home security. Send for our free home protection leaflet plus details of your nearest stockist.

Union Locks Limited,
P O Box 15, Willenhall,
West Midlands. WV13 1JS.

 a member of the Chubb Group

WINDOWS

Two-thirds of all burglaries take place through insecure ground floor windows, normally at the rear of the house where a burglar will not be easily seen or disturbed. In some instances the window will have been left open for ventilation; in other cases it will have been left open 'for the cat'. Every window, even those that at first sight appear too small or inaccessible, needs protecting: bathroom windows, often situated by drainpipes; and those next to flat roofs, garages, trees or dividing walls are all vulnerable. Any window which is not overlooked by your neighbours or which cannot be seen by passers-by is an ideal target for the burglar.

WINDOW LOCKS

While many burglars are prepared to break a small part of a window pane in order to reach in and slip the catch, they will think twice about trying to take out the whole pane and climb in: it is not easy, it takes time, it is noisy, it can be dangerous and it will only increase the risk of their being seen or heard. In so many cases, the simplest of security window locks will prevent the window from being easily opened, even if the glass has been broken.

Locking windows (shutting them is just not enough) needs to become as much a reflex action as locking the door when you leave your home. Window locks for every type of window – sash, casement, wood and metal – are readily available.

If you have louvre windows fitted you must be especially careful as they are particularly vulnerable; burglars can simply remove the slats of glass.

THE TRICK

Their security can be improved by gluing the slats to their frames with a strong epoxy resin; but the best advice, if you are thinking of fitting them, is 'Don't'.

FITTING

Before you start fitting locks to all your windows, check the condition of the frames. It is pointless installing powerful locks on rotting wood where the screws will just pull out when any force is exerted (see page 52 for repairing windows).

Window locks always come with detailed installation instructions and you should follow these carefully. However the basic principle is usually the same. You place the key in the lock and offer up the lock in its final position, tapping the key gently with a hammer to mark the sash. Using the correct sized drill, bore a hole in the sash to take the reception stud. It is very important that you use the right-sized drill for the job and, indeed, for all lock fitting. A loosely fitting lock is an insecure lock. Screw in the reception stud until it is flush with he sash.

Next, you lock the lock into the reception stud and check that the lock has a firm fit onto the window frame. Adjustments can be made by moving the lock up or down, or by turning the reception stud slightly. Finally mark the screw positions of the lock on the frame, start the holes with a gimlet or bradawl and screw the lock into position.

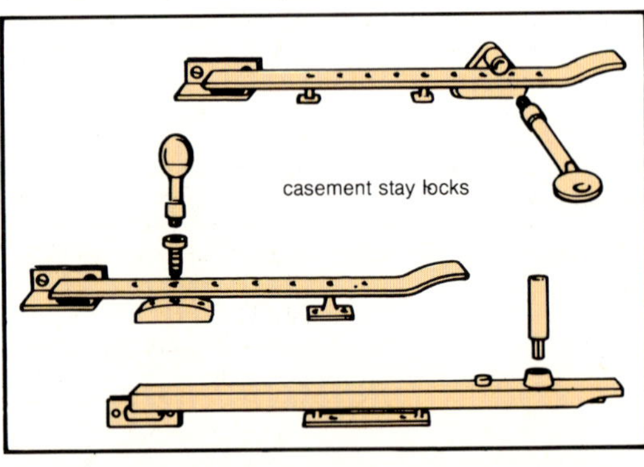

SAFETY PRECAUTIONS

It is always advisable to hang the key to the window lock near to it, so that, in case of fire, it is easily found. However, it must not be visible to a potential thief. A small cuphook, screwed into the windowsill behind the curtain return, is probably the least obvious but most accessible place.

BARS AND GRILLS

There are certain types of windows where even a window lock will not make them totally secure. This is particularly the case with louvre windows (see above) and leaded lights, where a single pane can easily be pushed in. In such cases, or if you live in a sub-basement or ground floor flat in a high-risk area, you should consider installing permanent bars or security grills.

Bars should be of steel rods, set not more than 125mm (5in.) apart, and firmly embedded in the structure of the walls if they are outside the window. These bars will prevent you escaping in event of a fire, so it is probably wiser not to fit them on bedroom windows.

A safer choice for such a room would be the moveable (folding) grills which can be either raised or lowered or moved from side to side. They look rather like old fashioned lift gates and have to be made specially for each window. On non-opening windows a decorative iron grill would be cheaper and less obtrusive. If you install one of these, make sure you use reasonable length woodscrews to attach it to the door or window frame (35mm (1½in.) would generally be all right).

OTHER PRECAUTIONS

If you have the misfortune to be burgled and have to replace a large pane of glass, you might consider installing shatterproof or Security (with a wire net inside it) glass. You can also buy security film (made of polycarbonate plastic) which is attached to the inside of the glass. Double glazing is also a deterrent because of having to get through two panes.

Skylights are probably best protected by being double-glazed (an important insulation point too as a lot of heat escapes through the roof (see page 127)). With a proper lock securing a sound frame to a sound sash, that would probably deter all but the most determined burglar.

Upper floor windows near drain pipes can be additionally protected by painting the pipes with 'anti-climb' paint. It has the special quality of staying permanently as a slippery jelly-type surface.

THE TRICK

This should not be used lower than 2.5m. (9ft) above the ground so as to avoid it accidentally getting on people's clothes.

Patio doors are particularly vulnerable to burglars as they are usually at the back of a building and are fitted by being lifted into place on the rails.

THE TRICK

Any patio lock should be fitted at both head and foot of the door and should include a bolt to the rails.

Many french windows have an 'espagnolette' lock which is easily burgled by breaking out one pane near the handle; you should fit head and foot locks as well on the door that closes last.

DOORS 1

There are many types of lock, from simple, face-fitting locks, poorly made and only for casual use, to solid, burglar-proof ones, mortised into the thickness of the door and having combinations of deadlocking bolts, spring night latches and special keying security. In between are the variations of the basic cylinder lock, where the keying system is set into the door and the mechanical parts contained within a box screwed to the door inner face. These locks are also available in heavy burglarproof form, and with variations of latch, lock and keying systems.

Each lock type must have a plunger deadbolt, or 'tongue', which (on locking) moves out to engage into a slot or 'keeper' set into the door frame. Incorporated into the keeper there may be a striking plate, which eases the spring latch into its slot as the door closes. Unfortunately the majority of locks originally fitted by builders are grossly inadequate. All exit/entry doors should be fitted with a five-lever mortise deadlock to B.S.3621. The normal two-lever deadlocks, as fitted by builders, have less than a dozen different keys, whereas a five-lever mortise lock has one thousand different keys.

A deadlocking action is perhaps the most important characteristic of a good lock, because it means that it can only be opened with a key once it has been locked. Unlike a simple rim-latch, a deadlock cannot be opened by a burglar forcing a piece of plastic between the edge of the door and the frame. Nor would a burglar be able to unlock the door by slipping his hand through your letter-box or through a broken glass panel in the door. If he has entered your home through the rear, a deadlocked front door will prevent him from walking out 'unnoticed' with your valuable possessions.

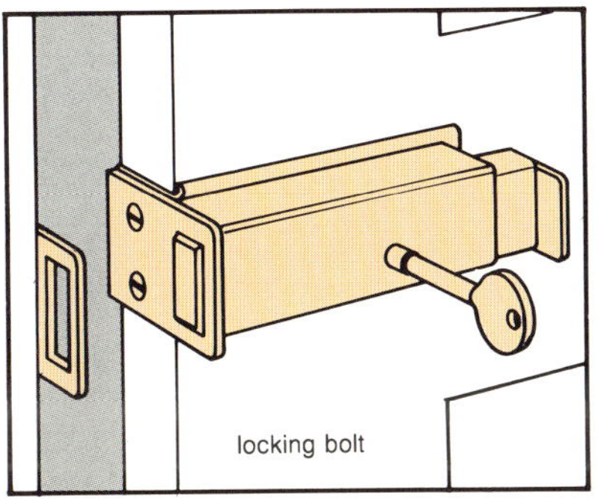
locking bolt

mortise rack bolt

FITTING

There must be no pressure on either face of the lock tongue to resist the turning of the key – nor on the top or bottom. The first job, then, is to check the door (or other hinged piece) for good fitting. Check that:

1. The door closes evenly all round;
2. It shuts closely to the jamb;
3. It is not rubbing at the top, bottom or sides;
4. It is not 'hinge-bound' (see page 45); and
5. All hinge screws are tight and that their heads are not meeting as the door is closed.

The above check is just a visual one but, if the lighting is poor, make a mechanical one, as follows:

THE TRICK

Close the door and look for light filtering through the cracks. If light is not showing fully, rub lipstick or carbon paper onto suspected high spots and close the door again. When you open the door a marker will be left at the high spots.

Leave them well clear as they must later be repainted.

THE TRICK

To check mechanically, use a thin tongue of plastic and slide and probe it to identify high spots.

Ease the high spots where the probe will not slide.

A word of warning: if the job involves an outside door and you are doing it in winter, don't make an excess clearance. The following summer the wood will shrink and in the autumn the door will start to rattle.

Don't forget that, as with your windows, the lock that you fit can only be as good as the frame into which it is fitted. So check that your door frames are also in good condition.

OTHER PRECAUTIONS

Those external doors that are not used as main exit points can be secured from the inside by fitting strong bolts at the top and bottom of the door. These should be mortised into the door and key-operated. Strong surface-mounted bolts can also be used, but the small flimsy bolts sometimes fitted by builders are of little use and should be replaced.

You can also get hinge (or dog) bolts which protect the door by strengthening the hinge side. They are particularly useful on doors that open outwards, because they are most susceptible to having the hinges tampered with. They should be screwed on near the top and bottom of the hinge side of the door and the striking plate must be mortised into the frame.

Not all unwelcome callers will come when your home is unoccupied. The elderly are susceptible to the doorstep conman. A door-chain or door-limiter fitted to your front door will allow you to check the identity of callers before letting them into your home. Some door chains have a key-operated lock which can be operated from outside. They are not an acceptable substitute for a proper mortise lock on a final exit door. Don't forget that any chain is probably considerably stronger than the door, its frame or the screws which hold it in place. A really determined effort to enter would probably succeed. You might consider a door-viewer, although its use will be limited to daylight hours unless you have an outside light.

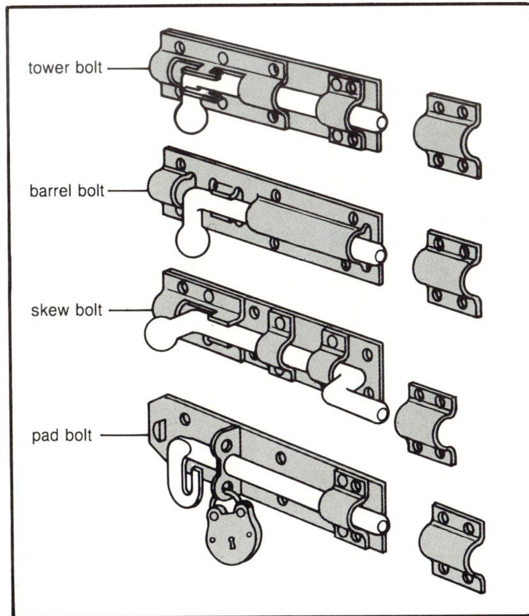

Always ask to see official proof of identification before allowing a stranger into your home. Meter readers, VAT officials, council staff, etc should all carry an identity card. Policemen should have a warrant card. If the policeman is in plain clothes and you are dubious about the warrant card, shut the door and ring the police station to check. A genuine policeman will never mind you doing this.

THE TRICK

If you let a salesman into your house and he sells you something on hire purchase that you later consider you don't want, get in contact with your local Citizens' Advice Bureau. You can withdraw from such a contract if you do it within five days of receiving the contract from the finance house; they must send it to you within seven days of you signing the initial agreement. You therefore have 12 days to change your mind.

Always be very sceptical of 'antique dealers' trying to buy from you. In 99 per cent of such cases, they will offer you a minute proportion of the item's real value or are 'casing the joint' for a future burglary.

THE TRICK

Sotheby's, Christie's, Phillips or Bonhams (all in London) will value items for you. Any reputable local jeweller can value jewellery, silver, etc, so make sure that you are not cheated out of its true value.

For fitting mortise locks, see page 55. For fitting cylinder locks, see page 330.

DOORS 2

CYLINDER LOCKS

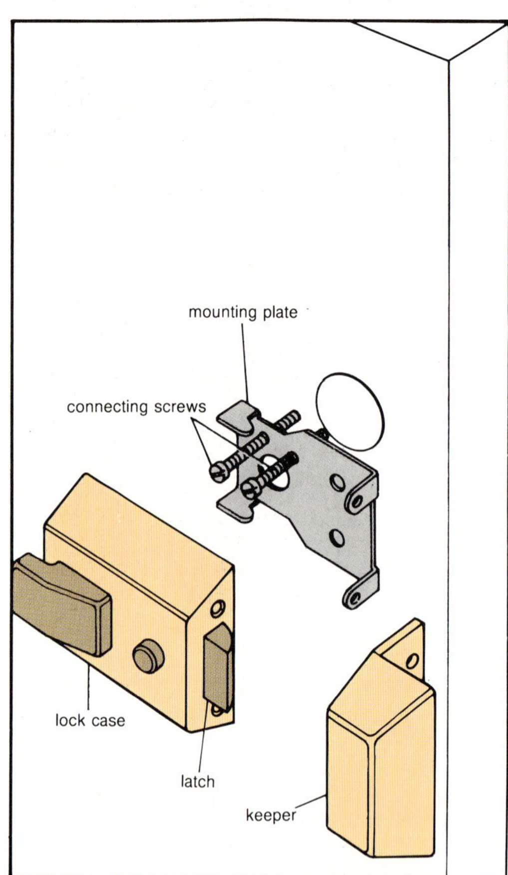

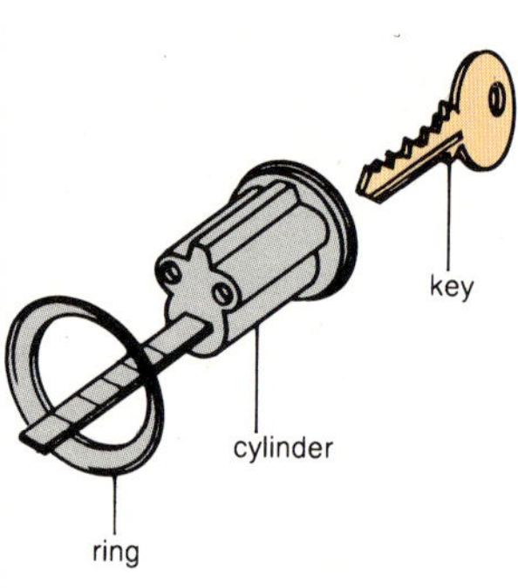

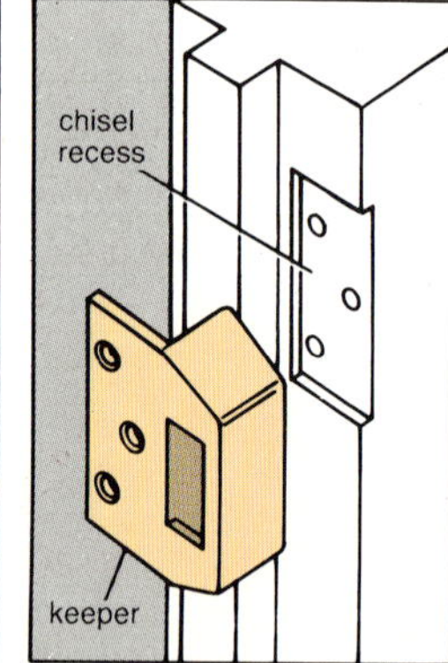

FITTING CYLINDER LOCKS

Cylinder rim locks fit flush to the room side of the door, and take a Yale-type key from the outside.

The general method of fixing is to bore a hole for the barrel, or cylinder, completely through the door. The back plate has a raised circular portion which fits into the hole in the inner face of the door and is held by the same screws that hold the cylinder.

From the rear of the cylinder a tongue projects, which rotates as the key is turned. As it projects into the lock mechanism, it causes the latch to be drawn back into the lock casing, so releasing the door. The lock casing fits into the back plate and is screwed through securely to the door.

Some cylinder rim locks have a front lip that must be cut in to the door edge and screwed there. There are many variations of function, but the fitting procedure is almost identical for the lock part of any make.

Ascertain the size of the backset from the package or paper templet provided. The backset is the distance of the vertical centre line of the large hole to the edge of the door, and is usually either approximately 60mm (2⅜in.) or 45mm (1¾in.). Do check because locks vary. If you have got a paper templet, place it on the door as instructed and mark through it for the hole centres.

Using a 32mm (1¼in.) diameter wood bit, bore completely through the door. Bore from one side until the centre spur shows, then bore the remaining web of wood out using as a centre the pilot hole just made.

Insert the cylinder into the rose (ring or bezel) and push the cylinder into the door. The operating tongue should project no more than 10mm (⅜in.) for most locks, but the instructions on the packet will give the precise length. This tongue must be hacksawn to the correct length.

Fit the back plate over the tongue, with the raised circular section locating into the hole. Check the long screw lengths, and cut them if they are too long. Use these to attach the cylinder and back plate firmly through the back-plate into the rear of the cylinder front boss. Use two short screws to fix the plate into position.

The latch (the whole lock) may be screwed to the back-plate, or it may need to be cut into, and screwed to the door edge: follow the instructions on the packet. However, with all locks of this type, the tongue from the cylinder must be carefully fed into the latch slot as the latch is closed with the back-plate.

If the face of the latch projects beyond the door edge (with the uncut type), slightly slacken the screws and tap the lock with a block of wood. There is usually enough free space in the various holes to allow some adjustment. With cut-in latches, the recess must be made slightly deeper.

The staple (striking plate or keeper) must now be fitted to the jamb. The details can vary enormously – it is therefore not possible to describe the steps here, but do mark out and cut very carefully. The lipstick trick (see page 329) may help to gauge the precise height position of the latch tongue.

Cylinder locks need to be fitted even more accurately than do mortise locks (see page 55), as most of them are based on night rim latches – latches which will close and lock the door without the use of a key. An improved version of the cylinder lock incorporates a deadlock sliding bolt as well as a spring latch. Alternatively it may have a very small second tongue controlling the mechanism within the lock that prevents the spring latch from being forced back into the lock by a stiff piece of plastic (such as a credit card) inserted into the crack of the door from its outer face.

This kind of lock can also be set up in such a way that, if the key is inserted from the inside of the door and turned, it sets an anti-thief device which prevents the knob being turned by hand if a burglar breaks a pane of glass and puts his hand through. If these safeguards are going to work properly, the tongue of the spring latch must close accurately into its keeper, so careful fitting is therefore vital.

Whatever the design, the basic procedure is the same: careful marking, cutting and fitting. Some cylinder locks come with a paper templet which can be laid on the door to pin-point all holes. The only essential tools are a sharp chisel, a large boring bit, usually 32mm (1¼in.) diameter, a bradawl and suitable screwdrivers. Fitting cylinder locks usually entails cutting a shallow recess into the door jamb for the staple (a striking plate) and sometimes into the door edge for the lock case lip to fit into.

OTHER DOOR LOCKS

Other door locks found are surface-fitting night or spring latches, with a key-turned dead bolt. They require little skill in fitting, other than accurate marking for the positions of the holes to take the handle-shank and key. These locks have an extended front end to the case which projects at right angles, and it must be cut into the door edge. Allow for this recess when marking for the two holes.

Striking plates for these rim locks are screwed into the door jamb, but you may need to mark and chisel a recess into the frame and into any architrave.

Where shallow out-cuts and recesses have to be cut through moulded architraves, use the tip of a fine saw (or broken hacksaw) to cut a series of cuts across the moulding before you do any chiselling. Avoid chisel blows along the grain because they split the moulding.

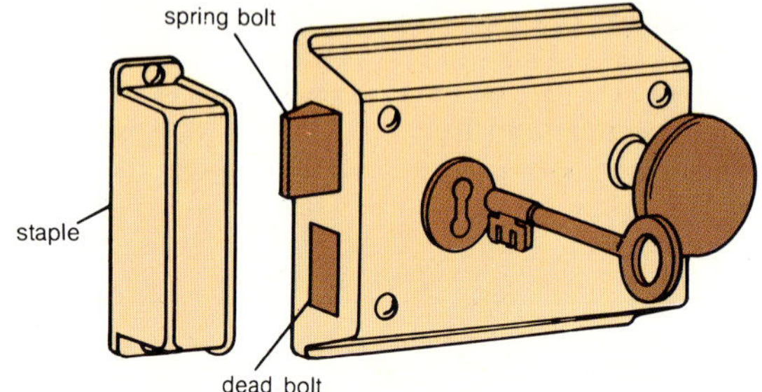

A cylinder lock without a deadlock can be opened with as simple a tool as a piece of plastic (like a credit card) or a kitchen palette knife. A metal 'anti-jemmy' plate, hammered into the door stop moulding will make it almost impossible for the lock to be opened with a plastic strip and make things considerably more difficult with other tools.

Remember with locks that you get what you pay for. Economise now and you may well regret it later.

BURGLAR ALARMS

There are many different systems available either in a d-i-y kit form, or as a specifically designed system from a professional installer. A sophisticated system will require regular maintenance and testing, and any system purchased should conform to B.S.4737. To find a reputable local security company, you can approach one of the following:

British Security Industry Association (BSIA)
68 St James Street, London SW1A 1PH (01–493 6634)
Aims to promote and encourage a high standard of ethics, service and equipment within the industry as a whole. It represents about 90 per cent (by volume) of the British security industry.

National Supervisory Council for Intruder Alarms (NSCIA)
St Ives House, St Ives Road, Maidenhead, Berks. SL6 1RD (0628 37512)
Aims to improve the standard of service and maintenance of intruder alarm installations and inspects installations to ensure they comply with the NSCIA Code of Practice and requirements from B.S.4737. They also investigate complaints against their members and maintain a roll of approved installers.

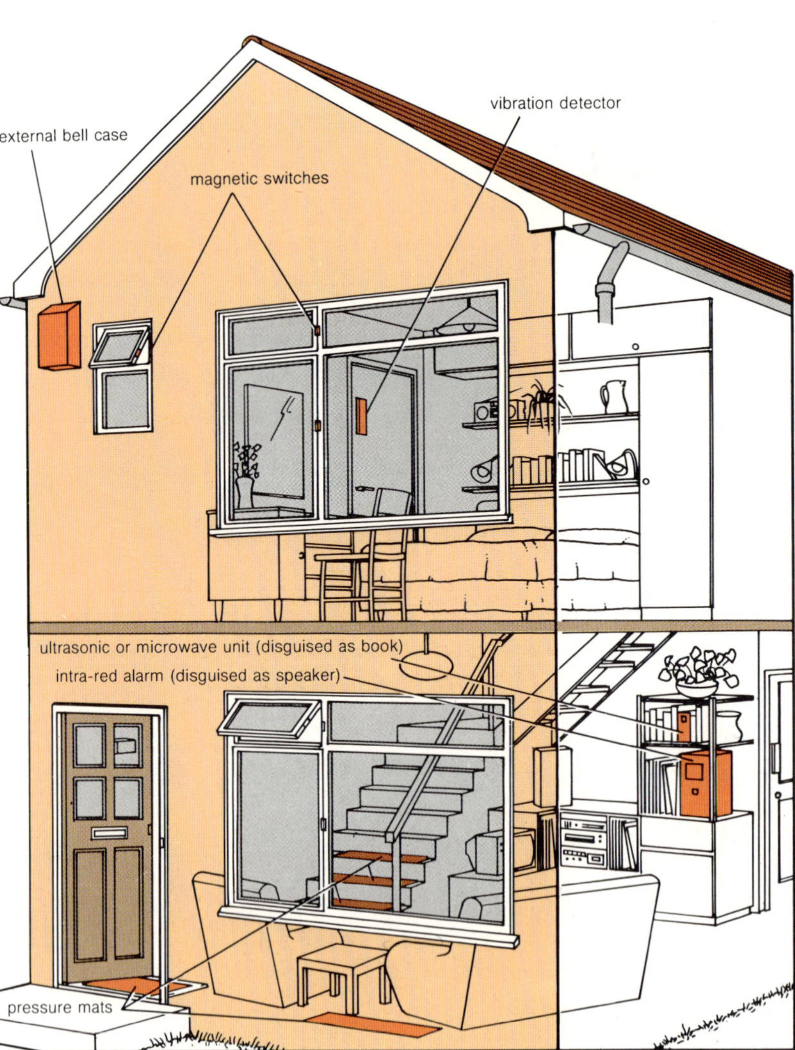

TYPES OF SYSTEM

A typical system has a range of sensors which detect the presence of an intruder. These are linked by wires to the control unit which then either sets off an alarm of some description or/and alerts the police direct.

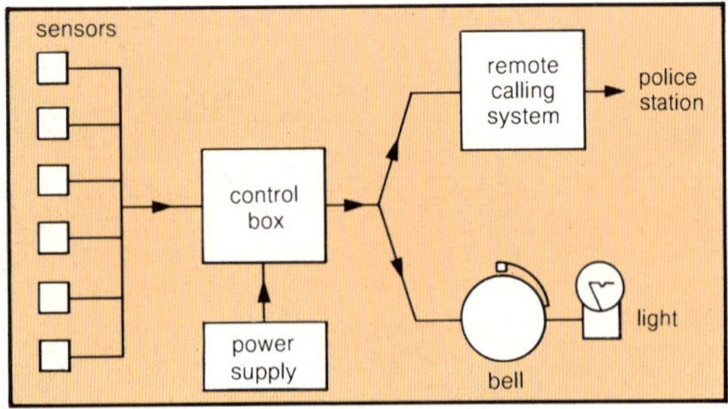

SENSORS

These divide into two types: those that indicate a penetration of the perimeter of the building (i.e. via a door or window) and those that indicate an intrusion of a specific area of the building. The former is probably of more use in a family dwelling to minimize the risk of confrontation with an intruder and allow maximum movement within the building while the alarms are set.

Broken Glass Detectors
These either work by vibration (when the glass breaks) or by hearing the noise of the glass breaking.

Continuous Wiring
This is rather obtrusive in a private home as it requires metal foil to be stuck all along the glass to be protected. Many shops use this system nowadays.

Magnetic Switches
The most commonly used device – its contacts are held together by a magnet mounted on the moving part of a door or window. When the door or window is opened, the switch is opened and the alarm sounds. However, if the glass of a window is broken through, the alarm will not go off.

Vibration or Inertia Detectors
These work in a similar way to magnetic switches, with weights instead of magnets. During a forced entry, the vibration will dislodge the weight for a second and so sound the alarm. Many buildings shake heavily as a result of passing traffic, high winds, etc; it is therefore important that the system can differentiate between these and a break-in.

Beam Interruption Detectors
A more sophisticated form of tripwire, using infra-red rays, which can protect quite large areas. The beam is focused onto a receiver; if the beam is broken the alarm sounds. Sunlight on the receiver can set it off accidentally.

Pressure Mats
These work by having two pieces of foil metallic in close proximity. Weight pushing them together sets the alarm off. They are useful on staircases and in front of purloinable articles.

If you use them on a staircase, be sure to use them on three treads in a row. That way the thief is unlikely to miss all of them. Don't put them under furniture as the weight will set them off eventually. Pets have also been known to activate them.

Movement Detectors
There are various types of sensor around based on infra-red, microwave and ultrasonic monitors respectively. They are reasonably good for covering a high-risk area like a sittingroom or a wall or floor safe. However, they require careful siting to avoid accidental triggering and are best installed by an expert.

THE CONTROL UNIT

When switched on, this constantly monitors the sensors and sets off the alarm if they are disturbed. B.S.4737 specifies that any control unit should have an anti-tamper system to prevent the thief from bypassing it. The B.S. also says it should be wired into a fused connector unit (see page 86) and should have a standby-battery backup system. It should have a high security key or keypad for the owner's special code and must permit you to enter and/or exit the building when it is activated, without setting off the alarm. This often involves the installation of a 'shunt lock' on the final exit door. A shunt lock has a built-in switch, which when unlocked, bypasses the magnetic switch on the door.

THE SIGNALLING SYSTEM

This can either be direct to the police or via a bell and/or a strobe light to passersby and neighbours. B.S.4737 requires that the bell should have its own power system and should continue to function if its wires are cut, is removed from its mounting or tampered with, and if its external power supply is cut off.

A recent Code of Practice suggests that the bell should cut out after 20 minutes; but that a flashing light should continue to signal the alarm.

There are three main types of remote signalling, all aim to pass a message to the police station directly.

Direct Line System
The most expensive, but most reliable, this does not depend on accessible telephone lines which might be cut. It is also easier to test and there can be no doubt as to where the alarm is from. It requires renting a direct line from the property to the police station from British Telecom.

Auto Dialling Equipment (ADE)
This uses magnetic tape to dial '999' using public lines. It then plays back a pre-recorded message for the police. Attach to an out-going calls only line.

Digital Communicators
Uses digital techniques to dial and send a message to a special receiver in a manned central station. From there the operator phones the police. The machine can dial more than once and register that the call has got through. It should be connected to an out-going calls only line so that it cannot be jammed by an incoming call. Some have the facility to send different messages indicating fire, freezing pipes, burglary, etc.

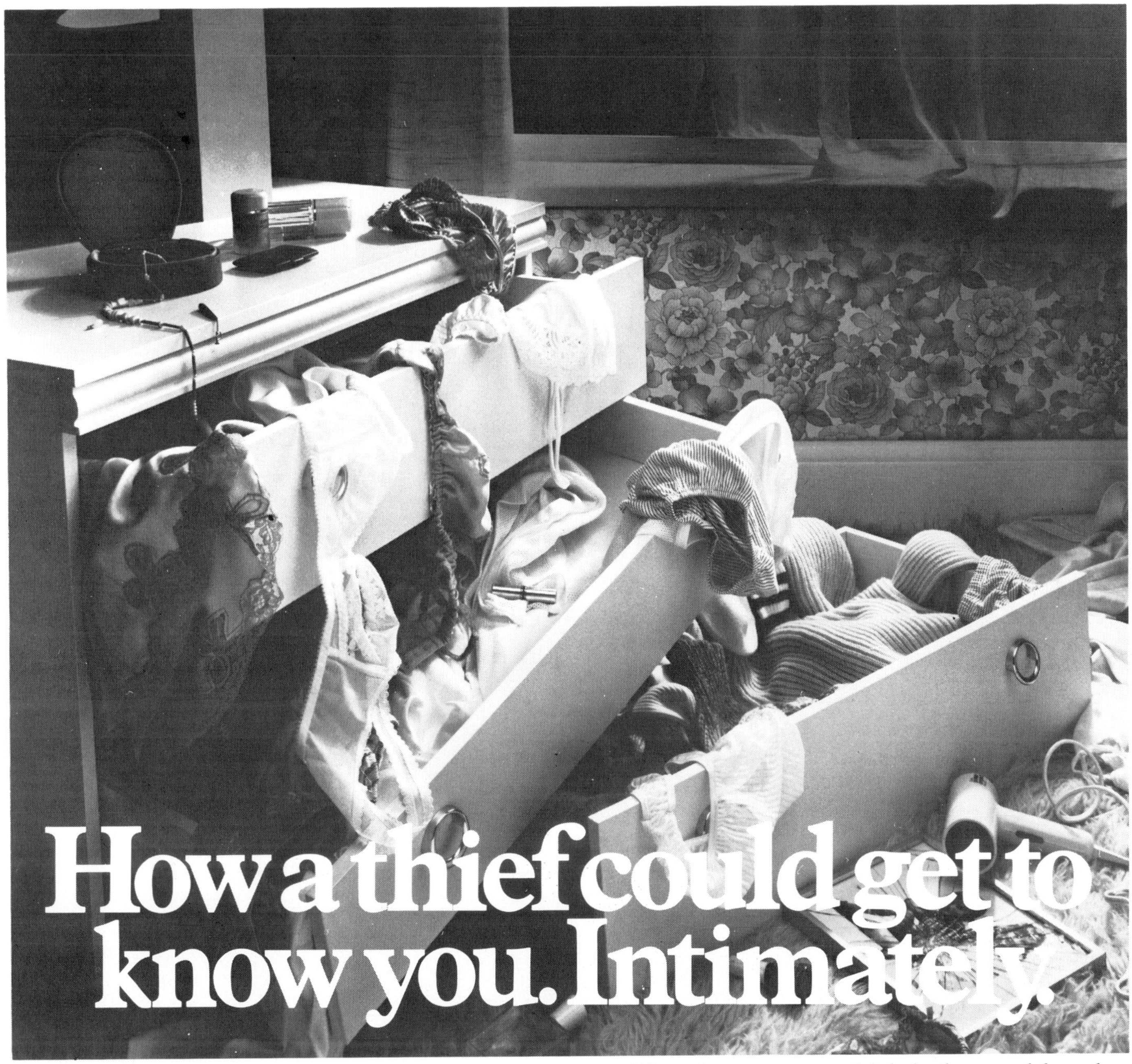

How a thief could get to know you. Intimately.

A window without window locks is an open invitation to a thief.

All too easily he can let himself in and start looking through your personal belongings.

But he can be discouraged by window locks, like those we've illustrated.

Take the simple lock designed for wooden sash windows. They cost £4 a pair and take only minutes to fit if you do it yourself.

The window security bolt is sold at most D.I.Y., hardware shops and builders' merchants in a choice of colours, so it won't spoil the looks of your window frames.

The push lock is specifically designed for side or top hung casement windows, whether they're aluminium or wood.

And the transom lock is made to protect metal and wooden windows.

If you're not sure which locks would make your windows most secure, ask the Crime Prevention Officer at your local Police Station.

His advice is free and he'll be pleased to help you avoid letting a burglar get to know you.

A window is always open to a thief. Unless it's locked.

ISSUED BY THE HOME OFFICE.

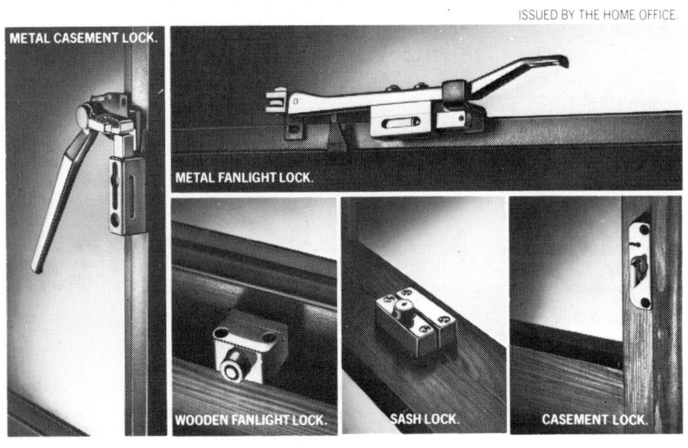

INSURANCE

Statistics tell us that something like one in every four households have no insurance of the contents; of those other three households, probably two have insurance which represents about half of the actual value of the contents. Contents insurance usually covers furnishing, furniture, kitchen equipment, electrical goods, household goods, food and drink, jewellery – in fact just about anything that would go in the furniture van if you moved.

Insurance is not something to be bought 'off the peg' and you would be wise to consult an insurance broker or to get quotations from two or three companies before deciding. If you have problems, or require additional advice, contact:

The British Insurance Association
Aldermary House, Queen Street, London EC4N 1TU
(01–248 4477)
They produce various leaflets about estimating your contents insurance and generally protecting your home.

POLICY BASIS

There are various forms of recompense for a loss and you will have to decide which you want.

INDEMNITY OR MARKET VALUE

If you are insured on an indemnity basis, you will be paid the cost of replacing what has been stolen or destroyed, or of repairing damaged articles less an amount for wear and tear. Electrical goods depreciate at about 1/10 of their value per year, while a picture would probably be rated at two per cent depreciation per year.

NEW FOR OLD

This type of policy will pay the full cost of repairing or replacing the stolen or destroyed objects at today's prices. However make sure that your total sum insured reflects current prices.

ALL-RISKS

This tackles the problem from the other way round and instead of stating all the events under which you are covered by the insurance while anything not mentioned is excluded (as in a Household Contents policy), it covers, subject to certain exclusions, damage or loss caused by anything which may happen. It usually requires each item to be valued separately and is most useful for jewellery, furs, portable electrical goods that you take out of the house, etc.

Jewellery should be valued by a professional valuer – most reputable jewellers will do this, but check the cost; it can be expensive. Keep receipts for large purchases like a video.

Don't forget that you must keep updating the value of your property year by year. Add in any large purchases made during the year, plus an allowance for inflation. If you have a stamp collection, etc, that should be valued separately.

CONVERSION TABLES

TO IMPERIAL

centimetre × 0.394 = inch
metre × 3.281 = foot
metre × 1.094 = yard
kilometre × 0.621 = mile

sq.centimetre × 0.155 = sq.inch
sq.metre × 10.764 = sq.foot
sq.metre × 1.196 = sq.yard
hectare × 0.405 = acre
sq.kilometre × 0.386 = sq.mile

gramme × 0.0353 = ounce
kilogram × 2.205 = pound
tonne × 0.984 = ton

cu.centimetre × 0.352 = cu.inch/fl.oz
litre × 0.568 = pint
litre × 0.22 = gallon

C° × 1.8 + 32 = F°

TO METRIC

inch × 2.54 = centimetre
foot × 0.305 = metre
yard × 0.836 = metre
mile × 1.609 = kilometre

sq.inch × 6.452 = sq.centimetre
sq.foot × 0.093 = sq.metre
sq.yard × 0.836 = sq.metre
acre × 2.471 = hectare
sq.mile × 2.59 = sq.kilometre

ounce × 28.35 = gramme
pound × 0.454 = kilogram
ton × 1.016 = tonne

cu.inch/fl.oz × 28.413 = cu.centimetre
pint × 1.761 = litre
gallon × 4.546 = litre

F° − 32 × 1.8 = C°

LENGTH: IMPERIAL/METRIC

Fractions of 1 inch in millimetres

in	*mm*
1/32	0.8
1/16	1.6
3/32	2.4
1/8	3.2
5/32	4.0
3/16	4.8
7/32	5.6
1/4	6.3
9/32	7.1
5/16	7.9
11/32	8.7
3/8	9.5
13/32	10.3
7/16	11.1
15/32	11.9
1/2	12.7
17/32	13.5
9/16	14.3
19/32	15.1
5/8	15.9
21/32	16.7
11/16	17.5
23/32	18.3
3/4	19.0
25/32	19.8
13/16	20.6
27/32	21.4
7/8	22.2
29/32	23.0
15/16	23.8
31/32	24.6
1 inch	25.4

inches/millimetres

in		*mm*
0.04	**1**	25.4
0.08	**2**	50.8
0.12	**3**	76.2
0.16	**4**	101.6
0.20	**5**	127.0
0.24	**6**	152.4
0.28	**7**	177.8
0.31	**8**	203.2
0.35	**9**	228.6
0.39	**10**	254.0
0.43	**11**	279.4
0.47	**12**	304.8
0.51	**13**	330.2
0.55	**14**	355.6
0.59	**15**	381.0
0.63	**16**	406.4
0.67	**17**	431.8
0.71	**18**	457.2
0.75	**19**	482.6
0.79	**20**	508.0
0.83	**21**	533.4
0.87	**22**	558.8
0.91	**23**	584.2
0.94	**24**	609.6
0.98	**25**	635.0
1.02	**26**	660.4
1.06	**27**	685.8
1.10	**28**	711.2
1.14	**29**	736.6
1.18	**30**	762.0
1.22	**31**	787.4
1.26	**32**	812.8
1.30	**33**	838.2
1.34	**34**	863.6
1.38	**35**	889.0
1.42	**36**	914.4
1.46	**37**	939.8
1.50	**38**	965.2
1.54	**39**	990.6
1.57	**40**	1016.0
1.97	**50**	
2.36	**60**	
2.76	**70**	
3.15	**80**	
3.54	**90**	
3.94	**100**	
7.87	**200**	
11.81	**300**	
15.75	**400**	
19.68	**500**	
23.62	**600**	
27.56	**700**	
31.50	**800**	
35.43	**900**	
39.37	**1000**	

feet/metres

ft	*in*		*m*
3	3	**1**	0.30
6	7	**2**	0.61
9	10	**3**	0.91
13	1	**4**	1.22
16	5	**5**	1.52
19	8	**6**	1.83
23	0	**7**	2.13
26	3	**8**	2.44
29	6	**9**	2.74
32	10	**10**	3.05
65	7	**20**	6.10
98	5	**30**	9.14
131	3	**40**	12.19
164	0	**50**	15.24
196	10	**60**	18.29
229	8	**70**	21.34
262	6	**80**	24.38
295	3	**90**	27.43
328	1	**100**	30.48

FURTHER READING

TOOLS AND SAFETY

The Complete Book of Tools A. Jackson & D. Day (Michael Joseph, 1978)
Manual of First Aid (British Red Cross Society & St John Ambulance, 1981)
Safety in the Home A. Acland (HMSO, 1971)

CARPENTRY

Home Carpentry F.E. Sherlock (Pelham Books, 1980)
The Home Woodworker J. Worthington (ed.) (Orbis, 1982)
Working in Wood (Reader's Digest Basic Guide, 1979)

DESIGNING & FITTING A KITCHEN

The Kitchen and Bathroom Book J. Manser (Pan, 1982)
The Kitchen Book T. Conran (Mitchell Beazley, 1977)

ELECTRICAL WIRING

Electrical Wiring B. Tattersall & G. Burdett (Pelham Books, 1980)
Home Electrics J. Worthington (ed.) (Orbis, 1981)
Manual of Home Electrics G. Burdett (David & Charles, 1981)
Understanding Practical Electrics (Reader's Digest Basic Guide, 1979)

PLUMBING

The Home Plumber D. Thomas (Orbis, 1981)
Home Plumbing (Reader's Digest Basic Guide, 1978)
Manual of Home Plumbing E. Hall (David & Charles, 1982)
Plumbing E. Hall (Pelham Books, 1979)

HEATING & INSULATION

Central Heating E. Rudinger (WHICH?, 1975)
Domestic Heating and Insulation W.H. Johnson (Pelham Books, 1982)
Home Heating and Fireplaces R. Tattersall (Stanley Paul, 1977)
Home Insulation R. Ball (ed.) (Orbis, 1983)
Keeping Warm for Half the Cost J. Colesby & P. Townsend (Prism Press, 1981)
Microbore Central Heating Systems (Wednesbury Tube Co, 8th ed., 1982)

EXTERIOR MAINTENANCE

Exterior House Maintenance H. & E. King (Pelham Books, 1981)
Flat Roofs Technical Guide (Property Services Agency, DOE; 2nd ed., 1981)
Looking After Your Garden (Reader's Digest Basic Guide, 1978)
Looking After Your House (Reader's Digest Basic Guide, 1977)
The Weekend Builder J. Worthington (ed.) (Orbis, 1981)
Working with Bricks, Concrete and Stone (Reader's Digest Basic Guide, 1978)

FLOORING

Carpet and Linoleum Laying Manual (Carpet Review, 1967)
Flooring R. Tattersall (Pelham Books, 1978)
Tile It! D. Messecar (Collins, 1983)

DECORATING

Decorating R. Tattersall (Pelham Books, 1978)
The Decorating Book M. Gilliatt (Michael Joseph, 1981)
Paint It! D. Messecar (Collins, 1983)
Paint Magic J. Innes (Windward/Berger Paints, 1981)
Paper It! D. Messecar (Collins, 1983)

CURTAINS & BLINDS

Book of Home Furnishings A. Fishburn (B.T. Batsford, 1982)
Curtains and Blinds H. O'Leary (Pelham Books, 1982)
Soft Furnishings for Your Home (Marshall Cavendish, 1975)

UPHOLSTERY & CANEWORK

Upholstering M. Flitman (B.T. Batsford, 1972)
Upholstery: a Beginner's Guide T. Ward (Stanley Paul, 1981)
Upholstery and Canework M. Edwards (Pelham Books, 1982)

PICTURE FRAMING

Picture Framing and Hanging L. Blonstein (Pelham Books, 1980)

HOME SECURITY

Home Protection T. Waters (Newnes Technical Books, 1982)
Safety and Security in the Home Barty, White & Burall (Design Centre, 1980)

GENERAL

Complete Do-It-Yourself Manual (Reader's Digest Books, 4th ed., 1976)
Encyclopedia of Home Maintenance J. Worthington (ed.) (Orbis, 1981)
Finishes A. Everell (B.T. Batsford, 1979)
Good Housekeeping Book of Home Improvements A. Jackson & D. Day (Ebury Press, 1977)
Good Housekeeping: Simply Fix It A.T. Jackson & D. Day (Ebury Press, 1979)
The House Book T. Conran (Mitchell Beazley, 1974)
Practical Living C. Evans (ed.) (Circle Books, 1981)
Repairing Houses T. James (Sphere Books, 1981)
The Reluctant Handyman P. Keegan & I. Layzell (*Cased*: Whittet/Windward, 1981; *Paperback*: Papermac, 1983)
The WHICH? Book of Do-It-Yourself R. Davies (ed.) (Consumer's Association/Hodder & Stoughton, 1981)

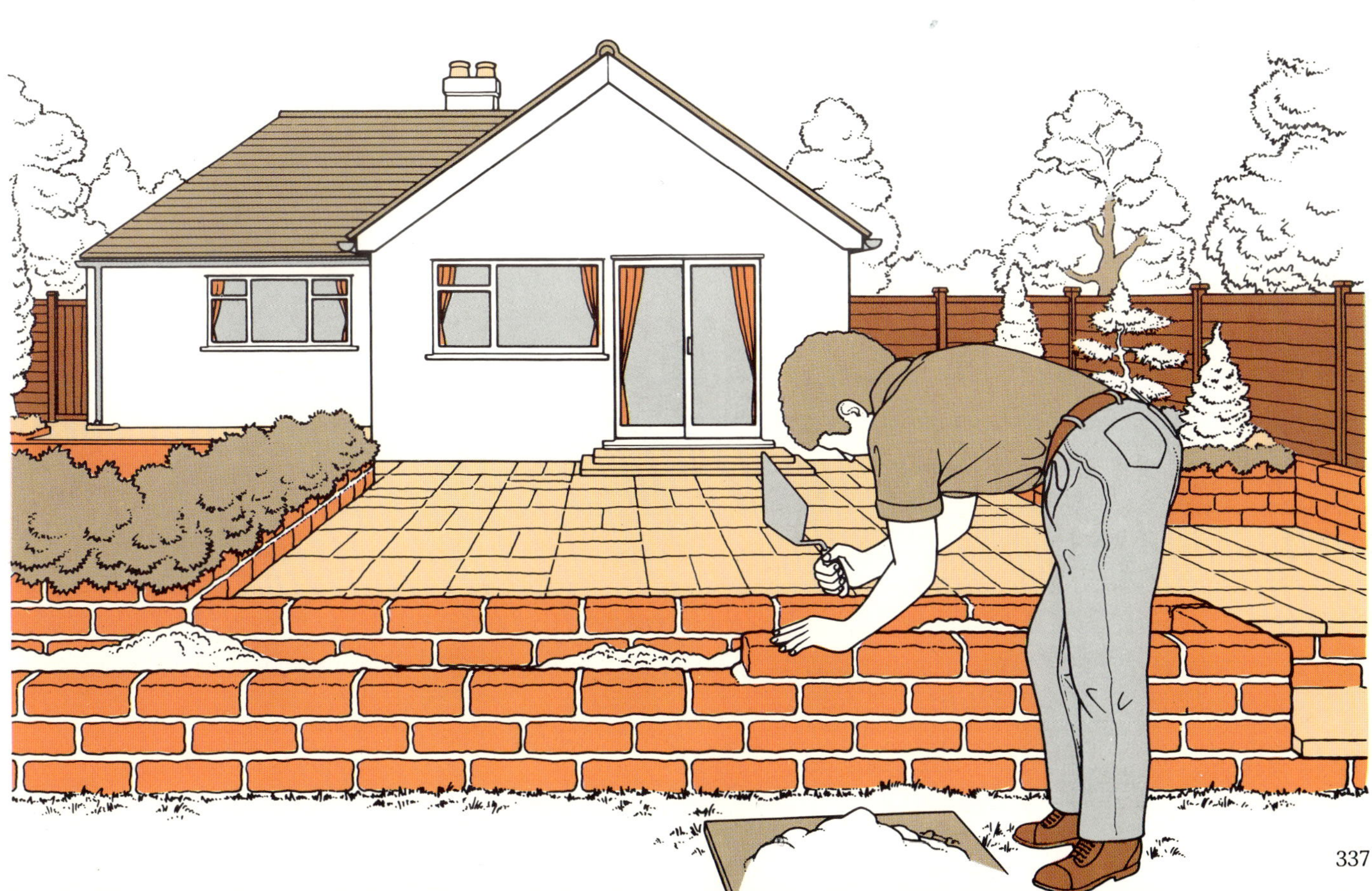

INDEX

INDEX

INDEX